PLACE NAMES OF HAWAII

Place Names of Hawaii

Mary Kawena Pukui
Samuel H. Elbert
Esther T. Mookini

REVISED AND ENLARGED EDITION

The University Press of Hawaii
Honolulu

Second edition 1974; paperback 1976, 1981

Copyright © 1974 by The University Press of Hawaii
First edition copyright 1966 by University of Hawaii Press
Library of Congress Catalog Card Number 73–85582
ISBN 0–8248–0524–0
Manufactured in the United States of America

Book design by Roger Eggers

*Ua hala nā kūpuna, a he ʻike kōliʻuliʻu wale nō kō keia lā,
i nā mea i ke au i hope lilo, iō kikilo.*

The ancestors have passed on; today's people see but dimly
times long gone and far behind.

CONTENTS

In this book the authors endeavor to provide the people of the State of Hawai'i with a glossary of important place names in the State, including names of valleys, streams, mountains, land sections, surfing areas, towns, villages, and Honolulu streets and buildings.

The first edition of *Place Names of Hawaii* contained only 1,125 entries. The coverage is expanded in the present edition to include about 4,000 entries, including names in English. Individual entries have been lengthened, especially for important places or those rich in legendary or historical associations, for example, 'Io-lani, Ka-huku, Ka-lihi, Ka-wai-a-Ha'o, Moana-lua, and La Pérouse. As in the earlier volume, meanings of the Hawaiian names are given when possible, as well as background information and, in some instances, references that may be consulted for verification and further information.

Approximately 800 more names are included in this volume than appear in the *Atlas of Hawaii* (see References). The difference is due to the inclusion here of names of surfing areas, streets, and buildings, and of rocks and spots for which legends exist.

The names in the Glossary are arranged in alphabetical order and, except for well-known towns, are located by quadrangles on Hawai'i, Maui, Moloka'i, and O'ahu, and by districts on Kaua'i. The quadrangles and districts are shown on maps 2, 3, 4, and 5. Honolulu streets are located by sections of the city (map 6).

Following the Glossary is an Appendix containing an analysis of the place names.

A major endeavor of the compilers has been to record the pronunciation of the place names as spoken by elderly Hawaiians who are fluent in the language. For this purpose the traditional orthography has serious limitations. For example, 'Alae (as in Wai-'alae) and 'Ala-'ē (a place on the Kona coast of Hawai'i) are both commonly written Alae, but one is the word for a mudhen and the other, for a sweet smell. It is easy, however, to indicate the approximate pronunciation used by knowledgeable Hawaiians if three modifications are made in the traditional spelling: a reversed apostrophe for the glottal stop, a macron over vowels that are long and stressed regardless of position in the word, and hyphens or spaces (as in Ka-lihi Uka) separating individual words that make up many of the names.

How many place names are there or were there in the Hawaiian Islands? Even a rough estimate is impossible: a hundred thousand? a million? Hawaiians named taro patches, rocks and trees that represented deities and ancestors, sites of houses and *heiau* (places of worship), canoe landings, fishing stations in the sea, resting places in the forests, and the tiniest spots where miraculous or interesting events are believed to have taken place. And an important element—one virtually unknown in Euro-American culture—that added zest to the use of place names and encouraged their proliferation is the pleasure they provided the poet and the jokester, as discussed in section 8 of the Appendix.

Place names are far from static, and their numbers increase more rapidly than most parts of an individual's total lexicon. Names are constantly being given to new houses and buildings, land holdings, airstrips, streets, and towns, and old names are replaced by new ones. The change from rural to urban living in Hawai'i, the rapid increase in population by birth and immigration, the development of new towns and the expansion of old ones, with attendant obliteration of natural landmarks, and the gradual disappearance of the Hawaiian language, have brought many additions and changes in the names of places, as well as changes in other aspects of island life.

It is all the more essential, then, to record the names and the lore associated with them now, while Hawaiians, such as the senior compiler, are here to lend us their knowledge. And, whatever the fate of the Hawaiian language, the place names will endure, in some shape or form, as a part of the English language.

Faced with an ever-increasing body of names, compilers of gazetteers are forced to choose the names to be included. They may decide to list all the names on certain maps, or only those of towns of a certain size, or of land areas of a specified magnitude, or those names deriving from a given language, or those

x

containing words of particular semantic areas, or those deemed romantic, poetic, or picturesque.

Early in this study we decided not to focus in any such way, but rather to list samples of all sorts of names: small places and large ones, high mountains and tiny valleys, Honolulu streets and buildings, surfing areas, and even stones. We have attempted to show what places the Hawaiians, both early and contemporary, considered worthy of naming—by no means everything in a given category, but the most often heard representatives of all the categories.

Hundreds of names mentioned in published legends and chants cannot be found on maps. These were excluded unless they were well known to one of the compilers. Also excluded were alternate spellings used by explorers and others before the present orthography was adopted in 1826. Cook, for example, wrote Hawai'i as Owy-hee (the Tahitian pronunciation today is Vaihī), Maui as Mowee, O'ahu as O-ahoo, Kaua'i as Atowai, and Ni'ihau as Neehau. Vancouver in 1794 wrote the same names Owhyee, Mowee, Woahoo, Attowai, and Onehow. Such spellings are of historic and linguistic interest, but the present study focuses on today's usages. In a few instances, however, outmoded forms are given, as Lā-hainā for the present Lahaina.

Names of winds and rains were not included, nor those of streets outside Honolulu unless they seemed of special interest or importance. In general only those Honolulu street names were included that have meanings not easily discoverable in the *Hawaiian Dictionary*.

The important difference between place names in Hawai'i and those on the United States mainland is that in Hawai'i about 86 percent of the names are in the language of the aboriginal population—a single language that is phonetically simple and easily identifiable by the paucity of sounds and the lack of closed syllables and consonant clusters. On the Mainland, place names have been taken from a great many languages—some of them European—but a large proportion are from the languages of the first inhabitants, the American Indians. These languages, some of which are extinct, number many dozens, and some of them are of a bewildering phonetic complexity that is not revealed in the spelling. The place names are in daily use, but their meanings are known only to experts and in many cases not **xi** even to them. Furthermore, most of the stories behind the names have been lost, distorted, and sentimentalized.

The Hawaiian names, in contrast, usually have understandable meanings, and the stories illustrating many of the place names are well known and appreciated. Pele, the volcano goddess who turned so many luckless people into stones, is still feared and revered; sharks are sometimes considered protective; and the mischievous, sexually insatiable pig-man, Kama-puaʻa, delights and amuses. Most places on the Mainland seem, by comparison, barren and bereft of traditions older than those introduced by the European and African immigrants. Whereas the Indians were considered savages and were slaughtered for their land, the Hawaiians were respected as people. Hawaiian kings and queens maintained their sovereignty almost until the present century. Intermarriage was and is extremely common. Not only does the Hawaiian past still live, it dates back a thousand years or more, whereas on most of the Mainland, traditions go back only a few centuries or even less. The land there seems lacking in history. Who were the Indians? What was their culture? Most persons do not know.

One of the pleasures of living in Hawaiʻi is the presence of Hawaiians, with their ancient language and traditions. The place names provide a living and largely intelligible history.

The Hawaiian world extended from Nihoa Island beyond Kauaʻi to South Point at the farthest tip of Hawaiʻi. This study covers a somewhat wider area, including all the Northwest (Leeward) Hawaiian Islands as far west as Midway.

Uniform coverage of all the islands was not possible. Areas in which the compilers had special interest or knowledge, and for which adequate published sources are available, are covered in more detail than other places. Molokaʻi, for example, is extremely well treated, Kauaʻi least well.

The Hawaiians, like Polynesians in other areas, considered themselves very much a unified whole, and they loved to express in sayings the eastern and western limits (never the northern and southern) of their domain, usually with reference to the passage of the sun:

Mai ka lā ʻōʻili i Haʻehaʻe ā hāliʻi i ka mole o Lehua. From the sun's appearance at Haʻehaʻe until [it] lies spread forth at the roots of Lehua.

Mai ke kai kuwā e nū ana i ka ulu hala o Keaʻau ā ka ʻāina kāʻili lā o lalo o Wai-kūʻau-hoe. From the noisy sea murmuring to the pandanus groves of Keaʻau to the land that snatches away the sun at Wai-kūʻau-hoe.

Samuel H. Elbert

ACKNOWLEDGMENTS

This book is the result of many years of research; space does not permit mention of everyone who answered our innumerable questions.

The entire manuscript, some 900 pages, was reviewed at an earlier stage, with particular attention to the islands of Moloka'i and O'ahu, by Catherine C. Summers, associate researcher in anthropology at the Bernice P. Bishop Museum. As coauthor of *Sites of Oahu* and as author of the recent *Molokai: a Site Survey,* she is especially qualified to review place names of these two islands.

The Committee for the Preservation of Hawaiian Language, Art, and Culture financed a large part of the manuscript preparation, including preparation of the maps. We wish to express our appreciation to the committee and particularly to its chairman at the time, Thomas Nickerson.

Officials at Iolani School, Punahou School, St. Andrew's Priory, the University of Hawai'i, and the Ka-mehameha Schools (especially Donald D. Mitchell) kindly furnished detailed background information about the buildings on their respective campuses. The various county boards of parks and recreation supplied the names of parks and trails throughout the State.

The program for IBM computer 360/65 was prepared by Ann M. Peters and Robert W. Hsu. Their recommendations as to types of information that could be recovered via computer were most helpful.

Much information over the years was provided by Edwin H. Bryan, Jr., of the Bishop Museum, who has his own collection of 25,000 Hawaiian place names.

The *Honolulu Star-Bulletin* kindly gave us permission to quote from the series of articles on Honolulu streets written by Clarice B. Taylor in cooperation with George Miranda, and published in 1956 in the newspaper.

Informants for names of present-day surfing sites were John Kelly, founder of the Save Our Surf movement, and Donald

Acknowledgments

M. Topping, also a veteran surfer. Kelly described types of waves, indicated the seasons when surfing is best in certain localities, and explained the rationale for some of the peculiar new English names.

A great many other persons contributed information and references. We wish particularly to thank Elizabeth Bushnell, Elizabeth Ball Carr, Agnes Conrad, Frances Damon Holt, Gavan Daws, Yasuto Kaihara, Edgar C. Knowlton, Jr., Gordon A. Macdonald, the Reverend Mary Numele Moku, Edwin H. Mookini, Zelie D. Sherwood, and Eleanor Williamson.

The Preface and Appendix were reviewed by Albert J. Schütz, and we are grateful for his many practical suggestions and comments.

None of those named, of course, is in any way responsible for the shortcomings and incompleteness of our work.

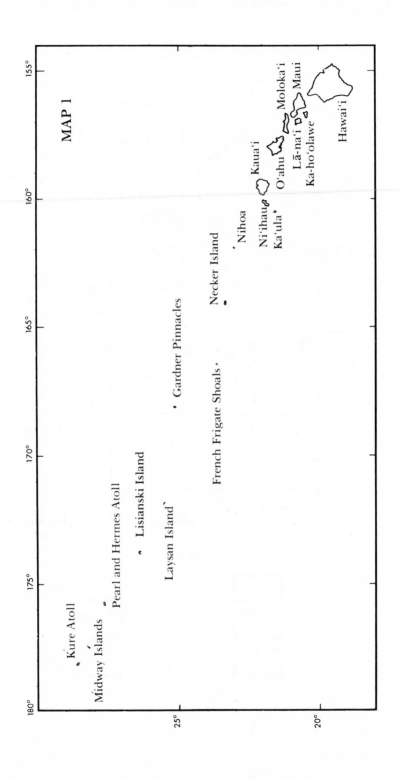

MAP 1

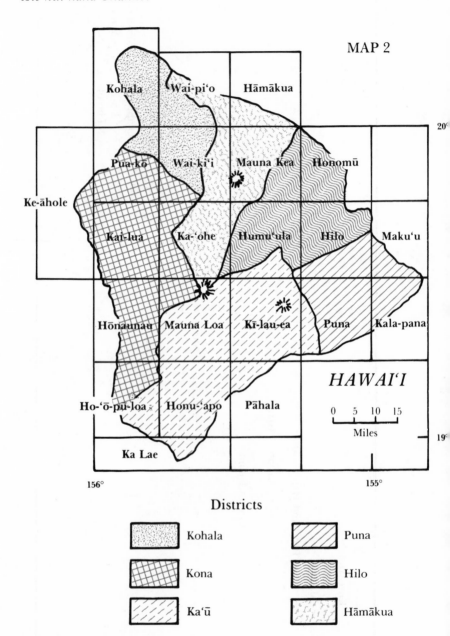

MAP 2

Kohala Wai-pi'o Hāmākua

20°

Pua-kō Wai-ki'i Mauna Kea Honomū

Ke-āhole

Kai-lua Ka-'ohe Humu'ula Hilo Maku'u

Hōnaunau Mauna Loa Kī-lau-ea Puna Kala-pana

HAWAI'I

Ho-'ō-pū-loa Honu-'apo Pāhala

0   5   10   15

Miles

19°

Ka Lae

156°   155°

Districts

Kohala		Puna	
Kona		Hilo	
Ka'ū		Hāmākua	

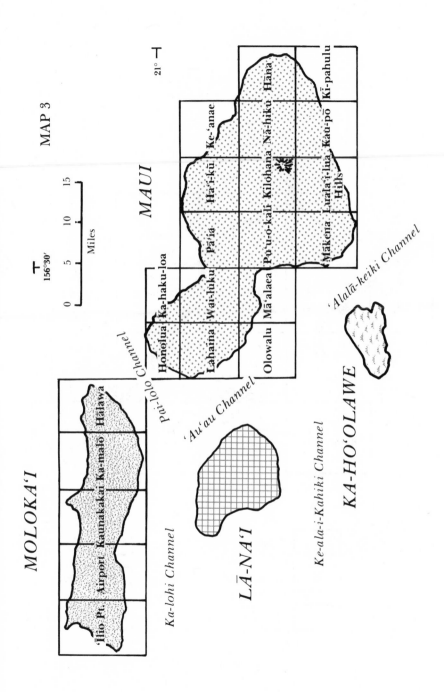

MAP 3

MOLOKA'I

'Īlio Pt. Airport Kaunakakai Ka-malō Hālawa

Pai-'lolo Channel

Ka-lohi Channel

MAUI

156°30′   Miles

0   5   10   15

21°

Honolua Ka-haku-loa

Lahaina Wai-luku Pā'ia Ha'i-kū Ke'anae

Olowalu Mā'alaea Pu'u-o-kali Kilohana Nā-hiku Hāna

Mākena Luala'i-lua Kau-pō Kī-pahulu
Hills

LĀ-NA'I

'Au'au Channel

Ke-ala-i-Kahiki Channel

'Alalā-keiki Channel

KA-HO'OLAWE

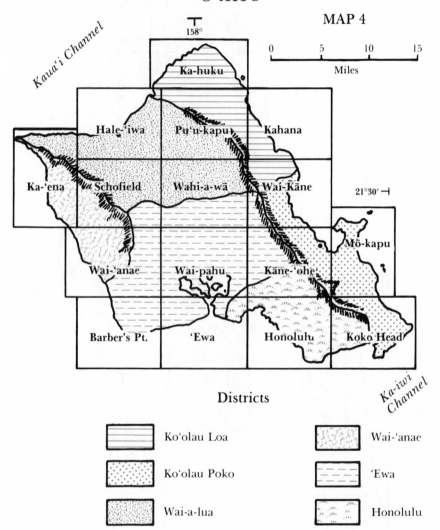

O'AHU

MAP 4

0   5   10   15

Miles

Kaua'i Channel

158°

21°30′

Ka-huku

Hale-'iwa   Pu'u-kapu   Kahana

Ka-'ena   Schofield   Wahi-a-wā   Wai-Kāne

Mō-kapu

Wai-'anae   Wai-pahu   Kāne-'ohe

Barber's Pt.   'Ewa   Honolulu   Koko Head

Ka-iwi Channel

Districts

▤ Ko'olau Loa	▨ Wai-'anae
▦ Ko'olau Poko	▤ 'Ewa
▦ Wai-a-lua	▦ Honolulu

MAP 5

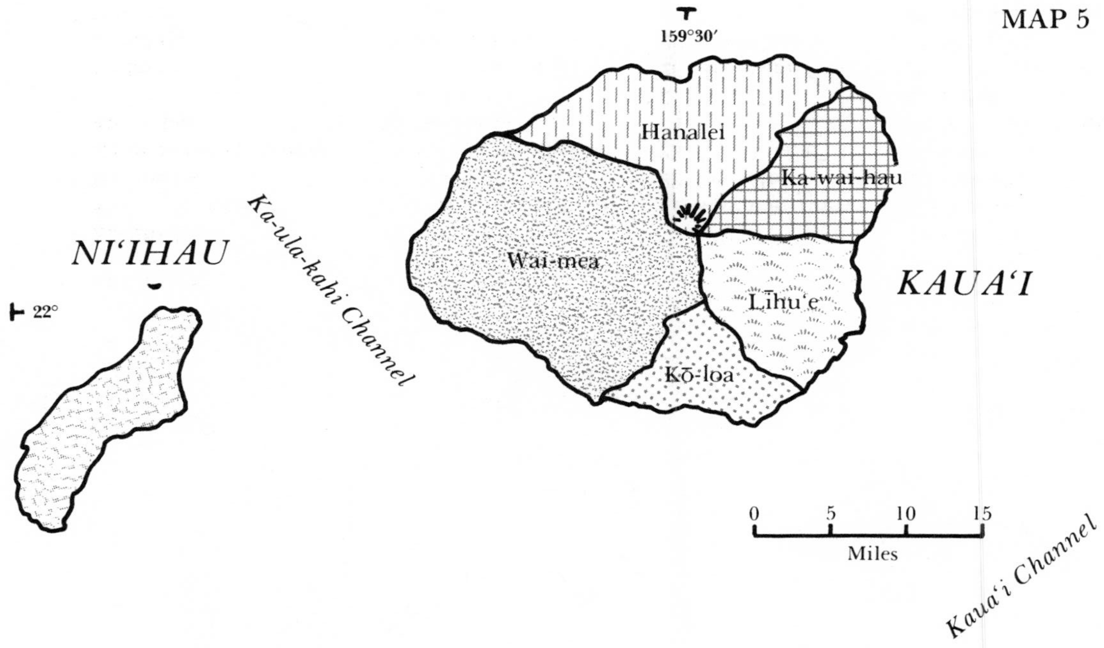

KAUA'I

159°30'

Hanalei

Ka-wai-hau

Līhu'e

Kō-loa

Wai-mea

Ka-ula-kahi Channel

Kaua'i Channel

NI'IHAU

22°

Miles

0   5   10   15

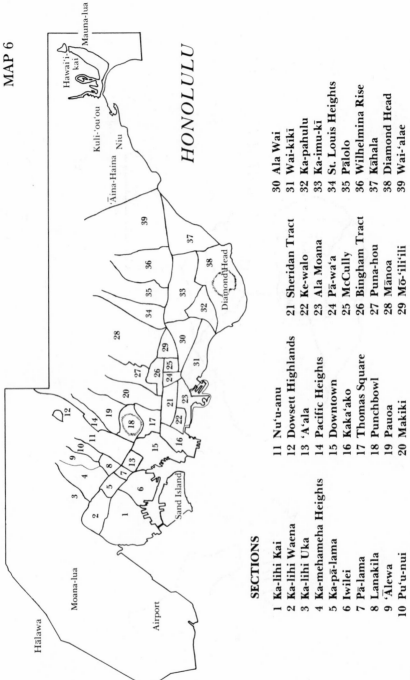

MAP 6

HONOLULU

SECTIONS

1 Ka-lihi Kai
2 Ka-lihi Waena
3 Ka-lihi Uka
4 Ka-mehameha Heights
5 Ka-pā-lama
6 Iwilei
7 Pā-lama
8 Lanakila
9 ʻAlewa
10 Puʻu-nui

11 Nuʻu-anu
12 Dowsett Highlands
13 ʻAʻala
14 Pacific Heights
15 Downtown
16 Kakaʻako
17 Thomas Square
18 Punchbowl
19 Pauoa
20 Makiki

21 Sheridan Tract
22 Ke-walo
23 Ala Moana
24 Pā-waʻa
25 McCully
26 Bingham Tract
27 Puna-hou
28 Mānoa
29 Mō-ʻiliʻili

30 Ala Wai
31 Wai-kīkī
32 Ka-pahulu
33 Ka-imu-kī
34 St. Louis Heights
35 Pālolo
36 Wilhelmina Rise
37 Kāhala
38 Diamond Head
39 Wai-ʻalae

GLOSSARY

Hawaiian Words Used in the Glossary

ahupuaʻa, land section, usually extending from the uplands to the sea

ʻaumakua, 'personal or family god'

heiau, ancient place of worship

hōlua, ancient sled or sled course down an incline

hula, 'Hawaiian dance'

kahuna, 'priest, sorcerer, master of an art'

kapu, 'taboo, sacred, forbidden'

kīpuka, an "island" of land (where there may be greenery) left surrounded by a lava flow

kōnane, old Hawaiian game resembling checkers

kuhina nui, executive officer during the Monarchy

kukui, 'candlenut'

kuleana, 'land holding'

kupua, 'demigod'

lei, 'garland'

lua, a type of hand-to-hand fighting

maika, ulu maika, old Hawaiian game similar to bowling

mana, 'supernatural power'

Menehune, legendary race of small people who worked at night building fishponds, roads, ditches, and temples

moʻo, supernatural being living usually in water; many were dangerous, some benevolent

pali, 'cliff'

poi, Hawaiian staff of life—cooked taro pounded and mixed with water

Of the above, hula, lei, and Menehune are not italicized in the Glossary.

For gods and demigods frequently mentioned, see Appendix 6.6.

Abbreviations and Symbols Used in the Glossary

For.	Fornander, *Hawaiian Antiquities* (e.g., For. 5:176 means Fornander, Volume 5, p. 176)
For. Sel.	Elbert, *Selections from Fornander*
HM	Beckwith, *Hawaiian Mythology*
Indices	*Indices of Awards*...
Kuy. 1, 2, 3	Kuykendall, *The Hawaiian Kingdom,* Volumes 1, 2, 3
Lit.	literally
PE	Pukui and Elbert, *Hawaiian Dictionary*
PH	Emerson, *Pele and Hiiaka*
qd., qds.	quadrangle, quadrangles (maps 2–4)
RC	Kamakau, *Ruling Chiefs*
TM	Taylor and Miranda, "Honolulu Street Names"
UL	Emerson, *Unwritten Literature*...
*	Pronunciation and meaning uncertain

See References for complete citations.

For other references the author's name is given (followed by a date if more than one work by the same author is listed) and a page number.

AaAaAa

'A'ahoaka. Hill, a *kīpuka,* Līhu'e district, Kaua'i (Macdonald and Abbott 390).

'A'ahu-wela. East slope of Mauna Kea, Hawai'i. *Lit.,* hot garment (perhaps so called because of volcanic eruptions).

'A'aka. Ridge, Wai-mea district, Kaua'i. Ancient surfing area, Lahaina, Maui. (Finney and Houston 28.) *Lit.,* roiled.

'A'aka-ki'i. Gulch, Pu'u-kapu qd., O'ahu.

A'a-kukui. Gulch and old *heiau* for human sacrifices, Wai-mea district, Kaua'i. *Lit.,* candlenut root.

'A'ala. Lane, park, street, and section 13 of Honolulu (map 6). *Lit.,* fragrant (said to be named for the sweet smell of nearby laundries; TM).

'A'ama-kāō. Gulch, Kohala qd., Hawai'i. *Lit.,* crowds [of] black crabs.

'Ā'ā-manu. Land section, Hāmākua qd., Hawai'i. *Lit.,* birds panic stricken.

'A'awa. Ancient surfing area near Wai-ehu, West Maui. (Finney and Houston 28.) *Lit.,* wrasse fishes.

'A'awa Iki. Small island (0.35 acres, 40 feet elevation), Ka-haku-loa qd., Maui. *Lit.,* small 'A'awa.

'A'awa Nui. Small island (0.09 acres, 40 feet elevation), Ka-haku-loa qd., Maui. *Lit.,* large 'A'awa.

'Ā'ā-wela. Mountain, Hanalei district, Kaua'i. *Lit.,* hot clinkery lava.

Adams. Ball park, Ka-huku, O'ahu, named for Andrew Adams, Kahuku Plantation manager 1904–1921. Lane, downtown Honolulu, officially named in 1850 in honor of Captain Alexander Adams, who commanded the sandalwood fleet under Ka-mehameha I. He was buried in Nu'u-anu cemetery. (Clark 16.)

Adelaide. Street, Ka-lihi Waena, Honolulu, named for Adelaide Fernandez, a prominent Mormon. (TM.)

Agee. House, upper Mānoa, Honolulu, formerly the home of Hamilton P. Agee, agriculturalist, now used as a studio for graduate students of the University of Hawai'i art department.

'Aha-'ino. Land divisions, gulch, and peak, Hālawa qd., south Moloka'i. *Lit.,* unpleasant assembly.

'Ahana. Street, Sheridan Tract, Honolulu, named for a Chinese merchant who lived there. (TM.)

Ahe-kolo. Street, Pauoa, Honolulu. (TM.) *Lit.,* creeping breeze.

'Āhihi. Point, Līhu'e district, Kaua'i. Bay, Mākena qd., Maui. Street, Ka-lihi Uka, Honolulu. *Lit.,* entwined.

Ahiki. One of the three peaks (the least pointed one) of Mount Olomana, near Kai-lua, O'ahu, on the Wai-mānalo side, named for the overseer *(konohiki)* of Ka-'ele-pulu and Ka-wai-nui ponds. (Sterling and Summers 5:266–267.) See Olo-mana.

'Ahina. Street, Diamond Head, Honolulu. *Lit.,* gray.

'Āhinahina. Plain near Kīholo, Hawai'i. Street, Pālolo, Honolulu. *Lit.,* gray.

Ahi-pu'u. Street, Nu'u-anu, Honolulu. *Lit.,* hill fire (a bonfire was kept laid here ready to warn chiefs of invaders from Ko'olau; Sterling and Summers 6:191.)

Āhole. Rock islet (0.15 acres, 40 feet elevation), Kī-pahulu qd., East Maui. *Lit., Kuhlia sandvicensis* (a fish).

Ahrens. School, Wai-pahu, O'ahu, named for August Ahrens, first manager of Oahu Sugar Company.

Āhua. Ancient surfing area off Coconut Island, Hilo, Hawai'i (Finney and Houston 26). Point, 'Ewa qd., O'ahu. Street, Moana-lua, Honolulu, named for an ancient fishpond in the area (TM). *Lit.,* heap.

Āhua-ka-moku-kō-lau. Hill (3,557 feet high), Kī-lau-ea Crater, Hawai'i. Probably *lit.,* the net-dragging district [has] heaps.

Āhua-loa. Land area on Hawai'i just southeast of Honoka'a on the old road to Kamuela. *Lit.,* long heap.

Ahu-a-Lupua. Resting place near the beach at Mahai'ula and Ka'ele-huluhulu, Kona, Hawai'i. *Lit.,* pile of Lupua (a chiefess).

Ahu-a-Moemoe. Mound back of Ke-ka'a rock on the grounds of the Sheraton-Maui Hotel near the golf course, Lahaina qd., West Maui. See Ke-ka'a. *Lit.,* mound of Moemoe.

Ahu-a-'Umi. Small hill south of Ka-huku, Ka'ū; *heiau,* Kai-lua qd., Hawai'i. *Lit.,* altar [used] by 'Umi. (For. Sel. 174; RC 35.)

Ahu-'ena. *Heiau* for human sacrifices (RC 180) restored by Ka-mehameha I, adjoining his residence at Ka-maka-honu, Kai-lua, North Kona, Hawai'i. (Ii 122, 123.) A *heiau* formerly at Hālau-lani, O'ahu. *Lit.,* red-hot heap.

'Āhui. Street, Kaka'ako, Honolulu. *Lit.,* cluster (as of bananas).

'Āhui-manu. Land division, stream, ranch, and subdivision, Kāne-'ohe qd., O'ahu. In 1845 Ka-mehameha III granted a tract of land in this area to the Catholic mission for the first Catholic school in the Islands. Each street name in the subdivision combines *Hui-* (flock) with the name of a bird. See 'Āhuli-manu. *Lit.,* bird cluster (perhaps so called because the birds from nearby Moku-manu were caught here and tied together in bunches).

Ahu-kini. Coastal land section and landing north of Nā-wiliwili, Kaua'i, named for a son of La'a-mai-Kahiki, who came from Tahiti. Former *heiau* at Kāne-'ohe, O'ahu. *Lit.,* altar [for] many [blessings].

'Ahulili. Peak, Kī-pahulu Forest Reserve, Kau-pō qd., Maui. (For a song, see Elbert and Mahoe 29–30.) Perhaps formerly 'Ā-hulili, *lit.,* glowing, dazzling.

'Āhuli-manu. Pool at 'Āhui-manu, O'ahu. *Lit.,* birds looking [for water].

Ahu-loa. Area in Ho'ō-pū-loa qd., South Kona, Hawai'i. *Lit.,* long heap (a cave here was used for storage).

Ahu-moa. Land section, Wai-ki'i qd., Hawai'i. *Lit.,* gathering [of] chickens.

Ahu-o-Laka. Islet (3.1 acres, awash at high tide), off Kaha-lu'u, Kāne-'ohe Bay, O'ahu. *Lit.,* altar of Laka.

Ahupai. Hill (1,470 feet high), Pā'ia qd., East Maui.

Ahu-pū. Bay and gulch, Ka-ho'olawe. *Lit.,* heap together.

Ahu-pū Iki. Bay and gulch, Ka-ho'olawe. *Lit.,* small Ahu-pū.

Ahu-pū Nui. Bay, Ka-hoʻolawe. *Lit.*, large Ahu-pū.

ʻAhuʻula. Street, Ka-lihi Kai, Honolulu. *Lit.*, feather cape.

Ahu-wale. Street and place, ʻĀina-Haina, Honolulu. *Lit.*, exposed.

ʻAiea. Land sections, mill, village, bay, stream, field, recreation center, and schools, west of Honolulu, Oʻahu. (RC 169). *Lit., Nothocestrum* tree.

ʻAi-hua-lama. Stream tributary to Mānoa Stream, and the area near Puʻu-pueo, Mānoa, Honolulu, where Ka-uhi killed Ka-hala-o-Puna, whom he suspected of having an affair with Kiʻi-helei. (Westervelt, 1964*b*:129; for another version, see Poha-kea; see also Awaawa-Kiʻihelei.) An owl *ʻaumakua* (personal god) saw the murder, dug up the girl's body, and resuscitated her.

ʻAi-kahi. Land section, street, elementary school, subdivision, shopping center, and playground, Kai-lua, Oʻahu. Street names in the subdivision begin with *ʻAi-*. *Lit.*, eat scrape (as the sides of a *poi* bowl; thus, to eat all).

ʻAi-kanaka. Land division, Hanalei district, Kauaʻi, perhaps named for a legendary oppressive chief who was defeated by Ka-welo (For. Sel. 32-113.) An ancient name for Pū-koʻo harbor, Molokaʻi, where inhabitants were washed into the ocean by a Kona storm and eaten by sharks (Jarrett 21). Pandanus groves here produced fine fruit (*Ka Leo o Ka Lahui,* February 22, 1894). *Lit.*, man-eating.

ʻAi-koʻolua. Gulch, Ka-malō qd., south Molokaʻi. *Lit.*, eat together (of two).

ʻAila. Street, Moana-lua, Honolulu, *Lit.*, oil.

ʻAimakapā. Fishpond, Kai-lua qd., Hawaiʻi, recommended for preservation. (Emory and Soehren).

ʻĀina-Haina. Subdivision of Honolulu, shopping center, playground, and elementary school, mostly developed after World War II. *Lit.*, Hind's land (named for Robert Hind, who started the Hind-Clarke Dairy there in 1924).

ʻĀina-hau. Home and land of Princess Ka-ʻiu-lani at the site of the present Princess Ka-ʻiu-lani Hotel, Wai-kīkī, Honolulu. (For a song, see Elbert and Mahoe 30–31.) See Ka-puni. *Lit., hau* tree land.

ʻĀina-hou. Land divisions, Humuʻula and Puna qds.; Shipman ranch, Kī-lau-ea qd., Hawaiʻi. Site of Irwin Park, downtown Honolulu; street, Hawaiʻi-kai, Honolulu. (Ii 30, 82; RC 418.) *Lit.*, new land.

ʻĀina-kea. Land section, Kohala qd., Hawaiʻi. Ka-mehameha I was trained here by Kaukōkō in Oʻahu fighting methods. A hero, Kukui-pahu, and 3,200 men were killed here and their feather cloaks taken (HM 419). Way, Ka-pahulu, Honolulu. *ʻAina-kea* is a kind of sugar-cane.

ʻĀina-koa. Subdivision, playground, and avenue, Wai-ʻalae, Honolulu. *Lit.*, soldiers' land. (The subdivision was opened up after World War II.)

ʻĀina-moana. State park, a man-made peninsula at the Wai-kīkī end of Ala Moana Park, usually called Magic Island. *Lit.*, sea land.

ʻAina-pō. Upland section, Kī-lau-ea qd., Hawaiʻi. *Lit.*, darkened land (often heavy with fog).

ʻAi-noni. Volcanic cone and stream, Kai-lua, Oʻahu. *Lit.*, eat *noni* (*Morinda citrifolia*) fruit.

'Ai-'ōpio. Fishpond, Kai-lua qd., Hawai'i, recommended for preservation. (Emory and Soehren.) *Lit.,* youth eating.

'Ai-pa'a-kō. Street, Lanakila section, Honolulu. A land parcel of this name was awarded in 1853. (Indices 704).

'Ai-pō. Summit swamp, Wai-'ale'ale, Kaua'i. Street, Hawai'i-kai, Honolulu. *Lit.,* eating [by] dark.

'Ai-wohi. Ancient surfing area, Wai-kīkī, O'ahu. (Finney and Houston 28.) *Lit.,* royal ruler.

'Akahi. Hill (1,538 feet high), Hālawa qd., south Moloka'i. Street, Ka-lihi Uka, Honolulu. *Lit.,* one.

'Akahi-pu'u. Hill near Hu'ehu'e, North Kona, Hawai'i. Three Menehune tried to remove the top of this hill but were prevented by a cock's crow. On the second night they traced the crowing to a cave. There they found a cock which they killed and roasted in an oven (reported still there in 1924). Again they tried to remove the hilltop, but again heard crowing. They opened the oven, but it was empty. The god Kāne has resuscitated the cock and removed it. The Menehune gave up their attempt. Later, a legendary strong man, Ka-lei-kini, thrust a *kauila* stick into the hill to secure the peak that had been almost severed. *Lit.,* one hill.

'Akaka. Falls (422 feet high) and State park near Hilo, Hawai'i. When a stone here called Pōhaku-a-Pele (stone of Pele) is struck by a *lehua-'apane* branch, the sky darkens and rain falls. A large stone in midstream about 70 feet above the falls is named Pōhaku-o-Kāloa.

Akāka. Projecting spur of the mountain range at the head of Mānoa Valley; a street near the Chinese cemetery, Mānoa, Honolulu, named for the mountain that is said to be the grandparent of the Mānoa princess, Ka-hala-o-Puna (HM 152). *Lit.,* clearness.

Aka-koa. Point, Wai-pi'o qd., Hawai'i. *Lit.,* brave reflection.

'Ākala. Street, Sheridan Tract, Honolulu. *Lit.,* raspberry.

Aka-lua Iki. Land section, Honolua qd., West Maui. *Lit.,* small Aka-lua (pit shadow).

Aka-lua Nui. Land section, Honolua qd., West Maui. *Lit.,* large Aka-lua.

'Akamu. Street, Nu'u-anu, Honolulu. *Lit.,* Adams (named for Annie K. Adams, owner of the subdivision; TM).

Akani-kōlea. Land near Kī-lau-ea Crater, Hawai'i, where Kama-pua'a taunted Pele. (PH 225.) *Lit.,* plover cry.

*'Aki. Land division, Lahaina qd., Maui.

'Akihi. Mountain, Honu-'apo qd., Hawai'i. *Lit.,* petrel.

'Akina. Street in Ka-lihi Kai, Honolulu, named for Representative Joseph A. 'Akina, speaker of the first Territorial House of Representatives. (TM.)

'Ako's Gulch. See Ka-hulu-'īlio.

'Alae. Land section, Honomū qd.; pit crater near Kī-lau-ea Crater, Puna qd., Hawai'i, active in 1969 (Macdonald and Abbott 101). Land sections and homesteads, Pu'u-o-kali qd., Kula, Maui. Peak (2,000 feet high), above Ka-laupapa peninsula, Moloka'i. *Lit.,* mudhen.

'Ala-'ē. School and land sections, Ke-ala-ke-kua, Hawai'i. *Lit.,* strange fragrance.

'Alae Iki. Land section near Kī-pahulu, East Maui. *Lit.,* small 'Alae.

ʻAlae-loa. Land division and point, Honolua qd., Maui. *Lit.,* distant mudhen.

ʻAlae-loa Iki. Coastal area, Honolua qd., Maui. *Lit.,* small ʻAlae-loa.

ʻAlae Nui. Land section near ʻAlae Iki, Kī-pahulu, East Maui. *Lit.,* large ʻAlae.

Alahaka. Bay and cliff near Hōnaunau, South Kona, Hawaiʻi. *Lit.,* plank bridge.

Ala-kahi. Land section and stream, Honomū qd.; stream and waterfall, Wai-piʻo qd., Hawaiʻi. *Lit.,* one way.

Alakaʻi. Swamp and trail, Wai-mea district, Kauaʻi. (PH 45.) *Lit.,* to lead.

Ala-kea. Street, downtown Honolulu. *Lit.,* white street (this street, leading to Honolulu Harbor, was once paved with white coral stones; Clark 9).

Ala-koa. Street, Wai-ʻalae, Honolulu. (TM.) *Lit.,* soldiers' street.

Ala-kukui. Point near Wai-lua Bay, Kauaʻi. A *heiau* here was named Kūhua. *Lit.,* torch path.

Alāla. High point between Kai-lua beach and Lani-kai, Oʻahu. A tall stone at the point is used by fishermen as a landmark to locate a fishing station at sea. *Lit.,* awakening.

ʻAlalā. Hill at Kulaʻi-mano, Hawaiʻi. *Lit.,* wailing.

ʻAlalā-keiki. Cave near Kamāʻoa, Kaʻū, Hawaiʻi. Channel between Ka-hoʻolawe and Maui. *Lit.,* child's wail (believed heard here).

Ala-mihi. Two places, one on each side of Mānoa Valley, Honolulu. On the death of a Mānoa native, a rainbow spanned the valley from one Ala-mihi to the other. *Lit.,* path [of] regret.

Ala Moana. Boulevard, shopping center, beach park, harbor, section 23 of Honolulu (map 6), and surfing area (Finney, 1959*a*:108). A "left-slide" surfing area seaward of the Ala Wai yacht harbor is called Ala Moana Bowl today; Hawaiʻi State surfing championships are held here. *Lit.,* ocean street.

Ala-muku. Street, ʻĀina-Haina, Honolulu. *Lit.,* cut-off street.

Alani. Drive, Woodlawn, upper Mānoa, Honolulu, perhaps named for a tree *(Pelea sandwicensis).*

Alanui-kīkeʻekeʻe-a-Māui. An ancient trail connecting Ke-kaʻa Point and Ka-haku-loa, West Maui; only the two ends of the trail are visible. *Lit.,* Māui's winding road.

Alanui-puhi-paka. Ridge and road, Hālawa qd., Molokaʻi. See Puʻu-pā. *Lit.,* smoke tobacco road (said to be a place where people pause to smoke and rest).

Ala-ʻoli. Street, Foster Village subdivision, Hālawa, Wai-pahu qd., Oʻahu. Name suggested by Mary Kawena Pukui in 1956. *Lit.,* happy path.

Alapaʻi. Coastal area, Ka-malō qd., north Molokaʻi, probably named for Alapaʻi-nui, leader of the Hawaiʻi forces that invaded Maui in 1738 and combined with the Molokaʻi forces to defeat Oʻahu invaders. See Ka-wela. Street on the boundary between downtown and Thomas Square sections, Honolulu, named for a chiefess who was a companion of Nā-ahi-ʻenaʻena (daughter of Ka-mehameha I) and the wife of John Young II. (RC 74, 340, 342; TM.)

A

Ala-pali. Place, Diamond Head section, Honolulu. *Lit.,* cliff street.

Ala-papa. Gulch, Ka-haku-loa qd., Maui. *Lit.,* level path *or* paved pathway.

Alapi'i. Point, northwest Kaua'i. *Lit.,* ascent.

'Ā-lau. An island (4.5 acres, 40 feet elevation) off Hane-o'o, East Maui; believed to have been formed by Pele. Headland, Ka-laupapa peninsula, Moloka'i. *Lit.,* many rocks.

Alaula. Way, Mānoa, Honolulu. *Lit.,* early dawn light.

Ala Wai. Boulevard, section 30 of Honolulu (map 6), parkway, canal, boat harbor, clubhouse, golf course, playground, field, elementary school, and promenade. The canal was constructed 1919-1928 with funds appropriated for the Wai-kīkī Reclamation Project "to reclaim a most unsanitary and unsightly portion of the city." See Wai-kīkī, Wai-kolu. *Lit.,* freshwater way.

'Ale'ale. Land section, south coast, Ka-ho'olawe. *Lit.,* ripple.

'Ā-le'ale'a. *Heiau* near Hale-o-Keawe, Hōnaunau, South Kona, Hawai'i. This *heiau* was used for sports and games after Hale-o-Keawe became the major *heiau. Lit.,* light [of] joy.

'Aleamai. Land section, Pā'ia qd., Maui. (HM 19.)

'Ale-koki. Pool (no longer in existence) in Nu'u-anu Stream, Honolulu. (For a song, see Elbert and Mahoe 30–31; UL 108.) *Lit.,* short ripples.

'Ālele. Land area in the approximate center of Kai-lua, O'ahu, formerly a plain called Kula-o-'Ālele, a sports area.

Alencastre. Street and place, St. Louis Heights, Honolulu, named for the Catholic bishop of Arabissus and vicar apostolic for Hawai'i 1924–1940. (TM.) He was born in Madeira but was reared in Hawai'i.

'Ale-nui-hāhā. Channel between Hawai'i and Maui. *Lit.,* great billows smashing.

'Ale'o. Street, Mānoa, Honolulu. *Lit.,* tower.

'Ālewa. Drive, playground, and section 9 of Honolulu (map 6). *Lit.,* suspended (on a height).

Alexander. Street near Puna-hou School, Honolulu, named for the missionary William Patterson Alexander (1805–1884) who came to Hawai'i in 1832 and served until his death. (TM.) A house built in 1899 for his third son, S.T. Alexander (1836–1904), Makiki, Honolulu (the house still stands, 1970). S.T. Alexander's widow donated funds for Alexander Field on the Puna-hou campus in 1908. See Olinda.

Alexander and Baldwin Building. Built in 1929 in downtown Honolulu as a memorial to the firm's founders, S.T. Alexander and H.P. Baldwin, sugar planters.

Alexander Hall. Puna-hou School building built in 1933 and named for William DeWitt Alexander (1833–1913), son of William Patterson Alexander and president of Puna-hou 1864–1871. Professor Alexander was the author of a Hawaiian grammar and a history of Hawai'i.

Alexander Young Building. Honolulu hotel built in 1903, now an office building. Dr. Robert W. Wood, who arrived in Honolulu in 1866, had an office and a home at this site; they were demolished when the hotel construction began in 1900.

Ālia-manu. Schools, playground, and crater near Salt Lake, Honolulu. *Lit.,* bird salt-pond. (The goddess Pele and her family lived here once. When they left, Pele dropped some salt, and the pet bird of Hi'iaka, Pele's favorite sister, escaped. Birds gathered here.)

Ālia-pa'akai. Salt Lake, O'ahu, said to have been dug by Pele on her first circuit of the islands. Some of the viscid matter from her eyes dropped and formed salt. Hawaiians believed that the lake was connected to the sea by a hole in the center of the lake. (*Ka Nupepa Kuokoa,* March 28, 1874.) *Lit.,* salt pond.

Alice Cooke Spalding House. See Spalding.

Ali'i. Fishpond, Kaunakakai qd., south Moloka'i. Surfing beach, Hale-'iwa, O'ahu, used by Oceanic Foundation for experimentation. *Lit.,* chief.

Ali'i-koa. Former *heiau,* Kaha-lu'u, O'ahu. (Sterling and Summers 5: 82a.) *Lit.,* brave chief.

Ali'i-ō-lani. Elementary school, Ka-imu-kī, Honolulu, and judiciary building, downtown Honolulu, constructed 1871–1874; both were named for Ka-mehameha V. This was one of his names, probably a contraction of Ali'i-iō-lani, chief unto heavens (one·of heavenly repute). (Kuy. 2:174–175.)

'Alika. Avenue, Dowsett Highlands, Honolulu. *Lit.,* Alec (named for Alec Dowsett, grandson of Samuel Dowsett; see Dowsett).

'Ali-kā. Volcanic cone (7,843 feet), Mauna Loa qd., Hawai'i, now called 'Ālika. Probably *lit.,* dig, thrust.

'Aliomanu. Stream and land section, Ka-wai-hau district, Kaua'i.

Allan. Street, upper Nu'u-anu, Honolulu, named for George T. Allan, an Englishman who managed Honolulu's Hudson's Bay Company store 1834–1847; he lived in upper Nu'u-anu. (TM.)

Allen. See 'Ele'ele.

Aloha Tower. Built in 1925, the ten-story building houses offices and provides a vantage point for Honolulu Harbor control.

'Ālo'i. Crater active in 1969 and 1970, Puna qd., Hawai'i, perhaps named for Kahawali's pig, 'Ālo'i-pua'a. Kahawali, an expert in hula and *hōlua* riding, refused to race an unknown woman. She was Pele, and in the form of fire she chased him toward the sea. He fled to Pu'u-kea hill (Wai-ki'i qd.), said goodbye to his wife and children and his favorite pig, and escaped from Pele in a canoe. See Ka-hōlua-o-Kahawali.

Alphonse. Street, St. Louis Heights, Honolulu, named for Brother Alphonse, a teacher at St. Louis College. (TM.)

'Alu. Street, Ka-lihi Uka, Honolulu. *Lit.,* depression.

Aluea. Rock islet (0.14 acres, 40 feet elevation), Ke-'anae qd., East Maui.

'Alula. Bay, Kai-lua qd., North Kona, Hawai'i.

***Amalu.** Stream, Lahaina qd., West Maui.

'Ama'u. Street, Kāhala, Honolulu. (TM.) *Lit.,* fern.

'Amauulu. Section in the town of Hilo, Hawai'i.

'Amikopala. Hill on Mauna Loa, Moloka'i. On a hill east of here was a

11

long *maika* course that was destroyed when pineapples were planted. (Cooke 120.)

'Anae-ho'omalu. Village, bay, and development area, well known for spectacular petroglyphs (Cox and Stasack 85), Pua-kō qd., North Kona, Hawai'i. Bishop Museum archaeologists in 1971 believed the site was occupied in A.D. 800 but that most of the petroglyphs date from after 1500. See Pōhaku-kū-lua. *Lit.*, restricted mullet.

Ana-haki. Gulch, Airport qd., Moloka'i. *Lit.*, broken cave.

Anahola. Mountain, land section, village, bay, ditch, river, and weir, Ka-wai-hau district, Kaua'i. See Ka-nahā-wale.

Anahulu. Stream, Wai-'alua, O'ahu. (Ii 98.) *Lit.*, ten days.

Ana-ka-luahine. Gulch, Honolua qd., West Maui. *Lit.*, cave [of] the old lady.

'Analū. Street, Pu'u-nui, Honolulu, named for Judge Lorrin Andrews (1795–1868), associate justice of the Supreme Court and judge of the probate court, the author of a Hawaiian dictionary and grammar and many translations into Hawaiian. His home was on Nu'u-anu Avenue. (TM.)

Ana-noio. Coastal area, Ka-malō qd., north Moloka'i. *Lit.*, noddy tern cave.

'Anapa. Street, Foster Village subdivision, Hālawa, Wai-pahu qd., O'ahu. Named suggested by Mary Kawena Pukui in 1956. *Lit.*, flash of light.

*Anapalau. Point, Ka-wai-hau district, Kaua'i.

Ana-puka. Shore cave, 'Īlio Pt. qd., Moloka'i. *Lit.*, cave with holes (fishermen tied their canoes in these holes).

Andrews. Lane, Pauoa, Honolulu, named for John Andrews, proprietor of Andrews Express. (TM.) Amphitheater, Mānoa Campus, University of Hawai'i, Honolulu, completed in 1935 and named for Dean Arthur L. Andrews (1871–1945), professor of English in 1910, first dean of the College of Arts and Sciences in 1920, and dean of faculties 1930–1936.

'Ānela. Street, Woodlawn, upper Mānoa, Honolulu. *Lit.*, angel.

Aniani-keha. Land section, Kaunakakai qd., Moloka'i. *Lit.*, blowing [on the] heights.

Aniani-kū. Street, Pauoa, Honolulu, named for Aniani-kū Stillman, wife of James Robinson Holt II. Their son, Valentine Holt, gave this name to the first hybrid hibiscus developed in Hawai'i. (TM.) *Lit.*, stand beckoning (a Papa-kōlea girl stood at this place beckoning to a girl in Mānoa who was chanting).

'Anini. Stream and beach, Hanalei district, Kaua'i; also called Wanini. *Lit.*, dwarfish, stunted.

'Ano-lani. Stream in Ka-puna-hala subdivision that enters Ka-mo'o-ali'i Stream, Kāne-'ohe, O'ahu; now called Ka-puna-hala. *Lit.*, chief-like nature.

Anuanu-kūlua. Hill in uplands of Ka-'ahakea, Hawai'i, said to have been elevated by a turtle. *Lit.*, doubly cool.

'Ānuenue. School in Ka-imu-kī; street, Mānoa, Honolulu. *Lit.*, rainbow.

'Ao'ao. Street, Ka-lihi Uka near the approach to the Wilson tunnel, Honolulu. *Lit.*, side.

Ao-lani. Street, Mānoa, Honolulu. *Lit.*, heavenly cloud.

Ao-lele. Street, Honolulu airport, named by Mary Kawena Pukui. *Lit.,* flying cloud.

Ao-lewa. Street, Honolulu airport, named by Mary Kawena Pukui. *Lit.,* floating cloud.

Ao-loko. Street, Honolulu airport, named by Mary Kawena Pukui. *Lit.,* inner cloud.

Ao-wena. Street, Honolulu airport, named by Mary Kawena Pukui. *Lit.,* rosy cloud.

ʻĀpaʻapaʻa. Old settlement area near Lapa-kahi, Kohala qd., Hawaiʻi, excavated by Bishop Museum archaeologists in 1968; named for a strong Kohala wind.

ʻĀpana. Valley, central Niʻihau. *Lit.,* section.

Apio. Lane, Nuʻu-anu, Honolulu, named for John K. Apio, caretaker of Oʻahu Cemetery for about 50 years. (TM.)

Apole. Point, Kau-pō qd., Maui. Also known as Lae o Apole. (Coulter.)

ʻĀpua. Land division, Wai-piʻo qd.; land division and point, Puna qd., Hawaiʻi (a lava flow with voluminous fountains from ʻĀloʻi and ʻAlae craters reached this point in June 1969; Macdonald and Abbott 102); ancient village in Puna that was swept away in the 1868 tidal wave (Hawaii Natural History Association Guide 14–16). Flat land area, Kua-loa, Koʻolau Poko, Oʻahu (UL 52). *Lit.,* fish basket.

ʻĀpua-kea. Land division, Kāne-ʻohe, Oʻahu, probably named for a local rain. *Lit.,* white fish basket.

ʻĀpua-kēhau. Point, Mākena qd., Maui. Old stream that debouched near the present Moana Hotel, Wai-kīkī, probably named for a rain. (For. Sel. 53; Ii 93.) *Lit.,* basket [of] dew.

ʻĀpuʻu-iki. Gulch, Hālawa qd., Molokaʻi. *Lit.,* small mound.

Arcadia. See Frear.

Armed Services YMCA. David L. Gregg (U.S. Commissioner 1853–1862) had a home on this site at Hotel and Ala-kea streets; it was demolished in 1882 to build the first YMCA building.

Armstrong. Street, lower Mānoa, Honolulu, named for the Reverend Richard Armstrong (1805–1860) who arrived in 1832; he replaced Bingham temporarily at Ka-wai-a-Haʻo Church 1840–1843. In 1848 he left the mission and became minister of public instruction. He died in a horseback riding accident. Fort Armstrong, built in 1907 on Ka-ʻakau-kukui Reef, Honolulu waterfront, was named for his son, Brigadier General Samuel C. Armstrong (1839–1893). (King 2–3.) Sick persons took cleansing baths just off the reef near here at a place called Ka-lehua-wehe. Armstrong Hall, Puna-hou campus, built in 1925, was also named for General Armstrong.

Artesian. Street, Bingham section, Honolulu, named for the first artesian well dug in 1880 in that area (TM), probably on the property of Dr. A. Marques (Kuy. 3:67).

Ashford. Street, Ka-lihi Kai, Honolulu, named for C.W. Ashford, attorney general under Ka-lā-kaua appointed in 1887. (TM.)

Asing. Playground, ʻEwa, Oʻahu, named for John M. Asing, Honolulu supervisor 1942.

Atherton. Street, lower Mānoa, Honolulu, named for J. B. Atherton (1837–1903), financier who arrived in Hawaiʻi in 1858, married Juliette M. Cooke, and became president of Castle and Cooke, Ltd. **13**

He was active in developing the sugar industry. (TM.) Men's dormitory, Honolulu YMCA, near the University of Hawai'i Mā-noa campus, completed in 1932 as a gift of the Atherton family and named for Charles Henry Atherton (1867–1928), a son of J.B. Atherton. See College Hill, Fernhurst.

Atkinson. Drive, Ala Moana, Honolulu, named for A.T. Atkinson, editor of the *Hawaiian Gazette* (1881), inspector general of schools (1887), census taker (1898), and member of the 1898 House of Representatives. (TM.)

A

'Au'au. Hill, northeast Kaua'i. Channel between Maui and Lā-na'i. *Lit.,* bathe.

'Au'au-lele. Land section, Ka'ū, Hawai'i. *Lit.,* flying bath (rain).

'Au-hau-kea-'ē. Land section and ancient surfing area, Kai-lua qd., Hawai'i. (Finney and Houston 26.)

'Auhuhu. Point, Kohala qd., Hawai'i, named for a small legume with pods used for poisoning fish. The plant grew wild here, and the residents traded it, along with taro, for fish from the coast.

'Au-kai. Street and lane, Kāhala, Honolulu, named for Edward K. Aukai, caretaker of the Judd property at Haki-pu'u, O'ahu (Clark 20); beach park, Kahana qd., O'ahu. *Lit.,* seafaring.

Auld. Lane, Ka-pā-lama section, Honolulu, named for William Auld, who lived in the area. He was the son of the Scottish seaman Alexander Auld, who settled in Hawai'i in 1810 with Captain Alexander Adams, commander of Ka-mehameha's sandalwood fleet. (TM.)

'Auli'i. Street, 'Ālewa Heights, Honolulu. (TM.) *Lit.,* neat.

Au-Moa'e. Street, 'Ālewa Heights, Honolulu. *Lit.,* time [of the] tradewinds.

Austin. Lane, Iwilei, Honolulu, named for Lono Austin. (TM.)

Auwahi. Land section, Mākena qd., Maui. *Lit.,* smoky glow.

'Auwai-a-ke-kua. Gulch and spring between Ke-'ā-muku lava flow and Pu'u-anahulu, North Kona, Hawai'i. *Lit.,* watercourse of the god.

'Auwai-o-limu. Playground and street, Punchbowl, and an area near the mouth of Pauoa Valley, Honolulu. Long hair of a *mo'o* woman (some say she was Ka-hala-o-Puna), bathing there at a ditch, resembled moss. *Lit.,* ditch of moss. (The name may once have been 'Auwai-o-ka-limu.)

Avalanche. A deep-water winter surfing area off Hale-'iwa, O'ahu, named for its large combers.

Awaawa-Ki'ihelei. Ridge and gulch on the eastern side of upper Mā-noa Valley, Honolulu. *Lit.,* Gulch of Image-with-drawn-down-eyelids. (Ki'ihelei boasted of having an affair with Ka-hala-o-Puna. As punishment, gods turned him into the ridge and gulch. See 'Ai-hua-lama.)

Awaawa-loa. Peak in the Ko'olau Range, O'ahu, above Mauna-wili. *Lit.,* long valley.

'Awa'awa-loa. Pond near Moana-lua, Honolulu, and street named for it. (TM.) *Lit.,* too salty.

'Awa'awa-lua. Valley, southeast Ni'ihau. *Lit.,* doubly bitter. (An alternative interpretation is Awaawa-lua, double valley.)

Awa-'awapuhi. Valley and trail, Hanalei district, Kaua'i. *Lit.,* ginger valley.

'Awahua. Bay west of Ka-laupapa peninsula, Moloka'i. *Lit.,* bitterness.

Awa-ke'e. Bay and land section, Ke-āhole qd., North Kona, Hawai'i. See Manini-'ōwali. *Lit.,* bent harbor.

'Awa-lau. Gulch, Ka-haku-loa qd., West Maui. *Lit.,* young kava plant *or* many branches.

Awa-lua. Land sections, Ke-āhole, Kai-lua, and Kohala qds., Hawai'i. Coastal area, Lahaina qd., Maui. Ancient surfing area, Honolulu (Finney and Houston 28). *Lit.,* double harbor.

'Awapuhi. Street, Mānoa, Honolulu. *Lit.,* ginger.

Awāwa-malu. See Wāwā-malu. *Lit.,* shady valley.

'Āwehi. Stream, Hilo and Honomū qds., Hawai'i. Gulch, east Lā-na'i, and alternate name for Lōpā surfing area, Lā-na'i.

'Āwili. Point, Ho'ō-pū-loa qd., South Kona; ancient surfing area, Puna district, Hawai'i (Finney, 1959*a:*51). See Kawili. *Lit.,* swirl.

'Āwini. Land section and gulch, Kohala qd., Hawai'i. See Nae-'ole. Falls and stream, Wai-mea district, Kaua'i.

BbBbBb

Baby Ala-Moana. Surfing area off Hawai'i-kai, Honolulu. The waves suggest those at the Ala Moana site called Ala Moana Bowl.

Baby Hale-'iwa. Surfing area off the Wai-kīkī end of Ala Moana Park, Honolulu, perhaps so called because of resemblance of the breaking surf to that at Hale-'iwa.

Baby Pipeline. See Pipeline.

Baby Queen's. Beginners' surf off the Ka-pahulu pier, Wai-kīkī, Honolulu.

Bachelot. Street, St. Louis Heights, Honolulu, named for a French priest, the Reverend Alexis Bachelot, apostolic prefect and leader of the first Roman Catholic missionaries who came to Hawai'i in 1827. He was expelled in 1831 but returned in 1837 and died the same year. (Kuy. 1:139, 142, 150.)

Bachman Hall. Administration building, Mānoa campus, University of Hawai'i, Honolulu, completed in 1949 and named for Paul S. Bachman (1901–1957), fifth president of the University 1955–1957.

Bailey House. Historical Society museum at Wai-luku, Maui. It was originally the main portion of the Wai-luku Female Seminary built in 1837. In 1839 a single-story wing was added. The Reverend Edward Bailey was in charge of the seminary 1841–1849. Mr. and Mrs. Bailey were members of the eighth missionary company, which sailed from Boston in 1836. Also called Hale-hō'ike'ike.

Baldwin. Museum, Lahaina, residence of Dr. and Mrs. Dwight Baldwin 1835–1870; student dormitory, Mauna-'olu College, formerly the residence of Henry Perrine Baldwin, son of Dwight Baldwin; high school at Pu'u-one Hills, Wai-luku, that opened on January 8, 1940, also named for H.P. Baldwin; parks, lower Pā'ia and Pu'u-nēnē, Maui, named for H.A. and F.F. Baldwin, sons of Henry Perrine Baldwin. A house built at 1302 Nehoa Street, Makiki, Honolulu, in 1899 for Henry Perrine Baldwin.

Ball. Mountain, Lahaina Luna, West Maui. See Pa'upa'u.

Bannister. Street and place, Ka-lihi Kai, Honolulu, named for Andrew Bannister, a part-Hawaiian carpenter and contractor who lived there. (TM.)

Banyan. Street, Pā-lama, Honolulu, named for a banyan tree growing near Kau-maka-pili Church. (TM.)

Banzai Pipeline. Surfing beach south and west of Sunset Beach, O'ahu. "Pipeline" refers to the curl of the fast-breaking waves. "Banzai" is the Japanese war cry, suggesting the surfer's risk as he rides (Finney and Houston 81).

Barber's Point. Quadrangle, southwest tip of O'ahu; surfing place (Finney, 1959a:108), beach park, golf course, naval air station, navy housing, elementary school, and oil refinery, all named for Captain

Henry Barber who, on October 31, 1796, was wrecked there on a coral shoal. (Howay 39.) Formerly Ka-lae-loa.

Barking Sands. Beaches, Wai-mea district, Kaua'i (see Ke-one-kani-o-Nohili), and Wai-'anae district, O'ahu (see 'Ōhiki-lolo), so called because the sand sounds loudly when walked upon.

Barron. Lane, Nu'u-anu, Honolulu, named for Charles Barron, active in politics in the early 1900s. (TM.)

Barwick. Playground, Puna-hou School, Honolulu, named for Frank Barwick, a shipwrecked sailor who remained in Hawai'i and was superintendent of grounds and buildings at Puna-hou for 38 years.

Bates. Street, Nu'u-anu, Honolulu, named for attorney A.B. Bates, who arrived in Hawai'i in 1849 and for a short time was tutor to princes Lot and Alexander.

Bay View. Golf center, Kāne-'ohe, O'ahu.

Beckley. Place and street, Ka-lihi Waena, Honolulu, named for Frederick K. Beckley who was chamberlain under Ka-lā-kaua.

Beckwith. Street, Mānoa, Honolulu, named for the Reverend Edward G. Beckwith, principal of Royal School 1852–1854, president of Puna-hou School 1854–1859, pastor of Central Union Church 1887–1894.

Bellows. Air force base and beach park, Wai-mānalo, Ko'olau Poko, O'ahu, named for Lt. F.B. Bellows.

Belser. Street, Ka-imu-kī, Honolulu, named for John J. Belser, a partner in the contracting firm Lord and Belser, active in the 1920s and 1930s.

Beretania. Principal street, Honolulu, a name adopted in 1850. *Lit.,* Britain. *Eng.*

Bertram. Street, St. Louis Heights, Honolulu, named for Brother Bertram (Gabriel Bellinghausen, 1848–1933), a German, first director of St. Louis College. He taught in the school for 22 years beginning in 1881 when the school was located on Nu'u-anu Stream in downtown Honolulu. (Paulin and Bender 17–45.)

Bethel. Street, downtown Honolulu, named for the Seamen's Bethel mission, at King and Bethel streets; destroyed by fire in 1886.

Bilger Hall. Chemistry building, Mānoa Campus, University of Hawai'i, Honolulu, completed in 1951 and named for Dr. Leonora N. Bilger (1893–) and Dr. Earl M. Bilger (1898–1964), professors of chemistry.

Bijou. Place, downtown Honolulu, named for the Bijou Theater located there in the early 1900s. It showed silent moving pictures.

Bingham. Street and section 26 of Honolulu (map 6), often called Bingham Tract, and named for the Reverend Hiram Bingham (1789–1869), leader of the first company of missionaries, who arrived in 1820. Mr. Bingham obtained from the chiefs the land on which Puna-hou School was built by the missionaries. Bingham Hall on the Puna-hou campus was built in 1883 and named for Mr. and Mrs. Bingham. The original Bingham Hall was replaced in 1959.

Bishop. Important street, downtown Honolulu, named for Charles Reed Bishop (1822?–1915), banker, financier, philanthropist, and public official. He married Princess Bernice Pau-ahi and established the Bishop Museum in her honor. The couple lived for many years near the site of the present Bishop Trust building. Bishop Street was cut through their property. Mr. Bishop lived in Hawai'i from 1846 to 1894. In 1858 he founded Bishop and Company Bank, now the First Hawaiian Bank. Charles R. Bishop Hall, built in 1901 and replaced in 1972, was donated by him to Puna-hou School.

B

Bishop Estate Building. Built in 1896 in downtown Honolulu to house the offices of the Bishop Estate, the C.R. Bishop Trust, and the Bernice Pauahi Bishop Museum. The estate offices have been moved, and the building now houses other offices.

Bishop Museum Complex. Charles Reed Bishop established the Bernice Pauahi Bishop Museum in 1889 at Ke-one-'ula in Ka-lihi Waena, Honolulu, as a memorial to his wife, a Hawaiian princess of the Ka-mehameha family. The complex has three buildings: Bishop Hall, built in 1891, was the boys' department of the Ka-mehameha Schools and became a part of the Bishop Museum complex in 1941 when the schools moved. Museum Hall, built in 1899, and Hawaiian Hall, in 1903, are the exhibit areas of the Museum. See Hale-hō'ike-o-Kamehameha.

Black Gorge. Valley, tributary to 'Ī-ao Valley, Wai-luku qd., West Maui.

Black Point. Road, place, point, and surfing area opposite the point, Diamond Head section, Honolulu, also known as Kūpikipiki'ō; lava flow resting on Diamond Head tuff (Macdonald and Abbott 373).

Black Rock Point. A popular "right-slide" surfing area south of Kāne-'īlio Point, Wai-'anae, qd., O'ahu.

Black Sands. See Kala-pana.

Blowhole. See Hālona, Kawelo-hea.

Boiling Pots. Pools in the Wai-luku River, Hilo, Hawai'i, and the favorite kite-flying spot of Māui (Westervelt, 1910:87).

Booth. Road and park, Pauoa, Honolulu, dedicated in 1950 and named for Charles W. Booth (1866–1910) who gave part of the land to the park. (*Honolulu Advertiser,* October 17, 1947.)

Bowers. Street, downtown Honolulu, named for W.W.L. Bowers, a police captain who settled here in 1893 and died in 1915. (TM.)

Bowers Hall. Faculty apartments, Puna-hou campus, Honolulu, built in 1948 and named for Mr. and Mrs. Francis Bowers, long-time supporters of Puna-hou.

Boyd. Street, Punchbowl, Honolulu, named for Robert N. Boyd, grandson of James Boyd, who settled in Hawai'i in 1794 as Ka-mehameha's ship builder. Robert Boyd and Robert W. Wilcox were sent by King Ka-lā-kaua to Italy for a military education. (TM.)

Brennecke. Beach east of Po'ipū Beach Park, Kō-loa district, Kaua'i, famous for body surfing, so named because it fronts the home of Dr. Marvin Brennecke.

Brewer. Building near the foot of Fort Street, Honolulu, opened in 1930, the 104th anniversary of C. Brewer and Company, on the site of an earlier store dating from 1910.

Brewery. On Queen Street, Honolulu, built in 1900 for Primo, and later Royal, beer; last used in 1960; usually called Royal Brewery.

Brigham. Street near the Bishop Museum named for W.T. Brigham, hired by Charles Reed Bishop in 1895 to organize the Bishop Museum and serve as director. (TM.)

Brokaw. Street, Ka-pahulu section, Honolulu, named for the captain of the J.D. Spreckels and Brothers tug *Fearless,* which operated out of Honolulu Harbor in the 1890s and towed sailing vessels into the harbor. (TM.)

Brown. Beach park, Kala-pana qd., Puna, Hawai'i, named in 1953 for Harry Kaina Brown, Hawai'i county auditor. Way, Mānoa, Honolulu, named for Mrs. Marie D. Brown, principal of Mānoa School 1898–1928 *(History of Mānoa School);* she was a descendant of the Beckley and Montano families (TM); golf course, named for Francis Ii Brown, 'Aiea, Wai-pahu qd., O'ahu.

Brown's Reef. Surfing area east of Diamond Head, Honolulu.

Buck. See Peter Buck.

Burbank. Street, Nu'u-anu, Honolulu, named for Mary Burbank, daughter of Judge Samuel Burbank, a lawyer from Maine who settled here in about 1850. Miss Burbank was librarian at the Library of Hawai'i 1891–1903. (TM.)

Bush. Lane, Punchbowl, Honolulu, named for John E. Bush, part-Hawaiian publisher of *Ka Leo o ka Lahui* in 1893; he was governor of Kaua'i in 1877. (TM.)

Byron Ledge. A broad, flat-topped ridge separating Kī-lau-ea from Kī-lau-ea Iki craters, Hawai'i, named for Lord (George Anson) Byron, a cousin of the poet and captain of H.M.S. *Blonde,* which in 1824 brought back the bodies of Ka-mehameha II and his queen, Ka-māmalu, who had died in England. (Olson 17.) Byron camped here in 1825 (Macdonald and Abbott 72).

Byron's Bay. Bay, Wai-ākea, Hilo, Hawai'i. Named for Lord Byron (see Byron Ledge).

CcCcCc

C

Camel's Back. Same as Ka-'āpahu.

Campbell. Avenue, Ka-pahulu section, Honolulu, named for James Campbell who came to Hawai'i in 1858 and died here in 1900. He married Abigail Kuaihelani Ma'i-pinepine (sick often) and was the father of former Territorial senator Ka-mō-kila (the majestic *mo'o*) and Abigail, who married Prince David Ka-wānana-koa. Campbell Avenue was the old approach road to the Campbell summer house. They owned the land that is now Ka-pahulu. (TM.) School named for James Campbell and industrial park owned by the Campbell Estate, near Barber's Point, O'ahu.

Canoes. Name of a surfing area off central Wai-kīkī, Honolulu.

Captain Cook. Town, South Kona, Hawai'i, named for Captain James Cook, who was killed at Ke-ala-ke-kua Bay in 1779. Street, Thomas Square section, Honolulu.

Carlos Long. Street, Pālolo, Honolulu, named for the man (a tax assessor) who opened the tract, and who was the son of an Italian, Charles Appianni; he was adopted and reared by Captain Long. (TM.)

Carnation. Street, Wilhelmina Rise, Honolulu, named for the carnations formerly grown there for the lei business. (TM.)

Cartwright. Park in Makiki and road in Wai-kīkī named for Alexander Joy Cartwright, Jr., whose house was at the site of the present Fort DeRussy. He settled in Honolulu in 1849 as a commission merchant and assisted in many civic enterprises. He died in 1893 and was buried in Nu'u-anu valley. (*Honolulu Star-Bulletin,* May 29, 1954; TM.)

Castle. Hospital, Kai-lua, O'ahu, named for Harold K.L. Castle who donated the land. High school, Kāne-'ohe, O'ahu, and street, Ka-pahulu, Honolulu, named for financier James Bickness Castle (1857–1918), father of Harold K.L. Castle and son of the lay missionary Samuel N. Castle (1808–1894), a founder of the mercantile firm Castle and Cooke. (TM.) Trail, Hau-'ula Forest Reserve, beginning at Puna-lu'u and following the ridge on the Kāne-'ohe side of Ka-lua-nui Stream, Kahana qd., O'ahu. See Kakela, Pu'uhonua.

Castle Hall. Puna-hou School building, Honolulu, built in 1913 with funds donated by the Mary Castle Trust in honor of Mr. and Mrs. Samuel N. Castle. Another Puna-hou building, James B. Castle Hall, was built in 1923.

Castle Memorial Hall. Preschool and primary units, College of Education, University of Hawai'i Mānoa campus, Honolulu, constructed in 1941 as a gift of the Castle Foundation.

Castle's. Deepwater surfing area a mile off-shore, Wai-kīkī, Honolulu, formerly called Ka-lehua-wehe; named for the Castle estate called Kai-nalu which was razed in 1958 for the construction of the Elks clubhouse. Waves at Castle's break from 10 to 25 feet or more in the summer.

Cavendish. Golf course, Lā-naʻi City, Lā-naʻi, built in 1947 and named for Edwin B. Cavendish, builder and designer of the course.

Central Union. Congregational church that was organized in 1887 as a merger of two older churches, Bethel Church (1833–1866) and Fort Street Church (1856–1892); meetings were held at the latter. A new church at Richards and Beretania streets was dedicated in 1892, and the present one at Puna-hou and Beretania in 1924. (Andrade; *Historical Glimpses of Central Union Church 1887–1937.*) The Hawaiian name was Kau-ke-ano.

C

Chain of Craters. Land section and road, Puna qd., Hawaiʻi. Recent eruptions here involving ʻĀloʻi, Alae, Kāne-nui-o-Hamo, Maka-o-puhi, and Nā-pau craters have covered much of the upper section of the road.

Chamberlain. Road, Fort Shafter, Honolulu; street, Puna-hou section, Honolulu, named for Levi Chamberlain (1792–1849), who came to Hawaiʻi in 1823 as a lay missionary; he was business manager of the mission and built Chamberlain House on the mission grounds near Ka-wai-a-Haʻo Church; he was one of the founders of Puna-hou School. (TM.) Chamberlain Field and Chamberlain Drive, Puna-hou School, were named for his grandson, William W. Chamberlain, a financier and former trustee of the school.

Chaminade. College, St. Louis Heights, Honolulu, named for Father William Joseph Chaminade of France, who founded the Society of Mary in 1817. See Kaminaka.

Chaplain. Lane, downtown Honolulu, named for the Reverend Samuel Damon, chaplain of the Seamen's Bethel. (Clark 17.)

Chinaman's Hat. Same as Moko-liʻi.

Chinatown. The area bounded by the Honolulu waterfront, River and Beretania streets, and Nuʻu-anu Avenue. Chinese plantation laborers moved here as early as 1860 after having completed their contracts. In 1900 a fire started by the Board of Health to eradicate bubonic plague broke out of control and swept through twelve blocks. The area was rebuilt as before, with a conglomeration of residences and shops.

Chun (or Chung) Hoon. Lane, ʻAʻala section, Honolulu, named for William Chun Hoon, bookkeeper for the hardware business of E.O. Hall and Son; father of William Chun Hoon, Jr., for many years City and County treasurer. (TM.)

Chun's Reef. Surfing area near the highway between Hale-ʻiwa Park and Wai-mea, Oʻahu.

Church. Lane, Mō-ʻiliʻili, Honolulu, that led to the old Protestant church in the area. (TM.)

Church College of Hawaiʻi. A Mormon college at Lāʻie, Oʻahu, started in 1955; it had about 1,300 students in 1971, many from Pacific islands. See Polynesian Cultural Center.

Clark. Street, Bingham section, Honolulu, named for the Reverend Ephraim W. Clark (1799–1878), pastor of Ka-wai-a-Haʻo Church 1848–1863. (TM.)

Claudine. Street, Wilhelmina Rise, Honolulu, named for an Inter-Island steamer. (TM.)

Cleghorn. Street, Wai-kīkī, Honolulu, named for A.S. Cleghorn, who settled here in 1851 and married Miriam Ka-pili Likelike (sister of Ka-lā-kaua); Princess Ka-ʻiu-lani was their daughter.

C

Clement. Street near Metcalf and Wilder streets, lower Mānoa, Honolulu, named for Father Clement Evrard, a Belgian, who in 1881 was in charge of St. Louis College. See Marques.

Clio. Street, Makiki, Honolulu, named for Clio Newton Chamberlain; she had been given this name by Queen Emma, probably for the ship that carried Emma to England in 1865. Mrs. Chamberlain was a trustee of Luna-lilo Home 1925–1928. (TM.)

Coconut Island. Island in Hilo Bay, Hawaiʻi. See Moku-ola. Island (23.8 acres, 40 feet elevation) in Kāne-ʻohe Bay, Kāne-ʻohe qd., Oʻahu, formerly owned by Chris Holmes, now the location of the Hawaiʻi Institute of Marine Biology of the University of Hawaiʻi, and used for marine research programs of the University. See Moku-o-Loʻe.

Coelho. Way, Nuʻu-anu, Honolulu, named for Senator William Joseph Coelho, who in 1907 introduced in the legislature the resolution that led to the founding of the College of Hawaiʻi, now the University of Hawaiʻi. (TM.)

Colburn. Street, Ka-lihi Kai, Honolulu, named for John F. Colburn, an auctioneer who settled here in 1850. His son was a lawyer and estate manager. (TM.)

College Hill. Residence of the president of the University of Hawaiʻi, built in 1902 for Frank C. Atherton (a son of J.B. Atherton), a gift to the University of Hawaiʻi in 1964 from the Atherton family. College Hill was formerly the name of the area behind Puna-hou School, which was known for a time as Oʻahu College. See Atherton.

College Walk. Street, ʻAʻala section, Honolulu, that led to old St. Louis College. (TM.)

Collins. Street, Diamond Head section, Honolulu, named for George M. Collins, trustee of Bishop Estate, 1928. (TM.)

Community Church of Honolulu. This was formerly the home of E. Faxon Bishop and was built in about 1900 above Nuʻu-anu Stream overlooking Ka-pena Falls.

Cone. Crater and peak (3,653 feet high), Kī-lau-ea qd., Hawaiʻi.

Cooke. Street, Kakaʻako, Honolulu, named for the missionary teacher Amos Starr Cooke (1810–1871) who settled in Hawaiʻi in 1837. He and Mrs. Cooke were in charge of the Chiefs' Children's School (downtown Honolulu) founded in 1839 and in 1846 renamed Royal School; Caucasian students were admitted in 1851. Five of the future rulers of Hawaiʻi were educated here; it is now a public school. (Richards 357.) Later, Cooke went into business and helped found the firm of Castle and Cooke. Cooke Hall (built in 1909) and Cooke Library (1964) on the Puna-hou School campus were both endowed by the Cooke family. See Hana-hau'oli, Honolulu Academy of Arts, Monte Cooke, Spalding.

Coolidge. Street, Mō-'ili'ili, Honolulu, cut through in President Coolidge's time and named for him. (TM.)

Coombs. Lane, Ka-lihi Kai, Honolulu, named for Jack Combs, a realtor and land owner; apparently the street name is misspelled. (TM.)

Cooper. Road, Mānoa, Honolulu, named for Henry E. Cooper, member of the Provisional Government Advisory Council, secretary of the Republic of Hawai'i, and circuit court judge. He built a stone house in Mānoa. (TM.)

Cooper Ranch. See Maka-luhi.

Correa. Road, Mānoa campus, University of Hawai'i, named for Senator Sylvester Philip Correa (1876–1948), printer and politician; he was a Territorial senator in 1917–1919 when Hawai'i College became a university. (TM.)

Coyne. Street, Sheridan Tract, Honolulu, named for Arthur J. Coyne who founded a furniture store in 1899. (TM.)

Craigside. Small street, Nu'u-anu, Honolulu, named for the Theo. H. Davies home that stood there. (TM.)

Crane. Playground, Ka-imu-kī, Honolulu, named for Charles S. Crane, mayor of Honolulu 1935–1938.

Crater. Reservoir and village, Lahaina qd., Maui.

Crawford Hall. Social science building, Mānoa campus, University of Hawai'i, Honolulu, completed in 1938 and named for David Livingstone Crawford (1889–1974), third president of the university 1927–1941.

Crescent Beach. Same as Papa-oneone.

Cromwell's. Surfing area opposite the home of Doris Duke Cromwell at Black Point, Honolulu.

Crouching Lion. See Ka-uhi-'īmaka-o-ka-lani.

Cummins. Street, Ke-walo section Honolulu, named for John Adams Cummins, prominent Hawaiian of the Ka-lā-kaua dynasty and minister of foreign affairs under both Ka-lā-kaua and Lili'u-o-ka-lani. (TM.)

Cunha's. Surfing area, Wai-kīkī (Finney 108), named for the Emanuel S. Cunha estate at Ka-pahulu and Ka-lā-kaua avenues.

Cunha's Alley. Alley connecting Merchant and King streets, just west of Fort Street, downtown Honolulu, named for Emanuel S. Cunha, who kept a saloon here from 1879 until his death in 1918; it became the site of an appliance warehouse in 1968. (Greer.)

Curtis. Street, Kaka'ako, Honolulu, named for Curtis Perry Ward, businessman who built Old Plantation on King Street; he died in 1882. Curtis Street is near the site of his first home. (TM.) See Honolulu International Center, Ward.

DdDdDd

D

Damien. Monument, Ka-laupapa, north central Moloka'i. Kaunakakai qd. Plaza in front of Our Lady of Peace Cathedral, Fort Street Mall, downtown Honolulu, named for Father Damien, the Belgian priest who worked at the leper settlement on Moloka'i and died there of leprosy in 1889. Statues of him stand in the Hawai'i State Capitol and in the United States Capitol in Washington. (Yzendoorn 197–221.)

Damon. Street, Mānoa, Honolulu, named for the Reverend S.C. Damon (1815–1885), for 42 years pastor of the Seamen's Bethel and founder of the church newspaper, *The Friend*. See Chaplain, Moana-lua. (TM.)

Davenport. Place and street, Makiki, Honolulu, named for the Davenport Hotel. (TM.)

Day. Street, Ka-lihi Waena, Honolulu, named for C.J. Day, who established a grocery store on Fort Street in 1892. (TM.)

Dayton. Lane, Nu'u-anu, Honolulu, named for David Dayton, who lived there in 1900 and was marshal of the kingdom of Hawai'i. (TM.)

Dean Hall. General science building, Mānoa campus, University of Hawai'i, Honolulu, completed in 1928 and named for Arthur L. Dean (1878–1952), second president of the university 1914–1927.

DeCorte. Playground, Ka-lihi Uka, named for Manuel DeCorte, teacher and playground director in Ka-lihi; he died in 1947. (*Honolulu Star-Bulletin,* May 3, 1952.)

Dement. Street, Ka-lihi Waena, Honolulu, named for Charles Dement, associated with the Inter-Island Steamship Company. (TM.)

DeRussy. Military reservation, Wai-kīkī, Honolulu, named for Brevet Brigadier General René E. DeRussy, superintendent of the U.S. Military Academy 1833–1838. (Addleman 7.)

Desha. Lane, Pā-lama, Honolulu, named for Isaac Desha, founder of a well-known part-Hawaiian family of Hilo and Honolulu. He settled in Honolulu in 1860 and was first steward of the Queen's Hospital. (TM.)

DeSilva. School, Hilo, Hawai'i, opened in 1959, named for Ernest B. DeSilva, district superintendent, Department of Education, Hawai'i.

Devil's Throat. Small pit crater formed in about 1921 on the east rift zone of Kī-lau-ea volcano, Hawai'i. (Macdonald and Abbott 38.)

Diamond Head. World-famous tuff crater that was formed on O'ahu by violent steam explosions some 100,000 years ago. The highest point is Lē'ahi Peak (760 feet); the rim averages about 400 feet. (Macdonald and Kyselka 18.) It was named for calcite crystals in the rocks that suggested diamonds. The mountain is a State monument. Formerly called Lae-'ahi and sometimes Diamond Hill (Kaimana-Hila) in the 1800s. It was used for *holua* sliding (Wilkes 46).

Circle, road, beach park, and Section 38 of Honolulu (map 6). Surfing area off Diamond Head.

Dillingham. Boulevard, Ka-lihi Kai and Iwilei, Honolulu, named for Benjamin F. Dillingham, a sea captain who settled in Honolulu in 1865; he died in 1918. He promoted land development and was founder of the Oʻahu Railway and Land Company. (TM.) His descendants have been prominent in the development of Honolulu.

Dillingham Hall. Auditorium, Puna-hou School campus, Honolulu, donated by the Dillingham family in 1929.

Dillingham Tennis Courts. Courts on Puna-hou School campus, Honolulu, given by the Walter Dillinghams in honor of their son, Gaylord, killed in World War II. See Gail.

Dillingham Transportation Building. Built in 1929 as an office building in the Bishop Street mercantile district, downtown Honolulu.

Disappearing Sands Beach. A name adopted in 1971 for the beach between Kai-lua and Ke-au-hou, Kai-lua qd., North Kona, Hawaiʻi.

Dole. Street running through the Mānoa campus, University of Hawaiʻi, Honolulu, named for Sanford B. Dole, son of the missionary Reverend Daniel Dole, born in Honolulu in 1844. He was jurist, president of the Provisional Government 1893–1894, president of the Republic of Hawaiʻi 1895–1898, and first governor of the Territory of Hawaiʻi 1898–1903. He died in 1926. A relative, James Dole, planted the first pineapples for canning in 1900 on land acquired from the government at Wahi-a-wā, Oʻahu; in 1901 he organized the Hawaiian Pineapple Company. He had a simple frame house on Dole Street, Wahi-a-wā, and in 1919 he bought the George Davies home on Green Street, Honolulu, distinguished by a circular turret.

Dominis. Street, Makiki, Honolulu, named for John Owen Dominis, governor of Oʻahu under Ka-lā-kaua, and consort of Queen Liliʻu-o-ka-lani. (TM.)

Donaghho. Street on the Mānoa campus, University of Hawaiʻi, Honolulu, named for John S. Donaghho, professor of mathematics and astronomy at the university 1908–1934. (TM.)

Doris. Place, Mānoa, Honolulu, named for Mrs. Doris Owen, wife of C.G. Owen, superintendent of the Pacific Guano and Fertilizer Company. It was named by Robert Booth who owned and subdivided the Mānoa property in 1915. (TM.)

Dow. Street, Nuʻu-anu, Honolulu, named for the brothers C.S. and A.J. Dow who lived there in the early 1900s. (TM.)

Dowsett. Avenue, Dowsett Highlands, Honolulu, named for Captain Samuel James Dowsett, who settled in Hawaiʻi in 1828, the first of the well-known Dowsett family. His eldest son, James Isaac, was the first white child, other than those of missionary parents, to be born in Hawaiʻi. (TM.)

Dowsett Highlands. Section 12 of Honolulu (map 6). See Dowsett.

Dreier. Street, Kakaʻako, Honolulu, named for August Dreier, industralist, who founded ʻEleʻele Plantation on Kauaʻi in 1884. He built a residence in Honolulu and donated property to the Catholic Church. (TM.)

Dudoit. Lane, Wai-kīkī, Honolulu, named for the family of Captain

D

Duke Ka-hana-moku

Jules Dudoit, who came to Hawai'i in 1833, served as French consul 1837–1845, assisted in the founding of the Catholic mission, and managed an early coffee plantation on Kaua'i. He was murdered in 1866. (TM.)

Duke Ka-hana-moku. See Ka-hana-moku.

Duval. Street, Ka-pahulu section, Honolulu, named for Albert Duval, a chemist with the Pacific Guano and Fertilizer Company. (TM.)

D

EeEeEeE

Eckert. Road on the Mānoa campus, University of Hawai'i, named for C.F. Eckert, director of the Hawaiian Sugar Planters' Association experiment station 1909–1913, and a university regent. (TM.)

Edmondson Hall. Zoology building, Mānoa campus, University of Hawai'i, Honolulu, completed in 1962 and named for Charles Howard Edmondson (1876–1970), professor of marine zoology 1920–1942.

'Ehakō. Street, Nu'u-anu, Honolulu. (TM.) *Lit.,* dove.

'Ēheu. Street, Pu'u-nui, Honolulu. (TM.) *Lit.,* wing.

'Ehu-kai. Streets, Wai-mānalo, and between Maka-pu'u and Koko Head, Honolulu; beach park and surfing area, Lā-ie qd., O'ahu. *Lit.,* sea spray.

'Ēkaha. Street, Wilhelmina Rise, Honolulu. (TM.) *Lit.,* bird's-nest fern.

'Ēkaha-nui. Land section, wind, and cave near the head of Lepelepe Gulch, Ka-malō qd., south Moloka'i. Gulch, Honouliuli, O'ahu. *Lit.,* large bird's-nest fern.

'Eke. Land section, Wai-pi'o qd., Hawai'i. Crater and peak (4,480 feet high), near the border between Lahaina and Wai-luku qds., West Maui.

'Ekekela. Avenue, Pu'u-nui, Honolulu. (TM.) *Lit.,* Esther.

'Ekela. Avenue, Ala Wai section, Honolulu. *Lit.,* Ethel.

Ēkoa. Street, 'Āina-Haina, Honolulu. (TM.) *Lit.,* false *koa* tree.

'Eleao. Land section, Wai-kāne qd., O'ahu. *Lit.,* plant louse.

'Ele'ele. Village, ditch, small-boat harbor, landing, and elementary school, Kō-loa district, Kaua'i; Port Allen was called 'Ele'ele Landing until 1909 when it was renamed in honor of a Honolulu merchant, Samuel Cresson Allen (Stroup 35). Land section, Wai-luku qd., West Maui. *Lit.,* black.

'Ele-hāhā. Stream, tributary of Wai-mea Stream, O'ahu. *Lit.,* black stalk (as of taro).

'Elelū. Land section, Hālawa qd., Moloka'i. *Lit.,* cockroach.

'Ele-lupe. Road, Kuli-'ou'ou, Honolulu.

'Elena. Street, Nu'u-anu, Honolulu. (TM.) *Lit.,* Ellen.

'Elepaio. Street, Kāhala, Honolulu. *Lit.,* flycatcher (a Hawaiian bird, *Chasiempis sandwichensis*).

'Ele-uweuwe. Hill (1,145 feet high), Kaunakakai qd., north Moloka'i. *Lit.,* swaying blackness.

Elizabeth. See Fort Elizabeth.

Elks Club. Building and surfing area, Wai-kīkī, Honolulu. (Finney, 1959a:108–109.)

'Elua. Street, Ka-lihi Uka, Honolulu. (TM.) *Lit.,* two.

'Eluwene. Street, Ka-lihi Kai, Honolulu. (TM.) *Lit.,* Edwin.

'Emekona. Place, Woodlawn, upper Mānoa, Honolulu. *Lit.,* Emerson. (Named for Nathaniel B. Emerson [1839–1915], author of *Unwrit-*

ten Literature of Hawai'i and *Pele and Hiiaka,* who owned property there. He was the son of the Reverend John S. Emerson, a missionary who arrived in 1832; TM.)

Emerson. Street, Thomas Square section, Honolulu, named for Mrs. Joseph S. Emerson (1843–1930), whose husband was the brother of Nathaniel B. Emerson (see 'Emekona), a surveyor and writer on Hawaiian ethnology who lived there.

E

Emma. See Queen Emma.

Emmeline. Place, Ka-lihi Uka, Honolulu, named for Emmeline Afong Magoon, daughter of Chun Afong and his wife Julia Fayerweather Afong, and wife of John Magoon. (TM.)

Emmeluth. Lane, Ka-pā-lama section, Honolulu, named for John F. Emmeluth, who had a plumbing establishment on the site of the former Bishop Trust Building on King Street until his death in 1898. (TM.)

'Ena. Road, Wai-kīkī, Honolulu, named for the son of John 'Ena (a Chinese merchant) and High Chiefess Ka-iki-lani; the son was privy councillor under Queen Lili'u-o-ka-lani and cofounder and president of the Inter-Island Steamship Company. (TM.)

Enchanted Lake. Subdivision, school, and park, Kai-lua, O'ahu, formerly called Ka-'ele-pulu Pond.

Enos. Lane, Puna-hou section, Honolulu, named for Joe Enos, a house painter of the early 1900s. (TM.)

'Eu. Lane, Iwilei, Honolulu. (TM.) *Lit.,* rascal.

Eugene. Street, St. Louis Heights, Honolulu, named for Brother Eugene (John Merkel), an instructor at St. Louis College who came in 1898. (Cf. TM.)

'Ewa. Plantation, plantation town, elementary school, and quadrangle west of Pearl Harbor, O'ahu. *Lit.,* crooked. (Kāne and Kanaloa threw a stone to determine district boundaries. The stone was lost but was found later at Pili-o-Kahe. See PE, *'ewa'ewa;* Ii 98; Sterling and Summers 1:8; UL 84.)

'Ewa Beach. A new name for an elementary school and for the beach between Pu'u-loa and One-'ula beaches, O'ahu.

FfFfFfFf

Farr. Lane, Ka-lihi Waena, Honolulu, named for George William Farr (1864–1948), treasurer and director of Von Hamm-Young Company; he married Sarah Ka-lei-kau, a full-blooded Hawaiian, and was father of George M. Farr, a deputy police chief. (TM.)

Farrington. Street, Bingham and Mānoa sections; high school, Ka-lihi Kai, Honolulu; and highway, Pearl City to the leeward coast, O'ahu; all named for Wallace Rider Farrington, governor of Hawai'i 1921–1929, and publisher of the *Honolulu Star-Bulletin* 1929–1933; he was the father of Joseph Rider Farrington, a Territorial delegate to Congress. (TM.)

Farrington Hall. Former University of Hawai'i theater, Honolulu, completed in 1930 and named for Wallace Rider Farrington, governor of the Territory of Hawai'i 1921–1929, and chairman of the university's board of regents 1914–1920. The building is scheduled for demolition (1972).

Federal Building. Built in 1922 in downtown Honolulu to house the offices of Federal agencies, now including post office, customs, and U.S. Attorney.

Felix. Street, St. Louis Heights, Honolulu, named for Brother Felix (John Rost), an instructor at St. Louis College. (Cf. TM.)

Ferdinand. Street, Mānoa, Honolulu, named in 1898 for Ferdinand Schnack, son of the subdivider of the area, John H. Schnack. (TM.)

Fern. Elementary school and playground, Ka-lihi Waena, named for Joseph J. Fern, first mayor of Honolulu 1909–1919; street, Pā-wa'a and McCully sections, Honolulu, named for George Fern, brother of Mayor Joseph Fern. (TM.)

Fernandez. Street, Ka-lihi Waena, Honolulu, named for Abraham Fernandez, a full-blooded Hawaiian born in 1857 to Ka-lama Māhoe and adopted by her second husband, Peter Fernandez. Abraham married Minerva Davis; both were workers in the Mormon mission. (TM.) Their son, E[dwin] K[āne] Fernandez, was for many years a well-known carnival and circus entrepreneur for all the Islands. He died in 1970.

Fern Grotto. Cave-like grotto, Wai-lua River, Kaua'i.

Fernhurst. YWCA residence at Wilder and Puna-hou streets, Honolulu, completed in 1952 and named for the residence at King and Alapa'i streets of J.B. Atherton. The Atherton home was given to the YWCA and later sold to the Honolulu Rapid Transit Company. The present Fernhurst is on the site of the old Pleasanton Hotel, which had been the family home of Paul Isenberg of H. Hackfeld and Company. (*Honolulu Star-Bulletin,* March 28, 29, 1952.)

Fireworks Cliff. Same as Makana.

First Break. Farthest offshore Wai-kīkī surfing area. (Finney and Houston 83.)

F

First Chinese Church of Christ. Originally located on Fort Street, downtown Honolulu. In 1929, on the fiftieth anniversary of the church in Hawai'i, the congregation moved into a new building, designed by Hart Wood, at 1054 South King Street. The building has Chinese features: a pagoda-like bell tower, clay roof tiles, and a stucco-over-stonework finish.

First Church of Christ Scientist. Built in 1923 on Puna-hou Street, the church was designed by Hart Wood, who pioneered in adapting traditional architectural styles and building materials to Hawai'i's climate and heritage.

Flies. Surfing area on the town side of the incinerators, Kaka'ako, Honolulu, named for unsanitary conditions at the City dump.

Fleming's Beach. A beach named for David Thomas Fleming (1881–1955). See Kapa-lua.

Ford Island. Island in Pearl Harbor and golf course, named for a former owner, Dr. S.P. Ford (1818–1866), a Honolulu physician during the 1850s and 1860s. In 1862, when roads were coming into existence on the island, local newspapers reported that he often drove in a carriage to the other side of O'ahu. (McClellan, 1937.) See Moku-'ume'ume, Poka 'Ailana.

Forrest Hall. Puna-hou School building, Honolulu, named in honor of Aileen Forrest, former alumni executive secretary.

Fort. Principal street, downtown Honolulu. At its foot was the fort at Honolulu Harbor built in 1816 and destroyed in 1857. The Hawaiian name Pāpū (fort) was adopted in 1850. (TM.) Most of the street was converted into a pedestrian mall in 1968.

Fort Elizabeth. State park, Wai-mea Kaua'i. On this land donated by Ka-umu-ali'i, Georg Anton Scheffer began construction of a fort in 1816 called Fort Elizabeth in honor of the consort of the Russian Emperor Alexander (Kuy. 1:58; Pierce). The fort was attacked during a local rebellion in 1824 (Kuy. 1:118).

Fort Ruger. State park and military reservation, Diamond Head, Honolulu. See Ruger.

Fort Shafter. Military reservation and golf course, Moana-lua, Honolulu. See Shafter.

Foster Botanic Garden. City park at Nu'u-anu Avenue and Vineyard Boulevard, downtown Honolulu. In 1855 Queen Ka-lama (wife of Ka-mehameha III) sold the original property to Dr. William Hillebrand, botanist and physician at the Queen's Hospital 1851–1871. The estate was purchased in 1890 by Captain and Mrs. Thomas Foster, and in 1930 Mrs. Foster (Mary E. Foster) willed six acres to the City and County of Honolulu. (*Honolulu Star-Bulletin,* January 3, 1931.) See Wood.

Foster Tower. Hotel in Wai-kīkī, Honolulu developed by and named for T. Jack Foster, Sr., in 1962.

Foster Village. Subdivision, Hālawa, Wai-pahu qd., O'ahu, developed by and named for T. Jack Foster, Sr., in 1957.

Frank. Street, St. Louis Heights, Honolulu, named for Brother Frank (Francis Herold), an instructor at St. Louis College who came to Hawai'i in 1883. (Cf. TM.)

Frear. Street, Thomas Square section, Honolulu, named for Walter Francis Frear, governor of Hawai'i 1907–1913. He married Mary Dillingham; their home was a mansion named Arcadia on Puna-hou Street, now the site of a retirement home of the same name.

Frear Hall. Women's dormitory, Mānoa campus, University of Hawai'i, Honolulu, completed in 1952 and named for Mary Dillingham Frear, daughter of B.F. Dillingham, university regent for 23 years.

Freeland. Street, Thomas Square section, Honolulu, so named because the land was "free" to be sold in fee simple lots. (TM.)

French Frigate Shoals. An atoll reef in the Northwest (Leeward) Hawaiian Islands, with about 16 small sand islets and a 120-foot-high rock, La Pérouse Pinnacle (*or* Rock). Total land area is about 0.09 square mile. These islets were officially annexed to the Republic of Hawai'i in 1895, and are now part of the City and County of Honolulu. They were discovered and surveyed by the French navigator La Pérouse on March 6, 1786. He almost lost his two frigates here. (Bryan, 1942:175–178; Macdonald and Abbott 403.)

Frog. Lane, Nu'u-anu, Honolulu, named for the many frogs in the taro patches there. (TM.)

Funchal. Street, Nu'u-anu, Honolulu, named by the Portuguese who settled there for the capital of their old home in the Azores. (TM.)

F

GgGgGg

G

Gail. Street, Diamond Head section, Honolulu, named for Gail Dillingham, granddaughter of Walter Dillingham, subdivider of the tract. (TM.)

Gardner Pinnacles. Two islands, now a bird sanctuary, in the Northwestern (Leeward) Hawaiian Islands, with an approximate area of 0.005 square mile and a maximum elevation of about 170 feet. They were discovered on June 20, 1820, by the American whaler *Maro* of Nantucket, under the command of Captain Joseph Allen. They were annexed to Hawai'i in 1898 and are now a part of the City and County of Honolulu. (Bryan, 1942:179–182; Macdonald and Abbott 403–404.)

Gartley. Place, Nu'u-anu, Honolulu, named for Alonzo Gartley, a Navy officer who settled in Hawai'i in 1900 and became an industrialist (manager of Hawaiian Electric Company until 1910 and vice-president of C. Brewer and Company until his death in 1921). (TM.) He was chairman of the first board of regents of the University of Hawai'i; Gartley Hall on the Mānoa campus, completed in 1922, was named for him.

Gateway House. Dormitory, Mānoa campus, University of Hawai'i, Honolulu, completed in 1963. It was the first dormitory in Hawai'i built for graduate students and also the first coed dormitory.

George Hall. Former library, Mānoa campus, University of Hawai'i, Honolulu, completed in 1924. After Sinclair Library was completed in 1956, the building was remodeled for the art department and was named for William H. George (1878–1949), dean of the College of Arts and Sciences 1930–1938.

George Washington Stone. See Kahiki-lani.

Gertz. Lane, Ka-lihi Waena, Honolulu, named for Christian Gertz, proprietor of Gertz Shoe Store, located in the 1880s at the corner of King and Fort streets. (TM.)

Gilmore Hall. Agriculture building, Mānoa campus, University of Hawai'i, Honolulu, completed in 1935 and named for John W. Gilmore, professor of rural economy and agronomy, and first president of the College of Agriculture and Mechanic Arts 1908–1913. In 1919 the college became the University of Hawai'i.

Glenwood. Village, Hilo qd., Puna district, Hawai'i, built in 1901 as a terminal of the Hilo Railroad. See Ka-pu'e-uhi.

Green. Street, Thomas Square section, Honolulu, named for William Lowthian Green, merchant and statesman. He was minister of foreign affairs and later, minister of finance under Ka-lā-kaua until his retirement in 1889. (TM.)

Green Lake. Same as Wai-a-Pele.

Gregory. Street near Bishop Museum, Ka-lihi Waena, Honolulu, named for Herbert E. Gregory, geologist, and trustee and director of the museum 1920–1936. (TM.)

Grey's Beach. Small beach just Diamond Head of the Hale-kū-lani Hotel, Wai-kīkī, Honolulu. The reef was opened here for a boat landing. The Hawaiian name was Ka-wehewehe (the opening up). The sick bathed here as a treatment.

Griffiths. Street, Bingham section, Honolulu, named for Arthur Floyd Griffiths, principal of Puna-hou School 1902–1921. (TM.) Griffiths Hall, Puna-hou School, built in 1957, was also named for him.

G

Grove Farm. Sugar plantation, Līhu'e, Kaua'i, started in 1864 by George N. Wilcox (1893–1933), planter and philanthropist; he was a son of the missionaries Abner and Lucy Wilcox. (Krauss.) See Wilcox.

Gulick. Street, Ka-lihi Kai and Ka-lihi Waena, Honolulu, named for Charles T. Gulick (TM), minister of interior under Lili'u-o-ka-lani and nephew of Peter J. Gulick, missionary in the third (1828) company (Kuy. 3:268n).

Gulston. Street, St. Louis Heights, named for the Most Reverend Gulston Ropert (1839–1903), Catholic bishop, fourth vicar apostolic of the Hawaiian mission 1892–1903. He was born in France. (Yzendoorn 228–233.)

Gump Building. Wai-kīkī building, especially designed and constructed to house the Gump collection of art treasures, opened in 1929. It now houses offices and a restaurant.

HhHhHh

Ha'aheo. Coastal area and elementary school, Hilo qd., Hawai'i. *Lit.,* pride (Ka-mehameha I ordered his people to plant a large area in taro in a single day; they did so, and he told them he was "proud" of them).

Ha'akoa. Land section and stream near Lau-pāhoehoe village, Hawai'i. *Lit.,* low *koa* tree *or* warrior-like.

Ha'akula-manu. Old name for Sulfur Banks, Kī-lau-ea volcano, Hawai'i. *Lit.,* like a birds' gathering place.

Ha'alele-pa'akai. Mountain summit, east Lā-na'i. *Lit.,* salt left (bags of salt were left here when travelers mistook dew at Pālāwai for salt; Emory, 1924:20).

Ha'alili-a-manu. Old section of Honolulu near the Hotel Street bridge over Nu'u-anu Stream. *Lit.,* fluttering by birds.

Hā'ao. Spring, land section, and church in Wai-'ōhinu, Honu-'apo qd., Ka'ū, Hawai'i (RC 158), named for a Ka'ū rain and a supernatural girl. Valley, central Ni'ihau.

Ha'eha'e. Land division near Kumu-kahi, Maku'u qd., Hawai'i. *Ka hikina a ka lā i Ha'eha'e* (PH 189), the rising of the sun at Ha'eha'e. See Kumu-kahi.

Hā'ele'ele. Ridge and valley near Poli-hale, Wai-mea district, western Kaua'i. *Lit.,* blackish.

Hā'ena. Land section and village, Kohala qd.; land section and village, Maku'u qd.; land section, Ka'ū district, Hawai'i. Land section, village, *heiau,* caves, point, and beach park, Hanalei, Kaua'i. Drive, Mānoa, Honolulu; *heiau* of Ka-mehameha I at 'Ewa, O'ahu (RC 173). *Lit.,* red hot. *A Lohi'au-ipo i Hā'ena lā, 'ena'ena ke aloha ke hiki mai* (UL 249), and Lohi'au-ipo at Red-hot, hot the love that comes.

*Haha. Falls, Ka-malō qd., south Moloka'i.

Hahae-ule. Hill (1,674 feet high), Kaunakakai qd., north Moloka'i. *Lit.,* tear [the] penis.

Haha'i-one. Elementary school, park, and street, Hawai'i-kai, Honolulu; valley, and the name of the Ka-mehameha Schools farm, Koko Head qd., O'ahu. The eastern part of Sandy Beach, O'ahu, also is called Haha'i-one; in whaling days ships anchored off this beach. *Lit.,* sand broken.

Hāhā-kea. Land division and gulch, Lahaina qd., West Maui. Perhaps *lit.,* white stalk.

Hāhā-lawe. Gulch, Kī-pahulu qd., East Maui, *Lit.,* break carry.

Haia-moa. Stream, Wai-he'e, O'ahu. *Lit.,* chicken chased.

Ha'i-kū. Land division and point, Honomū qd., Hawai'i. Land section, Līhu'e district, Kaua'i. Quadrangle, land section, village, elementary school, park, reservoir, ditch, East Maui. Valley, Kāne-'ohe qd., O'ahu. *Lit.,* speak abruptly *or* sharp break.

Ha'i-kū Gardens. A restaurant, Kāne-'ohe qd., O'ahu. The land was originally a part of Ka-limu-kele and was awarded to Hawaiians in the Great Mahele. It was owned by Edwin Baskerville until his death in 1924, then was sold to Oliver Stillman in 1926, and to Wilhelmina Tenney in 1927. She maintained a home here until her death in 1951. See Wilhelmina Rise.

Ha'i-kū Uka. Land section, Ha'i-kū qd., East Maui. *Lit.,* upland Ha'i-kū.

Haili. Forest area near Hilo, Hawai'i; timber was brought from here to build a church of the same name, said to have been built by Kua-kini (RC 390). Road, Pacific Heights, Honolulu. *Lit.,* loving memory.

*Haina. Land section, Hāmākua qd., Hawai'i.

Hainoa. Crater and hill, Kai-lua qd., North Kona, Hawai'i. A house platform formerly here was said to mark the home of the god Kū and his wife Hina. An *'ohi'a* tree called Kū-'ohi'a-laka grew here; it was the tree form of Kū. A large furrow marks the position of the tree.

Haipua'ena. Stream, Ke-'anae qd., East Maui.

Haka. Drive, Ka-mehameha Housing area, Ka-lihi Kai, Honolulu. (TM.) *Lit.,* shelf, perch (as for chickens).

Hāka'a'ano. Coastal flat, Hālawa qd., north Moloka'i.

Haka-kau-pueo. Congregational church at Huelo, Ha'i-kū qd., East Maui. *Lit.,* owl-resting perch (owls perched in a pandanus grove here).

Haka-lau. Village, land division, bay, gulch, and stream, Honomū qd.—the 1946 tsunami waves reached heights of 37 feet here and destroyed a sugar mill (Macdonald and Abbott 257–258); elementary school in the town of Hilo, Hawai'i. *Lit.,* many perches.

Hakina. Gulch, 'Īlio Pt. qd., south Moloka'i. See Pu'u-hakina. *Lit.,* broken piece.

Haki-o-awa. Bay and land area, north Ka-ho'olawe, where the fish demigod 'Ai'ai set up an altar *(kū'ula)* on a bluff looking out to sea (HM 22). *Lit.,* breaking of [the] harbor.

Haki-pu'u. Valley, land division, and stream, Wai-kāne qd., O'ahu. Kaha'i, a famous navigator, lived here and traveled to Samoa to bring back seeds and breadfruit; he was so respected that Ka-mehameha I in 1795 lowered the sail of his canoe in honor of his memory. (Sterling and Summers 5:38a.) *Lit.,* hill broken.

Haku-he'e. Point, Ka-haku-loa qd., Maui. Probably *lit.,* fleeing lord.

Haku-ola. Gulch, Pūpū-kea, Ka-huku qd., O'ahu. *Lit.,* living lord.

Hala. Drive, Ka-mehameha Heights, Honolulu. (TM.) *Lit.,* pandanus.

Hala'ea. The name of the current coming from the east at Ka Lae (South Point), Hawai'i, which meets a current from the west named Kāwili; the two currents go out to sea together. Hala'ea was named for a chief. A stone on the shore nearby, Pōhaku-o-ke-au (stone of the time), is believed to turn over in strong seas, an omen of coming change. (For a saying, see Appendix 8.1.)

Hāla'i. Hills, Hilo, Hawai'i. Hina, Māui's mother, gave this area to her daughter, Hina-ke-ahi, goddess of fire. A famine occurred and Hina-ke-ahi ordered her people to dig an earth oven. She placed herself in the oven and lit the fire. She then sank through the oven stones down to the underworld and became a gushing stream. On

35

the second day she emerged as a pool near the sea, and on the third day a spring burst forth. She washed herself and returned to the oven, ordering the people to open it. They found abundant food (Westervelt, n.d.: 157–161). See Pōhaku-nui, Puʻu-honu. *Lit.*, peaceful.

Hala-kaʻa. Land division, Lahaina qd., Maui. Probably *lit.*, rolling pandanus.

H

Halāliʻi. Cinder cone, Hale-a-ka-lā Crater, East Maui. Land section and lake, south central Niʻihau, named for its owner and famous for sugarcane growing in the sand with only leaves protruding. (See PE, *kō;* UL 101.) Hālāliʻi is the name of an Oʻahu trickster demigod (HM 430).

Hala-pē. Area and trail, Puna qd., Puna district near the Kaʻū boundary, Hawaiʻi. *Lit.*, crushed missing. (Gourds growing here were completely buried by shifting winds; people not knowing of them would "miss" them, hence the saying *I Hala-pē aku nei paha,* maybe at Hala-pē, said when things were not found. Also said of drunks, with *pē* in this case meaning 'soaked'.)

Hala-pepe. Drive, ʻĀina-Haina, Honolulu, named for a native tree.

Hālau-a-lolo. *Heiau,* Kai-lua, Mō-kapu qd., Oʻahu. *Lit.*, house of brains.

Hala-ʻula. Land section and village, Kohala qd., Hawaiʻi. Areas, Hanalei and Ka-wai-hau districts, Kauaʻi. *Lit.*, red pandanus.

Hālau-lani. Land division near the Pineapple Research Institute, Wai-piʻo, Wai-pahu qd., Oʻahu; ʻAhu-ʻena *heiau* was formerly here (Sterling and Summers 1:94–95). *Lit.*, high-born chief's large house.

Hālawa. Land section, village, gulch, and mill, Kohala qd., North Kohala, Hawaiʻi (Ii 13). Land section, peak, village, beach park, bay, point, stream, cape, and quadrangle, east Molokaʻi. (For 12 wind names here, see For. 5:102–103.) Land section, district park, elementary school, town, and stream, Wai-pahu qd., Oʻahu (Ii 70). *Lit.*, curve.

Hālawa Iki. Gulch, Hālawa qd., north Molokaʻi. *Lit.*, small Hālawa.

Hale. Beach park, Kala-pana qd., Puna district, Hawaiʻi, named in 1951 for Isaac Hale of Puna, Hawaiʻi, killed in action in Korea. *Lit.*, house.

Hale-ʻaʻama. *Heiau* at Kaha-luʻu, North Kona, Hawaiʻi. *Lit.*, loosening house.

Hale-ʻaha. Land division and gulch, Kamuela qd., Hawaiʻi. Land section, Kahana qd., Oʻahu (see also For. Sel. 222). *Lit.*, meeting house.

Hale-a-ka-lā. National park (established in 1961), volcano, crater, peak, ranch, and visitor center, East Maui; homesteads, Kahului qd., Maui. *Lit.*, house [used] by the sun (the demigod Māui was believed to have lassoed the sun here in order to lengthen the day, and permit his mother, Hina, to dry her tapa). Name of the home of Mr. and Mrs. Charles R. Bishop at the site of the Bishop Trust Building at Bishop and King streets; classroom building (built in 1931) at Ka-mehameha Schools, Honolulu.

Hale-ʻauʻau. Gulch, Wai-a-lua, Oʻahu. (For. Sel. 278; Ii 97; PH 100.) See Ka-lena. *Lit.*, bathhouse.

Hale-ʻauhau. State government building, Department of Taxation. *Lit.*, tax house.

Hale-haku. Bay, gulch, land section, and point, Haʻi-kū qd., Maui. *Lit.*, master house.

Hale-hōʻikeʻike. Historical Society museum at Wai-luku, Maui. See Bailey House. *Lit.*, exhibition house, museum.

Hale-hōʻikeʻike-o-Kamehameha. Hawaiian name of Bernice P. Bishop Museum, Honolulu. *Lit.*, exhibition house of Ka-mehameha.

Hale-ʻiwa. Town, elementary school, beach park, surfing beach (Finney, 1959*a*:108), and quadrangle, Oʻahu. *Lit.*, house [of] frigate bird (*ʻiwa* birds were admired for their beauty). See PE, *ʻiwa.*

Hale-kahawai. Women's dormitory, Mānoa campus, University of Hawaiʻi, Honolulu, completed in 1963. *Lit.*, river house (Mānoa Stream is behind the building).

Hale-ka-mahina. Hill and land sections, Makuʻu and Kala-pana qds., Puna, Hawaiʻi. *Lit.*, house [of] the moon.

Hale-kamani. Street, Niu, Honolulu. (TM.) *Lit.*, *kamani*-tree house.

Hale-kauwila. Street, downtown Honolulu, named in 1875 for the thatched house built here of *kauwila* wood in the 1820s on land now belonging to American Factors. (Clark 13.) The wood of the house is said to have been taken from the rafters in the sacred house of Līloa at Wai-piʻo, Hawaiʻi, a burial place of chiefs. (*The Friend,* May 1890, p. 34.)

Hale-kiʻi. Land section, Kai-lua qd., South Kona, Hawaiʻi. Alternate name for the *heiau* at Pihana, Maui. *Lit.*, image house.

Hale-koa. Drive and place, Wai-ʻalae, Honolulu. *Lit.*, soldiers' house (referring to a Bishop Estate subdivision for veterans in the area). (TM.) ʻIo-lani Barracks on the Palace grounds in downtown Honolulu was once known as Hale-koa.

Hale-kou. Coastal area east of Pelekunu Bay, Molokaʻi. Fishpond, Mō-kapu, Oʻahu. *Lit.*, *kou*-wood house.

Hale-kua. Stream, Wai-mea district, Kauaʻi. *Lit.*, tapa-beating house.

Hale Kuahine. Women's dormitory, East-West Center, University of Hawaiʻi, Honolulu, completed in 1962; named for the Kuahine (sister) rain of Mānoa Valley.

Hale Kula. Elementary school at Schofield Barracks, Oʻahu, and way near Puna-hou School, Honolulu. *Lit.*, school house.

Hale-kū-lani. Hotel, Wai-kīkī, Honolulu, dating from 1917. Before that time, Mr. and Mrs. Robert Lewers had a residence and hotel there named Hau Tree (the *hau* tree there is said to be between 150 and 200 years old). See Lewers. *Lit.*, house befitting royalty.

Hale-lani. Drive, upper Mānoa, Honolulu. (TM.) *Lit.*, chief['s] house.

Hale Laulima. Women's dormitory, Mānoa campus, University of Hawaiʻi, Honolulu, completed in 1969. *Lit.*, cooperative house.

Hale-leʻa. Land division and forest reserve, Hanalei district, Kauaʻi. Street, Mānoa, Honolulu. *Lit.*, joyful house.

Hale-lena. Place and former land section, Mānoa, Honolulu. *Lit.*, yellow house. (See Indices 740 for awards.)

Hale-loulu. Spring near Puʻu-kolekole, Ka-malō qd., Molokaʻi. *Lit.*, house thatched [with] *loulu* palm.

Hale-lua. Land section, Pāhala qd., Kaʻū; land section, gulch, and surf- **37**

ing area of ancient Hawai'i, Kohala qd., Hawai'i (Finney and Houston 26), home of the beautiful Kama-lālā-walu when she lived with Kū-moho (For. Sel. 271). Ancient surfing area, Lahaina, West Maui (Finney, 1959a:52, 1959b:347). *Lit.,* pit house.

Hale-mano. Same as Hele-mano. (For. Sel. 250; RC 207, 424; UL 242.) *Lit.,* many houses.

H

Hale Mānoa. Dormitory, East-West Center, University of Hawai'i, Honolulu, completed in 1962 and named for Mānoa Valley.

Hale-manu. Peak and stream, Wai-mea district, Kaua'i. *Lit.,* bird house.

Hale-ma'uma'u. Crater (3,646 feet elevation), also known as the fire pit, within the larger Kī-lau-ea Crater, and trail, Kī-lau-ea qd., Hawai'i. *Lit.,* fern house.

Hale-mau'u. Trail, Hale-a-ka-lā Crater, East Maui. *Lit.,* grass house.

Hālena. Gulch and shore area, 'Īlio Pt. qd., south Moloka'i. Cream-colored beach rock, valuable for flagstones, is common here (Stearns and Macdonald, 1947:27). *Lit.,* yellowish.

Hale-nānahu. Stream and reservoir, Līhu'e district, Kaua'i. *Lit.,* charcoal house.

Hale-o-Kāne. *Heiau* near Ka-loko, Hawai'i, recommended for preservation. (Emory and Soehren.) *Lit.,* house of Kāne.

Hale-o-Kapuni. *Heiau* site near Ka-wai-hae, Hawai'i, to be restored. Ka-mehameha I is said to have used this *heiau,* and sharks were fed here. Rocks from here may have been used to build Pu'u-koholā *heiau. Lit.,* house of Kapuni (a high priest of the chief Keawe).

Hale-o-Keawe. *Heiau* at Hōnaunau, North Kona, Hawai'i, built by Chief Keawe as a mausoleum, now a part of City of Refuge National Historical Park. (Ii 138; RC 203, 285.) *Lit.,* house of Keawe.

Hale-ola. Street and place, Niu, Honolulu, named for Hale-ola Hart, Jr., the only grandson of Edmund and Annie Love Hart; Congregational church, Mānoa; infirmary built in 1940, Ka-mehameha Schools, Honolulu. *Lit.,* house [of] life.

Hale-o-Lono. Land section, Hōlei Pali, Hawai'i. In ancient times the rain was so heavy here that it washed away all growing plants. The angry people caught some rain, put it in an oven, and saw it escape as a cloud at Pu'u-kapukapu. *(Hawaii Natural History Association Guide* 12.) See Kūkae-'ula'ula. On all the islands there are ancient *heiau* of this name for worship of Lono, including ceremonies to bring rain and growth; one overlooks Hāmoa Beach, Maui. Bay, northwest Lā-na'i. Land section and site of a former village, 'Īlio Pt. qd., southwest coast of Moloka'i; a harbor was built here in the late 1950s; canoe races to O'ahu start here. (For. Sel. 254; Ii 57.) *Lit.,* house of Lono.

Hale-one. Hill, Hālawa qd., south Moloka'i. Land section, Hanalei district, Kaua'i. *Lit.,* sand house.

Hale-palaoa. Landing, east Lā-na'i. *Lit.,* whale house.

Hale-pōhāhā. Hill, Honu-'apo qd., Hawai'i. *Lit.,* bursting house.

Hale-pōhaku. Two stone cabins in Mauna Kea State Park, at 9,220 feet elevation on Mauna Kea, Hawai'i, built in 1936 and 1939 by the Civilian Conservation Corps and named by L.W. Bryan, district forester. Mountain (3,786 feet high), Lahaina qd., West Maui. *Lit.*, stone house.

Hale-puaʻa. Land section near Kahu-wai, Hawaiʻi. *Lit.*, pig house.

Hale-uluhe. The name of Ka-mehameha II's house in Honolulu where St. Andrew's Priory now stands. *Lit.*, fern house.

Hāliʻi. Stream and falls, Līhuʻe district, Kauaʻi. *Lit.*, strewn.

Hāliʻi-maile. Land division, village, and Congregational church at Kāheka, Pāʻia qd., East Maui. Area in downtown Honolulu near the present Library of Hawaii, former name of the palace grounds and the home of Boki and Liliha and other royalty. (Ii 148; RC 271–272.) *Lit., maile* vines strewn.

Hāliʻi-noni. A spring on Lehua Island. *Lit.*, spread *noni (Morinda citrifolia).*

Hāliʻi-pālala. Land section near Hīlea, Kaʻū, Hawaiʻi. Natural rock salt was procured here. An old wagon trail for hauling salt is still visible. *Lit.*, spread wide.

Halina. Street, Ka-lihi Uka, Honolulu. *Lit.*, appearance.

Hālō. Land section, Kaunakakai qd., north Molokaʻi. *Lit.*, to peer.

Hā-loa. Hill (4,084 feet high), Wai-piʻo qd.. Hawaiʻi. Drive, Foster Village subdivision, Hālawa, Wai-pahu qd., Oʻahu, a name suggested by Mary Kawena Pukui in 1958; it is the name of the son of Wākea, the first man. Translations are 'long breath' or 'long life'.

Hāloku. Falls, Ka-malō qd., north Molokaʻi. *Lit.*, to ripple.

Hālona. Land sections, Kala-pana and Makuʻu qds., Hawaiʻi. Point, southeast Ka-hoʻolawe. Stream inland of Lahaina, Maui, mentioned in the Lahaina Luna song "Alma Mater," and in the Lahaina song "Hālona" (Elbert and Mahoe 40). Cove and blowhole lookout, Koko Head qd., and land section and hill (836 feet high), Wai-ʻanae qd., Oʻahu; street, Ka-pā-lama section, Honolulu. *Lit.*, peering place.

Hālūlā. Place, Mānoa, Honolulu. (TM.) *Lit.*, stillness.

Halulu. *Heiau* in Puna, Hawaiʻi, and at Kaunolū, Lā-naʻi (HM 92, 496). Land division and lake, south central Niʻihau. Probably named for the legendary man-eating bird *halulu.*

Hālupa. Street, Foster Village, Hālawa, Wai-pahu qd., Oʻahu. Name suggested by Mary Kawena Pukui in 1958. *Lit.*, flourishing (as plants).

Hāmākua. Quadrangle, district, ditch, ditch trail, golf course, forest reserve, and mill, northeast Hawaiʻi. Ditch, Haʻi-kū qd., East Maui. Poetic (Hawaiʻi): *kuhi loa,* long corner. (UL 122.)

Hāmākua Loa. Former district and land division, Haʻi-kū qd., Maui. *Lit.*, long Hāmākua.

Hāmākua Poko. Former district and land division, Haʻi-kū qd., Maui. *Lit.*, short Hāmākua.

Hāmama. Stream, Wai-heʻe, Oʻahu. *Lit.*, open.

Hamilton Library. Graduate library, Mānoa campus, University of Hawaiʻi, Honolulu, completed in 1968 and named for Thomas H. Hamilton (1914–), seventh president of the university 1963–1968.

Hammer. Point, ʻEwa qd., Oʻahu.

39

H

Hāmoa. Village, beach, bay, surfing area, and land division, Hāna, Maui. This is perhaps a shortening of Haʻamoa, an old name for Samoa.

Hamohamo. Area near ʻŌhua Avenue, Wai-kīkī, Oʻahu, once belonging to Queen Liliʻu-o-ka-lani. *Lit.,* rub gently (as the sea on the beach). *Aia akula paha i Wai-kīkī i Hamohamo i ka ʻimi ʻahuʻawa,* maybe just at Wai-kīkī at Hamohamo looking for ʻahuʻawa sedge (disappointment, failure; all one does is ʻrub' and this is ʻbitter' [ʻawa]). See ʻŌhua; Appendix 8.1.

Hamu-wai. Cliff separating Wai-lau and Pū-koʻo valleys, Hālawa qd., Molokaʻi. *Lit.,* gulp water.

Hana-. Prefix of many place names (also *Hono-*). See Appendix 5.2.

Hāna. Quadrangle, village, bay, surfing area, elementary and high school, beach park, district, forest reserve, plantation, and road, East Maui. Queen Ka-ʻahu-manu was born here at a place called Pōnaha-ke-one (circle [of] the sand). Poetic: *ʻāina ua, lani haʻahaʻa* (PH 210), rainy land, low-lying sky. (Ii 172.) See Nā-nuʻa-lele.

Hanahana-puni. Hill, Līhuʻe district, Kauaʻi. *Lit.,* surrounding warmth.

Hana-hauʻoli. Private elementary school, Honolulu, founded by Mr. and Mrs. George P. Cooke in 1918. (A new name.) *Lit.,* joyous work.

Hānai-a-ka-malama. Queen Emma's summer home, upper Nuʻu-anu, Honolulu, named for a demigoddess, probably built in 1847 by H.A. Peirce and sold to John Young II, uncle of the queen and son of John Young, adviser to Ka-mehameha I. Queen Emma inherited the property and used it as a summer retreat and social center. In 1890 it was sold to the Hawaiian government and in 1911 the surrounding area was made a public park. In 1915 the Daughters of Hawaiʻi renovated the house and now maintain it as a museum open to the public for a fee. (HM 214, 220; PH 138.) *Lit.,* the foster child of the light (*or* moon).

Hana-kahi. A part of the city of Hilo, Hawaiʻi, named for a chief who was a symbol of profound peace (UL 60–61). Hilo is called Hilo Hana-kahi. (For a song, see Elbert and Mahoe 50.) *Lit.,* single task.

Hanakaʻieʻie. Island beyond Nihoa mentioned in old chants. *Lit.,* bay [with] the rise and fall [of sea].

Hanakamanene. Valley, southeast Niʻihau. *Lit.,* bay [of] the shudder.

*Hanakanaea. Coastal area and bay, west Ka-hoʻolawe.

Hanakaʻōʻō. Land division, reservoir, point, and cemetery, Lahaina qd., West Maui. *Lit.,* the digging stick bay.

Hanakāpīʻai. Valley, stream, falls, trail, and beach, Hanalei district, Kauaʻi. *Lit.,* bay sprinkling food.

*Hanakaoe. Land section, Ka-huku qd., Oʻahu. (Sterling and Summers 4:31.)

Hanakauhi. Peak, Hale-a-ka-lā Crater, East Maui. *Lit.,* the cover bay.

Hanakealoha. Place, Pālolo, Honolulu. *Lit.,* love-making.

Hanakeaumoe. Island beyond Nihoa mentioned in old chants. *Lit.,* the late night bay.

Hanakoa. Land section, stream, falls, and trail, Hanalei district, Kauaʻi. *Lit.,* bay [of] *koa* trees *or* of warriors.

40 **Hanalei.** Land division, village, elementary school, bay, district, river, and valley, Hanalei district, Kauaʻi. See Pōhaku-Hanalei, Wyllie. (For. Sel. 96; PH 65; UL 155; for a song, see Elbert and Mahoe 41.) *Lit.,* crescent bay.

Hanalilolilo. Hill and trail in the forest area above Wai-kolu, Molokaʻi. *Lit.,* disappearing place (it is said that as one approaches this hill, either walking or in a car, it seems always to be receding—perhaps an optical illusion).

Hana-lima. Place, Nuʻu-anu, Honolulu. (TM.) *Lit.,* hand work.

Hanaloa. Point and fishpond, Wai-piʻo peninsula. Oʻahu. See Kū-mele-wai. *Lit.,* long bay.

Hanamalo. Point and cape, Hoʻō-pū-loa qd., Hawaiʻi. Probably *lit.,* loincloth bay.

*Hanamanioa. Cape and lighthouse, Mākena qd., southwest Maui.

Hanamāʻulu. Landing, land section, village, bay, ditch, river, beach park, and birthplace of the hero Ka-welo, Līhuʻe district, Kauaʻi. (For. Sel. 32, 102.) Street, Hawaiʻi-kai, Honolulu. *Lit.,* tired (as from walking) bay.

Hānana. Place, Puʻu-nui, Honolulu. *Lit.,* overflow.

Hanapēpē. Land section, town, bay, ditch, falls, stream, valley, and ancient surfing place (Finney and Houston 30), southern Wai-mea district, Kauaʻi. (For. Sel. 102.) *Lit.,* crushed bay (due to land-slides).

Hanaʻula. Mountain (4,616 feet high) and gulch near Uku-mehame, West Maui. A priest, Hua, quarreled with his prophet Lua-hoʻomoe and burned his house down. The priest died or was killed (HM 380), or a drought followed in which the chief died. *Lit.,* red bay.

Hanaʻula Iki. Hill (2,956 feet high), near Hanaʻula. *Lit.,* small Hanaʻula.

Hanauma. Beach park, bay, underwater park, and marine life conservation district created in 1967, Koko Head qd., Oʻahu (pronounced ha-nau-ma). The sand consists predominantly of green olivine crystals (Macdonald and Abbott 201). (Ii 104.) *Lit.,* curved bay *or* hand-wrestling bay.

Hanawana. Point and stream, Haʻi-kū qd., Maui. *Lit.,* sea urchin bay.

Hanawī. Stream, Ke-ʻanae qd., Maui.

Hane-oʻo. Land section, gulch, and large fishpond reportedly built in 1808 near Hāna, Maui. A female *moʻo* was sometimes seen here. *Lit.,* mature soul.

Hani. Lane, Ka-lihi Waena, Honolulu. (TM.) *Lit.,* to step lightly.

Hā-niu-malu. Area at Kau-nā-mano, Kaʻū, Hawaiʻi, where Mary Ka-wena Pukui was born. *Lit.,* shelter [of] coconut leaves (a supernatural woman, Hina, made a coconut-leaf shelter here). A later name is Pali-wai-ʻole (cliff without water), so called because after the plantation was established the water dried up.

Hānō. Point, Hālawa qd., Molokaʻi. *Lit.,* wheezing.

Hanohano. Site of Wai-pahu High School, Oʻahu. *Lit.,* majestic.

Hanu. Lane, Ka-lihi Waena, Honolulu. *Lit.,* breath. (TM.)

Hao. Place and street, ʻĀina-Haina, Honolulu, named for the Hind property on Hawaiʻi. (TM.) *Lit.,* to gather up.

Haona-pā-ipu. Ancient planting area on Puʻu-anahulu, Kona, Hawaiʻi. *Lit.,* receptacle food bowl (referring to crops raised here).

Hāʻoʻū. Village south of Hāna, Maui.

Hāpai-aliʻi

H

Hāpai-aliʻi. *Heiau* at Kaha-luʻu, Kona, Hawaiʻi. *Lit.,* elevating chief.

Hāpapa. Gulch, Puʻu-o-kali qd., Maui. Mountain, Wai-ʻanae Mountains, Oʻahu. *Lit.,* rock stratum.

Happy Valley. Village, Wai-luku, Maui.

Hāpuna. Bay, beach, State park, and land division, Pua-kō qd., Hawaiʻi. *Lit.,* spring.

Hardesty. Street, Pālolo, Honolulu, named for Samuel Clinton Hardesty, a contractor and member in 1912 of the Honolulu Board of Supervisors; he died in 1935. (TM.)

Harding. Important avenue, Ka-imu-kī, Honolulu, built during President Harding's administration and named for him.

Harvey. Lane, Ka-lihi Waena, Honolulu, named for Senator Frank Harvey who was a member of the Honolulu Board of Supervisors at the time the lane was named; he was shipping superintendent of the Inter-Island Steamship Company and lived in Ka-lihi Valley; he died in 1910. (TM.)

Hassinger. Street, Makiki, Honolulu, named for John F. Hassinger, chief clerk in the Department of the Interior under Ka-lā-kaua, and deputy customs collector during the Republic. (TM.)

Hau. Street, Ka-lihi Kai, Honolulu. (TM.) *Lit., Hibiscus tiliaceus.*

Haua. Gulch, east Lā-naʻi. *Lit.,* smitten.

Hau-ākea. Pali and peak, Airport qd., Molokaʻi.

Hau-ani. Gulch, Wai-piʻo qd., Hawaiʻi. *Lit.,* blowing cold.

Hau-iki. Sea area near the wharf at Hilo, Hawaiʻi. Street, Ka-lihi Uka, Honolulu. *Lit.,* small *hau* tree.

Hau-koe. Point, Lahaina, Maui. Perhaps *lit.,* remaining dew.

Hau-koʻi. Land section, Wai-piʻo qd., Hawaiʻi; see Hōkū-ʻula. Coastal area, north shore, Ka-malō qd., Molokaʻi. *Lit.,* smite [with] adze.

Hau-kulu. Road, upper Mānoa, Honolulu, and the site of the Lyon Arboretum. *Lit.,* dripping dew.

Hauna. Fishpond on inner side of Loko-Waka pond, Ke-au-kaha, Hawaiʻi. *Lit.,* fishy smell.

*Hauna-kea. Point and area, Hālawa qd., Molokaʻi.

Hāuna-pō. Lane and former land area, Ka-lihi Kai, Honolulu; name of a *heiau* in Ka-lihi; see ʻUmi. *Lit.,* night striking.

Haunu-nā-niho. Hill and former place of refuge, Wai-mānalo, Oʻahu. *Lit.,* binding the teeth.

Hau-ola. Ridge, Wai-mea qd., Kauaʻi. Gulch, northeast Lā-naʻi. Ancient surfing area, Lahaina, Maui (Finney and Houston 28); an offshore stone here is believed to have been a woman who was fleeing from her enemies when the gods turned her into a stone. See Hikina-a-ka-lā. *Lit.,* dew [of] life.

Hauʻoli. Streets, Pā-waʻa section, Honolulu, and Kai-lua, Oʻahu. *Lit.,* happy.

Hāʻupu. Peak and ridge, Līhuʻe district, Kauaʻi (PH 107), probably named for a demigod (see Pōhaku-o-Kauaʻi), also called Hoary Head. Bay, peak, and ridge, Pelekunu Valley, Ka-malō qd., Molokaʻi, the fortress of Ka-peʻe-ka-uila who abducted Hina (HM 464); she was rescued by her sons Kana and Nīheu. The hill stretched, but Kana defeated it by using five stretching bodies: human, rope, convolvulus vine, banana, and spider web (HM 466).

The hill was lifted up by turtles. Also called Hā'upu-kele. About 200 yards into the bay are some rocks as much as 100 feet high. It is said that a giant, Kana, walked down the ridge after defeating an enemy and kicked these stones into the water (Jarrett 21). See Ke-olo-'ewa, Kūka'i-wa'a, Mō-koholā. Land section, Pearl City, O'ahu. *Lit.,* recollection.

Hausten. Street, Mō-'ili'ili, Honolulu, named for Henry T. Hausten, founder of the Willows restaurant on this street. (TM.) See Willows.

Hau-'ula. Land section, village, forest reserve, homesteads, settlement, stream, elementary school, beach park, and playground, Kahana qd., O'ahu. *Lit.,* red *hau* tree.

Hawai'i. Largest island in the Hawaiian group, 76 miles wide, 93 miles long, with an area of 4,038 square miles and a population in 1970 of 63,468. Hilo is the major town and county seat. County and collective name for the entire island group (1970 population 769,913). This name occurs in many parts of Polynesia (Havaiki: New Zealand, North Marquesas; 'Avaiki: Cook Islands; Savai'i: Samoa). In some areas, but not in Hawai'i, it is the name of the homeland, or of the underworld to which the dead went. Epithets for the island of Hawai'i: *Hawai'i nui a Keawe,* great Hawai'i of Keawe (a chief); *Hawai'i kua uli* (PH 222), green-backed Hawai'i.

Hawaiian Gazette Building. Office building, Merchant Street, downtown Honolulu, built in 1881 for the *Hawaiian Gazette* newspaper. See Atkinson.

Hawai'i Hall. First permanent building of the Mānoa campus, University of Hawai'i, Honolulu, completed in 1912; it now houses the School of Social Work and the Department of Political Science.

Hawai'i Institute of Geophysics. Geophysics building, Mānoa campus, University of Hawai'i, Honolulu, completed in 1964.

Hawai'i-kai. Subdivision of Honolulu developed by Henry J. Kaiser, including golf course, recreation center, and drive. Streets here are named for localities on other islands. *Lit.,* sea Hawai'i.

Hawai'i-lānui. Gulch, north Lā-na'i. *Lit.,* holiday Hawai'i.

Hawai'i-loa. Ancient surfing area, Hanalei district (?), Kaua'i (Finney, 1959*a*:52). College on the Kai-lua side of the Nu'u-anu Pali, O'ahu, established by four Protestant churches and incorporated in 1963; first classes were held in 1967. In 1971 there were 170 students. See Pu'u-Hawai'i-loa. Ridge and street, Niu, Honolulu. Channel northwest of Nihoa Island. *Lit.,* long (*or* distant) Hawai'i.

Hāwea. Point and station, Lahaina qd., Maui, perhaps named for the famous drum brought by La'a-mai-Kahiki from Kahiki. (HM 356.)

Hāwelewele. Gulch, Kau-pō qd., Maui. *Lit.,* thin (as thread).

Hāwī. Village and land section, Kohala qd., Hawai'i. (PH 89.)

Hayden. Street, Ka-pahulu section, Honolulu, named for Jesse B. Hayden, a streetcar conductor for the Honolulu Rapid Transit Company; he died in 1920 at the age of 35. (TM.)

He-aka-lani. *Heiau,* Lahaina, Maui. *Lit.,* a heavenly shadow.

He'eia. Land division and bay noted for surfing, Kai-lua qd., Hawai'i. This is probably the He'eia in the song composed for Ka-lā-kaua: *Aia i He'eia lā, ka nalu e he'e ai,* there at He'eia, the waves to surf on. A *holua* sled course ended here. Village, elementary school,

H

playground, land divisions, stream, and fishpond covering 88 acres, Kāne-'ohe and Mō-kapu qds., O'ahu. During a battle with people from Leeward O'ahu, a tidal wave is said to have washed *(he'e 'ia)* the natives out to sea and back, after which they were victorious, thus fulfilling a prophecy. In ancient times, souls were judged here and divided into two groups: the white, who went to He'eia-kea, and the black, who went to He'eia-uli. He'eia is also the name given by the goddess Haumea to her foster child, the grandson of 'Olopana. (PH 90.)

He'eia Kea. Land division, He'eia, O'ahu. *Lit.*, white He'eia. (Sterling and Summers 5:90.)

He'eia Uli. Land division, He'eia, O'ahu. *Lit.*, dark He'eia. (Sterling and Summers 5:90.)

Heiau. Land section, northeast Ka-ho'olawe. *Lit.*, place of worship.

Heiheiahulu. Hill, Kala-pana qd., Hawai'i.

Hekili. Point, Olowalu qd., Maui. *Lit.*, thunder.

He-lani. Area near Ke-au-hou, Kona, Hawai'i; name of a Congregational church there. Ridge, Ka-malō qd., south Moloka'i. *Lit.*, a sky, *or* a royal chief.

Hele-a-ka-lā. Hill at Nānā-kuli, Wai-'anae qd., O'ahu. *Lit.*, snare by the sun (the hill blocks the rays of the setting sun).

Helele'i-ke-'ōhā. Stream, Hāna qd., Maui. Probably *lit.*, the taro sprout falls.

Hele-loa. Tract, Mō-kapu qd., O'ahu. *Lit.*, far travels.

Hele-mano. Stream, elementary school, reservoir, ditch, and camps, Wahi-a-wā and Hale-'iwa qds., O'ahu. *Lit.*, many snared *or* many going. See Hale-mano.

Helo. Place, Pālolo, Honolulu. (TM.) *Lit.*, red.

Helu. Mountain (4,400 feet), Lahaina qd., Maui. *Lit.*, scratch *or* count.

Helu-moa. Old land division near the Royal Hawaiian Hotel at Helu-moa Street, Wai-kīkī, and site of a *heiau* where Ka-hahana was sacrificed. *Lit.*, chicken scratch. (Chickens scratched to find maggots in the victim's body. The supernatural chicken, Ka'au-hele-moa, flew here from Ka'au Crater in Pālolo. Ii 17, 93.)

Hema. Place, 'Āina-Haina, Honolulu. *Lit.*, south, left.

Hemenway Hall. Student union building, Mānoa campus, University of Hawai'i, Honolulu, completed in 1938 and named in 1940 for Charles Reed Hemenway (1875–1947), member of the board of regents 1910–1940.

Hemolele. Place, 'Ālewa Heights, Honolulu. *Lit.*, holy.

Henke Hall. An agricultural science building, Mānoa campus, University of Hawai'i, Honolulu, completed in 1956 and named for Louis A. Henke (1889–), professor of agriculture 1916–1954.

Herman. Street, St. Louis Heights, named for either Brother Herman, a teacher at St. Louis College when it was located on River Street, or for the Most Reverend Herman Koeckeman, bishop of Albo and vicar apostolic of the Hawai'i Catholic Mission 1881–1892. (TM.)

He-ulu. Street, Makiki, Honolulu, perhaps named for a chief living at the time of Ka-mehameha (RC 312).

Hi'aloa. Street, 'A'ala section, Honolulu. *Lit.*, balding temple.

Hickam. Air Force base, village, elementary school, and golf course, Honolulu, named for Lt. Colonel Horace M. Hickam who was killed in an airplane accident at Fort Crockett, Texas, in 1934. (Addleman 55.)

Hīhīmanu. Peak, Hanalei district, Kaua'i. (For. Sel. 75.) *Lit.,* beautiful.

Hihi-nui. Falls, Wai-mea district, Kaua'i. *Lit.,* much entanglement.

Hi'i. Flats, east Lā-na'i. *Lit.,* carry.

Hi'iaka. Crater, Kī-lau-ea, Hawai'i, named for Pele's many sisters called Hi'iaka, the most famous being Hi'iaka-i-ka-poli-o-Pele (Hi'iaka in the bosom of Pele), who journeyed to Kaua'i to fetch Pele's dream lover, Lohi'au (PH). This name is spelled Heake on some maps.

Hi'iaka-noho-lae. A rock beyond the seawall (between the Kona Inn and the end of the wall) at Kai-lua Village, Kona, Hawai'i. (For. Sel. 14–15.) *Lit.,* Hi'iaka living [at] point. (One of Pele's Hi'iaka sisters lived here. In one legend the stone is the shark form of a priest turned to stone in response to an enemy's prayer to Pele. See Ka-iwi.)

Hi'ilani. Street, Tantalus, Honolulu. (TM.) *Lit.,* praise.

Hi'ilani-wai. Stream, Kāne-'ohe, O'ahu. *Lit.,* cherished water.

Hi'i-lawe. Falls, Wai-pi'o Valley, Hawai'i. This is the highest free-fall waterfall in Hawai'i and one of the highest in the world, with a vertical drop of about 1,000 feet. The fall is now usually dry, as the stream is diverted for irrigation. (Macdonald and Abbott 174; for songs, see Elbert and Mahoe 49, 94; UL 120.) Street, Pacific Heights, Honolulu. *Lit.,* lift [and] carry.

Hikauhi. Coastal area, gulch, fishpond, and reef passage, Airport qd., south Moloka'i. This was the name of the daughter of Chief Ho'olehua and his wife 'Īloli. She became the wife of Pāka'a and mother of the famous Kū-a-Pāka'a. (Nakuina 33; RC 37; Rice 77; Summers 63.) See Kau-manamana. For meaning, see PE, *hikauhi.*

Hiki. Street, Ka-lihi Uka, Honolulu. *Lit.,* to come *or* to be able.

Hiki-au. A *luakini* (*heiau* where human sacrifices were made) of Ka-mehameha I at Ke-ala-ke-kua, Hawai'i; Captain Cook was received here as the god Lono; now a State monument. (RC 256 for text and drawing; UL 36.) *Lit.,* moving current (surfing was famous here).

Hiki-lei. Valley, Wai-mea district, Kaua'i. *Lit.,* fetch lei.

Hiki-moe. Ridge and valley, Wai-mea district, Kaua'i. *Lit.,* resting place.

Hikina. Lane, Iwilei, Honolulu. (TM.) *Lit.,* east.

Hikina-a-ka-lā. Place of refuge (*pu'uhonua*) near the mouth of the Wai-lua River, Kaua'i; also called Hau-ola. *Lit.,* rising of the sun.

Hīlea. Village, gulch, and land division, Honu-'apo qd., Ka'ū, Hawai'i. (See PE.) *Lit.,* careless.

Hīlea Iki. Land section below Maka-nau hill, Honu-'apo qd., Ka'ū, Hawai'i. *Lit.,* small Hīlea.

Hīlea Nui. Land section, Honu-'apo qd., Ka'ū, Hawai'i. *Lit.,* great Hīlea.

Hīlia. Offshore area extending from Pā-kanaka Pond through Ka-lama-'ula, south central Moloka'i. *Lit.,* smitten. (Mullet were so numerous that fishermen kicked them ashore with the sides of their feet [*kā wāwae*].)

Hilina. *Pali, pali* trail and road, and peak (2,249 feet high), Kī-lau-ea qd., Hawai'i. (Macdonald and Abbott 316.) *Lit.,* struck (as by wind).

Hilo. City (1970 population 26,353), bay, district, harbor, golf courses, schools, and ancient surfing area (Finney and Houston 26), Hawai'i. Three sections of Hilo town are: Hilo-one (sand Hilo), near the sea; Hilo-Hanakahi, an inland section toward Ke-au-kaha, named for a chief famous in song (Elbert and Mahoe 50; PH 27); and Hilo-pali-kū (Hilo of the upright cliff), east of the Wai-luku River (PH 29). (See PE, *Kani-lehua.*) Perhaps named for the first night of the new moon or for a Polynesian navigator. Forest reserve in Hilo and Hāmākua districts; trail in Hilo and Puna districts. (For a saying, see Appendix 8.1.) Street, Wilhelmina Rise, Honolulu, named for Hilo crab grass (TM).

Hilole. Ancient surfing area, Lā-na'i. (Finney 53.)

Himalayas. A winter surfing area west of Ka-wai-loa, O'ahu.

Hina. Falls at 3,250 feet elevation, Ka-malō qd., Moloka'i, named for the goddess Hina, the mother of Moloka'i. See Ke-ana-o-Hina.

Hina-i-uka. A rock or peak also known as Queen Victoria's Profile on Mt. Hā'upu, Līhu'e district, Kaua'i. *Lit.,* Hina in [the] uplands. (Pele's sister Hi'iaka and Hina competed to win chief Kāhili; Hina won because her sarong was so highly scented with *mokihana* berries. The name Hina is said to be engraved as a petroglyph, sometimes awash, at Kīpū Kai, Kaua'i.)

Hina-kahua. Former site for dancing, *maika,* the *kilu* sexual game (RC 106), and fighting *(mokomoko),* Kapa'au, Hawai'i. *Lit.,* Hina's arena.

Hina-lele. Falls (280 feet drop), Hana-lei qd., Kaua'i. *Lit.,* Hina's leap.

Hīnalenale. Point, Hālawa qd., north Moloka'i. *Lit.,* sickly, weak.

Hīnalo. Place, Nu'u-anu, Honolulu. (TM.) *Lit.,* male pandanus flower (variant of *hīnano*).

Hinana-ulua. Point, Airport qd., north Moloka'i. *Lit.,* inspired [by a god] *hinana* fish.

Hīnano. Street, Ka-pahulu section, Honolulu. *Lit.,* male pandanus flower.

Hinau. Cinder cone (6,252 feet high), Hualālai, Hawai'i.

Hind. Drive, 'Āina-Haina, Honolulu; named for Robert Hind. See 'Āina-Haina.

Hi'olani. Place, Pauoa, Honolulu. *Lit.,* slumber.

Hi'ona-'ā. Land section between Pu'u-makani and Ka-'alā-iki, Ka'ū, Hawai'i. *Lit.,* rocky appearance.

Hipa-wai. Street and area in lower Mānoa, Honolulu. A *heiau* near here where human sacrifices were offered had this name (Sterling and Summers 6:133). For three awards, see Indices 740. *Lit.,* water foolishness.

Hī-puapua. Falls, Hālawa Valley, Moloka'i. *Lit.,* tail flowing.

Hiram. Lane, Pā-lama, Honolulu, named for a part-Hawaiian employee of the old Honolulu Iron Works. (TM.)

Hiu. Stream, Wai-'anae Valley, O'ahu. *Lit.,* throw violently.

Hi'u. Street, Ka-lihi Waena, Honolulu. (TM.) *Lit.,* fish tail.

Hō'ae'ae. Land section and point, 'Ewa, O'ahu. *Lit.,* to make soft or fine. A stone called Pōhaku-pili (clinging rock) is on the edge of the cliff on the boundary of Hō'ae'ae and Wai-kele; it belonged to the gods Kāne and Kanaloa.

Hoaka. Point, Wai-mea district, Kaua'i. *Lit.,* crescent.

Hoaka-lei. See Kualaka'i.

Hoa-koa. Place, Wai-'alae, Honolulu. (TM.) *Lit.,* soldier friend.

Hō'alu. Place, Makiki Heights, Honolulu. (TM.) *Lit.,* depression, bent.

Hoana. Place, 'Āina-Haina, Honolulu. *Lit.,* porcupine fish.

Ho'ānuanu. Old name for Maka-weli, Kaua'i. *Lit.,* to cause cold.

Hoa-pili. Lane, 'A'ala section, Honolulu, named for David K. Hoa-pili, Sr., an employee of Theo. H. Davies and Company. (TM.) *Lit.,* close friend.

Hoary Head. An English name for Hā'upu mountain, Kaua'i.

Hō'awa. Lane, McCully and Bingham sections, Honolulu, named for native trees and shrubs of the genus *Pittosporum*.

Hobron. Point, Wai-luku qd., Maui. Lane near the yacht harbor, Wai-kīkī, named for Coit Hobron, a sea captain who settled in Hawai'i during the Monarchy; his brother, T.H. Hobron, built the Hobron Building formerly at the corner of King and Fort streets. (TM.)

Hō'ea. Land section and stream, Kohala qd., Hawai'i. (For. Sel. 114.) Valley, Wai-mea district, Kaua'i. *Lit.,* to arrive.

Hoe-nui. Street, Ka-lihi Waena, Honolulu. (TM.) *Lit.,* big paddle.

Hō'eu. Ancient surfing area, Kai-mū, Hawai'i (Finney and Houston 26), now called Kai-mū. *Lit.,* mischief.

Ho'ina-kāuna-lehua. Stream, Līhu'e district, Kaua'i. *Lit.,* return [of] four *lehua* blossoms.

Hōkū-kano. Land sections, Kai-lua and Honu-'apo qds., Hawai'i; named for a star called Hōkū-pōkano. *Heiau,* Ka-malō qd., south Moloka'i.

Hōkū-lani. Elementary school, Mānoa, Honolulu. *Lit.,* heavenly star (a new name).

Hōkuli. Place near Lau-pahoehoe, Hawai'i, where 'Umi hid his god when he was living incognito and in poverty. (For. Sel. 126.)

Hōkū-nui. Peak, Līhu'e district, Kaua'i. *Lit.,* large star.

Hōkū-o-Betelehema. Congregational church at Pa'auilo, Hawai'i. *Lit.,* star of Bethlehem.

Hōkū-'ula. Hill (4,115 feet high), Hau-ko'i, Hawai'i, said to have been lifted out of the sea by a turtle and where Lono-i-ka-makahiki of Hawaii defeated Kama-lālā-walu of Maui (For. Sel. 188). Hill (1,400 feet high), Līhu'e district, Kaua'i. Coastal area, Hāna qd.; hill (2,504 feet high), Lahaina qd.; land division, Maka-wao, Maui. *Lit.,* red star.

Hōkū-welowelo. *Heiau* on cliff of Ka-luahine, Hawai'i. See Koa'e-kea. *Lit.,* shooting star.

Hōlei. *Pali* and ancient village, Puna qd., Hawai'i. A supernatural rat, 'Āpua, lived here; he was shot by Pikoi-a-ka-'alalā. Street,

Diamond Head section, Honolulu. (TM.) *Lit., Ochrosia sandwicensis,* a native tree.

Hole-lua. Place, Pā-lama, Honolulu. *Lit.,* wavering.

Hollinger. Street, Wai-kīkī, Honolulu, named for Tom Hollinger, a blacksmith and father of Supervisor Ben Hollinger, who served on the Honolulu Board of Supervisors 1914–1933. The senior Hollinger came to Hawai'i in 1884 and died in 1922. (TM.)

H

Holmes Hall. Engineering building, Mānoa campus, University of Hawai'i, built in 1972 and named for Wilfred Jay Holmes (1900–), dean emeritus, College of Engineering, and retired captain, U.S. Navy.

Holoholo-kū. *Heiau* at Wai-lua River, Kaua'i, said to be the oldest on the island and to be named for a foster parent of Ka-welo; it was a place of refuge (Ii 138), restored by the Kaua'i Historical Society and Bishop Museum in 1933. Hill, Wai-ki'i qd., Kohala, Hawai'i. *Lit.,* to run [and] stand.

Holoi-nā-wāwae. Stream, Hāna qd., Maui. *Lit.,* wash the feet.

Holo-ka-hana. Lane, Lanakila section, Honolulu. *Lit.,* success.

Hōlua. Cabin and cave on the Hale-mau'u Trail, Hale-a-ka-lā Crater, Maui. Way, Ka-lihi Uka, Honolulu. *Lit.,* sled.

Hōlua-loa. Village, elementary school, land sections, and bay, Kai-lua qd., Hawai'i. (Ii 6.) *Lit.,* long sled course.

Hō-mai-ka-wa'a. Stream and land division, Ka-wai-hau district, Kaua'i. *Lit.,* give me the canoe.

Home-la'i. Congregational church at Hāna, Maui. *Lit.,* peaceful home.

Home-lani. Cemetery at Hilo, Hawai'i. Place, Nu'u-anu, Honolulu. *Lit.,* heavenly home.

Homerule. Street, Ka-lihi Kai, Honolulu, named for a political party at the time of annexation which merged with the Democratic Party. (TM.)

Honalo. Land section, Kai-lua qd., Kona, Hawai'i. A *heiau* here was called Kualani (chiefly back). (For. 4:588.)

*****Honapu.** Surfing area, Ka-wai-hae, Kohala qd., northwest Hawai'i. (Finney, 1959a:108.)

Hōnaunau. Quadrangle, land section, village, bay, surfing areas (summer south-swell and winter north-swell), forest reserve, and elementary school, South Kona, Hawai'i. See Hale-o-Keawe.

Hone. Lane, Ka-pā-lama section, Honolulu. *Lit.,* soft and sweet.

Hongwanji Mission. See Honpa Hongwanji Mission.

Hono-. Prefix to many place names (also, *Hana-*). (Appendix 5.2.)

Hono-a-Pi'ilani. Highway around southwest Maui. *Lit.,* bays [acquired] by [Chief] Pi'i-lani. Six West Maui bays whose names begin with *Hono-* (bay) and the islands seen from them (Ka-ho'olawe, Lā-na'i, Moloka'i) were ruled by Pi'i-lani and are famous in song; the six bays are Honokahua, Honokeana, Honokōhau, Honokōwai, Honolua, Hononana. Pi'i-lani's daughter, Pi'i-kea, married 'Umi in the early 1500s. See Kiha-a-Pi'ilani.

Honohina. Village, Honomū qd., land sections, Honomū and Mauna Kea qds., Hawai'i. *Lit.,* gray bay *or* Hina's bay.

Honohono-nui. Land section inland from Loko-Waka, Hilo qd., Hawai'i. *Lit.,* much *honohono* grass.

Honoipu. Land section, landing, school, and ancient surfing area, Kohala qd., Hawai'i. (Finney and Houston 26.) *Lit.,* gourd bay.

Honoka'a. Town and elementary and high school, Hāmākua qd., Hawai'i. *Lit.,* rolling [as stones] bay.

Honokāhau. Village, bay, and ancient surfing area (Finney and Houston 26), Ke-āhole qd., Hawai'i. House sites, fishponds, and *heiau* have been found here. *Lit.* bay tossing dew. Same as Honokōhau.

Honokaheka. Point, Kohala or Wai-pi'o qd., Hawai'i. *Lit.,* sea-pool bay.

Honokahua. Land division, point, stream, village, and bay, Honolua qd., West Maui; cinder cone, Hale-a-ka-lā Crater, East Maui. See Hono-a-Pi'ilani. *Lit.,* sites bay.

*Honokala. Gulch, Kai-lua or Ka-'ohe qd., Hawai'i.

Honokalā. Point, gulch, and land section, Ha'i-kū qd., Maui. *Lit.,* the sun bay.

Honokalani. Land section, Hāna qd., Maui. *Lit.,* the royal chief bay.

Honokāne. Land division and stream, Wai-pi'o qd. (PH 62; UL 51); gulch, Ka'ū, Hawai'i, where there was a medical *heiau.* See Ke-kua-lele. *Lit.,* Kāne's bay.

Honoka'ope. Bay, Pua-kō qd., Hawai'i. *Lit.,* the bundle bay.

Honoka'upu. Land section, Pelekunu, Moloka'i. Former land section along the waterfront beyond the seaward end of Ala-kea Street, downtown Honolulu; it was an old surfing area (Finney and Houston 39) and one-time site of a coconut grove named for a chief. This name is on an 1810 map of Honolulu *(Honolulu in 1810).* (See Ke-kai-o-Māmala; Westervelt, 1964b:52–54.) *Lit.,* the albatross bay.

Honoke'ā. Valley and stream, Wai-pi'o qd., Hawai'i. *Lit.,* the volcanic rock place.

Honokeana. Land division and bay, Honolua qd., West Maui. *Lit.,* the cave bay.

Honokoa. Gulch, Kohala qd., Hawai'i. Bay and point, Ka-ho'olawe. Place, Wai-'alae, Honolulu. *Lit.,* brave bay.

Honokōhau. Village, school, surfing areas, and land sections, Ke-āhole and Kai-lua qds., Hawai'i (PH 69). Land division, village, stream, falls, ditch, tunnel, bay, and hill (305 feet high), Honolua qd., West Maui (Ii 172; PH 69–70). *Lit.,* bay drawing dew.

Honoko'i. Gulch, Hālawa qd., Moloka'i. *Lit.,* adze bay.

Honokōwai. Land section, ditch, point, stream, beach park, Lahaina qd., Maui. *Lit.,* bay drawing water.

Honokua. Land section and lava flow of 1950, Hōnaunau qd., Hawai'i.

Honoli'i. Cove, landing, stream, and gulch, Honomū qd., Hawai'i, where it is said Māui was killed. He chased a girl who climbed a tree; he changed himself into an eel and climbed after her; a priest came and killed the eel (Westervelt, n.d.: 151; PH 60, 61.) *Lit.,* little valley.

Honolua. Land section, village, landing, bay, winter surfing area, stream, mountain (2,627 feet), and quadrangle, Lahaina district, Maui. (PH 69.) *Lit.,* two harbors.

Honolulu. Bay and sand hill, land section, and former landing, Puna qd., Hawai'i. Capital of the State of Hawai'i (map 6). The city had a population in 1970 of 324,871; the City and County of Honolulu population (the island of Oʻahu and the Northwestern [formerly Leeward] Hawaiian Islands) was 630,528. Old names for the harbor were Kou and Māmala. The Bishop Museum has published a map of the city as of 1810. Sections of the town in the 1820s are described in RC 271–272. *Lit.,* protected bay.

Honolulu Academy of Arts. Museum, Thomas Square section, Honolulu, housing art collections, library, and educational facilities. A gift of Mrs. C.M. Cooke, it was built in 1927 on the site of her former home; many of the art objects which she had collected form the basis of the present collection. See Spalding.

Honolulu Hale. Honolulu's city hall, built in 1927, housing offices of the mayor, city council, and principal staff agencies. Ka-mehameha III is said to have built a government office building of the same name on Merchant Street in 1835; it was destroyed in about 1853. *Lit.,* Honolulu house.

Honolulu International Airport. Prior to 1932 the airport was called John Rodgers Airport, named for Commander John Rodgers who made the first flight to Hawaiʻi from the Mainland in 1925 (TM). It then comprised 885 acres, 766 of which were under water. In 1947, at that time one of the largest in the United States, its name was changed to Honolulu Airport. In 1951, the name was again changed—to Honolulu International Airport.

Honolulu International Center. Auditorium, exhibit hall, and sports arena complex just seaward of Thomas Square, Honolulu, built on the site of Old Plantation (see Curtis; Ward; and Elbert and Mahoe 83); it was opened in 1964. Renamed Blaisdell Center (1976).

Honolulu Nui. Bay, Nā-hiku qd., Maui. *Lit.,* large Honolulu.

Honomāʻele. Land division, Hāna qd., Maui. *Lit.,* numb bay. (PH 64.)

Honomakaʻu. Village and land section, Kohala qd.; land section, Honomū qd., Hawaiʻi. *Lit.,* harbor [of] fear.

Honomalino. Land division, bay, and forest area, Hoʻō-pū-loa qd., Kona, Hawaiʻi. (UL 66.) *Lit.,* calm bay.

Honomanū. Land division and bay, Ke-ʻanae qd., Maui. (PH 72.)

Honomū. Village, stream, and quadrangle, Hilo district, Hawaiʻi; a surf beyond the mill here was named Koʻo-kā (push strike). *Lit.,* silent bay.

Honomuni. Gulch, Hālawa qd., south Molokaʻi. See Ka-ulu-wai.

Hononana. Bay near Honolua Bay, West Maui. See Hono-a-Piʻilani. *Lit.,* animated bay.

Honono. Point, Hanalei district, Kauaʻi.

Hono-o-nā-pali. A remote and unfrequented area at the northwest end of the Alakaʻi Swamp, Kauaʻi. *Lit.,* brow of the cliffs.

Honopou. Stream and valley, Haʻi-kū qd., Maui. *Lit.,* post harbor.

Honopū. Uninhabited valley and trail, Hanalei district, northwest coast, Kauaʻi. It is called "valley of the lost tribe" in reference to a legendary little people called Mū-ʻai-maiʻa-o-Lāʻauhaele who lived at Lāʻau at the headwaters of Wai-niha Stream where wild bananas, their food, grew; they stole campers' food. (HM 326; PH 159.) Bay and gulch, west Lā-naʻi. Probably *lit,* conch bay.

Honopue. Land section and stream, Wai-piʻo qd., Hawaiʻi.

Honopueo. Land section, Kohala qd., Hawai‘i, named for an owl *‘aumakua* (personal god) who led a Kaua‘i hero, Ko‘olau-a-Mano, to find his mother. *Lit.,* owl bay.

Honouli Malo‘o. Land division and stream, Hālawa qd., south Moloka‘i. *Lit.,* dry Honouli (dark bay).

Honouliuli. Land division, village, forest reserve, and gulch, Wai-pahu qd., O‘ahu. *Lit.,* dark bay.

Honouli Wai. Land division and stream, Hālawa qd., south Moloka‘i. Phosphorescence *(maka-ihu-wa‘a)* was seen here. *Lit.,* wet Honouli.

Hono-wae. Bay, northwest Lā-na‘i. *Lit.,* chosen bay.

Honowai. Elementary school and playground, Wai-pahu, O‘ahu. Perhaps a new name.

Honowewe. Coastal area, Hālawa qd., Moloka‘i. *Lit.,* pouring bay [of rain].

Honpa Hongwanji Mission. Built in Honolulu (Nu‘u-anu section) in 1918 to commemorate the 700th anniversary of the founding of the Shin sect of Buddhism, now the headquarters of the sect in Hawai‘i.

Honua. Street, Kāhala, Honolulu; stream, Wai-‘anae district, O‘ahu. *Lit.,* land.

Honua-‘ino. Land sections, Kai-lua qd., Hawai‘i. (RC 105.) *Lit.,* bad land. (This is said to be the only place in the area without a canoe landing.)

Honua-kaha. Old section of Honolulu near Ka-wai-a-Ha‘o cemetery. (Ii 93.)

Honu-‘apo. Land section, quadrangle, village, and bay, Ka‘ū, Hawai‘i. (UL 191.) *Lit.,* caught turtle.

Honua-‘ula. Cove and land sections, Kai-lua, Kona; *heiau* for human sacrifices, Wai-pi‘o Valley, Hawai‘i (For. Sel. 158; RC 14). Valley, Wai-mea district, Kaua‘i. Point, north Lā-na‘i. Congregational church at Ka-naio and a nearby land division, Mākena qd., Maui (Coulter map, p. 229; RC 85). Valley, southeast Ni‘ihau. (Ii 119.) See Pu‘u-honua-‘ula. *Lit.,* red land.

Ho‘okēkē. Area in upper Kohana-iki, Kona, Hawai‘i. See Mai‘a-loa. *Lit.,* crowded.

Ho‘okena. Land section, village, elementary school, and beach park, Hōnaunau qd., Kona, Hawai‘i. (For a song, see Elbert and Mahoe 68–69.) *Lit.,* to satisfy thirst.

Ho‘okipa. Beach park and surfing area (Finney, 1959a:108) near Pā‘ia, Maui; surfing areas here are known as Ho‘okipa Lefts and Rights. Way, Ka-imu-kī, Honolulu. *Lit.,* hospitality.

Ho‘okomo. Land section, Humu‘ula qd.; hill, Hilo district, Hawai‘i. *Lit.,* entrance.

Ho‘oku‘i. Street, Punchbowl, Honolulu. *Lit.,* collision. (The street was so named because of the frequent accidents on its curved route.) (TM.)

Ho‘ola‘i. Street, Sheridan Tract, Honolulu. *Lit.,* to enjoy peace.

Ho‘olana. Ancient surfing area, Kohala district, Hawai‘i. (Finney, 1959a:51.) *Lit.,* to cause to float.

Ho‘olawanui. Stream, Ha‘i-kū qd., Maui. *Lit.,* make great sufficiency.

Ho‘olehua. Village, land divisions, and Hawaiian homestead area near

51

the Moloka'i airport, said to be named for a chief (see Hikauhi). *Lit.,* acting the expert.

Ho'olulu. Land division, Kona, Hawai'i. Valley and stream, northwest coast, Kaua'i. (UL 118.) Street, Ka-pahulu, Honolulu, named by Auhea Crowningburg, owner of the tract, for her ancestor, who may have hidden the bones of Ka-mehameha near Ka-loko, Hawai'i (RC 215). (TM.) *Lit.,* to lie in sheltered waters.

Ho'omaha. Way, Mānoa, Honolulu. *Lit.,* to rest.

Ho'omaika'i. Street, 'Ālewa Heights, Honolulu. *Lit.,* to give thanks.

Ho'omo'a. Channel between Lehua and Nihoa islands. *Lit.,* to cook.

Ho'onanea. Street, Mānoa, Honolulu. *Lit.,* to relax.

Ho'ope'a. Ancient surfing area, Hanalei, North Kaua'i. (Finney, 1959*a:* 53.) Probably *lit.,* to cross.

Ho'opōuli. Falls, Hanalei district, Kaua'i. *Lit.,* darkened.

Ho'ō-pū-loa. Quadrangle, land section, bay, and village, Kona, southwest Hawai'i; site of a lava flow in 1926. *Lit.,* put together [for a] long [time]. (Omoka'a and his wife Okoe lived here; any travelers entering their house were put into an oven, where they "stayed together a long time." Finally Omoka'a and Okoe were pushed into a net by Ka-miki and his brother. They were spared when they promised not to harm travelers again. See Okoe, Omoka'a.)

Hopaka. Street, Ke-walo section, Honolulu. (TM.) *Lit.;* Hobert.

Hope-loa. Place, Kāhala, Honolulu. *Lit.,* very last.

Hōpoe. Stone formerly in the sea at Kea'au, Maku'u qd., Hawai'i, believed to be Hi'iaka's companion turned to stone by Pele; it was moved by the tidal wave of 1946. (For. Sel. 216; PH 2; UL 88.)

Hopu-wai. Area at Honohina, Mauna Kea qd., Hawai'i, 6,425 feet elevation. *Lit.,* water catchment.

Horner. Reservoir, Lahaina qd., Maui. Street, Ka-lihi Kai, Honolulu, named for Robert Horner who had a furniture store; he was on the Honolulu Board of Supervisors in 1915 and chairman of the police commission. (TM.)

Hosmer. Grove and nature trail, Hale-a-ka-lā National Park, Maui, named for Ralph S. Hosmer, the first Territorial forester 1904–1914, who planted the grove in 1910.

Hotel. Street, downtown Honolulu, named in 1850; Hokele in Hawaiian. (TM.)

Houghtailing. Street, Ka-mehameha Heights and between Ka-lihi Waena and Ka-pā-lama, Honolulu, named for George W. Houghtailing who arrived in 1850 and was proprietor of the Bay Horse Saloon on Bethel Street; he died in 1887. (TM.)

Hua. Hill, northwest Kaua'i. *Lit.,* fruitful.

Hualālai. Large volcano, Kailua qd., North Kona, Hawai'i; it last erupted in 1801. See Hu'ehu'e, Ka-'ū-pūlehu, Lua-o-Milu, Puhi-a-Pele.

Huali. Street, Punchbowl, Honolulu. *Lit.,* bright.

Huanu. Street, Pauoa, Honolulu. *Lit.,* Juan.

Hua-wai. Small bay, south Lā-na'i. *Lit.,* water gourd.

Hu'ehu'e. Village and ranch, Pua-kō qd., Hawai'i. The last flow from Hualālai erupted in 1801 below the ranch at about 1,500 to 1,800 feet elevation and flowed to the sea (Macdonald and Abbott 51–52).

Hawaiians thought Pele started the flow because she wanted *awa* fish from Kīholo and Ka-'ū-pūlehu, *aku* fish from Ka'ele-huluhulu, and breadfruit from the uplands of Hu'ehu'e, and because she was jealous of Ka-mehameha's wealth and honor. Ka-mehameha, on the advice of a Pele seer *(kāula)*, offered sacrifices and the flow stopped. (RC 184–186; UL 124.) See 'Akahi-pu'u. *Lit.*, overflowing.

Hue-lani. Drive, upper Mānoa, Honolulu. *Lit.*, royal gourd (referring to the well for Ka-'ahu-manu's home). See Pū-'ahu'ula, Puka-'ōma'o.

Huelo. Village, stream, and point, Ha'i-kū qd., Maui (see Haka-kau-pueo). Islet 3.1 acres, Ka-malō qd., north Moloka'i. A game, originated by Papio, was played here; *loulu* palm leaves were woven into hammocks upon which players were laid and then tossed into the sea. See Leina-o-Papio. (*Ka Nupepa Kuokoa,* July 6, 1922.)

Huene. Street, Pu'u-nui, Honolulu. *Lit.*, wheezing.

Huia. Ancient surfing place, Hilo district, Hawai'i. (Finney and Houston 26.) Name of a wave for surfing (Beckwith, 1919:505).

Hui-aloha. Congregational church at Kau-pō, East Maui. *Lit.*, meeting [of] compassion.

Huihā. Surf opposite the Kona Inn, Kai-lua, Kona, Hawai'i, considered dangerous for surfing but used in ancient days.

Huikau. Hill, Humu'ula qd., Hilo district, Hawai'i. *Lit.*, confused.

Hui-lua. Fishpond (200 acres), Kahana, O'ahu, fed by freshwater springs and attributed to Menehune. Some believed it was connected by an underground passage dug by a shark to a pond at Kua-loa Point, as fish sometimes appear and disappear and believed to escape at the Kua-loa pond. (Newman; Sterling and Summers 4:138.) *Lit.*, twice joined.

Huina. Street, Nu'u-anu, Honolulu. *Lit.*, intersection.

Hula-ku'i. Drive, Moana-lua, Honolulu, apparently named for a type of hula dance.

Hulā-'ia. Old name for Hulē'ia Stream, Līhu'e district, Kaua'i. (PH 190.) *Lit.*, pushed through (Kama-pua'a ravished Pele here).

Hulali. Place, Ka-lihi Waena, Honolulu. *Lit.*, sparkling.

Hulē'ia. See Hulā-'ia.

Huli. Street, Nu'u-anu, Honolulu. *Lit.*, to seek *or* turn.

Huli-he'e. Palace at Kai-lua, Kona, Hawai'i, built in 1838 by Kua-kini, governor of Hawai'i and brother of Ka-'ahu-manu, and said to be named for a brother. Princess Ruth lived here for a time. Ka-lā-kaua redecorated it and used it as a summer palace, changing its name to Hiku-lani Hale (seventh ruler house) after himself. Later the house belonged to Jonah Kū-hiō Ka-lani-ana-'ole. In 1927 the palace was restored as a museum by the Daughters of Hawai'i. See Ka-lāke'e. *Lit.*, turn flee.

Huli-wai. Gulch, Wai-'anae and Wai-pahu qds., O'ahu. *Lit.*, water search.

Hulopo'e. Beach and surfing area, southeast Lā-na'i, named for a man.

Hulu. Islet (1.5 acres, 80 feet elevation), Ka-haku-loa qd., Maui. *Lit.*, feather.

Huluhulu-nui. Ridge, Wai-mea district, Kaua'i. *Lit.*, many rootlets.

Huluhulu-pueo. Stream, Wai-luku district, Maui. *Lit.*, owl feathers.

Humu'ula. Quadrangle; land sections, sheep station (6,700 feet elevation), road, and trail—all mostly in Mauna Kea and Humuʻula qds., Hawaiʻi. *Lit.,* jasper stone.

Huna. Tidal freshwater spring, Hīlea, Kaʻū, Hawaiʻi. *Lit.,* small.

Hūnā. Street, Nuʻu-anu, Honolulu. (TM.) *Lit.,* hidden

Huna-kai. Street, Kāhala, Honolulu. (TM.) *Lit.,* sea spray.

Hūnāna-niho. Land division, Hāmākua, Hawaiʻi. *Lit.,* tooth concealment (here ʻUmi's mother hid the *lei palaoa* given her by her lover, Līloa, for the child she might bear).

Hunehune. Gulch, Honouliuli, Oʻahu. *Lit.,* tiny.

Hunnewell. Street and place, Mānoa, Honolulu, named for James Hunnewell, who set up a trading company in 1817; he was a founder of C. Brewer and Company. (TM.)

Hyde. Street, Mānoa, Honolulu, named for the Reverend Charles McEwen Hyde (1832–1899). He was principal of the North Pacific Missionary Institute, secretary of the board of the Hawaiian Evangelical Association, and trustee of five educational institutions.

H

ʻIamo. Coastal area, northeast Lā-naʻi. *Lit.,* leaping.

ʻĪ-ao. Stream, valley, peak (2,250 feet high), park, and one-time sacred burying place of chiefs (Jarrett 22), Wai-luku qd. (see Kūkae-moku); intermediate school, Wai-luku, Maui. Lane, Pā-lama, Honolulu. *Lit.,* cloud supreme.

Iʻaukea. Street, Pauoa, Honolulu, named for Curtis Piʻehu Iʻaukea, chamberlain to Queen Liliʻu-o-ka-lani and administrator of her estate; as Ka-lā-kaua's envoy he attended the coronation of the Russian czar; and he accompanied Queen Ka-piʻo-lani to England to attend the jubilee of Queen Victoria in 1887. (TM.) He died in 1940.

ʻIeʻie. Playground, ʻAiea, Oʻahu. *Lit., Freycinetia* vine *or* a taro.

ʻĪ-emi. Spring and pond near the mouth of Moana-lua Valley, Oʻahu, the source of a water course that fed the taro patches of the bottom lands. *Lit.,* less great.

ʻIhiʻihi-lau-ākea. Crater west of Hanauma Bay, and bridge over ravine between Blowhole and Hanauma Bay, Oʻahu. *Lit.,* wide-leafed *ʻihi-ʻihi* (an extinct or unknown plant said to have grown at this site).

Iholena. Street and place, lower ʻĀlewa Heights, Honolulu, named for a kind of banana.

ʻĪʻī. State government building housing the Bureau of Conveyances, perhaps named for Papa ʻĪʻī, guardian of Liholiho (RC 220), and uncle of John and Daniel ʻĪʻī.

ʻĪʻī-lewa. Small crater, Kala-pana qd., Hawaiʻi, formerly called ʻIeʻie-lewa (swinging *ʻieʻie* vine).

ʻIʻiwi. Street, Kāhala, Honolulu, named for the *ʻiʻiwi* (scarlet honeycreeper).

I-lalo. Street, Kakaʻako, Honolulu. (TM.) *Lit.,* below.

Ilaniwai. Street, Kakaʻako, Honolulu.

ʻIliahi. Hill, Hanalei qd., Kauaʻi. Street, Nuʻu-anu, Honolulu; elementary school and playground, Wahi-a-wā, Oʻahu. *Lit.,* sandalwood.

Iliau. Trail, Wai-mea Canyon, northwest Kauaʻi, a native-plant preserve; of special interest is the *iliau,* a relative of the silversword, endemic to this region of Kauaʻi.

ʻIliʻili-kā. Land section, Kaunakakai qd., north central Molokaʻi. A trail began here leading down to Ka-laupapa peninsula; a bullock pen was at the head of the trail in the 1880s. *Lit.,* clashing pebbles.

ʻIliʻili-ʻōpae. *Heiau,* Mapulehu, southeast Molokaʻi, the largest *heiau* on Molokaʻi and said to be the oldest on the island. It is a platform-type *heiau,* 286 by 87 feet, and 11 to 22 feet high; it was used for human sacrifice. (Summers, Site 200.) Stones for the *heiau* were allegedly brought by Menehune, passing them hand-to-hand from Wai-lau Valley. Several legends concern the partial destruction of the *heiau.* In one (HM 134–135), the two sons of the *kahuna,* Ka-malō, were killed for playing on temple drums in the *heiau.* Ka-malō

55

sought the aid of the shark god Kauhuhu, who caused a storm to destroy the *heiau* and wash all the people out to sea except Ka-malō and his household. An old name for the *heiau* is 'Ili'ili-'Opoe. 'Opoe is said to be the name of a stream tributary to Wai-lau, from whence the Menehune brought the stones *('ili'ili)*. They insisted on being paid with whole *i'a* (seafood) rather than with portions and were therefore paid with shrimps *('ōpae)*. Still another interpretation is 'Ili'ili-o-Pae (pebbles of [Chief] Pae).

'Ili'ili-'ula. Stream, Līhu'e qd., Kaua'i. *Lit.,* red pebbles.

'Ilikai. Apartment hotel, Wai-kīkī, Honolulu. *Lit.,* surface [of the] sea.

'Ilio. Point and quadrangle, West Moloka'i. See Ka-lae-o-ka-'īlio. *Lit.,* dog.

'Ilio-pi'i. Cape and bay, Ka-laupapa peninsula, north central Moloka'i. Perhaps *lit.,* climbing dog.

'Ī-lo'i. Pond at Nīnole, Ka'ū, Hawai'i, formed by Pū-hau spring. A *heiau* is still visible above the pond. *Lit.,* supreme pond.

'Īloli. Three land divisions, Kaunakakai and Airport qds., Moloka'i. (PH 188.) See Hikauhi. *Lit.,* yearning.

I-luna. Place, Ka-lihi Uka, Honolulu. (TM.) *Lit.,* upper.

'Imi-ola. Congregational church at Wai-mea, Kohala, Hawai'i, established by Father Lyons. *Lit.,* seek salvation.

Imu-kālua-ua. Land section, Puna, Hawai'i. *Heiau,* Kaunakakai qd., north Moloka'i. *Lit.,* rain-baking oven. (It is believed that raindrops were caught and baked in the oven. Rain sent by a mischievous brother prevented Pauulea from drying her tapa. She built the *heiau* to stop the rain so that she might dry her tapa. The area has been arid ever since. Rice, 109). Also known as Ka-imu-kā-lua-ua, Nā-imu-kālua-ua.

Inamo'o. Walk, Sheridan Tract, Honolulu, named for a chief acting as regent of Kaua'i (in place of Ka-'eo) for the young chief, Ka-umu-ali'i, seen by Vancouver in 1792, 1793, and 1794. He died in 1794. (TM and Kuy. 1:48n.)

Inari Jinsha Shrine. Shinto shrine built in Kaka'ako, Honolulu, in 1914 and moved to its present location on King Street in 1918. It is associated with the fox and is painted red.

Incinerators. Surfing area off the city incinerator near Ke-walo Basin, Honolulu.

Infinities. A famous beach and surfing area, difficult of access, at Pā-ka-lā, Kaua'i, said to have this name because it is "infinitely" beautiful.

'Ino'ino. Gulch, Wai-pi'o qd., Hawai'i. *Lit.,* bad.

'Io. Street, Ka-pā-lama section, Honolulu, named for the 'io hawk, a symbol of royalty because it flies to great heights.

'Io-lani. The royal palace (Hale Ali'i) built for Ka-mehameha III in 1845 was given the name 'Io-lani in 1863 upon the request of Ka-mehameha V that the palace be named Alexander for his brother, Ka-mehameha IV, who had died a week earlier. The Privy Council preferred one of Alexander's Hawaiian names, 'Io-lani, and Ka-mehameha V agreed. (Ka-mehameha II was also named 'Io-lani.) In

1879 the cornerstone for the present palace was laid on the site of the earlier building; some of the stones for the foundation were brought from Kū-ki'i *heiau,* Puna, Hawai'i. Ka-lā-kaua and Lili'u-o-ka-lani lived here. Queen Ka-pi'o-lani probably planted the huge banyan tree on the grounds sometime after 1882. Lili'u-o-ka-lani was imprisoned here in 1895.

'Io-lani Barracks was built in 1871 at the present State Capitol site, and was moved to the palace grounds in 1965.

Episcopal boys' school on the Ala Wai Canal, Honolulu; this school was first established at Lua-'ehu, Lahaina, Maui, in 1863. In 1871 it was moved to Pauoa Valley in Honolulu and later was named 'Io-lani, perhaps for Ka-mehameha IV, a supporter of the Episcopal church. After several more moves, the school occupied its present location in 1953.

Avenue near Punchbowl, Honolulu. Ka-mehameha Schools dormitory built in 1940. *Lit.,* royal hawk (the high flight of the hawk signified royalty).

'Iole. Land division, Kohala qd., Hawai'i, named for a legendary rat. Mountain and stream, Līhu'e district, Kaua'i. *Lit.,* rat.

'Iole-ka'a. Valley and stream, He'eia, O'ahu. *Lit.,* rolling rat. (Rats of the area lured other rats to a slippery stone on the *pali* and caused them to fall to their deaths in the pool below. In another version, a rat shot by Pikoi-a-ka-'Alalā, a legendary hero, rolled down a cliff and lodged on a ledge known as 'Iole-ka'a.)

Irma's. A rocky near-shore surfing area, Wāwā-malu Beach Park, Sandy Beach, O'ahu, named for a weekend lunch wagon.

Iroquois Point. See Ka-nuku-o-Pu'uloa.

Irwin. Waterfront park, Honolulu, named for Bill Irwin, a businessman during the reign of Ka-lā-kaua; the park was given to the nation by his daughter, Helene I. Fagan. See 'Āina-hou.

Isenberg. Street, Mō-'ili'ili, Honolulu, named for Daniel Paul Rice Isenberg, son of Paul and Hannah Rice Isenberg and owner of the Wai-'alae Ranch, which is now a golf course. He was president of the Mō-'ili'ili baseball league when the street, leading to the old baseball park, was opened. He died in 1919. See Fernhurst. (TM.)

Ishii Garden. Formerly the house and garden of Yukichi Ishii, now a teahouse and restaurant overlooking Nu'u-anu Stream.

I-waho. Place, Ka-lihi Uka, Honolulu. (TM.) *Lit.,* outside.

'Iwa-lani. Place, Ka-imu-kī, Honolulu, named for an Inter-Island steamer. (TM.) *Lit.,* heavenly frigate bird.

Iwi. Way, Wilhelmina Rise, Honolulu. *Lit.,* bone *or* land boundary.

Iwilei. Road and section 6 of Honolulu (map 6) near the pineapple cannery, formerly a center of prostitution and the home of Sadie Thompson (in Somerset Maugham's *Rain*). *Lit.,* collarbone *or* a unit of measurement.

Izumo Taishakyō Mission. A branch of the Izumo Taisha Shintō sect of Japan. The mission was built in 1923 by a master shrine carpenter brought from Japan; it is now a part of the Kukui redevelopment area, Pā-lama, Honolulu.

JjJjJjJjJj

J

Jack. Lane, Nuʻu-anu, Honolulu, named for Jack Kalākiela, a police clerk. (TM.)

Jackass Ginger. Pool and mud slide, Judd Trail, upper Nuʻuanu, Honolulu, named by local youths in the early 1900s for a donkey that was tethered nearby and for the yellow ginger growing by the pool. See Kahua-i-lana-wai.

James. Street, Ka-imu-kī, Honolulu, named for the partner in the real estate firm of James and Jane that opened a tract in Ka-imu-kī in about 1915. (TM.)

Jefferson. Elementary school, Wai-kīkī.

Jefferson Hall. Administration building, East-West Center, University of Hawaiʻi, Honolulu, completed in 1962 and named for Thomas Jefferson.

John Rodgers. See Honolulu International Airport.

Johnson. Lane, ʻAʻala section, Honolulu, named for Fred Johnson, manager of Love's Bakery when it was located at Nuʻu-anu and Pau-ahi streets. His sister was Mrs. Robert Love. (TM.)

Johnson Hall. Men's dormitory, Mānoa campus, University of Hawaiʻi, Honolulu, completed in 1957 and named for Major John A. Johnson of the 100th Battalion, graduate of the University of Hawaiʻi, an outstanding athlete who was killed in action on January 25, 1944.

Judd. Street, Nuʻu-anu, Honolulu, and residence of several members of the family of Dr. Gerrit Parmele Judd (1803–1873), missionary doctor who arrived in 1837 and became an important adviser to Kamehameha III. His residence, "Sweet Home," was at Nuʻu-anu and Judd streets. (TM.) Trails and forest grove named in 1953 in honor of Charles S. Judd, Territorial forester 1915–1939, who planted the grove.

KkKkKk

Kaʻa. Point, northeast Lā-naʻi. Coastal area, Pāʻia qd., Maui. Hill and gulch, ʻĪlio Pt. qd., Molokaʻi. *Lit.,* rolling.

Ka-ʻā. Large land section, west Lā-naʻi. *Lit.,* the burning *or* the rock.

Ka-ʻaʻawa. Land section, village, elementary school, point, and stream, Wai-Kāne and Kahana qds., Oʻahu. The 1.5-acre beach park here was donated by Mrs. F.M. (Julie Judd) Swanzy in 1921. See Ka-ʻahuʻula, Swanzy. *Lit.,* the wrasse fish.

Ka-ʻaha. Point, Kohala qd.; coastal area, Kaʻū, Hawaiʻi. Peak, Waimea district, Kauaʻi. Street, Mō-ʻiliʻili, Honolulu, named for John Kaʻaha (died about 1940), principal of Ka-lihi Kai School; he built a home at Mō-ʻiliʻili quarry. (TM.) *Lit.,* the assembly.

Ka-ʻahakea. Land division, Hāmākua, Hawaiʻi. *Lit.,* the ʻahakea tree.

Ka-ʻahu. Ancient surfing area, Wai-luku qd., Maui. *Lit.,* the garment.

Ka-ʻahu-kūʻula. Land division, Līhuʻe district, Kauaʻi. *Lit.,* the fish-god garment.

Ka-ʻahu-manu. Church, Wai-luku, Maui. Elementary school, Beretania Street, and Ka-mehameha Schools gymnasium, Honolulu, named for Queen Ka-ʻahu-manu, favorite wife of Ka-mehameha I, who was later *kuhina nui* (executive officer), and who died a Christian in 1832. See Queen Ka-ʻahu-manu. *Lit.,* the bird [feather] cloak.

Kaʻahumanu-pōhaku. A large stone near ʻĀ-le-aleʻa platform in the Hōnaunau place of refuge, Kona, Hawaiʻi, where Ka-ʻahu-manu hid until her pet dog's barking gave her hiding place away. According to RC (p. 315) she swam to this area from Keʻei because of her grief when Ka-mehameha took another wife. In another version, she hid here to escape Ka-mehameha's jealous wrath, and some say that she first hid under nearby stones called Pōhaku-o-kau (stone of season). Also called Pōhaku-o-Kaʻahumanu. *Lit.,* Ka-ʻahu-manu's stone.

Ka-ʻahuʻula. Spring, Ka-ʻaʻawa, Oʻahu. *Lit.,* the feather cloak.

Kāʻai. Street, Wai-lupe, Honolulu. (TM.) *Lit.,* belt.

Ka-ʻai-kukui. Gulch, Honouliuli, Oʻahu. *Lit.,* the candlenut food.

Ka-ʻailana. Valley, southeast Niʻihau. *Lit.,* the buoyancy.

Ka-ʻai-pū. Avenue, Mānoa, Honolulu, named for a stone under which lived a supernatural woman. Three land parcels of this name were awarded in the early 1850s. (Indices 318, 319.) *Lit.,* the eating together.

Kaʻakaʻa-niu. Beach and land section, Hanalei district, Kauaʻi, famous for the *limu kohu* seaweed. *Lit.,* rolling coconut.

Ka-ʻākau-kukui. Filled-in reef, Honolulu Harbor. See *Atlas of Hawaii.* *Lit.,* the right (*or* north) light.

Ka-ʻākau-lua. Gulch, Mākena qd., Maui. *Lit.,* the double north *or* double right. An alternate pronunciation is Kaʻa-kaulua (rolling side-by-side).

59

Ka'ākau-pōhaku. Ancient surfing area, Wai-luku qd., Maui. (Finney, 1950*b*:345.) *Lit.,* the north (*or* right-hand) stone.

Ka-'ako-pua. Land section, part of which is now occupied by Central Intermediate School, Honolulu. Princess Ruth's home, Ke-ō-ua Hale, was here. *Lit.,* the flower picking.

Ka'ala. Mountain (3,938 feet), Wai-pi'o qd. (see Pu'u-ka'ala); land section and stream, Hāmākua and Mauna Kea qds., Hawai'i. Gulch and highest mountain (4,020 feet) on O'ahu, Wai-'anae range (PH 100; UL 242); playground and elementary school, Wahi-a-wā. Street, place, and way, Mānoa, Honolulu, probably named for Mt. Ka'ala (TM).

K

Ka-'ala'ala. Land sections and gulch on the southwest slope of Kī-lau-ea, in Kī-lau-ea, Mauna Loa, and Pāhala qds., Hawai'i. *Lit.,* scrofulous scar.

Ka-'alaea. Land division, Ha'i-kū qd., Maui. Coastal area, Hālawa qd., Moloka'i. Valley, land division, and stream, Wai-Kāne qd., O'ahu. *Lit.,* the ocherous earth.

Ka-'alā-iki. Land section, Honu-'apo qd., Hawai'i. *Lit.,* small lava rock.

Ka'alaina. Gulch, Mā'alaea qd., Maui.

Ka-'alā-kei. Valley, Koko Head qd., O'ahu. *Lit.,* the proud water-worn stone.

Ka-'alā-wai. Land division, former fishing right, street, and place, Diamond Head, Honolulu. (RC 135.) *Lit.,* the water basalt.

Ka-'ali. Cliff, northeast Ni'ihau. *Lit.,* the scar.

Ka-'ali'ali-nui. Valley, northeast Ni'ihau. *Lit.,* the greatly scarred.

Ka-'alo. Bend in the coast west of South Point, Hawai'i; fishing is good here in calm weather; a pier built here some years ago against the advice of local Hawaiians was soon destroyed by the elements. *Lit.,* the avoidance.

Ka-'a-loa. Street, Mō-'ili'ili, Honolulu, named for Samuel K. Ka'a-loa, a clerk with the law firm Marx, Prosser, Frear and Anderson for 40 years. He died in 1945. (TM.) *Lit.,* much traveled.

Ka-'alu'alu. Bay and point east of Ka Lae, Hawai'i, a surfing area with tradewind and summer south swell. (For a saying, see Appendix 8.1.) *Lit.,* the wrinkle (seen from out at sea, the fissures in the rock suggest wrinkles).

Ka'amola. Land division, Ka-malō qd., south Moloka'i. *Lit.,* loose, unsteady.

Kā'ana. Land section, Wai-mea district, Kaua'i. Hill, Airport qd., Moloka'i, famous for *lehua.* According to Emerson (UL 45), a rock here is the body of Kapo, a hula goddess and sister of Pele. The hill is said to be the site of the original school where the ancients learned hula dancing of every kind. Above the hill lived Kū-a-Pāka'a, the punster and hero; he taught men to farm, build houses, and fish. (*Ka Nupepa Kuokoa,* September 14, 1922.) *Lit.,* division.

Kā'ana-pali. Landing, village, district, and golf course, Lahaina qd., Maui. Also called Pōhaku-Kā'ana-pali and Kā'anapali-pōhaku. (PH 83.) *Lit.,* Kā'ana cliff.

Kā'anapali-pōhaku. Old name for Pōhaku-Kā'anapali.

Ka-'āpahu. Stream, Hanalei district, Kaua'i. Land area, central Lā-na'i. Hill on the eastern rim of Ka-malō gulch, south Moloka'i, known as the Camel's Back (Stearns and Macdonald, 1947:Plate 2). *Lit.,* the truncation.

Ka'a-pīpā. Point near Kī-pahulu, Hāna district, Maui. *Lit.,* passing edge.

Ka-'ā-poko. Stream, Hanalei district, Kaua'i. *Lit.,* the short stone.

Ka'a-puna. Land section, village, and ranch, Hōnaunau qd., Kona, Hawai'i. *Lit.,* wipe pumice (as in cleaning gourd containers).

Ka'au. Crater near the head of Pālolo Valley, Honolulu, said to have been formed when Māui's hook fell there after dropping Pōhaku-o-Kaua'i at Ka-'ena Point (PH 104); perhaps named for Ka'au-hele-moa, the supernatural chicken of Pālolo that flew to Helu-moa. See Helu-moa. Street, Pālolo, Honolulu. (TM.) *Lit.,* forty.

Ka-'auhuhu. Land section, Kohala and Wai-pi'o qds., Hawai'i. *Lit.,* the 'auhuhu plant *(Tephrosia purpurea).*

Ka-'aumakua. Peak, Honouliuli, O'ahu. *Lit.,* the family god.

Ka-'auwai. Place, Ka-pā-lama section, Honolulu. *Lit.,* the watercourse.

Ka-'awa-kō. *Heiau* at summit of Wai-'ale'ale, Kaua'i. *Lit.,* the kava drawn along.

Ka-'awa-loa. Village, land section, point, lighthouse, and site of the monument to Captain Cook, Hōnaunau and Kai-lua qds., Hawai'i. *Lit.,* the distant kava (runners went to Puna or Wai-pi'o to get kava for chiefs).

Ka-'awa-loha. Gulch, Kohala qd., Hawai'i. *Lit.,* the drooping kava.

Kā'awe-iki. Valley, Wai-mea district, Kaua'i. *Lit.,* tie a little.

Ka-'āwikiwiki. Land section and stream, Hāmākua qd., Hawai'i. (For. Sel. 116.) *Lit.,* the 'āwikiwiki vine.

Ka'ea. Cape, southwest Lā-na'i. Point, Honolua qd., Maui. Also called Ka-lae-o-ka'ea.

Ka'ele-huluhulu. Rocks in the sea at Mahai'ula; land section and fishpond, Ke-āhole qd., North Kona, Hawai'i, belonging to Ka-mehameha I and destroyed by Pele who wanted the *aku* fish there. (For. Sel. 287; Westervelt, 1963:148.) *Lit.,* frayed hull (canoes were dragged over the rocks at Mahai'ula at low tide, fraying the keels; they were used in fishing for bonito).

Ka-'ele-ki'i. Point, Lahaina qd., Maui. *Lit.,* the image blackness.

Ka-'elekū. Land section near Hāna, Maui. *Lit.,* the basaltic rock.

Ka-'ele-pulu. Pond (former fishpond), stream, and playground, now called Enchanted Lake, Kai-lua, O'ahu. *Lit.,* the moist blackness.

*Kaelua. Islet (0.9 acres, 40 feet elevation), Ke-'anae qd., Maui.

Ka-emi. Islet (2.5 acres, 120 feet elevation), Ka-haku-loa qd., Maui. *Lit.,* the ebbing.

Ka-'ena. Point and land section, Puna qd., Hawai'i. Northwesternmost point, Lā-na'i (see North End). 'Ai'ai, the fish demigod, marked a stone here that then turned into the first Hawaiian turtle. (HM 22.) See Poli-hua. Land division, quadrangle, and northwesternmost point, O'ahu, said to be named for a brother or cousin of Pele who accompanied her from Kahiki. (PH 100, 106, 157.) See Kua-o-ka-lā. *Lit.,* the heat.

Ka-ʻena Iki. Point south of Ka-ʻena, Lā-naʻi. *Lit.*, small Ka-ʻena.

Ka-ʻeo. Hill, ʻĪlio Pt. qd., north Molokaʻi, quarried for rock for stone adzes. (Stearns and Macdonald, 1947:Plate 2.) Hill (1,018 feet high), Niʻihau. See Puʻu-ʻeo, Puʻu-ka-ʻeo.

Kaʻe-wai. Place and elementary school, Ka-lihi Uka, Honolulu. (TM.) *Lit.*, water edge.

Ka-haʻakea. Gulch, Hālawa qd., north Molokaʻi. *Lit.*, the paleness.

K

Ka-hāhā-wai. Ancient surfing area (Finney and Houston 28), Ka-haku-loa qd., Maui; name of a chief and intimate friend of Ka-hekili, ruling chief of Maui (RC 124); name of a young Hawaiian killed in Honolulu during the Massey episode. *Lit.*, the broken rivulets.

Kāhai. Street, Ka-lihi Kai, Honolulu. (TM.) *Lit.*, belt, sash.

*Ka-hai-awa. Beach or point, ʻĪlio Pt. qd., Molokaʻi. (See Appendix 3.)

Kaha-ʻino. Pond, southwest Niʻihau. *Lit.*, stormy place [in the rough sea].

Kaha-ka-ʻau-lana. Old name for Sand Island, Honolulu. (RC 416.) *Lit.*, the floating swimmers pass by. (Reference is perhaps to fishermen's containers that floated by while the people fished, as for crabs and seaweeds.)

Ka-haku-loa. Land division, quadrangle, point, stream, bay, village, and homesteads, West Maui. *Lit.*, the tall lord.

*Kahala. Point, Kō-loa district, Kauaʻi. A *heiau* here was called Kū-hāhā-pō (Kū feeling [at] night).

Kāhala. Avenue, elementary school, field, and section 37 of Honolulu (map 6). *Lit.*, amberjack fish.

Ka-hala-iʻa. Ancient surfing area near Haʻaheo, Hawaiʻi. (Finney and Houston 26.) *Lit.*, the sin of eating forbidden fish or meat.

Ka-hālau. Islet (0.3 acres), Haʻi-kū qd., Maui. *Lit.*, the large house.

Ka-hale-lani. Hill, ʻĪlio Pt. qd., Molokaʻi. *Lit.*, the royal house.

Ka-hale-makani. Gulch, Lualaʻi-lua qd., Maui. *Lit.*, the windy house.

Ka-hale-pōhaku. Land section, ʻĪlio Pt. qd., south Molokaʻi. *Lit.*, the stone house.

Ka-hale-ʻula. Ancient surfing area, Ke-āhole qd., Hawaiʻi. (Finney and Houston 26.) *Lit.*, the red house.

Ka-hale-uluhe. See Pā-o-Pelekane.

Kaha-loa. Beach area between the Royal Hawaiian and Hale-kū-lani hotels, Wai-kīkī, noted for its fragrant *līpoa* seaweed; street, upper Mānoa, Honolulu. Ka-uʻi-o-Mānoa, a sister of the rat demigod Pikoi-a-ka-ʻalalā, lived here with her husband, Pā-waʻa, a Mānoa chief (Westervelt, 1964b:158). *Lit.*, long place.

Kaha-luʻu. Village, park, land division, bay, forest reserve, county beach park, and surfing area (Finney and Houston 26), Kai-lua qd., Kona, Hawaiʻi. A *kūʻula* (stone god of fishermen) was brought here from Ka-naio, Maui, and named Pōhaku-o-Kanaio. See Kuʻemanu. Valley, land division, elementary school, park, stream, and fishpond, Wai-kāne qd., Oʻahu, associated with the Ua-pō-ʻai-hale (house-encircling rain; Appendix 8.1; PH 90); perhaps named by fishermen who used to dive here for fish (Jarrett 23). A series of wet taro terraces here are said to be the largest on Oʻahu. See Ka-honua. *Lit.*, diving place.

*Kahamainui. Stream, Kahana qd., O'ahu.

Kahana. Stream and valley, Wai-mea district, southwest Kaua'i. Land division, camp, point, and stream, Honolua qd., Maui. Land section, quadrangle, village, valley, State park, bay, beach park, and stream, Kahana and Wai-kāne qds., O'ahu; 'Āhiu is the associated wind. *Lit.,* cutting.

Ka-hana-hāiki. Land division, Ka-'ena qd., O'ahu.

Ka-hana-hou. See Ka-loko-hana-hou. *Lit.,* the remaking.

Kahana Iki. Gulch, Honolua qd., Maui. Land section and stream, Mō-kapu qd., O'ahu. *Lit.,* small Kahana.

Ka-hana-moku. Beach at the Hilton Hawaiian Village Hotel, Wai-kīkī, Honolulu, named for Duke Ka-hana-moku (1890–1968), former Olympic swimming star and for many years sheriff of Honolulu. Duke was named for his father who was named by Bernice Pau-ahi Bishop to commemorate the visit of the Duke of Edinburgh to Hawai'i. Swimming pool, Mānoa campus, University of Hawai'i, completed in 1964.

Ka-hana-nui. Land division, stream, and gulch, Kaunakakai and Ka-malō qds., Moloka'i. Probably *lit.,* the great work.

Ka-hanu. Street, Ka-lihi Kai, Honolulu, named for William Ka-hanu, a blacksmith who worked for the Wright Carriage Company on Union Street. (TM.) *Lit.,* the breath.

Kaha-nui. Land sections, Airport, Kaunakakai, and Ka-malō qds., Moloka'i. *Lit.,* large place.

Ka-haoa. Beach area, Ka'ū, Hawai'i. *Lit.,* the scorching heat.

Kaha-pa'akai. Land division, upper Nu'u-anu, O'ahu, a stopping place for cattle being driven over the Pali to Honolulu. *Lit.,* salt place.

Ka-hau. Gulch, Ka-malō qd., south Moloka'i. *Lit.,* the *hau* tree *or* the dew.

Ka-hau-a-Le'a. Land division and village, Puna qd., Hawai'i. *Lit.,* the *hau* tree (*or* dew) of Le'a.

Ka-hau-iki. Gulch, Honolua qd., Maui. Land section and stream west of Ka-lihi Valley, O'ahu, that formerly irrigated extensive taro terraces (Sterling and Summers 6:309); street and place (TM), Ka-lihi Wae-na, Honolulu, named for the land section. (For a song, see Elbert and Mahoe 78.) *Lit.,* the small *hau* tree.

Ka-hau-komo. Hill above the sacred rock, Ka-pōhaku-luahine, in Ka-mana Nui Valley, Moana-lua, O'ahu, named for a *kahuna,* the grandfather of a famous chanter, Nā-maka-helu, who died in 1940 at the age of 83. A *heiau* may have been here. A young chief, Ka-moku-lani-ali'i, was strangled in a stream near here because he refused to fight the invader, Ka-mehameha I. *Lit.,* the *hau* trees begin.

Ka-hau-loa. Two land divisions near Nā-po'opo'o and a small bay south of there, Hōnaunau qd., Hawai'i. (For. 4:588.) Ka-hau-loa and her brother Kama-a-lau came from Kahiki and overslept after playing the sexual game, *kilu.* They were turned to stones in a stream, she a flat one and he an upright one. Crater, and site of a rifle range, Koko Head qd., O'ahu. *Lit.,* the tall *hau* tree.

Ka-hau-nui. Land section at Fort Shafter, Honolulu. *Lit.,* the large *hau* tree.

K

Kahawai-iki. Stream and gulch, Hālawa qd., Moloka'i. *Lit.,* small stream.

Kahawai-li'ili'i. Gulch, Hāmākua and Mauna Kea qds., Hawai'i. *Lit.,* small stream.

Kaha-walu. Drive, Dowsett Highlands, Honolulu, named for a Maui chief. *Lit.,* eight marks.

Kahe. Land section, point, beach park, and power plant, Wai-'anae qd., O'ahu. See 'Ewa. *Lit.,* flow.

Ka-he'a. Gulch, east Lā-na'i. *Lit.,* the red stains.

Kāhea-wai. Old name for a place in south Ka'ū, Hawai'i. *Lit.,* water calling (a chief here shouted loudly when he wanted water).

Kāhei. Point, Hālawa qd., Moloka'i. *Lit.,* to gird on.

Kāheka. Village and road, Ha'i-kū qd., Maui. Gulch, Ka-la'e, Kaunakakai qd., Moloka'i; a cave here was believed to be the home of the heroine of the Pu'u-ka-pe'elua legend (Cooke 102). Street, Sheridan Tract, Honolulu. *Lit.,* shallow pool.

Ka-hekili. Highway and diving place, West Maui. Highway, windward O'ahu. Both are named for an important Maui chief who ruled for 27 years on Maui beginning in 1766, and for nine years on O'ahu from 1782 (RC 82). See Pākaikai. *Lit.,* the thunder.

Kahekili's Leap. Cove, Mō-kapu qd., O'ahu, from which spies sent torch signals to Moloka'i with information for Chief Ka-hekili of Maui. (Sterling and Summers 5:178.) See Ka-leina-a-Kahekili.

Ka-helo. Land area at Puapua'a, Kona, Hawai'i, where horse- and foot-races were held in the 1880s; Ka-lā-kaua attended. *Lit.,* going to and fro.

Ka-helu. Ridge, Wai-mea district, Kaua'i. *Lit.,* the number *or* the scratch.

Ka-helu Nui. Valley, Wai-mea district, Kaua'i. *Lit.,* big Ka-helu.

Kahe-manō. Beach area, southeast Lā-na'i. *Lit.,* school of sharks.

Kahena-wai. Hill, 'Īlio Pt. qd., north Moloka'i. See Kāne-wai.

Ka-heu. Gulch, 'Īlio Pt. qd., Moloka'i. Probably *lit.,* the fuzz.

Kahe-wai. Place, Mānoa, Honolulu. *Lit.,* water flowing.

Kahiki-kolo. Inland area, Kaua'i, perhaps legendary, famous for a trunkless tree, *lā'au kumu 'ole.* (For. Sel. 232.)

Ka-hiki-lani. Rock near Pau-malū (Sunset Beach), O'ahu, named for a surfer whose wife gave him *lehua* leis every day; once he returned from surfing with '*ilima* leis given by another woman; the wife called on her '*aumakua* (family god) and the husband was turned to stone. (Sterling and Summers 4:20–23; for a variant, Finney and Houston 40.) Also known as George Washington Stone. *Lit.,* The arrival [of] chief.

Kahiki-nui. Land division and forest reserve, Luala'i-lua Hills qd., Maui. (UL 124.) *Lit.,* great Tahiti.

Kahikolu. Congregational church at Nā-po'opo'o, Kona, Hawai'i. *Lit.,* trinity.

Ka-hiku-o-nā-lani. Church at Pearl City, O'ahu. *Lit.,* the seventh of the kings (Ka-lā-kaua, the seventh king, helped build this church).

Kāhili. Land division, peak (3,016 feet high), falls, and park, Wai-mea district, Kaua'i. Coastal land section, Ka-laupapa peninsula, Molo-ka'i. *Lit.,* feather standard.

Kāhili-loa. Land area, Wai-mea district, Kaua'i. Point, Ka-malō qd., south Moloka'i. *Lit.,* long feather standard.

Kāhili-pali. Cliff and point, Honu-'apo qd., Ka'ū, Hawai'i, named for an ancient priest of that name. *Lit.,* [wind-] swept cliff.

Ka-hilu. Assembly hall, Wai-mea, Hawai'i, named for Thelma Ka-hilu-o-nā-pua-o-Pi'ilani (the quiet one of the descendants of Pi-'ilani) Parker Smart.

Ka-hinahina. Ridge, east Lā-na'i. *Lit.,* the Florida moss.

Ka-hīnano. Land section, Honomū qd., Hawai'i. *Lit.,* the male pandanus flower.

Ka-hina-a-ka-lani. Coastal land section, Airport qd., north Moloka'i. Probably *lit.,* the grayness of the sky, heaven.

Kahina-pōhaku. Fishpond (now in ruins), Hālawa qd., Moloka'i, (Summers 150.) Probably *lit.,* stone carving.

Kā-Hina-pōki'i. Stream entering the sea south of Mau-lua Gulch, Honomū qd., Hawai'i. *Lit.,* Hina's younger sibling.

Kā-Hina-wai. Gulch, 'Īlio Pt. qd., south Moloka'i. *Lit.,* Hina's water.

Kahipa. Same as Ka-lae-o-Kahipa.

Ka-hi'u. Point, Ka-laupapa peninsula, Moloka'i. *Lit.,* the fish tail. Also called Lae-o-Kahi'u.

Ka-hiwa. Gulch and falls (1,700 feet, the highest in the State), Hālawa qd., north Moloka'i. A cliff is called Ka-pali-a-Kahiwa. *Lit.,* the chosen one (perhaps the name of a person).

Ka-hoa-ea. Land section near the border between Kō-loa and Līhu'e districts, Kaua'i. (For. Sel. 233.) *Lit.,* coming up [of] the companion.

Ka-hoaloha. Valley, Wai-mea district, Kaua'i. *Lit.,* the friend.

Ka-hoana. Valley, Wai-mea district, Kaua'i. *Lit.,* the whetstone.

Ka-hola-iki. Bay near Pelekunu, north Moloka'i. *Lit.,* the small fish poisoning.

Ka-hola-loa. Former reef, Honolulu Harbor. An island accumulated here; it was enlarged by dredging and is now Sand Island. *Lit.,* the long extension.

Ka-holo. Cliff, southwest tip of Lā-na'i. (Macdonald and Abbott 198.) *Lit.,* the running.

Ka-holo-a-ke-āhole. Old waterfront section of Honolulu seaward of Kaka'ako. *(Honolulu in 1810.) Lit.,* the running of the *āhole* fish.

Ka-holo-a-Pele. Peak (4,691 feet high) between Kumu-'eli and Wai-lau, Ka-malō qd., Moloka'i. *Lit.,* Pele's landslide (Pele is said to have dug here).

Ka-holo-kuaiwa. Cliff, Wai-pi'o, Hawai'i. *Lit.,* the ninth movement (landslide).

Ka-holo-po'o-hina. Elevated land section (3,400 feet high), Wai-pi'o qd., Hawai'i. *Lit.,* the gray head slide.

Ka-hōlua-manu. The highest cliff of Wai-mea Valley, Kaua'i. *Lit.,* the slide [of] birds.

Ka-hōlua-o-Kahawali. Crater, and cinder and spatter cone on Kī-lau-ea volcano's east rift zone, Kala-pana qd., Hawai'i. *Lit.,* the sledding

K

course of Kahawali. (Chief Kahawali refused to race his sled with Pele, disguised as an old woman. She chased him down the mountain to the sea, where he managed to escape. A line of small spatter cones marks Kahawali's path, with Pele's barrage of hot rocks following him. HM 191; Macdonald and Abbott 50. See Ālo'i.)

Ka-homa. Site of petroglyphs, valley, stream, tunnel, ditch, and reservoir, Lahaina qd., Maui. *Lit.*, the thin one.

Ka-honua. Old name for Kaha-lu'u fishpond, Wai-Kāne qd., O'ahu. *Lit.*, the earth.

*Ka-ho'okama-kea. Gulch, Hālawa qd., Moloka'i.

Ka-ho'olawe. Island in Maui County, 11 miles long, 6 miles wide, with an area of 45 square miles. It is uninhabited and is used as a bombing target by the U.S. Navy. See Kohe-mālamalama. *Lit.*, the carrying away (by currents).

Ka-ho'olei-nā-pe'a. Land division near Kō-loa, Kaua'i. *Lit.*, the flying [of] the kites (the kite of the Kaua'i hero, Ka-welo, was entangled here with that of his rival cousin; For. Sel. 35).

Ka-ho'olewa. Ridge, Lahaina qd., Maui. *Lit.*, the swing.

Ka-ho'opulu. Stream, Ka-wai-hau district, Kaua'i. *Lit.*, the wetting.

Ka-ho'opu'u. Stream, Kohala, Hawai'i. *Lit.*, the heaped up.

*Kahua. Gulch, north Lā-na'i.

Ka-hua. Land sections, Lahaina qd.; land section and shelter, Mākena qd., Maui. *Lit.*, the fruit.

Ka-huā. Ranch, Kohala qd., Hawai'i. See Kai-'ōpae. *Lit.*, the jealousy.

*Kahuaawi. Gulch, Kaunakakai qd., Moloka'i. Just south of this gulch, before the point where it joins with Ka-lua-lohe Gulch, is the last remaining *maika* course. (Perhaps this is a misspelling of Ka-hua-wai.)

Ka-hua'i. Land section, Kau-pō qd., Maui. *Lit.*, the pouring forth.

Ka-hua-iki. Stream, Kāne-'ohe qd., O'ahu. *Lit.*, the small fruit.

Kahua-i-lana-wai. Pool, upper Nu'u-anu, Honolulu, perhaps the one now called Jackass Ginger. (Sterling and Summers 6:237–238.) *Lit.*, site of tranquil water.

Ka-hua-lele-pulu. Land section, Kaunakakai qd., south central Moloka'i.

Ka-hua-lewa. House-site area in the adze quarry on Mauna Loa, west Moloka'i.

Kahua-ma'a. Flats, northwest Kaua'i. *Lit.*, sling site.

Ka-hua-wai. A small waterfall on Ka-lau-ao Stream, O'ahu, once a favorite resting place exclusively for chiefs. Also called Ka-hue-wai (the water gourd).

Ka-hue. Land division, point, and ancient village destroyed in the 1868 tidal wave (Hawaii Natural History Association Guide 16), Puna qd., Hawai'i. A lava flow from the 'Ālo'i-'Alae crater area reached the sea about 1,000 feet west of here on September 21, 1970. *Lit.*, the gourd.

Ka-hue-wai. Same as Ka-hua-wai.

Ka-huku. Land sections, Honomū qd.; ranch, Honu-'apo qd., Ka'ū, Hawai'i. Ka-huku Pali is a fault scarp 2.5 miles northwest of South Point; it has a maximum height of about 600 feet, extends inland about 10 miles, and can be traced out to sea 18 miles (Macdonald

K

and Abbott 41). In Ka'ū two young chiefs raced with Pele on *hōlua* sleds but became afraid and refused to race with her when they discovered who she was; Pele chased them, devastating the once fertile area and creating Nā-pu'u-a-Pele (the hills of Pele). (Westervelt, 1963:23–26.) Village, land division, northernmost point, golf course, ranch, schools, forest reserve, and surfing beach (Finney, 1959a:108), O'ahu. The point here was cut off from the island by Lono-ka-'eho (Lono the stone), a chief with eight stone foreheads (see Ka-lae-o-Kahipa). A lone rock here, Kū's Rock Spring, was said to give forth pure spring water (Sterling and Summers 4:53; see Wai-pahu). O'ahu was believed to have consisted of two islands ruled by a brother and sister who locked fingers to pull the islands together. They did this at a pool called Pō-lou, perhaps a shortening of Pou-lou (hooked post). (Sterling and Summers 4:49–50a.) *Lit.,* the projection.

Ka-hului. Bay and land section south of Kai-lua, Hawai'i. Town, elementary school, port, bay, railroad, and surfing area known as Kahului Breakwater (Finney, 1959a:108), Maui. Probably *lit.,* the winning.

Ka-hulu-'īlio. Gulch, East Maui, now called Ako's Gulch. *Lit.,* the dog fur.

Ka-hulu-o-manu. Lower part of Ka-mana Nui Valley, Moana-lua, O'ahu, and site of a golf course. *Lit.,* the feather of [the] bird.

Ka-hūnā. Lane, Mō-'ili'ili, Honolulu. (TM.) *Lit.,* the hidden one.

Ka-huna-li'i. Valley, north central Ni'ihau. *Lit.,* the tiny fragment.

Kahu-wai. Crater near Hale-pua'a, Puna, Hawai'i. *Lit.,* water tender.

Ka-i'a. Point, Honolua qd., Maui. Street, Pauoa, Honolulu. *Lit.,* the fish (perhaps a part of a person's name).

Kai-aka. Point and bay, Hale-'iwa qd., O'ahu, said to be named for a person. *Lit.,* shadowed sea.

Kai-a-ke-akua. Sandy beach at Kai-lua Bay, Kona, Hawai'i. *Lit.,* sea of the god.

Kai-a-Kekua. Beach area near Ke-ala-ke-kua, Hawai'i, where the first missionary ship, the *Thaddeus,* arrived on March 30, 1820. *Lit.,* seashore of Kekua (short for Ke-ala-ke-kua).

Kai-i'a-li'u. Street, Mō-'ili'ili, Honolulu. *Lit.,* the salted fish.

Kai-'ama. Road, Mauna-lua, Honolulu. (TM.) *Lit.,* mullet sea (the old name of the valley in which it is located).

Kai-a-miki. Land section *(lele)* at Kumu-'eli, Ka-malō qd., Moloka'i. *Lit.,* sea of [the] receding.

Kaiapa-o-ka-'īlio. Land section, Wai-luku qd., Maui. The meaning of the first part of the name is not clear. The last part means 'of the dog'.

Kai-ehu. Point, Airport qd., Moloka'i. A bluff shelter at the southeast end of the point was excavated by Bishop Museum archaeologists in 1953. It was used primarily by fishermen. A radiocarbon date of 1408 ± 300 years was obtained from charcoal at the lowest level of the shelter. *Lit.,* sea spray.

Ka-'ie'ie. Land section and stream, Honomū qd., Hawai'i. Former *heiau* at Ka-lihi, Honolulu. *Lit.,* the '*ie'ie* vine.

67

K

Ka-'ie'ie Loko. Channel between O'ahu and Kaua'i. *Lit.*, inner Ka-'ie'ie.

Ka-'ie'ie Waena. Channel between O'ahu and Kaua'i. *Lit.*, middle Ka-'ie'ie.

Ka-'ie'ie Waho. Channel between O'ahu and Kaua'i. *Lit.*, outer Ka-'ie'ie. (This is the common name for the channel; For. Sel. 46.)

Kai-halulu. Beach area at base of Ka-'uiki Head, Hāna, Maui. *Lit.*, roaring sea.

Kai-he'e. Street, Makiki, Honolulu.

Ka-'ihi-kapu. Street, Moana-lua, Honolulu, and name of a fishpond at Māpunapuna. (TM.) *Lit.*, the taboo sacredness.

Ka-iholena. Hill behind Pā-kua, Honu-'apo qd., Ka'ū, Hawai'i. The local rain god, Kū-mauna, had a field of *iholena* bananas here.

Ka-ihu-kiako. Hill (1,875 feet high), Lahaina qd., Maui.

Ka-ihu-o-kala. Hill inland from Ka'uiki, Hāna, Maui. *Lit.*, the nose of surgeonfish. (The hill was thought to resemble the back and head of the *kala* fish. The article *ke* was probably lost between *o* and *kala*.)

Ka-ihu-o-ka-pua'a. Land sections at Koko Head and at Wai-mano, O'ahu; also a stone at Wai-mano. *Lit.*, the snout of the pig (Kama-pua'a).

Ka-ihu-o-Pala'ai. West Loch, Pearl Harbor, O'ahu. Pala'ai was a woman from here who married a Lā'ie man; she sent her husband from Lā'ie to fetch mullet from Honouliuli; mullet followed him as far as Kai-papa'u and then turned back—as they do today. *Lit.*, the nose of Pala'ai.

*Kaikaina. Hill (305 feet high), Ka-haku-loa qd., Maui.

Kaiko'o. Hilo bayfront redevelopment project, Hawai'i. Place, Black Point, Honolulu, named for the country home of Mrs. George R. Carter, used as a convalescent home for servicemen during World War II. The estate, which bordered the ocean, has since been subdivided. *Lit.*, strong sea.

Kai-kū'ono. Place, Black Point, Honolulu. *Lit.*, sea [and a] cove.

Ka-'ili. Stream and land, Kī-pahulu qd., Maui, owned by Ka-'ahu-manu and made into a place of refuge *(pu'uhonua)* by Ka-mehameha I. *Lit.*, the pebble.

Kā'ili. Small land section, Hālawa Valley, Moloka'i, with a place of refuge *(pu'uhonua)* of the same name. Street, Ka-lihi Waena, Honolulu, perhaps named for Ka-mehameha's feather god, Kū-kā'ili-moku (island-snatching Kū). According to TM, the Hutchinson family who lived here kept the name Kā'ili Kapu in honor of this god. *Lit.*, snatch.

Ka-'ili'ili. Land section and village, Puna; bay at Hīlea, Ka'ū, Hawai'i. Ridge and stream, Ka-malō qd., north Moloka'i. Land area on the Maka-pu'u side of the beach park at Sandy Beach, O'ahu. *Lit.*, the pebble. (Stones at Ka'ū, Hawai'i, were used for pathways and house flooring.)

Kā'ili-kahi. *Heiau*, Kaha-lu'u, O'ahu. *Lit.*, snatch once.

Kā'ili-kaula. Stream, Wai-pi'o qd., Hāmākua, Hawai'i. *Lit.*, snatch away rope.

Kā'ili-ki'i. Spot in Ka Lae qd., south Ka'ū where chief Ka-lani-'ōpu'u tried to get water by pounding a cliff; failing to get water, the *kahuna* adviser (Nā-ono-'āina) was hanged. Ka-lani-'ōpu'u lived nearby at Wai-'Ahukini until his death in 1782. *Lit.*, snatch away image.

Ka-'īlio. Point, Hanalei district, Kaua'i. *Lit.,* the dog.

Ka-'ili-'ula. Land section, Kī-lau-ea qd., Ka'ū, Hawai'i. Land division and gulch, Hālawa qd., south Moloka'i. *Lit.,* the red skin.

Kai-lua. Village, school, bay, and ancient surfing area (Finney and Houston 26), Kona, Hawai'i. Land division, land section, ditch, village, hill (1,269 feet high), gulch, Pā'ia area; stream, Ha'i-kū area, East Maui. Second largest city in the Hawaiian Islands (33,783 population in 1970), land division, schools, bay, beach park, field, ditch, and stream, Mō-kapu qd., O'ahu. *Lit.,* two seas (probably currents, especially on Hawai'i).

Kai-ma'ema'e. Point on southwestern part of Ford Island, O'ahu. *Lit.,* clean sea.

Kaimana-hila. Diamond Head, O'ahu. See Lae-'ahi. *Lit.,* diamond hill.

Kaimanawai. Place, Kāhala, Honolulu.

Kai-mū. Stream, Wai-pi'o qd.; land section and village, Kala-pana qd., Hawai'i, noted for its surf and its black sand beach. The black sand was formed by steam explosions that occurred when a lava flow entered the ocean (Macdonald and Abbott 44) in about 1750. The surfing site was formerly called Hō'eu and Ka-poho, but now is called Kai-mū. (For a pun, see PE, *mū.*) *Lit.,* gathering [at the] sea [to watch surfing].

Ka-imu-kālua-ua. Same as Imu-kālua-ua.

Ka-imu-kī. Intermediate and high schools, recreation center, and section 33 of Honolulu (map 6). The area is a small shield volcano; the summit, seaward of the Ka-imu-kī fire station, is indented by a crater about 30 feet deep (Macdonald and Abbott 374; PH 186). *Lit.,* the *ti* oven (the Menehune cooked *ti* roots in ovens here).

Ka-imu-loli. Area near Kau-pō, Maui, named for an ancient chief's fondness for oven-cooked *loli* (sea slug); Kau-pō people are sometimes humorously called *loli* eaters *('ai loli). Lit.,* the *loli* oven.

Ka-imu-manō. Land section, Hālawa qd., south Moloka'i. *Lit.,* the shark oven. (A cannibal shark-man, Nanaue, was caught at Kai-nalu and dragged up the gulch and hill. His body left a shallow ravine and, near the top of Kai-nalu hill, henceforth known as Pu'u-manō [shark hill], there is a rock with a deep groove entirely around it. The people cut up Nanaue with pieces of bamboo and burned his flesh. His father, Ka-moho-ali'i, was angry and henceforth bamboo growing here is dull. Summers 206–207; Thrum, 1907:265–268.) The exact location of the oven is not known.

Ka-imu-o-Hema. Place, Nu'u-anu, Honolulu, and original name of this land section. (TM.) *Lit.,* the oven of Hema.

Ka-'ina. Street, Wai-kīkī, Honolulu. (TM.) *Lit.,* the sea urchin.

Ka'ina-limu. Bay, Hāna qd., Maui. *Lit.,* seaweed procession.

Kainaliu. Village, Kailua qd., Kona, Hawai'i; formerly Kā-i-nā-liu (bail the bilge), the name of a canoe bailer for Keawe-nui-a-'Umi.

Kai-nalu. Land division and gulch, Hālawa qd., south Moloka'i. Abner Pākī, father of Bernice Pau-ahi Bishop was born here. See Ka-imu-manō, Pu'u-manō. Drive, elementary school, and new subdivision, One-awa land section, Kai-lua, O'ahu. *Lit.,* billowy sea.

Kā-i-nā-'ohe. Fishpond, Ka-malō qd., south Moloka'i. *Lit.,* cast with the bamboos.

K

Ka'inapau. Place, Kāhala, Honolulu, named for the chief who owned the land. (TM.)

Kai-nehe. Gulch and stream, Hāmākua qd., Hawai'i. Ke-ō-ua is said to have hidden here behind a rock called Pōhaku-o-Keōua during his battle with Ka-mehameha. *Lit.,* whispering sea.

Ka-inoa. Place, 'Āina-Haina, Honolulu. *Lit.,* the name.

Kai-'oli. School, Honolulu. *Lit.,* joyous sea.

Kaiolohia. Bay, north Lā-na'i. Plain east of Mo'omomi, Moloka'i. *Lit.,* tranquil sea.

Kai-'olu. Street, Wai-kīkī, Honolulu. (TM.) *Lit.,* cool ocean.

Kaiona. Beach park, Wai-mānalo, O'ahu, said to be named for a benevolent relative of Pele. *Nani ke kula a Kaiona i ka ho'ola'i a nā 'iwa,* the plain of Kaiona is pretty as the frigate birds soar.

Kaio'o. Drive, Wai-kīkī, Honolulu. *Lit.,* strong sea.

Kai-'ōpae. Gulch and point, Kohala qd., Hawai'i. *Lit.,* shrimp sea (warriors were as numerous as shrimps in the battle in which Lono-i-ka-makahiki killed Kanaloa-nui-o-ke-aka-waiea).

Kai-palaoa. Ancient surfing area, Hilo, Hawai'i (Finney and Houston 26). Land at foot of Wai-ānuenue Street, Hilo, Hawai'i. Ka-mehameha I often called here. Kamakau (RC 188) mentions a battle fought at Kai-palaoa and a *heiau* of the same name where Liholiho's navel cord was ceremonially cut in 1797 (RC 220). A boy riddling expert (For. 4:574–595) had the same name. *Lit.,* whale sea.

Kai-papa'u. Forest reserve, land section *(ahupua'a),* gulch, stream, hill, point, former quadrangle, Pu'u-kapu qd., O'ahu. See Ka-ihu-o-Pala'ai, Ma'akua. *Lit.,* shallow sea.

*Kaipoioi. Gulch, Mākena qd., Maui.

Ka-ipu-ha'a. Land section, Kohala qd., Hawai'i. *Lit.,* the low calabash.

Ka-ipu-kai-Hina. Coastal area, Mā'alaea qd., Maui. *Lit.,* Hina's meat dish.

Kai-puka-ulua. Gulch, Hālawa qd., Moloka'i. *Lit.,* sea [where] *ulua* fish appear.

Kaiser's. Surfing area opposite Kaiser Hospital, Wai-kīkī, Honolulu.

Ka-'iu-lani. Hotel and avenue, Wai-kīkī, named for Princess Ka-'iu-lani (1875–1899); playground, Ka-lihi Uka; elementary school, Kalihi Kai, Honolulu. See 'Āina-hau. *Lit.,* the royal sacred height.

Ka-'iwa. Stream, Hanalei district, Kaua'i. Peak and ridge above Lani-kai, O'ahu, where frigate birds *('iwa)* are often seen.

Ka-'iwa-loa. Well-preserved *heiau* at Olo-walu, Maui. *Lit.,* the long fern.

Ka-iwi. Land points near Kai-lua, Kona, Hawai'i, and farther north in the same district. At one of the points is a rock believed to be a petrified shark, the shark form of a priest (Ka-lua-lapa-uila). When the priest was about to be burned at 'Ōhiki, a legendary hero, Ka-miki, prayed to Pele and a terrible storm arose. The priest's shark form was turned to stone as it tried to enter the *heiau* to save the human form of the priest. One of Pele's sisters, Hi'iaka-noho-lae (Hi'iaka living [at the] point), came to live here, making the place sacred and forbidden to Pele. In the story of Punia, the shark Kai-'ale'ale, who had swallowed Punia, came here and was cut open by the people; Punia came out alive but was bald (For. Sel. 15). Channel (25 miles wide), separating Oʻahu from Molokaʻi. Road and cave, Mauna-lua, Honolulu. (TM.) *Lit.,* the bone.

Ka-iwi-keʻe. Stream, Heʻeia, Oʻahu. *Lit.,* the bent bone.

Kai-wiki. Land sections, stream, school, water system, and park, Hāmākua, Mauna Kea, and Honomū qds., Hawaiʻi. *Lit.,* quick sea.

Ka-iwi-koʻele. Stream near the boundary between Koʻolau Loa and Wai-a-lua districts, Oʻahu, and tributary to Wai-mea Stream. *Lit.,* the rattle bones.

Ka-iwi-lahilahi. Land section and stream, Honomū qd., Hawaiʻi. Two rocks on the banks of the stream are the beautiful Ke-anini and her lover; the girl did not leave before the cock crowed, and both were changed to stones. *Lit.,* the frail bone.

K

Ka-iwi-o-Pele. A cinder hill, Hāna qd., Maui. *Lit.,* the bone of Pele. (Pele's bones were left here after her battle with her older sister, Nā-maka-o-Kahaʻi. Lono-muku left the top of this hill to go to live on the moon. This hill is the principal landmark for Poʻo, a fishing station off Kī-pahulu. Kama-puaʻa ravished Pele here; HM 213.)

Ka-iwi-poʻo. Mountain, Kāne-ʻohe qd., Koʻolau range, Oʻahu. *Lit.,* the skull.

Ka-iwi-ʻula. Street, Ka-lihi Kai, Honolulu, and the part of Honolulu where the Bishop Museum is located. (Elbert and Mahoe 34, 35, 77, 78.) *Lit.,* the red bone.

Kākā. Point, Ka-hoʻolawe. *Lit.,* to hew.

Kakaʻako. Gulch, ʻĪlio Pt. qd., north Molokaʻi. Near the head of the gulch, at about 1,300 feet elevation on the east side, *kālai-pāhoa* trees *(nīoi, aʻe, ʻohe)* are said to grow. (PE 386.) Section 16 of Honolulu (map 6).

Kakaʻa-ʻuʻuku. Gulch, Airport qd., north Molokaʻi. *Lit.,* small rolling.

Kakaha-iʻa. Inland fishpond, Ka-malō qd., south Molokaʻi. *Lit.,* fish slicing.

Kakaʻina-pāhaʻo. Rainfall station, Airport qd., Molokaʻi. *Lit.,* mysterious procession.

*Kakaka-wawai. Land section, Ka-malō qd., Molokaʻi.

Kākala-hale. Hill (1,280 feet high), Kaunakakai qd., Molokaʻi. In the valley just southeast is the beginning of the 5-mile irrigation tunnel to Wai-kolu Valley. *Lit.,* ridge house.

Kākalaioa. Rock in the sea off Maka-puʻu, Oʻahu. *Lit.,* gray nickers (a rough bramble; the rocks here are as sharp as *kākalaioa* thorns).

Kā-kea. Upper part of Round Top, Honolulu.

Kākela. Drive and place, lower Mānoa, Honolulu, named for George P. Castle (1851–1932), a son of Samuel Northrup Castle, who lived there. He was president of Castle and Cooke 1903–1916. *Lit.,* castle. (TM.)

Kākīwai. Coastal area, Kaʻū, Hawaiʻi.

Kala. Place, Kāhala, Honolulu. (TM.) *Lit.,* surgeonfish.

Ka-laʻalāʻau. Valley, south central Niʻihau. *Lit.,* the twigs.

Ka Lae. South Point, Hawaiʻi, the southernmost point in all the fifty states; quadrangle, south Hawaiʻi. A rock in the sea here called Pōhaku-waʻa-Kauhi (Kauhi canoe stone) is believed to have been a canoe from Kahiki. See Wai-luku. (For a saying, see Appendix 8.1.) *Lit.,* the point.

Ka-laʻe. Village and land area in Kaha-nui, north central Molokaʻi. The people here were noted for their failure to observe the taboos of others: *He Ka-laʻe au, he ʻaʻe kū,* I am from Ka-laʻe, a taboo breaker. See Wai-a-ka-laʻe. *Lit.,* the clearness.

Ka-lae-ʻā. Point, Ka-laupapa peninsula, Molokaʻi. Also called Ka-lae-ʻaʻā. (*Ka Lahui Hawaiʻi,* September 27, 1877.) *Lit.,* the rocky point.

Ka-lae-āhole. Point, northwest Lā-naʻi. *Lit.,* the *āhole* fish point.

Ka-lae-ʻāmana. Point, northeast Kauaʻi. *Lit.,* the crosspiece point.

Ka-lae-kapu. Point, Hālawa qd., Molokaʻi. *Lit.,* the sacred point.

Ka-lae-kīki. Point, Kō-loa district, Kauaʻi. *Lit.,* the stifling point (from *(ikiiki).*

Ka-lae-kilo-iʻa. Coastal area, Ka-malō qd., north Molokaʻi. *Lit.,* the fish-observing point.

Ka-lae-kiʻona. Point, Wai-mānalo, Oʻahu. *Lit.,* the dung-heap cape.

Ka-lae-loa. Point, Mākena qd., Maui. Harbor and sandspit, Ka-malō qd., south Molokaʻi. Old name for Barber's Point, Oʻahu, where Captain Henry Barber went aground in 1796. See Barber's Point. *Lit.,* the long point.

Ka-laʻe Loa. Same as Ka-laʻe. *Lit.,* long Ka-laʻe. (UL 239.)

Ka-lae-mamo. Point near Nā-poʻopoʻo lighthouse, Kona, Hawaiʻi. *Lit.,* the *mamo* fish point.

Ka-lae-māmane. Point, Mākena qd., Maui. *Lit.,* the *māmane* tree point.

Ka-lae-manō. Point near Kīholo, Kona, Hawaiʻi. *Lit.,* the shark point.

*Ka-lae-mau. Point, Ka-laupapa peninsula, Molokaʻi.

Ka-lae-milo. Points at Ka-laupapa peninsula and Wai-lau, Molokaʻi. *Lit.,* the twirling point *or* the *milo* tree point.

Ka-lae-o-kaʻea. See Kaʻea.

Ka-lae-o-ka-hano. Point, southeast Lā-naʻi. *Lit.,* the point of the fame.

Ka-lae-o-Kahipa. Ridge and gulch near Ka-huku, Oʻahu. Two mountains here resemble the breasts of Lewa, a mythical woman. A point here was cut off from the island by Lono-ka-ʻeho, a fighter with eight stone foreheads. *Lit.,* the point of Kahipa. (UL 205.)

Ka-lae-o-ka-ʻīlio. Points at Kona, Hawaiʻi; Kau-pō, Maui; northwest Molokaʻi (also called ʻĪlio and Ka-ʻīlio). *Lit.,* the cape of the dog. (At the Kona point in a sea pool is the body of Anahulu, a supernatural dog that was changed to stone by Pele. See Puʻu-anahulu.)

Ka-lae-o-ka-lāʻau. Point, southwest tip of Molokaʻi named for the famous club (*lāʻau*) of Palila, the Kauaʻi hero who, with a spear given him by the gods, leapt to Kiha-a-Piʻilani, a Molokaʻi hill, and there attracted all the women; the angry and jealous Molokaʻi men fought him. His club lost its mana to the gods of Molokaʻi, and so he threw it away; it landed on this cape. (*Ka Nupepa Kuokoa,* July 6, 1922.)

Ka-lae-o-ka-ʻōʻio. Point and beach park, also called Ka-lae-ʻōʻio, at Kua-loa, Oʻahu, the boundary point between Koʻolau Poko and Koʻolau Loa. *Lit.,* the cape of the bonefish.

Ka-lae-o-Kowali. Point, Hanalei district, Kauaʻi. *Lit.,* the point of Kowali (a person).

Ka-lae-paʻa. Drive, Ka-lihi Uka, Honolulu. *Lit.,* the solid point *or* solid forehead.

Ka-lae-pōhaku. Land section, Ka-hului area, Maui. Area in Honolulu where St. Louis-Chaminade Education Center stands, playground, and nearby street and gulch. *Lit.,* the stone promontory.

Kala-haku. Cone, cliff, and overlook, Hale-a-ka-lā Crater, East Maui. *Lit.,* proclaim [the] lord.

Ka-lā-heo. Land section, gulch, elementary school, and town, Kō-loa district, Kaua'i. Land section, subdivision, school, avenue, and playground, Kai-lua, O'ahu. Street names in the subdivision begin with *'Ili-* (surface, skin). (Today, commonly pronounced Kalaheo.) *Lit.,* the proud day.

Ka-lā-hiki. Land section and beach, Hōnaunau qd., South Kona, Hawai'i. *Lit.,* the sunrise.

Ka-lā-hiki-ola. Land division and Protestant church built at Nunulu, Hawai'i in 1855 by Elias Bond. *Lit.,* the life-bringing sun *or* the day bringing salvation.

Ka-lā-hū. Point northwest of Hāna, Maui. *Lit.,* the overflowing sun.

Ka-lā-hua-pueo. Land section, Ka-malō qd., Moloka'i. Perhaps this is a garble for Ka-lāhui-pueo (the owl family). *Lit.,* the day [of the] owl's eggs.

Ka-lāhui-pua'a. Land division, Pua-kō qd., Kohala, Hawai'i. *Lit.,* the family [of] pigs.

Ka-la'i-a-ka-manu. Area near Kaunakakai, Moloka'i, perhaps the site of Ka-mehameha V's home, Malama. *Lit.,* the peace [made] by the bird. (UL 239.)

Kālai-moku. Street, Wai-kīkī, Honolulu, a variant name for Ka-lani-moku, adviser and prime minister for Ka-mehameha I and Queen Ka-'ahu-manu. He died in 1827. He was also called William Pitt. (TM.) *Lit.,* island carver.

Ka-la'i-'ōpua. Place, Tantalus, Honolulu. *Lit.,* the peace of the horizon cloud.

Kālai-pā-loa. Point, Kahana qd., O'ahu.

Kalaiwa. Way, Ka-lihi Uka, Honolulu. (TM.) *Lit.,* driver.

Kalakala. Land division, northeast Lā-na'i. *Lit.,* rough.

Ka-lā-kaua. Avenue and parkway, Wai-kīkī; intermediate school and recreation center, Ka-lihi Kai, Honolulu; golf course, Schofield, O'ahu, named for King Ka-lā-kaua (1836–1891). (UL 117.) *Lit.,* the day [of] battle.

Ka-lāke'e. Site of Huli-he'e Palace, Kai-lua, Kona, Hawai'i. This was Ka-mehameha's first residence in Kona and was called Papa (Ii 110). *Lit.,* the bend.

Ka-lā-kohi. Gulch, West Maui.

Ka-lālani. Ancient surfing place, Puna district, southeast Hawai'i. (Finney, 1959a:51.) *Lit.,* the row.

Ka-lalau. Land section, Hilo and Honomū qds., Hawai'i. Stream, valley, trail, land section, and beach, northwest Kaua'i. (For. Sel. 81; UL 102). *Lit.,* the straying. (On Hawai'i, two beautiful girls were seen swimming here, and when the viewers pushed through jungle or stream to find them, they had strayed [*lalau*]. *Aia akula i Ka-lalau,* there at Straying—said of one who behaves foolishly.)

Kalalea. Well-preserved fishing shrine at Ka Lae, Hawai'i; it was taboo to women. Offerings are still placed there. A stone nearby is called Pōhaku-o-ke-au, which may be translated 'stone of the cur-

K

rent' (referring to intersecting currents; see Hala'ea) or 'stone of the times,' referring to the belief that the stone turned over if there was to be a change in the government. Hill inland of Anahola, Ka-wai-hau, Kaua'i, which has a conspicuous hole near the top said to have been pecked open by Hulu, a supernatural bird, who wanted to see Anahola on the other side. Hulu could also change himself into man and *mo'o*. Another version, perhaps later, is that the Kaua'i hero, Ka-welo, threw his spear through this hole. According to another story (HM 419), Ka-pūnohu cast the spear. *Lit.,* prominent.

Kala-loa. Ancient surfing area, Puna district, Hawai'i. (Finney, 1959a: 51.) *Lit.,* very rough.

Kalalua. Crater, east rift zone, Kī-lau-ea, Hawai'i. (Macdonald and Abbott 98.)

Ka-lama. Coastal section, south central Ka-ho'olawe. Stream, Ka-wai-hau district, Kaua'i. Beach park, Pu'u-o-kali qd., Maui, named for Samuel E. Kalama, Maui County Chairman 1913–1933. Valley, young lava flow, and cinder cone (about 35 feet high with a crater 50 feet deep in its summit), Koko Head qd., O'ahu (Macdonald and Abbott 378); beach club and street, Mō-kapu qd., O'ahu. Street, Ka-lihi Waena, Honolulu; Ka-mehameha Schools dining hall, Honolulu, built in 1954, and named for the wife of Ka-mehameha III.

Ka-lama-. Five land sections near Ke-ala-ke-kua Bay, Kona, Hawai'i, probably named for a family. The names are Kalama-kumu (source Kalama), Kalama-'Umi, Kalama-kowali (swinging Kalama), Kala-ma-kāpala (staining Kalama), Kalama-wai-'awa'awa (bitter water Kalama). (For. 4:588–589.)

Ka-lama Iki. Gulch, west Lā-na'i. *Lit.,* small Ka-lama.

Ka-lama-kū. Street, Pauoa, Honolulu. (TM.) *Lit.,* the upright torch.

Ka-lama-'ula. Variant name for Kau-ka-hōkū, Kona, Hawai'i. Land division and the first Moloka'i homesteads, Kaunakakai qd., south Moloka'i. *Lit.,* the red torch *or* red *lama* tree.

*Kalanai. Point and site of a fishing shrine, as for *kala* and *enenue*, Lā-'ie, O'ahu. (Sterling and Summers 4:72.)

Ka-lana-o-kua-iki. *Pali,* Kī-lau-ea qd., Hawai'i.

Ka-lani. Beach, Airport qd., north Moloka'i. High school, Wai-'alae; street in Ka-lihi Kai, Honolulu, named for the family of Corbett Ka-lani (TM). *Lit.,* the sky *or* the royal chief.

Ka-lani-ana-'ole. Elementary and intermediate school at Pāpa'i-kou, Hawai'i. First tract of homesteads under the Hawaiian Homes Commission Act, Kaunakakai qd., south Moloka'i (Cooke 77). Highway and park, Honolulu. Beach park, Nānā-kuli, O'ahu. All were named for Prince Jonah Kū-hiō Ka-lani-ana-'ole. *Lit.,* the royal chief without measure. See Kū-hiō.

Ka-lani-kāula. *Kukui* grove and hill (734 feet high), Hālawa qd., Moloka'i, named for a seer or *mo'o*-slaying prophet who lived here; he was killed by Palo (or in another version, Ka-welo) of Lā-na'i by sorcery, and was buried under the *kukui* trees where he had made his home *(Puka La Kuokoa,* March 23, 1893). He is celebrated in the song "Moloka'i nui a Hina": *'O ku'u pua kukui, aia i Lani-kāula,* my *kukui* flower is at Lani-kāula. (See also UL 130.) This place is also known as Ulu-kukui-o-Lanikāula *(kukui* grove of Lani-kāula). The grove was considered sacred because of the reverence in which the seer was held. Nuts from the grove were considered superior. *Lit.,* the royal prophet.

Ka-lani-puʻu. Hill, Nā-wiliwili, Kauaʻi, formerly a calling hill *(puʻu kāhea)* from which the movements of fish were called out. Pele's older sister, Nā-maka-o-Kahaʻi, planted kava and bananas here. *Lit.,* the royal hill.

Ka-laoa. School, Kai-lua; land section, Honomū qd., Hawaiʻi, said to be named for Kalaoa Puʻumoi, sister of Ka-palaoa, the mother of the riddling expert, Kala-pana. Land section, stream, homesteads, Kai-lua qd., Kona, Hawaiʻi. Valley, southeast Niʻihau. (For a saying, see Appendix 8.1.) *Lit.,* the choker (as a stick for catching eels).

Kalapakī. Beach, Līhuʻe district, Kauaʻi.

Ka-lapa-kono-manu. Land section, Ka-malō qd., Molokaʻi. *Lit.,* the bird-catcher ridge.

Ka-lapa-moa. Ridge, Ka-malō qd., south Molokaʻi. *Lit.,* the chicken ridge.

Kala-pana. Land sections, quadrangle, trail, village, and park, Puna district, Hawaiʻi, famous for its black sand (see Kai-mū). Pele was attacked near here by Kama-puaʻa, the pig man (see Puaʻa-kanu; HM 187). A priest of Pele may have been named for Kala-pana. He had vowed that only Pele might cut his hair. On his way to the volcano he encountered a storm and went back to the shore. People got him drunk on kava. When he fell asleep they cut his hair. Later a woman appeared at the door and said that he would always remain there. He was turned to a stone, said to be still there by a pool not far from a Catholic church. (For. Sel. 276.) See Ka-laoa. Probably *lit.,* announce noted place.

Ka-lapa-wai. Land division, Kai-lua, Oʻahu. *Lit.,* the water ridge.

Ka-lapu. Ancient surfing area, Ke-au-hou, North Kona, Hawaiʻi. (Finney and Houston 26.) *Lit.,* the ghost.

Kala-pueo. Area near Maka-puʻu, Oʻahu. *Lit.,* owl proclamation (owls called on others here to battle).

Ka-lau-ao. Land section and stream, Wai-pahu qd., Oʻahu. A battle was fought in the area between here and ʻAiea Heights from November 16 to December 12, 1794; Ka-lani-kū-pule defeated and killed Ka-ʻeo-kū-lani, chief of Maui, Molokaʻi, Lā-naʻi, and Kauaʻi (RC 168–170). See Ka-hua-wai. *Lit.,* the multitude [of] clouds.

Kalaunu. Street, Ka-lihi Uka, Honolulu. *Lit.,* crown.

Ka-lau-o-ka-lani. Way, Wai-kīkī, Honolulu, named for David Ke-ola Ka-lau-o-ka-lani, clerk of the City and County of Honolulu for more than 20 years beginning in 1905; in 1900 he was secretary to Robert W. Wilcox, first delegate to Congress. (TM.) Probably *lit.,* the multitude of the royal chief.

Ka-lau-o-nā-kukui. *Heiau,* Ka-malō qd., south Molokaʻi. *Lit.,* the multitudes of lights.

Ka-laupapa. Village, peninsula, and land division, Molokaʻi; present site of the leper settlement on Ka-laupapa peninsula. The source of the lava that formed the peninsula was a small shield volcano against the cliff, rising to an altitude of 405 feet. Its top is indented by Ka-uha-kō Crater, a quarter of a mile across and more than 450

Ka-lā-wahine

feet deep, containing a pool of brackish water. (Macdonald and Abbott 351.) *Lit.,* the flat plain.

Ka-lā-wahine. Place, above Roosevelt High School, Honolulu, named for a deity who guarded water sources. (TM.) In the last century 25 land parcels with this name were awarded to Hawaiians. *Lit.,* the day [of] women.

Kala-wao. Land division, district, village, and county, Moloka'i; original site of the leper settlement on Ka-laupapa peninsula. Street and place, Woodlawn, Mānoa, Honolulu. *Lit.,* announce mountain area.

Kale. Place, Ka-lihi Uka, Honolulu. *Lit.,* Charles. (TM.)

Ka-leholeho. Ancient surfing area, Ka-hului area, Maui. *Lit.,* the callus.

Ka-lehua. Land section, Hāmākua qd.; ancient surfing area, Puna, Hawai'i (Finney and Houston 26). Ancient surfing area, Lahaina, West Maui (Finney, 1959a:52). Street and land area, Mānoa, Honolulu (TM). *Lit.,* the expert.

Ka-lehua-hakihaki. Peak (3,548 feet high), Wai-mea district, northwest Kaua'i. *Lit.,* the broken *lehua.*

Ka-lehua-wehe. Name for an ancient surfing area at Wai-kīkī (Finney and Houston 38; For. Sel. 35), now called Castle's. Sick persons were brought here for cleansing baths. *Lit.,* the removed *lehua* lei. (Pīkoi, the rat killer, went to Wai-kīkī wearing a *lehua* lei. He asked a surfing chiefess for her board. She refused because the board was taboo. They surfed and he gave her his lei. Finney and Houston 46, 47; PH 175.)

Ka-lei. Road, Mānoa, Honolulu. *Lit.,* the lei.

Ka-le'ia. Beach, Mā'alaea qd., Maui. *Lit.,* the abundance.

Ka-lei-kini. Ancient surfing area, Kaha-lu'u, North Kona, Hawai'i. (Finney and Houston 26.) See 'Akahi-pu'u. *Lit.,* the many leis.

Ka-leina-a-Kahekili. Area, southwest Lā-na'i. *Lit.,* the leap of Kahekili (whether this is the Maui chief who lived in the time of Kamehameha I is not known). See Kahekili's Leap.

Ka-leina-a-ka-'uhane. Area west of the Sheraton-Maui Hotel, Lahaina qd., Maui. *Lit.,* the leaping of the spirit (into the nether world).

Ka-lei-o-Papa. Dormitory, Ka-mehameha Schools, built in 1940 and named for Ka-mehameha III; his other names included Kau-i-ke-aouli (place in the blue firmament) and Ka-lei-o-Papa (the beloved child of Papa [the wife of Wākea]).

Ka-lele. Road, lower Mānoa, Honolulu. (TM.) *Lit.,* the flight *or* the altar.

Ka-lele-iki. Stream, Pūpū-kea, O'ahu. *Lit.,* the short leap.

Kalemela. Congregational church at Pā-'auhau, Hāmākua qd., Hawai'i. *Lit.,* Carmel.

Ka-lena. Land section and peak near Schofield Barracks, O'ahu; drive, Ka-lihi Uka, Honolulu. *Lit.,* the lazy one.

*Kā-leo-lehua-'ula. Land section, Ka-malō qd., Moloka'i.

Kālepa. Land section, Hāmākua qd.; point, South Kona, Hawai'i. Ridge, forest reserve, and trail, Līhu'e, Kaua'i. Land division, gulch, point, Kau-pō qd.; gulch, Wai-luku qd., Maui. See Merchant. *Lit.,* trade.

Kālepa-lehua. Gulch and stream, Hāna, Maui. *Lit.,* expert tradesman.

Ka-lepe-a-moa. Point, south Ka'ū, Hawai'i. Land division extending above Hāmoa, East Maui. See Kū-lepe-a-moa. *Lit.,* the comb [acquired] by [a] chicken.

Ka-lepolepo. Land division and beach near Kīhei, Maui. *Lit.,* the dirt. La Pérouse called the bay now named for him Keriporepo (Healy 30–31).

Kālia. Road, Wai-kīkī, Honolulu; stream, Wai-he‘e, O‘ahu. *Lit.,* waited for.

*****Kalialinui.** Land division and gulch, Pu‘u-o-kali qd., Maui.

Kaliawa. Street, Ka-lihi Kai, Honolulu.

Ka-lihi. Point, Honomū qd.; land section, South Kona, Hawai‘i, so named ("the edge") because it was a small area between two large ones. Land sections, Mākena and Hale-a-ka-lā qds., Maui. Land section, channel, stream, valley, elementary school, field, street, and shopping center, Honolulu, said to have been named by Prince Lot (afterwards Ka-mehameha V) in 1856. Ka-lihi in Honolulu is famous in legend as the home of Pele's sister Kapo (HM 186), and of Haumea, Pele's mother who is identified with Papa, the wife of Wākea. She had many adventures at Ka-lihi and saved her husband Wākea, who was being taken away for sacrifice, by embracing him. His bonds loosened and the two disappeared into a tree. Ka-‘ie‘ie was a *heiau* here for her worship. (HM 278–283.)

Ka-lihi Kai. Beach and beach park, Hanalei district, Kaua‘i. Elementary school and section 1 of Honolulu (map 6). *Lit.,* seaward Ka-lihi.

Ka-lihi Uka. Elementary school, park, and section 3 of Honolulu (map 6). *Lit.,* inland Ka-lihi.

Ka-lihi Waena. Elementary school, playground, and section 2 of Honolulu (map 6). *Lit.,* central Ka-lihi.

Ka-lihi Wai. Village, land division, bay, landing, and stream, Hanalei district, north Kaua‘i. *Lit.,* Ka-lihi [with a] stream.

Ka-lili. Place, Punchbowl, Honolulu. (TM.) *Lit.,* the jealousy.

Ka-limu-kele. Stream and land section, Kāne-‘ohe qd., O‘ahu. See Ha‘i-kū Gardens. *Lit.,* the watery seaweed.

Ka-li‘u. Hill, Kala-pana qd., Hawai‘i. (PH 22.) *Lit.,* the well salted.

Ka-liu-wa‘a. Valley, stream, and falls (Sacred Falls), Hau-‘ula, O‘ahu. A short distance below the falls is a trough-like gouge up the cliff where the pig demigod, Kama-pua‘a, is believed to have leaned against the cliff so that members of his family might climb up his body and escape their enemies. The stream and valley are called also Ka-lua-nui. (For. Sel. 202; Macdonald and Abbott 166; Sterling and Summers 4:102–113.) *Lit.,* the canoe hold *or* canoe leak.

Kāloa. Way, Mānoa, Honolulu, probably named for the twenty-fourth, twenty-fifth, and twenty-sixth days of the Hawaiian month.

Kalo‘alu-iki. Place, Mānoa, named for a god of taro patches. (TM.)

Ka-loa-o-ka-‘oma. Ancient surfing area, Ke-au, Maku‘u qd., Hawai‘i. (Finney and Houston 26.) *Lit.,* the length of the oven.

Kalo-haka. Stream, Kaha-lu‘u, O‘ahu. *Lit.,* hollow taro.

Ka-lohi. Channel between Moloka‘i and Lā-na‘i, 9 miles wide. *Lit.,* the slowness.

Ka-lo‘i. Gulch, Honouliuli, ‘Ewa, O‘ahu. (Sterling and Summers 1:161a.) *Lit.,* the taro patch.

Ka-loko. Land section and fishpond near Kai-lua, North Kona, Ha-

K

wai'i. Ka-mehameha's bones may have been hidden near here (RC 215); the Ka-mehameha family reserved the pond for themselves in 1848. A Bishop Museum archaeological survey in 1970 reported the existence of burial caves, petroglyphs, house structures, and other remains. Coastal area near Maka-pu'u, O'ahu; lane, downtown Honolulu. *Lit.*, the pond.

Ka-loko-'eli. Fishpond, Kaunakakai qd., coastal south Moloka'i. *Lit.*, the dug pond.

Ka-loko-hana-hou. Fishpond, Kāne-'ohe, O'ahu. The old name for this pond was Ka-hana-hou. *Lit.*, the repaired pond.

Ka-loko-loa. Cove near Kealakehe, North Kona, Hawai'i. *Lit.*, the long pond.

Kaloli. Point, Maku'u qd., Hawai'i.

Ka-lona. Gulch, Ka-malō qd., southeast Moloka'i. *Lit.*, the canoe resting block.

Ka-lona-iki. Walk, Ka-lihi Kai, Honolulu. (TM.) *Lit.*, the small canoe-supporting block.

Ka-lōpā. Land sections, gulch, church, and State recreation area, Hāmākua and Mauna Kea qds., Hawai'i. (For. Sel. 129). *Lit.*, the tenant farmer.

Ka-lou. Marsh, Waiale'e, O'ahu. *Lit.*, the hook.

Ka-lua. Place and road, Pālolo, Honolulu. *Lit.*, the pit.

Ka-lua-'aha. Land division, gulch, and place of refuge, Ka-malō qd., south Moloka'i. The first Christian mission on Moloka'i was established here in 1832 by the Reverend H.R. Hitchcock; it is also the site of a Catholic church (Our Lady of Sorrows) built in 1874 by Father Damien. *Lit.*, the gathering pit.

Ka-lua-āhole. Coastal area, Hālawa qd., Moloka'i. *Lit.*, the *āhole* fish pit.

Ka-lua-a-puhi. A fishpond still being used (1971), Airport qd., coastal southwest Moloka'i. *Lit.*, the pit of [the] eel.

Ka-lua-hā'ula. Ridge, Wai-mea district, northwest Kaua'i. *Lit.*, the reddish pit.

*Ka-lua-hauoni. Dome (3,288 feet elevation), Ka-malō qd., Moloka'i.

Ka-luahine. Cliff and falls near Wai-pi'o Bay, Hawai'i. *Lit.*, the old lady.

Ka-lua-hole. Coast between Wai-kīkī and Black Point, Honolulu. (For. Sel. 37.) *Lit.*, the *āhole* fish cavern.

Ka-lua-i-hākōkō. Point, Pu'u-o-kali qd., Maui. *Lit.*, the pit [for] wrestling. Hakōkō is said to have been the name of a chief.

Ka-lua-iki. Cinder cone, Hale-a-ka-lā Crater, East Maui. *Lit.*, the small pit.

Kālua-kanaka. A balancing stone in the Wai-luku River at Hilo, Hawai'i; it was believed connected by a tunnel to Coconut Island, and that persons falling over the stone into the stream would drown. Land section, Airport qd., south Moloka'i. *Lit.*, oven-baking man.

Ka-lua-kau. Land section, Airport qd., south Moloka'i. *Lit.*, the elevated pit.

Ka-lua-kauila. Gulch, Lā'ie; stream, Ka-'ena qd., O'ahu. *Lit.*, the *kauila* tree pit.

Ka-lua-ko'i. Land division and gulch, Airport qd., Moloka'i, the largest *ahupua'a* on Moloka'i, with an area of 46,500 acres. *Lit.*, the adze pit. (There are adze quarries on Mauna Loa extending over an area of 30 acres and also in the area just west of Mo'omomi.)

*Kalualea. Mountain, Kō-loa district, Kaua'i.

Ka-lua-lohe. Gulch, Kaunakakai qd., central Moloka'i. Tunnels here tap groundwater. (Map in Stearns and Macdonald, 1947.)

Ka-lua-makani. Land area, Mauna Kea qd., Hawai'i. *Lit.*, windy pit.

Ka-lua-nui. Ditch, Ha'i-kū qd., Maui. Cape, Kaunakakai qd., north Moloka'i. Ridge, Koko Head; land section and stream, northeast O'ahu (see Ka-liu-wa'a). According to Westervelt (1964*b*:249), the pig god, Kama-pua'a, was born here, apparently as a foetus; he was thrown away by an older brother but rescued by his mother, Hina. *Lit.*, the big pit. (For. Sel. 200.)

Ka-lua-nūnū. Land division, Ko'olau, Kaua'i. *Lit.*, the trumpetfish hole.

Ka-lua-'ōhiki. Land section, Ko'olau, Kaua'i. *Lit.*, the sand crab hole.

Ka-lua-o-Kapi'ioho. *Heiau,* Ka-malō qd., south Moloka'i, probably named for Ka-pi'i-oho (the curly hair), the O'ahu chief defeated in the battle at Ka-wela. See Ka-wela. *Lit.*, the pit of Ka-pi'i-oho.

Ka-lua-o-ka-wahine. Land section, Airport qd., south Moloka'i. *Lit.*, the pit of the woman (probably Pele).

Ka-lua-o-ke-li'i. A sea cavern at Kaha-lu'u, North Kona, Hawai'i, below the *heiau* of Ke'e-kū and Hāpai-ali'i. It was believed that a shark chief lived here but did not disturb divers for sea urchins *(wana). Lit.*, the cavern of the chief.

Ka-lua-'Ōlohe. Land section in Pālolo Valley, Honolulu, the name commemorating the defeat in *lua* fighting of cruel 'Ōlohe, a chief. (Sterling and Summers 6:100.)

Ka-lua-o-Pele. Crater, Wai-mānalo, O'ahu. *Lit.*, the pit of Pele.

Kālua-pe'elua. Gulch, Airport qd., Moloka'i. *Lit.*, baked caterpillar. (A caterpillar infestation was ended by baking the caterpillars. For another version, see Pu'u-ka-pe'elua.)

Ka-lua-pepeiao. Gulch, Hālawa qd., south Moloka'i. *Lit.*, the ear pit.

Ka-lua-puhi. Land section, Honu-'apo qd., Ka'ū, Hawai'i. Land area, Wai-mea qd., Kaua'i. Fishpond, Mō-kapu, O'ahu. *Lit.*, the eel pit (in a cave was an eel-shaped rock).

Ka-lua-pulani. Gulch, Pu'u-o-kali qd., Maui.

Kā-lu'e. Coastal area, Kī-lau-ea qd., Hawai'i. *Lit.*, hanging loose.

Kalukalu. Land sections and ledge, Kai-lua qd., North Kona, Hawai'i, named for a kind of grass said to grow only here.

Ka-lulu. Land section, southwest Lā-na'i. *Lit.*, the shelter.

Kā-luna-wai-Ka'ala. Stream, Pūpū-kea, O'ahu. *Lit.*, water from the heights [of] Ka'ala.

Ka-lu'u-o-ka-'ō'ō. Cinder cone, Hale-a-ka-lā Crater, East Maui. *Lit.*, the plunge of the digging stick.

Kama. Lane, Ka-pā-lama, Honolulu, named for John Kama, Republican politician during the 1900s. (TM.) *Lit.*, child.

*Kamaha. Hill, Hanalei district, Kaua'i.

Kama-hale. Land area, Pu'u-o-kali qd., Maui. *Lit.*, house child.

Ka-māhu'ehu'e. Fishpond, Ka-malō qd., south Moloka'i. *Lit.*, the openings.

Kama-iki. Point, southeast Lā-na'i. *Lit.*, small person.

Ka-maile. *Heiau,* plain, and spring, Ka-'ena qd., O'ahu. *Lit.,* the *maile* vine.

Ka-maile-'unu. Ridge and peak (1,312 feet high), Ka-'ena qd., O'ahu. *Lit.,* the stripped *maile.*

Ka-mā'ili. Homesteads, Kala-pana qd., Puna, Hawai'i. *Lit.,* the pebbles.

Kama-'ino. Area, Ni'ihau. *Lit.,* naughty child.

Kama-kahi. Gulch near the border between 'Īlio Pt. and Airport qds., Moloka'i. *Lit.,* single child.

K

Ka-maka-honu. Land division and home of Ka-mehameha I, Kai-lua, Hawai'i; he died here in 1819 (Ii 110, 118, chapter 9; RC 210). See Ahu-'ena. *Lit.,* the turtle eye.

Ka-maka-i'a. Land section, peak (2,633 feet high), and hills, Kī-lau-ea qd.; ancient surfing place, Kai-lua and Ke-āhole qds. (Finney and Houston 26), Hawai'i. *Lit.,* the fish eye.

Ka-māka'i-pō. Land section, gulch, and sandy beach, 'Īlio Pt. qd., Moloka'i. *Lit.,* the night guard.

Ka-makaīwa. Ancient surfing area, Ka-pa'a, Ka-wai-hau district, Kaua'i. (Finney and Houston 20.) *Lit.,* the mother-of-pearl eyes.

Ka-makou. Peak (4,970 feet high), the highest point on the East Moloka'i volcano, Ka-malō qd. (Stearns and Macdonald, 1947:3.) *Lit.,* the *Peucedanum* herb.

Ka-makua-mau-loa. Church, Ka-lihi Kai, Honolulu. *Lit.,* the everlasting father.

Kāmala. Point, Kō-loa district, Kaua'i. *Lit.,* hut.

Kamali'i. Hill, Kohala qd., North Hawai'i. Ridge, Ke-ālia Forest Reserve, Ka-wai-hau district, northeast Kaua'i. Park, Ka-hului, Maui. Park, downtown Honolulu. *Lit.,* children.

Ka-malino. Bay, land section, and site of an abandoned village, southwest Ni'ihau. *Lit.,* the calm.

Ka-malō. Harbor, land division, village, quadrangle, and gulch, southeast Moloka'i; originally Ka-malo'o (the dry place). A *kahuna* was named for the place: see 'Ili'ili-'ōpae.

Ka-malo-malo'o. Stream, Ka-wai-hau district, Kaua'i. *Lit.,* the dry loincloth.

Ka-māmalu. State office building, avenue, playground, and Ka-mehameha Schools classroom building built in 1967, all named for Victoria Ka-māmalu (1838–1866), the sister of Ka-mehameha V. See Ke-kū-anaō'a. *Lit.,* the protector.

Ka-mana Iki. The eastern and smaller tributary of Moana-lua Valley, O'ahu. *Lit.,* small Ka-mana.

Ka-mana-iki. Mountain and stream, Kāne-'ohe qd., O'ahu. Street, Ka-lihi Uka, Honolulu. *Lit.,* the small branch.

Ka-mana-kai. Gulch, Airport qd., Moloka'i. *Lit.,* the sea power *or* the sea branch.

Ka-mana Nui. The western tributary of Moana-lua Valley, O'ahu. *Lit.,* large Ka-mana.

Ka-mana-nui. Land section and ditch, Schofield Barracks, O'ahu. A forest grove here was called Pō-loa (long night). Stream tributary to Wai-mea Stream, and playground, Hale-'iwa, O'ahu. *Lit.,* the large branch.

80   **Ka-mana-wai.** Gulch, Mā'alaea qd., West Maui. *Lit.,* the stream branch.

Kamane. Coastal area, Honolua qd., West Maui.

Ka-mānele. Park, on University Avenue above the Mānoa campus of the University, Honolulu, named for chiefess Ka-ʻuaʻu-moku-o-ka-mānele, the daughter of Kua-kini, governor of Hawaiʻi. She died in 1834 at about 20 years of age. (RC 339.) *Lit.,* the sedan chair.

Ka-manoni. Land division, Hālawa qd., south Molokaʻi.

Ka-manu. Mountain, Līhuʻe district, Kauaʻi. *Lit.,* the bird.

Ka-manu-wai. Old name for a part of Honolulu near lower Nuʻu-anu Stream, named for a bird (some say a duck) who flew away with the foster child of the god Kāne. The child was named Ka-hānai-a-ke-akua (the foster child of the god) and was raised near Wao-lani in upper Nuʻu-anu Valley. Liholiho made his usual residence here (RC 271). (For a song, see Elbert and Mahoe 78.) See Kau-maka-pili. *Lit.,* the water bird.

Kamāʻoa. Plain near Ka Lae (South Point), Kaʻū, Hawaiʻi, a place noted for red dust; people jumped from a cliff (Kau-maea-lele-kawa) near here into a dust heap in imitation of the sport of leaping from a cliff into water *(lele kawa).* (For a saying, see Nakuina 44.) See ʻAlalā-keiki.

Kama-ohi. Gulch, Māʻalaea qd., West Maui. *Lit.,* young child.

Kama-ʻole. Land section, homesteads, and beach parks, Mākena qd., Maui. *Lit.,* childless.

Ka-maʻo-liʻi. Cinder cone, Hale-a-ka-lā Crater, East Maui. *Lit.,* the small *maʻo* shrub *or* a thrush.

Ka-maʻomaʻo. Plain near Puʻu-nēnē, Maui. Ghosts are believed to have wandered here. *Lit.,* the greenness.

Kāmaulele. Peak, Līhuʻe district, Kauaʻi.

Ka-mehame. Ridge, Koko Head qd., Oʻahu. *Lit.,* the *hame* tree.

Ka-mehameha. Highway around Oʻahu from Honolulu to Castle Junction; schools for Hawaiian children, field, Ka-lihi Waena; all named for Ka-mehameha I (1758?–1819). Fort Ka-mehameha is a military reservation at the entrance to Pearl Harbor established in 1909, today an Army family housing area. *Lit.,* the lonely one.

Ka-mehameha III. Elementary school, Lahaina, Maui, named for Ka-mehameha III and built on the grounds of his palace there.

Ka-mehameha IV. Road, Ka-lihi Valley, Honolulu. See ʻIo-lani.

Ka-mehameha V. Highway, southeast Molokaʻi. Ka-mehameha V had a home, Malama, near the Kaunakakai wharf. Post office built in 1871 at Merchant and Bethel streets, downtown Honolulu, as the principal Honolulu post office until the present federal building was constructed in 1922.

Ka-mehameha Heights. Section 4 of Honolulu (map 6).

Ka-mehame Iki. Land division, Puʻu-o-kali qd., Maui. *Lit.,* small Ka-mehame.

Ka-mehame Nui. Land divisions, Ka-hului and Mākena qds., Maui. *Lit.,* large Ka-mehame.

Ka-miki. Ridge, east Lā-naʻi. *Lit.,* the activeness.

Ka-milo. Point, Ka Lae qd., Hawaiʻi. *Lit.,* twisting (of current). Two places here were called Ka-milo-pae-aliʻi (Ka-milo landing [of] chiefs) and Ka-milo-pae-kānaka (Ka-milo landing [of] commoners). Drowned commoners washed in at the latter, chiefs at the former.

Ka'ū people traveling to Puna cast leis tied with loincloths and pandanus clusters into the sea at Puna; when the leis drifted back to Ka-milo, the Ka'ū people knew that the travelers had reached Puna. Points, Līhu'e district, Kaua'i, and Kī-pahulu qd., Maui. Kaua'i and Maui points, probably *lit.*, the *milo* tree.

Ka-milo-holu. Land division, Puna, Hawai'i. *Lit.*, the swaying *milo* tree.

K

Ka-milo Iki. Valley and elementary school, Koko Head qd., O'ahu. *Lit.*, small Ka-milo.

Ka-milo-loa. Two land divisions, road, and gulch, Kaunakakai qd., Moloka'i. *Lit.*, the tall *milo* tree.

Ka-milo Nui. Valley, Koko Head qd., O'ahu. *Lit.*, large Ka-milo.

Kaminaka. Drive near Chaminade College, Honolulu. *Lit.*, Chaminade.

Kammy's. Surfing area west of Sunset Beach, O'ahu.

Ka-moa. Point and ancient surfing area, Kai-lua qd., Hawai'i. (Finney and Houston 26.) Peak (4,038 feet high), inland in Ke-awa Nui, Ka-malō qd., Moloka'i. *Lit.*, the chicken *or* plant names.

Ka-moamoa. Land section, campground, picnic area, and site of ancient village destroyed in the 1868 tsunami (Hawaii Natural History Association Guide 1), Puna qd., Hawai'i.

Ka-moa-o-Pele. Cinder cone, Hale-a-ka-lā Crater, East Maui. *Lit.*, the chicken of Pele.

Ka-mōhio. Bay, south coast of Ka-ho'olawe. A large fishing shrine here, excavated in 1913, is described by McAllister (1933*b*:13).

Ka-moho-ali'i. Street, Ka-lihi Uka, Honolulu, named for Daniel Ka-moho-ali'i Ka-umu-ali'i. He and his father, Solomon, were named for the chief of the shark gods and brother of Pele, their family deity. *Lit.*, the chiefly chosen one.

Ka-mō-'ili'ili. See Mō-'ili'ili.

Ka-moku. Land section in Wai-pi'o and Wai-ki'i qds., Hawai'i. Hill, Hanalei district, Kaua'i. Land section, west Lā-na'i. Flats, Kaunakakai qd., Moloka'i. Street, Ala Wai, Honolulu. *Lit.*, the district *or* the cut-off portion.

Ka-moku-'ākulikuli. Old name for Sand Island. *Lit.*, the '*ākulikuli* (a succulent plant) island.

Ka-mole. Land section, Pā'ia qd.; gulch, Luala'i-lua Hills qd., East Maui. *Lit.*, the main root.

Ka-mo'o-ali'i. Lava flow, Kī-lau-ea and Pahala qds., Ka'ū, Hawai'i. Stream, Kāne-'ohe qd., O'ahu, site of a subdivision flooded in February 1969. Sometimes spelled Kamoalii. *Lit.*, the chiefly *mo'o*. (Many *mo'o* stories concern this area. In one, a chiefess from Maui was to meet a local chief here. A handsome man approached who she thought was the chief; but the chief arrived and the stranger turned into a *mo'o* and carried her into the stream. Sterling and Summers 5:140.)

Ka-mo'o-ho'opulu. Ridge, Ka-wai-hau district, Kaua'i. *Lit.*, the wet ridge.

Ka-mo'o-lā-li'i. Stream, Kāne-'ohe, O'ahu. *Lit.*, the *mo'o* [with a] small fin.

Kamuela. Name for the Wai-mea post office, Hawai'i, named for Samuel Spencer, a former postmaster, or, according to some, for

Samuel Parker, son of the founder of the Parker Ranch. Avenue, Ka-pahulu section, Honolulu, named for Samuel Wilder King (later, governor of the Territory) by his real estate partner, Frank James (see Palani); drive, upper Nuʻu-anu, Honolulu, named for Samuel ʻAi-kanaka Dowsett (TM). *Lit.,* Samuel.

Kanaʻana Hou. Congregational church at Ka-laupapa, Molokaʻi. *Lit.,* new Canaan.

Ka-naele. Swamp, central Kauaʻi. *Lit.,* the bog.

Ka-nahā. Wildlife sanctuary and pond near Ka-hului, Maui, said to have been built by Chief Kiha-a-Piʻilani, brother-in-law of ʻUmi (HM 387) who lived about A.D. 1500. (See Kiha-a-Piʻilani.) Nearly 500 native Hawaiian stilts *(āeʻo)* have been counted here at one time, about a third of the known total. Some 50 kinds of birds have been seen here, including herons, geese, ducks, owls, plovers, sandpipers, tattlers, coots, pheasants, and doves. Stream near La-haina, Maui. Rock islet (1.2 acres, 100 feet elevation) and point, Hālawa qd., Molokaʻi. Valley, central Niʻihau. Stream beginning on Tantalus, Honolulu. *Lit.,* the shattered [thing].

Kanahau. Land section and old *heiau* site, Kai-lua, Oʻahu. A tall stone at the north end of the *heiau* was called Pōhaku-Hiʻiaka (Hiʻiaka's stone). *Lit.,* marvelous.

Ka-nahā-wale. Ancient surfing area, Anahola, Ka-wai-hau district, northeast Kauaʻi. (Finney and Houston 30.) *Lit.,* easily broken.

Ka-naʻina. Avenue, Ka-pahulu section, Honolulu, and former Archives building (now used for State offices) on ʻIo-lani Palace grounds, downtown Honolulu, named for Charles Ka-naʻina, a friend of Ka-mehameha II, who gave Ka-naʻina his own fifth wife, Ke-kā-ulu-ohi, in 1821 (she had also been a wife of Ka-mehameha I). (RC 253.) In 1834 Ke-kā-ulu-ohi bore, by Ka-naʻina, her first male child, who became King Luna-lilo (RC 394). In 1837 Ka-mehameha III married Ka-naʻina's adopted daughter, Ka-mālama, in Ka-naʻina's home (RC 341). *Lit.,* the conquering.

Ka-naio. Coastal area, Māʻalaea qd.; land division, homesteads, village, and Congregational church, Mākena qd., Maui. See Honua-ʻula, Kaha-luʻu. *Lit.,* the bastard sandalwood tree.

Kanaka-leo-nui. Hill (8,250 feet high) inland from ʻŌ-ʻōkala village, Mauna Loa qd., Hawaiʻi. *Lit.,* loud-voiced person. This was the name of a retainer of ʻUmi-a-Līloa, a chief who is said to have had a house at the top of Mauna Kea with doors facing each of the six districts of Hawaiʻi. If the chief wanted the Hilo people to bring supplies, he called from the Hilo door to Kanaka-leo-nui, who shouted the orders from the top of the hill bearing his name.

Kanaka-loloa. Burial site, east side of Manukā State Park, South Kona, Hawaiʻi. Hill, Kaunakakai qd., north Molokaʻi. *Lit.,* tall person (long bones of four skeletons were found at the Kona, Hawaiʻi, site during bulldozing for the park).

Kanaka-nui. Street, Ka-lihi Kai, Honolulu, named for Samuel M. Kanaka-nui, who surveyed Ka-lihi Kai lands. (TM.) *Lit.,* big man.

Kanakea. Old name for Reeds Bay, near Wai-ākea, Hilo, Hawaiʻi. *Lit.,* wide stream.

Ka-nalo. Valley, northeast Niʻihau. *Lit.,* the housefly *or* the lost one.

Kanaloa

Kanaloa. Coastal land section, Mākena qd., Maui. Probably named for the god.

Ka-nalo Iki. Valley, northeast Ni'ihau. *Lit.*, small Ka-nalo.

Ka-nalu-kaha. Beach, 'Īlio Pt. qd., south Moloka'i. *Lit.*, the passing wave.

Ka-nani. Place, Nu'u-anu, Honolulu. (TM.) *Lit.*, the beauty.

*Kanapalu. Gulch, Hālawa qd., south Moloka'i.

Kanapou. Bay, east coast, Ka-ho'olawe.

Ka-nā'ū. Street, Niu, Honolulu. (TM.) *Lit.*, the yellow gardenia.

Ka-nāueue. Land sections, Kai-lua qd., Kona, Hawai'i, said to be named for a chief. The name of a fishpond once located near the site of the old O'ahu Railway station, Iwilei, Honolulu. *Lit.*, the rotating. This name was used in a risqué song: *Aia i Kū-wili 'o Ka-nāueue, nāue a'e kāua 'eā i ka 'ai ho'opau,* there at Stand Aswirl is Rotation, we rotate and eat everything up.

Kāne-'ai-moa. Point, Ka-malō qd., north Moloka'i. *Lit.*, chicken-eating Kāne.

Kāne-'ākī. Agricultural *heiau* at Mākaha, one of the best-preserved O'ahu *heiau,* restored 1969–1970. *Lit.*, hair-switch Kāne.

Kāne-ali'i. Avenue, Pauoa, Honolulu, named in 1915 for Robert M. Kāne-ali'i, a police officer. (TM.) *Lit.*, chief Kāne.

Kāne-ana. Large cave (formerly taboo) in Pu'u-o-Hulu hill, near Mā-kua, Wai-'anae district, O'ahu, where Māui and his grandmother lived. In other versions a shark man lived here. Mākua cave nearby is sometimes called Kāne-ana. (Sterling and Summers 2:97–100; Westervelt, n.d.:119.) *Lit.*, Kāne's cave.

Kāne-'āpua. A rock islet (0.09 acres, 50 feet elevation), east of Ka-holo cliff, Lā-na'i, named for a shark brother of Pele and of Kāne and Kanaloa; he was also a trickster and fish god (see HM 448–449 for his adventures). *Lit.*, Kāne fish trap.

*Kaneha. Ditch, reservoir, and weir, Ka-wai-hau district, east Kaua'i.

Kāne-hoa. Hill, Wahi-a-wā qd., O'ahu, named for a god said to be the father of Pele. (UL 49.) *Lit.*, companion [of] Kāne.

Kāne-hoa-lani. Mountain ridge, Wai-kāne qd., Kua-loa, O'ahu, named for a god ancestor of Pele; his female companion was said to be Ka-papa islet nearby. (PH XIII, 91.) *Lit.*, Kāne royal companion.

Kāne-i-kapōlei. See Kāne-kapōlei.

Kāne-'īlio. Point, Wai-'anae qd., O'ahu; a *heiau* here was dedicated to Kū-'īlio-loa, a legendary giant man-dog. See Black Rock Point. *Lit.*, dog Kāne.

Kāne-kapōlei. Street, Wai-kīkī, named for Marion Kāne-kapōlei Guerrero Diamond, who moved there in the early 1930s when the street, as yet unnamed, was a blind alley. Mrs. Diamond was named for the wife of Ka-lani-'ōpu'u (Kuy. 1:18, 31), who was also a wife of Ka-mehameha I (Ii 7); also the name of a god of flowers (PH 141). Compare Kāne-i-kapōlei, the name of a classroom building at the Ka-mehameha Schools, Honolulu, built in 1954.

Kāne-loa. Gulch, south central Ka-ho'olawe. Road and land area, Wai-kīkī, Honolulu. (TM.) *Lit.*, tall Kāne.

Ka-nenelu. Flats, Pāhala qd., Ka'ū, Hawai'i. *Lit.*, the bog. (A supernatural woman was believed to live here; people coming to draw water saw her combing her hair; then she would sink from sight into the pool. For a saying, see Appendix 8.1.)

Kāne-nui-o-Hamo. Crater near Kī-lau-ea Crater, Hawai'i. This may be the crater described by Wilkes (p. 183) as "the largest pit crater" except Kī-lau-ea, and written Kanemuo-kamu.

Kāne-'ohe. Quadrangle, land section, playground, village, bay, beach park, harbor, school, ranch, stream, county park, Marine Air Corps station, and golf course, O'ahu. *Lit.,* bamboo husband (according to one account, a woman compared her husband's cruelty to the cutting edge of a bamboo knife).

K

Kāne-pu'u. Ridge, central Lā-na'i. *Lit.,* Kāne's mountain.

Kāne-wai. Hill, northwest point of Moloka'i, covering about one-half square mile. (Stearns and Macdonald, 1947:24. U.S. Geological Survey and Summers call this Kahena-wai.) Street, playing field, and underground pool (believed to contain healing water; Sterling and Summers 6:112), Mānoa, Honolulu. *Lit.,* water [of] Kāne.

Kani-a-Hiku. Homesteads, Kala-pana qd., Hawai'i. *Lit.,* call of Hiku.

Kaniela. Place, Kuli-'ou'ou, Honolulu. *Lit.,* Daniel. (TM.)

Kani-kū. Hill, lava flow, and rock at Wai-nānā-li'i, North Kona, Hawai'i. (For. Sel. 182.) *Lit.,* upright sound.

Kani-moe. Rock at Wai-nānā-li'i, North Kona, Hawai'i. *Lit.,* prostrate sound.

Ka-nīnau-ele. Land division, Ko'olau, O'ahu. *Lit.,* the frivolous question (*ele* is short for *nīele*).

Ka-noa. Street, 'A'ala section, Honolulu, named for a family descended from High Chief Ka-iki-o-'Ewa. Paul Ka-noa and his son were governors of Kaua'i.

Kānoa. *Heiau* and land section, Honomū qd., Hawai'i. (RC 16.) Ridge, Wai-luku qd., Maui. Fishpond, Kaunakakai qd., Moloka'i. *Lit.,* bowl (as for kava).

Ka-noe-lani. Road, Ka-lihi Waena, Honolulu. *Lit.,* the heavenly mist.

*****Kanola.** Land section, Ka-malō qd., south Moloka'i.

Ka-noni. Point above Hōnaunau, Kona, Hawai'i. *Lit.,* the *noni* tree.

Kano-uli. Valley, southeast Ni'ihau. *Lit.,* dark stalk.

Ka-nounou. Point, Honolua qd., Maui. *Lit.,* the pelting (as of the sea).

Ka-nuku-awa. Fishpond, Ka-malō qd., south Moloka'i. *Lit.,* the harbor entrance.

Ka-nuku-o-ka-manu. Ancient surfing area (Finney and Houston 26), Wai-ākea, Hilo qd., Hawai'i. (For. Sel. 162.) *Lit.,* the beak of the bird (the place was thought to be shaped like a bird's beak).

Ka-nuku-o-Pu'uloa. Old name for Iroquois Point, near Pearl Harbor, O'ahu. *Lit.,* the entrance of Pu'u-loa.

Ka-nupa. Peak (1,962 feet high), Hālawa qd., Moloka'i. *Lit.,* the luxuriant growth.

Kaoaini. See Kaoini.

Ka-'ō-hala. Ancient surfing area, Wai-lua, Kaua'i. (Finney and Houston 30.) *Lit.,* the thrust passing.

Ka-'ōhao. Old name for Lani-kai, O'ahu. *Lit.,* the tying (two women were tied together here with a loincloth after being beaten in a *kōnane* game; For. 4:314–315).

Ka-'ohe. Quadrangle; land sections in Hāmākua, Humu'ula, Ka-'ohe,

85

and Wai-kiʻi qds.; homesteads, Kala-pana qd.; tract and ranch, Hōnaunau qd., Hawaiʻi. Area in ʻI-ao Valley, Maui. *Lit.,* the bamboo.

Kāohi-ka-ipu. Islet (a tuff cone, 11 acres, 40 feet elevation) near Rabbit Island, Oʻahu. A native reports that the island was formerly called Moku-hope (island behind), and that a rock that projects at low tide was Kāohi-ka-ipu (hold back the container), so called because the rock blocked sea-swept matter.

K

Kāʻohi-nani. Drive, upper Nuʻu-anu, Honolulu. (TM.) *Lit.,* gathering beauty (said to refer to bountiful harvest taxes).

Ka-ʻō-iki. *Pali* and series of faults separating Kī-lau-ea and Mauna Loa volcanoes, Hawaiʻi. *Lit.,* the small thrust.

*Kaoini. Fishpond, Kaunakakai qd., south Molokaʻi, also called Kaonini (Summers). A doubtful spelling is Kaoaini.

Ka-ʻōʻio. Same as Ka-lae-o-ka-ʻōʻio. *Lit.,* the bonefish.

*Kaonihu. Coastal area, Hālawa qd., north Molokaʻi.

Ka-ʻonina-puhi. Cliff at Puʻu-kawiwi, Oʻahu. *Lit.,* the writhing eel (marks on the cliff wall are said to have been made by a man who could turn himself into an eel; he was fleeing from an enemy).

*Kaonini. Same as Kaoini.

Kaʻonohua. Gulch and hill (2,689 feet high), Māʻalaea qd., Maui.

Ka-ʻono-ʻulu. Land division, gulch, peak (3,051 feet high), Mākena qd., Maui. *Lit.,* the desire [for] breadfruit.

Ka-ʻōpala. Coastal area and gulch, Honolua qd., Maui. See Nā-ʻōpala. *Lit.,* the rubbish.

Ka-ʻōpapa. Point on the coast below Ke-awe-iki, Kona, Hawaiʻi. *Lit.,* the flats.

Ka-ʻope-a-Hina. Fishpond, Hālawa qd., south Molokaʻi, perhaps named for an owner of the pond. *Lit.,* Hina's bundle.

Ka-paʻa. Land section and beach park, Kohala qd., Hawaiʻi. Land section, town, ditch, elementary school, weir, and beach park, Ka-wai-hau district, Kauaʻi. Land division, Kai-lua, Oʻahu, and a quarry there worked in the 1950s. *Lit.,* the solid *or* the closing. (The area with the quarry may have been so named because of the solid rock there.) *Ka laulā mauka o Ka-paʻa ē, mai paʻa i ka leo* (UL 40), the upland expanse of the closure, do not close your voice (an appeal for hospitality).

Ka-paʻakea. Land division, Ke-ʻanae qd., Maui; also called Paʻa-kea. Land section, homesteads, gulch, road, and a former inland fishpond, Kaunakakai qd., Molokaʻi. Area, pool, and lane, Mō-ʻili-ʻili, Honolulu. A street of that name, near the present Queen's Hospital, was named for the father of Ka-lā-kaua and Liliʻu-o-ka-lani (TM). See Hausten, Paʻakea, Willows. *Lit.,* the coral or limestone surface.

Kapaʻau. Land section, Kohala qd., Hawaiʻi. See Hina-kahua. *Lit.,* elevated portion of *heiau.*

Ka-pae-kahi. Ancient surfing area, Wai-ʻanae district, Oʻahu. (Finney, 1959a:51.) *Lit.,* the single landing.

Kapa-ʻeleʻele. A fishing shrine on the Puna-luʻu side of Kahana Bay, Oʻahu. *Lit.,* black border.

86 **Ka-pāhili.** Gulch near Hanapēpē, Kauaʻi. See Pāhili. *Lit.,* the blowing.

Ka-pahu. Street, Pauoa, Honolulu, named for Ka-pahu Keopua, one of the first three Hawaiians to be awarded lots in this homestead area. (TM.) *Lit.,* the box, drum, coffin, *or* push.

Ka-pahu-kapu. Ancient surfing area (Finney and Houston 26), Nā-poʻopoʻo, Hawaiʻi. See Manini. *Lit.,* the taboo drum.

Ka-pahulu. Avenue and section 32 of Honolulu (map 6). Ka-pahulu pier in Wai-kīkī is at the end of the avenue. *Lit.,* the worn-out soil.

Ka-paia. Village, stream, and reservoir, Līhuʻe district, Kauaʻi. Street, Hawaiʻi-kai, Honolulu. *Lit.,* the walls *or* bowers.

*Ka-pai-loa. Cape, Ka-malō qd., north Molokaʻi.

Ka-paka. Mountain, Hanalei district, Kauaʻi. Land section and point, Kahana qd., Oʻahu. (For. Sel. 196.) *Lit.,* the raindrop.

Kapakahi. Gulch, Wai-ʻalae, Honolulu. *Lit.,* crooked.

Ka-paka Nui. Falls (280 feet high), Hanalei district, Kauaʻi. *Lit.,* large Ka-paka.

Ka-pā-kule. Old name for a fishpond built by Menehune and dredged when Pearl Harbor was developed; home of Ka-ʻahu-pāhau. *Lit.,* the *akule* fish enclosure *(kule* is short for *akule).*

Ka-palaʻe. Upper cave, Hāʻena, Kauaʻi.

Ka-pā-lama. Section 5 of Honolulu (map 6), canal, and elementary school. *Lit.,* the *lama* wood enclosure (high chiefs were protected here; Elbert and Mahoe 78).

Kapalaia. Land section and ranch, Maka-wao, Maui; perhaps formerly Kāpala-ʻia, decorated, stained, designed.

Ka-paluoa. Land section, Pua-kō qd., Kona, Hawaiʻi (For. Sel. 182). Peak (3,436 feet high), south central Kauaʻi. Cabin, Hale-a-ka-lā Crater, East Maui. Land and sea areas across from the court house, Hau-ʻula, Oʻahu. Kāne and Kanaloa sent a whale here to pick up their worshiper, Makua-kau-mana (older perching branches) (Sterling and Summers 4:97) and take him to the legendary floating land Kāne-hūnā-moku to live with Kāne and Kanaloa in the "deathless land of beautiful people" (HM 69). *Lit.,* the whale *or* the whale tooth.

*Ka-pā-lau-oʻa. Headland, Airport qd., northwest Molokaʻi.

Ka-pale. Gulch, Kaunakakai qd., north Molokaʻi. *Lit.,* the defense.

Ka-pali-hiolo. Headland, Hālawa qd., Molokaʻi. *Lit.,* the collapsed cliff.

Ka-pali-kōī. Hill, ʻĪlio Pt. qd., Molokaʻi. *Lit.,* the sliding cliff.

Ka-pali-loa. Cliff, Hālawa qd., north Molokaʻi. *Lit.,* the long cliff.

Ka-pā-loa. Stream, Lahaina qd., Maui. Ridge, east side of Pelekunu Valley, Molokaʻi. *Lit.,* the long fence *or* long enclosure.

Ka-palu. Street, Pauoa, Honolulu. *Lit.,* the bait *or* relish *or* an individual's name.

Kapa-lua. Fleming's Beach, Honolua qd., Maui. *Lit.,* two borders.

Ka-pā-o-Lono. Playground, Ka-imu-kī, Oʻahu. *Lit.,* the enclosure of Lono.

Ka-papa. Offshore island (14 feet elevation), Wai-kāne qd., Oʻahu. A fishing shrine is here. See Kāne-hoa-lani. *Lit.,* the flat surface.

Kāpapa. *Pali,* Ka-malō qd., Molokaʻi. *Lit.,* unity.

*Ka-papaki-kane. Land section, Ka-laupapa peninsula, Molokaʻi.

K

Ka-papa-kōlea. Old name for Papa-kōlea, and a hill on Damon property, Moana-lua, Honolulu. (Ii 95; Sterling and Summers 6:332–333.) *Lit.,* the plover flats.

Ka-pāpala. Land section, Kī-lau-ea and Mauna Loa qds., Hawai'i. *Lit.,* the *Charpentiera* shrub. (UL 39.)

Ka-pāpale. Ancient surfing area, Wai-a-lua, north O'ahu (Finney, 1959*a:*51). *Lit.,* the crest.

Ka-pā-'ula. *Heiau,* Poli-hale State Park, Wai-mea district, west Kaua'i. *Lit.,* the red enclosure.

Ka-pe'a. Stream, Hālawa qd., north Moloka'i.

Ka-pehu. Stream, Honomū qd., Hawai'i. *Lit.,* the swelling.

Kapena. Street, downtown Honolulu, named for John Makini Kapena (1843–1887), "one of Hawaii's greatest orators, [who] held many offices in the Kalakaua regime. At this time [1887] in his short and tragic life he was suffering from alcoholism, bankruptcy, and the death of his wife" (Adler).

Ka-pena. Falls and pool, Nu'u-anu Stream, Honolulu, mentioned in the well-known song "Alekoki" (Elbert and Mahoe 33; UL 108). *Lit.,* the package.

Ka-pewa-o-ka-manini. Small harbor, Kona, Hawai'i. *Lit.,* the tail of the *manini* fish. On one side of this bay, the *manini* are said to be fat, but on the other side they are thin.

Kāpī. Fishpond at Ka-wela Bay, O'ahu. *Lit.,* sprinkle with water (or salt).

Ka-pilau. Ridge (4,426 feet elevation), Wai-luku qd., West Maui. *Lit.,* the stench.

Ka-pili. Street, Wai-kīkī, Honolulu, one of Princess Likelike's names; she lived at 'Āina-hau. (TM.) *Lit.,* the relationship *or Heteropogon contortus,* a grass.

Ka-pi'o-lani. Elementary school, Hilo, Hawai'i. Boulevard, county regional park (within which are the beach park center, driving range, natatorium, aquarium, bandstand, Wai-kīkī Shell, zoo, flower garden, nursery, etc.), Wai-kīkī, named for Queen Ka-pi'o-lani (1834–1899), wife of Ka-lā-kaua. *Lit.,* the arch [of] heaven (rainbows signified the presence of royalty).

Ka-pi'o-lani Maternity Home. Maternity and gynecological hospital on Puna-hou Street, Honolulu, named for Queen Ka-pi'o-lani, first president of the society, Ho'oulu a Ho'ōla Lāhui (propagate and perpetuate nation), that sponsored the hospital, established in 1890 at Beretania and Makiki streets. The present building and location date from 1929. It has been greatly expanded since then and serves all races.

Kapi'olani-nui. Dormitory constructed in 1931, Ka-mehameha Schools, Honolulu, named for the chiefess who defied Pele at Kī-lau-ea in 1824 (RC 382). *Nui,* not a part of her name, was added to distinguish her from Queen Ka-pi'o-lani and indicates seniority. *Lit.,* great Kapi'olani.

Kāpī-wai. Way, Pauoa, Honolulu. A land parcel of 1.25 acres by this name was awarded in 1853 (Indices 715). *Lit.,* sprinkling water.

Ka-pōhaku-luahine. Sacred boulder (11 feet long, 8.7 feet wide, and 3 feet high) now on the edge of Moana-lua Stream, O'ahu (McAl-

K

lister, 1933*a:*100-101). A child cried during a taboo ceremony, and to save the child from death the mother hid with it by this stone. Several petroglyphs, including birds and a *kōnane* board, are on the stone. (Sterling and Summers 6:356–357.) Offerings are still placed here. *Lit.,* the stone [of the] old lady.

Ka-poho. Land section and cone, Kala-pana and Maku‘u qds., Hawai‘i; a village here was buried in the 1960 eruption of Kī-lau-ea. Ancient surfing area in Kala-pana, now called Kai-mū. Gulch, southeast Lā-na‘i. Point, Mō-kapu peninsula, O‘ahu, where salt was formerly obtained by evaporation of sea water. *Lit.,* the depression.

Kapo-lei. Cone (166 feet high), on the southeast slope of the Wai-‘anae range, ‘Ewa qd., O‘ahu. *Lit.,* beloved Kapo (a sister of Pele).

Ka-poli. Spring, Mā‘alaea qd., Maui. *Lit.,* the bosom.

Ka-pua. Land area and gulch, southeast Lā-na‘i. Lane, Pā-lama, Honolulu. (TM.) Ancient surfing area, Wai-kīkī, O‘ahu (Finney and Houston 28); it is now filled in and a part of Ka-pi‘o-lani Park. Probably *lit.,* the flower.

Ka-pu‘a. Land sections, Ho‘ō-pū-loa and Kohala qds.; gulch, Kohala qd. (For. Sel. 288); ancient surfing area (Finney and Houston 26), Kaha-lu‘u, Kai-lua qd., Hawai‘i. An oppressive chief, Koi-hala, lived here and was stoned to death by people who were ordered to bring food from Ka‘ū. Land division, Wai-mānalo, O‘ahu. *Lit.,* the whistle.

Kā-pua. Small bay near the boundary between Kahana and Kā‘ana-pali, Honolua qd., Maui. *Lit.,* strike spawn (*lai* and *manini* fish spawned here; people kicked them ashore with their feet).

Kapuahi-a-Pele. Coastal land section, Kaunakakai qd., north Moloka‘i. *Lit.,* fireplace of Pele.

Ka-pua‘i. Ancient surfing area, bay or district, Hāna, Maui. (Finney 1959*a:*52.) *Lit.,* the flow [of water].

Kapua‘i-a-Kana. A place at Kē‘ē, Kaua‘i, believed to show the footprint of the stretching demigod, Kana, as he stepped from Ni‘ihau to Kaua‘i. *Lit.,* footprint of Kana. (Jarrett 24.)

Ka-pua-‘ilima. Ancient surfing area, Ka-wai-hae, Kohala qd., Hawai‘i. *Lit.,* the *‘ilima* flower.

Kapu-āiwa. Coconut grove near Kaunakakai, Moloka‘i, planted in the 1860s by Ka-mehameha V, who lived nearby. It is said that the grove was once 10 acres in area and contained a thousand trees, but it is now greatly reduced in size. State government building in Honolulu built in 1884, housing the land and tax appeal courts, and named for Ka-mehameha V; Ka-mehameha Schools dormitory built in 1940. *Lit.,* mysterious taboo.

Ka-pua-lei. Same as Kapu-lei. *Lit.,* the flower [for the] lei.

Ka-pū‘ali. Coastal area, Lahaina qd., Maui. *Lit.,* the warrior.

Ka-pua-o-Ko‘olau. Land division and gulch, Ka-malō qd., south Moloka‘i. *Lit.,* the flower of [the] windward. An alternate spelling is Ka-pū-o-Ko‘olau, the conch trumpet of [the] windward.

Ka-pueo-kahi. Port and harbor of Hāna, Maui. (Ii 172; Elbert and Mahoe 81-82.) *Lit.,* the single owl.

Ka-pu‘e-uhi. Old name for Glenwood, Puna qd., Hawai‘i. *Lit.,* the yam mound.

Ka-puhi. Stream, Ka-malō qd., Moloka‘i. *Lit.,* the eel.

Ka-puhi-kani. Point, 'Īlio Pt. qd., Moloka'i. *Lit.,* the sounding eel.

Ka-puka-a-Māui. Natural bridge, Wai-luku River, Hilo, Hawai'i, where Māui thrust his spear through the lava rocks to reveal Kuna's hiding place (Westervelt, n.d.:151). See Wai-kuna. *Lit.,* the hole [made] by Māui.

*****Kapuka'amoi.** Point, Hanalei district, Kaua'i.

Ka-puka-'ana. Congregational church between Ke-ālia and Ho'okena, East Maui. *Lit.,* the Exodus.

Kapūkakī. Old name for Red Hill and Makalapa Crater near Pearl Harbor, O'ahu. See Nape-hā.

Kapukapu. Ancient surfing area, Nā-po'opo'o, Kona, Hawai'i. (Finney and Houston 26.) *Lit.,* regal appearance.

Ka-puka-paia. Ridge, Wai-mea district, Kaua'i. *Lit.,* the wall hole.

*****Kapukapuahakea.** Land section, Hālawa qd., south Moloka'i. A land area here was called a *heiau* although it had no stone structure.

Ka-puka-ulua. Coastal area, Pā'ia qd.; point, Hāna qd., Maui. Coastal area, Ka-malō qd., south Moloka'i. *Lit.,* the *ulua* fish hole.

Kapu-kini. Coastal area, Nīnole, Ka'ū, Hawai'i. *Lit.,* many taboos.

Ka-puku-wahine. Coastal area, 'Īlio Pt. qd., Moloka'i. *Lit.,* the gathering place [of] females.

Kapu-lei. Land division, gulch, and battlefield, Ka-malō qd., south Moloka'i, also known as Ka-pua-lei. See Ka-wela. Street, Pauoa, Honolulu, named for the owner of the land at the time it was subdivided. *Lit.,* lei sacredness.

Kapulena. Plantation, Wai-pi'o qd., Hawai'i, named for the king shark of Hāmākua (Jarrett 24).

Ka-puna. Land section, road, stream, and spring, Kaunakakai qd., Moloka'i. *Lit.,* the spring.

Ka-puna-hala. Land section, road, elementary school, subdivision, stream formerly called Ano-lani, and playground, Kāne-'ohe qd., O'ahu. *Lit.,* the pandanus spring.

Ka-puna-hou. Old name for Puna-hou.

Ka-puna-kea. Land section, Lahaina qd., Maui. *Lit.,* the clear spring *or* the white coral.

Ka-puni. Ancient surfing area (Finney and Houston 28), street and former land area, Wai-kīkī, O'ahu. *Lit.,* the surrounding (perhaps named for the spreading banyan tree on the 'Āina-hau estate of A.S. Cleghorn).

Ka-pū-o-Ko'olau. See Ka-pua-o-Ko'olau.

Ka-pu'u-kolo. Old section of Honolulu bounded by Nu'u-anu Stream and Honolulu Harbor. (*Honolulu in 1810;* RC 271, 417.)

Ka-pu'u-lua. Crescent beach, Hālawa qd., Moloka'i. *Lit.,* the double hill.

Ka-pu'u-one. Ancient surfing area, Ka Lae qd., Hawai'i. (Finney and Houston 26.) *Lit.,* the sand hill.

Ka-pu'u-po'i. Point, Hālawa qd., Moloka'i. *Lit.,* the point [of] cresting [waves] (canoes were smashed in the seas here).

Karratti. Lane, Makiki, Honolulu, named for John Karratti, an Indian from Singapore who settled in Hawai'i in about 1830. He owned 300 acres of land in Makiki where he operated a dairy. He had ten children by Mary Ke-aloha Ka-ua-'awa. (Cf. TM.)

K

Kau. Place between Wai-'ōhinu and South Point, Ka'ū, Hawai'i. *Lit.,* to place.

Ka'ū. District, desert, elementary and high school, trail, and peak (2,082 feet high), Hawai'i. Poetic: *Ka'ū kua makani* and UL 65. (For sayings, see Appendix 8.1.) See Ka'ū-loa. Ka'ū is an ancient name, with cognates in Samoa (Ta'ū) and Mortlock Islands (Takuu): see Appendix 9. Small point and bay, Kī-pahulu qd., Maui.

Kaua. Ancient surfing area, Wai-mea, southwest Kaua'i. (Finney and and Houston 30.) *Lit.,* war.

Kaua'i. Island and county (33 miles long, 25 miles wide, with an area of 553 square miles and a 1970 population of 29,524). Līhu'e is the major town and the county seat. Epithet: *Kaua'i o Manokalanipō,* Kaua'i of Manokalanipō (an ancient chief; *lit.,* the innumerable dark heavens). Channel between Kaua'i and O'ahu. Street, Pu'u-nui, Honolulu. (For the meaning of Kaua'i, see Appendix 6.8.)

Ka-ua-i-ka-nanā. Stream and valley, Nā-pali coast, Hanalei district, Kaua'i. *Lit.,* the rain defied. (During a storm, a man found shelter in a small cave; his companion stood under a tree and shouted: *Ua 'oe ē ka ua, ka ua o ka nanā keia,* rain on, O rain, a rain defied is this. The man in the cave thought his companion had better shelter and ran out to see. The man under the tree then went into the cave.)

Kaua'i Surf. Hotel and golf course, Līhu'e, Kaua'i.

Kaua-kahi-a-ka-ho'owaha. Sacred hill, Kua-loa, Wai-kāne qd., O'ahu, named for a chief. *Lit.,* single battle of the despised.

Ka-ua-kinikini. Site of the church and school, Pu'uwai village, Ni'i-hau. *Lit.,* the abundant rain.

Ka-ua-lau-kī. *Heiau,* He'eia, Kāne-'ohe qd., O'ahu. Perhaps *lit.,* the ti-leaf rain.

Ka-ua-lehu. Caves at Ka'ū, Hawai'i, and at He'eia, O'ahu. *Lit.,* the ash rain.

Ka-ua-nui. Ancient surfing place, Wai-a-lua, north O'ahu. (Finney, 1959a:51.) *Lit.,* the big rain.

Ka-ua-o-Hā'ao. A Congregational church at Wai-'ōhinu, Ka'ū, Ha-wai'i. *Lit.,* the Hā'ao rain. This rain name was used in poetic expressions and made famous by the chant of Kua-kāhela announcing the killing of the Ka'ū chief, Ke-ō-ua-kuahu-'ula, by Ke'e-au-moku: *ku'u haku i ka ua o Hā'ao,* my lord in the Hā'ao rain. Kua-kāhela was Ke-ō-ua's *kahuna.*

Ka-ua-nono-'ula. Area around the intersection of Merchant and Ala-kea streets, Honolulu, said to be named for a chiefess fond of playing *kōnane.* Another version is that when Kaulana-i-ka-pōki'i came here from the legendary land, Kuaihelani, rainbows attested her rank, hence the name of the place. *Lit.,* the dark red rain.

Ka-ua-'ōpu'u. Hill (1,054 feet high) and stream, Wai-'anae, O'ahu.

*Kauapea. Beach, Hanalei district, Kaua'i.

Ka-ua-'ula. Land division, stream, tunnel, reservoir, and ditch, La-haina qd., Maui. *Lit.,* the red rain.

Ka-uha-kō. Land section, bay, and village near Hōnaunau, Kona, Hawai'i. *Lit.,* the dragged large intestines (a chief forced his people to pull him up and down a hill on a sledge; they became exhausted and in revenge killed him by dragging or dumping). Crater, Ka-laupapa peninsula, Moloka'i; lava flows from this crater built the shield volcano of the peninsula long after the main volcano had ceased activity (Macdonald and Abbott 350–351). A small brackish pool on the crater is said to have been the first crater dug by Pele on Moloka'i (*Ka Leo o ka Lahui,* January 9, 1893); after striking water, Pele went on to Maui. Street, Hawai'i-kai, Honolulu.

Kau-hana. Street and place, Pālolo, Honolulu. *Lit.,* work season.

Ka-'uhane. Street, Pauoa, Honolulu, named for Supervisor Noble K. Ka-'uhane, who helped push appropriations to develop this homestead area. (TM.) *Lit.,* the soul.

Ka-uhao. Ridge and valley, Wai-mea district, Kaua'i. *Lit.,* the scooping.

Ka-uhi-'īmaka-o-ka-lani. A rock on a mountain near Kahana Bay, O'ahu. A demigod (*kupua*) came from Kahiki with his relative, Pele, and was turned to stone; he asked Hi'iaka to free him, and when she refused he tried to tear himself loose and rose to a crouching position; today he is called "Crouching Lion." *Lit.,* the observant cover of the heavens. (PH chapter 20.)

Ka-uhi-koa. Mountain (1,227 feet high), and ditch, Ha'i-kū qd., Maui. *Lit.,* the koa tree cover.

Kauhola. Point, Kohala qd., Hawai'i. (For. Sel. 268–269.)

Kauholo. See Kaulolo.

Kau-i-ke-ō-lani. Children's hospital, Honolulu, founded by Albert S. Wilcox, son of missionary teachers Abner and Lucy Wilcox, and named for his wife, Emma Kau-i-ke-ō-lani. In 1908 Wilcox donated land and $50,000 for a children's hospital. *Lit.,* place in the skies [of] heaven.

Ka-'uiki. Head, point, and lighthouse, Hāna, Maui, home of the demigod Māui, and birthplace of Ka-'ahu-manu. Battles were fought at a fortress here between Maui defenders and invaders from Hawai'i. (Ii 172; RC 80, 160; Westervelt, n.d.:7.) See Pu'u-ki'i. *Lit.,* the glimmer.

Kauila. Street, Nu'u-anu, Honolulu; the name is that of a number of species of hardwood trees; see PE, *kauila.*

Kauka. Homesteads and land section, Kala-pana and Puna qds., Hawai'i.

Kau-ka-hōkū. Land division, Kai-lua qd., North Kona, Hawai'i, formerly called Ka-lama-'ula. *Lit.,* the star appears.

Kau-ka-moku. Gulch, north central Ka-ho'olawe. *Lit.,* place [on] the island.

Kau-ka-mōlī. See Kukui-lamalama-he'e.

Kau-ka-'ōpua. Mountain, Hanalei district, Kaua'i. *Lit.,* the horizon clouds alight.

Kaukau-'ai. Gulch, Kī-pahulu qd., Maui. *Lit.,* food prayer.

Kau-ke-ano. Hawaiian name for Central Union Church, Puna-hou, Honolulu; also the name of the area at Beretania and Richards streets where the first Central Union Church was located. *Lit.,* awe-inspiring (the awe rests).

Kau-kini. Ridge, Ka-haku-loa qd., West Maui. *Lit.,* placing multitude.

Kaukonahua. Gulch and stream (the longest in the State: 33 miles), Wahi-a-wā, Schofield, and Hale-'iwa qds., O'ahu. According to one explanation the name means "place his testicles" (a man's testicles were cut off here so that he could leap). A more likely explanation is Kau-kōnāhua (place fatness). See Kōnāhua-nui.

Ka-'uku. Volcanic cone on the eastern slope of Mauna Kea from which two lava flows reached the sea; the southern one formed Pepe'ekeo Point, Hawai'i. (Macdonald and Abbott 303.) *Lit.,* the louse.

Ka'ula. Valley and stream, Hāmākua and Mauna Kea qds., Hawai'i. Rocky islet (540 feet elevation) 22 miles southwest of Ni'ihau. The island is a tuff cone built on the submerged eroded remnant of an ancient shield volcano (Macdonald and Abbott 21, 199, 400, 401). It abounds with seabirds and is said to be named for one—which one is not known. A *heiau* called Pōhaku-pio (captured stone) is said to have been on the western side. The shark god Kū-hai-moana, a brother of Pele, lived here. The domain of the hero Ka-welo extended from Hanalei to Ka'ula: *'Ai lā 'oe i ka manu o Ka'ula* (For. Sel. 97), you then rule the birds of Ka'ula. (See PE, *puaea;* PH 177; RC 80.)

Kaula-huki. Hill and rough road, Ka-malō qd., central Moloka'i. *Lit.,* rope pulling (cattle were lassoed here).

Kaula'i-nā-iwi. Islet (about 40 feet elevation, 0.35 acres) beyond Coconut Island, Hilo, Hawai'i. *Lit.,* dry the bones (bones of chiefs were dried here). See Moku-ola.

Ka-ula-kahi. Channel between Kaua'i and Ni'ihau. *Lit.,* the single flame (streak of color).

*Ka-ula-lewelewe. Mountain (2,980 feet elevation), Lahaina qd., Maui.

Kaulana. Bay, Ka Lae qd., Hawai'i. Coastal area and gulch, northeast Ka-ho'olawe. *Lit.,* [boat] landing.

Kaulana-mauna. Land section, Ho'ō-pū-loa qd., South Kona, Hawai'i; there was food here, and it was a place where mountain travelers rested. *Lit.,* mountain resting place.

Kaulana-pueo. Church and land section, Huelo, Ha'i-kū qd., Maui. *Lit.,* owl perch.

Ka-'ula'ula. Valley, Wai-mea district, Kaua'i.

Ka-ule. Cape, east Ka-ho'olawe. See Lae-o-ka-ule. *Lit.,* the penis.

Ka-ule-kola. Land division near Hawai'i Loa College on the road to Kāne-'ohe town, O'ahu. *Lit.,* the sexually excited penis.

Ka-ule-o-Lī. Land sections near Hōnaunau, South Kona, Hawai'i. *Lit.,* the penis of Lī (he traded his penis for someone else's).

Ka-ule-o-Nānāhoa. Hill and phallic rock, Kaunakakai qd., central Moloka'i. See Nānāhoa, Pu'u-lua. *Lit.,* the penis of Nānāhoa (a legendary character and symbol of sexuality).

Ka'ū-loa. A stone formerly in Ka'ū, Hawai'i, between Nā-'ā-lehu and Wai-'ōhinu, believed to have been brought from Tahiti; in ancient poetry, Ka'ū is called Ka'ū-loa. *Lit.,* long Ka'ū.

*Kaulolo. Land section, Kaunakakai qd., central Moloka'i. On a 1922 map this place was spelled Kauholo.

Kaulu. Land section, Honomū qd., northeast Hawai'i; *pali,* Honu-'apo qd., south Hawai'i; ancient surfing area, Ke-au-hou, Kai-lua qd., North Kona, Hawai'i. (Finney and Houston 26.) *Lit.,* ledge.

Ka-'ulu. Land section near Hō'ae'ae, O'ahu, named for chief Ka-'ulu-hua-i-ka-hāpapa (the breadfruit bearing fruit on the flats) from Puna, Hawai'i.

K

Ka-ulu-lā'au. Street, Pauoa, Honolulu, named for Ka-ulu-lā'au Wright, the first Hawaiian to be awarded a homestead lot here. He was called the mayor of Papa-kōlea. (TM.) Ka-ulu-lā'au was a chief who was banished from Maui; he went to Lā-na'i where he destroyed trouble-making ghosts.

Ka-ulu-o-Laka. A *heiau* for hula dancers not far from Ka-ulu-Paoa *heiau,* both below Kē'ē cliff, Hā'ena, Kaua'i. *Lit.,* the inspiration of Laka (goddess of the hula). A large stone nearby was named Ki-lioe for a *mo'o* goddess; umbilical cords of infants were deposited here.

Ka-ulu-Paoa. *Heiau* at the foot of Kē'ē cliff, near Hā'ena, Kaua'i. *Lit.,* the inspiration [of] Paoa (Lohi'au and his friend Paoa trained in hula here).

Ka-ulu-wai. Hill (1,530 feet high), Kaunakakai qd., north Moloka'i. Ka-mehameha I is said to have camped for a year on the slopes of the hill while preparing to attack O'ahu. He raised taro at Pā-i-ka-lani patch in Honomuni Gulch. (Cooke 111–112.) *Lit.,* the water growth.

Ka-ulu-wela. Lane, elementary school, and playground (the gift of Mr. and Mrs. Theodore Richards), 'A'ala section, Honolulu. (TM.) *Lit.,* the hot stick for spreading oven stones.

Kau-maea-lele-kawa. Leaping mound of earth near Kamā'oa and inland of Pai-a-ha'a, Ka'ū, Hawai'i. *Lit.,* placing stench leaping place (perspiration and dust). See PE, *lele kawa.*

Kaumaha-loa. Land area, Wai-mea district, Kaua'i. *Lit.,* very heavy *or* very sad.

Kau-mahina. Park overlooking Hāna coastline, East Maui. *Lit.,* moonrise.

Kau-mai-ka-'ohu. Hill inland of Puna-lu'u, Ka'ū, Hawai'i. *Lit.,* the mist rests.

Kau-mai-luna. Place, 'Ālewa Heights, Honolulu. *Lit.,* place above.

Ka'u-maka. Land division near Hanalei, Kaua'i. *Lit.,* give me eye (referring to the cry of two boys who were fond of fish eyes and were killed by a shark sent by a sorcerer).

Kau-makani. Elementary school and coastal land section, Maka-weli, Kaua'i. Land section, Kī-pahulu qd.; mountain (4,576 feet high), Hāna qd., Maui. Street, Hawai'i-kai, Honolulu. *Lit.,* place [in] wind.

Kau-maka-pili. Congregational church and area in Honolulu. The present church is at Ke-one-'ula; the old site was at Beretania and Smith streets. Lowell Smith was the founder and first pastor; the first services were held in 1837. *Lit.,* perch [with] eyes closed. (The favorite bird, Ka-manu-wai, of the demigod 'Ai'ai, son of Kū-'ula, perched here. The bird was fed on bonitos caught with a magic lure [*pā*]; when the bird was hungry it closed its eyes. For. 4:557.)

Kaumalapau. Harbor (since 1926) and light, southwest Lā-na'i; originally Kau-māla-pa'u (soot [from burning] placed [in] gardens).

Ka-ūmana. Caves, land division, and elementary school above Hilo, Hawai'i.

Kau-manamana. Bay, reef passage, and former fishpond, Airport qd., south Moloka'i. Pāka'a, skilled navigator and seer, lived here (RC 37). See Hikauhi. *Lit.*, place branching out.

Kau-mō'ali. Gulch, Hāmākua and Mauna Kea qds., Hawai'i. *Lit.*, groove placed (the gods Kāne and Kanaloa lived here, and their canoe, being dragged to sea, cut out a groove; For. Sel. 268).

Ka-umu-ali'i. Coconut grove area in the Wai-lua River State Park, Līhu'e district, Kaua'i, probably named for the Kaua'i chief who gave Vancouver hogs and yams and took in exchange the name George, in honor of the British king and who became ruling chief of Kaua'i in 1794 (RC 162, 169). Street, Ka-lihi Kai, Honolulu, named for Solomon Kama Ka-umu-ali'i, a descendant of Ka-umu-ali'i-kālua-loa-o-ke-ō-ua-kuahu-'ula (the royal oven long baked the rainy cloud [of the] sacred altar), better known as Ke-ō-ua. The long commemorative name was given Ke-ō-ua after he was killed by Ke'e-au-moku, father-in-law of Ka-mehameha I. (TM.)

Ka-umu-honu. Valley, central Ni'ihau, and bay, south Ni'ihau. *Lit.*, the turtle oven.

Kaunā. Point, Ho'ō-pū-loa qd., Ka'ū, Hawai'i. (For a chant, see PE, *lulumi.*)

Kauna-kahakai. Old name for Kaunakakai, Moloka'i. *Lit.*, beach landing. (For. 4:575.)

Kaunakakai. Principal town on Moloka'i, also a quadrangle, land division, gulch, harbor, elementary school, and beach park. There are several surfing sites with summer swells on both sides of the harbor. See Kauna-kahakai.

Ka-unala. Land division, ridge, and stream, Ka-huku and Pu'u-kapu qds., O'ahu. *Lit.*, the plaiting.

Kauna-lā. Bay and gulch, 'Īlio Pt. qd., Moloka'i. *Lit.*, placing sun.

Kauna-lewa. Bay and gulch, 'Īlio Pt. qd., Moloka'i. Land section and ridge, Wai-mea district, Kaua'i; a famous coconut grove was here (HM 519). *Lit.*, swaying place (perhaps referring to coconuts).

Kaunalu. Gulch and bay, 'Īlio Pt. qd., Moloka'i. This is sometimes written Kaunala.

Kau-nā-mano. Land sections, Hāmākua and Honu-'apo qds., Ka'ū, Hawai'i. See Hā-niu-malu, Ke-kua-lele. *Lit.*, multitudes are placed [here].

Kauna'oa. Beach and point near Mauna Kea Beach Hotel, Pua-kō qd., Hawai'i. *Lit.*, native dodder *or* a mollusk.

Kauniho. Land division, Wai-pi'o qd., Hawai'i.

Kau-noa. School, Spreckelsville, Pā'ia qd., Maui. *Lit.*, place without taboo.

Kaunolū. Land division and bay, southeast Lā-na'i, and site of a deserted Hawaiian village. (For. 4:575.)

Ka-unu-a-Kahekili. *Heiau* near Wai-'alae, O'ahu. *Lit.*, the altar of Ka-hekili.

Ka-unu-loa. See Ke-kupua.

Ka-unu-nui. Point, north central Ni'ihau; ancient surfing area, west Ni'ihau. *Lit.*, the large altar.

Ka-unu-o-Hua. Ridge, Wai-mea district, Kaua'i. Peak (4,535 feet high), Pelekunu Valley, Ka-malō qd., Moloka'i. The body of Pele is said to

Ka-unu-o-Pou

K

lie here. The name is abbreviated in some chants as Unu-o-hua. *A aloha wale 'ia kā ho'i 'o Ka-unu-o-Hua, he pu'u wale nō*, even Ka-unu-o-Hua is loved, just a hill [how much more so a human being!]. (PH 115.) A ridge in Mā'alaea qd., West Maui, spelled Ka-uno-a-Hua, should perhaps be Ka-unu-o-Hua. Probably *lit.*, the altar of Hua (a war leader of Moloka'i; RC 70).

Ka-unu-o-Pou. Point, northeast Ni'ihau. *Lit.*, the altar of Pou.

Ka-unu-pahu. Ridge, Hālawa qd., Moloka'i. Perhaps *lit.*, the drum altar.

Kaupaku-hale. Hill, Schofield qd., O'ahu. *Lit.*, house ridgepole *or* roof.

Kaupaku-lua. Land section, point, and village, Ha'i-kū qd., East Maui. *Lit.*, two ridgepoles.

***Kau-piki-awa.** Point, Ka-laupapa peninsula, Moloka'i.

Kau-pō. Quadrangle, village, old district, homesteads, trail, and gap, East Maui. A peninsula and once a fishing village northwest of Maka-pu'u Point, O'ahu, now the site of a beach park and of Sea Life Park. The point of land was formed by lava which flowed to the sea from a vent about 200 feet up the cliffside; this was perhaps the most recent of the secondary eruptions on O'ahu. (For. Sel. 275; Macdonald and Abbott 377–378.) See Ko'o-nā-pou. *Lit.*, landing [of canoes] at night.

***Kaupoa.** Former land section, 'Ilio Pt. qd., west coast of Moloka'i. The bay here was given this name by Mr. and Mrs. George P. Cooke who had their beach home on the bay. It is now a rainfall station. See Pu'u-ka-heu.

Ka-'ū-pūlehu. Land division near the sea, Kai-lua and Pua-kō qds., North Kona, Hawai'i. The Ka-'ū-pūlehu lava flow of 1801 started above here at 5,500 to 6,000 feet on Hualālai and flowed to the sea. (Macdonald and Abbott 51–52.) *Lit.*, the roasted breadfruit ('*ū* is short for '*ulu*). Pele met two girls, Pā-hinahina and Kolomu'o, roasting breadfruit here (known then as Manu-ahi). Only Pā-hinahina shared her breadfruit. That night Hualālai erupted near Hu'ehu'e and destroyed the village, but spared the home of Pā-hinahina. See Hu'ehu'e. In another legend, the name is a contraction of Ka-imu-pūlehu-a-ke-akua (the roasting oven of the god).

Kau-puni. Stream, Wai-'anae Valley, Ka-'ena qd., O'ahu. *Lit.*, place around.

Kauwahi-pōuli. Gulch at head of Mānoa Valley, Honolulu. *Lit.*, dark place (the first area darkened by the setting sun).

Kauwalu. Islet (0.3 acres, 40 feet elevation), Ke-'anae qd., East Maui. Gulch, Pu'u-kapu qd., O'ahu.

Kāwā. Bay and springs near Hīlea, Hawai'i; ancient surfing areas, Puna-lu'u and Honu-'apo qds., south Hawai'i, and at Ke-olonā-hihi, Kai-lua qd., Hawai'i. *'Ili'ili hānau o Kō-loa, ka nalu ha'i o Kāwā*, birth pebbles of Kō-loa, breaking waves of Kāwā. (Finney and Houston 26.) *Lit.*, distance.

Ka-wa'a. Bay, Honu-'apo qd., south Hawai'i. *Lit.*, the canoe.

Ka-wa'a-a-Pele. A long rock in the sea east of Maka-pu'u, O'ahu. *Lit.*, the canoe [used] by Pele.

Ka-wa'a-loa. Bay, Airport qd., north Moloka'i. According to Coulter, this is Ka-wai-loa (the long stream). *Lit.*, the long canoe.

Ka-wa'a-o-Māui. Double rock lying in Hilo Bay said to be Māui's magic canoe. (Westervelt, n.d.:151.) *Lit.,* the canoe of Māui.

Ka-waena. Place, Pauoa, Honolulu. *Lit.,* the middle *or* the garden.

Ka-wa'ewa'e. Hill, Ni'ihau. *Heiau,* Kāne-'ohe, O'ahu. According to Thrum, it was built at the beginning of the twelfth century (Sterling and Summers 5:194). 'Olopana brought Kama-pua'a here to be sacrificed, but he escaped.

*Kawahuna. Land section, Airport qd., north Moloka'i. Many burials are located here.

Ka-wai. Point, Līhu'e district, Kaua'i. *Lit.,* the water.

Ka-wai-a-Ha'o. Congregational church of coral block, downtown Honolulu, begun in 1837 and dedicated in 1842. (Four thatched churches had stood at or near the present site, the last seating 4,500 people.) The Reverend Hiram Bingham drew the plans for the church. More than a thousand people worked on the building. Coral reef rock was cut with blunt axes by men diving 10 to 20 feet. Logs cut in Ko'olau Loa were brought by canoe to Kāne-'ohe and hauled over the Pali (RC 291). The name Ka-wai-a-Ha'o was first used to designate the church itself in 1853. The grounds, assigned to the mission in 1820 and formally deeded by Ka-mehameha III in 1840, include two cemeteries, the adobe school house built in 1835, and the Luna-lilo mausoleum built in 1879 (Luna-lilo was buried here in 1874). Likeke Hall, named for Dr. Theodore (Likeke) Richards, was dedicated in 1941. Many important events have occurred here. Ka-mehameha III spoke at a service of thanksgiving for the restoration of the kingdom in 1843; he is said to have used the words which have become Hawai'i's motto: *Ua mau ke ea o ka 'āina i ka pono,* the life of the land is preserved in righteousness. The coronation of Ka-mehameha IV in 1854 and his wedding to Emma in 1856 took place in this church (Kuy. 2:83). Ka-lā-kaua made important speeches here in 1874 and 1881; Lili'u-o-ka-lani had a special pew (Kuy. 3:479). The pastors have been Hiram Bingham, Richard Armstrong, E. W. Clarke, H. H. Parker, Akaiko Akana, William Kamau, Edward Kahale, and Abraham K. Akaka. In 1965 Ka-wai-a-Ha'o Church was designated a national historic landmark. Ka-wai-a-Ha'o Street begins at the church grounds. *Lit.,* the water [used] by Ha'o. Ha'o was a chiefess who was carried frequently from her home in Mō-'ili'ili for ceremonial bathing and purification in a spring located perhaps near the present News Building. J. F. G. Stokes (unpublished notes, Bishop Museum) has written that the spring was not at the church site; however, a stone was transported from the spring to the churchyard, and when the church was restored in about 1926 the stone was set up in the present newly made artificial pool that is supplied by piped water. Some accounts say that Ha'o was a chief. (Ii 93.)

Ka-wai-hae. Land sections and road, Kohala and Wai-pi'o qds.; village, bay, harbor, lighthouse, trail, uplands, and surfing area, Kohala qd., Hawai'i. Nearby is Mauna Kea Beach Hotel. *Lit.,* the water [of] wrath (people are said to have fought for water from a pool in this arid area).

Ka-wai-hāpai. Land division between Wai-a-lua and Ka-'ena, O'ahu. It is believed that Menehune lights are seen here. *Lit.,* the carried

Ka-wai-hau

water (water is said to have been carried here by a cloud in answer to the prayers of two priests).

Ka-wai-hau. District, Kaua'i. *Lit.,* the ice water. This was the name of a glee club started by Prince Lele-iō-hoku, brother of Ka-lā-kaua; the name was given in honor of an American missionary lady who (unlike the club members) drank only ice water. This name was later taken by an association of farmers in the district. Makana-limu was the old name. Bay, 'Īlio Pt. qd., north Moloka'i.

Ka-wai-hoa. Point, Ni'ihau (PH 210). Point beyond Portlock Road, Honolulu; the god Kāne brought forth water here (HM 64). *Lit.,* the companion's water.

Ka-wai-ho'eo. Street, Ka-lihi Kai, Honolulu. *Lit.,* the winning water.

Ka-wai-holo. Street, Ka-lihi Kai, Honolulu. (TM.) *Lit.,* the running water.

Ka-wai-hū-a-Kāne. A spring, perhaps near Wai-ki'i, Hawai'i.

Ka-wai Iki. Stream, Wai-pi'o qd., Hawai'i. River, Wai-mea district, Kaua'i. Stream, Ka-malō qd., north Moloka'i. Street and former land area, Pā-lama, Honolulu; a 1.02-acre *kuleana* of this name was awarded in 1852 (Indices 719). Stream, Wai-a-lua, O'ahu. *Lit.,* small Ka-wai (the water).

Ka-wai-kapu. Land division, gulch, and trigonometric station, Hālawa qd., south Moloka'i. *Lit.,* the sacred (*or* forbidden) water.

Ka-wai-kilo-kanaka. Same as Wai-aka, a pool on the Kai-lua side of the Nu'u-anu Pali, O'ahu; also called Ka-wai-kilo-kohe. *Lit.,* the water [for] spying on people.

Ka-wai-kilo-kohe. Same as Ka-wai-kilo-kanaka. *Lit.,* the water [for] spying on vagina.

Ka-wai-kini. Highest peak (5,243 feet) on Wai-'ale'ale, central Kaua'i. (PH 109; UL 40, 135.) *Lit.,* the multitudinous water.

Ka-wai-kōī. Stream inland of Wai-mea Canyon, northwest Kaua'i. *Lit.,* the flowing water.

Ka-wai-ku'i. A place near South Point, Hawai'i, where Ka-mehameha ordered a *kahuna* to try to get water (*wai*); the *kahuna* pounded (*ku'i*) the earth to no avail, and he was hanged for his failure. Street in Niu Valley, Honolulu, named for an ancient spring there.

Ka-wai-lena. Stream, Ka-malō qd., Moloka'i. *Lit.,* the yellow water.

Ka-wai-lewa. Land area, peak, and stream, Hanalei district, Kaua'i. *Lit.,* the suspended water.

Ka-waili'ulā. Land section near Kamuela, Hawai'i. *Lit.,* the mirage.

Ka-wai-loa. Bay, Līhu'e district, Kaua'i. Bay, northwest Moloka'i. Land sections, Koko Head qd.; hill (610 feet high), beach, village, camps, ranch house, station, Hale'iwa qd.; land section, forest reserve, gulch, and stream, Pu'u-kapu qd., O'ahu. (UL 241.) See Kukui. *Lit.,* the long water.

Ka-wai-nā'uke-po'o-o-ka-hā. Streamlet formerly leading to Wai-'ōhinu, Ka'ū, Hawai'i. *Lit.,* the stream delousing the head of the water course (a chief was deloused here).

Ka-wai Nui. Land sections, Honomū and Kai-lua qds.; streams, Honomū and Wai-pi'o qds., Hawai'i. Two streams, Ka-malō and Hālawa qds., Moloka'i. Stream, Pu'u-kapu qd.; swamp, fishpond (once the largest inland pond on Oʻahu), and canal, Mō-kapu qd., Oʻahu. See Puʻu-ka-Pele. (UL 82.) *Lit.,* the big water.

Ka-wai-paka. Same as Ka-wai-poko. *Lit.,* the drops [of] water.

Ka-wai-papa. Valley, Wai-mea district, Kauaʻi. Land section and gulch near Hāna, Maui, where the chief Kiha-a-Piʻilani built a path paved with stones (For. 5:176). See Kiha-a-Piʻilani. *Lit.,* the stratum stream.

Ka-wai-poko. Stream, Ka-malō qd., Molokaʻi. *Lit.,* the short stream.

Ka-wai-pūʻolo. Spring, said to have been near Hale-ʻiwa, Oʻahu. *Lit.,* bundle water. (The spring disappeared and after a long search was discovered by a *kilo* [seer] near Ka-ʻena Point; Menehune carried the water there in ti and taro leaves; Thrum's Annual, 1904:102–103.)

Ka-waiū. Gulch, southeast Lā-naʻi. *Lit.,* the milk.

Ka-wai-ʻula. Valley, northwest Kauaʻi. *Lit.,* the red water.

Ka-wai-uliuli. Elevation or peak, Hālawa qd., Molokaʻi. *Lit.,* the dark water.

Ka-wā-kiu. Gulch, ʻĪlio Pt. qd., Molokaʻi. (Cooke 120.) *Lit.,* the spy time *or* spy place.

Ka-wā-kiu Iki. Bay, ʻĪlio Pt. qd., north Molokaʻi. *Lit.,* small Ka-wā-kiu.

Ka-wā-kiu Nui. Bay, ʻĪlio Pt. qd., north Molokaʻi. *Lit.,* large Ka-wā-kiu.

Kā-wala. Land section, Kaʻū, Hawaiʻi, extending from Kāhili-pali. *Lit.,* strike backwards.

Kawa-luna. Land section, Ka-laupapa peninsula, Molokaʻi. (*Ke Au Okoa,* October 17, 1867.) For an Oʻahu *heiau* of this name, see Wao-lani. *Lit.,* high leaping place.

Ka-wānana-koa. Place, school, playground, and land area, Nuʻu-anu, Honolulu, where the second engagement of the battle of Nuʻu-anu is said to have been fought; Ka-hahana lived here (RC 135). The playground and school were named for Prince David Ka-wānana-koa (1868–1908). *Lit.,* the fearless prophecy.

Kawa Nui. Diving places in Kaʻū and in Kai-lua qd., Kona, Hawaiʻi. At Kaʻū, an easier diving place for children, in a cove on the Kona side, was called Kawa Iki. Bay, southwest Niʻihau. *Lit.,* big leaping place.

Ka-wao. Park, Pālolo, Honolulu. *Lit.,* the inland region.

*Kaweea. Land section, Ka-malō qd., Molokaʻi; spelled Kaweoa on a 1922 quadrangle map.

Ka-wehewehe. Reef entrance and channel off Grey's Beach, just east of the Hale-kū-lani Hotel, Wai-kīkī, Honolulu. The sick were bathed here as treatment. The patient might wear a seaweed (*limu-kala*) lei and leave it in the water as a request that his sins be forgiven, the lei being a symbol. *Lit.,* the removal.

Ka-wēkiu. Way, Kuli-ʻouʻou, Honolulu. (TM.) *Lit.,* the summit.

Ka-wela. Land divisions, Hāmākua, Wai-piʻo, Honu-ʻapo, and Ka Lae qds., Hawaiʻi. Land division, Hāna qd., Maui. Land division, place of refuge, gulch, and salt flats, Ka-malō qd., south Molokaʻi. In 1736 invading Oʻahu forces fought here the combined forces from Molo-kaʻi and Hawaiʻi under Alapaʻi-nui. The Oʻahu chief, Ka-piʻi-oho-o-ka-lani (the head curls of the royal chief) was killed and his forces routed after a five-day battle. (RC 70.) Numerous burials were here.

Stone walls here were built in the time of Ka-mehameha V to keep cattle out of the gardens. Bay, land section, gulch, and stream, Ka-huku qd., Oʻahu. *Lit.,* the heat.

Ka-weli-koa. Point, Līhuʻe·district, Kauaʻi. *Lit.,* the terror [of the] warriors.

Kawelo-hea. Blowhole, Honu-ʻapo, Hawaiʻi. *Lit.,* calling Ka-welo (Ka-welo was murdered by her husband, and her bones were placed in this hole).

K

Ka-welo-lani. Place, Wilhelmina Rise, Honolulu. *Lit.,* the royal breed (it is unlikely that the reference is to the legendary hero Ka-welo).

Kaweoa. See Kaweea.

Ka-weo-nui. Point, Hanalei district, Kauaʻi. *Lit.,* the large redness.

Kāwī. Stream, Ka-wai-hau district, Kauaʻi.

Kāwili. Point, Ke-āhole qd., Hawaiʻi; ancient surfing area, Hilo qd., Hawaiʻi (Finney and Houston 26); current coming from the west to Ka Lae (South Point), south Hawaiʻi. See Halaʻea. *Lit.,* twist.

Ka-wiʻu. Fishpond, Ka-malō qd., south Molokaʻi. *Lit.,* the entanglement.

Kawiwi. Mountain, Schofield qd., Oʻahu, believed to have been a place of refuge in war. (Sterling and Summers 2:72–77.)

Keaʻā. Land sections, Hāna qd., Maui, and Honu-ʻapo and Wai-piʻo qds., Hawaiʻi.

Ke-aʻa-hala. Stream, land sections, and playground, Kāne-ʻohe qd., Oʻahu. *Lit.,* the pandanus root.

Ke-aʻa-lau. Land division and fishpond, Kāne-ʻohe, Oʻahu. *Lit.,* the many roots.

Keaʻau. Land sections, intermediate and elementary school, and villages, Hilo, Makuʻu, and Puna qds., Hawaiʻi. (For. Sel. 18; UL 62.) Land section, village, forest reserve known as Keaʻau Makua, peak, and beach park, Ka-ʻena qd., Oʻahu.

Ke-aʻa-ulu. Gulch, Ka-huku qd., Oʻahu. *Lit.,* the growing root.

Ke-Aʻe-loa. Lane, Nuʻu-anu, Honolulu, named for a wind.

Ke-ʻahakea. Land section, Wai-piʻo qd., Hawaiʻi. *Lit., Bobea* trees and shrubs.

Ke-ahi. Street and place, Mānoa, Honolulu, and point west of Pearl Harbor, Oʻahu, noted for ʻōʻio fish and as a surfing site. *Lit.,* the fire.

Ke-ahi-a-Kahoe. Same as Puʻu-ke-ahi-a-Kahoe.

*Ke-ahi-a-ka-lio. Hill, Halāwa qd., north Molokaʻi.

Ke-ahi-a-Laka. Land section and village, Makuʻu qd., Hawaiʻi, where Pele dug a crater. (PH 211.) *Lit.,* the fire [made] by Laka (a hula goddess).

Ke-ahi-ʻā-loa. Hill (3,548 feet high), Wai-luku qd., West Maui. *Lit.,* the fire long burning.

Ke-ahi-kano. Mountain (2,013 feet high), Honolua qd., West Maui. *Lit.,* the hard fire.

Ke-ahi-kauō. Hill (3,003 feet high), Wai-luku qd., West Maui. *Lit.,* the dragged fire.

Ke-āhole. Quadrangle; land sections, Ke-āhole and Puna qds.; point and airport, Ke-āhole qd., Hawaiʻi. *Lit.,* the *āhole* fish.

Ke-āhua. Stream, Hanalei district, Kauaʻi. Land division, village, and road, Pāʻia qd., Maui. *Lit.,* the mound.

Ke-ahu-'aiea. Land section, Mākena qd., Maui. *Lit.,* the heap of *'aiea* trees and shrubs.

Ke-āhua-iwi. Gulch, Pu'u-o-kali qd., Maui. *Lit.,* the bone pile.

Ke-ahu-o-Kū. Hill, Hālawa qd., Moloka'i. *Lit.,* the altar of Kū.

Ke-ahu-o-Lū. Land section and point, Kai-lua and Ke-āhole qds., Hawai'i. *Lit.,* the heap of Lū.

Ke-ā-ina. Bay and gulch, Hālawa qd., Moloka'i. *Lit.,* jibber jabber.

Ke-aīwa. Land sections, Kī-lau-ea. Mauna Loa, and Pāhala qds.; gulches, Honu-'apo, Mauna Loa, and Pāhala qds.; lava flow, spring, and site of the mudflow of 1868, Pāhala qd., south Hawai'i; see Wood. State park and *heiau* above 'Aiea, O'ahu; the *heiau,* probably medicinal, is said to have been built in the time of Kākuhihewa. Nearby, Thomas R. L. McGuire planted a grove of Norfolk Island pines in 1928. The site was rededicated in 1951, but before that time, people had hauled away stones from the *heiau. Lit.,* the mystery (said to be the name of an early priest and to refer to his mysterious healing powers).

Ke-aka. Drive, Ālia-manu, Honolulu. (TM.) *Lit.,* the shadow.

Ke-ā-ka-manu. Hill above Hāmoa, East Maui. *Lit.,* the noise [of] the bird (bird catchers snared birds here). This name is sometimes spelled Keakaamanu.

Ke-ākea. Hill, Hanalei district, northeast Kaua'i. *Lit.,* the breadth.

Ke-ākea-lani. Elementary school, Volcano, Hawai'i. Street, 'Āina-Haina, Honolulu, named for a chiefess who ruled, in name only, over Kohala, Kona, and Ka'ū. Her son was the famous Ke-awe (RC 63-64). *Lit.,* breadth [of] heaven.

Ke'ā-kū. A large cave on the south slopes of Hale-a-ka-lā, Maui.

Ke-akua-'umi. Coastal area at Ke-ono-kū-'ino, Ka-malō qd., south Moloka'i. *Lit.,* the strangled ghost.

Ke-ala-a-ka-'iole. Area near Molo-a'a, Kaua'i. *Lit.,* the trail [made] by the rat (a supernatural rat was occasionally seen here).

Ke-ala-hou. Land divisions, homesteads, school, Pu'u-o-kali qd., Maui. *Lit.,* the new pathway.

Ke-ala-i-Kahiki. Channel between Lā-na'i and Ka-ho'olawe through which voyages to foreign lands (Kahiki) were begun; western point of Ka-ho'olawe. See Lae-o-ke-ala-i-Kahiki. *Lit.,* the way to foreign lands.

Ke-ala-kaha. Land section and stream, Hāmākua qd., Hawai'i, the birthplace of 'Umi, son of Līloa by 'Akahi-a-Kuleana. (For. Sel. 124.) *Lit.,* the turning road.

Ke-alaka'i. Street, 'Ālewa Heights, Honolulu. *Lit.,* the leader.

Kealakehe. Homesteads and elementary school, Kai-lua and Ke-āhole qds., Hawai'i.

Ke-ala-ke-kua. Land section, Hōnaunau and Kai-lua qds.; village, Kai-lua qd.; bay (where Captain Cook was killed), trail, and underwater State park (315 acres) extending from Ka-'awa-loa lighthouse to Manini Point, Hōnaunau qd., Hawai'i. *Lit.,* pathway [of] the god. There were many *heiau* on the road from Ke-ala-ke-kua to Kai-lua; Thrum listed 40 (Restarick). It was believed that a god slid down a cliff here leaving an imprint, and that the gods often slid here in order to cross the bay quickly (Wilkes 90, 184).

K

Ke-ala-kīpapa. Trail from Wāwā-malu to Maka-puʻu, Oʻahu. *Lit.,* the paved road.

Ke-ala-komo. Land division and ancient village, Puna qd., Hawaiʻi. William Ellis (pp. 183–190) described a weekend visit here in 1823: the village was "populous"; two-thirds of the people were "intoxicated"; his party suffered from thirst. A lava flow from Mauna Ulu vent poured into the sea near here in 1971 and created 97 acres of new land. *Lit.,* the entrance path.

Ke-ala-kō-waʻa. *Heiau* near Kai-lua, Hawaiʻi, said to be for canoe builders. *Lit.,* the way [for] dragging canoes.

Ke-ala-loloa. Ridge, Māʻalaea qd., Maui. *Lit.,* the long pathway.

Ke-ala-ʻolu. Avenue, Kāhala, Honolulu. *Lit.,* the cool road.

Ke-ala-pūpū-a-Kiha. Coast area, ʻĪlio Pt. qd., north Molokaʻi. *Lit.,* the shell pathway of Kiha. (The Maui chief, Kiha-a-Piʻilani, built a shell pathway near here; For. 5:176. See Kiha-a-Piʻilani.)

Ke Alaula o ka Mālamalama. Church, Cooke Street, Honolulu. *Lit.,* dawn light of enlightenment. (The translation as given at the church is The Bright Morning Rays of the Church of Reasonable Services.)

Ke-ālia. Land division, Hōnaunau qd., Kona, Hawaiʻi. Forest reserve, village, land section, landing, plantation, river, Ka-wai-hau district, Kauaʻi. Pond near Kīhei, Maui. Old name for Meyer Lake, Kaunakakai qd., Molokaʻi. Land division, Ka-ʻena qd., Oʻahu. Drive, Kamehameha Heights, Honolulu (TM). The place in Kona, according to one informant, was not named for its salt: a chief (Ka-lei-paʻihala) was so absorbed watching boxing, spear throwing, and *kōnane* that he kept saying to his impatient wife, *"Alia nō, a napoʻo ka lā,"* just wait until the sun sets (this is a saying told to persons who stay too long). See Meyer Lake. *Lit.,* the salt encrustation.

Ke-ālia-aupuni. Land section, south Lā-naʻi. *Lit.,* the government salt encrustation.

Ke-ālia-kapu. Land section, central Lā-naʻi; there are numerous petroglyphs on a boulder here. *Lit.,* the sacred salt encrustation.

Ke-aliʻi. Point and stream, Haʻi-kū qd.; gulch, Lahaina qd., Maui. *Lit.,* the chief.

Ke-aliʻi Iki. Land division, Haʻi-kū qd., Maui. *Lit.,* small Ke-aliʻi.

Ke-aliʻi Nui. Land division, Haʻi-kū qd., Maui. *Lit.,* large Ke-aliʻi.

Ke-aloha. Beach park, Hilo, Hawaiʻi, named in 1963 for James Ke-aloha, former chairman and executive officer of the County of Hawaiʻi and the first elected lieutenant governor of the State of Hawaiʻi. Street and place, Ka-lihi Waena, Honolulu. *Lit.,* the compassion.

Ke-alohi. Hill and point, Heʻeia, Oʻahu. *Lit.,* the shining (perhaps formerly Ke-ʻalohi).

Ke-alohi-lani. Avenue, Wai-kīkī, and name of Queen Liliʻu-o-ka-lani's seaside cottage, Honolulu. *Lit.,* the royal brightness (perhaps formerly Ke-ʻalohi-lani). The Queen's home may have been named for a mythical land in the heavens to which a girl traveled for four months and ten days (HM 530), and where a house was built of clouds for Ke-ao-melemele (the yellow cloud), a daughter of Kū and Hina.

Ke-ama. Place, Mānoa, Honolulu. (TM.) *Lit.,* the outrigger float.

Ke-ʻā-muku. Lava flow, Wai-kiʻi and Ka-ʻohe qds., Kona, Hawaiʻi. *Lit.,* cut-off lava. Another explanation is that women, children, and the aged hid in caves here during wars; they had to stifle any burning ('*ā muku*) fire if an enemy appeared.

Ke-ana. Land division and fishpond, Kāne-'ohe qd., O'ahu; the old name for Koko-kahi; land section, Lā'ie; cave near the sugar mill, Ka-huku, O'ahu, containing two stones that were boys turned to stone for disobeying their mother's instruction not to make any sound during thunderstorms. (PH 233.) *Lit.,* the cave.

Keana'āwī. Ridge and falls, Hanalei district, Kaua'i.

Ke-ana-bihopa. Land section, Hilina Pali, Kī-lau-ea qd., Hawai'i. *Lit.,* the bishop's cave.

Ke-'anae. Quadrangle, land section, village, elementary school, park, lookout, homesteads, point, landing, stream, valley, peninsula, East Maui. Here, the god Kāne, accompanied by Kanaloa, thrust his *kau-ila* staff into solid rock, and water gushed forth. (HM 64.) *Lit.,* the mullet.

Ke-'anae Uka. Land section, Ke-'anae qd., Maui. *Lit.,* upland Ke-'anae.

Ke-ana-haki. Cliff and bay, south Ni'ihau. *Lit.,* the broken cave.

Ke-ana-ka-'iole. Gulch, Airport qd., south Moloka'i. *Lit.,* the cave [of] the rat.

Ke-ana-kāko'i. Ancient quarry (at 12,400 feet elevation), Mauna Kea; pit crater (at 3,468 feet elevation), Kī-lau-ea Crater, Hawai'i. An adze quarry in the pit crater was buried by lava erupted in 1877. *Lit.,* the adze-making cave.

Ke-ana-ka-pua. Bay, Hālawa qd., Moloka'i. Probably *lit.,* the bay [of] the baby fish.

Ke-ana-koholua. Ridge, Ka-malō qd., south Moloka'i. *Lit.,* the lance cave.

Ke-ana-kolu. Land section behind Pāhala, Ka'ū, Hawai'i. *Lit.,* the triple cave (three caves connected by tunnels are said to be here).

Ke-ana-kua. Coastal area, Ka-malō qd., north Moloka'i. *Lit.,* the back cave.

Ke-ana-o-Hina. A shallow cave on the east side of Moloka'i-nui-a-Hina Gulch, Moloka'i. This was the home of Hina, the second wife of Wākea, the first man, and the mother of Moloka'i. According to a saying, one doesn't know Moloka'i until he visits the cave, which is called the base (*kumu*) of Moloka'i; he must approach with reverence (HM 219) and wear a flower lei and a ti leaf around his neck for protection. Navels of infants were buried here. (Cooke 152.) *Lit.,* the cave of Hina.

Ke-ana-o-ka-manō. See Manō, Wao-lani.

Ke-ana-o-ke-akua-pōloli. A cave at Maka-pu'u, O'ahu, visible only from the sea. (PH 87–89.) *Lit.,* the cave of the hungry god. (A goddess lived here; the area was too dry to grow food.)

Ke-ana-pa'akai. Coastal area, Mā'alaea qd., Maui. *Lit.,* the salt cave.

Ke-'ānapanapa. Point, northwest Lā-na'i. *Lit.,* the flash.

Ke-ana-papa. Point, Lā-na'i. *Lit.,* the flat cave.

Ke-ana-pa'ū. A place near Maka-pu'u, O'ahu. *Lit.,* the wet cave.

Ke-ana-pua'a. Cave near Pearl Harbor, O'ahu. *Lit.,* the pig's cave (Kama-pua'a slept here).

Ke-ana-puhi. Large cave, Pelekunu, Moloka'i. *Lit.,* the eel's cave. (A shark who lived here went to Kahiki and on returning found an eel

K

occupying the cave. He covered the cave's mouth, but the eel bored a hole and got out. *Ka Nupepa Kuokoa,* July 6, 1922.)

Ke-ana-puka. Land area, Hanalei district, Kaua'i. Cave, Hālawa qd., north Moloka'i. *Lit.,* the cave [with a] hole.

Ke-ana-uhi. Valley, north central Ni'ihau. *Lit.,* the cave cover.

Ke-aniani. A ridge inland of Ka-hulu-o-manu in Ka-mana Nui Valley, Moana-lua, O'ahu, named for a seer who defied the taboos of Ka-lani-kū-pule and removed the taboo sticks that guarded the valley. *Lit.,* transparent.

Ke-'anini. Ancient surfing area, Hāna Bay, East Maui (Finney and Houston 28).

Ke-anu. Street, Pālolo, Honolulu, named for a family living there when the tract was opened. (TM.) *Lit.,* the coolness.

Ke-anu-'i'o-manō. Land division and stream, Wai-pi'o qd., Hawai'i. *Lit.,* the coldness of shark flesh.

Keaoi. Islet (about 2.5 acres, 240 feet elevation), Kī-lau-ea qd., Hawai'i.

Ke-ao-lele. Place, Pālolo, Honolulu. *Lit.,* the flying cloud.

Ke-ā-pōhina. Area in Ka'ū, Hawai'i, on the border between Honu-'apo and Mauna Loa qds. *Lit.,* the gray lava.

*Keapuka. Land section and stream, Kāne-'ohe qd., O'ahu.

Ke-au. Land section, Honu-'apo qd.; coastal area, Maku'u qd. (see Ka-loa-o-ka-'oma), Hawai'i. *Lit.,* the current.

Ke-au-hou. Land sections, Hilo, Hōnaunau, Humu'ula, Kai-lua, Ka-'ohe, Kī-lau-ea, Mauna Loa, and Puna qds.; ancient village washed away in the 1868 tsunami (*Hawaii Natural History Association Guide* 16), ranch, point, and landing, Kī-lau-ea qd.; village, bay, school, and surfing area (Finney and Houston 26), Kai-lua qd. (in this area is one of the longest and best preserved *hōlua* slides), Hawai'i. Usually pronounced Ke-ou-hou (*au* to *ou* is a frequent change in fast speech). *Lit.,* the new era *or* the new current.

Ke-au-hou Kona. Golf course, Kai-lua qd., Kona, Hawai'i.

Ke-au-kaha. Hawaiian homestead area, elementary school, waterfront park and residential district, Hilo, Hawai'i. *Lit.,* the passing current.

Ke-awaawa-iki. Land area, Wai-a-lua, O'ahu. *Lit.,* the small valley.

Ke-awa-iki. Village and bay, Pua-kō qd., Kona, Hawai'i. Lighthouse, Lahaina, Maui. *Lit.,* the small passage.

Ke-awa Iki. Coastal area, Ka-malō qd., Moloka'i. *Lit.,* small Ke-awa.

Ke-awa-ka-lani. Beach, 'Īlio Pt. qd., south Moloka'i. *Lit.,* the channel [of] the royal chief.

Ke-awa-kapu. Coastal area between Kīhei and Mākena, East Maui. *Lit.,* the sacred (*or* forbidden) harbor.

Ke-awa-la'i. Congregational church at Mākena, East Maui. *Lit.,* the tranquil haven.

Ke-awa-lua. Coastal area and stream, Honolua qd., West Maui. *Lit.,* the double channel.

Ke-awa-nui. Landing, Wai-mea district, northwest Kaua'i. Bay, northeast Ni'ihau. Hill, northeast end of Mō-kapu peninsula, O'ahu. *Lit.,* the big bay.

Ke-awa Nui. Fishpond, gulch, land division, Ka-malō qd., south Moloka'i. The fishpond was built in about 1500, before the time of

Kiha-a-Pi'ilani, and has been in continual use since then. *Lit.,* big Ke-awa.

Ke-awa-'ula. Cave, land division, and beach park, now known as Yokohama Bay, Wai-'anae, O'ahu. It was believed that spirits of the newly dead would come to a place here called Ka-ho'iho'ina-Wākea (Wākea's turning-back place); if the personal god (*'aumakua*) thought the person was not ready to die, he would turn the spirit back to re-enter the body. The goddess Hi'iaka opened a cave here to get water. (PH 157.) *Lit.,* the red harbor (said to be named for numerous cuttlefish [*mūhe'e*] that color the water). The O'ahu Railroad train stopped here to let Japanese fishermen off; so many came that the bay was called Yokohama Bay. A challenging "left-slide" summer surfing site here is now called Yokohama.

Ke-awāwa. Area at Mauna-lua, O'ahu. *Lit.,* the valley.

Keawe. Street, Kaka'ako, Honolulu, named for a chief.

Ke-awe-iki. Coastal land area on a small bay below Ke-ala-ke-kua Bay, Hawai'i. *Lit.,* the small streak.

Keawe-kāheka. Bay and point, Hōnaunau qd., South Kona, Hawai'i. *Lit.,* Keawe's sea pool.

Keawe-wai. Stream and gulch, Wai-manu Valley, Wai-pi'o qd., Hawai'i. *Lit.,* water [belonging to] Ke-awe.

Kē'ē. Beach and cliff west of Ha'ena, Kaua'i. After Lohi'au died of love for Pele, his body was sequestered in a cave on this cliff. Hi'iaka and her companion, Wahine-'ōma'o (green woman), climbed the cliff, and with herbs and long prayers Hi'iaka restored Lohi'au to life. Three rainbows appeared, and they all descended to earth. (PH 107–152, painting p. 160.) In sayings, Kē'ē represents great distances and trouble: *Aia i Kē'ē,* there at Kē'ē (too far to bother about). (For. Sel. 81.) *Lit.,* avoidance.

Ke'eaumoku. Important street, Makiki, Honolulu, extending seaward; probably named for a governor of Maui who bore the same name as his father, an ally and father-in-law of Ka-mehameha I. See Moku-'ōhai.

Ke'ehi. Lagoon and beach park east of Honolulu International Airport. *Lit.,* tread upon.

Ke'ei. Land sections, village, coastal area, and ancient surfing area, Hōnaunau qd., Hawai'i. (Finney and Houston 26.) The battle of Moku-'ōhai was fought here. See Ka'ahumanu-pōhaku.

Ke'eke'ehia. Hill near 'Ulu-pala-kua, East Maui. A *heiau* once stood here. *Lit.,* trodden upon.

Ke'elikōlani. State office building, Honolulu, named for Princess Ruth Ke'elikōlani (1826–1883), daughter of Pau-ahi and Ke-kū-anaō'a (RC 347); also Ka-mehameha Schools swimming pool built in 1964.

Ke'e-kū. *Heiau,* perhaps a *luakini* (temple for human sacrifices), at Hīlea, Ka'ū, Hawai'i; an impressive site enclosed with massive stone walls. Also a *heiau* at Kaha-lu'u, Kona, Hawai'i. *Lit.,* abrupt turn.

Ke'elināwī. Land section, southwest Ni'ihau.

Kēhau. Place, Pālolo, Honolulu. *Lit.,* dew.

Kehena. Land division, Kala-pana qd., Hawai'i, the birthplace of the Reverend J. W. Kanoa, a man of chiefly rank and the first Hawaiian missionary to the Gilbert Islands. *Lit.,* place for refuse.

Kei-ka-palani

K

Kei-ka-palani. Land section, Ka-haku-loa qd., Maui. *Lit.,* the *palani* fish boasts.

Keiki-lani. Circle, Wai-lupe, Honolulu. (TM.) *Lit.,* heavenly (or royal) child.

Keʻilu. Point, northeast Kauaʻi.

Ke-kaʻa. Black rock and area, site of Sheraton-Maui Hotel, Kāʻana-pali, West Maui. A man, Moemoe, insulted the demigod Māui; after lassoing the sun, Māui chased and killed Moemoe, who turned into this rock. (For. 5:538.) *Lit.,* the rumble (such sounds are said to be heard during storms).

Ke-kaʻa-lāʻau. Mountain (2,358 feet high), Honolua qd., Maui. *Lit.,* the twirling warclub.

Ke-kaha. Land area, North Kona, Hawaiʻi. Land section, elementary school, town, ditch, and plantation, Wai-mea district, southwest Kauaʻi. *Lit.,* the place.

Kekahi. Cape, Hālawa qd., Molokaʻi. *Lit.,* one. (Spelled Kehahi on some maps.)

Ke-kai-o-Māmala. The surf in the outer entrance of Honolulu Harbor, named for the chiefess Māmala who loved to play *kōnane,* drink *ʻawa,* and ride the surf. See Māmala.

Ke-kau. Place, Nuʻu-anu, Honolulu. Probably *lit.,* the summer season.

Ke-kaulike. Street, ʻAʻala section, Honolulu, named for the mother of David Ka-wānana-koa and Kū-hiō Ka-lani-ana-ʻole. She was a sister of Queen Ka-piʻo-lani. (TM.) *Lit.,* the equality.

Ke-kā-ulu-ohi. State government building housing the Archives of Hawaiʻi; Ka-mehameha Schools dormitory built in 1931, Honolulu. Ke-kā-ulu-ohi (1794–1845) was the wife, in turn, of Ka-mehameha I, Ka-mehameha II, and Ka-naʻina; by Ka-naʻina she bore Luna-lilo, afterwards king. She was *kuhina nui* for Ka-mehameha III. (RC 236, 394.) *Lit.,* the vine growing [with] shoots.

Keke. Hill, Kō-loa district, Kauaʻi.

Kekele. Land division at the foot of Nuʻu-anu Pali, Oʻahu, famous for the fragrance of *hala* flowers and fruits. *Lit.,* damp.

Kekepa. Islet off northern end of Mō-kapu peninsula, Oʻahu. *Lit.,* to snap at.

Ke-koa-lele. Ridge above Oʻahu Country Club and west of the Pali Highway, Honolulu. *Lit.,* the leaping warrior.

Ke-kua-ʻai-ʻopihi. Coastal area near the eastern point of Molokaʻi. *Lit.,* the god (or ghost) eating limpets.

Ke-kua-lele. Land section, hill, and stream, Hāmākua qd., Hawaiʻi. *Lit.,* the flying god (a stone god on a hillside between Kau-nā-mano and Honokāne in Kaʻū tired of this location and flew to Ke-kua-lele).

Ke-kū-anaōʻa. State government building named for the governor of Oʻahu in the 1840s and husband of Kīnaʻu; their children were Alexander Liholiho (Ka-mehameha IV), Lot Ka-mehameha (Ka-mehameha V), and Victoria Ka-māmalu. *Lit.,* the standing projections. (*Anaōʻa* is probably a variant spelling for *wanaōʻa.* The name is said to refer to ships' masts seen in the harbor when Ke-kū-anaōʻa was born.)

Ke-kua-nohu. Site of the fort for which Fort Street, Honolulu, was named. The fort was begun by Russians in 1816 and finished by Hawaiians after the Russians were banished. It was removed in 1857, and coral stones from its walls were used for a retaining wall along the waterfront.

Ke-kua-noni. Street and place, Pauoa, Honolulu, named for the chief who was granted a tract in the area during the Great Mahele, 1849. (TM.) *Lit.,* the *noni (Morinda citrifolia)* god.

Ke-kua-pio. Land division between Wai-ʻōhinu and Nā-ʻā-lehu, Kaʻū, Hawaiʻi. *Lit.,* the whistling spirit (spirits whistled at strangers here).

Ke-kua-waha-ʻulaʻula. Land area, Puʻu-o-kali qd., Maui. *Lit.,* the red-mouth god.

Ke-kū-hau-piʻo. Ka-mehameha Schools field house, built in 1949 and named for the favorite warrior of Ka-lani-ʻōpuʻu, who saved young Ka-mehameha's life in a Maui battle and later became Ka-mehameha's teacher in the arts of warfare. *Lit.,* the standing [of the] arched *hau* tree.

Ke-kupua. Valley near Maka-weli, Wai-mea district, Kauaʻi. Three *heiau* for human sacrifice were here: Kū-ana-lili, Aʻa-kukui, and Ka-unu-loa (the long pebble).

Kelawea. Village, Lahaina qd., Maui.

Keller Hall. University of Hawaiʻi building, Mānoa campus, Honolulu, completed in 1959, and named for Arthur R. Keller (1882–1961), a vice-president of the university and a dean of the College of Applied Sciences.

Ke-mamo. An area above Wai-piʻo Valley, Hawaiʻi. (For. Sel. 138.) *Lit.,* the descendant.

Kemole. Hill and gulch, Wai-kiʻi qd., Hawaiʻi.

Kemoʻo. Land division near Schofield Barracks, Oʻahu; usually pronounced Kīmū.

Kennedy Theatre. Theater building, Mānoa campus, University of Hawaiʻi, Honolulu, completed in 1963 and named for John Fitzgerald Kennedy. The second performance there (the satirical *Of Thee I Sing*) was scheduled for December 5, 1963. Upon the arrival of news of President Kennedy's assassination, the theater, originally named the East-West Theatre, was given his name, and *Of Thee I Sing* was replaced by a Kabuki play, *Benten the Thief,* and *Hamlet.*

Kē Nui. Road, Sunset Beach, Oʻahu. *Lit.,* big Kē (protest).

Kē-ō-kea. Land section and point, Hilo qd.; land section and village, Honomū qd.; land section, Kala-pana qd.; beach park and bay, Wai-piʻo qd., Kohala, Hawaiʻi. The meaning for the bay in Kohala is said to be ʻthe sound of white [caps]ʼ. Land section, village, and park, Puʻu-o-kali qd., Maui. *Lit.,* the white sand (*ō* is short for *one*).

Keoki. Place, Kuli-ʻouʻou, Honolulu. *Lit.,* George.

Ke-ola. Street, Ka-mehameha Heights, Honolulu. (TM.) *Lit.,* the life.

Ke-ola-o-ka-lani. Kindergarten building, Ka-mehameha Schools, Honolulu, built in 1954 and named for the son of Princess Ruth and Lele-iō-hoku; he died in infancy. *Lit.,* the life of the royal chief.

Ke-ō-lewa. Cinder cone (2,109 feet high), Kaunakakai qd., north Molokaʻi. Probably *lit.,* the shifting sand (*ō* is short for *one*).

Ke-olo-ʻewa. Peak (2,109 feet high), north central Molokaʻi, sometimes spelled Ke-ō-lewa. In some tales Ke-olo-ʻewa is a Molokaʻi chief who abducts Hā-ka-lani-leo (harsh the chief's voice) and takes her to Hāʻupu mountain, where she is rescued by her son, Kana. (HM 465.) In other stories he is the brother of the man who abducts Hina (PH 79). See Hāʻupu, Pāʻū-o-Nuʻakea. *Lit.,* the crooked hill.

Ke-olonā-hihi. *Heiau* and ancient surfing area, Kai-lua qd., Hawaiʻi, where Ka-mehameha I first learned to surf (Finney and Houston 55). See Kāwā. *Lit.,* the creeping *olonā* plant.

K

Keolu. Land section, subdivision, elementary school, drive, and playground, Kai-lua, Oʻahu.

Keomana. Land area, Kai-lua qd., Hawaiʻi.

Ke-omo. Point between Ke-ala-ke-kua Bay and Hōnaunau, Hawaiʻi. *Lit.,* the suction tube.

Ke-ō-muku. Village, central Lā-naʻi. *Lit.,* the shortened sand (*ō* is short for *one*).

Ke-onaona. Street, Nuʻu-anu, Honolulu. *Lit.,* the fragrance.

Ke-one. Bay, west Lā-naʻi. *Lit.,* the sand.

Ke-one-ʻeleʻele. A plain about 2 miles south of Pāhala, Kaʻū, Hawaiʻi. *Lit.,* the black sand.

Ke-one-hānau. Coastal area, ʻĪlio Pt. qd., north Molokaʻi. *Lit.,* the birth sands *or* the birthplace.

Ke-one-heʻeheʻe. Sliding Sands Trail, leading into the crater from the summit of Hale-a-ka-lā, Maui. *Lit.,* the sliding sand.

Ke-one-heheʻe. Peak, Mauna Kea area, Wai-kiʻi qd., Hawaiʻi. *Lit.,* the sliding sand (*i.e.,* cinders).

Ke-one-heleleʻi. Beach, Honolua qd., Maui. *Lit.,* the scattered sand.

Ke-one-kani-o-Nohili. Barking Sands, Wai-mea district, Kauaʻi. *Lit.,* the sounding sand of Nohili.

Ke-one-kū-ʻino. Land district, Ka-malō qd., south Molokaʻi. *Lit.,* the sand rises [in the] storm.

Ke-one-lele. Desert area, ʻĪlio Pt. qd., north Molokaʻi, said to have been a burial site. *Lit.,* the flying sand.

Ke-one-ʻōʻio. Land section and bay (also called La Pérouse Bay), Mā-kena qd., Maui. Gulch, Nānā-kuli, Oʻahu. (For. 4:574.) *Lit.,* the sandy [place with] bonefish.

Ke-one-poko. Coastal area, Hālawa qd., south Molokaʻi. *Lit.,* the short sand.

Ke-one-poko Iki. Land section, Makuʻu qd., Hawaiʻi. *Lit.,* small Ke-one-poko.

Ke-one-poko Nui. Land section, Makuʻu qd., Hawaiʻi. *Lit.,* large Ke-one-poko.

Ke-one-ʻula. Area in which are situated Ka-ʻiu-lani School and Kaumakapili Church, Honolulu. *Lit.,* the red sand.

Keoni. Street, Mānoa, Honolulu. *Lit.,* John.

Keoniana. Street, Wai-kīkī, Honolulu, named for the second John Young, the *kuhina nui* under Ka-mehameha II and minister of foreign relations under Ka-mehameha IV (Kuy. 2:36). See ʻOlohana, Young. *Lit.,* John Young.

Keoniki. Land division, Wai-piʻo qd., Hawaiʻi.

Ke-ōpū. Land section, Kai-lua qd., Kona, Hawai'i. *Lit.,* the bunching together.

Ke-'ōpua. Street, Pauoa, Honolulu, named for a settler in the area before it was opened to homesteaders. He was a stevedore and died in 1936. (TM.) *Lit.,* the cloud bank.

Ke-ō-puka. Land sections near Ke-ala-ke-kua Bay, Kona, Hawai'i. *Lit.,* the perforated sand (*ō* is short for *one*). Islet (1.7 acres, 120 feet elevation), Ke-'anae qd., Maui.

Ke-ō-puka Loa. Land division, Hālawa qd., Moloka'i. *Lit.,* long Ke-ō-puka.

Ke-ō-puka 'U'uku. Land division, Hālawa qd., Moloka'i. *Lit.,* small Ke-ō-puka.

Ke-ō-ua. Walk, Sheridan Tract, and classroom building at the Kamehameha Schools built in 1940, Honolulu, named for Ka-lani-kupu-a-pā-i-ka-lani-nui (the royal chief [who] grew and touched the great sky) Ke-ō-ua (the rainy cloud), the father of Ka-mehameha I by Ke-ku'i-'apo-iwa (the joining [of] nine circles, *i.e.,* nine families united in one person). (RC 123.)

Ke-ō-ua-hale. Princess Ruth's house, today the site of Central Intermediate School on Queen Emma Street, Honolulu. The site was called Ka-'ako-pua (the plucked flower).

Ke-pani-wai. Park, Wai-luku, Maui. *Lit.,* the water dam (Wai-luku Stream was choked with human bodies after the slaughter there; see Wai-luku.)

Ke-pono. Coastal area, Ka-malō qd., north Moloka'i.

Ke-po'o-koholua. Hill (1,555 feet high), Hālawa qd., Moloka'i. *Lit.,* the lance head.

Ke-puhi. Points at Kohala qd., and Nā-po'opo'o park, Kona, Hawai'i; at Hanalei, Kaua'i; and at Wai-'anae, O'ahu. Land area, northeast Hanalei district, Kaua'i. Coastal area and bay, 'Īlio Pt. qd., Moloka'i. Street, Diamond Head section, Honolulu.

Ke-puna. Gulch, Hālawa qd., Moloka'i. Perhaps this should be Ka-puna (the spring).

Ke-puni. Gulch, Luala'i-lua qd., Maui.

Kēwā. Land section near Wai-lua, Kaua'i. (UL 136.) Stream, Kāne-'ohe, O'ahu. *Lit.,* anticipation.

Ke-walo. Section 22 of Honolulu (map 6), basin (harbor), and surfing areas, one called Ke-walo (Diamond Head side of the channel) and another, Point Panic ('Ewa side). Outcasts (*kauwā*) intended for sacrifice were drowned here. *Lit.,* the calling (as an echo).

Kiaka. Bay alongside Wai-a-lua Bay, O'ahu.

Kī'ao. Land section, Honu-'apo qd., Ka'ū, Hawai'i. Land section, Hālawa qd., Moloka'i. The name may once have been Kia-ao (cloud pillar).

Kī-'apu. Land area, Kala-pana qd., Hawai'i. *Lit.,* ti-leaf drinking cup.

Ki'ei. Bay, southwest Lā-na'i. Land area near Kau-pō, Maui. *Lit.,* peer (a half-human shark [*manō kanaka*] peered at the land and seeing no growing taro remarked that the land was bare).

Ki'eki'e. Land division and ranch headquarters, Ni'ihau. *Lit.,* lofty.

K

K

Kiha-a-Pi'ilani. Hill, 'Īlio Pt. qd., south Moloka'i, named for an ancient Maui chief. See Hono-a-Pi'ilani, Ka-lae-o-ka-lā'au, Ka-nahā, Ka-wai-papa, Ke-ala-pūpū-a-Kiha. *Lit.,* Kiha [child] of Pi'i-lani.

Kiha-loko. Fishpond, Hālawa qd., south Moloka'i. *Lit.,* supernatural lizard pond *or* Chief Kiha's pond.

Kīhei. Village, plantation, elementary school, boat landing, beach park known as Mai-poina-'oe-ia'u, Mā'alaea qd., Maui. Place, Ka-pahulu section, Honolulu. *Lit.,* cape, cloak.

Kīhewa-moku. Islet off Lani-loa Point, Lā'ie qd., O'ahu.

Kīholo. Bay, Pua-kō qd., Kona, Hawai'i; also the name of a fishpond said to have been built by Ka-mehameha I; it was destroyed by a lava flow in 1859 because, the story goes, Pele was hungry for the *awa* and mullet there. (Westervelt, 1963:148.) See Hu'ehu'e, Lua-hine-wai. Street, 'Āina-Haina, Honolulu, named for Hind property at Kona, Hawai'i. *Lit.,* fishhook.

Ki'i. Point north of Alahaka Bay, south of Hōnaunau, Kona, Hawai'i. Areas near South Point, Ka'ū, and in Puna qd., Hawai'i. Landing, Ni'ihau. Reservoir, Ka-huku qd., and point, Mō-kapu qd., O'ahu. *Lit.,* image.

Ki'i-a-La'a. Valley, central Ni'ihau. *Lit.,* image [made] by La'a.

Ki'i-kau. Ancient surfing area, Ke-āhole qd., Hawai'i (Finney and Houston 26). *Lit.,* placed image.

Ki'i-kolu. Hill, Ka-laupapa peninsula, Moloka'i. *Lit.,* triple image *or* triple fetching.

Ki'i-lae. Bay, watercourse, and land section south of Hōnaunau, Kona, Hawai'i. *Lit.,* cape image.

Ki'i-nohu. Gulch, Ka-malō qd., south Moloka'i.

Kīkala. Land sections and homesteads, Kala-pana qd., Hawai'i. *Lit.,* hip.

Kikanē. Walk, Sheridan Tract, Honolulu. *Lit.,* Sidney.

Kīkēkē. Avenue, Ka-imu-kī, Honolulu. (TM.) *Lit.,* to knock.

Kīkepa. Point, northeast Ni'ihau. *Kīkepa* is the tapa or sarong worn by women with the top under one arm and over the shoulder of the opposite arm.

Kīkī. Land area near Koa'e, Puna, Hawai'i, named for the *kīkī* bird that nested together with a *koa'e* bird; the *koa'e* bird faced the area known as Koa'e, and the *kīkī* bird faced Kīkī. According to some, both birds stole wild taro until they were destroyed by the demigod Pīkoi-a-ka-'alalā.

Kīkī-'ae'ae. Small cone at about 5,000 feet elevation on Hualālai, Hawai'i. (Macdonald and Abbott 306.) Probably *lit.,* fine basket.

Kiki-a-ka-lā. Land section, Ka-malō qd., Moloka'i. Perhaps short for Ikiiki-a-ka-lā, heat of the sun.

Kīkī-a-Ola. Land division, small boat harbor, stream, and watercourse, Wai-mea, Kaua'i, now called Menehune Ditch. See Kīpapa-a-Ola. *Lit.,* container [acquired] by Ola. (Chief Ola ordered the Menehune to build a watercourse here; each brought a stone, and the ditch was finished in a single night; HM 328–329.)

Kīkī-hale. Old section of Honolulu bordered by Mauna-kea and King streets to Nu'u-anu Stream, named for the daughter of Chief Kou. (Honolulu in 1810.)

Kikilia. Place, Pālolo, Honolulu. *Lit.,* Cecelia.

Kiki-manu. Place near Wai-o-honu, East Maui.

Kiki-pua. Flat or point, Hālawa qd., north Moloka'i, said to be named for a female *mo'o* who lived here and was killed by Hi'iaka (PH 84–85). *Lit.,* young fish (*or* flower) basket.

Kiki-welawela. Land section, He'eia, O'ahu. Probably short for Ikiiki-welawela (stifling hot).

Kiko-'ula. Gulch, Hālawa qd., Moloka'i. *Lit.,* red dot.

Kila. Narrow strip of land at the top of the cliff at Kahana, O'ahu. (Sterling and Summers 4:144.)

Kilakila. Drive, 'Ālewa Heights, Honolulu. *Lit.,* magnificent.

Kīlau. Peak (4,080 feet high), Ka-malō qd., Moloka'i, probably named for a fern.

Kī-lau-ea. Active volcano on the flank of Mauna Loa, nearly continuously active 1823–1894 and 1907–1924; eruptions began again in 1952 and still continue (Macdonald and Abbott 74–77). Quadrangle, crater, gulch, State park, military camp, and forest reserve, Humu'ula, Kī-lau-ea, and Puna qds.; ranger station, Puna qd., Hawai'i. Village, land division, landing, bay, lighthouse, sugar plantation (1877–1971), elementary school, point, stream, falls, and tuff cone, Hanalei district, Kaua'i. Land division, park (Diamond Head section), and avenue (Wai-'alae, Ka-imu-kī, and Kāhala sections), Honolulu. *Lit.,* spewing, much spreading (referring to volcanic eruptions).

Kī-lau-ea Iki. A small crater just outside Kī-lau-ea Crater, Hawai'i. *Lit.,* little Kī-lau-ea.

Kīlea. Hill (269 feet elevation), Olowalu qd., Maui. *Lit.,* small but conspicuous hill.

Kili-hau. Street, Moana-lua, Honolulu, named for a fishpond that was once nearby. (TM.) *Lit.,* cold rain.

Kilioe. See Ka-ulu-o-Laka.

Kī-loa. Land section, former village, and spring near Ke-ala-ke-kua, Kona, Hawai'i. Land section, Ka-malō qd., Moloka'i. *Lit.,* long ti plant (good ti was found here).

Kilohana. Land divisions, Mauna Loa qd., south Hawai'i (UL 124); land division (at 9,620 feet), and Girl Scout camp, Wai-ki'i qd., north Hawai'i. Peak and crater, Līhu'e district, Kaua'i (Macdonald and Abbott 389, figure 260). A boy, Lahi, and his uncle, while hunting 'uwa'u birds on the summit, lured a giant into a hole and killed him; warriors came to catch the bird hunters, but Lahi hid at a pass and threw the men one at a time over a cliff (HM 331, Rice). Lookout, Wai-mea Canyon, Kaua'i (PH 183). Quadrangle, elementary school, and summit observatory, Hale-a-ka-lā, East Maui, now called White Hill. Summit of the mountain separating 'Uala-pu'e and Wailau; point near Ka-la'e overlooking Ka-laupapa; park and school, 'Uala-pu'e, Moloka'i. Peak at the head of Ka-lihi Valley, Honolulu. The sorceress Haumea (mother of Pele) lived here with her husband Wākea. While fishing at He'eia, she had a premonition of danger to her husband. She returned to Kilohana, left her fishing basket with its crabs and *pōhuehue* vines (which are still found there), and went down to Wai-ka-halulu (former reef off the Honolulu waterfront); men had tied up Wākea and were carrying him to Wai-kīkī for execu-

111

tion. She begged permission for one last embrace. At her touch the bonds fell away and the two disappeared into a tree (HM 281). In some versions the tree was a breadfruit. Street, Ka-lihi Uka, Honolulu. *Lit.,* lookout point *or* outer tapa *or* best, superior.

Kilo-lani. Congregational church at Kīhei, East Maui. *Lit.,* sky observing.

Kimo. Drive, Dowsett Highlands, Honolulu, named for the son of Henry Isaac Dowsett, pioneer settler and captain of his own vessel. *Lit.,* James.

Kimokeo. Street, 'Āina-Haina, Honolulu. (TM.) *Lit.,* Timothy.

Kīna'u. Cape, Mākena qd., Maui. Ka-mehameha Schools dormitory built in 1931, street parallel to Beretania, and State office building, named for the daughter of Ka-mehameha I and Ka-heihei-mālie, and wife of Ke-kū-'anaō'a; she was the mother of Ka-mehameha IV, Ka-mehameha V, Victoria Ka-māmalu, and Ke-kū-āiwa. After Ka-'ahu-manu's death she became *kuhina nui* for Ka-mehameha III, an office she held until her death in 1839 at the age of 35 (RC 348). In a chant in her honor, Kīna'u is said to have been named for a mythical bird, Ka-manu-kīna'u-a-Pae. *Lit.,* flaw.

King. Principal street, Honolulu, named in 1850 for Hawaiian kings; formerly called Mō'ī. (TM.) Intermediate and high school, Kāne-'ohe, O'ahu, named for Samuel Wilder King (1896–1959), delegate to Congress 1934–1942 and governor of the Territory of Hawai'i 1953–1957. Governor King lived in Kāne-'ohe.

King's Landing. New name for Pāpa'i, Maku'u qd., Hawai'i, in honor of Ka-mehameha's accident there. See Pāpa'i.

Kini. Place, Ka-lihi Uka, Honolulu; sacred rock that attracted fish, Wai-mānalo, O'ahu. *Lit.,* Jane, Jean, *or* multitudes.

Kini-hāpai. Stream, Wai-luku qd., Maui. *Lit.,* carry multitudes.

Kino-'ole. Street, Hilo, Hawai'i, named for the high chiefess Kino-'ole Pitman, wife of Benjamin Pitman, Sr. See Volcano House. *Lit.,* without body.

*Ki'oki'o. Coastal area, Hālawa qd., north Moloka'i.

Kiola-ka'a. Land sections and homesteads, Honu-'apo and Ka Lae qds., Hawai'i. *Lit.,* throw roll. (There was a bowling course here. The hero Ka-miki and his brother Maka-'iole were having a wit-matching contest [*ho'opāpā*]. Maka-'iole threw a *paua* taro to his sister, because *pa-* in the taro name would reveal to her that she was needed to come and help him *ho'opāpā*.)

Kī'olokū. Land section, Honu-'apo qd., Hawai'i.

Kī'ope. Pond on the grounds of Huli-he'e Palace, Kai-lua, North Kona, Hawai'i, where chiefs bathed. *Lit.,* bundle.

Kī-pāhoehoe. Land section by the sea near Hōnaunau, South Kona, Hawai'i. *Lit.,* much smooth lava. (It is said that the people here filled hollows on the shore with stones to make a smooth landing place for canoes. A spring was here.)

Kī-pahulu. Forest reserve, quadrangle, village, district, and valley, East Maui; home of Laka (UL 43), a god worshipped by canoe makers. *Lit.,* fetch [from] exhausted gardens (*kī* is short for *ki'i*).

Kīpapa. Land section, Mākena qd., Maui. Fishpond at Ke-one-kū-'ino

K

and ridge at Pelekunu, Ka-malō qd., Moloka'i. Ditch, gulch, junction, stream, elementary school, and park, Wahi-a-wā qd., central O'ahu. *Lit.,* placed prone (referring to corpses slain in the victory of O'ahu forces over those of Hawai'i in the fourteenth century; Alexander, 1891:96).

Kīpapa-a-Ola. Trail above Hanalei, Kaua'i. See Kīkī-a-Ola. *Lit.,* roadway [made] by Ola (a Kaua'i chief).

Kipona. Place, Pālolo, Honolulu. (TM.) *Lit.,* variegated colors.

Kīpū. Point northwest of Kumu-kahi, east Hawai'i. Land division, Līhu'e district, Kaua'i, visited by Kama-pua'a (For. Sel. 228). Point, village, land division, and petroglyph site, Kaunakakai qd., north Moloka'i. (Cox and Stasack 94; PH 110.) See 'Uhane-lele. *Lit.,* hold back.

Kīpuka-'āhiu. *Kīpuka* (see list of Hawaiian words, p. 3), Kī-lau-ea qd., Hawai'i. *Lit.,* wild *kīpuka.*

Kīpuka-'ākala. *Kīpuka,* Honu'apo qd., Ka'ū, Hawai'i. *Lit.,* raspberry *kīpuka.*

Kīpū Kai. Part of Kīpū seaward of Hā'upu, Kaua'i. *Lit.,* seaward Kīpū.

Kīpuka Kapā'ū. *Kīpuka,* Ka'ū, Hawai'i, seaward of Ka-huku, named for a man called Ka-pā'ū who lived here with his wife. A lava flow surrounded their house but left them alive.

Kīpuka-ke-ana-bihopa. *Kīpuka,* Kī-lau-ea qd., Hawai'i. *Lit.,* the bishop's cave *kīpuka.*

Kīpuka-kēkake. *Kīpuka,* seaward of Ka-huku, Honu-'apo qd., Ka'ū, Hawai'i. A donkey *(kēkake)* was saved here from a lava flow.

Kīpuka-kī. *Kīpuka,* Kī-lau-ea qd., Hawai'i. *Lit.,* ti *kīpuka.*

Kīpuka-kula-lio. *Kīpuka,* Kī-lau-ea qd., Hawai'i. *Lit.,* horse-pasture *kīpuka.*

Kīpuka-mauna-'iu. *Kīpuka,* Kī-lau-ea qd., Hawai'i. *Lit.,* lofty mountain *kīpuka.*

Kīpuka-nēnē. *Kīpuka,* picnic area, and campgrounds, Hawai'i Volcanoes National Park, Kī-lau-ea qd., Hawai'i. *Lit.,* goose *kīpuka.*

Kīpuka-noa. *Kīpuka,* Honu-'apo qd., Ka'ū, Hawai'i. *Lit.,* nonsacred *kīpuka.*

Kīpuka-o-Pele-iki. *Kīpuka,* Ka'ū, Hawai'i. *Lit.,* *kīpuka* of little Pele.

Kīpuka-pā-hipa. *Kīpuka,* Honu-'apo qd., Ka'ū, Hawai'i. *Lit.,* sheep-pen *kīpuka.*

Kīpuka-pakēkakē. Land section, Kī-lau-ea qd., Hawai'i. *Lit.,* brittle *kīpuka.*

Kīpuka-papālina-moku. *Kīpuka,* Kī-lau-ea and Puna qds., Ka'ū, Hawai'i. *Lit.,* cut-cheek *kīpuka.*

Kīpuka-pepeiao. *Kīpuka,* Hawai'i Volcanoes National Park, Kī-lau-ea qd., Hawai'i. *Lit.,* ear *kīpuka.*

Kīpuka-pua-ulu. *Kīpuka* known also as the Bird Park, Hawai'i Volcanoes National Park, Kī-lau-ea qd., Hawai'i. (Macdonald and Abbott 307.) *Lit.,* growing-flower *kīpuka.*

Kīpū Uka. Part of Kīpū inland of Hā'upu, Kaua'i. *Lit.,* inland Kīpū.

Kirkwood. Place, 'Āina-Haina, Honolulu, named for John Kirkwood Clarke, trustee of the Robert Hind Estate and of the Bishop Estate, and former vice-president of Bishop Trust Company. (TM.)

K

Klebahn. Place, Nuʻu-anu, Honolulu, named for F. W. Klebahn of Hackfeld and Company. (TM.)

Klum Gymnasium. University of Hawaiʻi gymnasium, Mānoa campus, Honolulu, completed in 1957 and named for Otto Klum, football coach 1921–1939.

Koa. Avenue, Wai-kīkī, Honolulu, named for Prince David Ka-wānana-koa. (TM.) *Lit.*, brave.

*Koʻa. Fishpond, east Lā-naʻi.

Koaʻe. Village and land section, Makuʻu qd., Hawaiʻi, perhaps named for Puna-ʻai-koaʻe (Puna, ruled by tropicbird), a supernatural being with a tropicbird form who once lived near here at Pū-ʻula; he is seen today flying over Kī-lau-ea Crater. See Kīkī. Cone, Kī-lau-ea qd., Hawaiʻi. Street, Wai-ʻalae-Kāhala, Honolulu. *Lit.*, tropicbird.

Koaʻe-kea. Cliff on the side of Wai-piʻo Valley, Hāmākua, Hawaiʻi. Kāne and various gods lived at the top of this cliff at a place called Hōkū-welowelo (comet); their conch sounded every night, to the annoyance of Chief Hākau, who ordered the thieving dog, Puapua-lenalena, to steal it. According to For. 4:558–561 the gods lived at Pua-kō, not at Hōkū-welowelo. (UL 67.) Land section, Hāna qd., Maui. *Lit.*, white tropicbird.

Kōʻai. Hill (2,585 feet high), Olowalu qd., Maui. *Lit.*, to stir, as with a circular motion of the hand.

Koaiʻe. Cove and former fishing village south of Māhukona, Kohala, Hawaiʻi; excavations in 1968 show that the village was inhabited until historic times. (Newman.) Stream, Wai-mea, Kauaʻi, named for the *koaiʻe* (*Acacia koaia*) tree that was uprooted by Nā-maka-o-ka-paoʻo, a Maui hero who made a war club of it.

Koa-kea. Area at Wai-piʻo, Hawaiʻi. *Lit.*, white *koa* tree. (For. Sel. 118.)

Koala. Gulch, east Lā-naʻi.

Koali. Land section, gulch, and village, Hāna qd., Maui. Place, lower St. Louis Heights, Honolulu, probably named for a morning glory. (TM.)

Koa-liʻi. Hill, Hālawa qd., Molokaʻi. *Lit.*, chiefly warrior.

Koʻa-lua. Ancient surfing area, Ka-paʻa, east Kauaʻi (Finney and Houston 30). Probably *lit.*, two coral heads.

Koʻa-mano. Reef, Heʻeia, Oʻahu. *Lit.*, many shrines.

Koʻa-manō. Stone at Hāʻena, Kauaʻi, representing a predatory shark. (Pronounced Koʻa-mano today.) *Lit.*, shark shrine.

Kō-ā-uka. Land division, Wai-piʻo, Hawaiʻi. *Lit.*, the uplanders.

Kō-ʻele. Land division, central Lā-naʻi. *Lit.*, dark sugarcane.

Koena-limu. Land division near Lae-hou, North Kona, Hawaiʻi. *Lit.*, remaining seaweed.

Kohā-i-ka-lani. *Heiau* erected by a chief of this name at Maka-nau, Kaʻū, Hawaiʻi. *Lit.*, resounding in the sky.

Kohā-kō-hau. Stream, Wai-piʻo qd., Hawaiʻi.

Kohala. District (famous for the ʻĀpaʻapaʻa wind), quadrangle, extinct volcano, land section, club, sugar plantation, elementary and high schools, ditch, trail, mill, mountains, forest reserve, post office, seminary, and village, all in northwest Hawaiʻi; point, Honomū qd., northeast Hawaiʻi.

Kohana-iki. Land sections, Kai-lua and Ke-āhole qds., North Kona, Hawai'i. *Lit.,* small barrenness.

Kohe-anu. Stream, Mau-lua Gulch, Hawai'i. *Lit.,* cold vagina.

Kohe-lepelepe. Old name for Koko Crater, O'ahu. (For the story of the formation of the crater, see Pua'a-kanu. Similar adventures began at Lele on Kaua'i and Wai-lua Nui on Maui.) *Lit.,* vagina labia minor.

Kohe-mālamalama. Ancient name for Ka-ho'olawe. (HM 189.) *Lit.,* bright vagina.

Kōheo. Point, Kō-loa district, Kaua'i. Land division, Pu'u-o-kali qd., Maui. Coastal area, formerly swamp, Kaunakakai qd., Moloka'i. *Lit.,* to show off *or* to twirl.

Kōheo-hala. Coastal area, northeast Ka-ho'olawe. Same as Puhi-kōheo-hala. Possibly *lit.,* missing show-off.

Koholā-lele. Land division and landing, Hāmākua and Mauna Kea qds., Hawai'i. Falls, Līhu'e district, Kaua'i. Fishpond, Kua-loa, O'ahu, believed dug by Menehune and still used commercially in 1971. (UL 39.) *Lit.,* leaping whale.

Kohola-loa. Old name for Sand Island, Honolulu. *Lit.,* long reef.

Kohua. Ridge, northwest Kaua'i.

Ko'i-ahi. Land section at Mākua, Ka-'ena qd., O'ahu, where finest *maile-lau-li'i* formerly grew. *Lit.,* fire adze.

Ko'iawe. Stream, Wai-pi'o qd., Hawai'i. *Lit.,* light, moving rain.

Kō-kea. Street and place, Ka-pā-lama section, Honolulu. (TM.) *Lit.,* white sugarcane.

Kōke'e. State park, natural history museum, land division, and stream, Wai-mea district, Kaua'i. *Lit.,* to bend *or* to wind.

Koki'o. Land section, Kohala qd., Hawai'i, named for a native hibiscus.

Kōkī-o-Wailau. Cliffs, Wai-lau Valley, Ka-malō qd., Molokai'i. 'Ai'ai, the son of a fishing god, Kū-'ula-kai, went to Moloka'i and found people neglecting to preserve the young fish. He hid all the fresh-water shrimps from other valleys in a small cave in a cliff. The full name of the mountain is Kōkī-o-Wailau-alapi'i-a-ka-'ōpae (the top of Wailau [is] the ladder to the shrimps). (HM 22.) *Ka pi'i nō ia ā Kōkī-o-Wailau,* he has climbed Kōkī-o-Wailau (he is successful). See Pōhaku-Kā'anapali.

Koko Crater and Koko Head. Modern names for two well-known tuff cones east of Honolulu; the old name for Koko Crater was Kohe-lepelepe. Koko was formerly the name of a small canoe landing at the Wai-'alae side of Koko Head, named for red earth, or for the blood (*koko*) of a man bitten by a shark. Today a City-County regional park area includes Koko Head District Park, Hālona Blow Hole, Koko Crater Botanic Garden, Koko Head Rifle Range, Hanauma Bay Beach Park, Koko Head Sandy Beach Park, and Koko Head Playground; nearby is Koko Head Elementary School.

Koko-iki. Land section near Mo'o-kini *heiau,* Kohala, Hawai'i, birthplace of Ka-mehameha I (Ii 3), said to be marked by a stone called Pōhaku-hānau-ali'i (stone [of] royal birth). *Lit.,* little blood.

Koko-kahi. YWCA Branch, Mō-kapu qd., O'ahu, founded in 1935 by the Reverend Theodore Richards (Likeke), who also gave the name.

K

Kokole

The old name of the area was Ke-ana. *Lit.*, one blood (a new name signifying that all races have similar blood and are hence equal). See Ka-wai-a-Haʻo.

Kokole. Point, Wai-mea district, Kauaʻi. *Lit.*, raw.

Kokololio. Gulch near Lāʻie Maloʻo, Oʻahu. *Lit.*, gusty.

Kokomo. Village, Haʻi-kū qd., Maui; said to have been originally Koa-komo, *lit.*, *koa* tree entering.

Kola-loa. Gulch, Puʻu-o-kali qd., Maui. *Lit.*, much sexual excitement.

Kole-aka. Area near Fort and School streets, Honolulu. *Lit.*, shadowed reddishness.

Kōlea-liʻiliʻi. Hill (1,254 feet high), Wai-ʻanae Valley, Oʻahu. *Lit.*, small plover.

Kolekole. Gulch, stream, and beach park, Wai-piʻo and Mauna Kea qds., Hawaiʻi. Mountains, Mākena qd., Maui. Pass and road from Schofield Barracks through the Wai-ʻanae Range, Oʻahu. A large stone at the pass on Oʻahu has been called a sacrificial stone, but it was probably never so used; others say the stone represents a woman named Kolekole who guarded the pass; students of *lua* fighting lay in wait here to practice their skill on travelers. In a battle here Maui forces killed the last of the Oʻahu people who had escaped the massacre at Niu-hele-wai. See Puʻu-kolekole. *Lit.*, raw, scarred. (In one explanation of the name, a woman on the pass saw an apparently blind man approaching; doubting his blindness, she exposed herself. He opened his eyes and exclaimed, *A ʻula, kolekole!* Red, raw!)

Kolo. Land section, Hōnaunau qd., Kona, Hawaiʻi (see ʻŌlelo-moana). Ridge near Mānā and hill in south central Kauaʻi, both in Wai-mea qd. Wharf, harbor, and gulch (said to be the legendary home of Pā-kaʻa and Kū-a-Pākaʻa), Airport qd., and ridge, Ka-malō qd., Moloka'i. *Lit.*, crawl *or* pull.

Koloa. Street, Kāhala, Honolulu. *Lit.*, native duck.

Kō-loa. Beach at Puna-luʻu, Kaʻū, Hawaiʻi, where birth stones *(ʻiliʻili hānau)* were said to reproduce. Town, park, land division, elementary school, district, reservoir, landing, and stream, southeast Kauaʻi. (For. Sel. 108.) According to one account, the district was named for a steep rock called Pali-o-kō-loa. The first successful sugar plantation in the Islands was started here in 1835. It became a part of Grove Farm in 1948. See Waitā.

Kolo-a-ka-pohu. Peak, Kō-loa district, Kauaʻi. *Lit.*, creeping of the calm.

Kolo-iki. Ridge, northeast Lā-naʻi. Old name for Reid's Island in the Wai-luku River, Hilo, Hawaiʻi. *Lit.*, little crawling.

Kolo-kea. Valley, Wai-mea district, Kauaʻi. *Lit.*, creeping white (mists).

Kolokolo. Point, Hanalei district, Kauaʻi. Sea cave, southwest Lā-naʻi. *Lit.*, creeping.

Kolomona. Place, Woodlawn, Honolulu. (TM.) *Lit.*, Solomon.

Kolo-pulepule. Section of the city of Hilo, Hawaiʻi, behind the armory. *Lit.*, aimless creeping.

Kolo-walu. Ridges on the east side of upper Mānoa, Honolulu. A trail along the ridge begins near the summit of St. Louis Heights and descends into Woodlawn, Mānoa. Another branch leads to Mt. Olympus. *Lit.*, eight creeping.

Kō-mai‘a. Street, lower Mānoa, Honolulu. Perhaps *lit.*, dragging bananas.

Kona. Leeward districts on Hawai‘i, Kaua‘i, Moloka‘i, Ni‘ihau, and O‘ahu. Poetic (Hawai‘i): *kai mā‘oki‘oki; kai ‘ōpua i ka la‘i; kai hāwanawana,* streaked sea; clouds [over the] sea in the calm; whispering sea. (See Appendix 9.) *Lit.*, leeward.

Kona Gardens. Real estate development, Ka‘ū, Hawai‘i.

Kōnāhua-nui. Peaks (3,105 and 3,150 feet high) above Nu‘u-anu Pali, O‘ahu. *Lit.*, large fat innards. In one story a giant threw his great testicles (*kona hua nui*) at a woman who escaped him. See Kaukonahua. Today the pronunciation is Konahua-nui.

Kona Waena. Elementary and high school; central Kona, Kai-lua qd., Hawai‘i. *Lit.*, central Kona.

Konia. Street, Ka-mehameha Heights, Honolulu, and Ka-mehameha Schools classroom building built in 1949 and named for the mother of Bernice Pau-ahi Bishop and foster mother of Lili‘u-o-ka-lani. She was the daughter of Ka-‘ō-lei-o-kū, the first son of Ka-mehameha I (RC 286). She died in 1857.

Konohiki. Stream, Ka-wai-hau district, Kaua‘i. *Lit.*, land overseer.

Ko‘o-ho‘ō. Place, Kai-lua, O‘ahu. *Lit.*, inserted post.

Ko‘o-kā. See Honomū.

Ko‘oko‘olau. Hill (also called Pu‘u-ko‘oko‘olau), Mauna Kea qd.; land section, Puna; crater, Kī-lau-ea qd., Hawai‘i, named for the plant (*Bidens* spp.) used by Hawaiians for tea.

Ko‘olau. Windward districts, Kaua‘i, East Maui, and Moloka‘i. Ditch and forest reserve, Nā-hiku qd.; gap, Kilohana qd., Maui. Windward mountain range, O‘ahu. (See Appendix 9.) *Lit.*, windward.

Ko‘olau-kani. Valley, east Ni‘ihau. *Lit.*, sounding [of the] Ko‘olau [wind].

Ko‘olau Loa. District, northern windward O‘ahu. *Lit.*, long Ko‘olau.

Ko‘olau Poko. District, southern windward O‘ahu. *Lit.*, short Ko‘olau.

Ko‘o-nā-pou. Old name for Kau-pō, Wai-mānalo, O‘ahu. *Lit.*, staff posts (posts supported thatched roofs of the stone houses in this village).

Kopala. Hill on the slopes of Mauna Loa, ‘Īlio Pt. qd., Moloka‘i, below which was a trail leading to Pāka‘a's (see Kau-manamana) sweet potato patches. (Cooke 119.)

Kope. Gulch, Wai-luku qd., Maui. *Lit.*, to rake.

Kopke. Street, Ka-lihi Kai, Honolulu, named for Ernest Kopke of Lī-hu‘e Plantation on Kaua‘i, who came to Hawai‘i from Germany in 1871; he invented, among other things, a centrifugal separator. (TM.)

Korean Christian Church. The front of this Liliha Street, Honolulu, church is a replica of the Kwang Wha Mun gate in Seoul, Korea. The Honolulu church was founded in 1918 by Syngman Rhee (leader in the struggle for free Korea, and the first president of South Korea), then in exile in Hawai‘i. The church was built in 1938.

Kou. Old name, until 1800, for Honolulu Harbor and vicinity, includ-

Kō-'ula

ing the area from Nu'u-anu Avenue to Ala-kea Street and from Hotel Street to the sea (Westervelt, 1964b:15), noted for *kōnane* (pebble checkers) and for *ulu maika* (bowling), and said to be named for the executive officer (*ilāmuku*) of Chief Kākuhihewa of O'ahu. (PH 168.) *Lit., kou* tree.

Kō-'ula. Valley and stream, Wai-mea and Kō-loa districts, Kaua'i. The tyrant 'Ai-kanaka, frightened of the hero Ka-welo, fled here from Nounou Hill (For. Sel. 100). Street near Ke-walo Basin, Honolulu, named for a land section. The O'ahu meaning is 'red sugarcane'.

Kōwā. Channel between Coconut Island and the main island at Hilo, Hawai'i. *Lit.,* channel.

Kowali-'ula. Area in Wai-ka'o, Hawai'i. *Lit.,* red morning glory.

Kō-wawā. Cliff on the Ka'ū side of Kī-lau-ea Crater, Hawai'i. (PH 38.) *Lit.,* prolonged echo.

Krauss. Street, Pauoa, Honolulu, named for Frederick George Krauss, agriculturist with the University of Hawai'i who was in charge of the experiment station located at the site of the present Robert Louis Stevenson School near Papa-kōlea Homestead at the time the area was settled (TM). Complex of buildings at 2500 Dole Street, Honolulu, formerly the Pineapple Research Institute, now (1972) housing University offices.

Kua. Gulch, Ka-malō qd., south Moloka'i. *Lit.,* back.

Kū-'aha. Peak, Wai-mea district, Kaua'i. *Lit.,* stand proudly.

Kuahiku-ka-lapa-o-Anahulu. Highest point of Pu'u-anahulu, Pua-kō qd., Hawai'i. *Lit.,* sevenfold ridges of Anahulu.

Kuahine. Drive, Mānoa, Honolulu, named for a Mānoa rain brought by a "sister." (TM.) *Lit.,* sister of a male.

Kuahiwi. Way, Ka-lihi Uka, Honolulu. *Lit.,* hill, mountain.

Kua-honu. Point, Kīpū-kai, Kaua'i. *Lit.,* turtle back.

Kū-āhua. Coastal land area, north Lā-na'i. Islet, Wai-pahu qd., O'ahu. *Lit.,* standing heap.

Kū-ahu-lua. Gulch, south Lā-na'i. *Lit.,* two altars standing.

Kū-a-kahi-unu. Ancient surfing place, Hanalei district, Kaua'i. (Finney, 1959a:30.) *Lit.,* standing like a fishing shrine.

Kū-a-ka-'iwa. See Lae-o-kū-a-ka-'iwa.

Kū-a-ka-moku. Islet (1.1 acres), northwest Ni'ihau. *Lit.,* resembling the island.

Kuakea. Gulch, Hālawa qd., south Moloka'i. (RC 74.) *Lit.,* faded, light-colored (perhaps named for a Maui chief).

Kua-kini. Hospital and street, Lanakila and Nu'u-anu sections, Honolulu, named for Ka-'ahu-manu's brother (1791–1844), a governor of Hawai'i Island and acting governor of O'ahu who enforced puritanical laws; he was also known as John Adams. Kua-kini was in charge of building Moku-'ai-kaua church in Kai-lua, Kona, Hawai'i, in 1823, and rebuilding it in 1836. (RC 388–391.) *Lit.,* multitudinous [high ancestors] behind.

Kuala. Hill, Hālawa qd., Moloka'i. *Lit.,* somersault.

Kuala-i-ka-pō-iki. Ancient surfing area, Wai-'anae qd., O'ahu. (Finney, 1959a:51.) *Lit.,* tumbling in the small night.

K

Kualaka'i. Area near Barber's Pt., O'ahu. A spring here is called Hoaka-lei (lei reflection) because Hi'iaka picked *lehua* flowers here to make a lei and saw her reflection in the water. *Lit., Tethys* (a sea creature).

Kualapa. Land area, Hanalei district, Kaua'i. Land section near Ke-one-'ō'io, East Maui. *Lit.,* ridge (referring to an inexhaustible sweet potato garden with heaped-up earth whose owner had talked to the farming god Maka-li'i).

Kuala-pu'u. Hill, elementary school, reservoir, and Del Monte pineapple cannery village, Kaunakakai qd., Moloka'i. See Wai-kolu. *Lit.,* hill overturned.

Kua-loa. Land division, point, and beach park, Wai-kāne qd., O'ahu, an area anciently considered one of the most sacred places on the island. When a chief was here, all passing canoes lowered their masts in recognition of his sacredness. A place of refuge was here. (Sterling and Summers 5:2–28). See Hui-lua, Koholā-lele, Pali-kū. *Lit.,* long back.

Kualono. Street, 'Ālewa Heights, Honolulu. (TM.) *Lit.,* mountain ridge.

Kua-lua. Ancient surfing area, Wai-mea district, southwest Kaua'i. (Finney and Houston 30.) *Lit.,* twice.

Kuamo'o. Land section, Kai-lua qd., Hawai'i, where Ke-kua-o-ka-lani (the god of the heavens), nephew of Ka-mehameha I, fought to preserve eating taboos, and where he was killed (RC 228). Ridge, north Lā-na'i. Street, Wai-kīkī, Honolulu, named for Mary Kuamo'o Ka-'oana-'eha, sister of Ke-kua-o-ka-lani and wife of John Young, adviser to Ka-mehameha. She was named in honor of the place where her brother was killed . (TM.) *Lit.,* backbone.

Kuamo'o-Kāne. Hill (642 feet high) above Hanauma Bay, O'ahu. *Lit.,* Kāne backbone.

Kuana. Ridge, Ka-malō qd., Moloka'i. Street, Wai-'alae, Honolulu. (TM.) *Lit.,* standing.

Kū-ana-lili. See Ke-kupua.

Kū-'ano-'auwai. Stream, Ka-'alaea, O'ahu. *Lit.,* similar [in] nature [to a] ditch.

Kua-o-ka-lā. Land section, forest reserve, and ancient *heiau* site overlooking Ka-'ena Point, O'ahu. *Lit.,* back of the sun.

Kuapā. Old name for Mauna-lua fishpond east of Honolulu, partly filled in for Hawai'i-kai subdivision; the remnants of the pond are now a marina. It was once believed that the pond was partly constructed by Menehune and was connected by a tunnel to Ka-'ele-pulu pond, Kai-lua, O'ahu. *Lit.,* fishpond wall.

Kua-pehu. Land section, Hōnaunau qd., Hawai'i. *Lit.,* swollen back.

Kū-ā-pōhaku. Drive, Ka-lihi Uka, Honolulu. *Lit.,* turn to stone.

Kū-a-pu'u-iki. Stream or spring, Hālawa qd., Moloka'i. *Lit.,* turned into (*or* like a) little hill.

Kū'au. Land division, Pā'ia qd., Maui. Rock at Mō-kapu peninsula, O'ahu, known today as Pyramid Rock; it is believed to have given birth to other stones. *Lit.,* handle.

Kūʻēʻē Ruins. Old village site with extensive house sites, within Hawaiʻi Volcanoes National Park, Pāhala qd., Hawaiʻi. *Lit.*, confrontation.

Kuʻele. Hill near Wai-ehu Point, northeast Molokaʻi. (Summers 176.)

Kuʻemanu. *Heiau*, now restored, at Kaha-luʻu, Hawaiʻi, where chiefs prayed for good surfing conditions. Nearby is a brackish pool where chiefs rinsed salt off their bodies after surfing.

Kū-heia. Coastal area and bay, north central Ka-hoʻolawe. *Lit.*, stand entangled.

K

Kū-hiō. Bay, Hilo; village, Wai-piʻo qd., Hawaiʻi. Elementary school, theater, hotel, beach park, avenue, housing area, and playground, Honolulu, named for Prince Jonah Kū-hiō Ka-lani-ana-ʻole (1871–1922), delegate to Congress and father of the Hawaiian Homes Commission Act. See Ka-lani-ana-ʻole.

Kūhiwa. Gulch and land section, Nā-hiku qd., Maui. The median annual rainfall is 365 inches. Kūhiwa is the name of a special taboo made by a chief.

*Kuholilea. Land division, Lahaina qd., Maui.

Kuhua. Land division, Lahaina qd., Maui. *Lit.*, to thicken.

*Kui. Point, Ka-malō qd., north Molokaʻi. Place, Ka-lihi Uka, Honolulu; channel, Mauna-lua Bay, Oʻahu.

Kuʻia. Shoal, northern Ka-hoʻolawe. Valley and stream, Wai-mea district, Kauaʻi. Land division, Lahaina qd., Maui. *Lit.*, obstructed.

Kū-i-Helani. Classroom building, Ka-mehameha Schools, Honolulu, built in 1954 and named for one of Ka-mehameha's chiefs. He died in 1827. *Lit.*, standing at Helani (a mythical land).

Kuʻikahi. Street, Wai-kīkī, Honolulu. (TM.) *Lit.*, agreement.

Kuikui. Cape, Ka-hoʻolawe. The name is a variant of *kukui* (candlenut *or* torch).

*Kui-lau. Ridge, Ke-ālia Forest Reserve, Ka-wai-hau district, Kauaʻi.

Kui-lei. Cliffs and lookout, Diamond Head; lane, Mō-ʻiliʻili, Honolulu (TM), *Lit.*, lei stringing.

Kuili. Hill near the beach, not far from Makala-wena, North Kona, Hawaiʻi. *Lit.*, memorized temple prayer.

Kui-lima. Point and resort hotel and golf course between Ka-huku Point and Ka-wela Bay, Oʻahu. *Lit.*, joining hands.

Kū-ʻīlio-loa. *Heiau* at tip of Kāne-ʻīlio Pt., Wai-ʻanae qd., Oʻahu, named for a legendary dog who protected travelers; later the qualities of a bad dog were unfairly attributed to him. In one story (For. Sel. 214) he is defeated by Kama-puaʻa. (HM 93.) *Lit.*, long dog Kū.

*Kuinihu. Cone, ʻĪlio Pt. qd., Molokaʻi.

Kuʻi-paʻakai. Lane, Ka-pā-lama section, Honolulu. *Lit.*, pounding salt.

Kūkae-moku. Old name for ʻĪ-ao Needle, West Maui. *Lit.*, broken excreta.

Kūkae-ʻulaʻula. Land section inland of Wai-ʻōhinu, Kaʻū, Hawaiʻi, formerly called Kū-kaʻe-ʻulaʻulaʻa (stand edge uprooted). A captured warrior who was to be sacrificed was imprisoned here. When the guards slept, an owl bit the cords that tied him to a post and led him toward Hale-o-Lono *heiau* for safety. The guards woke and gave chase. The man hid by crouching against some rocks at a spot called Poʻo-pueo (owl head), with the owl perched on his head. The guards thought the owl was looking for mice and went on. This happened several times, but finally the man reached the safety of the *heiau,* and he became a priest of Lono. *Lit.,* red excreta.

Kūkaʻi-au. Village, ranch, gulch, and land section near Pāpaʻa-loa, Hawaiʻi. *Lit.,* current appearing.

Kūkaʻi-manini. Island, Ka-wela Bay, Oʻahu. *Lit., manini* fish procession.

Kūkaʻi-waʻa. Point, Ka-malō qd., north Molokaʻi. *Lit.,* canoe extension. (The demigod Kana came to Hāʻupu to rescue his mother, Hina, in a canoe called Kau-mai-ʻeliʻeli; For. 4:442–444. He anchored the canoe's bow at Hāʻupu and the stern at Kūkaʻi-waʻa. See Hāʻupu.)

Kūkala-ʻula. Cliff, Kī-lau-ea qd., Hawaiʻi. *Lit.,* red proclamation (probably referring to a chief and his feather cloak).

Kū-ka-lau-ʻula. Cliffs, Kī-lau-ea and Pāhala qds., Hawaiʻi. *Lit.,* the red spear tips stand.

Kū-kani-loko. Walk, Ka-lihi Kai, Honolulu, named for the stones near Wahi-a-wā, Oʻahu, where royalty gave birth (Fornander believed that these birth stones were established in the twelfth century); also the name of an ancient chief. (TM.)

Kū-kanono. Subdivision, Kai-lua, Oʻahu. Street names here begin with *Manu* (bird). *Lit.,* stand strike.

Kū-kiʻi. Land division, Makuʻu qd., Hawaiʻi. Stones from a *heiau* here of the same name, said to have been built by ʻUmi (HM 391), were brought to Honolulu by Ka-lā-kaua in 1877 and used in construction of the foundation of ʻIo-lani Palace. Point and surfing area north of Nā-wiliwili Bay, Kauaʻi. (PH 158.) *Lit.,* standing image.

Kūkila. Street and place, Foster Village subdivision, Hālawa, Wai-pahu qd., Oʻahu. Name suggested by Mary Kawena Pukui in 1956. *Lit.,* majestic, regal.

Kū-kiʻo. Land section, North Kona, Hawaiʻi. See Manini-ʻōwali. Fish-pond, Ka-huku, Oʻahu. *Lit.,* settled dregs.

Kūkūau. Section of Hilo, Hawaiʻi, named for a grapsid crab.

Kukui. Village, Hilo qd.; beach, Kohala qd.; point, Honomū qd.; stream, Wai-piʻo qd.; ancient surfing areas, Nā-poʻopoʻo and Hōnau-nau qds. (Finney and Houston 26), Hawaiʻi. Peak (3,005 feet high) and trail, Wai-mea Canyon, Kauaʻi. Point, north Lā-naʻi. Peak (5,788 feet high), Lahaina qd., and bay, Kī-pahulu qd., Maui. *Heiau,* Ka-malō qd., south Molokaʻi; and elevation, Mauna Loa, Airport qd., Molokaʻi, where the men of Pā-lāʻau to the north were turned into *kauila* trees. In this story ʻUmi-a-Maka, a youth skilled in *mokomoko* (hand-to-hand fighting) who lived above ʻIloli hill at Ka-wai-loa, was challenged by an unknown from Kawahuna. On the advice of his *kahuna,* ʻUmi-a-Maka brought a small black pig to Kukui Hill. Its squealing drove away his opponents' gods and turned the people into *kauila* trees (*Ka Nupepa Kuokoa,* September 14, 1922). Area on

121

Kukui-aniani

the Maka-puʻu side of Pā-honu, Wai-mānalo, Oʻahu (For. Sel. 266). Downtown Honolulu lane and street named in 1856; the first street lamp *(kukui)* was at Fort and Kukui streets (TM). The State tree is the *kukui;* its oily nuts were used for lights. *Lit.,* candlenut lamp, light of any kind.

Kukui-aniani. *Heiau,* Wai-Kāne qd., Oʻahu. *Lit.,* flickering light.

Kukui-haele. Village above Wai-piʻo Valley, Wai-piʻo qd., Hawaiʻi. A healing god, Ka-maka-nui-ʻahaʻilono (the great eye messenger) once lived here. *Lit.,* traveling light (night marchers were seen here).

Kukui-hoʻolua. Islet off Lāʻie Point, Oʻahu. See Lani-loa. *Lit.,* oven-baked candlenut.

Kukui-kea. Land section, Honomū qd., Hawaiʻi. *Lit.,* white candlenut.

Kukui-kiʻikiʻi. Stream not far from Ke-ala-kaha, Hāmākua qd., Hawaiʻi. *Lit.,* tilted candlenut tree.

Kukui-lamalama-heʻe. Gulch and ridge, Hāmākua qd., Hawaiʻi. *Lit.,* torch lighting squid. (This was a derisive name used by Ka-mehameha I for the warriors of his foe, Ke-ō-ua.) An older name was Kau-ka-mōlī (place the straight line), so called because the gods Kāne and Kanaloa, who lived here, drew their canoes up the beach, making a groove; these gods prepared colors with which the fishes of the sea were tinted.

Kukui-nui. Ridge, Ka-malō qd., Molokaʻi. *Lit.,* large candlenut *or* large light.

Kukui-o-hāpuʻu. *Pali,* Kaha-nui, Kaunakakai qd., north Molokaʻi. *Lit.,* torch of fern. (At a *heiau* here of the same name signal fires to Oʻahu were set in time of war.)

Kukui-o-Kahoʻāliʻi. Land section, Kaunakakai qd., south Molokaʻi. *Lit.,* light (or *kukui* tree) of Ka-hoʻāliʻi (the one who was made a chief). Ka-hoʻāliʻi was an important god impersonated in certain ceremonies by a human being; at *makahiki* festivals he ate ceremonially the eye of a human sacrifice or of a fish (HM 49–50). The white *kaʻupu* bird, with bones removed, was a symbol of the god. (RC 180.)

Kukui-o-Kanaloa. Bluff, Kaunakakai qd., north Molokaʻi. *Lit.,* light of Kanaloa.

Kukui-o-Lono. Hill and site of a *heiau* in a private park near Port Allen, Kō-loa district, Kauaʻi. *Lit.,* Lono's light (said to be site of signal fires for seafarers).

Kukui-o-Napehā. Area seaward of 8th and 9th avenues, Ka-imu-kī, Honolulu, that was once a heap of rocks. *Lit.,* Napehā's light (*or* beacon).

Kukui-o-Paʻe. Land section and homesteads, Hōnaunau qd., South Kona, Hawaiʻi. *Lit.,* candlenut trees of Paʻe (a chief who planted them).

Kukui-pahu. Land section, Kohala qd., Hawaiʻi. (For. Sel. 268.) *Lit.,* pierced candlenut.

Kukui-palaoa. Islet (3.6 acres, 50 feet elevation), Ka-malō qd., north Molokaʻi. *Lit.,* whale [bone] lamp.

Kukui-pilau. *Heiau,* Kai-lua, Oʻahu. *Lit.,* stinking *kukui.*

K

Kukui-ʻula. Land section, harbor, and bay, Kō-loa district, Kauaʻi. Land section, gulch, and stream, Kī-pahulu qd., Maui. *Lit.,* red light.

Kukui-waluhia. Land section, Kohala qd., Hawaiʻi. *Lit.,* scraped candlenut.

Kūkūkū. Gulch, Airport qd., south Molokaʻi; a fishpond was located here.

Kukuluāeʻo. Tract formerly fronting Ke-walo Basin, Honolulu, containing marshes, salt pans, and small fishponds. *Lit.,* Hawaiian stilt (bird).

Kula. Land section, Makuʻu qd., Hawaiʻi. Elementary school, sanatorium, land area, forest reserve, and former district, Kilohana qd., Maui. (For a saying, see Appendix 8.1.) *Lit.,* plain.

Kula-ʻalamihi. Fishpond, Hālawa qd., south Molokaʻi. *Lit.,* crab source.

Kū-laha-loa. Gulch, Mapulehu, Hālawa qd., south Molokaʻi; also a "bell stone" here. The stone was named for a *kahuna* from Kaʻū, Hawaiʻi, who challenged Hina, the mother of the island. He was defeated and was turned into two stones, one resting on the other. When the upper stone is struck the two stones ring like a bell. (Cooke 152.) The upper stone slipped in a 1950 earthquake and the stone no longer rings loudly. *Lit.,* Kū known far.

Kulaʻi-ka-honu. Land section, Honomū qd., Hawaiʻi. *Lit.,* push over the turtle.

Kulaʻi-mano. An inland area, Honomū qd., Hawaiʻi; canoes were made here. *Lit.,* push over many (a legendary man pushed his foes over a cliff as they came up).

Kula-kōlea. Drive and place, Ka-lihi Uka, Honolulu. (TM.) *Lit.,* plover field. (An alternate interpretation is that the name is Kula-Kolea [*lit.,* Korean school], named for a Korean language school that was here, near a Korean settlement, until about 1953, when the subdivision was made.)

Kula-manu. Street and place, Black Point, Honolulu, named for Kula-manu Beatrice McWayne, who lived here until her death in 1943. (TM.) *Lit.,* bird plain.

Kulana-kiʻi. Land section and stream, Honomū qd., Hawaiʻi. *Lit.,* image position.

Kū-lani. Cone (5,518 feet high) on the eastern slopes of Mauna Loa, Humuʻula qd., Hawaiʻi; site of a prison camp. *Lit.,* like heaven.

Kū-lani-hākoʻi. Gulch, Puʻu-o-kali qd., Maui, named for a mythical pond in the sky land, Ke-alohi-lani. *Lit.,* agitated heaven that stands.

Kula-o-ka-ʻeʻa. Land section, Honolua qd., West Maui. *Lit.,* plain of dust.

Kula-o-ka-huʻa. Old name of a section of Honolulu between Alapaʻi and Puna-hou streets, inland of King Street. (Kuy. 3:204.) *Lit.,* plain of the boundary.

Kula-o-ka-lālā-loa. Land section, Honolua qd., Maui.

Kū-lepe-a-moa. *Heiau* and ridge, Koko Head qd., Oʻahu. *Lit.,* flapping of chicken.

Kuli-haʻi. Land section, Hāmākua qd., Hawaiʻi. *Lit.,* broken knee.

K

K

Kuli-'ou'ou. Land divisions, valley, forest reserve, section of the city, homesteads, road, and beach park, Honolulu. The first carbon-14 dating (A.D. 1000 ± 180) in Hawai'i was based on carbon taken from a cave here in 1950. *Lit.*, sounding knee (referring to a knee drum [*pūniu*] attached to the knee).

Kū-loa. Point, Kahana qd., O'ahu. *Lit.*, long Kū.

Kūloli. Elevation between Ka-unu-o-Hua and Pēpē-'ōpae, Ka-malō qd., inland central Moloka'i. *Lit.*, having no wife, children, or relatives. See PE, *kūloli*.

Kuloloia. Former beach extending from about the foot of Fort Street to Kaka'ako, Honolulu. (Ii 65, 90.)

Kū-lua. Cones on the northeast rift of Mauna Loa, Hawai'i. Gulch, 'Īlio Pt. qd., Moloka'i. *Lit.*, two standing.

Kulu'ī. Place, 'Āina-Haina, Honolulu; gulch, Koko Head qd., O'ahu, named for certain small trees and shrubs (*Nototrichium* spp).

Kū-mai-pō. Place and stream, Schofield qd., O'ahu. A trail here led to the top of the Wai-'anae ridge and then down to upper Mākaha. (Sterling and Summers 1:13.) *Lit.*, Kū from night.

Kū-Makali'i. Mountain, Wai-'anae range, O'ahu. *Lit.*, rising Pleiades.

Kū-mele-wai. Birthplace of John 'Ī'ī near Hanaloa fishpond, 'Ewa, O'ahu. (Ii 20.) *Lit.*, like water singing.

Kūmimi. Land division and point, Hālawa qd., Moloka'i, named for an anthid crab.

Kūmoho. Ancient surfing area, Kohala qd., Hawai'i (Finney and Houston 26). *Lit.*, to rise (as water).

Kumu. Site of a spring near Kūkūau, Hilo, Hawai'i. Children enjoyed diving and swimming here, but it is now filled in. *Lit.*, source.

Kumu-'eli. Land division and gulch, Ka-malō qd., south Moloka'i. *Lit.*, digging [for the] source.

Kumu-'iliahi. Area, Kilohana or Luala'i-lua Hills qd., Maui. *Lit.*, sandalwood tree.

Kumu-kahi. Easternmost cape, Hawai'i, named for a migratory hero from Kahiki who stopped here and who is represented by a red stone. Two of his wives, also in the form of stones, manipulated the seasons by pushing the sun back and forth between them. One of the wives was named Ha'eha'e. Sun worshipers brought their sick to be healed here. (HM 119.) Another Kumu-kahi, the favorite younger brother of Kama-lālā-walu, lived here or near here (For. Sel. 250). Also the name of a chief who pleased Pele but who ridiculed her; she heaped lava over him, thus forming the cape (Westervelt, 1963:28). Channel between Ni'ihau and Lehua islands. *Lit.*, first beginning.

Kumukumu. Land division, Ka-wai-hau district, Kaua'i. *Lit.*, stubs.

Kumu-mau. Point, 'Ewa qd., O'ahu. *Lit.*, eternal source.

Kūmū-nui-'ai-ake. Stream entering the sea near Pāpa'ikou, north of Hilo, Hawai'i. *Lit.*, great liver-eating *kūmū* fish (a supernatural fish).

Kū-naka. Coastal area, Hālawa qd., Moloka'i. *Lit.*, stand shivering.

Kuna-lele. Valley, Wai-mea district, Kaua'i. *Lit.*, leaping freshwater eel.

124   **Kuna-wai.** Lane, springs, and playground in the Liliha area, Lanakila section, Honolulu, named for a supernatural freshwater eel *(kuna)* who lived in a sacred pool *(wai)* here where wild ducks never swam. A chief, Ka-hānai-a-ke-kua, bathed here. He was reared at Wao-lani *heiau* by the gods Kāne and Kanaloa; he married his younger sister and became the ruling chief of Oʻahu with the Mū, Wā, and Menehune as his servants (HM 300, 365). Some believe that the water has healing qualities. Four *kuleana* of this name in the area were awarded to Hawaiians in the early 1850s. (Indices 723.)

Kunia. Land division, elementary school, road, and town near Scho-field Barracks, Oʻahu. *Lit.,* burned.

Kuolo. Area near Keaʻau, Puna, Hawaiʻi, where the Puna chief, Huaʻā, was defeated, thus giving control of Puna to ʻUmi (For. Sel. 168). *Lit.,* to rub.

Kū-paʻa. Gulch, Wai-luku qd., West Maui. Drive, Pālolo, Honolulu (TM). *Lit.,* steadfast.

Kūpā-ʻia. Ridge and gulch, Makakupaʻia, Ka-malō qd., Molokaʻi. *Lit.,* hewed out.

Kupa-nihi. Old name for Pacific Heights, the name of a supernatural pig who had a taro patch in Pauoa Valley, Honolulu, and who gave birth to a human. *Lit.,* native treated-with-respect.

Kū-paua. Valley, Koko Head qd., Oʻahu. *Lit.,* upright clam.

Kū-peke. Land division, gulch, and fishpond, Hālawa qd., Molokaʻi. *Lit.,* stunted.

Kūpikipikiʻō. Old name for Black Point, Oʻahu. *Lit.,* rough [sea].

Kupopolo. *Heiau* near Wai-mea, Oʻahu, largely in ruins.

Kure. Atoll 1,400 miles northwest of Honolulu, most distant of the Northwestern (Leeward) Hawaiian Islands, an oval atoll with maxi-mum diameter of 6 miles. Within the lagoon are three sand islands no more than 20 feet high and with a total area of about 0.47 square miles. It was discovered by a Russian navigator (for whom it is named), annexed to the Hawaiian Kingdom in 1886, and acquired by the United States in 1898; it is now a part of the City and County of Honolulu. At least four ships have been wrecked on the reef. The name is also spelled Cure. (Bryan 204–207.)

Kuroda. Field, Fort DeRussy, Wai-kīkī, named in honor of Staff Sergeant Robert T. Kuroda who died heroically in France in 1944.

Kurtistown. Village, Hilo qd., Hawaiʻi, named for A.G. Curtis, a pio-neer at ʻOlaʻa in 1902 when the ʻOlaʻa Sugar Company began operations. (Coulter 235–236.)

Kū's Rock Spring. See Ka-huku.

Kuʻuna-a-ke-akua. See Makala-wena.

Kuʻuna-honu. Coastal area, Hālawa qd., Molokaʻi. *Lit.,* turtle releasing.

Kūwili. Street, Iwilei, Honolulu, named for a fishpond once at the site of the old Oʻahu Railway depot. *Lit.,* stand swirling. See Ka-nāueue.

Kuykendall Hall. English department building, Mānoa campus, Uni-versity of Hawaiʻi, Honolulu, completed in 1964, and named for Ralph S. Kuykendall (1885–1963).

LILILILI

La'a. Old name for 'Ōla'a, Hawai'i, a legendary area for collecting bird feathers. (PH 34; UL 41.) Lane, Ka-pā-lama section, Honolulu, named for the John La'a family. (TM.) *Lit.,* dedicated.

La'a-kea. Street and place, Foster Village subdivision, Hālawa, Waipahu qd., O'ahu. Name suggested by Mary Kawena Pukui in 1956. *Lit.,* sacred light, as of sunshine, happiness, or knowledge.

La'a-loa. Land sections, Kai-lua qd., Hawai'i. A *heiau* here was called Lele-iwi (bone altar); the famous priest Hāwa'e, who served under chief Ehu-ka-ipo, lived here. *Lit.,* very sacred.

Lā'au. Ridge, Hanalei district, Kaua'i. See Honopū. Hill, Hāmākua, Hawai'i. Point, southwest tip of Moloka'i. Also called Ka-lae-o-ka-lā'au. (UL 240.) Street, Ala Wai section, Honolulu. *Lit.,* wood.

La'a-uhi-ha'iha'i. Land area, Kō-loa district, Kaua'i. *Lit.,* broken yam vine.

Lā'au-kahi. Peak, Kō-loa district, Kaua'i. *Lit.,* lone tree.

Lā'au-'ōkala. Point near Maka-weli, Kaua'i. *Lit.,* bristly tree.

Ladd. Lane, Nu'u-anu, named for William Ladd, a New Englander who founded Kō-loa Sugar Company on Kaua'i in 1835, and Ladd and Company in Honolulu. (TM.)

lae. 'Cape, point.' Some names are written either with or without *Lae-*, as Lae-o-Kīlauea and Kī-lau-ea, and with or without the article *ka-*, as Lā'au and Ka-lae-o-ka-lā-'au.

Lae. Street, Pauoa, Honolulu. *Lit.,* land point *or* forehead.

Lae-'ahi. Old name for Lē'ahi, O'ahu; the mountain was compared by Pele's younger sister, Hi'iaka, to the brow *(lae)* of the *'ahi* fish. (Ii 33.) See Lē'ahi.

Lae-'apuki. Land division, overlook, and ancient village site, Puna, qd., Hawai'i. *Lit.,* short point.

Lae-hī. Point, northeast Lā-na'i. *Lit.,* casting [for fish] point.

Lae-ho'olehua. Point, Ka-laupapa peninsula, Moloka'i. *Lit.,* strong point.

Lae-hou. Point, Pua-kō qd., Hawai'i. *Lit.,* new point.

Lae-kimo. Point, Honu-'apo qd., Ka'ū, Hawai'i, sometimes called Lae-o-kimo. *Lit., kimo* game point.

La'ela'e. Way, Ka-lihi Uka, Honolulu. (TM.) *Lit.,* bright.

Lae-līpoa. Point, Ka-wai-hau district, Kaua'i. See Līpoa. *Lit., līpoa* seaweeds point.

Lae-loa. Point south of Hōnaunau Bay, Hawai'i. *Lit.,* long point.

Lae-manō. Land section, Pua-kō qd., Hawai'i. *Lit.,* shark point.

Lae-nani. Beach park, Wai-kāne qd., O'ahu. *Lit.,* beautiful point of land.

Lae-noio. Point near Kealakehe, Hawai'i. *Lit.,* tern point.

Lae-o-Hālona. Same as Hālona.

Lae-o-Kahi'u. Same as Ka-hi'u. *Lit.,* point of the fish tail.

Lae-o-ka-huna. Point near Poho-iki, Puna, Hawaiʻi. *Lit.,* point of the secret place.

Lae-o-kai-liʻu. Point, Ka-wai-hau district, Kauaʻi. *Lit.,* point of salty sea.

Lae-o-Kākā. Point, southeast Ka-hoʻolawe. Same as Kākā.

Lae-o-Kama. Coastal area, Honolua qd., Maui. *Lit.,* point of Kama (perhaps Kama-puaʻa, the pig demigod).

Lae-o-ka-milo. Point, Ka Lae qd., Hawaiʻi. *Lit.,* point of the whirling (driftwood was piled here).

Lae-o-ka-ʻōnohi. Point, Hanalei district, Kauaʻi. *Lit.,* point of the eyeball *or* of the rainbow fragment.

Lae-o-ka-pahu. Point, Ka-malō qd., north Molokaʻi. *Lit.,* point of the drum.

Lae-o-ka-puna. Ridge, Ka-malō qd., south Molokaʻi. *Lit.,* point of the spring *or* of the coral.

Lae-o-ka-ule. Point, northeast Ka-hoʻolawe. *Lit.,* point of the penis.

Lae-o-Kealaikahiki. Point, west Ka-hoʻolawe. *Lit.,* point of Ke-ala-i-Kahiki.

Lae-o-Kealohi. Same as Ke-alohi.

Lae-o-kimo. Same as Lae-kimo. See Pā-ʻula.

Lae-o-Kūakaʻiwa. Point, south central Ka-hoʻolawe. Also called Kū-a-ka-ʻiwa.

Lae-o-kuikui. Point, northeast Ka-hoʻolawe. (*Kuikui* is a variant of *kukui,* candlenut *or* light.)

Lae-o-pali-kū. Point, Ka-wai-hau district, Kauaʻi. *Lit.,* point of steep cliff.

Lae-o-Pūhili. Point, Honu-ʻapo qd., Hawaiʻi. *Lit.,* Pūhili's point.

Lae-paʻakai. Points, Hōnaunau, Hawaiʻi, and south Lā-naʻi. *Lit.,* salt point.

Lae-pālolo. Point, north Lā-naʻi. *Lit.,* clay point.

Lae-paoʻo. Land section, Kala-pana qd., Hawaiʻi. *Lit.,* paoʻo fish point.

Lae-wahie. Rocky point, north Lā-naʻi. *Lit.,* firewood point.

Lahaina. District, quadrangle, town, roadstead, West Maui, formerly the gathering place for whalers, and the capital of the Islands from 1820 to 1845. Surfing sites on both sides of the harbor are known as Lahaina Lefts and Lahaina Rights. The associated wind is Ka-ua-ʻula. See Lā-hainā.

Lā-hainā. Old pronunciation of Lahaina. *Lit.,* cruel sun (said to be named for droughts).

Lahaina Luna. Stream, ditch, school, and high school established in 1831 above Lahaina, Maui. (RC 405.) The first Hawaiian newspaper was printed here in 1834. *Lit.,* upper Lahaina.

*Lahi-a-manu. Gulch, Ka-malō qd., south Molokaʻi.

Lā-hiki-ola. Same as Ka-lā-hiki-ola.

Lahilahi. See Lau-kī-nui, Mauna-lahilahi.

Laho-ʻole. Coastal area, Ka-haku-loa qd., Maui. *Lit.,* without scrotum.

Lāʻie. Small land division, Maka-wao; coastal area, Māʻalaea qd.; cave and hill, Hale-a-ka-lā Crater, Maui. Land section, town, elementary school, bay, point, and the site of the Church College of Hawaiʻi, Ka-huku qd., Oʻahu. Lāʻie-ka-wai is the traditional birthplace of the sacred princess Lāʻie-i-ka-wai (Lāʻie in the water).

Lāʻie Maloʻo

The princess was taken to the mythical paradise Pali-uli (green cliff) on Hawaiʻi. (Beckwith, 1919; HM.) See Mālaekahana. Wai-ʻāpuka. *Lit.*, *ʻie* leaf.

Lāʻie Maloʻo. That part of Lāʻie village, Oʻahu, toward Honolulu. *Lit.*, dry Lāʻie.

Lāʻie-puʻu. Hill, Hale-a-ka-lā Crater, East Maui. *Lit.*, *ʻie* leaf hill.

Lāʻie Wai. That part of Lāʻie village, Oʻahu, with the pond and streams. *Lit.*, wet Lāʻie.

Laiki. Place, Kai-lua, Oʻahu, the site of the country home of Arthur H. Rice built in about 1915. Mr. Rice planted ironwood trees as a windbreak and coconut palms as a copra plantation (some ironwoods and coconuts still remain). When the plantation failed he raised cattle here and at Mō-kapu. After his death in the 1950s, his home was demolished and the land subdivided. *Lit.*, Rice.

La-ʻimi. Road and old section of Nuʻu-anu Valley, Honolulu. (Sterling and Summers 6:213.) *Lit.*, day [of] seeking.

Lā-kapu. Road near the airport, Honolulu. (TM.) *Lit.*, taboo day.

Laki. Road, ʻAlewa Heights, Honolulu. (TM.) *Lit.*, lucky.

Laki-mau. Street, Ka-pahulu section, Honolulu, the nickname for Paul K. Strauch, whose father, P.E.R. Strauch, was the realtor who opened the tract. (TM.) *Lit.*, always lucky.

Lako-loa. Street, Honolulu airport. (TM.) *Lit.*, very wealthy.

Lālākea. Stream, gulch, and land section at the Kukui-haele side of Wai-piʻo Valley, Hawaiʻi, named for a kind of shark.

Lālā-koa. Land section, northeast Lā-naʻi. *Lit.*, *koa* tree branch.

Lālā-milo. Land division, Pua-kō qd., Hawaiʻi. *Lit.*, *milo* tree branch.

Lama-kū. Place, Pālolo, Honolulu. (TM.) *Lit.*, standing torch.

Lama-loa. Head and gulch, Hālawa qd., north Molokaʻi. *Lit.*, tall *lama* tree *or* torch.

Lamo. Land section, northeast Lā-naʻi.

Lana. Ancient surfing area, southwest Niʻihau. (Finney and Houston 30.) *Lit.*, floating.

Lā-naʻi. Island in Maui County, also known as Nā-naʻi, 13¼ miles long, 13 miles wide, with an area of 140 square miles and a 1970 population of 2,204; also elementary and high school. Lā-naʻi City (1,624 feet elevation) is the major town. Epithet: *Lā-naʻi o Kaululāʻau* (Lā-naʻi of Kaululāʻau). Perhaps *lit.*, day [of] conquest.

Lānaʻi-hale. Highest peak (3,379 feet) on Lā-naʻi. *Lit.*, house [of] Lā-naʻi.

Lanakila. Elementary school, street, playground, and section 8 of Honolulu (map 6). *Lit.*, victory (named in honor of Ka-mehameha's victory in the battle of Nuʻu-anu).

Lani-ākea. Cave and pool not far from Huli-heʻe Palace, Kai-lua, Hawaiʻi. The Thurston family, who lived near here, called their home Lani-ākea; the name may be cognate with Raʻi-ātea Island in the Society Islands (Appendix 9). Surfing area, Hale-ʻiwa qd., Oʻahu (Finney, 1959a:108), famous for long "right-slide" rides and named for a nearby residence. *Lit.*, wide sky.

Lani-hau. Land divisions, Kai-lua and Ke-āhole qds., Kona, Hawaiʻi. *Lit.*, cool heaven.

Lani-huli. Peak above Nuʻu-anu Pali, Oʻahu, and name of an ancient *mo'o* god of Lā'ie; drive and place, lower Mānoa, Honolulu. (For a song, see Elbert and Mahoe 86.) *Lit.,* turning royal chief.

Lani-kai. Section of Kai-lua, surfing beach, and elementary school, Mō-kapu qd., O'ahu. Development here began in 1924; the name was changed from Ka-'ōhao to Lani-kai, in the belief that it meant 'heavenly sea' (*Honolulu Advertiser,* August 15, 1948). This is English word order; in Hawaiian the qualifier commonly follows the noun, hence Lani-kai means 'sea heaven, marine heaven'.

Lani-kāula. Street, Mānoa, Honolulu. See Ka-lani-kāula.

*Lanikepu. Land division and gulch, Wai-pi'o qd., Hawai'i.

*Lani-lili. Hill (2,563 feet high), Wai-luku qd., West Maui.

Lani-loa. Road, Pacific Heights, Honolulu; land leading to Lā'ie Point, O'ahu. The five islets off the point were created when the demi-gods Kana and Nīheu chopped up the body of a *mo'o* and threw the pieces into the sea (see Kīhewa-moku, Kukui-ho'olua, Moku-'auia, Pule-moku). The hole where Kana severed the *mo'o* head has since then filled in. (PH 97; Sterling and Summers 4:83.) *Lit.,* tall majesty.

Lani-maumau. Stream, Wai-pi'o qd., Hawai'i. *Lit.,* increasing heaven.

Lani-pili. Place, Wilhelmina Rise, Honolulu. Probably *lit.,* clinging heaven. (Most streets on Wilhelmina Rise were named by non-Hawaiians. In Hawaiian, *lanipili* means 'cloudburst, heavy rain.')

Lanipō. Peak (2,621 feet high) back of Wilhelmina Rise and above Mauna-wili, O'ahu. *Lit.,* dense (as plant growth).

Lani-poko. Place, Wilhelmina Rise, Honolulu. *Lit.,* short heaven.

Lani-pū'ao. Rock, Kō-loa district, Kaua'i. *Lit.,* womb sky.

Lani-puni. Stream, Ka-malō qd., Moloka'i. *Lit.,* surrounding heaven.

Lani-wai. Land section, Ko'olau Poko, O'ahu. *Lit.,* water supremacy. (For a song, see Elbert and Mahoe 60–61.)

Lānui. Place, 'Ālewa Heights, Honolulu. (TM.) *Lit.,* holiday.

Lā-ola. Place, Nu'u-anu, Honolulu. (TM.) *Lit.,* day of life.

Lapa-iki. Gulch, northern Lā-na'i. *Lit.,* small ridge.

Lapa-kahi. Land section, Kohala qd., Hawai'i, site of 1968 archaeological diggings, an *ahupua'a*. (Newman.) *Lit.,* single ridge.

Lapa-kohana. Cinder cone (2,268 feet high), Ka-malō qd., south Moloka'i. *Lit.,* bare ridge.

Lapa-'ula'ula. Ridge, Hālawa qd., Moloka'i. *Lit.,* red ridge.

La Pérouse. Bay in Mākena qd. on the southwestern tip of Maui, also known as Ke-one-'ō'io. La Pérouse sailed along the coast on May 29, 1786, and was met by 150 canoes loaded with trading goods. The next morning La Pérouse and a party, well-armed, went ashore and exchanged gifts with the people. (Gassner.) Geologically, the bay resulted from the extension of the coast by the only historic Hale-a-ka-lā eruption, in about 1790 (Macdonald and Abbott 50). West of the bay are ruins of an ancient Hawaiian village. A rocky trail leads eastward to other ruins and an ancient Hawaiian well. (Stearns and Macdonald, 1942:Plate 2.) See French Frigate Shoals, Ka-lepolepo.

La Pérouse Pinnacle. See French Frigate Shoals.

La Pietra. Home of the Walter F. Dillinghams, built in 1921 on the slope of Diamond Head and modeled after the Italian villa of the same name in which the Dillinghams were married. The building is now the home of Hawai'i School for Girls.

Lau-iki. Street, Ala Wai section, Honolulu. (TM.) *Lit.,* small leaf.

Lau-kī-nui. Beach, Mākaha, O'ahu, now called Lahilahi Beach. *Lit.,* large ti leaf.

Lau-koa. Place, Pacific Heights, Honolulu. (TM.) *Lit., koa* leaf.

Laulā. Way, Ke-walo section, Honolulu. *Lit.,* wide.

Lau-lani. Street, Ka-lihi Uka, Honolulu. (TM.) *Lit.,* heavenly leaf.

Laulau-nui. Islet, Pearl Harbor, O'ahu. *Lit.,* large leaf package.

Laulau-poe. Gulch, Koko Head qd., O'ahu. *Lit.,* round leaf package.

Lau-mai'a. Land section (6,754 feet elevation), inland from Hilo, Hawai'i; a stone trail said to be made by 'Umi-a-Līloa was also so named. *Lit.,* banana leaf.

Lau-maile. Street, Ka-lihi Uka, Honolulu. (TM.) *Lit., maile* leaf.

Lau-maka. Street, Ka-lihi Kai, Honolulu. (TM.) *Lit.,* green leaf.

Lau-niu. Street, Wai-kīkī, Honolulu. (TM.) *Lit.,* coconut leaf.

Lau-niu-poko. Land section, hill (808 feet high), point, village, ditch, stream, State wayside park, Lahaina qd., Maui. *Lit.,* short coconut leaf.

Lau-pāhoehoe. Land sections, Hāmākua, Honomū, Mauna Kea, and Wai-pi'o qds.; stream, Hāmākua and Mauna Kea qds.; village, Honomū qd.; homesteads, Mauna Kea qd.; beach park, elementary and high school, point, and ancient surfing area (Finney and Houston 26), Honomū qd., Hawai'i, where 'Umi was bruised while surfing incognito before becoming a chief (For. Sel. 124). A man who came from Kahiki and thence to the canoe landing at Lau-pāhoehoe built a *heiau* here called Ule-ki'i (penis fetching). The man turned into a *pāo'o* fish, and his sister into an *'a'awa* fish. Fishermen who wanted to catch them were surprised to see them turn into human beings. *Lit.,* smooth lava flat.

Lau-'ula. Street, Wai-kīkī, Honolulu. (TM.) *Lit.,* red leaf.

Lau-'ulu. Trail, Hale-a-ka-lā Crater, Maui. *Lit.,* breadfruit leaf.

Lava Trees. State park with lava tree casts, Kala-pana and Puna qds., Hawai'i.

Lāwa'i. Village, land division, gulch, and stream, Kō-loa district, Kaua'i.

Lāwa'i Kai. Land area and bay, seaward of Lāwa'i, Kaua'i. *Lit.,* seaward Lāwa'i.

Laysan. Island of the Northwestern (Leeward) Hawaiian Islands (maximum elevation 40 feet, approximate area 1.56 square miles). In the center is a brackish lagoon. The island was discovered by Captain Stanikowitch on March 12, 1828; he named it Moller Island after his ship. Guano was collected here commercially from 1892 to 1904. A bird population close to 10 million was reported in 1902. It was annexed to Hawai'i in 1898 and is now a part of the City and County of Honolulu. (Bryan, 1942:183–189.)

Lē'ahi. Point, south Ni'ihau. Hospital and avenue, Honolulu; the highest peak in Diamond Head; a variant name for Lae-'ahi.

Lee. Place, Nu'u-anu, Honolulu, named for William L. Lee, Chief Justice of the Supreme Court of the Kingdom of Hawai'i under Ka-mehameha III and IV. He drew up a legal code, promulgated school laws, and served in the division of lands known as the Great Māhele. (TM.)

Leftovers. Surfing area west of Wai-mea, O'ahu.

Lehia. Street, Foster Village subdivision, Hālawa, Wai-pahu qd., O'ahu. Name suggested by Mary Kawena Pukui in 1958. *Lit.,* skilled.

Lehua. Island (291 acres, maximum elevation 710 feet) west of Ni'ihau, the westernmost island of the main Hawaiian chain (not including the Northwestern Hawaiian Islands); landing, northeast Ni'ihau. For a saying, see PE, *kā'ili. Lit., lehua* flower. (Pele's younger sister, Hi'iaka, accompanying Pele on her first trip to Hawai'i, left a *lehua* lei at this island when her brother, Kāne-'āpua, decided to stay there.) Elementary school, Pearl City, O'ahu. (PH 106; UL 258.)

Lehu-'ula. Elevation, Ka-malō qd., Moloka'i. *Lit.,* red ashes.

Lei-aloha. Avenue, Mānoa, Honolulu. *Lit.,* lei [of] love.

Leighton. Street, 'Āina-Haina, Honolulu, named for Robert Leighton Hind, eldest son of Robert Hind. See 'Āina-Haina. (TM.)

Lei-lani. Street, Pu'u-nui, Honolulu. *Lit.,* heavenly lei *or* royal child.

Lei-lehua. Plains, village, high school, and golf course, Wahi-a-wā, area famous for training in *lua* fighting; site of present Schofield Barracks; lane, downtown Honolulu (TM). *Lit., lehua* lei.

Lei-loke. Drive, Makiki, Honolulu. (TM.) *Lit.,* rose lei.

Lei-Lono. Land area, Moana-lua, Honolulu, one of the leaping places of ghosts to the nether world. *Lit.,* Lono's lei.

Leina-a-ka-'uhane. Land section near Ka-'ena Point, O'ahu, from which ghosts were thought to leap to the nether world. Similar places are reported on every island (HM 156). *Lit.,* leaping place of ghosts.

Leina-o-Papio. Point, Ka-malō qd., north Moloka'i. See Huelo. *Lit.,* Papio's leap.

Lei-no-Haunui. *Pali,* south Lā-na'i. *Lit.,* lei for Haunui (a person).

Lēkia. See Pōhaku-Hanalei.

Lele. Land division near Hā'upu, Kaua'i, probably named for an event similar to that which resulted in the O'ahu name Kohe-lepelepe. Old name for the Lahaina district, Maui, so called because of the short stay of chiefs there *(Pacific Commercial Advertiser,* 1857). See Malu-'ulu-o-Lele. *Lit.,* altar *or* flight.

Lele-a-Hina. *Heiau,* He'eia, O'ahu. *Lit.,* altar [made] for Hina.

Lelehune. Place, Mānoa, Honolulu. *Lit.,* fine rain, spray.

Lele-iwi. Cape, beach park, and point, Hilo qd., Hawai'i. A fish *heiau (heiau ho'oulu i'a),* named Pū-hala (pandanus tree) once was near here. (For. Sel. 22, 24, 278; PH 189; UL 60.) *Heiau* at La'a-loa, Kona, Hawai'i. Area, Hanalei district, Kaua'i. *Pali* and overlook, Hale-a-ka-lā Crater, Maui. *Lit.,* bone altar (poetically, a symbol of disaster or anger).

Lele-kawa. Sea arch, Puna, Hawai'i. (Hawaii Natural History Association Guide 9.) *Lit.,* jump from a high place into the water.

Lele-koa'e. Coastal area, Ka-malō qd., north Moloka'i. *Lit.,* flight of tropicbirds. (The name is a poetic phrase descriptive of cliffs where *koa'e* birds fly.)

Lele-mākō. Gulch, Hālawa qd., north Moloka'i. *Lit.,* rough leaping.

Lele-paua

Lele-paua. Inland fishpond at Moana-lua, O'ahu, said to have been built by chief Ka-'ihi-kapu-a-Manuia.

Lemon. Road, Wai-kīkī, Honolulu, named for James Silas Lemon, a Frenchman who came to Hawai'i in 1849; he owned the Commercial Hotel and opened the Ka-imu-kī tract. He died in 1882. (TM.)

Lenalena. Land section and landing, Ka-laupapa peninsula, Moloka'i. *Lit.*, yellow.

Lēpau. Point, Ka-malō qd., north Moloka'i. Perhaps short for Lele-pau (all flying).

Lepelepe. Land section, Ka-malō qd., south Moloka'i. *Lit.*, fringed.

Lewa-lani. Drive, Tantalus, Honolulu. (TM.) *Lit.*, heaven floating.

Lewers. Street, Wai-kīkī, Honolulu, named for Christopher H. Lewers, a merchant who arrived in Hawai'i in 1850 and founded the firm of Lewers and Dickson, which later became Lewers and Cooke. He died in 1870. (TM.) According to another account, the street was named for Mr. and Mrs. Robert Lewers who had a residence and hotel at the site of the present Hale-kū-lani Hotel. See Hale-kū-lani.

Libert. Street, St. Louis Heights, Honolulu, named for the Most Reverend Libert Boeynaems (1857–1926), bishop of Zuegma and vicar apostolic of the Hawaiian Catholic mission 1903–1926. (TM.) He was born in Belgium.

Libby. Street, Ka-lihi Kai, Honolulu, running to the former Libby, McNeill, and Libby pineapple cannery. (TM.)

Lighthouse. Surfing area, Diamond Head, Honolulu, named for the Diamond Head Lighthouse. (Finney, 1959a:108.)

Liha. Hill (3,671 feet high), Lahaina qd., Maui. Probably *lit.*, to shudder.

Līhau. Mountain (4,197 feet), Lahaina qd., Maui. *Lit.*, gentle cool rain (considered lucky for fishermen; UL 241).

Lihi-kai. Elementary school, Ka-hului; park, Wai-ka-pū, Maui. *Lit.*, sea edge.

Liholiho. Dormitory, Ka-mehameha Schools, built in 1940; school, Ka-imu-kī; and street, Makiki, Honolulu, named for Ka-mehameha II, who was also called Ka-lani-nui-kua-liholiho-i-ke-kapu (the great chief [with the] burning-back taboo), referring to the taboo against approaching him from the back. *Lit.*, glowing (see PE, *liholiho*).

Līhu'e. City and district, Kaua'i. Former land division near Schofield Barracks, O'ahu (UL 242). *Lit.*, cold chill.

Lī-hu'i. Cemetery, Mā'alaea qd., Maui. *Lit.*, aching chill.

*Liilioholo. Coastal area, Pu'u-o-kali qd., Maui.

Likeke Hall. See Ka-wai-a-Ha'o, Koko-kahi.

Likelike. Highway and elementary school, Honolulu, named for Princess Miriam Likelike (1851–1887), the younger sister of Ka-lā-kaua and Lili'u-o-ka-lani.

Likini. Street and place, Moana-lua, Honolulu. (TM.) *Lit.*, rigging.

Liliha. Street along the western border of section 11 of Honolulu (map 6), named for the wife of Governor Boki of O'ahu; after Boki's disappearance in 1829 she became governess of O'ahu and in 1831 tried unsuccessfully to organize a revolt against Ka-mehameha III. *Lit.*, rich, oily.

Līlīnoe. Peak (12,956 feet), Mauna Kea qd., Hawai'i, also called Pu'u-Līlīnoe, named for a goddess of mists (Līlīnoe), sister of the more famous Poli-ahu, goddess of snow. Street, Wilhelmina Rise, Honolulu. *Lit.,* mists.

Lili'u-o-ka-lani. Park, Hilo waterfront, Hawai'i. State government building, elementary school, gardens, and avenue, Honolulu, named for Queen Lili'u-o-ka-lani (1838–1917), last queen of Hawai'i. *Lit.,* smarting of the high-born one (at the time of Lili'u's birth, her foster mother's aunt, Kīna'u, was suffering from eye pain; hence the name). See 'Io-lani, Paoa-ka-lani, Ulu-hai-malama, Washington Place.

Līloa Rise. Street, Mānoa, named for the father of 'Umi-a-Līloa of Hawai'i. (TM.)

Lima-huli. Falls, stream, and valley near Ka-lalau, Kaua'i. *Lit.,* turned hand.

Lima-loa. Gulch, Nānā-kuli, O'ahu. Lima-loa is the name of a luckless lover in the Kama-pua'a legend (For. Sel. 226, 230). *Lit.,* long arm.

Limu-koko. Point, Hōnaunau qd., Hawai'i, named for a kind of seaweed better known as *limu-kohu.*

Lina-puni. Street and elementary school, Ka-lihi Waena, Honolulu.

Lincoln. Elementary school, 'Auwai-o-limu Street, Honolulu; building housing East-West Center institutes, University of Hawai'i, Honolulu, completed in 1962 and named for Abraham Lincoln.

Līpe'epe'e. Street, Wai-kīkī, Honolulu, named for a seaweed. (TM.)

Lipioma. Way, Mānoa, Honolulu. *Lit.,* small adze.

Līpoa. Point, Honolua qd., Maui, named for certain brown seaweeds. See Lae-līpoa.

Lisianski. Island in the Northwestern (Leeward) Hawaiian Islands chain (maximum elevation 20 feet, approximate area 0.7 square miles). The island was discovered by Captain Urey Lisiansky when his ship, the *Neva,* went aground here on October 15, 1805. The islet was annexed to Hawai'i in 1857 and is now a part of the City and County of Honolulu. (Bryan, 1942:190–194.)

Līwai. Street, 'Āina-Haina, Honolulu, named for a Kona family.

Lo'alo'a. *Heiau* at Kau-pō, Maui, attributed to Ke-kau-like and re-dedicated by Liholiho when he was still a child. (RC 66, 188.) *Lit.,* pitted.

Lohe-nā. Area in Ka'ū, Hawai'i; shrimps found nowhere else in the world were discovered here by A.H. Banner and named Lohe-nā shrimps. *Lit.,* hear wails.

Lo'i. Street, upper Mānoa, Honolulu. *Lit.,* patch (as of taro or rice).

Lo'i-loa. Spring, Wai-lau trail, Ka-malō qd., north Moloka'i, discharging approximately 750,000 gallons of water daily. (Stearns and Macdonald, 1947.) *Lit.,* long taro patch.

Lo'i-pūnāwai. Spring east of Kaunakakai, Moloka'i. *Lit.,* spring pond.

Lokelani. Street, Ka-lihi Uka, Honolulu. *Lit.,* red rose.

Loko-a-Mano. Name of a filled-in pond at the site of the Pearl Harbor Navy yard, O'ahu. *Lit.,* Mano's pond.

Loko-ea. Old fishponds near Wai-a-lua and Wai-pahu, O'ahu. *Lit.,* rising pond.

Loko-'eo. Fishpond, Pearl Harbor, O'ahu.

Loko-pa'akai. Lake in Ālia-manu area, O'ahu. *Lit.,* salt lake.

Loko-wai-aho. A fishpond near Pearl Harbor, O'ahu. *Lit.,* fishline water pond.

Loko-Waka. Pond at Ke-au-kaha, Hilo, Hawai'i. *Lit.,* Waka's pond (Waka, a *mo'o,* dived into the pool to escape Pele who was jealous of Waka's interest in a man).

Long. Lane, Ka-pā-lama section, Honolulu, named for Captain Elias Long, a trader who settled in Pā-lama. (TM.)

Lono. Place, Mānoa, Honolulu, named for the god Lono.

Loomis. Street, Mānoa, Honolulu, named for Edward Backus Loomis, assistant City and County engineer and assistant Territorial surveyor with the Bishop Estate beginning in 1912. (TM.)

Lōpā. Gulch and summer south-swell and trade-wind surfing area, east Lā-na'i. Also called 'Āwehi. *Lit.,* tenant farmer.

Lopeka. Place, Dowsett Highlands, Honolulu. (TM.) *Lit.,* Roberta.

Lopez. Lane, Ka-pā-lama section, Honolulu, named for Antone J. Lopez, a Portuguese whaler who settled in Hawai'i in about 1860 and died at Pā-lama in 1908. He owned a ranch at Lei-lehua and a dairy at Pā-lama. (TM.)

L'Orange. Playground and baseball field, Wai-pahu, O'ahu, dedicated in 1972 and named for Hans P.F. L'Orange, manager of O'ahu Sugar Company 1937–1957.

Loulu. Street, Mānoa, Honolulu, named for the native fan palm.

Lowell. Place, Ka-pā-lama section, Honolulu, named for the Reverend Lowell Smith. (TM.) See Smith.

Lower Pā'ia. Town, Pā'ia qd., Maui.

Lowrie. Irrigation canal, Pā'ia qd., Maui, named for William J. Lowrie, manager of the Hawaiian Commercial and Sugar Company plantation. The canal was started in 1899 and completed in 1900.

Lowrey. Avenue, Mānoa, Honolulu, named for F. Lowrey, a former president of Lewers and Cooke. He was elected to the Territorial House of Representatives in 1920. (TM.)

lua. 'Pit, crater, hole'.

Lua-'alaea. Stream and land section, Mānoa, Honolulu. *Lit.,* pit [of] red earth.

Lua-ali'i. See Mākao.

Lua-'ehu. Area at Lahaina, Maui, where an Episcopal school, known as Lua-'ehu School, was established in 1862. The school was moved to Honolulu in 1871 and renamed 'Io-lani. *Lit.,* red-head pit (a red-haired *mo'o* lived here).

Luahine-wai. Seashore area near Kīholo, Kona, Hawai'i. It is said that chiefs bathed here in a cool, deep pool and that opening into the pool was a secret cave where bones of ancient chiefs are hidden. *Lit.,* old lady's water (a supernatural *mo'o* lived here).

Lua-hohonu. Pit crater near the caldera of Moku-'āweoweo on the summit of Mauna Loa, Hawai'i. *Lit.,* deep pit.

Lua-hou. Pit crater near the caldera of Moku-'āweoweo, Mauna Loa, Hawai'i. *Lit.,* new pit. (The name is misleading because this is shown on Wilkes' 1840 map; whereas Lua-hohonu was not shown and hence is the newer one; Macdonald and Abbott 54.)

Luakaha. Street and land section, upper Nu'u-anu, Honolulu, and the site of and name of the country home of Ka-mehameha III. *Lit.,* place for relaxation.

Lua-ke-ālia Lalo. Land section, Ka-ho'olawe. *Lit.,* lower pit [of] the salt encrustation.

Lua-ke-ālia Luna. Land section, Ka-ho'olawe. *Lit.,* upper pit [of] the salt encrustation.

L

Lua-ko'i. Hill (3,000 feet high) and ridge, Lahaina qd., Maui. See Ka-lua-ko'i. *Lit.,* adze pit.

Luala'i-lua. Quadrangle, hills, and land division, east Maui. *Lit.,* two-fold tranquility.

Lualualei. Land section, forest reserve, homesteads, reservoir, and beach park, Wai-'anae qd., west O'ahu. (Sterling and Summers 2:19.)

Lua-Mākālei. Lava tube shelter near South Point, Hawai'i, studied by Bishop Museum archaeologists 1967–1968, who believed it was the site of a large settlement. See Mākālei, Wai-'Ahukini. *Lit.,* pit [of] Mākālei.

Lua-makika. The highest point (1,477 feet) on Ka-ho'olawe, the eroded remnant of the crater of a shield volcano. (Macdonald and Abbott 337.) *Lit.,* mosquito pit.

Lua-manu. Pit crater, Kī-lau-ea qd., Hawai'i. *Lit.,* bird pit.

Lua-mo'o. Land section, He'eia, O'ahu. *Lit.,* mo'o pit.

Lua-nā-moku-'iliahi. Trench far inland of Ka-milo-loa, Moloka'i, believed to have been dug on the orders of chiefs and filled with sandalwood logs which were then sold to fill ships having the same dimensions as the trench. Also called Sandalwood Boat. (LeBarron; Summers 90.) *Lit.,* pit [of] the sandalwood ship.

Lua-o-Milu. A deep legendary pit said to be on the summit of Hualālai, Hawai'i. *Lit.,* pit of the underworld.

Lua-pala-lau-hala. Pit crater near Ka-huku Ranch, Ka'ū, Hawai'i. *Lit.,* pit [of] yellowed pandanus leaves.

Lua-pō'ai. Pit crater along the crest of the Ka-huku fault scarp near Ka-huku Ranch, Ka'ū, Hawai'i. (Macdonald and Abbott 308.) *Lit.,* circular pit.

Lua-pū'ali. Pit crater along the crest of the Ka-huku fault scarp near Ka-huku Ranch, Ka'ū, Hawai'i. (Macdonald and Abbott 308.) *Lit.,* irregularly shaped pit.

Lua-wai. Land section, Kai-lua qd., Hawai'i. Street and place, Ka-imu-kī, Honolulu. *Lit.,* water hole.

Luhi. Beach, north Kaua'i. *Lit.,* tedious, tired. (The saying, *Ho'i i ke one o Luhi,* go back to Tired Beach, refers to one returning to an unpleasant task; Appendix 8.1.)

Luina-koa. Street, Wai-'alae, Honolulu. *Lit.,* marine (member of the U.S. Marine Corps).

Lukela. Lane, Ka-lihi Waena, Honolulu, named for Joe Lukela, a fisherman. (TM.) *Lit.,* Luther.

Luke-Pane. Avenue, Ala Wai section, Honolulu. Frank L. James de-

veloped the area in 1926 and named this street for his wife—Luke-
Pane is the Hawaiianized version (invented by him) of his wife's
name, Frances Lucy.

Luluku. Land section and stream, Kāne-'ohe area, O'ahu. *Lit.*, destruction.

*Lulumahu. Stream, Pauoa, Honolulu.

Lumaha'i. Land division, canyon, stream, and beach, Hanalei district,
Kaua'i. Breadfruit trees here are said to have been planted by a
Menehune named Weli (Rice 38).

Luna-lilo. Street laid out in 1874 and named for King Luna-lilo, who
had died that year (Clark 12); cross-town freeway; home for aged
Hawaiians, established by the will of Luna-lilo; Ka-mehameha
Schools dormitory built in 1940; and elementary school, all in
Honolulu. *Lit.*, very high (of royalty).

Luna-lilo Home Road. Street leading to the Luna-lilo Home (see
Luna-lilo), Hawai'i-kai, Honolulu.

Lunaville. Village, Lahaina qd., Maui. *Lit.*, foreman town.

Lū-pehu. Land division, Hālawa qd., Moloka'i. *Lit.*, scatter swelling.

Lurline. Drive, Wilhelmina Rise, Honolulu, named for a Matson passenger liner that had been named for Captain William Matson's
daughter, Lurline Roth. (TM.)

Lusitana. Street, Punchbowl, Honolulu, named for a Portuguese Wel-
fare Society whose members were largely immigrants from the
Azores who arrived in 1883. (TM.) Lusitania is the ancient name
of West Hispania, and now a poetic name for Portugal.

Lydgate. State park, section of Wai-lua River Park, Kaua'i, named for
the Reverend J.M. Lydgate (1854–1922), founder and first pastor
of the Līhu'e English Union Church, and, in 1896, pastor of the
Kō-loa church.

Lyon Arboretum. The arboretum (123 acres, from 300 to 1,800 feet
elevation) was established in 1907 at the head of Mānoa Valley
on the land known as Hau-kulu. It was eventually named for Harold
L. Lyon (1879–1957), director of the arboretum 1919–1957. In 1953
formal presentation was made to the University of Hawai'i. Some
6,000 kinds of plants grow there.

L

MmMmM

Mā. Way, Wahi-a-wā, Oʻahu.

Maʻakua. Gulch inland of Hau-ʻula, Puʻu-kapu qd., Oʻahu, where a *hilu* fish dammed the water of Kai-papaʻu Stream and caused a flood that washed the people of Hau-ʻula out to sea.

Māʻalaea. Quadrangle, bay, village, and small boat harbor, Maui isthmus. Southeast of the boat harbor is a fringing reef, south-swell summer surfing area. Adjacent to the jetty is a surfing site known as Māʻalaea Rights. Road, ʻĀlewa, Honolulu. Perhaps a contraction of Maka-ʻalaea (ocherous earth beginning). (Ii 10.)

Ma-ʻā-lehu. Land section, Kaunakakai qd., north Molokaʻi. (Perhaps the name is garbled; the last part means ʻashed burnedʻ.)

Māʻalo. Land section and gulch near Kau-pō, Maui; a *hau* tree grove here was famed for illicit love affairs. *Lit.,* pass by.

Machado. Street, Ka-lihi Uka, Honolulu, named for Manuel Machado, an early Portuguese settler. (TM.)

MacKenzie. State park, Puna district, Hawaiʻi, established in 1934, and named for Albert J. MacKenzie, forest ranger.

MacNeil Hall. Observatory and Science Center, Puna-hou School campus, Honolulu, built in 1956 and named for Wilbur MacNeil who taught science at Puna-hou for more than thirty years.

Māeaea. Beach and landing near Wai-a-lua, Oʻahu. (Ii 98.) *Lit.,* stench.

Māʻeliʻeli. Small land area, Kaʻū, Hawaiʻi. Cliff, Kāne-ʻohe qd., Oʻahu. *Lit.,* digging (the gods Kāne and Kanaloa raced up the cliff, digging in their fingers and toes as they climbed).

Maʻemaʻe. Elementary school and hill, Nuʻu-anu, Honolulu. *Lit.,* clean (Elbert and Mahoe 33; UL 108.)

Magazine. Street, Thomas Square section, Honolulu. In the days of the monarchy a path here led up Punchbowl to a magazine where gunpowder was stored for firing salutes from the Punchbowl guns. (TM.)

Magellan. Avenue, Thomas Square section, Honolulu, named for the Portuguese explorer.

Magic Island. Same as ʻĀina-moana; also a surfing site here.

Mahaiʻula. Coastal area, bay, village, and ancient surfing area (Finney and Houston 26), Ke-āhole qd., Hawaiʻi. A stone fish goddess about a fathom from the shore was named Pōhaku-o-Lama; she was brought gifts by fishermen except during May, June, and July. During these months the sea thereabout turned yellowish and the people thought the deity was menstruating. (For. Sel. 286.) Land section, Pua-kō qd., Hawaiʻi.

Maha-lani. Cemetery, Wai-ehu village, Maui. *Lit.,* heavenly rest.

*****Mahana.** Hill (1,800 feet high), Honolua qd., Maui. Locality, Air- **137**

port qd., Moloka'i. The Moloka'i Ranch, which in 1908 had 17,000 sheep, had a shearing shed here. The ranch stopped raising sheep in the 1920s.

Mahana-loa. Valley, Wai-mea district, Kaua'i. *Lit.,* very warm.

Mā-hā'ule-pū. Land section and road, Kō-loa district, Kaua'i. *Lit.,* and falling together.

M

Mahelona. Memorial hospital at Ke-ālia, Kaua'i, named in 1915 for Samuel Mahelona (1884-1912), son of Albert S. Wilcox. *Lit.,* Mahlon (Biblical).

Mahi. Place, lower Mānoa, Honolulu, named for a Hawaiian who owned much of the land. (TM.) *Lit.,* strong.

Mahi'ai. Street and place, Ala Wai section, Honolulu, named for the Chiefess Ke-ali'i-mahi'ai, daughter of Nā-haku-'elua Pua of Mō-'ili'ili. (TM.) See Nā-haku. *Lit.,* farmer.

Māhie. Point east of Kahana Bay, O'ahu. Street and place, Foster Village subdivision, Hālawa, Wai-pahu qd., O'ahu. Name suggested by Mary Kawena Pukui in 1958. *Lit.,* delightful, charming, pleasant.

Mahi-kea. Islet (one acre in area, 40 feet elevation), Hilo qd., Hawai'i.

Mahiki. Land division, Wai-mea, Hawai'i, named for a horde of *mo'o* killed by Hi'iaka. (PH chapter 12.) *Lit.,* leap.

Mahina-akaaka. Gulch, Kohala qd., and former *heiau* at Ke-ahi-a Laka, Puna, Hawai'i. *Lit.,* clear moon.

Māhinahina. Land divisions, plantation, and point, Honolua qd., Maui. A *heiau* of this name, now destroyed, was near the shore at Kaunakakai, Moloka'i. *Lit.,* silvery haze (as of moonlight).

Mahina-nui. Islet (0.6 acres, 40 feet elevation), Ka-haku-loa qd., Maui. *Lit.,* large moon *or* large plantation.

Mahina-uli. Gulch, Maka-weli, Kaua'i. *Lit.,* dark moon.

Mahi-nui. Mountain, fishpond, and stream, Mō-kapu qd., O'ahu, named for a legendary hero who was defeated by Olo-mana, and whose body was cast from Mount Olo-mana to the present location of the mountain. *Lit.,* great champion.

Mahohuli. Fishpond, Wai-ākea park, Hilo, Hawai'i.

Mahuka. Bay, Pāhala qd., Ka'ū, Hawai'i. *Lit.,* flee.

Māhu-kona. Land section, village, harbor, and beach park, Kohala qd., Hawai'i. Street, Ala Moana section, Honolulu. *Lit.,* leeward steam.

Mahulili. Land section, Kaunakakai qd., north Moloka'i.

Mai'a-loa. Pit at Ho'okēkē in upper Kohana-iki, Kona, Hawai'i. *Lit.,* long banana.

Maigret. Street, St. Louis Heights, Honolulu, named for the Catholic bishop of Arathia, Louis Maigret, a church pioneer. (TM.) See St. Louis.

Mā'ihi. Land division, Kai-lua qd., Hawai'i, named for Ma'ihi-'ala-kapu-a-Lono (fragrant sacred Mā'ihi, [child] of Lono), a wind goddess.

Mai-hiwa. Ancient surfing area, Wai-kīkī, O'ahu (Finney and Houston 28).

Maile. Land section, Schofield qd., O'ahu, probably named for the *maile* vine.

Maile Flat. Trail and forested area of heavy undergrowth of *maile,* northwest Kaua'i.

Maile-hahai. High point on the ridge between Ka-mana Nui and Ka-mana Iki, Moana-lua Valley, O'ahu, site of the former Damon mountain home "Top Gallant."

Maile-kini. Ancient *heiau* near Ka-wai-hae, Hawai'i, near Pu'u-koholā, soon to be restored. (Ii 17.) *Lit.,* many *maile* vines.

Maile-li'i. Land section, Ka-malō qd., south Moloka'i. *Lit.,* small *maile.*

Maile-pai. Land division and stream, Honolua qd., Maui.

Mā'ili. Town, beach park, surfing area, playground, point, stream, and elementary school, Wai-'anae qd.; hill (1,510 feet high), Schofield qd., O'ahu. *Lit.,* pebbly.

Mā'ili'ili. Hill and stream, Lualualei, O'ahu. Also called Pu'u-Mā'ili'ili. *Lit.,* pebbly.

Māilo. Peak, Wai-mānalo, O'ahu, said to be named for a strong chief (Sterling and Summers 5:338). *Lit.,* thin.

Ma'ino. Land section, Hāna, Maui. *Lit.,* defacement. (A nearby cliff was called Pali-pilo [stinking cliff] because of deposits there of human excrement.)

Mai-poina-'oe-ia'u. Beach park dedicated in 1956 to the memory of World War II service men, Kīhei, Maui. *Lit.,* forget me not.

maka. 'Point, eye'.

Maka-'ai-kū-loa. Surfing beach and point, Kī-pahulu qd., southeast Maui. 'Ai'ai set up a stone of victory *(pōhaku-o-lanakila)* here to commemorate the victory of his father, Kū'ula, over a giant eel. (HM 20.) *Lit.,* eye eating standing long.

Maka'ala. Street, Moana-lua, Honolulu. (TM.) *Lit.,* alert.

Maka-'alae. Area on northwest Ka-ho'olawe. Point and land section near Hāna, Maui; tobacco was grown here in the 1860s. *Lit.,* mudhen's eyes.

Maka-'eha. Land division, Pu'u-o-kali qd., Maui. *Lit.,* sore eye.

Maka-'ele'ele. Gulch, Hālawa qd., Moloka'i. *Lit.,* black eye *or* black point.

Mākaha. Point, ridge, and valley, Wai-mea district, Kaua'i. Dwelling place of the demigods Hina and Māui at Ka-haku-loa, West Maui (Jarrett 24). Land section, village, valley, point, elementary school, playground, beach park, stream, hotel, and two golf courses (called Mākaha Valley East and Mākaha Valley West), Ka-'ena and Schofield qds., O'ahu; the area is famous today for surfing (annual international championships are held here) and as a resort; in ancient days, famous for robberies. (Ii 97.) *Lit.,* fierce.

Maka-hana-loa. Cape and land division, Honomū and Mauna Kea qds., Hawai'i; an ancient leaping place for souls. A sacred bamboo grove called Hō-mai-ka-'ohe (hand me the bamboo) was planted here by the god Kāne; bamboo knives used for circumcision came from this grove. (PH 189.)

Maka-hanu. *Pali* (at 1,200 feet elevation), Kī-lau-ea qd., Hawai'i. *Lit.,* breathing face.

Maka-hau-'ena. Point, southwest Ni'ihau. *Lit.,* point smiting rage.

M

M

Maka-hoa. Point, Hanalei Bay; ridge and *heiau* near Kauna-lewa, Kaua'i. Point near Lā'ie, O'ahu. *Lit.,* friendly point.

Maka-hū-'ena. Point near Po'ipū Beach, Kaua'i. Possibly *lit.,* eyes overflowing heat.

Maka-huna. Gulches in Kohala qd., Hawai'i, and Mā'alaea qd., Maui. Ancient *heiau* at Diamond Head, Honolulu, dedicated to Kāne and Kanaloa. *Lit.,* hidden point *or* hidden eyes.

Māka'i-koa. Street, Wai-'alae, Honolulu. (TM.) *Lit.,* military police.

Makaīwa. Bay, Pua-kō qd., Hawai'i. Ancient surfing area (Finney and Houston 30), Wai-lua, Kaua'i. Ka-'ili-lau-o-ke-koa, Moikeha's granddaughter, rode the curving surf of Makaīwa (HM 538). Land area, east Lā-na'i. Bay and land divisions, Ke-'anae qd.; beach near Lahaina, Maui. Gulch, Barber's Point, O'ahu; street, Kāhala, Honolulu. *Lit.,* mother-of-pearl eyes (as in an image).

Maka-kilo. Crater, land area, gulch, subdivision, elementary school, and playground, Wai-'anae qd., O'ahu. See Pu'u-maka-kilo. *Lit.,* observing eyes.

Maka-kilo-i'a. Fish observation point at the top of Ka-'uiki Hill, East Maui, facing Hawai'i. A stone was placed here as a lookout for *akule* fish by 'Ai'ai, the legendary hero (HM 22) who marked out fishing grounds on nearly all the islands. Hill (664 feet high), Kaunakakai qd., south Moloka'i. *Lit.,* fish-observing point.

Makakupa'ia. Two land divisions and road, Kaunakakai qd., south Moloka'i; a game-management area.

Maka-kupu. Old name for a part of Wood Valley, Kī-lau-ea qd., Hawai'i.

Maka-lapa. Old crater, park, elementary school, and Naval officers' housing area, near Pearl Harbor, O'ahu; formerly called Kapū-kakī. *Lit.,* ridge features.

Makalapua. Place, downtown Honolulu, perhaps named for the song of this name (Elbert and Mahoe 75–76) honoring Queen Lili'u-o-ka-lani. (TM.) *Lit.,* profuse bloom.

Makala-wena. Village and land section, Ke-āhole and Pua-kō qds., Hawai'i. The legendary hero Ka-miki destroyed some ghosts fishing here at a spot called Ku'una-a-ke-akua (net-setting of ghosts); these ghosts made mullet *('anae)* and goatfish *(weke)* bitter. *Lit.,* release [of] glow.

Maka-leha. Stream and mountains, Ka-wai-hau district, Kaua'i. Stream, Hale-'iwa qd., and valley, Schofield qd., O'ahu. *Lit.,* eyes looking about as in wonder and admiration.

Mākālei. Place, Diamond Head section, Honolulu, named either for a fishing temple on the flanks of Diamond Head (TM), or for a fish-attracting branch believed owned by the goddess Hau-mea, mother of Pele (HM 276–287). See Pāpala-ho'omau.

Makaleka. Avenue, Ala-wai section, Honolulu, named for Margaret James by her father, Frank L. James, who developed the area in 1926. *Lit.,* Margaret.

Makalena. Street, 'Āina-Haina, Honolulu, named for Solomon Maka-lena, a police officer whose family had a homestead here. *Lit.,* muslin *(Eng.).* An alternate interpretation is Maka-lena (eyes askance).

Makalihua. Hill, Ka-malō qd., south Moloka'i.

Makali'i. Points, Ka-laupapa peninsula, Moloka'i, and Kahana qd., O'ahu. *Lit.,* tiny *or* Pleiades.

Maka-lina. Ravine, Ka-haku-loa qd., Maui. *Lit.,* scarred face.

Makālua-puna. Point, Honolua qd., Maui. *Lit.,* spring hole (as for planting taro).

Maka-luhi. Site of Cooper Ranch, near Hau-'ula, O'ahu. *Lit.,* tired eyes ('Olopana's warriors rested here while searching for Kama-pua'a).

M

Makamaka-'ole. Land section between Honu-'apo and Nā-'ā-lehu, Ka'ū, Hawai'i, named for a *heiau* formerly there. Stream and cliff near Kā'ana-pali, Maui. *Lit.,* without friends (so named in Ka'ū because a woman chanted a lament here for her departed husband).

Makana. Cliff near Hā'ena Point, Hanalei district, Kaua'i, from which firebrands were hurled; known today as Fireworks Cliff. *Lit.,* gift.

Makana-limu. An old name for Ka-wai-hau district on Kaua'i; an upland *heiau* of this name was built by Ka-umu-ali'i, Ka-meha-meha's rival who finally submitted to him. *Lit.,* gift [of] seaweed.

Makana-lua. Peninsula, Ka-laupapa, Moloka'i. *Lit.,* double gift.

Makanani. Drive, Ka-mehameha Heights, Honolulu, named for the three McInerny brothers who owned the land when it was sub-divided. (TM.) *Lit.,* McInerny.

Maka-nau. Hill above Hīlea, Ka'ū, Hawai'i, and former plantation camp. A *heiau* on the brow of the hill was named Kohā-i-ka-lani (resound in the sky) for the chief who ordered his men to carry the famous birth pebbles *('ili'ili hānau)* from Puna-lu'u to be used in construction of the *heiau* so that it would be unique. After building the *heiau* the men were ordered to fell an *'ōhi'a* tree for an image; they then killed the chief. He was the grandfather of chiefs mentioned in the 'Umi story. The *heiau* was later destroyed when sugarcane was planted there. *Lit.,* surly eyes.

Makani-ka-hio. Land section, Wai-pi'o qd., Hawai'i. *Lit.,* wind [of] the gust.

Makani-'olu. Place, Kuli-'ou'ou, Honolulu. (TM.) *Lit.,* cool wind.

Maka-noni. Large stone near Cape Kumu-kahi, Puna, Hawai'i. (UL 197.) Probably *lit.,* mixed (speckled) face.

Maka-nui. Place, Pālolo, Honolulu. *Lit.,* large eye.

Mākao. Land section near Hau-'ula, O'ahu, named for Macao, China. A *heiau* here, named Lua-ali'i (royal pit), contained a pond within its walls, and around the pond were placed images. (Sterling and Summers 4:99–101.)

Maka-oe. Lane, Wai-kīkī, Honolulu. *Lit.,* haughty eye.

Maka-o-Hule. Point, Kohala qd., Hawai'i. *Lit.,* eyes (*or* point) of Hule.

Maka-o-Kaha'i. Point, Kō-loa district, Kaua'i, named for Pele's older sister.

Maka-o-puhi. Large double pit crater, active in 1969, one of the Chain of Craters, Puna qd.; land section, Ka'ū, Hawai'i. *Lit.,* eye of eel (a green rock in Ka'ū suggests an eel's eye).

Maka-pala. Land section and village, Kohala and Wai-pi'o qds., Hawaiʻi; a *heiau* here was named Kua-pālaha (broad back). *Lit.*, sore beginning to heal.

Maka-puʻu. Pool and land division, Hāna qd., Maui (Ii 172). Avenue, Ka-imu-kī, Honolulu; beach park, point, headland, and surfing beach (Finney, 1959*a:*108), Koko Head qd., Oʻahu. *Lit.*, hill beginning *or* bulging eye (the name of an image said to have been in a cave known as Ke-ana-o-ke-akua-pōloli; PH chapter 19).

M

Makaua. Land section and beach park, Kahana qd., Oʻahu. *Lit.*, unfriendly.

Makau-a-Māui. A place name on Coconut Island, Hilo, Hawaiʻi. *Lit.*, Māui's hook (this was the first island snared by the demigod when he attempted to bring the islands together).

Makauhelehele. Coast locality, Kai-lua qd., Hawaiʻi.

Maka-ʻUkiu. Point, Makuʻu qd., Hawaiʻi. Coastal area, Ka-malō qd., north Molokaʻi, perhaps named for a north wind. (Summers 159.) *Lit.*, ʻŪkiu end.

Maka-ʻula. Land section, Kai-lua and Ke-āhole qds., Kona, Hawaiʻi. *Lit.*, red eye (so named because of a fire there).

Makawa. Ancient surfing place, Hanalei district, Kauaʻi. (Finney, 1959*a:*53.)

Maka-wao. Land section, village, park, elementary school, district, and forest reserve, Haʻi-kū qd., Maui. Land section and stream, Kai-lua, Oʻahu. *Lit.*, forest beginning.

Maka-weli. Landing, land division, and river, Wai-mea district, south coast of Kauaʻi; formerly called Hoʻānuanu. (UL 110.) *Lit.*, fearful features.

Make-āhua. Gulch, Kohala qd., Hawaiʻi. *Lit.*, dead [in a] heap.

Makee. Road, Wai-kīkī, Honolulu, named for James Makee (pronounced McKee), trader, rancher, and captain of whaling ships. He came to Hawaiʻi in 1843 and stayed until his death in 1879. (TM.) He is celebrated in the well-known *Hula o Makee* about a ship named for him (Elbert and Mahoe 55).

Mākena. Land section, Kala-pana qd., Hawaiʻi. Village, bay, landing, school, and quadrangle, East Maui. *Lit.*, abundance.

Makiki. Place, street, heights, stream, valley, and section 20 of Honolulu (map 6), probably named for a type of stone used as weights for octopus lures.

Makiki Christian Church. Honolulu church built in 1932 to resemble a Japanese castle; the gold dolphins atop the tower signify salvation.

Mākila. Point, land division, reservoir, and ditch, Lahaina qd., Maui. *Lit.*, needle.

Mākini. Street, Ka-pahulu section, Honolulu.

*Makiwa. Gulch, Olowalu qd., Maui.

Makoe-wai. Stream near Pepeʻekeo, Hawaiʻi.

Mākole. Land area, northwest Kauaʻi. Land section and point, southeast Lā-naʻi. *Lit.*, red-eyed.

Mākole-ʻā. Point, Ke-āhole qd., Hawaiʻi. *Lit.*, glowing red eye.

Mākole-lau. Land division, Ka-malō qd., south Molokaʻi, and trail to Pelekunu Valley. *Lit.*, many red eyes.

142 **Makoloaka.** Islet (0.39 acres, 80 feet elevation), Ke-ʻanae qd., Maui.

Mākua. Land section, village, cave, stream, valley, surfing beach (Finney, 1959a:108), Ka-ʻena qd., Oʻahu; the traditional haunt of expert *lua* fighters. (Ii 98; UL 203.) See Kāne-ana. *Lit.,* parents.

Makuahine-me-ke-kaikamahine. See Nā-wāhine-waʻa.

Makua-iki. Ridge, Nā-pali coast, Kauaʻi. (UL 114.) *Lit.,* small parent.

Makuleia. Bay, Honolua qd., Maui.

Makuʻu. Land sections, Hōnaunau, Kala-pana, Makuʻu, and Puna qds.; quadrangle, Puna district, Hawaiʻi. (For. Sel. 256.) Probably *lit.,* canoe end-pieces.

Māla. Land division and port, Lahaina qd., Maui. *Lit.,* garden.

Malae. *Heiau* near mouth of Wai-lua River, Kauaʻi. See Poli-ʻahu.

Mālaʻe. *Heiau* and gulch, Ka-malō qd., south Molokaʻi. Peninsula east of Kāne-ʻohe, Oʻahu. *Lit.,* clear.

Mālaekahana. Land division and stream, Puʻu-kapu and Ka-huku qds., Oʻahu, the name of the mother of Lāʻie-i-ka-wai (see Lāʻie; HM 526), and also the name of an image that enraptured *(hoʻohihi)* Kumu-kahi, the rascal child in the Hale-mano legend (For. Sel. 260).

Malaeola. Islet (0.09 acres, 80 feet elevation), Hāna qd., Maui.

Māla-ihi. Road, Wai-luku qd., Maui. *Lit.,* sacred garden.

Malalo-wai-a-ole. Gulch, Māʻalaea qd., Maui.

Malama. Inland crater, sea area, land section, and homesteads, Kala-pana qd., Hawaiʻi. (PH 20.) Name of Ka-mehameha V's home at Kaunakakai, Molokaʻi (see Ka-mehameha V). Place, Mānoa, Honolulu. *Lit.,* month *or* moon.

Malama-kī. Forest area, Kala-pana qd., Hawaiʻi. *Lit.,* bright ti plant. (It is said that the game *hoʻolele kī* was played here. A ti leaf was held in the hand while the player chanted *ʻO kēlā kī, ʻo keia kī, na Ka-moho-aliʻi kaʻu kī, lele!* that ti, this ti, my ti is for Ka-moho-aliʻi, fly! Then the leaf was hurled, and if the chant had been said correctly and the wind was right, it returned to the sender. This game was played only here. Ka-moho-aliʻi, a celebrated shark deity, was Pele's older and favorite brother.)

Mālamalama. Land section, Kai-lua, Oʻahu. *Lit.,* enlightened.

Mālamalama-iki. Land section, Honomū qd., Hawaiʻi. Peak (2,010 feet high), northeast Kauaʻi. *Lit.,* little light.

Malanai. Street, Pā-waʻa section, and place, Pā-lama, Honolulu, named for a gentle breeze.

Malele-waʻa. Point at Wai-lau, Hālawa qd., Molokaʻi. (*Ka Lahui Hawaii,* September 27, 1877; Nakuina 51.) A place of this name said to be on Kauaʻi is mentioned in a song for Ka-ʻahu-manu: *E pua ana ka makani i nā hala o Malele-waʻa,* the wind blows upon the pandanus of Malele-waʻa. *Lit.,* scattered canoes.

Malia. Street, Wai-ʻalae, Honolulu. *Lit.,* Mary. (The street passes Star of the Sea School and is named for Mary, the Mother of Christ, patron saint of the school.)

Malia-ka-malu. Catholic church, Fort Street, Honolulu. *Lit.,* Mary [of] the peace.

Mālie. Place, Ka-imu-kī, Honolulu. *Lit.,* calm.

Malihini. Cave formerly used as a shelter for travelers, Ka-malō qd., Moloka'i, said to have been destroyed by a landslide (Summers 178). *Lit.,* visitor.

Māliko. Gulch and bay, Pā'ia qd., Maui. *Lit.,* budding.

Malino. Place, lower 'Ālewa Heights, Honolulu. *Lit.,* calm.

Maliu. Point, Ke-āhole qd., Hawai'i, once famous for surfing. (For. Sel. 268.) Street, Ka-lihi Uka, Honolulu. *Lit.,* look upon.

Malo. Land section, Honolua qd., Maui. *Lit.,* loincloth.

Mālua. Drive, 'Ālewa Heights, Honolulu. *Lit.,* depression.

Maluhia. Boy Scout camp, Ka-haku-loa qd., Maui. Street, Pālolo; State convalescent hospital, Ka-mehameha Heights, Honolulu. *Lit.,* peaceful.

Maluna. Street, Moana-lua, Honolulu. *Lit.,* upward.

Malu-ō. Cliff along the Wai-manu side of Wai-pi'o Valley, Hawai'i. *Lit.,* ever shady.

Malu-'ulu-o-Lele. Park, Lahaina, Maui. *Lit.,* breadfruit shelter of Lele. (This is a poetic epithet for Lele, as in the song *He Aloha nō 'o Honolulu.* Lele was an old name for the Lahaina district.)

Mamaewa. Gulch, Kamuela qd., Hawai'i.

Māmaki. Bay and point, southeast Lā-na'i, named for certain native trees, the bark of which was used for tapa; *heiau* east of Kaunolū, Lā-na'i, now a rocky enclosure at a cliff edge (Titcomb 19).

Māmala. Bay, Honolulu Harbor to Pearl Harbor, O'ahu, named for a shark woman who lived at the entrance of Honolulu Harbor and often played *kōnane.* She left her shark husband, 'Ouha, for Hono-ka'upu. 'Ouha then became the shark god of Wai-kīkī and of Koko Head (Finney and Houston 39; Westervelt, 1964*b*:15, 52–54). In the song "Nā ka Pueo" (Elbert and Mahoe 81), the name of the bay is juxtaposed to *mālama,* to protect: *Ma ka 'ilikai a'o Māmala, mālama iho ke aloha,* on the surface [of the sea] of Māmala, protect the love. See Ke-kai-o-Māmala.

Māmalahoa. Belt road, Hawai'i. Peak, Hanalei district, Kaua'i (For. Sel. 80). Stream, Kāne-'ohe; place, Nu'u-anu, Honolulu. Probably named for the law of the splintered paddle, *māmala hoe* (see PE); *hoa* (friendship) has replaced *hoe* (paddle).

Mamalu. Bay near Kau-pō, Maui. Street and place, 'Ālewa Heights, Honolulu. *Lit.,* shady.

Māmane. Place, Puna-hou district, Honolulu, named for a native tree.

Mana. *Heiau,* Hālawa qd., Moloka'i. Place, Wilhelmina Rise, Honolulu. *Lit.,* supernatural power.

Mānā. Land division, Ka'ū, Hawai'i; land divisions and home of the owners of the Parker Ranch, Wai-pi'o qd., Hawai'i. Dry western end of Kaua'i, where an older sister of Pele, Nā-maka-o-Kaha'i (the eyes of Kaha'i), introduced the *kauna'oa* dodder. (Ii 150; PH 159; UL 79.) *Lit.,* arid.

Manahoa. Rock islet (0.35 acres, 40 feet elevation), Ke-'anae qd., Maui.

Mānai. Land section, Hāmākua qd., Hawai'i. *Lit.,* lei-making needle.

Mana-iki. Place, Ka-lihi Uka, Honolulu. *Lit.,* small branch.

Ma-nā-ka'a. Stone, beach, and hill at the eastern end of Wai-ka-puna, Ka'ū, Hawai'i. The stone was a man named Ma-nā-ka'a who was turned to stone by Pele as he grieved over the loss of his children, Kanoa and Pōpō-'ohai.

Mana-lau. Ancient surfing area, Hanalei, Kaua'i. (Finney, 1959*b*:347.) *Lit.,* many branches.

Mānalo. Gulch, Airport qd., north Moloka'i. Bishop Museum archaeologists excavated a shelter cave here in 1952. Street, Pā-wa'a section, Honolulu, named for a spring that existed near McKinley High School (TM). *Lit.,* potable.

Manamana. Site of Queen's Hospital, Honolulu; place and street, Woodlawn, upper Mānoa, Honolulu. *Lit.,* branching.

Mānana. Offshore island, also known as Rabbit Island, a tuff cone (67 acres, 200 feet elevation), Koko Head qd.; land division, elementary school, and stream at Pearl City, O'ahu.

Mānana-uka. Area now called Pacific Palisades, Wai-pahu qd., O'ahu. *Lit.,* inland Mānana.

Mana-nole. Stream, Wai-luku qd., Maui. *Lit.,* weak branch.

Manauwea. Street, 'Āina-Haina, Honolulu, named for a type of edible seaweed. (TM.)

Mana-wai. Land division, Ka-malō qd., Moloka'i. A *heiau* here is named for Chief Kumu-ko'a, whose daughter Ka-lola married Kamehameha I (RC 109). *Lit.,* water branch.

Mana-wai-nui. Land division, coastal area, and gulch, Luala'i-lua Hills qd.; land division, valley, and stream below 'Ahulili, Kau-pō qd.; gulch, Mā'alaea qd., Maui. Gulch, Airport qd., south Moloka'i. *Lit.,* large water branch.

Mana-wai-pueo. Gulch, Mā'alaea qd., Maui. *Lit.,* owl stream branch.

Mānele. Harbor and bay, south Lā-na'i. Street, downtown Honolulu, probably named for the same chiefess as was Ka-mānele Park. *Lit.,* sedan chair.

Mane'o-papa. Gulch, Airport and Kaunakakai qds., Moloka'i.

Māniania. Cliff, Honu-'apo qd., Ka'ū, Hawai'i. Ditch, Wai-luku qd., Maui. Waterfall above Moa-'ula falls, Hālawa qd., Moloka'i. *Lit.,* a shuddering sensation. (At Ka'ū, Hawai'i, a man called Ni'auepo'o attempted to climb a coconut tree named Niu-loa-hiki. As he climbed, the tree, in its eel form, lifted itself skyward. The man called down to his mother, *Ē Hina ē, ē Hina ē, māniania mai nei o'u mau wāwae,* Hina, O Hina, my feet have a shuddering feeling.)

Mānienie. Land section and gulch, Hāmākua and Mauna Kea qds., Hawai'i. *Lit.,* Bermuda grass.

Mānienie-'ula. Ridge, Wai-mea district, Kaua'i. *Lit.,* red Bermuda grass.

Manini. Beach near the south end of Ke-ala-ke-kua Bay, Hawai'i, said to be a new name; the old names were Ka-pahu-kapu (the sacred drum) and Wai-'ama'u. Reef, East Maui. Gulch and cliff near Ka-'ena Point, O'ahu, named for the *manini* fish: a man who had been ordered by a chief on pain of death to find an answer to a riddle offered Hi'iaka a *manini* fish in return for the answer. Way and street, Ka-lihi Uka and Wilhelmina Rise, Honolulu (the street was probably named for the Matson freighter *Manini*). *Lit.,* surgeonfish.

Manini-holo. Dry cave, Hanalei district, Kaua'i. *Lit.,* traveling *manini* fish.

M

Manini-ʻōwali. Land section, Ke-āhole and Pua-kō qds.; undersea spring and rock between Awa-keʻe and Kū-kiʻo, Hawaiʻi. A girl named Manini-ʻōwali was betrothed as a child to Ulu-weuweu because their parents were close friends. When the wedding day approached the boy became ill. A *kahuna* made the diagnosis that he was in love with someone else. The *kahuna* prayed for the girl, but the gods turned both young people into rocks that can be seen at low tide. *Lit.,* weak *manini* fish.

Manō. Ridge in upper Ka-mana Nui Valley, Moana-lua, Oʻahu. A shark man lived in a cave here; both the man and the cave were called Ke-ana-o-ka-manō (the cave of the shark). The man followed bathing parties to the sea and killed them, but he was finally killed. He cultivated kava and yams *(uhi)*. *Lit.,* shark.

Mānoa. Stream, Nā-pali coast, Kauaʻi. Land section, stream, waterfall, valley, field, elementary school, and section 28 of Honolulu (map 6). Part of the floor of Mānoa Valley was covered with a lava flow from Sugarloaf cone 10,000 to 20,000 years ago. The Mānoa campus of the University of Hawaiʻi is built on this flow, and Mō-ʻiliʻili quarry has been excavated in it. (Ii 158; Macdonald and Abbott 376.) *Lit.,* vast.

Mānoa-aliʻi. Land division on the ʻEwa side of Mānoa Valley (west of a line from Puʻu-luahine to Rocky Hill), Honolulu. *Lit.,* royal Mānoa (chiefs lived here).

Mānoa-kanaka. Land opposite Mānoa-aliʻi, Honolulu. *Lit.,* commoners' Mānoa (commoners lived here).

Mano-hua. The highest point on the islet of Ka-ʻula. A wooden image is said to have stood at the top but it was carried away by Congregational visitors. *Lit.,* many words *or* many fruits.

Mano-wai. Land section, west Molokaʻi. *Lit.,* water source.

Mano-wai-nui. Land division, Kaunakakai qd., north Molokaʻi. *Lit.,* great water source.

Mano-wai-ʻōpae. Land section, stream and pool near Pāpaʻa-loa, Honomū qd., Hawaiʻi. *Lit.,* source [of] shrimp stream.

Manuʻa. *Heiau* that once stood on what are now the Queen's Hospital grounds, Honolulu. This name is perhaps cognate with Manuʻa in American Samoa. (Appendix 9.)

Manuʻa-kepa. Land section, Hanalei, Kauaʻi. (See PE, *limu-kā-kanaka;* PH 5; UL 133.)

Manu-ahi. Old name for Ka-ʻū-pūlehu, Kona, Hawaiʻi. Stream and valley, south Kauaʻi. Ridge, Ka-malō qd., north Molokaʻi, where the stretching demigod, Kana, lived with his brother Nīheu. *Lit.,* firebird.

Manu-honohono. Hill (499 feet high), Kō-loa district, Kauaʻi. *Lit.,* bad-smelling bird.

Manukā. Land section, State park, and house, Hoʻō-pū-loa qd., Hawaiʻi, named for a legendary robber. See Kanaka-loloa. *Lit.,* blundering.

Manu-ʻōhule. Coastal area, Māʻalaea qd., Maui. Probably *lit.,* bird [of the] meeting point of receding and incoming waves.

Manuwā. Drive, Moana-lua, Honolulu. (TM.) *Lit.,* man-of-war (ship).

Manu-wai-ahu. Gulch, Schofield Barracks, O'ahu. *Lit.*, bird water pool.

Ma'o. Lane, Ka-lihi Waena, Honolulu. (TM.) See Wai-'aha. *Lit.*, green.

Mā'oi. Place, Pālolo, Honolulu. *Lit.*, bold.

Mapulehu. Land division, stream, and former place of refuge, Hā-lawa qd., south Moloka'i; perhaps a contraction of *māpu* (wafted scent) and *pūlehu* (broil).

Māpunapuna. Place, road, and spring-fed fishpond formerly at Moana-lua, Honolulu. *Lit.*, bubbling.

M

Maria, Hōkū o ke Kai. Catholic church, Kala-pana, Puna, Hawai'i, built by Father Evarist Gielen who came to Hawai'i in 1927 and decorated the church's interior with religious paintings (Franken-stein 27–37). *Lit.*, Mary, Star of the Sea.

Maria Lanakila. Catholic churches, Ke-ālia, Kona, Hawai'i, and La-haina, Maui. The Ke-ālia church was built in 1860. In 1899 Father John Velghe painted the altar and interior decorations. The church was destroyed by an earthquake in 1950 (Frankenstein 9). The La-haina church was dedicated in 1858. *Lit.*, Mary [Our Lady of] Victory.

Marin. Street, downtown Honolulu, one of the oldest in the city, named for Francisco de Paula Marin, a Spaniard who came to Ha-wai'i in the early 1790s; he introduced many fruits and vegetables new to the Islands, and made wine. (Clark 16–17.) See Vineyard.

Mariposa. Drive, Wilhelmina Rise, named for a Matson steamer. (TM.)

Marmion. Street, Kaka'ako, Honolulu, named for Marmion Magoon, who was manager of the American Sanitary Laundry when it was located there. (TM.)

Maro Reef. Reef in the Northwestern (Leeward) Hawaiian Islands chain, generally covered with breakers. Discovered by Captain Allen of the American whaler *Maro* in 1820, it was annexed to Hawai'i in 1898 and is now a part of the City and County of Hono-lulu. See Gardner Pinnacles.

Marques. Street near Puna-hou School, Honolulu, named for August Jean Baptiste Marques (1841–1929), a French physician who arrived in 1878, edited the Portuguese language newspaper *O Luso Ha-waiiano* 1885–1888, taught French at Puna-hou School, was a mem-ber of the Hawai'i legislature 1890–1891, a consul of France 1912–1929, and consul of Russia, Panama, and Belgium. He championed the introduction of Portuguese laborers and may have established Marquesville, a Portuguese settlement where Father Clement said mass; see Clement. (Knowlton.)

Martin. Street, Ka-lihi Waena, Honolulu, named for the part-Hawai-ian caretaker for the old Ka-mehameha Schools in about 1900 when they were located next to the Bishop Museum. (TM.)

Mason. Place near St. Francis Hospital, Honolulu, named for John Mason Young, owner of the tract, who came to Hawai'i in 1908. He was an architect and a professor of engineering at the College

147

of Hawaiʻi. In 1930 he was president of the Honolulu Chamber of Commerce. (TM.)

Matlock. Street, Makiki, Honolulu, named for William Matlock Campbell who lived in Hawaiʻi prior to 1900. He built and sold many of the houses on Matlock, Davenport, and Young streets. (TM.)

Matsonia. Drive, Wilhelmina Rise, Honolulu, named for a Matson steamer. (TM.)

Matzie. Lane, Ka-pā-lama section, Honolulu, named for a seaman who came to Honolulu in about 1880 and told tall tales in exchange for drinks. (TM.)

Mau-hili. See Wai-komo.

Maui. Second largest island in the Hawaiian group, 48 miles long, 26 miles wide, with an area of 728 square miles and a population in 1970 of 38,691. Wai-luku is the major town and county seat. Maui High School is in Ka-hului. The county includes Maui, Lā-naʻi, Ka-hoʻolawe, and Molokaʻi islands. Epithet: *Maui o Kama,* Maui of Kama (a famous ancient chief, also called Kama-lālā-walu). The island was named for the demigod Māui (see Appendix 3).

maukele. Wet mountain areas, as at Wai-piʻo qd., Hawaiʻi. (See PE, *maʻukele.*)

Maʻulili. Bay, East Maui.

Mau-loa. Hill (198 feet high), south Niʻihau. *Lit.,* everlasting.

Mau-loku. Leaping place for souls, Nihoa. *Lit.,* continuous falling.

Mau-lua. Bay and gulch, Honomū qd., Hawaiʻi. *Lit.,* always depressed.

mauna. 'Mountain'.

Mauna-ʻala. Site of Royal Mausoleum, Nuʻu-anu, Honolulu. *Lit.,* fragrant mountain.

Mauna-alani. Hill (3,113 feet high), Wai-luku qd., Maui. Probably *lit.,* moss mountain.

Mauna-hilu. Place, Wilhelmina Rise, Honolulu. *Lit.,* quiet mountain.

Mauna-hina. Cinder cone, Hale-a-ka-lā Crater, Maui. *Lit.,* gray mountain.

Mauna Hoʻāno. Church at Paʻauilo, Hawaiʻi. *Lit.,* hallowed mountain.

Mauna-hui. Peak (2,828 feet high), Kaunakakai qd., Molokaʻi. *Lit.,* combined mountain.

Mauna-huʻihuʻi. Old name for Mountain View, Hawaiʻi. *Lit.,* chilly mountain.

Mauna-ʻihi. Place, Punchbowl, Honolulu, named in 1936 by Mrs. Manuel E. Reis; it was formerly a portion of Prospect Street. (TM.) *Lit.,* sacred mountain (named for a *heiau* above it).

Mauna-iki. Hill (3,032 feet high) and trail, Kī-lau-ea qd., Hawaiʻi. *Lit.,* small mountain.

Mauna-kapu. Hill, Līhuʻe district, Kauaʻi. Mountain in the Wai-ʻanae range separating Nānā-kuli and Honouliuli forest reserves, Oʻahu. *Lit.,* sacred mountain.

Mauna-kea. Important street, downtown Honolulu, probably named for an Inter-Island steamer. Leis were sold on the street (and still are), because the street led to a pier.

Mauna Kea. Highest mountain in Hawaiʻi (13,796 feet); quadrangle, State park, observatory, and forest reserve; land section, hotel, and golf course, Kohala qd., Hawai'i. See Ke-ana-kāko'i. *Lit.,* white mountain (often the mountain is snowcapped).

Mauna Ke'a. Congregational church in Kala-pana, Hawai'i. *Lit.,* mount [of the] cross.

Mauna-ki'eki'e. Slope at the base of Punchbowl behind Queen's Hospital, Honolulu. *Lit.,* tall mountain.

Mauna-kini. Mountain (1,437 feet), Ka-haku-loa qd., Maui. *Lit.,* many mountains.

Mauna-kū-wale. Mountain, Wai-'anae range, O'ahu. *Lit.,* mountain standing alone.

Mauna-laha. Stream, Makiki uplands, Honolulu. *Lit.,* flat mountain.

Mauna-lahilahi. Mountain and beach park west of Wai-'anae town, O'ahu. *Lit.,* thin mountain.

Mauna-lani. Hospital, circle, playground, and avenue, Wilhelmina Rise, Honolulu, named for a Matson ship. *Lit.,* heavenly mountain (a made-up name).

Mauna-lei. Gulch and land section, northeast Lā-na'i. Avenue, Ka-imu-kī, Honolulu, named for a Matson ship (TM). *Lit.,* lei mountain (clouds over the Lā-na'i mountain suggested a lei).

Mauna-loa. Avenue, Ka-imu-kī, Honolulu, probably named for an Inter-Island ship. Village, school, and highway, west Moloka'i. See also Mauna Loa.

Mauna Loa. Active volcano, second highest mountain in Hawai'i, and probably the largest single mountain mass on earth, rising 13,677 feet above sea level and about 29,000 feet above its base on the ocean floor (Macdonald and Abbott 54); also quadrangle and trails, central Hawai'i. Shield-shaped dome containing two separate peaks, one of which, Pu'u-nānā, is the highest point (1,381 feet) in west Moloka'i; the area was anciently famous for adze quarries, *hōlua* sliding, and the trees from which *kālai-pāhoa* sorcery images were made (see Kaka'ako). *Lit.,* long mountain.

Mauna-lua. Section of Honolulu now known as Hawai'i-kai; bay also known as Wai-'alae Bay, forest reserve, and beach park, Koko Head qd., O'ahu. (Ii 94.) See Kuapā. *Lit.,* two mountains.

Mauna-'ō-ahi. Ridge, Koko Head qd., O'ahu. *Lit.,* fire-hurling hill.

Mauna-'olu. College and land division, Pā'ia qd., Maui. *Lit.,* cool mountain.

Mauna-'olu'olu. Land section and gulch, Ka-malō qd., south Moloka'i. The Reverend H.R. Hitchcock (1800–1855) built a house here to escape the heat of Ka-lua-'aha. *Lit.,* cool mountain.

Mauna-pōhaku. Old name for St. Louis Heights and site of Lanakila School, Honolulu. *Lit.,* rock mountain.

Mauna-ulu. Small mountain, Hawai'i Volcanoes National Park, formed in the eruptions of the 1960s along the Chain of Craters and still being built in 1973. *Lit.,* growing mountain.

Mauna-una. Hill (1,769 feet high), Honouliuli, O'ahu. *Lit.,* mountain sent [on errands]. (Two servant *mo'o* who lived here had no keepers to supply their needs; Sterling and Summers 1:178a.)

Mauna-wai. Coastal area, Wai-mea Bay, O'ahu. *Lit.,* water mountain.

Mauna-wili. Land sections, ditch, ranch, stream, and valley, Koko

149

Head qd.; subdivision, elementary school, and playground, Kai-lua, O'ahu. Street names in the subdivision begin with *Luna* (overseer). *Lit.,* twisted mountain.

Mau-'oli'oli. Spring and land division near Hā'ao, Ka'ū, Hawai'i. *Lit.,* ever joyous.

Mau'u-mae. Ridge above Wilhelmina Rise, Honolulu. The O'ahu chief Kākuhihewa is said to have died here. Also, the name of a *heiau,* ridge, and cone, Pālolo Valley, Honolulu, where Kāne and Kanaloa wrestled and trampled down the grass so that it withered (Jarrett 28). *Lit.,* wilted grass.

Māwae. Place, 'Ālewa Heights, Honolulu. (TM.) *Lit.,* cleft.

McCandless. Lane, Ka-pā-lama section, Honolulu, named for three McCandless brothers (James S., John A., and Lincoln L.) who came to Hawai'i in 1880; their well-digging company developed more than six hundred artesian wells. (TM.) Office building, downtown Honolulu, built in 1906.

McCorriston. Street, Diamond Head section, Honolulu, named for the family of Dan and Hugh McCorriston who settled on Moloka'i in the 1880s and started Ka-malō sugar plantation. (TM.)

McCully. Important street and section 25 of Honolulu (map 6), named for Lawrence McCully, appointed associate justice of the supreme court by Ka-lā-kaua. He opened the Puna-hou tract as a subdivision. (TM.)

McGerrow. Village, Wai-luku qd., Maui.

McGregor. Point and landing, Mā'alaea qd., Maui. Lane, Pā-lama, Honolulu, named for Daniel McGregor, a sanitary inspector for the Territorial Board of Health. He was the father of Judge Calvin McGregor of the circuit court. (TM.)

McGrew. Lane, Nu'u-anu, Honolulu, named for Dr. John S. McGrew. After serving as a surgeon in the Civil War he came to Hawai'i to practice medicine. His office and home were at the site of the Alexander Young Building. He was an ardent annexationist leader. (TM.)

McKinley. Honolulu high school, and street in lower Mānoa, named for President McKinley. Annexation was consummated during his administration. (TM.)

Melchers Building. The oldest commercial building in Honolulu, built on Merchant Street, downtown Honolulu, in 1854 by the firm of Melchers and Reiner. It is now owned and used for offices by the City and County of Honolulu.

Melemele. Place, Woodlawn, upper Mānoa, Honolulu. (TM.) *Lit.,* yellow.

Menehune Ditch. See Kīkī-a-Ola.

Merchant. Historic street, downtown Honolulu, named in 1850; also called Kālepa (Merchant). (TM.)

Metcalf. Street, Mānoa and Bingham sections, Honolulu, leading to the Mānoa Campus of the university; named for Theophilus Metcalf, an Englishman, first marshall of the old fort in Honolulu, government surveyor, financier, and partner with A.H. Fayerweather in the 1830s in milling sugar on Hawai'i. (TM.)

Meyer Lake. Lake at the foot of Pu'u-'ōlelo, Kaunakakai qd., north

Moloka'i, probably named for R.W. Meyer or his descendants. A German, he came to Moloka'i in the 1840s, married a Hawaiian-Samoan, and raised many crops (including sugarcane); he was overseer of the leper settlement in the 1860s (Summers 22). The lake was formerly called Ke-ālia.

Meyers. Street, Fort Shafter, Honolulu, named for a military officer. (TM.)

Mīana. Points northeast of Hōnaunau Bay, Kona, Hawai'i, and at the base of Maka-pu'u, O'ahu. *Lit.*, urinal.

M

Midkiff. The Frank E. Midkiff Mānoa home was built in 1917 and is now the Honolulu Holiness Church. Mr. Midkiff was president of the Ka-mehameha Schools 1923–1934 and a former high commissioner of the Trust Territory of the Pacific Islands.

Mid-Pacific. Country club and golf course at Lani-kai, O'ahu. Mid-Pacific Institute is a private high school in Honolulu.

Midway Islands. Atoll about 1,309 miles northwest of Honolulu (maximum elevation 12 feet, approximate land area 2 square miles). Midway was discovered on July 8, 1859, by Captain N.C. Brooks of the Hawaiian bark *Gambia*; he named it Middlebrook Islands. The atoll has been under the jurisdiction of the U.S. Navy since January 20, 1903. (Bryan, 1942:199–203.) The Battle of Midway, June 1942, may have been the turning point in World War II.

Mikahala. Way, Wilhelmina Rise, Honolulu, named for an Inter-Island steamer (TM). *Lit.*, Mr. Hall.

Miki-lua. Land sections, Schofield and Wai-'anae qds., O'ahu. Perhaps *lit.*, two active persons.

Miki-ola. Subdivision, Kāne-'ohe, O'ahu, named for a filled-in fishpond there. *Lit.*, active [and] alive.

Miko. Lane, Moana-lua, Honolulu. *Lit.*, salted.

Mili-lani. Street, downtown Honolulu, the name of Princess Victoria Ka-māmalu's home in Honolulu near the Ali'i-ō-lani Building; earlier, it may have been John 'Ī'ī's home. Newly developed town, golf club, and cemetery near Wahi-a-wā, O'ahu; streets here are named for stars, days, and nights. (Ii x, 172.) *Lit.*, beloved place [of] chiefs.

Mili-lani Waena. Elementary school, Wahi-a-wā, O'ahu.

Miller. Street, downtown Honolulu, named for General William Miller, first British consul general 1844–1855; he negotiated a treaty in which England acknowledged the independence of Hawai'i. (TM.) His home was on the street named for him.

Miller Hall. Home economics building, Mānoa campus, University of Hawai'i, Honolulu, completed in 1939 and named for Dr. Carey D. Miller (1893–), chairman of the home economics department 1922–1946, and professor emeritus of foods and nutrition.

Milo. See Ka-lae-milo.

Milo-li'i. Land section, village, bay, landing, and beach park, Ho'ō-pū-loa qd., Hawai'i; fishing village on the Kona side of South Point, Hawai'i. Land sections, ridge, and valley, Nā-pali coast, Kaua'i. (UL 114.) *Lit.*, fine twist (as sennit cord). (The Hawai'i village was noted for its excellent sennit. According to one story the place was

M

named for an expert sennit twister who lived there.) An alternate interpretation is 'small swirling', as a current.

Mimo. Valley, Kaunakakai qd., north Moloka'i, site of terraces or platforms where hulas were performed. (Summers 33.) *Lit.,* deft.

Mission. Lane leading to the old mission houses behind Ka-wai-a-Ha'o Church, Honolulu, named in 1850. (TM.)

Mission Houses. Three houses, now a museum, near Ka-wai-a-Ha'o Church in Honolulu built between 1821 and 1841. The frame house is the oldest of its kind in the Islands and was the home of several early missionaries including Hiram Bingham, Gerrit Judd, and Elisha Loomis, printer. One coral-block house was built in 1841 as an addition to the frame house; the other (the Chamberlain House) was built in 1831 and was originally the storehouse for mission goods and home for the business agent, Levi Chamberlain (see Chamberlain).

Moa-kea. Land division, Hālawa qd., Moloka'i. The chiefess Kāne-alai is said to have planted a mountain apple *('ōhi'a-'ai)* tree here. (Summers 154.) *Lit.,* white chicken.

Moa-lepe. Ridge and stream, Ka-wai-hau district, Kaua'i. *Lit.,* chicken [with] comb.

Moa-li'i. Land division, Lahaina qd., Maui. *Lit.,* royal cock.

Moana Hotel. The first large tourist hotel in Wai-kīkī and now the oldest, built in 1901. The site was known as Ulu-kou, *kou*-tree grove, until the 1860s. *Lit.,* open sea.

Moana-lua. Land division, park, playground, golf course, residential area, shopping center, schools, and stream near Fort Shafter, Honolulu (map 6), said to be named for two encampments *(moana lua)* at taro patches, where travelers bound for Honolulu from 'Ewa rested. The site contains extensive gardens that are maintained as a public park. The buildings here are Ka-mehameha V cottage, a summer house built in 1867 and given to Samuel Damon in the 1880s, and the great hall built in 1906 by Samuel Damon; many parts of the great hall, including carvings, were sent from China. An ancient *maika* field near here was called Pueo-hulu-nui (much-feathered owl) because owls from Kaua'i and Ni'ihau were said to meet here to participate in the battle of the owls. In another story, a young chief, Kūla'i-i-'Aiea, fell in love with a girl bathing in 'I-emi pool. He cried out *Moana kā ho'i ka wai o kēnā lua wai,* how wide the water of that water hole. She accepted his offer of love. Much later, when Ka-hekili of Maui conquered O'ahu he placed his son, Ka-lani-kū-pule, in charge of Moana-lua. After the battle of Nu'u-anu, Ka-lani-kū-pule fled but was finally caught and sacrificed on an altar, probably at Pu'u-kapu. Ka-mehameha gave Moana-lua to Ka-me'e-ia-moku. Next the valley passed to his son, Hoa-pili, then to Hoa-pili's adopted son Lot (afterwards Ka-mehameha V), to Ruth Ke'elikōlani, and then to Bernice Pau-ahi, who willed the entire *ahupua'a* to Samuel M. Damon in 1884. At the present time (1974) the Damon family is offering the entire valley, including Ka-mana Nui and Ka-mana Iki, to the people of Hawai'i as a park of more than

3,000 acres for preservation of native Hawaiian flora and historic sites. For noted places see ʻĪ-emi, Ka-hau-komo, Ka-mana Nui, Ka-pōhaku-luahine, Manō, ʻUmi-mua, Wai-ola, Wai-puka.

Moana-wai. Place, Nuʻu-anu, Honolulu. *Lit.,* freshwater lake.

Moa-nui. Land section, East Maui, where taro was grown. Ka-meha-meha-nui, son of Ke-kau-like, was buried here. He was a very taboo chief (RC 4) who ruled Maui for a time in the early eighteenth century. Land division, stream, and sugar mill, Hālawa qd., Moloka'i. See Pākaikai. *Lit.,* big chicken.

Moa-nui-a-Hea. Place, Kai-lua qd., Kona, Hawaiʻi. Perhaps *lit.,* large chicken of Hea.

Moa-ʻula. Land sections and gulches, Honu-ʻapo, Mauna Loa, and Pāhala qds., Hawaiʻi; originally called Moʻa-ʻula (*lit.,* cooked red [by Pele's fires]). *Heiau,* Wai-piʻo, Hawaiʻi, dedicated by Ka-lani-ʻōpuʻu (RC 108). Hill (1,444 feet high), Ka-hoʻolawe; meaning not certain. Waterfall, Hālawa qd., Molokaʻi; when Queen Emma died in 1885, violent storms washed beach sand up Hālawa Valley as far as the pool at the base of the falls. Falls, stream, ridge, and *heiau,* Wai-kolu, Molokaʻi. A *heiau* at Kīpapa, Oʻahu. *Lit.,* red chicken.

Moʻa-ʻula. See Moa-ʻula.

Moe-au. Point on the Koko Head side of the base of Maka-puʻu headland. The point on the Wai-mānalo side is called Maka-puʻu. (PH 88.) *Lit.,* resting current.

*Moeauoa. Land section, Kai-lua qd., Kona, Hawaiʻi.

Mohi-ākea. Gulch, Schofield qd., Oʻahu.

Mōhihi. Road, river, falls, and divide, Wai-mea Canyon, Kauaʻi, probably named for a variety of sweet potato.

Moho. Coastal area, Ka-haku-loa qd., Maui. *Lit.,* chosen one.

Moho-kea. Land section, Honu-ʻapo qd., Kaʻū, Hawaiʻi. *Lit.,* white *moho* (Hawaiian rail, an extinct flightless bird).

Moho-pilo. Land section, Kaʻū, Hawaiʻi. *Lit.,* rail bird bad smell (so called because of rail droppings).

Moho-wae. Land section near Kamaʻoa, Kaʻū, Hawaiʻi. *Lit.,* selected champion (athletic contests were held here).

Mō-ʻiliʻili. Field, and section 29 of Honolulu (map 6). Kama-puaʻa chased two beautiful women here. They vanished and he rooted; water burst forth, almost drowning him. (Westervelt, 1964*b*:259–260.) Formerly, Ka-mō-ʻiliʻili. See Mānoa. *Lit.,* pebble lizard. (*Mō-* is short for *moʻo,* a lizard destroyed by Pele's younger sister, Hiʻia-ka; his body was cut to pieces and formed a hill across from Kū-hiō School.)

Moi-nui. Point north of Hōnaunau, South Kona, Hawaiʻi. *Lit.,* large threadfish.

Mō-iwi. Hill, Ka-hoʻolawe. *Lit.,* cut (*mō-* is short for *moku*) bone.

Mō-kapu. A bird islet (3.6 acres, 360 feet elevation), Ka-malō qd., north Molokaʻi. Peninsula, elementary school, point, quadrangle, and land division, Kai-lua, Oʻahu; originally named Moku-kapu (sacred district) because Ka-mehameha I met his chiefs here; it was "the

M

sacred land of Ka-mehameha" (Sterling and Summers 5:165). See North Beach. *Lit.,* taboo district (*mō-* is short for *moku*).

Mokauea. Island off Sand Island, Honolulu Harbor; street Ka-lihi Kai, Honolulu.

Mō-keʻehia. Islet (4.5 acres, 160 feet elevation), Ka-haku-loa qd., Maui. *Lit.,* trodden island (*mō-* is short for *moku*).

Mokihana. Valley and stream, Wai-mea district, northwest Kauaʻi. *Lit., Pelea anisata* (a tree found only on Kauaʻi; its flowers, strung in leis, represent Kauaʻi).

*Mokio. Two points, ʻĪlio Pt. and Ka-malō qds., Molokaʻi.

Mō-koholā. Large rock islet (0.36 acres, 50 feet elevation), off Pele-kunu, Molokaʻi. This island and Mō-kōlea were believed formed by rocks hurled at Kana's canoe while he attempted to rescue his mother, Hina, from Hāʻupu hill (Summers 210). For another version, see Hāʻupu. *Lit.,* cut (*mō-* is short for *moku*) whale.

Mō-kōlea. Points, Kī-lau-ea Bay, Kauaʻi, and Ka-haku-loa qd., Maui. Small stone islet (0.46 acres, 50 feet elevation), near Mō-koholā, Molokaʻi. Rock islet, Mō-kapu qd., Oʻahu. Possibly *lit.,* cut plover *or* plover island (*mō-* is short for *moku,* cut, *or* island).

Moko-liʻi. Islet in Kāne-ʻohe Bay off Kua-loa, Oʻahu, known also as Chinaman's Hat. Koholā-lele fishpond nearby is sometimes called Moko-liʻi. *Lit.,* little *moʻo* (a rare use of *moko* for *moʻo*). The lizard Moko-liʻi was destroyed by the goddess Hiʻiaka; its tail became the islet, its body the flat area near the old sugar mill (PH 91). In For. 5:370, a hero, Ka-ulu, grabbed the teeth of Moko-liʻi, an evil supernatural who preyed on passers-by, and flew into the sky with him; Moko-liʻi fell down and broke into pieces.

Mokomoko. Gulch, Kaunakakai qd., central Molokaʻi. *Lit.,* hand-to-hand fighting.

Moku. Coastal land section, Kaunakakai qd., south Molokaʻi. *Lit.,* district *or* islet *or* severed.

Moku-ʻaeʻae. Rock islet (0.3 acres, 104 feet elevation) off Kī-lau-ea, Kauaʻi. *Lit.,* fine (small) island.

Moku-ʻai-kaua. Forest area above Kai-lua, Kona, from which timber was taken to build the church of the same name at Kai-lua, Kona, Hawaiʻi. It was constructed by Kua-kini, governor of Hawaiʻi, with the cooperation of four thousand people. The roof was thatched with pandanus leaves, and, according to William Ellis, stones from an old *heiau* at the same spot were used for the foundation. Queen Ka-ʻahu-manu was present at the dedication, on December 10, 1823. The original church was destroyed by fire in 1835, and the present structure was completed in January 1837. *Lit.,* section won [during] war.

Moku-a-Kae. Small bay south of Ke-ala-ke-kua Bay, Kona, Hawaiʻi.

Moku-a-Kamohoaliʻi. Island beyond Nihoa. *Lit.,* island of Ka-moho-aliʻi (older brother of Pele).

Moku-ālai. Islet (0.74 acres, 10 feet elevation) off Lani-loa Point, Lāʻie, Oʻahu, part of the body of a lizard (see Lani-loa). *Lit.,* island standing in the way.

Moku-ʻauia. Largest islet (12.5 acres, 10 feet elevation) off Lani-loa

Point, Lāʻie, Oʻahu, part of the body of a lizard (see Lani-loa). *Lit.,* island to one side.

Moku-ʻāweoweo. Summit crater of Mauna Loa volcano, Hawaiʻi. *Lit., ʻāweoweo* fish section (the red of the fish suggests volcanic fires).

Moku-hala. Islet (0.18 acres, 40 feet elevation), Ke-ʻanae qd., Maui. *Lit.,* pandanus island *or* island passed by. Ridge in central Ka-mana Nui Valley, Moana-lua, Oʻahu. Probably *lit.,* pandanus grove.

Moku-hano. Rock islet off Ka-ʻuiki, Maui. *Lit.,* majestic island.

Moku-hau. Park and road, Wai-luku qd., Maui. *Lit., hau* thicket.

Moku-hōlua. Islet (0.18 acres, 40 feet elevation), Ke-ʻanae qd., Maui. *Lit.,* sled island.

Moku-honua. Land section, Hilo qd., Hawaiʻi. *Lit.,* land section.

Moku-hoʻoniki. Islet (10.6 acres, 203 feet elevation), Hālawa qd., Molokaʻi, famed for its two large pits, one a burial pit and the other a pig oven. (For. Sel. 288.) *Lit.,* pinch island (as a lover pinches).

Moku-hope. See Kāohi-ka-ipu. *Lit.,* island behind.

Moku-huki. Islet (0.35 acres, 40 feet elevation), Ke-ʻanae qd., Maui. *Lit.,* pulling island.

Moku-kāpapa. Islet in Kāne-ʻohe Bay off Kaha-luʻu, Oʻahu. *Lit.,* shoal island.

Moku-kapu. Same as Mō-kapu. *Lit.,* taboo district.

Moku-lau. Islet (0.9 acres, 40 feet elevation), stream, land area, landing, and ancient surfing place (Finney and Houston 28), Kau-pō qd., Maui. (For. Sel. 286.) *Lit.,* many islets (numerous rock islets are in the sea nearby).

Moku-lēʻia. Land section, beach park, surfing area, and station, Hale-ʻiwa qd.; land sections and forest reserve, Ka-ʻena and Schofield qds., northwest Oʻahu. The historian Kamakau was born here (RC vii). *Lit.,* isle [of] abundance.

Moku-lele. Elementary school, Hickam Air Force Base; drive and place, Kāne-ʻohe, Oʻahu. *Lit.,* airplane.

Moku-lua. Two islets (24.1 acres, 225 feet elevation) off Lani-kai, Oʻahu. *Lit.,* two islands.

Moku-mana. Islet (0.7 acres, 40 feet elevation), Ke-ʻanae qd.; gulch, Māʻalaea qd., Maui. *Lit.,* divided island *or* divided district.

Moku-manamana. Old name for Necker Island. *Lit.,* branching island.

Moku-manu. Islet (2.87 acres, 150 feet elevation), Ka-malō qd., Molokaʻi. Islets (16.6 acres, 225 feet elevation) off Mō-kapu, Oʻahu. *Lit.,* bird island.

Moku-moa. Street, Moana-lua, Honolulu, named for an ancient fishpond. (TM.) *Lit.,* chicken island.

Moku-naio. Islet, southwest Lā-naʻi. *Lit.,* bastard sandalwood island.

Moku-noio. Rock islet off Ka-ʻuiki, Maui. *Lit.,* tern islet.

Moku-ʻōhai. Site of a battle won by Ka-mehameha in 1782 over Kī-walaʻō and Ke-ō-ua, thus gaining control of Kona, Kohala, and Hāmākua, Hawaiʻi. The battle was fought in the village of Keʻei, near the bay listed on maps as Moku-a-Kae; this name is not known to local persons, and may be a garble for Moku-ʻōhai. Kiwalaʻō's throat was slit with a shark-tooth weapon *(leiomano)* by Ka-mehameha's ally, Keʻeaumoku (RC 121; Kuy. 1:38). *Lit., ʻōhai* tree grove.

*Moku-o-hua

*Moku-o-hua. Gulch, Ka-malō qd., south Molokaʻi.

Moku-o-Kahaʻilani. Rock island (0.9 acres, 40 feet elevation), Hoʻō-pū-loa qd., Hawaiʻi. *Lit.,* island of Kahaʻilani (a chief).

Moku-o-Kau. Islet (0.18 acres, 40 feet elevation), Haʻi-kū qd., Maui.

Moku-ola. Old name for Coconut Island, Hilo Bay, Hawaiʻi. *Lit.,* healing island. (People came here for spring water believed to have healing qualities; umbilical cords of infants were hidden here under a flat stone known as Papa-a-Hina [stratum of Hina] to protect them from rats. In another explanation, Moku-ola was a son of ʻUlu; see Wai-ākea. A sea pool to the right of the landing on the island was called Puaʻa-kāheka; see Kaulaʻi-nā-iwi; Appendix 8.1 for a saying; Ii 171.)

Moku-o-Loʻe. Old name for Coconut Island, Kāne-ʻohe Bay, Oʻahu. *Lit.,* island of Loʻe (Kahoe's sister who is said to have lived on the island; see Puʻu-ke-ahi-a-Kahoe).

Moku-one. Valley, Wai-mea district, Kauaʻi. Street, Hawaiʻi-kai, Honolulu. *Lit.,* sand island.

Moku-ʻopihi. See ʻOpihi.

Moku-pala. Islet (0.18 acres, 40 feet elevation), Kī-pahulu qd., Maui. *Lit.,* rotten island (probably referring to *limu*).

Moku-papa. Gulch and point, Haʻi-kū qd., Maui. *Lit.,* flat island.

Moku-papapa. Islet (0.72 acres, 50 feet elevation), Hālawa qd., Molokaʻi. On her first journey from Kahiki, Pele left her brother, Kāne-milo-hai, there to build up land (PH X). *Lit.,* flat island.

Moku-peʻa. Gulch, Honolua qd., Maui. *Lit.,* cross district.

Moku-pipi. Islet (1.08 acres, 80 feet elevation), Hāna qd., Maui. *Lit.,* pearl oyster island.

Moku-puku. Islet (1.50 acres, 40 feet elevation), Wai-piʻo qd., Hawaiʻi. *Lit.,* contracted island.

Moku-pūpū. Point, East Maui. *Lit.,* shell island.

Moku-ʻumeʻume. Old name for Ford Island, Pearl Harbor, Oʻahu. Water was brought for melons raised here. *Lit.,* ʻume game island (famous for this sexual game).

Mōlehu. Land area, southeast Kauaʻi. Drive, Foster Village subdivision, Hālawa, Oʻahu. Name suggested by Mary Kawena Pukui in 1956. *Lit.,* twilight.

Moleka. Stream, Makiki, Honolulu.

Mō-liʻi. Fishpond, Haki-puʻu, Oʻahu. *Lit.,* small section (*mō-* is short for *moku,* section).

Mōlī-lele. Cliff inland of Wai-o-ʻAhukini, Hawaiʻi. *Lit.,* leaping albatross.

Molo-aʻa. Land division, bay, volcanic cone, stream, and forest reserve, Hanalei and Ka-wai-hau districts, northeast Kauaʻi. *Lit.,* matted roots (said to be of the paper mulberry growing here).

Molokaʻi. Island, 38 miles long, 10 miles wide, 261 square miles in area, and having a 1970 population of 5,261. District, forest reserve, lighthouse, high school, airport, and hospital. Poetic names are *Molokaʻi nui a Hina* (great Molokaʻi, child of Hina) and *Molokaʻi pule oʻo* (Molokaʻi, powerful prayer). In legends Hina was the mother of Molokaʻi. The island was noted for sorcery and sports. (Elbert and Mahoe 78–79.)

Moloka'i-nui-a-Hina. Gulch, Hālawa qd., south Moloka'i. See Ke-ana-o-Hina. *Lit.,* great Moloka'i, [child] of Hina.

Molo-kini. Islet (150 feet elevation) between Ka-ho'olawe and Maui. When Lohi'au (Pele's dream lover) lived at Mā'alaea, Maui, he took to wife a *mo'o*, Pu'u-o-inaina (hill of wrath). Pele in anger bisected her; her tail became Pu'u-ō-la'i Hill, Mākena, Maui, and her head Molo-kini Islet. see Pu'u-ō-la'i. (For. 5:514–521; HM 189; PH 75.) *Lit.,* many ties.

Mololani. Crater, Mō-kapu peninsula, O'ahu. Here, the god Kāne drew a figure of the first man on the earth, and Kū and Lono caught a spirit of the air and made the drawing live. Kāne tore a woman from the man's side. (HM 47–48; for a song, see Elbert and Mahoe 61.) *Lit.,* well cared for; also the name of a rain.

*Momoualoa. Land division and gulch, Wai-pi'o qd., Hawai'i. (For. Sel. 190.)

Mona. Street, 'Āina-Haina, Honolulu, named for Mona Hind Holmes, daughter of Senator Robert Hind. (TM.)

Monsarrat. Avenue near the Diamond Head end of Wai-kīkī, probably named for Marcus Cumming Monsarrat, who came to Hawai'i from Ireland and Canada in 1850 and was at one time collector of customs. He died in 1871. His wife was Elizabeth Dowsett. The avenue may have been named for his son, Judge James Melville Monsarrat (1854–1943), a legal adviser of Hawaiian monarchs.

Montague Hall. Music school building, Puna-hou School, Honolulu, built in 1937, donated by the Atherton family in memory of Juliette Montague Cooke and her daughter, Juliette Montague Cooke Atherton. Both were interested in music.

Monte. Street, Ka-lihi Uka, Honolulu, leading to a small Catholic church where a statue of the Portuguese Lady of the Mount stands in a grotto. *Lit.,* mountain (a Portuguese loanword).

Monte Cooke. Place near the Bishop Museum named for Dr. Charles Montague Cooke, Jr., who was a trustee of the museum 1929–1948, president of the board of trustees 1941–1948, and curator of malacology 1946–1948.

Monterey. Drive and place, Wilhelmina Rise, Honolulu, named for a Matson steamer. (TM.)

Mo'oheau. Park, Hilo waterfront, Hawai'i, named for Chief Ka-'ai-'awa'awa-i-Mo'oheau (the bitter food of Mo'oheau), the son of Ho'olulu, who is said to have hidden Ka-mehameha's bones. Avenue, Ka-pahulu section, Honolulu, named by Auhea Crowningburg, through whose land the street ran, for Chief Mo'oheau, an ancestor. (TM.)

Mo'o-helāia. Unknown place, famous in chants, said to be near the summit of Mauna Loa, Moloka'i. *Noho ana Laka i ka uluwehiwehi, kū ana i luna i Mo'o-helāia, 'ōhi'a kū i luna o Mauna Loa* (UL 33), Laka lives in the verdure, stands at Mo'o-helāia, 'ohi'a trees stand on Mauna Loa.

Mo'o-kapu-o-Hāloa. Main ridge of Kāne-hoa-lani at Kua-loa, O'ahu. *Lit.,* sacred section of Hā-loa (a son of Wā-kea, the first man).

Mo'o-kini. *Heiau,* Kohala qd., Hawai'i, attributed to Pā'ao, a priest from Tahiti. In building the *heiau,* stones were passed hand to hand

M

for 9 miles from the seacoast. Stones near here were called Pā'ao's canoe, paddles, and fishhooks, and the fields he cultivated were called *nā mau'u o Pā'ao* (Pā'ao's grasses) and left untouched for fear of storms. (HM 370–371.) A stone east of the *heiau* was called Pōhaku-holehole-kānaka (stone [for] stripping human [flesh]). The flesh was removed from human sacrificial victims and the bones were made into fishhooks and other objects. Pahu-kini *heiau* at Kai-lua, O'ahu, was also called Mo'o-kini. *Lit.,* many *mo'o or* many lineages.

M

Mo'o-loa. Land section and falls, Ka-malō qd., south Moloka'i. *Lit.,* long lizard *or* long ridge.

Mo'o-moku. Land division, Lahaina qd., Maui. *Lit.,* severed ridge.

Mo'omomi. Beach and land area, Airport qd., Moloka'i.

Mo'o-muku. Place, Kuli-'ou'ou, Honolulu. (TM.) *Lit.,* cut-off land section.

Moore Hall. Building, Mānoa campus, University of Hawai'i, Honolulu, completed in 1969 and named for Charles Moore (1901–1967), professor of philosophy.

Mōpua. Village, Olowalu qd., Maui. *Lit.,* melodious (said to be the name of a legendary character).

Moreira. Street, Papa-kōlea, Honolulu, named for Benjamin Moreira, who built the first house on this street. (TM.)

Mormon Temple. The Church of Jesus Christ of Latter-day Saints was established in Lā-'ie, O'ahu in 1850; in 1920 the temple was dedicated—the first ever built outside Salt Lake City.

Morris. Lane, Ka-pā-lama section, Honolulu, named for a part-Hawaiian carpenter family who in 1890 owned property there. (TM.)

Mother Waldron. Park, Kaka'ako, Honolulu, named for Mrs. Margaret Waldron (1873–1939), teacher at Pohukaina School, and founder and director of the playground for 24 years.

Mott-Smith. Drive, Makiki, Honolulu, named for E.A. Mott-Smith, a lawyer who was a trustee of the Lunalilo Estate in 1926 when the Luna-lilo Home was moved from Makiki to Mauna-lua. (TM.)

Mott-Smith Building. Brick structure, downtown Honolulu, constructed in 1897 and named for Dr. John Mott-Smith, Honolulu dentist.

Mount Ball. See Pa'upa'u.

Mount Olympus. Mountain, Ko'olau Range between Mānoa Valley and Wai-mānalo, O'ahu. See Tantalus.

Mountain View. Village and elementary school, Hilo qd., Hawai'i, named for the Mountain View House, built in 1891 as a half-way house stop on the way to the volcano from Hilo (Olson 75). See Mauna-hu'ihu'i.

Muliwai. Land section and land division, Wai-pi'o qd., Hawai'i. Land section, Kau-pō qd., Maui. Lane, downtown Honolulu, named for Nu'u-anu Stream (TM). *Lit.,* river.

Muliwai-'ōlena. Stream, Wai-mānalo, O'ahu. *Lit.,* turmeric river *or* yellow river.

Mu'o-lau-lani. Site of the Queen Lili'u-o-ka-lani Children's Center,

Ka-pā-lama section, Honolulu. Liliʻu-o-ka-lani had a home here. *Lit.,* innumerable royal buds.

Mū‘olea. Point, village, and land section, Kī-pahulu qd., Maui. See PE, *limu-make-o-Hāna.*

Murray. Drive, Ālia-manu, Honolulu, named for a military officer. (TM.)

M

NnNnNn

N

Nā-ahi-ʻenaʻena. Building for primary students, Ka-mehameha Schools, Honolulu, built in 1954 and named for the daughter of Ka-mehameha I by Ke-ōpū-o-lani (the cluster of royal chiefs); usually spelled Nahienaena. *Lit.,* the burning fires.

Nā-ʻai. Street, Ka-lihi Uka, Honolulu, named for a chief. *Lit.,* the food.

Nā-ʻalae. Gulch, Puʻu-o-kali qd., Maui. *Lit.,* the mudhens.

Nā-ʻale. Street, Papa-kōlea, Honolulu. (TM.) *Lit.,* the billows (the sea can be seen from this street).

Nā-ʻā-lehu. Land section, village, and elementary school, Honu-ʻapo qd., Hawaiʻi. *Lit.,* the volcanic ashes.

Naʻau-kāhihi. Coastal land section, Airport qd., north Molokaʻi. *Lit.,* entangled intestine.

Nā-ʻehu. Peak, Ka-malō qd., Molokaʻi. *Lit.,* the red-heads.

Nae-ʻole. Walk, Sheridan Tract, Honolulu, named for the Kohala chief Nae-ʻole who snatched the child Ka-mehameha when he was born in about 1753 (RC 66–67) and is said to have taken him to ʻĀwini, Kohala, Hawaiʻi, to be reared. (TM.) *Lit.,* without gasping.

*Naha. Valley, east Lā-naʻi.

Nā-haku. Place, Ala Wai section, Honolulu, named for Nā-haku-ʻelua-pua (the weaving [of] two flowers), mother of Ke-aliʻi-mahiʻai. See Mahi-ʻai. *Lit.,* the lords.

Nā-hale-o-Koʻo. Land section (800 feet elevation) near Wai-mea Canyon, Kauaʻi. *Lit.,* the houses of Koʻo.

Nahienaena. See Nā-ahi-ʻenaʻena.

Nā-hiku. Village, ditch, homesteads, landing, and quadrangle, East Maui. (RC 80.) *Lit.,* the sevens (districts of this area).

Nā-hoko. Coastal area, east Lā-naʻi. *Lit.,* the fleshy body parts.

Nā-hua. Street, Wai-kīkī, Honolulu, named for a Hawaiian chiefess who owned property between the Royal Hawaiian Hotel and the Hale-kū-lani. *Lit.,* the fruits.

Nā-huku. Lava tube near Kī-lau-ea Crater, Hawaiʻi, now called Thurston Lava Tube. *Lit.,* the protuberances.

Nahu-māʻalo. Point, Kō-loa district, Kauaʻi. *Lit.,* bite [in] passing.

Naʻi-a-ka-ʻūlili. A spring on Niʻihau believed discovered by tattler birds. *Lit.,* sought for by the tattler.

Nā-ʻili-a-Kaʻauea. Lookout point, Kālepa Ridge Trail, Kālepa Forest Reserve, Līhuʻe district, Kauaʻi. (This name is sometimes spelled Nailiakuea.) *Lit.,* the pebbles of Kaʻauea.

Nā-imu-kālua-ua. Same as Imu-kālua-ua. *Lit.,* the rain-baking ovens.

Naio. Gulch, northeast Lā-naʻi. Street, ʻĀlewa Heights, Honolulu. *Lit.,* bastard sandalwood.

Nā-ʻiwa. Three land divisions, Kaunakakai qd., Molokaʻi. *Lit.,* the frigate birds (perhaps named for the beauty of the birds).

Nā-iwi-o-Pele. Hill near Hāna, Maui. *Lit.,* Pele's bones (Pele fought here with her sister Nā-maka-o-Kahaʻi; Pele escaped but left some of her bones).

Nā-kala-loa. Stream, Wai-luku qd., Maui. *Lit.,* the long [house] gables.

Nā-kālele. Point, Lahaina qd., Maui. *Lit.,* the leaning.

Nā-kalo-a-Ola. Small mountain area above Hanalei, Kauaʻi. *Lit.,* the taros of [Chief] Ola.

***Nakaohu.** Land section and point, Lualaʻi-lua Hills qd., Maui.

Nā-keiki-a-nā-ʻiʻiwi. Land area (600 feet elevation), Nā-pali coast, Kauaʻi. *Lit.,* children of the *ʻiʻiwi* birds.

Nā-keiki-a-Pua. Coastal area, Hālawa qd., Molokaʻi. *Lit.,* the children of Pua.

Na-keiki-ʻelima. Area, Wai-mea district, Kauaʻi. *Lit.,* the five children.

Nakele. Street, Nuʻu-anu, Honolulu. *Lit.,* rustling.

Nā-kiu. Street near Metcalf Street and the university, Honolulu. *Lit.,* the spies.

Nā-koʻokoʻo. Street, Ala Wai section, Honolulu, named for John K. Nā-koʻokoʻo, a clerk in the City and County building inspector's offices. (TM.) *Lit.,* the canes.

Nā-kuina. Street, Ka-lihi Waena, Honolulu, named for Emma Metcalf Nā-kuina (Mrs. Moses Nā-kuina) who wrote articles on ancient Hawaiian land and water rights. (TM.) Her husband, a minister, also wrote on Hawaiian subjects (see References). *Lit.,* the stitching together.

Nā-lāʻau-Hawaiʻi. Botanic garden for endemic dry-land plants, on the slope of Diamond Head, Wai-kīkī, Honolulu, created by George C. Munro and named by him in 1951. *Lit.,* the Hawaiian plants.

Nā-lani. Street, Ka-lihi Uka, Honolulu. *Lit.,* the heavens *or* royal chiefs.

Nā-lei-aloha. Place, Kuli-ʻouʻou, Honolulu. *Lit.,* the leis [of] love.

Nā-lima-wai. Coastal area, Lahaina qd., Maui. *Lit.,* the five waters.

Naluai. Lane, Ka-lihi Kai, Honolulu, named for Peter Naluai, an employee of the federal customs service. (TM.)

Naluea. Stream, Wai-piʻo qd., Hawaiʻi. *Lit.,* nausea.

Nalu-lua. Coastal land section, Kaunakakai qd., south Molokaʻi. *Lit.,* double wave.

Namahana. Peak (2,650 feet), land section, and valley, Hanalei district, Kauaʻi.

Nā-māhana. Street, Wai-kīkī, Honolulu, named for Lydia Pīʻia Nā-māhana, a daughter of Keʻeaumoku, and for a Maui chiefess also named Nā-māhana. The street was named by the subdivider, Bruce Cartwright. (TM.) *Lit.,* the twins.

Nā-makani-paio. Campground, Hawaiʻi Volcanoes National Park, Kī-lau-ea qd., Hawaiʻi. *Lit.,* the conflicting winds.

Nā-malu. Bay, Honolua qd., Maui. *Lit.,* the protections.

Nā-mana-o-ke-akua. Cinder cone, Hale-a-ka-lā Crater, East Maui. *Lit.,* the powers of the god.

Nā-mauʻu. Drive, Puʻu-nui, Honolulu, named for John Nā-mauʻu, clerk in the government offices during the monarchy. (TM.) *Lit.,* the grasses.

Nā-milimili. Street, Pauoa, Honolulu. *Lit.,* the favorite ones.

Nā-moho-kū. Land section, Hālawa qd., south Molokaʻi. *Lit.,* the selected upright ones.

N

Nā-moku. Islet (0.09 acres, 50 feet elevation), Ka-laupapa peninsula, Moloka'i. *Lit.,* the islands.

Nā-moku-'ehā. Street, Pauoa, Honolulu. *Lit.,* the four islands.

Nā-molo-kama. Mountain, Hanalei district, Kaua'i. (Elbert and Mahoe 41, 75; UL 133.) *Lit.,* the interweaving bound fast.

Nānāhoa. Islet off west Lā-na'i, said to have been a man named Nānā-hoa who abused his wife; both were turned into phallic stones. Of the four sea towers off west Lā-na'i (see Macdonald and Abbott 200), the one farthest out to sea is said to be female, and the others males (Emory, 1969:35). Stone near the top of a high spur dividing Ko'olau Poko and Ko'olau Loa, Haki-pu'u, O'ahu. The stone was formerly a taboo child not allowed to look upon a woman until he was married; however, he stared at a naked beauty sleeping on the beach and was turned to stone. See Ka-ule-o-Nānāhoa.

Nāna'i. Dialectal variant of Lā-na'i. (PH 115.)

Nānā-i-ka-pono. Elementary school and church at Nānā-kuli, O'ahu. *Lit.,* look toward righteousness (a new name).

Nānaina. Place, 'Ālewa Heights, Honolulu. *Lit.,* view.

Nānā-kuli. Land section, town, school, forest reserve, stream, valley, beach park, and surfing area, Wai-'anae qd., O'ahu. (Ii 29.) *Lit.,* look at knee (said to be named in honor of the tattooed knee of Ka-'ōpulupulu, a priest whose chief, Ka-hahana, turned a deaf [*kuli*] ear to his advice, and, when asked about his knee, told of his relationship with the chief, thus rebuking him); *or* look deaf (said because people in the area had not enough food to offer passersby; hence they looked at them and pretended to be deaf).

Nānā-wale. Subdivision near Pāhoa; forest reserves, land division, and bay, Maku'u qd., Hawai'i. Unsuccessful fishermen would say that their canoe landed at Nānā-wale (*lit.,* just look around): *ua pae ka wa'a i Nānā-wale.*

Nanea. Street, Pā-wa'a section, Honolulu. *Lit.,* to live at ease.

Nani-hale. Place, Woodlawn, upper Mānoa, Honolulu. *Lit.,* house beauty.

Nani-kai. Surfing area, Wai-'anae qd., O'ahu. (Finney, 1959a:108.) *Lit.,* marine beauty.

Nani-nani-kukui. Gulch, Airport qd., south Moloka'i.

Nā-ninini. Coastal area, Ka-malō qd., north Moloka'i. *Lit.,* the pouring forth.

Nā-niu. Place, Mānoa, Honolulu. *Lit.,* the coconuts.

Nā-niu-'apo. Stream tributary to Mānoa Stream, Honolulu. *Lit.,* the grasped coconuts.

Nā-niu-o-Kāne. Rocks in Hāna Bay, Maui. *Lit.,* the coconuts of Kāne.

Nā-nu'a-lele. Point at Hāna Bay, Maui. Stones were carried from here to Honua-uka, inland of Ka-'uiki, for Pi'i-lani-hale *heiau* being built by Kiha-a-Pi'ilani. A surfing area here is known as Hāna. *Lit.,* the altar heaps.

*Nao. Hill, Airport qd., Moloka'i.

Nā-'ohaku. Ancient surfing area, Kohala qd., Hawai'i. (Finney and Houston 26.) See Kūmoho.

Nā-ʻohe. Land division, Puna, Kauaʻi. Street, Hawaiʻi-kai, Honolulu. *Lit.,* the bamboos.

Nā-ʻōhule-ʻelua. Land section, Ka-ʻohe qd.; ancient surfing area, Kailua and Ke-āhole qds., Hawaiʻi. (Finney and Houston 26.) *Lit.,* the two bald heads.

Nā-one. Street, Pauoa, Honolulu, named for John Nā-one, contractor and painter who resided there. (TM.) *Lit.,* the sands.

Nā-ʻōpala. Lane, Ka-lihi Kai, Honolulu, named for Captain Moses Nā-ʻōpala, master of the Inter-Island steamer *Likelike* at the turn of the century. (TM.) See Ka-ʻōpala. *Lit.,* the rubbish.

Nā-pali. Overlook, Hōlei Pali, Kī-lau-ea qd., Hawaiʻi, which was covered by lava in the current (1968–) eruption of Kī-lau-ea. Coastal area, State park, forest reserve, and old district, northwest Kauaʻi. Place, Wilhelmina Rise, Honolulu. *Lit.,* the cliffs.

Nā-pau. Pit crater (erupted in 1963 and 1965) and trail, Puna qd., Hawaiʻi. *Lit.,* the endings.

Nape-hā. Deep pool and resting place (mentioned in Ii 95) on a trail to Kapūkakī; land division near ʻAiea, Oʻahu. *Lit.,* bend over breath (the chief Kū-aliʻi is said to have leaned over the pool to drink).

Nā-pili. Bay and land section, Lahaina qd., Maui. *Lit.,* the joinings *or* pili grass. (RC 74.)

Nā-pōhaku-a-Kāne-ame-Kanaloa. See Nā-wāhine-waʻa.

Nā-pōʻopoʻo. Lighthouse, village, school, and beach park, Hōnaunau qd. (RC 101; see Ka-pahu-kapu); land section, Wai-piʻo, Hawaiʻi. *Lit.,* the holes. (The Hōnaunau place is said to have been so named because persons in canoes in the bay looking ashore saw people peering out of holes that served as doors in the grass houses.)

Nā-pua-nani. Park, ʻAiea, Oʻahu. *Lit.,* the beautiful flowers.

Nā-pū-maiʻa. Area, Honu-ʻapo qd., Kaʻū, Hawaiʻi; formerly called Nā-pū-maiʻa-a-ka-lā (the banana clumps of the sunlight). Plants were offered on a *heiau* here in asking forgiveness for crimes. Nā-pū-maiʻa is also a family name.

Nā-puʻu. Inhabited and gardened area between Puʻu-anahulu and Puʻu-waʻawaʻa, Kona, Hawaiʻi. Chief Keawe-nui-a-ʻUmi appointed Ehu as supervisor, and Kona became known as *Kona, kai malino a Ehu* (Kona, calm seas of Ehu). Bananas, sugarcane, sweet potatoes, and yams were plentiful until the supernatural dog, Puapua-lenalena, began to steal. *Lit.,* the hills.

Nā-puʻu-a-Pele. Hills, Hoʻō-pū-loa qd., Hawaiʻi. See Ka-huku. *Lit.,* the hills of Pele.

Nā-puʻu-koiele. Hills, Wai-kāne qd., Oʻahu. *Lit.,* hills moving to and fro.

Nā-puʻu-kū-lua. Lava flows, Kī-lau-ea qd.; hills (3,200 and 3,000 feet high), Honu-ʻapo qd.; and hills (5,960 and 5,986 feet), Ka-ʻohe qd., Hawaiʻi. Hills above Pā-pōhaku, west Molokaʻi, with *hōlua* courses (Cooke 119); cinder cones, Ka-malō qd., south Molokaʻi. *Lit.,* the hills standing [in] twos.

Nā-puʻu-maiʻa. Peak (1,870 feet high), Nuʻu-anu, Honolulu. *Lit.,* the banana hills.

N

Nā-puʻu-o-nā-elemākule

Nā-puʻu-o-nā-ʻelemākule. Coastal hills west of ʻOpihi-nehe, Kaʻū, Hawaiʻi. *Lit.,* the hills of the old men.

Nāʻū. Gulch, Mauna Kea qd., Hawaiʻi. *Lit.,* yellow.

Naue. Place near Hāʻena, Hanalei district, Kauaʻi, famous for pandanus trees. (For a song, see Elbert and Mahoe 80–81.) *Lit.,* to move.

Nāulu. Place, Foster Village subdivision, Hālawa, Oʻahu. Name suggested by Mary Kawena Pukui in 1956. *Lit.,* shower clouds.

Nā-ulu. Forest and picnic area (cut off from the road and partially destroyed by lava flows in 1972), Puna qd., Hawaiʻi. *Lit.,* the groves.

Naupaka. Land section, west Lā-naʻi. *Lit., Scaevola* shrubs.

Nā-wāhine. Site of ancient fishing village, ʻAnae-hoʻomalu Bay, Kona, Hawaiʻi; two brackish wells are here. *Lit.,* the women.

Nā-wāhine-waʻa. Two rocks in the pineapple field east of Puʻu-ka-moʻo, Kaunakakai qd., north Molokaʻi. They are said to be a mother and her daughter who followed the spirit of the husband and father going to ʻUhane-lele. They heard a cock crow, turned, and were changed into stones (Cooke 103). It is said that people still leave offerings, such as liquor or money, on the rocks. Alternate names are Makuahine-me-ke-kaikamahine (mother and the daughter) and Nā-pōhaku-a-Kāne-ame-Kanaloa (the stones of Kāne and Kanaloa). (See picture preceding page 209, RC.) *Lit.,* the foolish women.

Nā-wai-hulili. Stream, Hālawa qd., Molokaʻi. *Lit.,* the sparkling waters.

Nā-waimaka. Valley, Wai-mea, Hawaiʻi. *Lit.,* the tears.

Nā-wāwae-o-ʻAlika. Land area, Puʻu-o-kali qd., Maui. This may be a new name. *Lit.,* the feet of Alex *or* the feet of Arctic.

Nā-wiliwili. Village, land division, port, stream, bay, and small boat harbor, Līhuʻe district, Kauaʻi. *Lit.,* the *wiliwili* trees.

Necker. Island of the Northwestern (Leeward) Hawaiian Islands (elevation 276 feet, approximate area 0.07 square mile). It was discovered by La Pérouse on November 4, 1786, and named after Jacques Necker, French minister of finance under Louis XVI. It was annexed to Hawaiʻi in 1894 and is now a part of the City and County of Honolulu. Hawaiian artifacts have been found here (Buck, Figure 315), as well as remains of fishponds, ditches, agricultural terraces, house platforms, and temple platforms (Macdonald and Abbott 403; Emory, 1928). The island is a bird sanctuary. (Bryan, 1942:171–174.) See Moku-manamana.

Nehe. Point, Wai-luku qd., Maui. Lane, Punchbowl, Honolulu. (TM.) *Lit.,* rustle.

Nehoa. Street and place, Makiki, Honolulu. *Lit.,* strong.

Nehu. Place and playground, ʻĀina-Haina, Honolulu. *Lit.,* anchovy.

Neka ʻAilana. Same as Necker Island (a new name). *Lit.,* Necker Island.

Nēnē. Street, Ka-lihi Waena, Honolulu, named for the Hawaiian goose. (TM.)

Nēnē-hānau-pō. Headland, Airport qd., north Molokaʻi. *Lit.,* goose born [at] night.

Nenue. Street, ʻĀina-Haina, Honolulu. (TM.) *Lit.,* pilotfish.

Neue. Bay at Wai-piʻo qd., Hawaiʻi.

Niʻau-pala. Fishpond, Hālawa qd., south Molokaʻi. *Lit.,* yellow coconut-leaf midrib.

Niepers. Lane, Ka-lihi Kai, Honolulu, named for Carl Niepers, a German missionary who married Susan Titcomb. He was the father of Bina Mossman and Dorothy Landgraf. (TM.)

Nihi-pali. Place, Wilhelmina Rise, Honolulu. *Lit.,* cliff edge *or* creeping [along the] cliff (as referring to rain).

Nihoa. Coastal land section, Kaunakakai qd., north Molokaʻi. (Summers 196.) Waterfront area in downtown Honolulu formerly owned by Ka-ʻahu-manu and named by her in honor of her visit to Nihoa Island (Ii 166). The island is the highest of the Northwestern (Leeward) Hawaiian Islands and the one nearest the main islands. It has a maximum elevation of 910 feet and an approximate area of 0.25 square miles. Discovered by Captain Douglas of the British ship *Iphigenia* on March 19, 1789, it was annexed to Hawaiʻi in 1898 and is now a part of the City and County of Honolulu. Kenneth P. Emory (1928) tells of 66 house sites on the island. Small stone images from there are in the Bishop Museum. The famous chant, "Ka Wai a Kāne," mentions the island (UL 257–259). (Bryan, 1942: 167–170; PH X–XII; RC 253.) See Mau-loku. *Lit.,* firmly set.

Niho-ʻoawa. Gulch, Hālawa qd., south Molokaʻi. *Lit.,* tooth gulch.

Niʻihau. Island in Kauaʻi County, 18 miles long, 6 miles wide, with an area of 73 square miles and a 1970 population of 237. Major village is Puʻuwai. Poetic: see PE, *kō, ʻulu.* (UL 212.)

Nikolo. Street, Diamond Head section, Honolulu. *Lit.,* Nicholas. (TM.)

Nimitz. Highway leading from downtown Honolulu to Pearl Harbor, named for Fleet Admiral Chester W. Nimitz (1885–1966), commander of the Pacific naval forces in World War II; elementary school, Pearl Harbor; beach park, Barber's Point, Oʻahu.

Niniko. Place, Dowsett Highlands, Honolulu, named for a cousin of Queen Pomare of Tahiti who was brought to Hawaiʻi in the 1830s to marry Prince Moses Ka-mehameha. The prince died before she arrived and she married John K. Sumner and lived at his estate in upper Nuʻu-anu until she died in 1898. (TM.) Niniko is Hawaiianized Tahitian.

Ninini. Point near Nā-wiliwili Harbor, Kauaʻi. *Lit.,* pour.

Ninini-wai. Plain west of Kuala-puʻu, Molokaʻi. *Lit.,* pour water. (Summers 37.)

Nīnole. Land section and village, Honomū qd.; land section, homesteads, village, cove, and gulch, Honu-ʻapo qd., Hawaiʻi. There are freshwater springs at the Nīnole in Honu-ʻapo; see Pū-hau. A cannibalistic *moʻo,* Kaikapū (hag), lived at the Honu-ʻapo Nīnole; her pretty granddaughter led travelers to her cave, where she ate them raw (HM 264). *Lit.,* bending.

Nioi. Place, Wilhelmina Rise, Honolulu, named for the red pepper plant or for a tree, *Eugenia molokaiana,* that when growing at Mauna-loa, Molokaʻi, was said to be poisonous. (TM.)

Niolopa. Place and old part of Nuʻu-anu Valley, Honolulu. (Sterling and Summers 6:189.)

N

Niolopua. Drive, upper Nuʻu-anu, Honolulu, named for Mrs. Rowena Niolopua Dowsett Turner. (TM.) *Lit.*, handsome, beautiful. Niolopua was a god of sleep.

Niu. Ridge and valley, Wai-mea district, Kauaʻi. Land division, Kau-pō, Maui. Subdivision of Honolulu, land division, valley, and intermediate school, Koko Head qd., Oʻahu. *Lit.*, coconut.

Niu-hele-wai. Old part of Honolulu, site of a battle in which Ka-hekili of Maui defeated Ka-hahana of Oʻahu; a stream here was choked with corpses (Alexander, 1891:123). (For. 4:575.) See Kolekole. *Lit.*, coconut going [in] water.

Niu Iki. Circle, Niu Valley, Honolulu. *Lit.*, little Niu.

Niu-kū-kahi. Ancient surfing area, Ka-hului qd., Maui. (Finney and Houston 28.) *Lit.*, coconut standing alone.

Niu-liʻi. Village, land division and stream, Kohala and Wai-piʻo qds., Hawaiʻi. Reservoir, Lualualei, Oʻahu. *Lit.*, small coconut.

Niu-malu. Small beach area just north of Huli-heʻe Palace, Kai-lua, Hawaiʻi (Ii 110, 118). Beach park and land division, Līhuʻe, Kauaʻi. Land sections, Kau-pō and Hāna qds., Maui. Before 1954 there was a hotel by this name near the site of the Hawaiian Village Hotel, Wai-kīkī, Honolulu. *Lit.*, shade [of] coconut trees.

Noble. Lane, Ka-pā-lama section, Honolulu, named for John Avery Noble, of English-Hawaiian ancestry, who was first a jockey for William Cornwell on Maui and later a salesman. His wife was Elizabeth Kapeka McCandless; they were parents of Johnny Noble, a musician and composer born in 1892. (TM.)

Noʻeau. Street, Wilhelmina Rise, Honolulu, named for an Inter-Island steamer. (TM.) *Lit.*, clever.

Noela. Street and place, Wai-kīkī, Honolulu. (TM.) *Lit.*, Noel.

Noe-lani. Elementary school, Mānoa, Honolulu. *Lit.*, heaven mist.

Nohili. Small area and point in Barking Sands beach, Kauaʻi. Street, Hawaiʻi-kai, Honolulu.

Noho-nani. Street, Wai-kīkī, Honolulu. *Lit.*, sit daintily (a poetic phrase in the famous name song for Liliʻu-o-ka-lani, "Liliʻu ʻē," and in a name song for Kīnaʻu; Elbert and Mahoe 45).

Nohona-o-Hae. Hill, Wai-kīʻī qd., Hawaiʻi. *Lit.*, dwelling of Hae.

Nohu. Street, ʻĀina-Haina, Honolulu, named for a fish with poisonous spines *or* a low, hairy plant.

Nōmilu. Cone and fishponds, Kō-loa, Kauaʻi, said to have been made by Pele and guarded by Puhi-ʻula (red eel) and Puhi-pakapaka (scaly eel), both supernatural eels. During volcanic activity on Hawaiʻi, sulphur is smelled in these ponds. Hawaiians gathering salt there placed salt offerings on leaves for Pele. Valley, southeast Niʻihau.

Nonopapa. Land section, west Niʻi-hau. Sheep were sheared in shacks here. *Lit.*, invalid.

Nono-ʻula. Crater west of Hanauma Bay, Oʻahu, said to be named for a mythical creature created by Pele. (PH 187.) *Lit.*, red sunburned.

North Beach. A 2-mile stretch of surfing and body-surfing areas east of Kāne-ʻohe Marine Corps Air Station, Oʻahu, once considered the best beaches in Hawaiʻi; known before World War II as Mō-kapu Beach.

North End. Winter north-swell and trade-wind surfing area, north Lā-naʻi, also known as Ka-ʻena.

Northwestern Hawaiian Islands. Islands extending northwestward from Nihoa to Midway and Kure, including Nihoa, Necker, Gardner Pinnacles, French Frigate Shoals, Laysan, Lisianski, Midway, and Kure. Until 1968 they were called the Leeward Islands. In 1909 all the islands except Midway and Kure were set aside as bird sanctuaries.

Notley. Street, Ka-lihi Waena, Honolulu, named for Charles K. Notley, son of Charles R. Notley, founder of Hāmākua Plantation, who surveyed the area. (TM.)

Nounou. Mountain (now known as Sleeping Giant), trail, and forest reserve, Ka-wai-hau district, Kauaʻi. The tyrant ʻAi-kanaka made his last stand on the mountain against the invader Ka-welo. Hula chant by Hiʻiaka (PH 109): *Ālai ʻia aʻela e Nounou, nalo Ka-ipu-haʻa i ka laulā mauka o Ka-paʻa,* Nounou is screened, The-low-calabash is lost in the wide expanse inland of Ka-paʻa. (For. Sel. 66.) See Kō-ʻula. *Lit.,* throwing.

Nū. Place, Lanakila section, Honolulu. *Lit.,* to roar, as wind.

Nuaʻailua. Stream and point, Ke-ʻanae qd., East Maui.

Nuʻa-lele. Land division, Hāna, Maui. *Lit.,* leaping heap.

Nuʻalolo. Valley, stream, land section, and trail, Nā-pali coast, northwest Kauaʻi, proposed as a State reserve area. The *iliau,* a relative of the silversword, grows here. Also called Nuʻulolo, Nuʻololo.

Nuʻalolo Kai. Beach and State park, Nā-pali coast, Kauaʻi. *Lit.,* seaward Nuʻalolo.

Nuku-ʻele. Point, Mākena qd., Maui. *Lit.,* black point.

Numana. Road, Ka-lihi Uka, Honolulu, named for Paul Newman, a lawyer who came from San Francisco to Hawaiʻi in 1884. He was made a noble by Ka-lā-kaua; later he was a member of Liliʻu-o-ka-lani's cabinet and defended her in her trial for treason. (TM.)

Number Threes. Surfing area out from the Hale-kū-lani Hotel, Honolulu.

Nunulu. Land division, Kohala qd., Hawaiʻi. *Lit.,* growl.

Nuʻololo. Same as Nuʻalolo, Nuʻulolo.

Nuʻu. Land section and landing, Lualaʻi-lua Hills qd., Maui. Land section, Ka-malō qd., Molokaʻi. *Lit.,* height.

Nuʻu-anu. Avenue, officially named in 1850 (TM), section 11 of Honolulu (map 6), valley, park, cemetery, stream, *pali* (cliff), elementary school, and State wayside park, Honolulu. In the famous battle of Nuʻu-anu in 1795, Ka-mehameha of Hawaiʻi drove the Oʻahu warriors up to the Pali; according to some accounts, three hundred survivors were driven over the cliff; others say the warriors jumped to their deaths rather than surrender. (Kuy. 1:47.) *Lit.,* cool height.

Nuʻulolo. Same as Nuʻalolo, Nuʻololo.

Nuʻu-pia. Fishpond, Mō-kapu qd., Oʻahu. *Lit.,* arrowroot heap.

OoOoOo

O

Oʻahu. Most populous of the Hawaiian Islands, 40 miles long, 26 miles wide, with an area of 608 square miles and a 1970 population of 768,561. Honolulu is the major city and State capital. See Appendix 6.8 for a refutation of a meaning often quoted, 'gathering place'. Epithets: *Oʻahu o Kākuhihewa,* Oʻahu of Kākuhihewa (an ancient chief); *Oʻahu a Lua,* Oʻahu [child] of Lua (Lua slept with Papa after Papa became angry about husband Wākea's infidelity; Lua gave birth to Oʻahu; HM 302).

Oʻahu Railway and Land Terminal. A former railway station on North King Street. The railway carried agricultural equipment, produce, and passengers (especially Navy personnel going to Pearl Harbor because there were no taxis). The station was abandoned in 1948 and is now State-owned and rented for offices and storage.

ʻOawa-kilikā. Gulch, Māʻalaea qd., Maui. *Lit.,* rain-washed gulch.

ʻŌhai. Lane, Pauoa, Honolulu, named for a native shrub.

ʻŌhai-kea. Land section between Mauna Kea and Hualālai, Hawaiʻi. (For. Sel. 190.) *Lit.,* light *ʻōhai* shrub.

ʻŌhai-ʻula. Beach, Ka-wai-hae, Hawaiʻi. Ridge, Wai-mea district, Kauaʻi. *Lit.,* red *ʻōhai* shrub.

Ohale. Cone (3,318 feet high), Kī-lau-ea qd., Hawaiʻi.

ʻOhe. Street, Kakaʻako, Honolulu. (TM.) *Lit.,* bamboo.

ʻOheʻo. Gulch, streams, pools, now called Seven (Sacred) Pools, Kī-pahulu qd., Maui. Menstruating women were not allowed to bathe here, hence it was considered taboo.

ʻŌhiʻa. Gulch, Haʻi-kū qd., Maui. Two holes in the gulch sides are said to have been made by the god Kāne who thrust in his spear to get water for himself and for Kanaloa (HM 65). Two land divisions and a gulch, Ka-malō qd., southeast Molokaʻi. Ancient surfing area, west Niʻihau (Finney and Houston 30). *Lit., ʻōhiʻa* tree.

ʻŌhiʻa-ʻai. Gulch, Puʻu-kapu and Lāʻie qds., Oʻahu. *Lit.,* mountain apple.

ʻŌhiʻa-lele. Area Hoʻō-pū-loa qd., Hawaiʻi. Ridge, Ka-malō qd., Molo-kaʻi. *Lit.,* leaping *ʻōhiʻa* tree (a vine suspended from an *ʻōhiʻa* tree was used as a swing).

ʻŌhiʻa-pilo. Land section, Kaunakakai qd., south Molokaʻi. *Lit.,* swampy *ʻōhiʻa* tree (a mangrove swamp is nearby).

ʻŌhiki. Land section, Kai-lua qd., Hawaiʻi. See Ka-iwi. *Lit.,* sand crab *or* to pry.

ʻŌhiki-lolo. Ridge, peak, land section, and beach sometimes called Barking Sands, Ka-ʻena qd., Oʻahu. (PH 157.) *Lit.,* prying out brains.

ʻŌhua. Avenue, Wai-kīkī, Honolulu. *Lit.,* retainer (Liliʻu-o-ka-lani's retainers lived here).

ʻŌ-ʻia-moi. Point, southeast Niʻihau. *Lit.,* pierced threadfish.

ʻŌʻili. Land area and loop, Wai-ʻalae, Honolulu. (TM.) *Lit.,* heart.

ʻŌʻili-puʻu. Cinder cone, Hale-a-ka-lā Crater, Maui. *Lit.,* hill appearing.

'Ō'io. Drive and old land section, 'Āina-Haina, Honolulu. Stream, Kahana and Lā'ie qds., O'ahu. See Ka-lae-o-ka-'ō'io. *Lit.,* bonefish.

'Ōkala. Islet (2.15 acres, 400 feet elevation) off Wai-kolu, Moloka'i. *Lit.,* bristling.

'Oki'oki-o-lepe. Fishpond, Pu'u-loa, O'ahu. Perhaps this should be 'Oki'oki-lepe. *Lit.,* cut strips.

Okoe. Bay, landing, village, and land section, Ho'ō-pū-loa qd., Hawai'i, named for a murderess. See Ho'ō-pū-loa.

*Okoli. Cone, 'Īlio Pt. qd., north Moloka'i. Coulter spelling is Okii.

'Ōkū. Point, north Ni'ihau. *Lit.,* to protrude.

'Oku'u. Hanauma Bay side of Sandy Beach, O'ahu. *Lit.,* crouch (people crouched by a healing stone).

Ola. Lane, Ka-lihi Waena, Honolulu. (TM.) *Lit.,* life.

'Ōla'a. Land divisions, Hilo, Humu'ula, Kī-lau-ea, and Puna qds.; flume, back road, plantation mill, and railroad, Hilo qd.; village, forest reserve, and forest park reserve Kī-lau-ea qd., Hawai'i; formerly called La'a. (Ii 83; UL 190.)

Ola-loa. Street, Foster Village subdivision, Hālawa, Wai-pahu qd., O'ahu. Name suggested by Mary Kawena Pukui in 1956. *Lit.,* long life, ever living.

'Ōlapa. Street, 'Āina-Haina, Honolulu, probably named for native trees. (TM.)

Old Man's. Surfing area opposite the Elks Club, Wai-kīkī.

Old School Hall. Oldest building on Puna-hou School campus, Honolulu, built in 1852. The stone was from Rocky Hill, coral from Kewalo Basin, timber from Mānoa, and the window glass and slate for the roof from New England.

'Ōlelo-moana. Land sections and homesteads, Hōnaunau qd., Hawai'i. *Lit.,* sea speaking. (Two fishermen at sea had broken their hooks, and one said: "There are two old men there on shore. Their bones will furnish material for new hooks." The men on land heard and crept away to the north to a place called Kolo [creep] and escaped.)

Olinda. Village, land area, reservoir, and prison camp at about the 4,000-foot level, Kilohana qd., Maui, said to have been the name of Samuel T. Alexander's home there, later sold to Harry Baldwin. Alexander is reported to have taken the name from a place in Spain. Gudde (1969) wrote that Olinda is a place in Shasta County, California, and that the name was brought there by Samuel T. Alexander from the Hawaiian Islands in the early 1860s. It is also the name of a Brazilian city, probably short for *O linda vista!* What a beautiful view! See Alexander.

'Ōlino. Street, Foster Village subdivision, Hālawa, Wai-pahu qd., O'ahu. Name suggested by Mary Kawena Pukui in 1956. *Lit.,* brilliant, shiny.

Oliver. Street, Bingham section, Honolulu, named for the Reverend Oliver P. Emerson (1845–1938), brother of Nathaniel B. and J.S. Emerson, and son of the missionary J.S. Emerson. He graduated from Puna-hou in 1865, went to Williams College, and was a minister on the mainland for 20 years. He returned to Hawai'i in 1888. (TM.)

olo-. 'Hill'.

'Olohana. Street, Wai-kīkī, Honolulu. *Lit.,* all hands. (This was the Ha-

waiian name of John Young, adviser and aide to· Ka-mehameha I;
as an English sailor and boatswain he had shouted this to his sailors.
See Young.)

Olohena. Land division and ridge, Ka-wai-hau district, Kaua'i. A
heiau for human sacrifices on the ridge was called Mahe-walu, short
for Māhele-walu, eight divisions. Olohena has no meaning, but may
be cognate with Olosenga, an island in the Manu'a group, Samoa.
Other sources say the *heiau* was named Kukui.

Olokele. Stream, canyon, and sugar plantation, Wai-mea district,
Kaua'i. Avenue, Ka-pahulu, Honolulu. *Lit.,* honeycreeper (another
name for the *'i'iwi*).

Olo-ku'i. Peak (4,602 feet high), Ka-malō qd., north Moloka'i, and fortress where Ka'ōhele, a member of the royal families of Moloka'i
and Maui, and famous as a fast runner and jumper, was caught by
the Oahuans (*Ka Elele Poakolu,* February 9, 1881). It became a
place of refuge during a battle between Maui and Moloka'i, when
the people of Pelekunu fled up this hill and threw stones, killing
their pursuers (*Ke Au Hou,* September 21, 1910). *Lit.,* tall hill.

Olo-mana. Peak (1,643 feet high), ridge, stream, school, and golf
course, Mō-kapu qd., O'ahu, named for a legendary giant who
jumped from Kaua'i to this peak. A sports field was nearby. The
nearby peaks are Ahiki (nearest Wai-mānalo) and Pāku'i (the central peak). See Mahi-nui. *Lit.,* forked hill.

Olonā. Lane, Lanakila section, Honolulu, named for a native shrub
from which cord was made. (TM.)

Olopua. Land section, Pā'ia qd., Maui. Street, Mānoa, Honolulu,
named for a native tree.

Olo-ua. Cave where fishermen found shelter, Puna, Hawai'i. *Lit.,*
sounding rain *or* rainy hill.

'Olo-'upena. Coastal area and falls, Ka-malō qd., north Moloka'i. *Lit.,*
hanging net.

Olowalu. Quadrangle, village, canyon, land division, shaft (well), ditch,
stream, and wharf, West Maui. More than a hundred Hawaiians
were treacherously killed here and many wounded on orders from
Captain Simon Metcalfe in 1790 (Kuy. 1:24). Many petroglyphs are
seen on a cliff face here (Cox and Stasack 11, 93). *Lit.,* many hills.

'Olu. Street, Ka-imu-ki, Honolulu. (TM.) *Lit.,* cool.

'Ōma'o. Valley, Wai-mea district, Kaua'i. Gulch, Pu'u-kapu qd., and
stream, Mō-kapu qd., O'ahu. *Lit.,* green.

*Ōma'o-pio. Land division, homesteads, and road, Mākena qd., Maui.
Perhaps *lit.,* whistling thrush.

Omoka'a. Land section, Ho'ō-pū-loa qd., Kona, Hawai'i, named for
the murderer who lived at Ho'ō-pū-loa.

'Onaha. Street, Kāhala, Honolulu. (TM.) *Lit.,* curve.

*Onau. Land section, Mākena, Maui.

One-ali'i. Beach park and homesteads, Ka-milo-loa, southeast Moloka'i.
Lit., royal sands.

One-awa. Land division and street, Kai-lua, O'ahu. *Lit.,* milkfish sand.
One-awa was famous for great quantities of *'ō'io,* and perhaps also
awa fish (Sterling and Summers 5:246). The ridge between Kai-lua
and Kāne-'ohe was named One-awa Hills in 1971.

One-'ele. Place, Makiki, Honolulu. (TM.) *Lit.,* black sand.

One-kahakaha. Beach and beach park near Hilo, Hawai'i. *Lit.,* drawing [pictures] sand.

One-loa. Bay, Honolua qd., Maui. *Lit.,* long sand.

One-o-Hilo. Gulch, 'Ilio Pt. qd., south Moloka'i. *Lit.,* sand of Hilo.

One-'ula. Beach park, 'Ewa qd., O'ahu. *Lit.,* red sand.

'Ōnini. Gulch, Kaunakakai qd., south Moloka'i. *Lit.,* breeze.

Onomea. Village, stream, and bay, Honomū qd., Hawai'i. A well-known sea arch here collapsed in 1958 (Macdonald and Abbott 199, 205).

*Ono-palani. Gulch, Airport qd., south Moloka'i.

Ono-uli. Land sections, Hōnaunau and Kai-lua qds., Kona, Hawai'i. *Lit.,* dark *ono* fish. (Another interpretation is Ō-no-Uli, rations for Uli; Uli was the grandmother of Kana, the stretching demigod, whom she reared, and his brother Nīheu; HM 464–477.)

Ōnū Iki. One of the Northwestern (Leeward) Hawaiian Islands beyond Nihoa. *Lit.,* small Ōnū (protuberance).

Ōnū Nui. One of the Northwestern (Leeward) Hawaiian Islands beyond Nihoa. *Lit.,* large Ōnū (protuberance).

'Ō'ō. Lane, Lanakila section, Honolulu. *Lit.,* black honeyeater (its yellow feathers were used for feather work).

O'o-hope. Fishpond, He'eia, O'ahu. *Lit.,* late maturity.

'Ō'ō-'ia. Fishpond, Airport qd., Moloka'i. *Lit.,* pierced.

'Ō'ō-kala. Village, Hāmākua qd., Hawai'i. *Lit.,* sharp digging stick.

'O'olā-maka-pehu. Gulch, Wai-pi'o qd., Hawai'i. *Lit.,* puffed-up hungry eyes.

'O'oma. Land sections and homesteads, Kai-lua and Ke-āhole qds., Kona, Hawai'i. *Lit.,* concave.

'Ō'ō-manō. Point, Wai-mea district, Kaua'i. *Lit.,* shark spear.

'Ōpae-ka'a. Falls and stream, Ka-wai-hau district, Kaua'i. *Lit.,* rolling shrimp.

'Ōpae-'ula. Pond a few miles north of Ke-āhole Point, Kona, Hawai'i, a wildlife sanctuary where ducks, coots, stilts, and other Hawaiian birds feed on the abundant shrimp. The pond was probably much larger before a large part of it was buried in lava; ancient fishpond stone walls are said to remain today. A *heiau* of this name on Moloka'i was destroyed in 1899 when a pier was built at Kaunakakai (Summers 84–85). Stream and reservoirs, Wai-a-lua, O'ahu (Ii 98). *Lit.,* red shrimp.

'Ōpae-wela. Valley, Wai-mea district, Kaua'i. *Lit.,* hot shrimp.

'Ōpana. Land section, Ka-wela, O'ahu. Perhaps related to *'ōpā,* squeeze.

'Opihi. Offshore rock near the north boundary of Ke-one-poko Nui, Maku'u qd., Puna, Hawai'i, sometimes called Moku-'opihi.

'Opihi-kao. Village, Kala-pana qd., Puna, Hawai'i. Formerly probably 'Opihi-kāō, *lit.,* crowd [gathering] limpets (because of robbers, people were afraid to gather *'opihi* alone).

'Opihi-nehe. Area, Pāhala qd., Ka'ū, Hawai'i. *Lit.,* rattling *'opihi* shells. (It was taboo to rattle *'opihi* shells here. If one did, a ghost was heard to ask, "Seaward or inland?" If the answer, from another ghost, was "seaward," the victim would be drowned; if "inland," he would have an accident on land.)

O

'Ōpua. Street, Foster Village subdivision, Hālawa, Wai-pahu qd., Oʻahu. Name suggested by Mary Kawena Pukui in 1956. *Lit.,* cloud bank.

Ōpū-nahā. Gulch, Māʻalaea qd., Maui. *Lit.,* broken cluster.

Orvis Auditorium. One of the music buildings, Mānoa campus, University of Hawaiʻi, Honolulu, completed in 1961, and named for Mae Zenke Orvis, the donor's wife.

O

Osorio. Place, Thomas Square section, Honolulu, named for Augusto Monteiro Osorio, born in Portugal, who came to Hawaiʻi in 1885. He established the firm of Osorio and Company in Hilo with three sons as partners. (TM.)

Oswald. Street, St. Louis Heights, Honolulu, named for Brother Oswald, an instructor at St. Louis College.

'Ouli. Land divisions and gulch, Pua-kō and Wai-piʻo qds., Kohala, Hawaiʻi, and name of a famous soldier of Ka-hekili's who was skilled with the sling. (For. Sel. 222, RC 87.) *Lit.,* omen.

Our Lady of Peace Cathedral. Built in 1843 and dedicated to Our Lady of Peace, it serves a large congregation as the cathedral of the Roman Catholic diocese of Honolulu; it faces on the Fort Street Mall, Honolulu.

Owaluhi. Gulch, Ka-haku-loa qd., West Maui.

Owāwa. Street, Ka-lihi Uka, Honolulu. (TM.) *Lit.,* gulch.

Owen. Street, Ka-lihi Kai, Honolulu, named for Clinton G. Owen, factory superintendent in the 1920s for the guano fertilizer works located there. (TM.)

'Owena. Street, Diamond Head, Honolulu, believed named for Owen Jones Holt, father of the mounted police officer Edward S. Holt, whose home was at Diamond Head. (TM.) *Lit.,* Owen.

PpPpPp

Pā'ā. Land section and cones, Kō-loa district, Kaua'i. *Lit.,* dry, rocky.

Pa'a-hana. Street, Ka-imu-kī, Honolulu, perhaps named for the lady at Mānana, 'Ewa, made famous in the long song, "Pa'a-hana" (Elbert and Mahoe 84). *Lit.,* hard working.

Pa'akea. Land section, gulch, and stream, Ke-'anae qd., Maui (also called Ka-pa'akea). Fishpond near Pearl Harbor, O'ahu. *Lit.,* coral bed, limestone.

Pa'a-la'a. Land section, Hale-'iwa qd., O'ahu. *Lit.,* sacred firmness.

Pa'ala'a Uka. Land division, Hale-'iwa qd., O'ahu. *Lit.,* inland Pa'ala'a.

Pa'alaea. Islet (0.16 acres, 40 feet elevation), Wai-pi'o qd., Hawai'i.

Pa'a-le'a. Street, Pālolo, Honolulu. *Lit.,* pleasure-loving.

Pā'ani. Street near lower University Avenue, Honolulu. *Lit.,* play, sport.

Pā-'au'au. Land areas, Honu-'apo, Mauna Loa, and Pāhala qds., Hawai'i. Formerly a pond and home, Pearl City peninsula, O'ahu, famous in song. *Lit.,* bath enclosure.

Pā-'auhau. Village, gulch, and land sections, Hāmākua, Mauna Kea, and Wai-ki'i qds., Hawai'i, and site of an indecisive battle between Ka-mehameha and Ke-ō-ua (RC 151). Site of a Maui battle (near Ka-lae-o-ka-'īlio) in which Ka-mehameha distinguished himself and saved the life of Ke-kū-hau-pi'o (RC 84). *Lit.,* tribute enclosure.

Pa'auilo. Village and elementary and high school, Hāmākua qd., Hawai'i.

Pa'a-wili. Land section, south Lā-na'i. *Lit.,* held twisting.

Pacheco. Playground, Pearl City, and street, Ka-lihi Waena, Honolulu, named for Manuel Caetano Pacheco (1874–1951), born in the Azores, a Democrat who for many years served as chairman of the Finance Committee of the Honolulu Board of Supervisors and was known as the "watchdog of the treasury"; he was a senator from 1919 to 1921 and then returned to the Board of Supervisors. He was foreman of the bookbinding department of the *Honolulu Star-Bulletin.* (*Honolulu Star-Bulletin,* June 8, 1951; TM.)

Pacific Heights. Road, heights, and section 14 of Honolulu (map 6); a carriage road was laid out in 1889; later there was a cable car. (TM.) See Kupa-nihi.

Pacific Palisades. Residential development, Wai-pahu qd., O'ahu, formerly called Mānana-uka.

Pae-ahu. Large land section in Honua-'ula, Mākena qd., Maui. *Lit.,* row [of] heaps.

Pae-māhū. One of four stones at the western end of Kū-hiō Beach Park, Wai-kīkī, Honolulu, believed to have been medical *kāhuna* from Tahiti that guarded this spot; formerly they were in the sea. Rocks at mouth of Wai-lua River, Kaua'i, believed to have been men turned to stone by Kapo. *Lit.,* homosexual row.

P

P

Paena-palaua. Gulch, Hālawa qd., Molokaʻi. Perhaps this name should be Paena-palaoa (whale landing).

Pāhala. Quadrangle and town, southwest Hawaiʻi. *Lit.*, cultivation by burning mulch.

Pā-hale. Stream, Honomū and Mauna Kea qds., Hawaiʻi. *Lit.*, house lot.

Pā-hālōna. Land section, Wai-kāne qd., Oʻahu. *Lit.*, peering wall.

Pā-hau. Point, southwest Niʻihau. Possibly *lit.*, *hau* enclosure.

Pāheʻeheʻe. Ridge and hill (652 feet elevation), Wai-ʻanae qd., Oʻahu. *Lit.*, slippery.

Paheʻe-o-Lono. Point, Molokini Islet. *Lit.*, Lono's slide.

Pā-hihi. Gulch, Kau-pō qd., Maui. *Lit.*, entangled enclosure.

Pāhili. Road, Puʻu-nui, Honolulu. (TM.) See Ka-pāhili. *Lit.*, to blow strongly.

*Pahiomu. Fishpond, Ka-malō qd., south Molokaʻi; also listed as Pahio-niu (Summers 98).

Pahipahi-ʻālua. Land section and gulch near Ka-wela, Oʻahu; there was a fishing shrine here.

Pāhoa. Village, elementary and high school, and junction, Kala-pana and Makuʻu qds., Hawaiʻi. Land section, Ke-ʻanae qd.; land section, Lahaina qd., Maui. Coastal area, Ka-malō qd., south Molokaʻi. Avenue, Ka-imu-kī, Honolulu, in some accounts named for a *moʻo* destroyed by Hiʻiaka; stream, Kaʻena qd.; land section, Wai-ʻanae qd., Oʻahu, where Kama-puaʻa was dragged by ʻOlopana's men; they desisted from butchering him with daggers *(pāhoa)* when Kama's friends said this would damage the body and make it a poor sacrifice. (For. Sel. 204.)

Pāhoehoe. Land section and stream, Honomū qd.; land sections, Kai-lua and Hōnaunau qds., Kona, Hawaiʻi. The Kona place was named for a chiefess, Pāhoehoe-wahine-iki-a-ka-lani (little woman [and] smooth lava of the chief). *Lit.*, smooth type of lava.

Pā-honu. Offshore pond (500 feet long, 50 feet wide), Wai-mānalo, Oʻahu, visible at low tide, said to be where captured turtles were kept for chiefs. (Sterling and Summers 5:340.) *Lit.*, turtle enclosure.

Pahu. Point. See Lae-o-ka-pahu.

*Pahualoo. Land section, Hālawa qd., Molokaʻi.

Pahu-kauila. Gulch, Ka-malō qd., south Molokaʻi. *Lit.*, *kauila* wood drum.

Pahu-kini. *Heiau* behind Ka-paʻa quarry, Kai-lua, Oʻahu; also called Moʻo-kini. (McAllister 182–183.) *Lit.*, many drums.

Pahu-kui. Street, Ka-lihi Waena, Honolulu.

Pahulu. Street, Ka-lihi Uka, Honolulu, probably named for the god of nightmares.

Pahu-o-Māui. Name of a *heiau* that stood at the site of the lighthouse below Diamond Head, Oʻahu. *Lit.*, Māui's drum.

Pāʻia. Quadrangle, village, bay, and school, East Maui. *Lit.*, noisy.

Pai-a-haʻa. Land division and ancient surfing area east of South Point, Kaʻū, Hawaiʻi. (UL 191.) *Lit.*, lift and sway [of waves].

Pāʻia-kuli. Reservoir (now abandoned), Wai-piʻo qd., Hawaiʻi. *Lit.*, deafeningly noisy.

Paia-loa. Fishpond (now filled in), Ka-malō qd., south Moloka'i. *Lit.,* long wall.

Pā-'ie'ie. Land near Pana-'ewa, Hilo, Hawai'i. *Lit.,* 'ie'ie vine enclosure. *Luhe i ka wai o Pā-'ie'ie,* drooping over the water of Pā-'ie'ie (comparing a drunk to drooping 'ie'ie vines).

Pā-i-ka-lani. Ancient taro patch, three acres in area, Honomuni Valley, southeast Moloka'i, said to have been set aside by Pi'i-lani, chief of Maui, and to have been used later by Ka-meha-meha I. A variant name is Pā-i-ka-hā-wai (reach the water flume). (Summers 142-144.) *Lit.,* reach the sky.

Paikō. Lagoon, peninsula, and drive, Kuli-'ou'ou, Honolulu, named for Pico, a part-Portuguese resident of the area.

Pai-lolo. Channel between Maui and Moloka'i, 8.5 miles wide; probably a contraction of *pai* (lift) and *oloolo* (shifting).

Pa'ina. Old name for Wilhelmina Rise, Honolulu. *Lit.,* crackle.

Pai-'olu'olu. Point, south side of Hanauma Bay, O'ahu. *Lit.,* lift gently.

Pākahi. Place, Wilhelmina Rise, Honolulu. (TM.) *Lit.,* first.

Pākaikai. Land section and wind name, Wai-a-lua, Moloka'i, where Ka-mehameha-nui (an older brother of Ka-hekili) was hidden as a child and raised on taro leaves. His bathing pool in a stream was known to older residents. Remnants of nearby taro terraces are said to be still visible. See Ka-hekili, Moa-nui, Welokā. (Summers 149.)

Pākākā. Old canoe landing, Honolulu Harbor *(Honolulu in 1810)*. Wharf built in 1827 at the same site. See Robinson. *Lit.,* to skim (as stones over water).

Pā-ka-lā. Village and point, Wai-mea district; points east of Kī-lau-ea, northeast Kaua'i; at one of these places was a *heiau* of the same name. See Infinities. *Lit.,* the sun shines.

Pakalalē. The 'Ewa side of Smith Street near Hotel Street, Honolulu, named for the British ship *Butterworth. Lit.,* Butterworth.

Pā-kanaka. Fishpond, Airport qd., south Moloka'i. (Summers 71-75.) *Lit.,* touched [by] commoners (it could be used by commoners).

Pā-kaua. Point, northwest Ni'ihau. *Lit.,* fortress.

Pākī. Avenue and playground alongside Ka-pi'o-lani Park; Ka-meha-meha Schools classroom built in 1960, Honolulu; all named for High Chief Abner Pākī, descendant of Maui kings.

Pākī-lehua. Valley, central Ni'ihau. *Lit.,* crush *lehua or* many experts.

Pā-kini. Land section, Ka Lae qd., Ka'ū, Hawai'i, once well populated. Street, Ālia-manu, Honolulu. (Ii 11.) *Lit.,* many enclosures.

Pā-kini Iki. Land sections, South Point, Hawai'i. *Lit.,* small Pā-kini.

Pā-kini Nui. Land sections near South Point, Hawai'i. Menehune built a *heiau* near here called Po'o-kanaka. A *heiau po'o kanaka* is one where human sacrifices were made; nevertheless, Pā-kini Nui was a *heiau ho'oulu 'ai* where offerings were made in the hope of increasing food production. *Lit.,* large Pā-kini.

Pākīpika. Pacific.

Pakohana. Street, Pacific Heights, Honolulu, named for an 'Ewa chiefess who was grandaunt of Lahilahi Webb. (TM.) *Lit.,* bare.

Pākolu. Place, Wilhelmina Rise, Honolulu. *Lit.,* threefold.

Pā-kua. Hill, Honu-'apo qd., Hawai'i. *Lit.,* back wall *or* enclosure.

Pāku'i. Peak (4,380 feet high), and *heiau* (Summers 119), Ka-malō qd., Moloka'i. Street, Pālolo, Honolulu; central peak of the three peaks of Mount Olo-mana, O'ahu, named for the keeper of the fishponds at Ka-'ele-pulu and Ka-wai-nui, a swift runner (Sterling and Summers 5:266–267). *Lit.,* attached.

P

Pākū-lena. Stream, Pūpū-kea, O'ahu. *Lit.,* yellow barrier.

Pala. Street, Lanakila section, Honolulu. *Lit.,* ripe.

Pā-lā'au. Three land divisions, Airport and Kaunakakai qds., north central and southwest Moloka'i; State park overlooking Ka-laupapa peninsula and containing the phallic stone Ka-ule-o-Nānāhoa. See Pu'u-lua. *Lit.,* wooden fence *or* enclosure.

Pala-hemo. A deep water hole inland from South Point, Ka'ū, Hawai'i, believed connected underground to the sea and haunted by a *mo'o* of the same name; in times of rain it was taboo to bathe there. Two sayings refer to Pala-hemo: *I 'ike 'oe iā Ka'ū a puni, a ike 'ole 'oe iā Pala-hemo, 'a'ole 'oe i 'ike iā Ka'ū,* if you have seen all Ka'ū, but have not seen Pala-hemo, you haven't seen Ka'ū. *E ho'i Ka'ū i Pala-hemo,* go back to Ka'ū and Pala-hemo (an insult, since Pala-hemo means 'loose dab of excreta', a name given because of markings on the walls of the hole suggesting excreta).

Pala-hinu. Rocky point, northwest Lā-na'i. *Lit.,* grease-daubed.

Pala'ie. Ancient surfing area, Lahaina qd., Maui. (Finney and Houston 28.) *Lit.,* inconstant.

Pālailai. Gulch, Barber's Pt. and Wai'anae qds., O'ahu. *Lit.,* the young *lai* fish.

Pala-lau. Coastal area, Mā'alaea qd., Maui. *Lit.,* yellow leaf.

*Palalupi. Cape, Hālawa qd., Moloka'i.

Pā-lama. Street and section 7 of Honolulu (map 6). *Lit., lama* wood enclosure. See Ka-pā-lama.

Pā-lama Fire Station. The brick firehouse at Pā-lama, Honolulu, built in 1901, is the oldest remaining public building constructed in Honolulu during Hawai'i's Territorial government period. It was declared outmoded as a firehouse, and the State has used it for offices since 1965.

Palamea. Lane, Pā-lama, Honolulu. *Lit.,* plump.

Palani. Avenue, Ala-wai section, Honolulu, named by Frank L. James, who developed the area in 1926 for his son, Francis Peter James. *Lit.,* Frank.

Palaoa. Point, southwest Lā-na'i. Place, Wai-kīkī, Honolulu. *Lit.,* whale (dead whales were sometimes washed ashore here; TM).

Palapala. Place, Ka-lihi Waena, Honolulu. *Lit.,* learning (the street is near the old Ka-mehameha School; TM).

Palapalai. Gulch, Kohala qd., Hawai'i. *Lit., palapalai* fern.

Palapū. Stream, Mō-kapu qd., O'ahu. *Lit.,* wound.

Palauea. Large land section, Mākena qd., Maui. Bishop Museum archaeologists have excavated here. *Lit.,* lazy.

Pālāwai. Land division and basin, south central Lā-na'i. Gulch, Wai-'anae qd., O'ahu.

Palea. Point, north side of Hanauma Bay, O'ahu. *Lit.,* brushed aside.

Pale-'a'ahu. Gulch, Mā'alaea qd., Maui. *Lit.,* clothing lining.

Pā-lehua. Inland area, central Kaua'i. Land division, hill (2,566 feet elevation), and road, Wai-'anae qd., O'ahu. *Lit., lehua* flower enclosure.

Pale-manō. Point near Ke'ei Village, Kona, Hawai'i. *Lit.,* shark defense. (Some say the pronunciation is Pale-mano, much defense, referring to the protection afforded by the point from the Ulu-mano wind.)

Palena. Street and place, Ka-lihi Waena, Honolulu. *Lit.,* border, boundary.

P

Pali. Famous precipice in the Ko'olau range (see Nu'u-anu), highway from Honolulu through tunnels of the same name to the Kai-lua area, and golf course at the foot of the cliff, O'ahu. *Lit.,* cliff.

Pali-a-Kāne. A cliff on Ka'ula Islet near the cave dwelling of Pele's shark brother, Kū-hai-moana. He was said to be 30 fathoms long and to be the husband of Ka-'ahu-pāhau. *Lit.,* cliff of Kāne.

Pali-'ele'ele. Cliff near Hale-le'a, Kaua'i. Nearby is Pali-kea. *Lit.,* black cliff.

Pali-ka-holo. Sea cliff, southwest Lā-na'i. *Lit.,* cliff [of] the landslide.

Pali-kapu-o-Kamohoali'i. A cliff at Kī-lau-ea, Hawai'i, allotted by Pele to her favorite brother Ka-moho-ali'i (the royal selected one). Regardless of wind direction, volcanic smoke is believed never to fly over this cliff. *Lit.,* sacred cliff of Ka-moho-ali'i.

Pali-kapu-o-Keōua. A cliff near Ke-ala-ke-kua, Hawai'i. *Lit.,* sacred cliff of Ke-ō-ua (Ka-mehameha's foe slain by Ke'eaumoku).

Pali-kea. Peak near Pali-'ele'ele, Hanalei district, Kaua'i. Stream, Hāna qd., Maui. Peak (3,098 feet high) above Lualualei in the Wai-'anae mountains, and another above Kai-lua in the Ko'olau range (near the Pali), O'ahu. *Lit.,* white cliff.

Pali-kilo. Place at Mō-kapu peninsula, O'ahu. *Lit.,* observation cliff.

Pali-koa'e. Coastal area, northeast Ni'ihau. See Lele-koa'e. *Lit.,* tropicbird cliff.

Pali-kolo. Bluffs, Mō-kapu peninsula, O'ahu, formerly a place of worship where prayers were said for fish and crops; at a lookout tower persons watched for fish and intruders. (Sterling and Summers 5:121.) *Lit.,* creeping cliff.

Pali-kū. Area and cabin, Hale-a-ka-lā Crater, Maui. The cliff that divides the Ko'olau Poko and Ko'olau Loa districts, O'ahu; also, the ancient name for the area on the Ko'olau Poko side now called Kua-loa. *Lit.,* vertical cliff.

Pali-lele-o-Kalihipa'a. Peak (3,268 feet elevation), Kī-lau-ea qd., Hawai'i. *Lit.,* leaping cliff of Ka-lihi-pa'a.

Pālima. Place, Ka-imu-kī, Honolulu, *Lit.,* fivefold.

Pali-malu. Drive, Dowsett Highlands, Honolulu. (TM.) *Lit.,* shady cliff.

Pali-o-Ka'eo. A cliff east of Ka-huku Ranch, Ka'ū, Hawai'i. *Lit.,* cliff of Ka'eo.

Pali-o-Pu'upā. Ridge on the south side of Hālawa Valley, Moloka'i. See Pu'u-pā.

Pali-o-Kūlani. Cliff near South Point, Hawai'i. *Lit.,* cliff of Kū-lani.

Pali-pilo. See Ma'ino.

P

Palisades. Elementary school, Pearl City, Oʻahu.

Pali-uli. A legendary paradise of plenty, usually thought to be in the Puna district, Hawaiʻi, the home of the sacred princess Lāʻie-i-ka-wai. Many Island places are named Pali-uli, including: a land section with a water cistern, Puna, Hawaiʻi; a cave near Hāna, Maui, where Ka-ʻahu-manu was born in 1768 (RC 309); a point, north central Niʻihau; a land section at Wai-kāne, and a *heiau* in lower Moana-lua, Oʻahu, now believed destroyed. Street, Ka-pahulu section, Honolulu (TM). *Lit.,* green cliff.

Pali-wai-ʻole. Same as Hā-niu-malu. *Lit.,* waterless cliff.

Pā-loa. Pond, Wai-a-lua, Oʻahu. *Lit.,* long enclosure.

Pālolo. Section 35 of Honolulu (map 6); homesteads, stream, valley, avenue, elementary school, and field, Honolulu. See Helu-moa, Kaʻau. *Lit.,* clay.

Paloma. Place, Wilhelmina Rise, Honolulu, named for the yacht *La Paloma* which was remodeled by Fred Smith and Robert W. Shingle in 1906 to enter the transpacific races. (TM.)

Pālua. Place, Wilhelmina Rise, Honolulu. *Lit.,* second.

Pā-moa. Site of St. Francis Convent, Mānoa, Honolulu; name of a street passing the convent. *Lit.,* chicken enclosure.

Pana-ʻewa. Land division, Hilo district, Hawaiʻi; legendary home of *moʻo* destroyed by Hiʻiaka. Poetic: *Pana-ʻewa nui, moku lehua* (PH 32), great Pana-ʻewa, *lehua* groves. (PH chapter 9.) Land division, Lahaina qd., Maui.

Pā-nāhāhā. Two fishponds, Ka-malō and Hālawa qds., south Moloka-ʻi. (Summers 95, 137.) Land section, Kāne-ʻohe, Oʻahu. *Lit.,* broken wall.

Pā-na-ka-uahi. Gulch and stream, Wai-pahu qd., Oʻahu. A talkative local god, Ke-akua-ʻōlelo (the speaking god), lived here. According to some accounts he betrayed secrets. In another story he saw a chiefess hide a *lei palaoa* (whale-tooth pendant) in a stone called Pōhaku-hūnā-palaoa (stone hiding whale-tooth pendant); he promised to tell only her descendants. *Lit.,* touched by the smoke.

Pānau. Land section, Puna qd., Hawaiʻi, said to be the home of ʻOpelukahi, a robber in the time of Ka-mehameha I who knew the art of *lua.* He robbed and murdered a Kohala man whose brother then swore revenge. The brother oiled his body and at Ke-ala-komo fought and killed ʻOpelukahi. (*Honolulu Star-Bulletin,* September 26, 1970.) A shark god born of humans here was Ka-ʻehu-iki-manō-o-Puʻuloa (the little shark red-head of Pearl Harbor), who was fed kava mixed with mother's milk. His cave is said to be here. *Lit.,* uneasy.

Pānau Iki. Land section, Puna qd., Hawaiʻi. *Lit.,* small Pānau.

Pānau Nui. Land section, Puna qd., Hawaiʻi. *Lit.,* large Pānau.

Pani-au. Place in south Kohala, Pua-kō qd., Hawaiʻi. *Lit.,* enclosed [by] current.

Pā-nīʻau. Peak (1,281 feet high), northeast Niʻihau. *Lit.,* touch mid-rib.

Pānini. Loop, Diamond Head section, Honolulu. *Lit.,* cactus.

Paniolo. Place, ʻĀina-Haina, Honolulu. *Lit.,* cowboy (from Spanish *español*).

Pā-nui. Street, Lanakila section, Honolulu, named for Kimokeo Pā-nui, a diver in the 1900s for Lyle's Marine Railway. (TM.) *Lit.,* large enclosure *or* wall.

Paoa-ka-lani. Street, Wai-kīkī, Honolulu, named for one of Queen Liliʻu-o-ka-laniʻs homes. The friend of Lohiʻau on Kauaʻi was named Paoa (PH 153). *Lit.,* the royal perfume. (For a song, see Elbert and Mahoe 72, 73.)

Pao-maʻi. Land section, north Lā-naʻi. *Lit.,* sick Pao. (Pao was a district overseer who exhausted himself running and swimming to Lahaina, Maui; Emory, 1969:20.)

Paopao. Point, north Lā-naʻi. *Lit.,* scooping.

Pā-o-Pelekane. Site of St. Andrew's Cathedral and Priory, once the site of the home of Ka-mehameha III, known as Ka-hale-uluhe (the fern house); when the land was given to the Church of England the name was changed. *Lit.,* enclosure of Britain.

Pāpā. Village, bay, and land sections, Hoʻō-pū-loa qd., Hawaiʻi. *Heiau,* Hālawa qd., north Molokaʻi (Summers 169). *Lit.,* forbidden.

Pā-paʻa. Bay and stream, Ka-wai-hau district, Kauaʻi. Fishpond, Kāne-ʻohe, Oʻahu. *Lit.,* secure enclosure.

Pāpaʻa-ʻea. Land section and stream, Haʻi-kū qd., Maui. Kiha-a-Piʻilani made a long paved road beginning here. *Lit.,* turtle-shell piece.

Papaʻa-koko. Land section on the Kahana side of Lāʻie, Oʻahu, the one-time site of a place of refuge. *Lit.,* secured blood.

Pāpaʻa-lā. *Pali,* Ka-malō qd., Molokaʻi. *Lit.,* sunburn.

Pāpaʻa-loa. Village near Lau-pāhoehoe, Hawaiʻi. *Lit.,* much burned.

Papa-hawahawa. Gulch near Hāna, Maui. See Wai-o-honu. *Lit.,* dirty flat.

Pāpaʻi. Land section, Makuʻu qd., Hawaiʻi, where Ka-mehameha I was struck on the head with a paddle while his foot was caught in a crevice (see PE, *māmala hoe); now* called King's Landing. (RC 125.) *Lit.,* crab.

Papa-iki. Land section, Ka-malō qd., Molokaʻi. *Lit.,* small flats.

Pāpaʻi-kou. Town, landing, and ancient surfing area (Finney and Houston 26), Honomū qd.; land sections, Honomū, Mauna Kea, and Honu-ʻapo qds., Hawaiʻi. The meaning of the Honu-ʻapo name is hut [in a] *kou* [grove] (a chief had a shelter here).

Papa-kāhulihuli. A stone in the Wai-luku River, Hilo, that tipped when stepped upon, dropping the stepper into a pit (Ka-lua-kanaka, the human pit) where he died unless he found the opening that led underground to Moku-ola (Coconut Island). *Lit.,* swaying rock.

Papaka Iki. Coastal area and gulch, northeast Ka-hoʻolawe. *Lit.,* small Papaka.

Papaka Nui. Coastal area and gulch, northeast Ka-hoʻolawe. *Lit.,* large Papaka.

Papa-kōlea. Beach 3 miles northeast of Ka Lae, Hawaiʻi, famous for its sand consisting predominantly of green olivine crystals.

P

Pāpala

(Macdonald and Abbott 201.) Playground and homesteads, Pauoa, Honolulu; formerly Ka-papa-kōlea. *Lit.,* plover flats.

Pāpala. Land section, valley, stream, and falls, Hālawa qd., north Molokaʻi. Street, Mānoa, Honolulu, named for a tree belonging to the amaranth family. (TM.)

Pāpala-hoʻomau. Congregational church at Kī-pahulu, Maui, said to be named for a fishhook of the hero, Hema, that was made of *mākālei* wood, which was believed to attract fish. *Lit.,* sticky pāpala tree.

Pāpala-ua. Coastal area and gulch, Māʻalaea qd., Maui. Valley and falls, Hālawa qd., Molokaʻi; a variant name is Pāpala. Because of the lack of sunshine here there was the saying *Pupuhi kukui o Pāpala-ua, he ʻino,* light the lights of Pāpala-ua, the weather is bad (said of any gloomy place where lights were lit in the daytime). (Summers 172–173.) *Lit.,* rain fog.

Papale-hau. Coastal area, Pāhala qd., Kaʻū, Hawaiʻi. *Lit.,* shield [from] cool breeze.

Papalekoki. Hill, Mauna Kea qd., Hawaiʻi.

Papa-lele. Land section and gulch, Hāmākua and Mauna Kea qds., Hawaiʻi. *Lit.,* leaping flats.

Papa-loa. Islet (0.4 acres, 40 feet elevation), Hāna qd., Maui. Coastal land section, Hālawa qd., Molokaʻi. *Lit.,* long flat.

Papamū-a-Kāne. A rock islet east of Ka-ʻuiki, Maui, perhaps the same as well-known ʻĀ-lau or Papa-loa. *Lit.,* Kāne's *kōnane* board.

Papa-nahoa. Gulch, Ka-haku-loa qd., Maui. *Lit.,* defiant flats.

Papanalahoa. Point, Ka-haku-loa qd., Maui.

Papa-nui. Deep-water summer surfing area about a mile seaward of Kū-hiō Beach, Wai-kīkī, Honolulu, named in 1930 by Duke Ka-hana-moku to honor the big boards that were ridden there (Finney, 1959*a*:108, 109). *Lit.,* big board.

Papa-nui-o-Kāne. Islet (3.13 acres, 40 feet elevation), Haʻi-kū qd., Maui. *Lit.,* great flat of Kāne.

Papa-o-haku. Beach, gulch, and roadstead, west Molokaʻi coast. *Lit.,* flats of [the] lord.

Papa-oneone. Beach, Mākaha, Oʻahu. Also known as Crescent Beach. *Lit.,* sandy shelf *or* reef.

Pāpapa-iki. Coastal area, Ka-malō qd., north Molokaʻi. *Lit.,* small flats.

Papa-ʻula. Point, Pāʻia qd., Maui. *Lit.,* red flats.

Papa-ulu-ana. Land section near Kī-pahulu, East Maui. Burial caves here are said to contain the bones of Wahie-loa (long fuel), a son of the hero Ka-haʻi, who lived here, but who after the birth of a son, Laka, went to Puna-luʻu, Kaʻū, Hawaiʻi, to obtain a birth gift. Here he was sacrificed. Laka later retrieved his bones. (HM 258.)

Papa-wai. Point and hill (381 feet high), Māʻalaea qd., Maui. (For. Sel. 274.) *Lit.,* water stratum.

Pāpio. Gulch, Hālawa qd., Molokaʻi, named for the young stage of *ulua* (crevally) fish.

Pā-pōhaku. Park, Wai-luku, Maui. Gulch and a 2-mile beach on the western shore of Molokaʻi. *Lit.,* stone fence.

Pāpū. Circle, Kāhala, Honolulu. *Lit.,* fort.

Pā-pua. Gulch, Honolua qd., Maui. *Lit.,* flower enclosure *or* baby fish enclosure.

Parker. Place, Mānoa, Honolulu, named for the Reverend Henry H. Parker (1834–1927), son of a missionary and pastor of Ka-wai-a-Haʻo Church for 54 years. He was coauthor of the Andrews and Parker Hawaiian Dictionary. Elementary school, Kāne-ʻohe, Oʻahu, named for the Reverend Benjamin W. Parker (1803–1877) of the sixth missionary company, father of Henry H. Parker; he opened the first school in Windward Oʻahu in 1837.

Parker Ranch. A 185,610-acre cattle ranch in northern Hawaiʻi started by John Palmer Parker in 1837.

Paty. Drive, upper Mānoa, named for two brothers, R. William Paty and Captain John Paty, who settled in Hawaiʻi in 1840 and who lived in the area. (TM.)

Pau. Street near the McCully bridge, Wai-kīkī, Honolulu, named by Bruce Cartwright who subdivided the area. (TM.) *Lit.,* finished (canoe races on the Ala Wai Canal finished here).

Pau-ahi. Land section and gulch, Wai-piʻo qd.; land section, Kai-lua qd.; pit crater, Puna qd., Hawaiʻi. Street, downtown Honolulu, named in memory of the great fire of 1886 and of the aunt of Bernice Pau-ahi Bishop (and mother of Princess Ruth) who had been named Pau-ahi because as a child she was saved from a fire. Building, Puna-hou campus, Honolulu, donated by Charles Bishop in memory of his wife, and built in 1894. The administration building at the Ka-mehameha Schools, built in 1964, was named for Princess Bernice Pau-ahi, the benefactress of the schools. The Bishop Museum entomology building, built in 1964, is named Pau-ahi Hall. *Lit.,* destroyed [by] fire.

*Paualaia. Point, Airport qd., north coast of Molokaʻi.

Pau-ʻeono. Point, Ka-malō qd., north Molokaʻi. On a 1922 quadrangle map the name was spelled Pauaono. *Lit.,* six destroyed.

Pā-uʻi. Place, ʻĀlewa Heights, Honolulu. (TM.) *Lit.,* enclosure [of] beauties.

Pau-ka-uila. Land section, Hale-ʻiwa, Oʻahu. *Lit.,* the lightning ceases.

Paukū-kalo. Homesteads, coastal area, and surfing area, Ka-hului, Maui. See Pihana. *Lit.,* taro piece.

Paukū-pahu. Land division near Hilo, Hawaiʻi. *Lit.,* section cut off short.

Pā-ʻula. Small beach east of the mouth of the Wai-luku River, Hilo, Hawaiʻi; Queen Liliʻu-o-ka-lani planted seaweed here; a surfing area here has the same name. *Lit.,* red enclosure. Beach west of Ka-haoa, Kaʻū, Hawaiʻi, named for a beautiful woman who played *kimo* (jacks) with Koaʻe, one of Pele's lovers; Pele turned the two of them to stone from the waist down; from the waist up their bodies were reduced to ashes. There was a large cave with a pool here, and a canoe landing called Pā-ʻula Kai. *Lit.,* red enclosure. Drive, Wilhelmina Rise, Honolulu.

Pau-malū. Land section, Girl Scout camp, satellite communication station, and surfing beach now known as Sunset Beach, Ka-huku qd., gulch and stream, Puʻu-kapu and Ka-huku qds., Oʻahu. *Lit.,* taken secretly (a shark bit off the legs of a woman who caught more squid than was permitted; Sterling and Summers 4:18).

Pau-nau. Land division, Lahaina qd., Maui. *Lit.,* completely chewed up.

Pauoa. Land section and bay, Pua-kō qd., Hawai'i. Valley, elementary school, flats, and section 19 of Honolulu (map 6).

Pā-ū-o-Nu'akea. Islet (0.72 acres, 50 feet elevation), Ka-malō qd., north Moloka'i, probably named for the daughter of Nu'akea and Ke-olo-'ewa, a Hā'upu chief. The daughter became an *'aumakua* (personal god), and Nu'akea became goddess of lactation. An alternate name is Pā'ū-a-Nu'akea. See Ke-olo-'ewa. *Lit.,* sarong of Nu'akea.

Pa'upa'u. Ditch and hill (2,561 feet high) near Lahaina Luna, Maui, now called Mount Ball, where David Malo is buried. (For a saying, see Appendix 8.1.) *Lit.,* drudgery (servants were weary of bringing water to bathe the chief's child).

Pau-walu. Land division, Hawai'i. Point, Ke-'anae qd., Maui. Village and harbor, Hālawa qd., Moloka'i. *Lit.,* eight destroyed. (A shark-man on Moloka'i killed seven children in a family. The eighth child was sent out as bait, and the shark was caught and killed; Summers 145.)

Pa'u-wela. Town, lighthouse, and point, Ha'i-kū qd., Maui. *Lit.,* hot soot.

Pā-wa'a. Section 24 of Honolulu (map 6); the Cinerama Theater here was formerly called Pā-wa'a. *Lit.,* canoe enclosure. (It is said that canoes were brought here from the sea by canal. But also see Kaha-loa.)

Pā-wale. Place, Mānoa, Honolulu. *Lit.,* easy to touch (TM) *or* a plant name.

Pāweo. Peaks, Ho'ānuanu, Wai-mea district, Kaua'i. *Lit.,* turn aside.

Pe'ahi-nā-i'a. Hill above Puna-lu'u, O'ahu. *Lit.,* beckon [to] the fish.

Pearl. City, peninsula, schools, park, playground, and recreation center, Wai-pahu qd., O'ahu. See Pu'u-loa.

Pearl and Hermes Atoll. Atoll about 1,050 miles northwest of Honolulu, with an elevation of 10 feet and approximate area of 0.47 square miles. It was discovered by the crews of two English whalers, the *Pearl* and the *Hermes,* both of which went aground on the reef on April 26, 1822. It was acquired by the United States in 1898 and is now a part of the City and County of Honolulu. (Bryan, 1942: 195–198.)

Pearl Harbor. The important U.S. Navy base on O'ahu attacked by the Japanese on December 7, 1941; named for pearl oysters formerly found there. A pond called Loko-a-Mano was filled in to build the Navy yard. The Hawaiian name is Pu'u-loa (long hill).

Pearl Harbor Kai. Elementary school near Pearl Harbor, O'ahu. *Lit.,* seaward Pearl Harbor.

Pearl River. See 'Ewa.

Pehu. Street, Pālolo, Honolulu. *Lit.,* swollen.

*Pekeo. Rainfall station east of Kuala-pu'u town, central Moloka'i.

Pekue. Ancient surfing area, Mokule'ia, Hale-'iwa qd., O'ahu (Finney and Houston 28).

Pele. Lane and street, Punchbowl, Honolulu, named for the legendary volcano deity, Pele, who searched for a home at Punchbowl on her way from the Northwest (Leeward) Islands to Hawai'i Island (PH xii).

Pelekane. Drive, upper Nu'u-anu, Honolulu, named for Captain James Isaac Dowsett, British officer of the Royal Navy who was called Pelekane (British) by the Hawaiians. (TM.) Stream, Kai-lua, O'ahu.

Pelekikena Hale. Home of the president of the Ka-mehameha Schools, built in 1939. *Lit.,* president's house.

Pelekunu. Valley, bay, stream, gulch, and land division, Ka-malō qd., north Moloka'i. (Summers 178-185.) *Lit.,* smelly (for lack of sunshine).

Pele-li'ili'i. Gulch, Kī-lau-ea qd., Hawai'i. *Lit.,* small lava flow.

Pele-'ula. Lane and old section of downtown Honolulu, named for a chiefess seer who lived here and who vainly tried to steal Lohi'au from Hi'iaka in a *kilu* game (PH xii, 169, chapter 31); many healing *heiau* were here (Ii 46). *Lit.,* red Pele.

Penguin Bank. Submarine platform west of Moloka'i. (Stearns and Macdonald, 1947:14.)

Pensacola. Street, Makiki, Honolulu, laid out in 1874 and named for the battleship that often visited Hawai'i in the 1860s and 1870s and carried King Luna-lilo to Hilo in 1873.

Pepe'ekeo. Village, point, and stream, Honomū qd., Hawai'i, formerly called Pepe'e-ke-ō (the food crushed, as by warriors in battle). A stream and rock here are named for Kama-pua'a, who tried unsuccessfully to drown Hina, mother of Māui, here. See Ka-'uku.

Pepeiao-lepo. Land division and bay, Hāna, Maui. *Lit.,* dirty ear (while diving, Kama-pua'a got mud in his ear).

Pēpē-'ōpae. Peak, Ka-malō qd., Moloka'i. *Lit.,* shrimp crushed.

Perry. Street, Ka-lihi Uka, Honolulu, named for Antone Perry, superintendent of the top department, Schuman Carriage Company, in the horse and buggy days; his residence was here. (TM.) Building at Nu'u-anu and Hotel streets built in 1889 by the widow of Jason Perry, Portuguese consul; it now houses offices.

Peter. Street, St. Louis Heights, Honolulu, named for St. Peter. (TM.)

Peter Buck. Street near the Bishop Museum, Honolulu, named for the museum's director from 1936 until his death in 1951; he was a Maori-Irish native of New Zealand who came to Hawai'i in 1927 and was world famous for Pacific anthropological studies, especially those concerned with material culture.

Peter Lee. Road, Kī-lau-ea qd., Hawai'i, named for the manager of Volcano House who built the first road from Pāhala to the Volcano House in 1891 (Olson 46).

Peterson. Lane, Ka-pā-lama section, Honolulu, named for I. D. Peterson, postmaster under Ka-lā-kaua and founder of the part-Hawaiian family of prominent musicians. (TM.)

Petrie. Playground, Ka-imu-kī, Honolulu, named for Lester Petrie, mayor of Honolulu 1941-1947.

Phallic Stone. See Ka-ule-o-Nānāhoa.

Pia. Gulch, Ka-malō qd., south Moloka'i. Street and place, Niu, Honolulu; valley, Koko Head qd., O'ahu. (TM.) *Lit.,* arrowroot, starch.

Pīhā. Land section, Mauna Kea qd., Hawai'i. *Lit.*, flotsam.

Pihana. Road and *heiau*, Wai-luku qd., Maui. According to HM 333, this *heiau* was built by Menehune in a single night from stones brought from Paukū-kalo beach; others say it was built by Chief Kahekili. A variant name is Hale-ki'i (image house). The Maui chief, Ke-kau-like, was brought here to die in 1736 (RC 69–70). *Lit.*, fullness.

Piha-pono. Cinder cone (5,200 feet high), Hualālai, Hawai'i. *Lit.*, completely full.

Pihea. Peak (4,150 feet high) and trail, Nā-pali coast, Kaua'i.

Pi'i-holo. Mountain (2,260 feet high), road, and Girl Scout camp, Ha'i-kū qd., Maui. *Lit.*, climb run.

Pi'i-honua. Land sections, Hilo, Honomū, Humu'ula, and Mauna Kea qds.; village, upland area, and ancient surfing place (Finney and Houston 26), Hilo qd., Hawai'i. *Lit.*, land incline.

Pi'i-kea. Gulch, Puna, Hawai'i. (For. Sel. 278.) One of 'Umi-a-Līloa's wives, a chiefess of Maui, had this name. Street and place, Foster Village subdivision, Hālawa, Wai-pahu qd., Honolulu. Name suggested by Mary Kawena Pukui in 1958. *Lit.*, to become light (as the day).

Pi'ikoi. Honolulu street running through the Makiki area probably named for David Ka-hale-pouli Pi'ikoi, father of David Ka-wānana-koa and Kū-hiō Ka-lani-ana-'ole. David Pi'ikoi's father, Jonah Pi'i-koi, owned a large section of the Ke-walo area and built the first two-story wooden house in that area near the present McKinley High School. (TM.) *Lit.*, lofty aspirations.

Pi'i-lani. Ditch, Lahaina qd., Maui. See Hono-a-Pi'ilani.

Pi'i-lani-hale. Ancient *heiau* near Hāna, Maui; probably the largest *heiau* in the State. *Lit.*, house [of] Pi'i-lani (a famous Maui chief).

Pīkake. Place, Nu'u-anu, Honolulu, named for the jasmine flower.

Pīkoi-lele. Old name for Villa Franca subdivision, Hilo, Hawai'i. *Lit.*, flying tripping-club.

Pila'a. Beach, Hanalei district, Kaua'i.

Pilau. Hill (2,158 feet elevation), Puna qd., Hawai'i. *Lit.*, stench.

Pilgrim. Chapel, Central Union Church, Honolulu, built in 1940 to commemorate the union with Pilgrim Church, which was formerly the First Protestant Portuguese Church, established in 1887 by Benjamin F. Dillingham and members of Central Union Church, and renamed Pilgrim Church in 1928 by the Reverend T. M. Talmadge. On April 2, 1971 after a fire at Queen's Hotel on Punchbowl Street, the cornerstone of the First Protestant Portuguese Church was found. In a box were copies of Portuguese and English newspapers, as well as the 1896 list of church members. (*Honolulu Advertiser,* April 2, 1971.)

Pili. Place, Wilhelmina Rise, Honolulu, probably named for *pili* grass used for thatching. (TM.)

Pili-a-mo'o. An area in Mō-'ili'ili, Honolulu. *Lit.*, cling, as a lizard.

Pili-kai. Street, 'Āina-Haina, Honolulu, named for a medicinal plant. (TM.)

Pili-lā'au. Playground, Wai-'anae, O'ahu, named for Herbert K. Pili-lā'au of Wai-'anae, Congressional Medal of Honor winner who was killed in Korea. (*Honolulu Advertiser*, July 4, 1952.) *Lit.*, close to wood *or* wooden shingle.

Pili-lani. Place, Makiki, Honolulu. (TM.) *Lit.*, close [to] heaven.

Pili-lua-nu'u. Hill, Kua-loa, O'ahu. *Lit.*, two heights joining.

Pili-o-Kahe. Land section, Wai-'anae qd., O'ahu. See 'Ewa. *Lit.*, clinging to Kahe.

Pili-o-koe. Gulch, Wai-'anae qd., O'ahu.

*Pilipili-lau. Stream, Ka-malō qd., Moloka'i.

Pili-wai. Area east of Ka-lua-a-puhi pond, Kaunakakai qd., south Moloka'i, where it is said Pe'e-lua, the ancestor of caterpillars, was chased for taking someone else's wife. He was caught in a deep sleep, set on fire, and kicked. Bits of him were scattered, and caterpillars became common. See Pu'u-ka-pe'elua and Pu'u-'enuhe. Street, Ka-lihi Uka, Honolulu. *Lit.*, close [to] water.

Pili-wale. Place near Nā-'iwa, Moloka'i. *Lit.*, cling needlessly.

Pilomena. Father Damien's Catholic church at Kala-wao, Moloka'i. *Lit.*, Philomena.

Pinao. Bay on the Ka'ū side of South Point, Hawai'i. Bishop Museum archaeologists excavated here in 1965. *Lit.*, dragonfly.

Pi'o. Place, Ka-lihi Waena, Honolulu. (TM.) *Lit.*, arch.

Pipeline. Same as Banzai Pipeline. A nearby surfing area is called Baby Pipeline.

Piper's Pali. Street, Puna-hou campus, Honolulu, named for Leo F. Piper, maintenance engineer for Puna-hou School. (TM.)

Pipi'o. Fishpond, Hālawa qd., south Moloka'i. *Lit.*, arched.

Pīpī-wai. Gulch, Hālawa qd., north Moloka'i. *Lit.*, sprinkling water.

Pō'ala. Elevation, Hālawa qd., Moloka'i. *Lit.*, to roll up.

Poamoho. Stream, trail, and camp, Wahi-a-wā, O'ahu.

Pō-'ele'ele. Stream, Kō-loa district, Kaua'i. *Lit.*, black night.

*Po'elua. Gulch and bay, Ka-haku-loa qd., Maui. Street near Mānoa School, Honolulu. (Pronunciation and meaning not certain: *po'e-lua* means '*lua*-fighting people', and *pō-'elua* means 'two nights').

Poepoe. Place, Ka-lihi Kai, Honolulu, named for Joseph M. Poepoe, editor of the Hawaiian language newspaper, *Ka Nupepa Kuokoa*, in the 1890s. He was a lawyer and member of the Legislature. (TM.)

Pohā. Lane, Bingham section, Honolulu. *Lit.*, cape gooseberry.

Pōhai-nani. Retirement home, Kāne-'ohe qd., O'ahu, named by Mary Kawena Pukui. *Lit.*, beauty surrounded.

Pōhākau-noho. Ridge, Ka-malō qd., Moloka'i. *Lit.*, resting seat.

Pōhā-kea. Homestead section, Ka'ū, and land section near South Point; homesteads, Hāmākua qd., Hawai'i. Peak, Hanalei district, Kaua'i. Gulch, Wai-luku qd.; hill (1,205 feet elevation), Mākena qd., Maui. Mountain and pass (2,200 feet elevation), Wai-'anae mountains, O'ahu; from here Hi'iaka saw by cloud omens that her *lehua* groves on Hawai'i had been burned by Pele, and that her friend Hōpoe had been turned to stone (PH 162-163); this is where Ka-uhi brutally murdered his wife, Ka-hala-o-Puna, because he thought she had been defiled (For. 5:188-193); see also 'Ai-hua-lama. Land section and rock off Kua-loa; elementary school, 'Ewa Beach, O'ahu. *Lit.*, white stone (*pohā* is short for *pōhaku*).

Pōhā-ki'iki'i. Land area, Ka-wai-hau district, Kaua'i. *Lit.*, tilted stone.

Pōhaku

Pōhaku. Street and place, 'Ālewa Heights, Honolulu. *Lit.*, rock.

Pōhaku-ao. Land section and former shrine, Nā-pali, Kaua'i. *Lit.*, day stone.

Pōhaku-eaea. Point, Mākena qd., Maui. (For. Sel. 20.) *Lit.*, stone [with] smell.

Pōhaku-Hanalei. Rock on one rim of Green Lake (Wai-a-Pele), Ma-ku'u qd., Hawai'i, named for Hanalei, a woman married to Lēkia, a rock on the opposite rim of the lake. A supernatural man, Ka-lei-kini, known for his destruction of other supernaturals, attempted to dislodge Lēkia. After he left, Hanalei chanted: *Lēkia ē, ē Lēkia ē, 'onia i pa'a,* Lēkia, o Lēkia, move and get firm. Ka-lei-kini was unable to dislodge him. In some accounts, Hanalei was a twin sister of Lēkia.

Pōhaku-honu. Stream, Hanalei district, Kaua'i. Gulch, Hālawa qd., Moloka'i. *Lit.*, turtle stone.

Pōhaku-ho'ohānau. Sacred stones near Holoholo-kū *heiau,* Wai-lua River, Kaua'i, where women of royalty came to give birth. *Lit.*, giving-birth stone.

Pōhaku-Kā'anapali. A large but not high rock (*pōhaku*) near the sea at the border of Māhinahina and Kahana, Honolua qd., Maui. A local boy knew how to climb up the concave side of this rock without using his hands. He and a Moloka'i boy, who bragged about Moloka'i mountains, wagered their lives on a climbing competition. The Mauian was able to climb Kōkī-o-Wailau, Moloka'i, but the Molo-ka'i boy could not climb Pōhaku-Kā'anapali. The Mauian did not claim his antagonist's life, however, and they became friends. Formerly called Kā'anapali-pōhaku; now called also Pōhaku-o-Kā'ana-pali.

Pōhaku-kū-lua. Two submerged stones in 'Anae-ho'omalu Bay, Kona, Hawai'i. One of the stones is said to be in the Kona district and the other in Kohala. *Lit.*, stones standing double.

Pōhaku-Lēkia. See Pōhaku-Hanalei.

Pōhaku-loa. Ranger station, section of Mauna Kea State Park, and land division in the saddle between Mauna Kea and Mauna Loa; land sections, Kai-lua and Wai-ki'i qds.; gulches, Kohala, Mauna Kea, and Wai-ki'i qds., Hawai'i. Cape, northeast Kaua'i. Point, north Lā-na'i. Land sections, Kau-pō, Ka-haku-loa, and Mā'alaea qds.; harbor, Hāna qd., Maui. Land sections, point, gulch, and hill, Hālawa and 'Ilio Pt. qds., Moloka'i. Land division, Wai-a-lua, O'ahu (PH 89). Large stone believed to bless expectant mothers and endow children with strength and wisdom, formerly outside the gate of Puna-hou School, Honolulu. It was moved from Round Top to Puna-hou only with the permission of Ka-mehameha III. It was finally broken up to permit widening of the road to Mānoa, and pieces were put into the nearby stone wall. *Lit.*, long stone.

Pōhaku-lua. Islet, 'Anae-ho'omalu Bay, Hawai'i. *Lit.*, double stone.

Pōhaku-māuliuli. Cone and gulch, 'Ilio Pt. qd., north Moloka'i. *Lit.*, dark stone.

Pōhaku-noho. Rocks near the sea at Ka-wai-hae, Hawai'i, said to have been used as a seat by Ka-mehameha and, earlier, by Alapa'i-kūpalu-manō (Alapa'i chumming shark) as they watched for sharks. The rock is now in three pieces; it is said to have been broken in the 1930s. *Lit.,* chair rock.

Pōhaku-nui. The southernmost of the Hālaʻi Hills, Hilo, Hawaiʻi and home of the ʻAlae (mudhen) family from whom Māui got the secret of fire (Westervelt, n.d.:64). Hill, Kaunakakai qd., north Molokaʻi. *Lit.,* large stone.

Pōhaku-o-Kaʻahumanu. Same as Kaʻahumanu-pōhaku.

Pōhaku-o-Kāʻanapali. Same as Pōhaku-Kāʻanapali.

Pōhaku-o-Kāne. Hill and *heiau,* Hanalei district, Kauaʻi. *Lit.,* hill of Kāne.

Pōhaku-o-kau. See Kaʻahumanu-pōhaku.

Pōhaku-o-Kauaʻi. Legendary stone at Ka-ʻena Point, Oʻahu, believed to have been hurled by a giant (Hāʻupu) from Kauaʻi (PH 104). When Māui attempted to draw the islands together, sea goddesses snagged his hook on this rock. Inland is a stone called Pōhaku-o-Oʻahu. *Lit.,* rock of Kauaʻi.

Pōhaku-o-ke-au. See Kalalea.

Pōhaku-o-Lama. See Mahaiʻula.

Pōhaku-o-Lēkia. A stone at Green Lake (Wai-a-Pele), Puna, Hawaiʻi. See Pōhaku-Hanalei.

Pōhaku-o-Oʻahu. Stone near Pōhaku-o-Kauaʻi. *Lit.,* stone of Oʻahu.

Pōhaku-paea. Islet (0.18 acres, 40 feet elevation), Mākena qd., Maui. *Lit.,* stone that lands [ashore].

Pōhaku-pālaha. Peak (8,105 feet elevation), Hale-a-ka-lā Crater, Maui. *Lit.,* flat rock.

Pōhaku-Pele. Peak, Hanalei district, Kauaʻi. *Lit.,* lava rock.

Pōhaku-pili. Peak, Hanalei district, Kauaʻi. Land division and gulch, Hālawa qd., Molokaʻi. *Lit.,* joined stone.

Pōhaku-pio. See Kaʻula.

Pōhā-kupu. Residential subdivision and park, Kai-lua, Oʻahu. *Lit.,* growing rock.

Pōhaku-puka. Land division, school, and stream, Honomū qd., Hawaiʻi. *Lit.,* perforated rock.

Pōhaku-pule. Coastal area and gulch, Honolua qd., Maui. *Lit.,* prayer rock.

Pōhaku-ʻulaʻula. Peak (3,976 feet elevation), inland between Pelekunu and Wai-lau valleys, northeast Molokaʻi. *Lit.,* red stone.

Pōhaku-waʻawaʻa. Land area, Kaʻū, Hawaiʻi. *Lit.,* corrugated rock.

Poho-iki. Coastal land section, possible future hotel development site, and surfing area, Kala-pana qd., Hawaiʻi. *Lit.,* small depression (Pele is said to have dug a crater here).

Poho-kinikini. Land sections, Kaʻū and Kohala, Hawaiʻi. *Lit.,* many hollows.

Poho-lua. Rainfall station near Mauna Huʻi, Kaunakakai qd., Molokaʻi. *Lit.,* pit hollow.

Pōhue-loa. Valley, northeast Niʻihau. *Lit.,* long gourd.

Pohukaina. School and street mostly in Kakaʻako, Honolulu; formerly, the area behind the Hawaiʻi State Library.

Point Panic. See Ke-walo.

Poʻipū. Land division and beach, Kō-loa district, Kauaʻi. *Lit.,* completely overcast *or* crashing (as waves).

P

Poka ʻAilana. Ford Island, Pearl Harbor. *Ua pau koʻu lihi hoihoi i ka nani o Poka ʻAilana,* all my delight in the beauty of Ford Island is gone (expression of disenchantment or anger). Formerly called Moku-ʻumeʻume. *Lit.,* Ford Island.

Pō-ka-ʻī. Land section, bay, beach park, boat ramp, and surfing place (Finney, 1959a:108), Wai-ʻanae qd., Oʻahu; once the site of a *heiau* and famous coconut grove. Today it is commonly called Pokai but is sung Pō-ka-ʻī. *Lit.,* night [of] the supreme one.

Pō-kele. Former name of the wharf at Queen and Nuʻu-anu streets, Honolulu. *Lit.,* muddy night.

Poki. Street near the Puna-hou School campus, Honolulu, probably named for Boki Ka-māʻuleʻule (the one who faints), governor of Oʻahu and husband of Liliha. He accompanied Ka-mehameha II to England. In 1829 he set off on an expedition to the New Hebrides in search of sandalwood, but his ship and all aboard disappeared. (RC 294–296.) Boki may have been named for Ka-mehameha I's pet dog, Poki (from English "boss"). At the time of Boki's birth, many dogs were named Poki, including dog guardians (*kiaʻi*).

Pōkiʻi. Ridge, Wai-mea district, Kauaʻi. The old name was Pōkiʻi-kauna (chanting youngest brother or sister). Kapo, Pele's sister, left her younger female relative, Moe-hauna (lie struck), here and she chanted a farewell. *Lit.,* youngest brother or sister.

Pōkole. Point and fishpond, Kaha-luʻu; street, Ka-imu-kī, Honolulu, Oʻahu. *Lit.,* short.

Pola Iki. Land division, Lahaina qd., Maui. *Lit.,* small Pola (flap, as of a *malo*).

Pola Nui. Land division, Lahaina qd.; elevated land section (3,000 feet high), Māʻalaea qd., Maui. *Lit.,* large Pola.

Polapola. Land section (*ʻili*), Kala-wao; village for lepers, Ka-laupapa peninsula, Molokaʻi, a *heiau* for the goddess Kapo once stood here. *Lit.,* improved in health. (The word is cognate with Borabora, the name of the island in the Society Islands, but this is probably a coincidence.)

Pō-leho. Coastal area, northeast Niʻihau. *Lit.,* cowry night.

Poli-ʻahu. Well-preserved *heiau* in a State park near Wai-lua, Kauaʻi, associated with Malae *heiau.* Land division on Mauna Kea, Hawaiʻi (UL 251), named for the snow goddess. *Lit.,* garment [for the] bosom (referring to snow).

Poli-hale. State park, beach, ridge, *heiau,* and land division, Wai-mea district, Kauaʻi, famous for its seaweed *(pahapaha)* used in leis (For. Sel. 102), a practice said to have been introduced by Pele's older sister, Nā-maka-o-Kahaʻi. *Lit.,* house bosom.

Polihiwa. Place, Dowsett Highlands, Honolulu; perhaps a garble of Polohiwa (glistening black). (TM.)

Poli-hua. Beach area, north Lā-naʻi. *Lit.,* eggs [in] bosom (turtles lay eggs here; see Ka-ʻena).

Poli-o-Keawe. Cliff, Puna qd., Hawaiʻi. *Lit.,* bosom of Keawe.

Polipoli. Peak, spring, cabin, campground, and park, Mākena qd., Maui.

Poli-wai. Gulch, Wai-kele, Oʻahu. *Lit.,* water bosom.

Poloke. Place, Tantalus, Honolulu. (TM; see Indices 740 for an award.)

Pololū. Large valley, Wai-pi'o qd., Hawai'i. *Lit.,* long spear.

Pō-lou. See Ka-huku.

Polū-lani. Place, Pauoa, Honolulu. *Lit.,* sky blue.

Polynesian Cultural Center. Center built at Lā'ie, O'ahu, by Mormons and opened in 1963; there are six model villages (Fijian, Hawaiian, Maori, Samoan, Tahitian, and Tongan). Most construction materials were brought from the various island groups, and native carpenters constructed the houses. In return for educational expenses, students from the Pacific islands who attend neighboring Church College of Hawai'i, talk to visitors about their island cultures, and participate in evening pageants. See Church College of Hawai'i.

Ponaha-wai. Land division, Hilo qd., Hawai'i. *Lit.,* water circle.

Ponimō'ī. Road, Diamond Head, Honolulu. *Lit.,* carnation.

Po'o. Ancient surfing areas, Ka-pa'a and Wai-mea districts (Finney and Houston 30); coastal area, Hanapēpē, Kaua'i. See Ka-iwi-o-Pele. *Lit.,* head.

Po'okela. Church at Maka-wao, East Maui. *Lit.,* foremost.

Po'o-kū. Land section and former *heiau,* Hanalei district, Kaua'i. *Lit.,* upright head.

Po'o-lau. Beach and gulch, 'Ilio Pt. qd., Moloka'i.

Po'o-lolo-'ole. Land area, Wai-mea district, Kaua'i. *Lit.,* head without brains.

Po'o-mau. Canyon and stream, Wai-mea district, Kaua'i. *Lit.,* constant source *or* constant head.

Po'onāhoahoa. Stream, Wai-luku qd., Maui.

Po'o-oneone. Point, southeast Ni'ihau. *Lit.,* sandy head.

Po'opo'o. Islet (0.5 acres, 40 feet elevation), south Lā-na'i. *Lit.,* hollow.

Po'opo'o-iki. Valley, northwest Kaua'i. *Lit.,* small depression.

Po'o-pueo. See Kūkae-'ula'ula.

Pope. Elementary school, Wai-mānalo, O'ahu, built in 1965 and named for Mrs. Willis T. Pope, commissioner of education 1928-1930, cofounder and first president of Hawai'i Congress of Parents and Teachers. The environmental laboratory in the St. John Plant Science Building (completed in 1971) at the Mānoa campus, University of Hawai'i, Honolulu, was named for Willis T. Pope, as was a nearby campus road. Pope was a dean of the College of O'ahu and (1908–1909) professor of botany and horticulture.

Popo-i'a. Flat islet off Kai-lua Beach Park, O'ahu (less than 4 acres in area and about 10 feet elevation), a bird refuge. *Lit.,* fish rot (so called because of fish bones left there; Sterling and Summers 5:283).

Pōpō-'ie. Ancient surfing area, Lahaina qd., Maui. (Finney and Houston 28.) *Lit.,* 'ie vine cluster.

Pōpō-kī. Land section, Maku'u qd., Hawai'i. (For. Sel. 256.) *Lit.,* ti leaf bundle.

Populars. Surfing area, Wai-kīkī, O'ahu, where beginners learn to surf. (Finney and Houston 80.)

Port Allen. See 'Ele'ele.

P

Portlock. Road and point near Koko Head, Honolulu, named for British explorer Captain Nathaniel Portlock who commanded the British vessels *King George* and *Queen Charlotte* that anchored off the coast of Oʻahu, May 31, 1786. He sent his men up Kuli-ʻouʻou Valley in search of water. (TM.) Surfing area named after the road (Finney, 1959a:108, 109).

Pou-hala. Fishpond and land division near Pearl Harbor, Oʻahu. *Lit.,* pandanus post.

Poupou. Land section, Puna district; stream, Honomū qd., Hawaiʻi. *Lit.,* stout.

Prince Edward. Street, Wai-kīkī, Honolulu, named by Bruce Cartwright for Prince Edward Ke-liʻi-aho-nui, brother of princes David Ka-wānana-koa and Kū-hiō Ka-lani-ana-ʻole. (TM.)

Princeville. Projected vacation and retirement development, Hanalei district, Kauaʻi. The area was so named in honor of a visit there in 1860 of Ka-mehameha IV and Queen Emma and their son, the prince Ka Haku o Hawaiʻi. It was then a sugar plantation owned by Robert Crichton Wyllie. Later it became a cattle ranch, and in 1968 it was sold for development. See Wyllie.

Pua. Lane, Nuʻu-anu, Honolulu, named for the father of Samuel K. Pua, sheriff of Hilo, Hawaiʻi. (TM.)

Puaʻa-hala. Land division and development area, Ka-malō qd., south Molokaʻi. *Lit.,* passing pig. (An alternate explanation: *pū-aʻa-hala,* clump of pandanus roots.)

Puaʻa-haʻu-nui. See Puahauni.

Puaʻa-kaʻa. Park, Hāna, Maui. *Lit.,* rolling pig.

Puaʻa-kanu. Land division, Puna district, Hawaiʻi, where Pele was attacked by Kama-puaʻa. Pele's sister Kapo sent her vagina to lure away the pig man. He followed it to Koko Crater, Oʻahu, where it left an imprint, and then flew off to Ka-lihi. The old name for Koko Crater is Kohe-lepelepe, vagina labia minor. See Kala-pana. *Lit.,* pig planting.

Pua-ʻala. Lane, Ka-lihi Uka, Honolulu. *Lit.,* fragrant flower. (TM.)

Puaʻa-laulau. Gulch, Hālawa qd., Molokaʻi. *Lit.,* wrapped pig.

Puaʻa-liʻiliʻi. Beach area at Wai-kīkī, Honolulu, approximately between ʻĀpua-kēhau (site of the Moana Hotel) and Helu-moa (site of the Royal Hawaiian Hotel). Ka-mehameha I's houses were here. *Lit.,* little pig.

Puaʻa-luʻu. Stream between Puʻu-haoa and ʻŌheʻo near Kī-pahulu, Maui. The pig demigod, Kama-puaʻa, dived here to escape his pursuers. A *heiau* here was called Poʻo-manini (*manini* fish head). *Lit.,* diving pig.

Pua-ʻena. Point and ancient surfing area (Finney and Houston 28), Wai-a-lua Bay, Oʻahu (for a song, see Elbert and Mahoe 68); place below the Mānoa campus, University of Hawaiʻi, Honolulu. *Lit.,* issue hot. (Pele lived at Wai-a-lua Bay before going to Hawaiʻi.)

Puahauni. Flat point, Hālawa qd., Molokaʻi; probably formerly Puaʻa-haʻu-nui (pig snorting much).

Pū-ʻahuʻula. Area in upper Mānoa, Honolulu, near Puʻu-luahine, site of Queen Ka-ʻahu-manu's home, Puka-ʻōmaʻo (green apertures); also the name of the spring in the area. The famous female *mo'o* Kiha-nui-lūlū-moku (great island-shaking *mo'o*) lived here; she had eel, lizard, and woman forms. She made plants thrive in Wa'a-loa ravine. Ka-'ahu-manu died here in 1832. See Hue-lani. *Lit.*, feather-cloak spring. (*Pū-* is short for *puna*.)

Pua'i-'ālua. Crater, Puna qd., Hawai'i. *Lit.*, to flow out twice.

Pua-ka-huahua. Coastal area, Honolua qd., Maui.

Pua-ka-lehua. Land section, Kī-lau-ea qd., Hawai'i. See Wood Valley. *Lit.*, the *lehua* blooms (a reference to the pretty girls there).

Pua-kea. Land section, point, ranch, and ancient surfing area (Finney and Houston 26), Kohala qd., Hawai'i. Land section, Mō-kapu qd., and *heiau* at Haki-pu'u (Sterling and Summers 5:35), O'ahu. *Lit.*, white blossom.

Pua-kō. Village, quadrangle, bay, point; land divisions and flume, Kohala and Wai-pi'o qds., Hawai'i. About 3,000 petroglyph units are in the Kohala area (Cox and Stasack 85). The dog thief, Pupua-lenalena, lived in one of these places (HM 349–351; For. 4:558–561). Two stones in the sea at an unidentified Pua-kō in the Ka'ū district would turn over upon the death of a chief. Shortly before the death of Ka-mehameha they turned completely over, and on the day of his death one of them, Pōhaku-o-kai, was deposited on dry land. On the day Queen Emma died, it was lifted by a wave to the water's edge. Pōhaku-o-kai (stone [from over-] seas) was believed to have come from Kahiki. The other stone was named Pōhaku-o-Hulu. A shark-man lived here, 'I-waha-'ou'ou (supreme one [with] projecting mouth). See Koa'e-kea. *Lit.*, sugarcane blossom.

Pua-kō Ke-'ā-muku. Trail, Pua-kō qd., Hawai'i.

Pua-kō-pāpapa. Beach near Wai-ka-puna, Ka'ū, Hawai'i, a favorite spot for catching *ulua* fish with a line but no pole (*pī ulua*). *Lit.*, flat dragging issue (reference to strong seas).

Pua-kō Wai-mea. Trail, Kohala qd., Hawai'i.

Pū-'āla'a. Land section, Kala-pana qd., Puna, Hawai'i, said to be named for the *'āla'a* tree, common here but rare elsewhere. An ancient and hitherto unrecorded village site was discovered here by Bishop Museum archaeologists in 1971. *Lit.*, *Planchonella* tree.

Pū-'alaea. Land section and cliff, Honomū qd., Hawai'i. *Lit.*, ocherous earth hill.

Pua-lanalana. Coastal area, Hālawa qd., Moloka'i. Possibly *lit.*, floating flower.

Pua-lani. Way, Wai-kīkī, Honolulu. (TM.) *Lit.*, heavenly flower.

Pualele. Place, Wilhelmina Rise, Honolulu. *Lit.*, sow thistle.

Pū'ali. Gulch, Hālawa qd., Moloka'i. *Lit.*, groove.

Pua-loke. Place, Pā-wa'a section, Honolulu. (TM.) *Lit.*, flower [of the] rose.

Pū-'ama. Coastal area, Ka-malō qd., south Moloka'i. *Lit.*, young mullet (*pū-* is short for *pua*).

Puanaiea. Point, northwest Kaua'i. *Lit.*, sickly, weak.

Pua-nani. Lane, Ka-lihi Kai, Honolulu. (TM.) *Lit.*, beautiful flower.

Pua'ō. Ancient surfing area, Ka-laupapa, north Moloka'i (Finney and Houston 30). *Lit.*, onslaught of dashing waves.

Puapua

Puapua. Land sections, Kai-lua qd., and in the Ka'ū district, Hawai'i. A lava tube where people hid in time of war is in the Ka'ū Puapua. Probably *lit.*, tail feathers.

Pua-pua'a. Land section, Kai-lua qd., North Kona, Hawai'i. See Ka-helo. *Lit.*, piglet (named for supposed resemblance of two large rocks to pigs).

Publics. Surfing area named for the public bath building, Wai-kīkī (Finney, 1959a:108).

Pu'e'a. Coastal area, Ka-malō qd., north Moloka'i.

Puehu. Ridge, Wai-mea district, Kaua'i. Fishpond site, Wai-'anae, O'ahu, where the hero Ka-welo struck an image that refused to sanction his sailing to Kaua'i to fight. (Sterling and Summers 2:52.) *Lit.*, scattered.

Pūehuehu. Pool in Nu'u-anu Stream near School and Liliha streets, Nu'u-anu, Honolulu, formerly popular for diving. (Ii 63.) Papa struck the earth with a rock here, thus creating the pool. (Sterling and Summers 6:172.) *Lit.*, spray scattered.

Pūehuehu Iki. Land division, Lahaina qd., Maui. *Lit.*, small Pūehuehu.

Pūehuehu Nui. Land division, Lahaina qd., Maui. *Lit.*, large Pūehuehu.

Pū-'elelū. Land division, Hālawa qd., south Moloka'i. *Lit.*, cockroach hill.

Pueo. Point, Ni'ihau. Street, Kāhala, Honolulu. See Pu'u-pueo. *Lit.*, owl.

Pueo-ao. Beach, 'Īlio Pt. qd., north Moloka'i. Probably *lit.*, daylight owl.

Pueo-hulu-nui. Land division above Wai-'ōhinu, Ka'ū, Hawai'i. (UL 67.) See Moana-lua. *Lit.*, well-feathered owl.

Puhā. Stream, Wai-mānalo, O'ahu. *Lit.*, a hollow (as in a tree).

Pū-hala. Rise, Mānoa, Honolulu. *Lit.*, pandanus tree.

Pūhā-loa. Fishpond, Ka-malō qd., south Moloka'i. *Lit.*, bursting forth long.

Pū-hau. Springs at Nīnole, Ka'ū, and in Kona, Hawai'i. *Lit.*, icy spring (*pū* is short for *puna*).

Pūhā-wai. Spring and area, Lualualei, O'ahu. *Lit.*, water bursting out *or* water hollow.

Pūhele. Ancient surfing area, Hāna, Maui (Finney and Houston 28), celebrated in poetry. *Lit.*, traveling hill.

Puhi. Village and stream, Lihu'e district, Kaua'i. A shark god, Ka-holi-a-Kāne (the sprouting [made] by Kāne) lived in a cave here. *Lit.*, blow.

Puhi-a-'Epa. Name of a blowhole at Ka-'auhuhu, Kohala, Hawai'i. *Lit.*, blowing by 'Epa (the 'E'epa were supernatural beings).

Puhi-a-Pele. Spatter cone visible from the highway, built around the vent of the 1801 eruption of Hualālai. (Macdonald and Abbott 52.) See Ka-'ū-pūlehu. *Lit.*, blown out by Pele.

Puhi-kōheo-hala. Same as Kōheo-hala.

Puhi-lele. Point, Kī-pahulu qd., Maui. *Lit.*, leaping eel.

Pūhili. Land section and point said to be named for a priest of the same name, Ke-āhole qd., North Kona, Hawai'i. *Lit.*, to thwart.

P

Puhi-mau. Crater (3,623 feet elevation), Kī-lau-ea qd., Hawai'i. *Lit.*, ever smoking.

Puhina-o-Lono. *Heiau* behind Captain Cook monument, Ke-ala-ke-kua, Hawai'i. *Lit.*, burning of Lono (that is, Captain Cook; his body was burned and the flesh stripped from the bones, which were then taken aboard ship; RC 103).

Puhi-'ula. Beach area, Ni'ihau. *Lit.*, red eel.

Pū'iwa. Road, lane, pool, and area, Nu'u-anu, Honolulu. A god of tapa makers, Maikohā, was buried here near the stream, and from his body grew the first *wauke* (paper mulberry) plants. (Westervelt, 1964: 20, but see HM 99.) *Lit.*, startled (Ka-mehameha I's guns startled the O'ahu enemy here).

Puka-'ana. Church built by Kua-kini between Ke-ālia and Ho'okena, South Kona, Hawai'i. Kua-kini, brother of Ka-'ahu-manu, was governor of Hawai'i in the 1830s. *Lit.*, Exodus.

Puka-'auhuhu. Land section, East Maui. *Lit.*, 'auhuhu plant hole.

Pū-ka'i. Gulch, East Maui. *Lit.*, parading trumpet.

Puka-lani. Village, Pā'ia qd., Maui. Street, Wilhelmina Rise, Honolulu. (TM.) *Lit.*, heavenly gate. (One report says the Maui name was originally Pu'u-ka-lani, hill [of] the heavens.)

Puka-'ōma'o. The name of Ka-'ahu-manu's home at Pū-'ahu'ula in upper Mānoa, Honolulu. See Hue-lani. *Lit.*, green opening (the queen's house had green shutters).

Puka-ulua. Point, Mō-kapu qd., O'ahu. *Lit.*, ulua fish opening.

Pūkele. Stream, avenue, and playground, Pālolo, Honolulu. *Lit.*, muddy.

Pūko'a. Gulch, Wai-pi'o qd., Hawai'i. Street, Kai-lua, O'ahu. *Lit.*, coral head.

Pū-ko'o. Two land divisions, harbor, gulch, village, and fishpond, Hā-lawa qd., south Moloka'i. Seaward of the fishpond is a surfing area with several summer south-swell and trade-wind sites. See Wai-lau. *Lit.*, support hill.

Pūla'a. Lane, Ka-lihi Kai, Honolulu, named for John Pūla'a, a carpenter and painter in the early 1900s. (TM.)

Pūlama. Land section, Puna qd., Hawai'i. *Lit.*, to cherish.

Pūlehu. Ridge, Wai-mea district, Kaua'i. Land division, road, and gulch, Pu'u-o-kali qd., Maui. *Lit.*, broiled.

Pūlehu Iki. Land division, Kilohana qd., Maui. *Lit.*, small Pūlehu.

Pūlehu Nui. Land division, Pu'u-o-kali qd., Maui. *Lit.*, large Pūlehu.

Pule-moku. Islet off Lani-loa Point, Lā'ie, O'ahu. *Lit.*, broken prayer.

Pū-lena. Stream, Ka-malō qd., Moloka'i. Perhaps *lit.*, yellow conch. Street, Mānoa, Honolulu, probably short for nearby Pu'u-lena.

Pulepule. Gulch, Honolua qd., Maui. *Lit.*, spotted with variegated colors.

Pumehana. Street, Pā-wa'a section, Honolulu. *Lit.*, warmth.

Puna. Quadrangle and district, southeast Hawai'i; land section and sugar mill, Kala-pana qd.; forest reserves, Kala-pana and Puna qds.; road, Hilo qd., Hawai'i. The Ka-wai-hau district, Kaua'i, was sometimes called Puna. Street, Ka-mehameha Heights, Honolulu. Poetic (Hawai'i): *paia 'ala i ka hala,* bowers fragrant with pandanus; *ka*

P

'*āina i ka houpo o Kāne* (PH 218), the land in the heart of Kāne.

Pū-nahā. Gulch, Honolua qd., Maui. Probably *lit.*, broken conch.

Punahele. Place, 'Āina-Haina, Honolulu. *Lit.*, favorite.

Puna-hoa. Land sections, Hilo qd., Hawai'i. *Lit.*, companion spring.

Puna-ho'olapa. Spring, Ka-huku, O'ahu. See Puna-manō. *Lit.*, restless spring.

Puna-hou. Private school, street, and section 27 of Honolulu (map 6), formerly called Ka-puna-hou. The school was established by Hiram Bingham in 1841, on property given at the request of Ka-'ahu-manu, for chiefs' children and missionary children. There were 34 students in the first class; in 1971 there were 3,500, from kindergarten through the twelfth grade. *Lit.*, new spring. (The god Kāne thrust his staff into the ground here to get water. According to another story, an old couple lived by a pandanus tree and each dreamed of a spring; when the man offered red fish and pulled up the pandanus tree, water oozed out. The seal of Puna-hou School depicts a pandanus tree, pool, and taro leaves.)

Puna-kou. Land section and gulch on the south side of Mauna Loa, Airport qd., south Moloka'i. The god Kāne brought forth fresh water here (HM 64). *Lit.*, *kou* tree spring.

Punākua. Hill, 'Īlio Pt. qd., south Moloka'i. *Lit.*, spring [of the] gods (from *puna akua*).

Puna-lau. Point, Honolua qd., Maui. Fishpond, Airport qd., south Moloka'i, now filled in (Summers 78–79). *Lit.*, many springs.

Puna-lu'u. Land sections and gulches, Honu-'apo and Pāhala qds.; harbor, landing, black sand beach and beach park, and ancient surfing area (Finney and Houston 26), Honu-'apo qd.; village and *heiau*, Puna qd., south Hawai'i. A cannibalistic *mo'o*, Kaikapū (hag), lived here; she was killed by Laka and his helpers (HM 263). Stream, Mauna Loa qd., Hawai'i. Fishpond, Kāne-'ohe, O'ahu. *Lit.*, spring dived for. Land sections, Kāne-'ohe, Kahana, and Wai-kane qds.; village, beach park, and point, Kahana qd.; stream, Kahana and Wai-kāne qds., east O'ahu. *Lit.*, coral dived for.

Puna-manō. Spring and swamp, Lā-'ie, O'ahu. A small shark was captured and kept in this pool. The husband and wife guardians asked the shark to guard the breadfruit on a nearby tree. The woman's brother came and picked some breadfruit, which fell into the pool. The man swam into the pool to get them and was killed by the shark. When husband and wife returned they saw a bloody trail on the water, which they followed for about a mile to Puna-ho'olapa spring, but they found neither brother nor shark. (Sterling and Summers 4:44–47.) *Lit.*, shark spring.

Puna-pōhaku. Stream, Ka-'ena qd., O'ahu. *Lit.*, rocky spring.

Puna-'ula. Land division and gulch, Hālawa qd., south Moloka'i. *Lit.*, red spring.

Pūnāwai. Coastal area, Hālawa qd., north Moloka'i. *Lit.*, water spring.

Pūnāwai-kohe-le'a. Former spring near Wahī-lau-hue, 'Īlio Pt. qd., Moloka'i. *Lit.*, spring [of] orgasm vagina.

Punchbowl. Posterosional tuff cone in Honolulu; section 18 of Honolulu (map 6). The National Cemetery of the Pacific is in the crater. See Pū-o-waina.

Pūniu-'ōhua Li'ili'i. Gulch, Hālawa qd., south Moloka'i. *Lit.,* small Pūniu-'ōhua (coconut-shell passenger) *or* young fish coconut shell.

Pūniu-'ōhua Nui. Gulch, Hālawa qd., south Moloka'i. *Lit.,* large Pūniu-'ōhua.

*Punolohi. Point, Hālawa qd., Moloka'i.

Pū'ō-hala. Land section, playground, and elementary school, Kāne-'ohe, O'ahu. *Lit.,* passing gust *or* passing blaze.

Pū-o-waina. Hawaiian name for Punchbowl and drive along the north slope of Punchbowl crater; section 18 (map 6), Honolulu. *Lit.,* hill of placing [human sacrifices] (for which this hill was famous).

Puopelu. See Pu'u-'ōpelu.

Pū-'ou. Land division, Lahaina qd., Maui.

Pū-pa'akai. Gulch, Hālawa qd., Moloka'i. *Lit.,* eat a little salt.

Pūpū-kea. Hill (552 feet high), surfing beach (Finney, 1959*a*:108), beach park, and homesteads, Ka-huku qd.; land section, homesteads, trail along the summit ridge of the Ko'olau mountains, forest reserve, and Boy Scout camp, Pu'u-kapu qd., north O'ahu. *Lit.,* white shell.

Pūpū-kea Pau-malū. Homesteads and forest reserve, Pu'u-kapu, Hale-'iwa, and Ka-huku qds., O'ahu.

Pūpū-'ōpae. Stream, Kai-lua, O'ahu. *Lit.,* gathering shrimp.

pu'u. 'Hill, mountain, cone, peak, elevation'. Some names are written either with or without *pu'u* (as Pu'u-kukui and Kukui). In a few names *pu'u* is shortened to *pū-* (as Pū-'alaea, Pū-ko'o, Pū-o-waina).

Pu'u. Ancient surfing area, Ke-olonā-hihi, Kai-lua qd., Hawai'i. (Finney and Houston 26.) *Lit.,* peak.

Pu'u-a-'a'o. Hill near Wai-'ōhinu, Honu-'apo qd., Hawai'i. *Lit.,* hill of *'a'o* bird. (The name was considered a bad omen; an earthquake in the 1860s dislodged a part of the hill.)

Pu'u-ahulili. See Ahulili.

Pu'u-'alaea. Peak, Hale-a-ka-lā Crater, Maui. *Lit.,* ocherous earth hill.

Pu'u-alalā. Hill (210 feet high), northeast Ni'ihau. *Lit.,* crow hill.

Pu'u-ali'i. Sand dune site near South Point, Hawai'i, excavated by Bishop Museum archaeologists at the same time as nearby Wai-'Ahukini. Hill, central Lā-na'i. Peak (4,222 feet high), Ka-malō qd., Moloka'i. *Lit.,* royal hill.

Pu'u-anahulu. Hill and land sections, Kai-lua, Pua-kō, Wai-ki'i, and Ka-'ohe qds., Kona, Hawai'i. *Lit.,* ten-day hill. (Perhaps named for a supernatural dog of that name; see Ka-lae-o-ka-'īlio. In some accounts, Anahulu was a priestess.)

Pu'u-anoano. Hill, Kaunakakai qd., north Moloka'i, with a *hōlua* course. (Cooke 121.) *Lit.,* mysterious hill.

Pu'u-anu. Hill (2,972 feet high), Mā'alaea qd., Maui. *Lit.,* cool hill.

Pu'u-'āpa'apa'a. Hill on northwest coast of Kohala qd., Hawai'i, named for a wind.

Pu'u-apalu. Hill, 'Īlio Pt. qd., north Moloka'i.

*Pu'u-au. Hill (2,372 feet high), Hālawa qd., Moloka'i.

Pu'u-'au'au. Hill, Kō-loa district, Kaua'i. *Lit.,* swimming hill.

Pu'u-'aukai. Hill, Kō-loa district, Kaua'i. *Lit.,* sea-travel hill.

Pu'u-ea. Ancient surfing area, Honomū qd., Hawai'i (Finney and Houston 26). *Lit.,* rising hill.

P

P

Pu'u-ehu. Hills, Ka-wai-hau district, Kaua'i, and Ha'i-kū qd., Maui. *Lit.,* dust hill.

Pu'u-'enuhe. Hill, Honu-'apo qd., Ka'ū, Hawai'i. *Lit.,* caterpillar hill. (A legendary caterpillar, Kumu-hea, married a girl here but visited her only at night and only in human form. He fed her his own food—sweet potato greens—but she wasted away on this diet. Kumu-hea's father, the god Kū, removed his ability to assume human form. The people appealed to Kāne, who cut Kumu-hea into pieces; these are the caterpillars of today, which Hawaiians do not injure; HM 135. See Pili-wai and Pu'u-ka-pe'elua.)

Pu'u-'eo. Pali, Kī-lau-ea and Puna qds.; elevated place in Hilo qd., where Ka-lani-'ōpu'u built the *heiau* of Kanoa (RC 108); land sections, Honomū and Ka Lae qds., Hawai'i. See Ka-'eo, Pu'u-ka-'eo.

Pu'u-epa. Land section, Kohala qd., Hawai'i. (For. Sel. 26.) Also spelled Pu'u-wepa.

Pu'u-'eu. Hill (2,747 feet high), Hanalei district, northwest Kaua'i. *Lit.,* rascal hill.

*Pu'u-haha. Hill, Ka-malō qd., Moloka'i.

Pu'u-hakina. Hill, 'Īlio Pt. qd., Moloka'i. See Hakina. *Lit.,* broken hill.

Pu'u-hale. Elementary school, Ka-lihi Kai, Honolulu. *Lit.,* house hill.

Pu'u-haoa. Land section, Kī-pahulu qd., Maui. *Lit.,* hot hill.

Pu'u-hau-kea. Cone, 13,441 feet elevation, Mauna Kea, Hawai'i. *Lit.,* white snow hill.

*Pu'u-hāuna-kō. Hill (627 feet high), Ka-haku-loa qd., Maui.

Pu'u-hau'oki. Cone, 13,640 feet elevation, Mauna Kea, Hawai'i. *Lit.,* frosty hill.

Pu'u-Hawai'i-loa. Hill, Mō-kapu qd., O'ahu. See Hawai'i-loa. *Lit.,* distant Hawai'i hill.

Pu'u-hele. Cemetery and hill behind Mā'alaea, Maui, believed once a *mo'o* (HM 189). See Pu'u-o-kali. Hill, Hāna qd., Maui. Hill, Kauna-kakai qd., central Moloka'i. *Lit.,* traveling hill.

*Pu'u-hewale. Stream, Honolua qd., Maui.

Pu'u-hinahina. Land division, South Kona, Hawai'i; the ruins of a *hōlua* sled course are still here. (RC 256.) Hill, Wai-mea district, Kaua'i. Perhaps named for one of the several *hinahina* plants.

Pu'u-hīna'i. Cinder cone, Pua-kō qd., Hawai'i. *Lit.,* basket hill.

Pu'u-Hipa. Hill (1,002 feet high), Lahaina qd., Maui. Hipa is said to have been a mythological character.

*Pu'u-hoi. Land section and ridge, Ka-malō qd., Moloka'i.

Pu'u-hōlei. Hill, Puna qd., Hawai'i. See Hōlei.

Pu'u-hona. Hill (905 feet high), Mā'alaea qd., Maui, probably named for a native tree.

Pu'u-honu. Hill in the Hāla'i Hills, Hilo, Hawai'i, where Hina-ke-ahi was baked in an *imu* (oven). See Hāla'i. Hill, Kohala qd., Hawai'i. *Lit.,* turtle hill.

Pu'uhonua. Westernmost point, City of Refuge National Historical Park, Hōnaunau, Kona, Hawai'i. Street, Mānoa, Honolulu, leading to the site of the old S.N. Castle home, and of an ancient place of refuge (*pu'uhonua*). (Sterling and Summers 6:128.)

Pu'uhonua-'ula. Spatter and lava cone built by a prehistoric eruption, Kala-pana qd., Hawai'i. (Macdonald and Abbott 86–87.) *Lit.*, red place of refuge.

Pu'u-Ho'olehua. Hill, Airport qd., south Moloka'i.

Pu'u-hou. Littoral cone (240 feet high) formed when the 1868 flow from Mauna Loa entered the ocean west of South Point, Ka'ū, Hawai'i. (Macdonald and Abbott 309.) *Lit.*, new hill.

Pu'u-hue. Ranch, Kohala qd., Hawai'i. (For. 4:586.)

Pu'u-huluhulu. Hills, Humu'ula qd. (6,758 feet high), Wai-ki'i qd. (6,005 feet), Ka Lae qd. (2,734 feet), Puna qd. (3,440 feet), and Wai-pi'o qd. (2,471 feet); gulch, Wai-ki'i qd., Hawai'i. *Lit.*, shaggy hill.

Pu'u-iki. Hills, Wai-pi'o qd. (3,768 feet high), Pua-kō qd. (3,417 feet), Kohala qd. (4,274 feet), and Honu-'apo qd. (5,399 feet), Hawai'i. Land division and village, Kī-pahulu qd.; land division, Lahaina qd., Maui. Land section, Wai-a-lua, O'ahu. *Lit.*, small hill.

Pu'u-'īloli. Hill, Airport qd., south Moloka'i. *Lit.*, hill of longing.

Pu'u-'io. Hill (2,842 feet high), Mākena qd., Maui. *Lit.*, hawk hill.

Pu'u-ka'ala. Peak (3,508 feet high), Wai-pi'o qd., Hawai'i. See Ka'ala.

Pu'u-ka-'aumakua. Hill in the Ko'olau range, O'ahu, where the Ko'olau Loa, Ko'olau Poko, and 'Ewa districts meet. *Lit.*, the family deity hill.

Pu'u-ka-'eo. Coastal hill (358 feet high), and inland hill (1,683 feet high), Honolua qd.; hill, Mākena qd., Maui. Dome (3,702 feet high), Ka-malō qd., Moloka'i. See Ka-'eo, Pu'u-'eo.

Pu'u-ka-hala. Hill (1,128 feet high), Pu'u-o-kali qd., Maui. *Lit.*, the pandanus hill.

Pu'u-kāhea. Land section, Hālawa qd., Moloka'i. Land section, Wai-'anae, O'ahu; site of Ka-hoa-li'i *heiau,* restored by Ka-hahana but destroyed in 1870 when its stones were used for fences. See Ka-lani-pu'u. *Lit.*, calling hill. (*Ke alanui hele mauka o Pu'u-kāhea la, e kāhea aku ka pono e komo mai 'oe i loko nei* [UL 39], the path going inland of Calling-hill, the right to call you to come within.)

*Pu'u-ka-heu. Hill near Kaupoa, west Moloka'i.

Pu'u-ka-hinahina. Hill (7,811 feet high), Mauna Kea qd., Hawai'i. Probably *lit.*, hill [of] the silversword.

Pu'u-kahua-uli. Peak, Moana-lua, Honolulu. *Lit.*, dark site hill.

Pu'u-kāhuli-'anapa. Hill (547 feet high), Ka-haku-loa qd., Maui. *Lit.*, overturned hill [that] shines.

Pu'u-ka-'īlio. Peak (1,965 feet high), Kolekole Pass, Wai-'anae range, O'ahu. *Lit.*, the dog hill.

Pu'u-ka'ina-pua'a. Peak (2,266 feet high), Ka-wai-loa Forest Reserve, north O'ahu. *Lit.*, pig procession hill.

Pu'u-ka-iwi-po'o. Hill, 'Aiea, O'ahu. *Lit.*, the skull hill.

Pu'u-kakanihia. Hill (3,157 feet high), just east of Wai-mea, Hawai'i. *Lit.*, noisy hill. (*Kakanihia* is a rare passive/imperative of *kakani*.)

Pu'u-Kākea. Cinder cone on the Ko'olau range on west side of Mānoa Valley, Honolulu, named for a storm wind associated with Mānoa; also called Sugarloaf. (Macdonald and Abbott 376.) See Mānoa.

Pu'u-kala. Land section, Kai-lua and Ke-āhole qds., Hawai'i, where

Pu'u-ka-lepe-a-moa

fishponds were destroyed by the lava flow of 1801. *Lit., kala* fish hill.

Pu'u-ka-lepe-a-moa. Hill (9,393 feet high), Mauna Kea qd., Hawai'i. *Lit.,* hill [of] the comb [acquired] by chicken.

Pu'u-ka-maha. Peak (4,016 feet high), Hanalei district, Kaua'i. *Lit.,* hill [of] the rest *or* hill [of] the severed portion.

Pu'u-ka-mana. Hill, Wahi-a-wā qd., O'ahu. *Lit.,* hill [of] the supernatural power.

Pu'u-Kamananui. Hill (870 feet high) at Ka-mana-nui, Wai-a-lua, O'ahu. *Lit.,* Ka-mana-nui hill.

Pu'u-ka-manu. Hill, Hanalei district, Kaua'i. *Lit.,* the bird hill.

Pu'u-ka-moa. Hill (3,439 feet high), Wai-pi'o qd., Hawai'i. *Lit.,* the chicken hill.

Pu'u-ka-mo'o. Hill (1,233 feet high), Kaunakakai qd., north Moloka'i. *Lit.,* hill [of] the *mo'o* (a lizard that tormented a girl was burned and small lizards burst forth from his body, thus introducing lizards to the Islands; Jarrett 31).

Pu'u-ka-naio. Hill on the slopes of Kuala-pu'u, Kaunakakai qd., Moloka'i. *Lit.,* the pinworm hill.

Pu'u-kanaka-leo-nui. Hill, Mauna Kea qd., Hawai'i. *Lit.,* loud-voiced man hill.

Pu'u-Kāne. Hill (3,721 feet high), Wai-luku qd., Maui. *Lit.,* Kāne's hill.

Pu'u-kānehoa. Peak (2,728 feet high), Honouliuli, 'Ewa, O'ahu, named for native shrubs.

Pu'u-Kānehoalani. A high cone-shaped peak behind Kua-loa, O'ahu, named for a god who "ruled the heavens" (Malo 83). According to some, he was the father of Pele. This hill was pierced by the legendary dog, Kū-'īlio-loa (HM 347). *Lit.,* Kānehoalani hill.

Pu'u-ka-'ōkū. Falls, Ka-malō qd., north Moloka'i. *Lit.,* the prominent hill.

Pu'u-kaone. Hill (787 feet high), Kī-lauea qd., Hawai'i.

Pu'u-ka-pe'elua. Hill, Kaunakakai qd., north Moloka'i. A beautiful girl lived in a cave near Ka-la'e. She was visited every night by a lover who left before daylight. The girl wasted away with worries about him. A *kahuna* advised her to attach a piece of white tapa to a wart on her lover's back. In the morning shreds of tapa helped to trace him to this hill, where a large caterpillar (*pe'elua*) was sleeping. The priest ordered the people to collect wood and set fire to him. His body broke and a myriad small caterpillars (or army worms) scattered over the plains, infesting them. (Cooke 102.) See Pili-wai and Pu'u-'enuhe. *Lit.,* hill [of] the caterpillar.

Pu'u-ka-Pele. Hill, Hāmākua, Hawai'i. Peak (3,657 feet high), Wai-mea Canyon, Kaua'i. Voices of Menehune here were believed audible on O'ahu: *Wawā ka Menehune i Pu'u-ka-Pele ma Kaua'i, pū'oho ka manu o ka loko o Ka-wai-nui ma Ko'olau-loa, O'ahu,* Menehune speak at Pu'u-ka-Pele, birds at Ka-wai Nui pond at Ko'olau Loa, O'ahu, are startled. (HM 329; UL 111.) Hill, Airport qd., northwest coast of Moloka'i. *Lit.,* the volcano hill.

Pu'u-kapu. Land division and homesteads, Kamuela, Hawai'i. Peak (1,350 feet high), and quadrangle, Ka-wai-loa, O'ahu. Hill (215 feet high), Moana-lua, Honolulu; chiefs and commoners are said to have met here to discuss important matters. *Lit.*, sacred hill.

Puʻu-kapuaʻi. Hill (1,047 feet high), Wai-ʻanae qd., Oʻahu. *Lit.*, footprint hill.

Puʻu-kapukapu. Hill (1,050 feet high), Kī-lau-ea qd., Hawaiʻi. See Hale-o-Lono. *Lit.*, regal hill.

Puʻu-kaua. Peak (3,127 feet high) in the Wai-ʻanae range, Oʻahu. *Lit.*, war hill *or* fort hill.

Puʻu-kauwā. Two hills and road, Kaunakakai and Ka-malō qds., north Molokaʻi. Perhaps *lit.*, outcast hill.

Puʻu-ka-waiwai. Hill (3,229 feet high), Wai-piʻo qd., Hawaiʻi. *Lit.*, the prosperity hill.

Puʻu-kawiwi. Same as Kawiwi.

Puʻu-kea. Hills, Mauna Kea, Makuʻu, and Wai-kiʻi qds., Hawaiʻi. See ʻĀloʻi. *Lit.*, white hill.

Puʻu-ke-ahi-a-Kahoe. Cliff, Kāne-ʻohe qd., Oʻahu, that overlooks Ka-mana Nui and Ka-mana Iki valleys. *Lit.*, the fire of Ka-hoe Hill. (Ka-hoe lived inland and traded vegetables for fish from his brother who lived by the sea. Because his brother was stingy, Ka-hoe in retaliation cooked his vegetables in a cave; the smoke went out the other end, and so when people came looking at the smoky end, he could hide his vegetables; Sterling and Summers 5:131.) Cf. Moku-o-Loʻe.

Puʻu-ke-ō-kea. Hill, Lualaʻi-lua Hills qd., Maui. *Lit.*, hill [of] white sand.

Puʻu-keʻokeʻo. Hill, Kaʻū, Hawaiʻi. *Lit.*, white hill.

Puʻu-kēpau-ʻula. Peak (2,678 feet high), Mākaha Valley, Oʻahu. *Lit.*, red gum hill.

Puʻu-kī. *Heiau* and land section, Kona; land division and hill (3,201 feet high), Wai-piʻo qd., Hawaiʻi. Hills, Hanalei and Wai-mea districts, Kauaʻi. *Lit.*, ti plant hill.

Puʻu-kiʻi. Islet (1.5 acres, 72 feet elevation) at the mouth of Hāna Harbor, East Maui, where Ka-ʻuiki Head light is located. *Lit.*, image hill *or* fetching hill. (On Ka-ʻuiki Head nearby, site of an ancient fort, ʻUmi erected a huge image to frighten attackers; For. 4:248.) On some maps the island is listed as Puʻu-kū (upright hill); some Hāna people use this name.

Puʻu-kīlea. Hill (732 feet high), Honolua qd., Maui. *Lit.*, small but conspicuous hill.

Puʻu-kilo-iʻa. Hill, Wai-mānalo, Oʻahu. *Lit.*, hill [for] observing fish.

Puʻu-kīpū. Cone (6,289 feet high), Humuʻula qd., Hawaiʻi. *Lit.*, holdback hill.

Puʻu-koa. Land section, Kī-lau-ea qd., Hawaiʻi. *Lit.*, *koa* tree hill.

Puʻu-koaʻe. Hill (3,250 feet high), Kī-lau-ea qd., Hawaiʻi. Islet (13 acres, 378 feet elevation), south central Ka-hoʻolawe. Hill (636 feet high), Ka-haku-loa qd., Maui. Hill, ʻĪlio Pt. qd., Molokaʻi. *Lit.*, tropicbird hill.

Puʻu-koholā. Hills, and *heiau* near Ka-wai-hae, Kohala, Hawaiʻi, constructed by Ka-mehameha I for his war god, Kū-kā-ʻili-moku. In 1966 it was declared a registered national historic landmark, and, in 1972, a congressionally authorized national historic site; it is to be

P

P

restored by the National Park Service. (Ii 17; Kuy. 1:37; RC 145, 154.) See Hale-o-Kapuni, Maile-kini. *Lit.*, whale hill.

Pu'u-kō-hōlua. Hill, Ka'ū, Hawai'i. *Lit.*, hill dragging *hōlua* sleds. (Present pronunciation, Pu'ukoholua.)

Pu'ukole. Land section, Kohala qd.; hill, Mauna Kea qd., Hawai'i. Islet, also known as Sand Bank, Ka-malō qd., south Moloka'i. Point, northeast Ni'ihau. *Lit.*, mons pubis.

Pu'u-kolekole. Mountain, trail, and road, Ka-malō qd., south Moloka'i. *Lit.*, scarred hill.

Pu'u-koli'i. Hill (1,263 feet high), camp, and reservoir, Lahaina qd., Maui. *Lit.*, koli'i shrub hill.

Pu'u-ko'oko'olau. Hill, Mauna Kea qd., Hawai'i. See Ko'oko'olau. *Lit.*, beggar-tick hill.

Pu'u-kū. See Pu'u-ki'i.

Pu'u-kūkae. Cinder cone, Ka-poho, Puna, Hawai'i. *Lit.*, excreta hill.

Pu'u-kukui. Peak (5,788 feet high), the highest point on West Maui, Lahaina qd. (Macdonald and Abbott 324.) *Lit.*, candlenut hill.

Pu'u-kū-Makali'i. Peak (2,572 feet high), Kolekole Pass, Wai-'anae range, O'ahu. Probably *lit.*, rising Pleiades hill.

Pu'u-kumu. Cinder cone, Hale-a-ka-lā Crater, Maui. *Lit.*, foundation hill.

Pu'u-ku'ua. Hill, Honouliuli, O'ahu; Pele's sister Kapo once left her flying vagina (*kohe lele*) there. See Kohe-lepelepe. *Lit.*, relinquished hill.

Pū-'ula. Congregational church and village near Koa'e, Puna, Hawai'i. In the early days, church service was announced by a red conch shell (*pū 'ula*). When a bell was obtained, the conch was buried and a funeral was held for it; later it was stolen. Pele's first landing in Puna was at Ke-awa-o-Pele near here; from there she went to Ke-ahi-a-Laka and Poho-iki, where she dug craters. See Koa'e.

Pu'u-la'alā'au. Hill, Kai-lua qd., Kona, Hawai'i. *Lit.*, twig hill.

Pu'u-la'ela'e. Hill (3,665 feet high), Wai-pi'o qd., Hawai'i. *Lit.*, clear hill.

Pu'u-Laimana. Cone built by the 1960 Ka-poho eruption, Hawai'i. *Lit.*, Lyman's hill (named for Richard Lyman, Jr., owner of the land).

Pu'u-laina. Hill (650 feet high), Lahaina qd., Maui.

Pu'u-lala. Hill, Wai-pi'o qd., Hawai'i. *Lit.*, diagonal hill.

Pu'u-lani. Peak, Wai-mea district, Kaua'i. *Lit.*, sky mountain.

*Pu'u-lanikepu. Hill (3,442 feet high), Wai-pi'o qd., Hawai'i.

Pu'u-lehua. Small cone at about 5,000 feet elevation on Hualālai, Kona, Hawai'i. (Macdonald and Abbott 306.) *Lit.*, lehua flower hill.

Pu'u-lena. Pit crater, Kala-pana qd., Hawai'i. (Macdonald and Abbott 314.) A wind coming from here has the same name. Ancient surfing area, Hanalei district (?), Kaua'i (Finney, 1959*b*:347). Hill at the upper end of the Chinese cemetery, Mānoa, Honolulu. (PH 193.) *Lit.*, yellow hill.

Pu'u-Lilīnoe. Same as Lilīnoe (the peak).

*Pu'u-lio. Hill (3,000 feet high), Wai-luku qd., Maui.

Pu'u-loa. Land section, Kai-lua qd., Kona; peak, Kohala qd.; land sections and camps, Mauna Kea qd.; old name for Queen's Bath and for mound with the most concentrated complex of petroglyphs in

Hawai'i (Cox and Stasack 21–24, 87), Puna qd., Hawai'i; the mound was used as a depository for umbilical cords *(piko)* of infants. Coastal area, Hālawa qd., Moloka'i. Land section, camp, salt works, station, street, playground, beach park, village, area east of Pearl Harbor, and old name for Pearl Harbor, O'ahu; it is said that breadfruit were brought here from Samoa. (PH 16.) *Lit.,* long hill.

Pu'u-lua. Gulch and a double hill *(pu'u lua)*, Hālawa qd., south Moloka'i; the weather station here has recorded the highest annual rainfall on Moloka'i—nearly 150 inches (Stearns and Macdonald, 1947:40). Cinder cone (1,666 feet high), Kaunakakai qd., Moloka'i. West of here are the phallic stone, Ka-ule-o-Nānāhoa (the penis of Nānāhoa), and two stone images of fertility, Kaunānāhoa and his wife, Kawahua. The *kahuna* told women who were barren to bring offerings to these images and to spend the night at the base of the stone; in the morning they would go home pregnant (*Ka Nupepa Kuokoa,* June 12, 1924). A *hōlua* course was here. See Pā-lā'au. *Lit.,* double hill.

Pu'u-luahine. Hill in Ka-lama-'ula, central Moloka'i, with what is believed to be the only remaining *maika* course on the island (Summers 86–87). Hill at the head of Mānoa Valley, Honolulu, named for a *mo'o* woman called Luahine (old woman), who moved here from Haha'i-one with her two sons, Kū-mauna (mountain upright) and Pae-hala (pandanus row). The sons were turned into stone, the mother into the hill.

Pu'u-lū'au. Hill (2,336 feet high), Mā'alaea qd., Maui. *Lit.,* taro tops hill.

Pu'u-māhana-lua. Hill, east Lā-na'i. *Lit.,* twin hill.

Pu'u-māhana-lua-nui. Hill, Lahaina qd., Maui. *Lit.,* large twin hills.

Pu'u-mahia. Point south of Puna-lu'u Beach Park, O'ahu. *Lit.,* pleasant hill.

Pu'u-māhoe. Cone, 13,154 feet elevation, Mauna Kea, Hawai'i. Hills in Mākena and Nā-hiku qds., East Maui. The last lava flow from Hale-a-ka-lā (about 1790) came from the Mākena hill at an altitude of 1,550 feet. It is believed that the flow was caused by Pele, who appeared incognito to a family and demanded a chicken; they refused, saying they had vowed it to Pele. Angry nevertheless, she turned the woman and the daughter to stone, said to be visible now. The husband and his small son ran to the sea, but Pele followed them and turned them into stones in the sea. (Stearns and Macdonald, 1942:103–107; Macdonald and Abbott 51–52.) *Lit.,* twin hill.

Pu'u-maile. Hill and stream, Wai-pi'o qd., Hawai'i. Cinder cone, Hale-a-ka-lā Crater, Maui. *Lit.,* maile vine hill.

Pu'u-Mā'ili'ili. Hill, Lualualei, O'ahu. See Mā'ili'ili, Pu'u-o-hulu. *Lit.,* pebbly hill.

Pu'u-maka-'ā. Land section, Honu-'apo qd., Ka'ū, Hawai'i, probably a man's name. *Lit.,* glowing eye hill.

Pu'u-maka-kilo. Hill near Honouliuli, O'ahu. *Lit.,* observing eyes hill.

Pu'u-maka-li'ili'i. Cinder cone, Ka-malō qd., Moloka'i. *Lit.,* small eyes hill.

Pu'u-mā-kanaka. Peak (12,414 feet high), Mauna Kea qd., Hawai'i. *Lit.,* hill crowded with people (*mā-* is short for *maka*).

P

Puʻu-makani. Hill, Honu-ʻapo qd., Hawaiʻi, now called Waiūbata (butter) because of a dairy there. *Lit.,* windy hill.

Puʻu-maka-wana. Coastal hill, Ka-haku-loa qd., Maui. *Lit.,* sea urchin face hill *or* spiked face hill.

Puʻu-makina. Hill, Honolua qd., Maui.

Puʻu-māmane. Cinder cone, Hale-a-ka-lā Crater, Maui. *Lit., māmane* tree hill.

Puʻu-manawahua. Peak (2,401 feet high), Nānā-kuli, Oʻahu. *Lit.,* great grief hill *or* nausea hill.

Puʻu-manini-kolo. Hill, Kaunakakai qd., south Molokaʻi. *Lit.,* hill [for] seining *manini* fish *or* creeping *manini* fish hill.

Puʻu-manō. Hill, Hālawa qd., Molokaʻi. See Ka-imu-manō. *Lit.,* shark hill.

Puʻu-manu. Hill (3,013 feet high), Wai-piʻo qd., Hawaiʻi. Hills, Hanalei district, Kauaʻi, and southeast Lā-naʻi. *Lit.,* bird hill.

Puʻu-mauʻu. Land sections in Wai-piʻo and Ka Lae qds., Hawaiʻi. *Lit.,* grass hill.

Puʻu-moe. Hill (2,433 feet high), Māʻalaea qd., Maui. *Lit.,* sleeping hill *or* prostrate hill.

Puʻu-mō-iwi. Hill (1,161 feet high), central Ka-hoʻolawe. *Lit.,* bone cut hill.

Puʻu-moʻopuna. Peak (1,548 feet high), Honouliuli, Oʻahu. *Lit.,* grandchild hill.

Puʻu-nāhāhā. Two land sections in Kona, one in Kaʻū, and one in Kohala, Hawaiʻi. *Lit.,* shattered hill.

Puʻu-naio. Prehistoric cinder cone near the 1790 lava flows at Mākena, East Maui. (Macdonald and Abbott 51.) *Lit.,* bastard sandalwood hill.

Puʻu-nānā. Peak on Mauna Loa dome, west central Molokaʻi. See Mauna Loa. *Lit.,* observation hill. (From here one can see the Hoʻolehua plain of east Molokaʻi, Maui, Lā-naʻi, and on very clear days, Hawaiʻi.)

Puʻu-nananana. Coastal area, Hālawa qd., Molokaʻi. *Lit.,* spider hill.

Puʻu-naue. Cinder cone, Hale-a-ka-lā Crater, Maui. *Lit.,* earthquake hill.

Puʻu-nēnē. Land sections, Kaʻū, Hawaiʻi, and Lā-naʻi. Town, hospital, elementary school and cinder pit, Pāʻia qd.; land section, Honolua qd., Maui. *Lit.,* goose hill.

Puʻu-nianiau. Hill (6,849 feet high), near Hale-a-ka-lā Crater, Maui. *Lit.,* peaceful hill.

Puʻu-noa. Point and village, Lahaina qd., Maui. *Lit.,* hill freed of taboo.

Puʻu-nole. Cinder cone, Hale-a-ka-lā Crater, Maui. *Lit.,* weak hill.

Puʻu-nui. Playground and section 10 of Honolulu (map 6). The matriarch of all *moʻo* supernaturals lived here in a clay pit that was later filled in by Caucasians to prevent animals from falling in. *Lit.,* big hill.

Puʻu-nukohe. Hill, Kāne-ʻohe qd., Oʻahu.

Puʻu-Oʻahu. Hill, Kaunakakai qd., south Molokaʻi. *Lit.,* Oʻahu hill.

Puʻu-o-hala. Village and park, Wai-luku qd., Maui. *Lit.,* hill of pandanus.

Pu'u-o-hāla'i. Land division, Hilo qd., Hawai'i. *Lit.*, hill of tranquility.

Pu'u-o-Hawai'i. Land division near the airport, Lā-na'i. *Lit.*, Hawai'i's hill (the island of Hawai'i can be seen from here). Hill, Moana-lua, Honolulu; Ka-mehameha is said to have isolated people from Hawai'i here so that they could not rebel. Many were buried here.

Pu'u-'ōhelo. Hill, Hālawa qd., Moloka'i. *Lit.*, 'ōhelo berry hill.

Pu'u-'ōhi'a. Mount Tantalus behind Honolulu. *Lit.*, 'ōhi'a tree hill.

Pu'u-o-Hoku. Land section, ranch, and cape, Hālawa qd., Moloka'i, mentioned in chants: *A ka lae o Pu'u-o-Hoku i kai, e luma'i 'ia ana lā e ka makani, ka ihu o nā moku i kai anoano;* at the cape of Pu'u-o-Hoku at the sea, beaten there by the wind, prows of ships in silent seas. *Lit.*, hill of Hoku (night of the full moon).

Pu'u-'ohu. Hill (3,934 feet high), Wai-pi'o qd., Hawai'i. *Lit.*, misty hill.

Pu'u-'ōhulehule. Peak, Wai-kāne, O'ahu. *Lit.*, joining-of-waves hill.

Pu'u-o-Hulu. Hill, Lualualei, O'ahu, said to be named for a chief who was in love with Mā'ili'ili, one of twin sisters; since he could not tell the sisters apart, a *mo'o* changed them both to mountains, and he still looks at them. See Pu'u-Mā'ili'ili. A cave (Kāne-ana) here was said to be the home of Māui and Hina (Westervelt, n.d.:120). *Lit.*, Hulu's hill.

Pu'u-o-Hulu Kai. Hill (856 feet high), Lualualei, O'ahu. *Lit.*, seaward Pu'u-o-Hulu.

Pu'u-o-Hulu Uka. Hill (715 feet high), Lualualei, O'ahu. *Lit.*, inland Pu'u-o-Hulu.

*Pu'u-o-ina. Finest example of platform-type *heiau* in Kona (Emory and Soehren 36), south shore of Honokōhau Bay, Hawai'i.

Pu'u-o-ka-'eha. Peak (3,732 feet high), Ka-malō qd., Moloka'i. *Lit.*, hill of the pain.

Pu'u-o-Kaha'i. Highest peak on Mō-kapu peninsula, O'ahu. *Lit.*, hill of Kaha'i (a hero).

Pu'u-o-kaha-nui. Bluff, Airport qd., south Moloka'i. *Lit.*, hill of big place.

Pu'u-o-ka-i'a. Land section, Pā'ia qd., Maui. *Lit.*, hill of the fish.

Pu'u-o-Kaiaka. Hill (110 feet high and covering about one-half square mile), on northwest coast, 'Īlio Pt. qd., Moloka'i. (Stearns and Macdonald, 1947:24.) U.S. Army bulldozers covered a *heiau* at the top of the hill in 1967 (Summers 50). *Lit.*, hill of Kaiaka (said to be a mythological character).

Pu'u-o-Kāka'e. Hill, East Maui. *Lit.*, hill of Kāka'e (a chief).

Pu'u-o-ka-lau-liko. Land section, Honolua qd., Maui. *Lit.*, hill of the budding leaf.

Pu'u-o-kali. Quadrangle and hill (1,481 feet high), Mā'alaea qd., Maui, believed once a *mo'o,* the wife of nearby Pu'u-hele; their child, Pu'u-o-inaina (hill of wrath) was placed on Ka-ho'olawe and later was a lover of Pele's sweetheart, Lohi'au. (HM 189.) *Lit.*, hill of waiting.

Pu'u-o-ka-'ōpu'u. Land section, Honolua qd., Maui. *Lit.*, the budding hill.

Pu'u-o-kapolei. Hill, Honouliuli, O'ahu. The pig-man demigod, Kama-pua'a, established his grandmother here as queen after conquering most of O'ahu. (Sterling and Summers 1:158.)

P

Puʻu-o-Kaupō. Hill, Wai-luku qd., Maui. *Lit.,* Kau-pō hill.

Puʻu-o-Kila. Mountain and lookout, Kōkeʻe State Park, Kauaʻi. *Lit.,* Kila's hill. (Kila, the favorite son of Moikeha, a ruling chief of Oʻahu and direct descendant of Wākea, the first man, is the hero of many legends, most of which recount a journey to Kahiki; in some versions [HM 357] he was a chief of Kauaʻi.)

Puʻu-o-Kīpahulu. Peak, Koko Head qd., Oʻahu.

Puʻu-o-koʻeke. Bluff, Ka-malō qd., Molokaʻi. *Lit.,* in-law hill.

Puʻu-o-Kona. Peak (2,200 feet high), above Wai-mānalo, Oʻahu. *Lit.,* hill of leeward.

Puʻu-ōlaʻi. Hill (998 feet high), Ka-haku-loa qd., Maui; beach and hill (360 feet), Mākena qd., Maui, believed to be the tail of a *moʻo* who angered Pele by becoming the wife of Lohiʻau. The *moʻo*'s tail became Molo-kini Islet. (HM 189.) See Molo-kini. *Lit.,* earthquake hill.

Puʻu-ʻōlelo. Hill (1,389 feet high), Ka-haku-loa qd., Maui. Cinder cone and *heiau* (Summers 113–114), Kaunakakai qd., Molokaʻi. *Lit.,* speaking hill.

Puʻu-ʻoli. Hill, Kaunakakai qd., Molokaʻi. Probably *lit.,* happy hill.

Puʻu-o-māhie. Ridge, Kahana, Oʻahu. (Perhaps this is Puʻumahia Point listed in Coulter.) (Ii 93.) *Lit.,* hill of pleasure.

Puʻu-o-mahuka. State park and well-preserved *heiau* near Wai-mea Bay, Oʻahu, credited to Menehune, and a place where chiefesses gave birth. It was probably at this *heiau* that three of Vancouver's crewmen were offered in sacrifice in 1794. The images here are said to have been destroyed by order of Ka-mehameha II in 1819. *Lit.,* hill of escape.

Puʻu-o-Mālei. Land section, Haʻi-kū qd., Maui. (PH 88.) *Lit.,* hill of Mālei (a *kupua* goddess).

Puʻu-o-Mānoa. Old name for Rocky Hill, Puna-hou, Honolulu. (Ii 93.) *Lit.,* hill of Mānoa.

Puʻu-ʻōmaʻo. Hill on the Honolulu side of Moana-lua Valley, Honolulu; now the site of a cemetery. *Lit.,* green hill.

Puʻu-o-Maui. Hill at Moana-lua, Honolulu, where Maui people were placed by Ka-mehameha I, so that they would not revolt. Many were buried here. *Lit.,* hill of Mauians.

Puʻu-o-Māui. Hill (8,133 feet high), Kilohana qd., Maui. *Lit.,* hill of Māui (the demigod).

Puʻu-o-Molokaʻi. Hill, Wai-mānalo, Oʻahu. *Lit.,* hill of Molokaʻi.

Puʻu-onale. Land section, Kohala qd., Hawaiʻi. (For. Sel. 274.)

Puʻu-one. Land section, Wai-luku qd., Maui. *Lit.,* sand hill.

Puʻu-ʻōʻō. Hills in Hilo, Kohala, and Pua-kō qds.; ranch, Humuʻula qd.; trail, central Hawaiʻi. *Lit.,* ʻōʻō (Hawaiian honeyeater) hill.

Puʻu-ʻōpae. Hill, Līhuʻe district, Kauaʻi. *Lit.,* shrimp hill.

Puʻu-ʻōpae. Cinder cone, Hale-a-ka-lā Crater, Maui. *Lit.,* hill of Pele.

Puʻu-ʻōpelu. Village, Wai-piʻo qd., Hawaiʻi. (Sometimes spelled Puo-pelu.) *Lit.,* ʻōpelu (mackerel scad) hill.

Puʻu-o-Pipika. Hill, Airport qd., Molokaʻi.

Puʻu-o-ʻUmi. Hill (634 feet high), Pāʻia qd., Maui. *Lit.,* ʻUmi's hill.

Puʻu-o-waha-ʻula. Peak (4,827 feet high), Ka-malō qd., Molokaʻi. See Waha-ʻula ʻ *Lit.,* hill of red mouth.

Puʻu-o-Wailau. Peak (4,547 feet high), Ka-malō qd., Molokaʻi. See Wai-lau. *Lit.,* hill of Wai-lau.

Puʻu-ʻowāʻowaka. Hill (3,449 feet high), Wai-piʻo qd., Hawaiʻi. *Lit.,* glittering hill.

Puʻu-o-weli. Hill (1,753 feet high), Puʻu-o-kali qd., Maui. *Lit.,* hill of fear.

Puʻu-pā. Hill, Wai-kiʻi qd., Kohala, Hawaiʻi. Old name for the *pali* end of the trail down the south side of Hālawa Valley, Molokaʻi, probably now called Alanui-puhi-paka. *Lit.,* wall hill.

Puʻu-pālailai. Land section, Wai-piʻo qd., Hawaiʻi. Hill (492 feet high), ʻEwa, Oʻahu. Probably *lit.,* young *lai* fish hill.

Puʻu-pane. Hill, Hanalei district, Kauaʻi. Peak, Schofield qd., Oʻahu. *Lit.,* answering hill.

Puʻu-pāpaʻa. Peak (540 feet high), Mō-kapu qd., Oʻahu. *Lit.,* scorched hill.

Puʻu-pāpaʻi. Cinder cone, Ka-malō qd., south Molokaʻi; a *heiau,* now destroyed, was here (Summers 85). *Lit.,* crab hill.

*Puʻu-peahinaia. Hill (1,623 feet high), Wai-a-lua, Oʻahu.

Puʻu-Pehe. Islet (1.1 acres, 50 feet elevation) off Lā-naʻi. A man hid his sweetheart, Pehe, here; later she was drowned. Now called Sweetheart Rock. *Lit.,* Pehe's hill.

Puʻu-pelu. Land section, Wai-piʻo qd., Hawaiʻi. *Lit.,* turned-over hill.

Puʻu-pia. Hill, upper Mānoa, Honolulu. *Lit.,* arrowroot hill.

Puʻu-piei. Mountain inland of Kahana, Oʻahu.

Puʻu-piha. Cemetery, Lahaina qd., Maui. *Lit.,* filled hill.

Puʻu-pili. Hill, Kohala qd., Hawaiʻi. Hill, Airport qd., north Molokaʻi. *Lit., pili* grass hill.

Puʻu-pilo. Hill inland of Wai-lua, Kauaʻi; it is a *kīpuka* (Macdonald and Abbott 390). *Lit.,* hill [of the] swampy odor *or pilo* plant hill.

Puʻu-Pīmoe. Hill (1,766 feet high), Mākena qd., East Maui. *Lit.,* Pīmoe hill (Pīmoe was a demigod who lived in the sea; in his *ulua* fish form he was hooked by Māui in his efforts to unite the islands).

Puʻu-pōā. Point, Hanalei Bay, Kauaʻi.

Puʻu-poepoe. Cone, 12,679 feet elevation, Mauna Kea, Hawaiʻi. *Lit.,* round hill.

Puʻu-pōhaku. Cone, 13,186 feet elevation, Mauna Kea, Hawaiʻi. Hill (705 feet high), Wai-pahu qd., Oʻahu. *Lit.,* rock hill.

Puʻu-poho-ʻulaʻula. Hill (4,596 feet high), Wai-piʻo qd., Hawaiʻi. *Lit.,* red depression hill.

Puʻu-pouli-hale. Hill, Honouliuli, Oʻahu. *Lit.,* dark house hill.

Puʻu-puaʻi. Peak (3,885 feet high), Kī-lau-ea qd., Hawaiʻi. *Lit.,* gushing hill.

Puʻu-pueo. Hill (969 feet high), Ka-ʻena Point; hill (645 feet), Wai-kāne qd., Oʻahu; a *heiau* here was named Kukui-aniani (flickering light); hill in Mānoa, Honolulu. A Mānoa beauty, Ka-hala-o-Puna, was killed three times by a jealous husband; each time she was resuscitated by an owl who lived on this hill. (Westervelt, 1964:128‒130.) *Lit.,* owl hill.

Puʻu-ʻuala-kaʻa. Hill and State park, Honolulu. See ʻUala-kaʻa. *Lit.,* rolling sweet potato hill.

P

P

Pu'u-'uao. Hill, Ka-laupapa peninsula, Moloka'i. *Lit.,* peacemaker hill.

Pu'u-'ua'u. Hill (1,656 feet high), 'Aiea, O'ahu. *Lit.,* dark-rumped petrel hill.

Pu'u-'ula. Hill, 'Īlio Pt. qd., Moloka'i; hill, Ka-malō qd., Moloka'i. *Lit.,* red hill.

Pu'u-'ula'ula. Cone and rest house at the 10,092-foot level on the trail to the summit of Mauna Loa, Kī-lau-ea qd. (also called Red Hill); Coulter lists places with this name at Humu'ula, Ka Lae, Ke-āhole, Pāhala, and Wai-ki'i qds., Hawai'i. Hill, southwest Lā-na'i. Observatory (at 10,023 feet), Hale-a-ka-lā, Maui. *Lit.,* red hill.

Pu'u-wa'awa'a. Land divisions, Honu-'apo, Pua-kō, and Kai-lua qds., and peak (3,824 feet high), Pua-kō qd., Hawai'i. *Lit.,* furrowed hill.

Pu'uwai. Village and point, Ni'ihau. *Lit.,* heart.

Pu'u-wai-hu'ena. Hill, Pūpū-kea, O'ahu. *Lit.,* flowing water hill.

Pu'u-wepa. See Pu'u-epa.

Pū-wāhi. Coastal land section, Ka-laupapa peninsula, Moloka'i. *Lit.,* broken conch.

Pyramid. Rock, Mō-kapu qd., O'ahu.

QqQqQq

Quarantine Island. See Sand Island.

Queen. Street, downtown Honolulu, named in 1850 for Queen Kā-lama, wife of Ka-mehameha III.

Queen Emma. Street and square near St. Andrew's Cathedral, downtown Honolulu, named for Queen Emma (1836–1885), wife of Ka-mehameha IV, granddaughter of John Young, adopted daughter of Dr. T. C. Rooke, and candidate for election as queen in 1875. She gave the cathedral site to the Episcopal Church. The street was named at the Privy Council meeting of November 10, 1856. (TM.) For Queen Emma's summer home, see Hānai-a-ka-malama.

Queen Ka-'ahu-manu. Highway leading to the Ke-āhole Airport, North Kona, Hawai'i. See Ka-'ahu-manu.

Queen's Bath. Large warm spring pool, Puna, Hawai'i, formerly called Pu'u-loa.

Queen's Hospital. Hospital, originally intended for indigent Hawaiians, established in the late 1850s largely through the efforts of Ka-mehameha IV and Queen Emma. A two-story stone building was completed at Beretania and Punchbowl streets in 1860 and named in honor of Queen Emma, an enthusiastic supporter. The hospital was built on land named Manamana (branching). It is now The Queen's Medical Center. (See Kuy. 2:69–71; Greer, 1969.)

Queen's Surf. Surfing area and beach park, Wai-kīkī, Honolulu, named for Queen Lili'u-o-ka-lani's beach house which stood there (Finney, 1959a:108–109). At one time Chris Holmes' home was there; it was a recreation center for service men in World War II and became a restaurant and night club in 1949. The building was torn down in 1970.

Queen Victoria's Profile. See Hina-i-uka.

Quincy. Place, St. Louis Heights, Honolulu, named by Paul Low and James Hara, subdividers of the heights. For this area they preferred Biblical names or names of Catholic dignitaries, but finding no name beginning with *Q*, they chose Quincy at random. (TM.)

Quinn. Lane, downtown Honolulu, named for the brothers Thomas and James M. Quinn who operated hacks from famous Hackstand 290. (TM.)

RrRrRrRr

R
Rabbit Island. See Mānana.
Rainbow. Falls, Wai-luku River, Hilo, Hawaiʻi. The cave under the falls was said to be the home of Hina, mother of Māui (Westervelt, n.d.:99). The Hawaiian name is Wai-ānuenue. Drive, Honolulu, just beyond Wai-ʻoli Tea Room, Mānoa, Honolu.u.
Ragsdale. Place, Dowsett Highlands, Honolulu, named for Annie Green Ragsdale, daughter of Alexander Ragsdale, who married James Isaac Dowsett. (TM.)
Rawlins. Lane, ʻAʻala section, Honolulu, named for William Joseph Rawlins of England who established a soap factory in Pā-lama in 1837. (TM.)
Red Hill. Hill and school, Hālawa, Wai-pahu qd., Oʻahu. Formerly, Kapūkakī. See Puʻu-ʻula-ʻula.
Reed. Lane, waterfront, downtown Honolulu, named for a skilled ship-builder. (TM.)
Reeds. Land section, bay, and beach park, Hilo qd., east Hawaiʻi. See Kanakea.
Regulars. One of approximately fifteen surfing areas off Sand Island, Honolulu, so called because of its popularity and because one can surf there in fairly calm seas.
Reid's Island. See Kolo-iki.
Rice. Hill (1,195 feet high), Māʻalaea qd., Maui. Athletic field, Puna-hou campus, Honolulu, named for the Rice family. See Laiki.
Richard. Lane, Ka-lihi Waena, Honolulu, named for Antone Richard. (TM.)
Richards. Street, downtown Honolulu, named in 1850 for the Reverend William Richards (1793–1847) who came with the second (1823) missionary company but left the mission to be an adviser to Ka-meha-meha III and first minister of public instruction. He translated large sections of the Hawaiian Bible.
Robello. Lane, Iwilei, Honolulu, named for Frank Robello who worked before 1900 for the McGuire Express Company. The lane was the site of Queen Liliʻu-o-ka-lani's Pā-lama home. (TM.)
Robert. Place, St. Louis Heights, Honolulu, named for Brother Robert, a well-known painter at St. Louis College.
Robinson. Lane, Nuʻu-anu, Honolulu, named for James Robinson, an English seaman who started the Robinson shipyard business at Pā-kākā, Honolulu Harbor. The lane leads to the family home. (TM.)
Rock City. Surfing area near Sunset Beach, north Oʻahu.
Rocky Hill. Hill behind Puna-hou School, Honolulu, formerly known as Puʻu-o-Mānoa.
Rodgers. See Honolulu International Airport.
Roland. Lane, downtown Honolulu, named for an English family who lived there. (TM.)

Rooke. Avenue, Puʻu-nui, Honolulu, named for Dr. T. C. B. Rooke, English physician and surgeon who settled in the Islands in about 1832 and became court physician and adviser to kings. He married Grace Kamaʻikui, daughter of John Young and the High Chiefess Ka-ʻōana-ʻeha. He was the adoptive father of Queen Emma, consort of Ka-mehameha IV. (TM.)

Rose. Street, Ka-lihi Waena, Honolulu, named for Sheriff Charles Henry Rose. (TM.) He was deputy sheriff in 1908 and sheriff in 1914.

R

Rosebank. Place, Nuʻu-anu, Honolulu, named for the home built in Nuʻu-anu Valley by Dr. Robert C. Wyllie. The estate was noted for its beautiful gardens and many rose bushes. (TM.) See Wyllie.

Round Top. See Tantalus, ʻUala-kaʻa.

Royal. Place, Black Point, Honolulu, named for a summer home of Queen Liliʻu-o-ka-lani in Kāhala. (TM.) Elementary school, downtown Honolulu (see Cooke).

Royal Brewery. See Brewery.

Royal Hawaiian Hotel. Famous Wai-kīkī hotel built in 1927, and sometimes referred to as the "pink palace." On the grounds, formerly known as Helu-moa, some of the coconut trees reputedly date back to an ancient grove already there when Ka-mehameha V built a beach house on the site in the 1870s.

Royal Kāʻana-pali. Golf course, Lahaina, Maui.

Royal Mausoleum. Built in 1865 by Honolulu's first architect, Theodore Heuck. The bodies of Ka-mehameha IV and his infant son were the first to be placed here, followed by the bodies of other descendants of the Ka-mehameha and Ka-lā-kaua families.

Royal Palm Drive. Entrance drive at Puna-hou School, Honolulu. The seeds were brought from Paris by Gerrit Judd and set out as four hundred seedlings by the class of 1894. Commonly called Palm Drive.

Royal Saloon. Built in 1890 on Merchant Street; a survivor of Honolulu's boisterous nineteenth-century waterfront.

Ruger. Military reservation, Diamond Head area, Honolulu, established in 1906 and named for Major General Thomas H. Ruger, superintendent of the U.S. Military Academy at West Point, 1871–1876. (Addelman 4.)

Russian Fort. See Fort Elizabeth.

Rycroft. Street, Sheridan Tract, Honolulu, named for Robert Rycroft who established a "soda works manufacturing plant" there in 1900 (TM.)

SsSsSsS

S

Sacred Falls. See Ka-liu-wa'a.

St. Andrew's Cathedral. Kamehameha IV and Queen Emma established the Episcopal Church in Hawai'i in 1861. The cornerstone of the cathedral in Honolulu was laid in 1867, but the church was not consecrated until 1902. It was named for the saint on whose feast day Ka-mehameha IV died (November 30, 1863). Cut stone for the arches, columns, and windows was brought from England. The front was extended to incorporate a stained glass wall in 1958. Next door is St. Andrew's Priory School, dedicated in 1867. In 1972 about 640 girls were enrolled in grades one to twelve.

St. Francis. Catholic hospital, Pu'u-nui, Honolulu, founded in 1927 and named for St. Francis of Assisi; convent and high school, Mānoa, Honolulu.

St. John. Plant science laboratory completed in 1971 on the Mānoa campus of the University of Hawai'i and named for Senior Professor Emeritus Harold St. John.

St. Louis. Drive, St. Louis Heights, Honolulu, named for St. Louis College (now St. Louis High School).

St. Louis Heights. Section 34 of Honolulu (map 6).

Salt Lake. See Ālia-pa'akai. Elementary school, Hālawa, Wai-pahu qd., O'ahu.

Sam Sing. Village, Pā'ia qd., Maui.

San Antonio. Avenue, Punchbowl, Honolulu, named for a benevolent society founded by early Portuguese immigrants. (TM.)

Sandalwood Boat. See Lua-nā-moku-'iliahi.

Sand Bank. Same as Pu'ukole, Moloka'i.

Sand Hill. Peak (3,700 feet high), Kī-lau-ea qd., Hawai'i. Land section, Wai-luku qd., Maui. Old name of area was Pu'u-one.

Sand Island. Flat island (641.27 acres, less than 10 feet in elevation) in Honolulu Harbor; the island was built up on Ka-hola-loa Reef, partly by dredging the harbor; originally it was the larger of two islands that were joined in 1940. The smaller island had a quarantine station in 1869 and was known as Quarantine Island or Mauli-ola (a god of health). The old name had been Ka-moku-'ākulikuli (the *'ākulikuli* plant island) or (rarely) Kaha-ka-'au-lana.

Sandy Beach. Beach and popular surfing area east of the Blowhole, O'ahu, also known as Wāwā-malu and 'Ōku'u.

Saratoga. Road, Wai-kīkī, Honolulu, named for Saratoga House, a hotel which stood on Hotel Street in the 1880s. (TM.)

Saul. Place, St. Louis Heights, Honolulu.

Schofield Barracks. Military reservation, Wahi-a-wā, O'ahu, constructed in 1909 and named for Lt. General John M. Schofield (1831–1906). He served as secretary of war under President Andrew Johnson. (Addleman 5.) Formerly called Lei-lehua.

School. Midtown street, Honolulu, first named School Lane in 1850. It led to the Royal School. (Clark 10–11.)

Scott. Elementary school, 'Aiea, O'ahu, named for Alvah A. Scott, (1888–1949), manager of 'Aiea sugar refinery, 1926–1939.

Secrets. Summer south-swell surfing area near 'Āina-Haina, O'ahu. Newly discovered sites are sometimes kept secret in order not to reveal their locations because of overcrowding. This site is no longer new but the name remains.

S

Self. Lane, Ka-lihi Kai, Honolulu, named for Captain Lui Self of the Inter-Island steamer *Iwalani*. (TM.)

Sereno. Street, Nu'u-anu, Honolulu, named for the Reverend Sereno E. Bishop (1827–1909), son of the missionary Artemus Bishop; he was the first missionary son to return to the Islands as a missionary. (TM.)

Seven Pools. (Formerly, Seven Sacred Pools.) See 'Ohe'o.

Shafter. Military reservation established in 1907, and elementary school, Moana-lua, Honolulu, named for Major General William R. Shafter (1835–1906) who won the Medal of Honor in the Civil War. (Addleman 5.)

Shepherd. Home built in 1897 on Puna-hou Street for Frank Dodge, then superintendent of the Bishop Estate, and purchased by Dr. Irwin Shepherd in 1916.

Sheridan Tract. Section 21 of Honolulu (map 6).

Sherman Park. Place, Pu'u-nui, Honolulu named for Union General William Tecumseh Sherman. (TM.)

Shingon Temple. Built in 1917 when the Shingon mission was established in Sheridan Tract, Honolulu.

Sierra. Drive, Wilhelmina Rise, Honolulu, named for the steamer *Sierra* which ran between San Francisco, Hawai'i, and New Zealand. (TM.)

Shipwreck. Beach, north coast of Lā-na'i.

Siloama. Congregational church for leprosy patients at Kala-wao, Moloka'i, named for Siloam, a spring and pool of water near Jerusalem where a blind man, on Jesus' bidding, washed and recovered his sight (John 9:7).

Silva. Street, Ka-lihi Kai, Honolulu, named for the father of Manuel Silva, the Hawaiian chanter and dancer. (TM.)

Simon. Street, Lanakila section, Honolulu, named for Captain Simon, skipper of a lumber ship which plied between the Islands and the northwest coast. (TM.)

Sinclair. Library, Mānoa campus, University of Hawai'i, Honolulu, completed in 1956, and named for Gregg M. Sinclair (1890–), fourth president of the university, 1942–1955.

Sing Loy. Lane, Ka-pā-lama section, Honolulu, named for a prominent Chinese merchant of the 1880s. (TM.)

Slade. Drive, Puna-hou School campus, Honolulu, named for John S. Slade, principal of the Puna-hou Junior Academy until 1933, and then dean. (TM.)

Slaughter House. Challenging rocky surfing area at Makuleia Bay, northwest coast of Maui.

Sleeping Giant. See Nounou.

Sliding Sands Trail. See Ke-one-he'ehe'e.

Smith. Street, downtown Honolulu, named in 1850 for the Reverend Lowell Smith (1802–1891). Smith established Kau-maka-pili Church in 1838, then a 30- by 65-foot grass house (TM.); he was pastor of the church for 30 years. See Kau-maka-pili, Lowell.

Snyder Hall. Department of Microbiology building, Mānoa campus, University of Hawai'i, Honolulu, completed in 1962, and named for Laurence H. Snyder (1901–), sixth president of the university 1958–1963.

S

Solomon. Elementary School, Schofield Barracks, O'ahu, named for Samuel K. Solomon, a soldier from Kohala, Hawai'i, who was killed in combat in Vietnam in 1965.

Sonoma. Street and place, Mānoa, Honolulu, named for the steamer *Sonoma,* sister ship of the *Sierra.* (TM.)

Spalding Hall. A University of Hawai'i building, Mānoa campus, Honolulu, housing the economics department and the graduate division, completed in 1961 and named for Philip E. Spalding, chairman of the board of regents 1943–1961.

Spalding House. Branch of the Honolulu Academy of Arts, Makiki Heights, Honolulu, named for the former owner, Alice Cooke Spalding (Mrs. Philip E. Spalding), who left the property to the Honolulu Academy of Arts in 1970 as a museum for Oriental art. It was built in 1927 by her mother, Mrs. C.M. Cooke, founder of the Academy of Arts.

Spartan. Reef, Pā'ia qd., Maui.

Spencer. Beach park, Pua-kō qd., Hawai'i, named for Samuel Mahuka Spencer, Hawai'i County chairman 1924–1944. (*Honolulu Advertiser,* March 1, 1960.) See Kamuela. Street, Punchbowl, Honolulu, named for Charles N. Spencer, minister of interior under Ka-lā-kaua. (TM.)

Spreckels. Street, Puna-hou section, Honolulu, named for the sugar industrialist, Claus Spreckels. (Clark 18.)

Stangenwald Building. Honolulu's first "skyscraper," a six-story structure on Merchant Street built in 1901 and probably named for Dr. Hugo Stangenwald, whose house on 'Iliahi Street, probably built in 1860, is still a residence. The doctor died in 1899.

Sugarloaf. Mountain behind Honolulu. See Pu'u-Kākea, Tantalus.

Sulphur Banks. See Ha'akula-manu.

Sunset Beach. See Pau-malū.

Swanzy. Five-acre beach park and playground, Ka-'a'awa, Kahana qd., O'ahu, named for Mrs. F.M. (Julie Judd) Swanzy, who donated the land in 1921. See Ka-'a'awa.

Sweetheart Rock. See Pu'u-Pehe.

TtTtTtTt

T

Tantalus. Mountain (2,013 feet high) behind Honolulu, named by early Puna-hou students for the Greek god who, always thirsty, was punished by being placed in a pool of water. When he tried to drink, the water receded. (Thrum's Annual, 1928:105–106.) Perhaps similarly, as the students climbed, the peak seemed always to recede. See Puʻu-ʻōhiʻa. The same students (including children of the Emersons and Gulicks) also named Olympus, Round Top, and Sugarloaf.

Thirty. Hill (3,224 feet high), Māʻalaea qd., Maui.

Thomas Square. Park and section 17 of Honolulu (map 6), named for British Rear Admiral Richard Thomas who, on orders from Queen Victoria, raised the Hawaiian flag at this site on July 31, 1843, thus returning Hawaiʻi to Ka-mehameha III after Lord George Paulet had seized and declared Hawaiʻi annexed to Britain on February 25, 1843. See Victoria.

Thurston Lava Tube. Lava tube, Kī-lau-ea, Hawaiʻi, named for the missionary Thurston family. The old name was Nā-huku.

Thurston Memorial Chapel. Completed in 1966 on the Puna-hou campus, Honolulu, given by the Thurstons in honor of their son, Robert S. Thurston, Jr., a 1941 graduate who was lost on a military mission in 1945 in the Pacific.

Tripler. Army hospital, Moana-lua, Honolulu; opened on North King Street in 1907 as a post hospital for Fort Shafter. In June 1920 it was officially named for Major General Charles Stuart Tripler (1806–1866), medical director during the Civil War. In 1948 a new Tripler general hospital was built on Moana-lua Ridge, Honolulu, and in July 1950, the name was changed to Tripler Army Hospital. It serves members of the armed forces and their dependents, veterans, and members of the Public Health Service.

Trousseau. Street, Ka-pahulu section, Honolulu, named for Dr. George Trousseau, a French physician who in 1873 advocated segregation of lepers (Kuy. 2:257).

Turtles. Surfing area on the fringing reef seaward of Hawaiʻi-kai, Oʻahu. Turtles are sometimes seen here.

UuUuUu

U

Ua. Drive, Pālolo, Honolulu. (TM.) *Lit.,* rain.

'Uala-ka'a. Old name for Round Top, Honolulu; now a street and State park, Puna-hou section, Honolulu. *Lit.,* rolling sweet potato (a rat bit a sweet potato, causing it to roll downhill and sprout; Ka-mehameha I planted many sweet potatoes here, which, on being dug, rolled downhill).

'Uala-pu'e. Land division and fishpond, Ka-malō qd., south Moloka'i. *Lit.,* hilled sweet potatoes.

*Ua-pa. Land section, Ka-malō qd., Moloka'i.

'Ūhā-'īlio. Ancient surfing area, Lahaina qd., Maui. (Finney and Houston 28). *Lit.,* dog's hindquarters.

'Uhane-lele. V-shaped gap in the Kīpū cliff walls, north Moloka'i, a leaping place for the spirits of the dead. (Cooke 102-103; Summers 34. *Lit.,* leaping soul.

Uhau-'iole. Stream and falls, Līhu'e district, Kaua'i. *Lit.,* rat-hitting.

Uhiuhi. Street, 'Āina-Haina, Honolulu, named for a hardwood tree. (TM.)

Uhu. Street, Ka-lihi Waena, Honolulu. (TM.) *Lit.,* parrotfish.

Uila. Street, Foster Village subdivision, Hālawa, Wai-pahu qd., O'ahu. Name suggested by Mary Kawena Pukui in 1956. *Lit.,* lightning.

U'i-lani. Place, Pālolo, Honolulu. *Lit.,* heavenly (*or* royal) beauty.

Ukali. Street, Foster Village subdivision, Hālawa, Wai-pahu, O'ahu, named for the planet Mercury, as suggested by Mary Kawena Pukui in 1958.

Ukana. Street, Ālia-manu, Honolulu. (TM.) *Lit.,* baggage.

'Uko'a. Fishpond, Wai-a-lua, O'ahu; believed inhabited by Lani-wahine, a *mo'o,* for whom offerings were left; she swam to the sea through a tunnel. Strange fish were sometimes found here—part mullet and part *weke,* or mullet on one side and *kūmū* on the other. When the fish were scaled, the colors were found to be deeply embedded. Unpredictably the fish might be fat or thin and hardheaded. (Ii 98; UL 205.)

Uku-mehame. Land division, canyon, gulch, stream, reservoirs, and shaft (well), Olowalu qd., Maui. (UL 197.) *Lit.,* paid *mehame* wood.

Ula. Street, Ka-lihi Waena, Honolulu. (TM) *Lit.,* lobster.

'Ula-'ino. Land section near Hāna, Maui. *Lit.,* stormy red.

'Ula-kua. Shore area and ancient surfing area (Finney and Houston 28) near the foot of Richards Street, downtown Honolulu. *Lit.,* back red.

Ulana. Street and place, Ka-lihi Uka, Honolulu. (TM.) *Lit.,* still, calm.

'Ula'ula. Hill, Mauna Kea qd., Hawai'i. Hill (3,078 feet high), Lahaina qd., Maui. *Lit.,* red.

Ule. Point, east Ka-ho'olawe. *Lit.,* penis.

Ule-hawa. Stream and beach park between Nānā-kuli and Lualualei,

O'ahu, said to be the birthplace of Māui and to have been named for a chief (Sterling and Summers 2:23, 35.) *Lit.,* filthy penis.

Ule-ki'i. See Lau-pāhoehoe.

'Ulili. Street, Kāhala, Honolulu. *Lit.,* wandering tattler (the bird).

Ulu-hai-malama. Name of Queen Lili'u-o-ka-lani's garden, Nu'u-anu, Honolulu, now called Lili'u-o-ka-lani Gardens. (For a song, see Elbert and Mahoe 72–73.) *Lit.,* inspiring offering [of] enlightenment.

Ulu-kou. Area in Wai-kīkī, Honolulu. (HM 342; Ii 93; RC 166.) See Moana Hotel. *Lit., kou* tree grove.

Ulu-kukui-o-Lanikāula. See Ka-lani-kāula.

'Ulu-maika. Street, Kāhala, Honolulu, named for the stone used in a game much like bowling. (TM.)

Ulu-mau. Hawaiian village, He'eia, O'ahu (formerly at the Wai-kiki end of Ala Moana Park, an area previously used for Aloha Week festivities), and moved in 1969 to He'eia. *Lit.,* ever-growing (a name suggested by Mary Kawena Pukui for the Aloha Week area).

Ulu-ma-wao. Peak (995 feet high), Kai-lua, O'ahu. (PH 86.) *Lit.,* growth at forest.

Ulu-niu. Avenue, Wai-kīkī, Honolulu. (See Indices 758 for two awards made to Ke-kū-ana-o'a.) *Lit.,* coconut grove.

'Ulu-pala-kua. Settlement and ranch, Mākena qd., Maui. *Lit.,* breadfruit ripening [on] back [of carriers].

Ulu-pa'u. Hill, Mō-kapu qd., O'ahu. *Lit.,* increasing soot.

Ulu-pō. Ancient *heiau* and now a historic site near Kai-lua, O'ahu; a large open platform was sometimes attributed to Menehune. *Lit.,* night inspiration.

Uluwehi. Place, Mānoa, Honolulu. *Lit.,* decorative growth.

'Ume'ume-lehelehe. Point, Ka-malō qd., north Moloka'i. *Lit.,* lips (*or* labia of vagina) pulling back and forth.

'Umi. Caverns, Mauna Loa qd.; peak, Wai-pi'o qd., Hawai'i. Land section, Ka-haku-loa qd., Maui. These places are probably named for the sixteenth-century chief of Hawai'i. Street and former land section, Ka-lihi Kai, Honolulu. *Lit.,* strangle. (The name is probably derived from the strangling of a victim used as a human sacrifice at the *heiau* Hāuna-pō which stood in the vicinity of the present street; TM.)

'Umi-koa. Village and ranch, Mauna Kea qd., Hawai'i. Perhaps *lit.,* brave 'Umi.

*Umi-lehi. Point near Pelekunu Bay, north Moloka'i.

'Umi-pa'a. Small land section, Kaunakakai qd., south central Moloka'i, formerly an inland fishpond. *Lit.,* stifle firmly.

'Umi-wai. Land division, Kohala, Hawai'i. (For. Sel. 254, 268.) *Lit.,* hold breath [in] water. (A brackish pool here was said to lead to a spring for which one had to dive. An alternate interpretation is 'water [of] 'Umi', the chief.)

Unu-o-Hua. Same as Ka-unu-o-Hua. *Lit.,* altar of Hua.

'Uo. Ancient surfing area, Lahaina qd., Maui. (Finney and Houston 28.)

'Upolu. Point, Kohala, Hawai'i. Cf. 'Upolu, an island in Samoa, Appendix 9.

Uwao. Stream, Wai-āhole, O'ahu. *Lit.,* peacemaking.

U

Uwē-kahuna. Volcano observatory, bluff, and cliff (PH 208, 221), Kī-lau-ea qd., Hawai'i, and name of one of Kaha-wali's priests who challenged Pele after Kaha-wali's defeat in *hōlua* sledding (see Ka-hōlua-o-Kahawali). A house stood over a pit here; when curious persons entered, the priest pulled ropes making the floor collapse, and they fell to their deaths in the pit. Ka-miki, a hero, set the house on fire and the priest wept *(uwē kahuna).* (Westervelt, 1963:44.)

U

Uwe-wale. Gulch, Kī-lau-ea qd., Ka'ū, Hawai'i. *Lit.,* crying without cause. (*Uwē wale* is a taunt to one weeping; twin brothers climbed a hill; the faster one teased the slower one who had started to cry: *Uwē wale 'uwā, ho'i i Wai-'ōhinu i ka 'ai mai'a pala,* silly crying oh, go back to Wai-'ōhinu to eat ripe bananas [considered bad luck; see PE *mai'a*].)

VvVvVvV

Vancouver. Drive and place, Mānoa, Honolulu, named for the British explorer, Captain George Vancouver, who wintered in Hawai'i three times between 1792 and 1794.

Varney Memorial Fountain. On Mānoa campus, University of Hawai'i, Honolulu, named for Ada S. Varney, teacher at the Territorial Normal Training School, 1911–1929; it was completed in 1934 from funds collected by her former students.

Velzeyland. Surfing area east of Sunset Beach, O'ahu, named for Velzey, a popular make of surfboard.

Ventura. Street, Mānoa, Honolulu, named for the steamer *Ventura,* sister ship of the *Sierra,* operated by the Oceanic Steamship Company. (TM.)

Victoria. Street, Thomas Square section, Honolulu. According to TM, the street was named for Princess Victoria Ka-māmalu, granddaughter of Kamehameha I and sister of Ka-mehameha IV and V. It may rather have been named for Queen Victoria, since it was through her orders that Hawaiian sovereignty was restored at adjacent Thomas Square. See Thomas Square.

Villa. Lane, Bingham Tract section, Honolulu, named for the Hotel Vida Villa, a popular family hotel during the early 1900s. (TM.)

Villa Franca. Section of Hilo, Hawai'i, formerly populated mainly by Portuguese. The old name was Pīkoi-lele.

Vineyard. Midtown boulevard and street, Honolulu, one of Honolulu's oldest streets; it ran to the vineyard of the Spaniard Don Francisco de Paula Marin which was there in the early 1800s.

Violet. Lake, Lahaina qd., Maui.

Volcano. Observatory (4,077 feet elevation), village, golf course, road, trail, and school, Ka'ū and Puna districts, Hawai'i.

Volcano House. Hotel on the brink of Kī-lau-ea caldera, Hawai'i. The first Volcano House was a hut built in 1846 by Benjamin Pitman, Sr. (Olson 23.) See Kino-'ole.

WwWwW

W **Wa'ahila.** Former land section, Mānoa; faculty housing, Mānoa campus, University of Hawai'i; ridge separating Mānoa and Pālolo valleys; State recreation area, 40 acres in area, St. Louis Heights; trail along Wa'ahila ridge ending in upper Mānoa Valley, Honolulu. Also the name of a beneficent Mānoa rain, and of a chiefess who excelled in a dance named for her. (PH 170.)

Wa'a-iki. Coastal area, bay, and gulch, northeast Kaho'olawe. *Lit.,* small canoe.

Wa'a-Kauhi. See Wai-luku.

Wa'a-loa. Way, place, ravine, and stream, Mānoa, Honolulu. (TM.) See Pū-'ahu'ula. *Lit.,* long canoe.

Wa'a-'ula. Trail and coastal area, Ka-malō qd., north Moloka'i. *Lit.,* red canoe.

Wahane. Gulch, northeast Lā-na'i. *Lit., loulu* palm nut.

Waha-'ula. Land section and a *luakini* (*heiau* where human sacrifices were offered) near Kala-pana, Hawai'i, attributed to Pā'ao, a priest from Tahiti in about the thirteenth century; originally called 'Aha-'ula (sacred assembly). It was used by Ka-mehameha I and dedicated to his war god, Kū-kā'ili-moku; it was also the last major temple where public worship was held. In one legend (HM 346; Westervelt, 1964a:2–13), a young chief crossed through the smoke of the *heiau* (believed to be the shadow of the *heiau* god and hence taboo); he was killed by the *Mū* people and his bones thrown into the bone pit. His spirit told his father, the high chief of Ka'ū, who recovered the bones to give them proper burial or to resuscitate the son. *Lit.,* red mouth.

Wahi-awa. Stream and *heiau,* Kō-loa district, Kaua'i. (For. Sel. 102.) *Lit.,* milkfish place.

Wahi-a-wā. Quadrangle, land section, city, district, forest reserve, public fishing area, homesteads, ditch, reservoir, schools, botanic gardens, and recreation center, central O'ahu. (PH 99.) *Lit.,* place of noise (rough seas are said to be heard here).

Wahi-kuli. Land sections, gulch, ditch, State wayside park, reservoir, and housing development, Lahaina, Maui. *Lit.,* noisy place.

Wahī-lau-hue. Gulch and land section, 'Īlio Pt. qd., north Moloka'i. A well here (Pūnāwai-kohe-le'a) which gave drinkable water is now filled in. *Lit.,* wrap gourd leaf.

Wahine-kapu. A bluff near Kī-lau-ea, Hawai'i and taboo residence of the god, Ka-moho-ali'i, Pele's brother (Jarrett 32). (PH 140, 184.) *Lit.,* sacred woman (Pele).

Wahine-koa. Place, Wai-'alae, Honolulu. (TM.) *Lit.,* female soldier.

Wahine-maka-nui. Islet (about 0.18 acres, 40 feet elevation), Puna, Hawai'i. *Lit.,* big-eyed woman.

218 **wai.** 'Fresh water of any kind, stream, river'. Four places on Maui beginning with *Wai-* are famous in song: Wai-ehu, Wai-he'e, Wai-ka-pū, Wai-luku.

Wai-'aha. Forest reserve and stream, Kai-lua qd., Hawai'i. A *heiau kālua ua* (to stop rain *or* to get rain) called Ma'o (green) was destroyed here when a road was built. *Lit.*, gathering water.

Wai-a-Hewahewa. Gulch and stream, Airport qd., south Moloka'i. *Lit.*, water of Hewahewa.

Wai-āhole. Land division, camp, ditch, tunnel, forest reserve, homesteads, elementary school, stream, village, and beach park, Wai-kāne qd., O'ahu. *Lit.*, mature *āhole* (a fish) water.

Wai-a-ho'okalo. Gulch, Hālawa qd., north Moloka'i.

Wai-ahu-akua. Valley and stream, Hanalei district, northwest Kaua'i.

Wai-'Ahukini. Lava-tube shelter and pool, formerly called Wai-o-'Ahukini, on the Kona side of South Point, Hawai'i, studied by Bishop Museum archaeologists, 1967–1968; they believed it was occupied by fishermen between A.D. 750 and 1250 or 1350. Fishhooks found there are similar to those in the Marquesas. See Kā'ili-ki'i. *Lit.*, water [of] 'Ahukini (a supernatural woman).

Waiahulu. Stream, Wai-mea district, Kaua'i. (For. Sel. 242.)

Wai-aka. Spring and pool on the windward side of Nu'u-anu Pali, O'ahu, famous for its clear reflections; now called Wai-kilo-kohe and Ka-wai-kilo-kanaka. *Lit.*, reflection water *or* shadowy water.

Wai-'aka. Land divisions, town, and gulch, Wai-pi'o qd., Hawai'i. Road and place, Mō-'ili'ili, Honolulu. (TM.) *Lit.*, laughing water.

Wai-a-ka-'alalā. Spring, Ka'ū, Hawai'i, said to have been discovered by Hawaiian crows after the 1907 lava flow. *Lit.*, water [found] by the crow.

Wai-a-ka-'ea. Pond and land division, Puna, Hawai'i. *Lit.*, water [used] by the turtle.

Wai-a-ka-'īlio. Bay, Kohala qd., Hawai'i. Land section, Kaunakakai qd., Moloka'i. *Lit.*, water [used] by the dog.

Wai-a-ka-la'e. Gulch, Kaunakakai qd., Moloka'i. See Ka-la'e. *Lit.*, water of the clearness.

Wai-a-ka-milo. Road and former land section, Ka-lihi Kai, Honolulu. *Lit.*, water of the *milo* tree.

Wai-a-ka-moi. Watershed, Ke-'anae qd., Maui. *Lit.*, water [acquired] by the threadfish.

Wai-a-Kanaloa. A wet cave at Hā'ena, Hanalei district, Kaua'i. (UL 249.) *Lit.*, water [used, made] by Kanaloa.

Wai-a-Kanapō. Coastal area, 'Īlio Pt. qd., Moloka'i. *Lit.*, water of Kanapō (perhaps the name of a person or place).

Wai-a-Kāne. Gulch, Airport qd.; south Moloka'i, where a spring, below high tide, is said to have been made by Kāne and Kanaloa (Summers 65); spring, Kaunakakai qd., north Moloka'i. Old name for Wai-kāne, O'ahu. *Lit.*, water [made] by Kāne.

Wai-a-ka-puhi. Islet (0.1 acres, 40 feet elevation), Maka-wao, Maui. *Lit.*, water [used] by the eel.

Wai-ākea. Village and land section, Maku'u qd.; land section and camp, Humu'ula qd.; land section, Hilo suburb, bay (another name is Byron's Bay), park (see Mahohuli), fishpond, forest reserve, mill, plantation, stream, and school, Hilo qd., Hawai'i. A legendary man,

'Ulu (breadfruit), lived here. He died of starvation and was buried near a running spring. Next morning a breadfruit tree laden with fruit was found there, ending the famine. See Ka-nuku-o-ka-manu, Moku-ola. (HM 98; PH 27; UL 60.) The tidal wave of 1960 greatly damaged the Hilo suburb of Wai-ākea. *Lit.,* broad waters.

Wai-a-ke-akua. Stream and gulch, Honolua qd., Maui. Stream, Hālawa qd., Moloka'i. Waterfall and stream, Mānoa Valley, Honolulu (said to be on the east side of the valley). *Lit.,* water [used] by the god. (Kāne and Kanaloa, after making Puna-hou spring, came to this pool. A goddess, Kāmeha'ikana—alternate name for Haumea—flirted with them. Her servant tried to stop her and was turned to stone. Kāne left his footprint on the stone at the pool's edge.)

Wai-a-koa. Land division, village, road, gulch, and homesteads, Pu'u-o-kali qd., Maui. *Lit.,* water [used] by warrior.

Wai-a-koa'e. Diving pool, Ka-lihi Stream, Honolulu. (Ii 45.) *Lit.,* water [used] by tropicbird.

Wai-'ākōlea. Pond at Kala-pana, Puna, Hawai'i. *Lit.,* fern water.

Wai-a-kuilani. Gulch, Ka-malō qd., south Moloka'i.

Wai-'alae. Stream, falls, and mountain (3,600 feet high), Wai-mea district, Kaua'i. Mountain (1,357 feet high), section 39 (map 6), country club, school, and avenue, Honolulu, said to be named for a spring. *Lit.,* mudhen water.

Wai-'alae Iki. Residential development area (the old name is Wiliwili-nui) and playground, Honolulu. *Lit.,* small Wai-'alae.

Wai-'alae Nui. Land division and gulch, Honolulu. *Lit.,* large Wai-'alae.

Wai-'alalā. Spring near Ka-la'e, Moloka'i. *Lit.,* screaming water.

Wai-Alapa'i. Gulch, Hālawa qd., Moloka'i, perhaps named for Alapa'i, a Hawai'i chief who assisted Moloka'i against invaders from O'ahu.

Wai-'ale. Reservoirs and drive, Wai-luku qd.; gulch, Kilohana qd., Maui. *Lit.,* rippling water.

Wai-'ale'ale. Land section, Wai-pi'o qd., Hawai'i. Highest mountain on Kaua'i (5,080 feet), with a mean annual rainfall of 476 inches. (PH 109; UL 40.) *Lit.,* rippling water *or* overflowing water.

Waiale'e. Land section, gulch, station, and beach, Ka-huku qd., O'ahu.

Wai-'ale-'ia. Valley and stream just east of Ka-laupapa peninsula, Moloka'i. *Lit.,* gulped water.

Wai-a-lua. Land division, peak, village, and valley, Hālawa qd., Moloka'i (sometimes spelled Wai-lua). Mill, town, railroad, bay, beach park, recreation center, district, golf course, reservoir, and elementary and high schools, Hale-'iwa qd.; plantation camp, Pu'u-kapu qd., northwest O'ahu. (PH 99.)

Wai-'ama'u. Same as Manini, Kona, Hawai'i. *Lit.,* fern water.

Wai-'anae. Quadrangle, mountain range, land division, town, valley, school, district, and homesteads, O'ahu. A lizard goddess named Pūhā-wai (water hollow) once lived inland at a place called Pūhā; she stole a woman's husband; the wind god, Makani-ke-oe, restored him to her. (PH 161.) *Lit.,* mullet water.

Wai-'anae Kai. Land division and forest reserve, Ka-'ena qd., O'ahu. *Lit.,* seaward Wai-'anae.

220 **Wai-'ānapanapa.** Lakes (6,800 feet elevation), Hāna Forest Reserve,

Nā-hiku qd.; State park and caves, Hāna qd., Maui. A cruel chief, Ka'akea, suspected his wife, Pōpō-'alaea (ball of ocherous earth), of having an affair with her younger brother. The wife hid in a cave, but the shadow of the *kāhili* waved by the attendant betrayed their hiding place, and Ka'akea killed them both. On the night of Kū, the water in the pool is said to run red. (HM 381.) *Lit.,* glistening water.

Wai-a-niu. Same as Wai-'ōniu. *Lit.,* water for coconut.

Wai-a-nui. Gulch, Kaunakakai qd., north Moloka'i. *Lit.,* very big water.

Wai-anu. Land section and stream, Wai-āhole, O'ahu. *Lit.,* cold water.

Wai-ānuenue. Old name for Rainbow Falls, Hilo, Hawai'i. *Lit.,* rainbow [seen in] water.

Wai-anu-kole. Coastal area, Lahaina qd., Maui. *Lit.,* red [with] cold water.

***Wai-a-o-oli.** Gulch, Airport qd., south Moloka'i.

Wai-a-Pele. Old name for Green Lake, Maku'u qd.; bay, Pāhala, Ka'ū, Hawai'i. A pair of twins whispered during a thunderstorm (taboo at the time) and were turned into stones; the male twin, Pōhaku-o-Hanalei, is on the ridge west of the bay, and the female twin, Pōhaku-o-Lēkia, on the opposite ridge. *Lit.,* water [made] by Pele.

Wai-a-pua'a. Valley, south central Ni'ihau. *Lit.,* water of [the] pig.

Wai-'āpuka. Pond near the highway, Lā'ie, O'ahu, formerly containing a secret cave where Lā'ie-i-ka-wai was hidden as an infant until maturity so that her father would not kill her, as he had vowed to do. *Lit.,* water coming out.

Wai-au. Lake (13,020 feet elevation) near the summit of Mauna Kea, Hawai'i. Streams, Wai-mea district, Kaua'i, and Hilo qd., Hawai'i. Land division and village, Wai-pahu qd.; place, Makiki, Honolulu, O'ahu. *Lit.,* swirling water.

Wai-'auia. Land area, Kai-lua, O'ahu. *Lit.,* water diverted.

Wai-awa. Land division, ditch, and stream, Wahi-a-wā, Wai-pahu, and Wai-kāne qds., O'ahu. *Lit.,* milkfish water.

Wai-'awa'awa. Site of reservoir, Ka-wai-hau district, and land section, Wai-mea district, Kaua'i. (For. Sel. 244.) *Lit.,* bitter water.

Wai-ehu. Point and stream, Honomū qd., Hawai'i. Land division, point, streams, village, beach, park, and golf course, Wai-luku qd., Maui. Peak, point, coastal area, and waterfalls, Ka-malō qd., north Moloka'i. *Lit.,* water spray.

Wai-'eli. Hill, 'Īlio Pt. qd., south Moloka'i, covering about one-half square mile. (Stearns and Macdonald, 1947:24.) Street, Kāhala, O'ahu. *Lit.,* dug water. (On some maps the Moloka'i hill is spelled Waiele.)

Wai-hali. Gulch, Ka-haku-loa qd., Maui. *Lit.,* fetch water.

Wai-hānau. Stream and valley, Ka-laupapa peninsula, Moloka'i (sometimes misspelled Wai-a-hānau). *Lit.,* birth water.

Wai-he'e. Land section, village, school, canal, point, reef, river, sugar company, farm, trail, park, canyon, and water tunnels, Wai-luku qd., Maui. Land section and stream, Kāne-'ohe and Wai-kāne qds.; old name for Wai-mea Falls, Wai-mea; street, Ka-lihi Uka, Honolulu, O'ahu. *Lit.,* squid liquid. (A mute, Ke-aka-o-Kū, the shadow of Kū, was told that his speech would be restored if he went to Kahiki to be married. On the way he was attacked by a huge squid which he killed and threw to Kaha-luʻu, Oʻahu. Slime flowed over the land; hence the name. [Sterling and Summers 5:64.])

Wai-hī. One of several streams originating in the high Koʻolau mountains behind Mānoa Valley, and debouching near or at Mānoa Falls, Honolulu. *Lit.,* trickling water.

W

Wai-hiʻi. Stream, Kaunakakai qd., north Molokaʻi; gulch and pipeline, Airport qd., Molokaʻi. *Lit.,* lifted water.

Wai-hilahila. Fishpond, Hālawa qd., south Molokaʻi. *Lit.,* bashful water.

Wai-hī-lau. Stream, Wai-piʻo qd., Hawaiʻi. *Lit.,* many trickling waters (as on a cliff face).

Wai-hiʻu-malu. Falls (400-foot cascade), Kī-pahulu qd., Maui.

Wai-hohonu. Hill and stream, Kō-loa district, Kauaʻi. A "hole" here was formed when a *kupua* hero, Palila, felled a forest of trees with a single stroke (HM 414–415). *Lit.,* deep water.

Wai-hoʻi. Valley, Hāna qd., Maui. *Lit.,* returning water.

Wai-hou. Street, ʻĀina-Haina, Honolulu. (TM.) *Lit.,* new water.

Wai-hū-a-Alapaʻi. Land section, Ka-malō qd., south Molokaʻi. *Lit.,* swollen waters of Alapaʻi. (Alapaʻi was a Hawaiʻi chief who aided Molokaʻi forces in their struggle against Oʻahu invaders.)

Wai-huna. Hill on the east side of Mahana, Airport qd., Molokaʻi. *Lit.,* hidden water.

Wai-ʻili-kahi. Stream, Wai-piʻo qd., Hawaiʻi. *Lit.,* water [with] single surface.

Wai-inu. Road, Wai-luku qd., West Maui. *Lit.,* drink water.

Wai-kā. Land section, Wai-mea, Hawaiʻi. (For a song, see Elbert and Mahoe 52.) Kō-loa Reservoir, Kauaʻi (pronounced Wai-tā). *Lit.,* cleared water.

Wai-ka-halulu. Gulch, Mauna Kea, Hawaiʻi. Bay, south Ka-hoʻolawe. Diving pool and waterfall, Nuʻu-anu Stream; the present waterfront area between Fort and Richards streets, formerly a reef that was filled in when the harbor was dredged in the early 1850s (Kuy. 2:20–23); lane, Nuʻu-anu, Honolulu. (Ii 63.) See Kilohana. *Lit.,* water [of] the roaring.

Wai-kahe. Place, Ka-lihi Kai, Honolulu. *Lit.,* stream.

Wai-kakala-ua. Land section and stream, Wai-kāne, Wahi-a-wā, and Wai-pahu qds., Oʻahu. *Lit.,* water rough [in] rain.

Wai-kakulu. Land section, Hālawa qd., south Molokaʻi.

Waikākuʻu. Village, Hōnaunau qd., Hawaiʻi.

Wai-ka-loa. Stream, Wai-piʻo qd., Hawaiʻi. *Lit.,* water [of] the length.

Wai-kahekahe. Land section, Hilo qd., Puna district, Hawaiʻi.

Wai-kahekahe Iki. Land section, Makuʻu and Puna qds., Hawaiʻi.

Wai-kahekahe Nui. Land section, Makuʻu qd., Hawaiʻi.

Wai-ka-lua. Land division and fishpond, Kāne-ʻohe, Oʻahu. *Lit.,* water [of] the *lua* fighter *or* of the pit.

Wai-ka-moi. Land section, stream, and ridge trail, Ke-ʻanae qd., Maui. *Lit.,* water [of] the *moi* taro.

Wai-Kanaloa. Wet cave, Hanalei, Kauaʻi. Same as Wai-a-Kanaloa. *Lit.,* Kanaloa's water.

Wai-Kāne. Village, quadrangle, land division, and stream, Oʻahu. (Ii 93.) *Lit.,* Kāne's water (old name was Wai-a-Kāne).

Wai-ka-palaʻe. Wet cave, Hanalei, Kauaʻi. Same as Wai-o-ka-palaʻe. *Lit.,* water [of] the lace fern.

Wai-ka-pū. Land section, village, ditch, stream, park, sugar company, water tunnels, valley, Wai-luku qd., Maui. *Lit.,* water [of] the conch. (A conch in a cave here could be heard everywhere in the Hawaiian Islands until it was stolen by a supernatural dog, Puapua-lenalena, yellow tail feathers.)

Wai-ka-puna. Bay, Honu-ʻapo qd., Kaʻū, Hawaiʻi. There are springs here below sea level and on shore. In one story, a beneficent shark god, Ke-aliʻi-kau-o-Kaʻū (the placed god of Kaʻū) married a girl here and she gave birth to a kindly green shark. A stone in the sea here was called Pōhaku-waʻuwaʻu-ʻili (skin-scratching stone). A boy or girl would take a sweetheart from elsewhere to this stone and scratch his or her skin so that others would know that he or she was taken. *Lit.,* water [of] the spring.

Wai-kau-malo. Land section, park, and stream, Honomū qd., Hawaiʻi. *Lit.,* placing loincloth water.

Wai-keʻekeʻe. Stream, Wai-kāne, Oʻahu. *Lit.,* crooked water.

Wai-kele. Land section, stream, and park, Wai-pahu qd., Oʻahu. *Lit.,* muddy water.

Wai-kiʻi. Village, quadrangle, and gulch, north central Hawaiʻi. A spring here was believed formed when a legendary hero, Ka-miki, carried water in a calabash from another spring (Ka-wai-hū-a-Kāne, the hidden water of Kāne). *Lit.,* fetched water.

Wai-kīkī. Section 31 of Honolulu (map 6), beach, park, elementary school, and tennis center, Honolulu. *Lit.,* spouting water (said to be named for swamps later drained to form Ala Wai Canal; also the name of a chiefess [PH 173]).

Wai-kilo-kohe. Same as Ka-wai-kilo-kohe. *Lit.,* water [for] spying on vaginas. Also called Wai-aka.

Wai-kina. Gulch, Paʻu-wela, East Maui. *Lit.,* persistent water.

Wai-koaʻe. Place and former land section, Ka-lihi Kai, Honolulu. *Lit.,* tropicbird water.

Wai-koali. Stream, northwest Kauaʻi. *Lit.,* morning-glory water.

Wai-koko. Stream and land section, Hanalei district, Kauaʻi. *Lit.,* blood water.

Wai-koloa. Land section, development area, and stream, Pua-kō and Wai-kiʻi qds.; land section, stream, and hill (2,800 feet high), Wai-piʻo qd.; ponds, Humuʻula qd., Hawaiʻi. *Lit.,* duck water. (This may be Wai-kō-loa, the name of a wind.)

Wai-kō-loa. Gulch near Schofield Barracks, Oʻahu. (For. Sel. 278.) Also, the name of a cold northwest wind (For. Sel. 282). *Lit.,* water pulling far.

Wai-koloa Iki. Land division, Wai-piʻo qd., Hawaiʻi. *Lit.,* small Wai-koloa.

Wai-kolu. Stream, Honomū qd., Hawaiʻi. Valley, land division, and stream, Ka-malō qd., Molokaʻi. A 5.5-mile water tunnel commencing in the north fork of Kaunakakai gulch ends on the western side of

Wai-kolu valley; the breach-through was made in 1960. In 1969 between 2 and 28 million gallons of water a day passed through into a 1.4-billion-gallon reservoir at Kuala-puʻu (Summers 25). Way, Wai-kīkī, Honolulu, named for the three waters emptying into Wai-kīkī before the Ala Wai Canal was dug (TM). *Lit.,* three waters.

W

Wai-komo. Stream, Kō-loa district, Kauaʻi. The sleeping forms of the gods Kāne and Kanaloa are said to be imprinted at Mau-hili pool in this stream (HM 65). Part of Mākua beach, Kaʻena qd., Oʻahu. *Lit.,* entering water.

Wai-koʻo-lihilihi. Pool at Puna, Hawaiʻi. *Lit.,* water supporting eyelashes. (*Lehua* flowers were fastened on reeds here in honor of visiting chiefs; when they kneeled to drink, the blossoms touched their eyelashes. The last royal person to visit here was Ke-oho-kālole, mother of Ka-lā-kaua and Liliʻu-o-ka-lani.)

Wai-kūʻau-hoe. Trickling waterfall *(wai hī)* on a cliff of the Nā-pali coast, Kauaʻi. Fishermen placed their paddle handles *(kūʻau hoe)* against the cliff and drank the trickling water. For a saying, see the Preface.

Wai-kulu. Land section, Honolua qd., Maui. *Lit.,* trickling water.

Wai-kuna. Pool in the Wai-luku River above Rainbow Falls, Hilo, Hawaiʻi, believed the home of Kuna (freshwater eel), a *moʻo* who tried to kill Māui's mother, Hina, who lived in a cave below the falls. Kuna threw a rock to dam the river and drown Hina. Hina called to Māui for help; he poured hot water into Kuna's home. They fought and Kuna was beaten to death and thrown over Rainbow Falls. (Westervelt, n.d.:100.) *Lit.,* eel water.

Wai-lana. Gulch, Hālawa qd., Molokaʻi. *Lit.,* floating water.

Wai-lani. Road, Pacific Heights, Honolulu. *Lit.,* heavenly water.

Wai-lau. Land section, Honu-ʻapo and Pāhala qds., Hawaiʻi. Valley, Wai-mea district, Kauaʻi. Valley, land division, trail, former village, and stream, Ka-malō qd., north Molokaʻi. In *Ka Nupepa Kuokoa* of August 2, 1912, are listed many place names along the trail from Pū-koʻo, Molokaʻi, up over the mountain and down to the bottom of Wai-lau Valley. *Lit.,* many waters.

Wai-Lea. Land areas, Honomū qd., Hawaiʻi, and Mākena qd., Maui. Point between Lani-kai and Wai-mānalo, Oʻahu. *Lit.,* water of Lea (canoe makers' goddess; also the name of a fish god that stands on this point).

Wailele. Falls, Ka-malō qd., north Molokaʻi. Gulch, Puʻu-kapu qd., Oʻahu; street, Ka-lihi Uka, Honolulu, named in 1865 by Prince Lot for a waterfall of the same name. (TM.) *Lit.,* waterfall.

Wai-lena. Gulch, Ka-haku-loa qd., Maui. *Lit.,* yellow water.

Wai-loa. Land section, Pāhala qd.; falls, river, and State park, Hilo qd.; river, Wai-piʻo qd., Hawaiʻi. *Lit.,* long water.

Wai-loku. Gulch, Hālawa qd., Molokaʻi. *Lit.,* surging water.

Wai-lua. Land division and stream, Honomū qd.; land division, Honu-ʻapo qd., Hawaiʻi. State park, land division, river, falls, valley, town, and golf course, Līhuʻe qd., Kauaʻi. *Heiau,* a place of refuge, and birth stones here are said to be in excellent condition. (UL 255.) See Ka-ʻō-hala. Bay, Ki-pahulu qd., Maui. *Lit.,* two waters.

Wai-lua Iki. Land division, Nā-hiku qd., Maui. *Lit.,* small Wai-lua.

Wai-lua Nui. Land division, Nā-hiku qd., Maui, where Kapo saved Pele from Kama-pua'a. Stones represent a vagina. See Kohe-lepe-lepe. *Lit.,* big Wai-lua.

Wai-luku. River and State recreation area, Hilo, Hawai'i. A rock here called Wa'a-Kauhi (canoe [of] Kauhi [a Maui chief]) is said to be the petrified canoe of the demigod Māui. See Ka Lae. Land division, elementary school, quadrangle, heights, city, point, sugar company, and stream, West Maui; site of the battle in the late eighteenth century in which the army of Ka-lani-'ōpu'u was nearly annihilated by Ka-hekili of Maui. (Kuy. 1:31; PH 57; RC 148.) See Ke-pani-wai. *Lit.,* water [of] destruction.

Wai-lupe. Land section, circle, place, beach park, valley, gulch, elementary school, playground, peninsula, and Naval radio station, seaward of 'Āina-Haina, Honolulu. A pond here was filled in by man to form Wai-lupe peninsula. *Lit.,* kite water (kites were flown only in prescribed places; this was one of them).

Wai-mā. Point, Pua-kō qd., and stream, Wai-pi'o qd., Hawai'i. *Lit.,* discolored water.

Wai-māha'iha'i. Coastal area, Mā'alaea qd., Maui. *Lit.,* broken water.

Wai-malu. Hill (1,450 feet high), land section, town, elementary school, playground, and stream debouching at Pearl Harbor, O'ahu; the Spaniard Francisco de Paula Marin had a home here (Ii 95). *Lit.,* sheltered water.

Wai-malu Uka. Land section near Wai-malu, O'ahu. *Lit.,* inland Wai-malu.

Wai-mana. Land section, Ka-malō qd., Moloka'i. *Lit.,* many waters.

Wai-mānalo. Land division, bay, beach, beach park, gymnasium, ditch, forest reserve, landing, stream, and school, Koko Head qd.; land division, road, and gulch, Barber's Pt. qd., O'ahu, and the site of the home of Chief Kākuhihewa (see Mau'u-mae). *Lit.,* potable water.

Wai-mano. Stream, trail, and land division near Pearl Harbor, O'ahu; the shark demigoddess Ka-'ahu-pāhau bathed here. *Lit.,* many waters.

Wai-manu. Land sections, village, bay, stream, horse and foot trail, gap (2,089 feet elevation), and valley, Wai-pi'o qd., Hawai'i. (UL 52.) Land section, Wai-mea district, Kaua'i. Falls, Ka-malō qd., north Moloka'i. Street, Kewalo section, Honolulu. *Lit.,* bird water.

Wai-mea. Village, homesteads, elementary and intermediate school, land division, tableland (3,000 feet elevation), and trail, Wai-pi'o qd., Hawai'i. Town, bay, canyon, district, school, ditch, plantation, landing, river, road, and land division, southwest Kaua'i, where Captain Cook first landed (1778). Land section, bay, reservoir, hill (251 feet high), falls (55 feet high), stream, beach, park; famous big-wave surfing area where winter waves break to 35 feet or more; Hale-'iwa and Pu'u-kapu qds., north O'ahu. The falls were formerly called Wai-he'e. After Captain Cook was killed at Ke-ala-ke-kua, Hawai'i, on February 14, 1779, his ships called here for water on February 27. Vancouver landed here in 1793; while drawing water in the stream, two of his men were killed by Hawaiians who wanted their weapons. Vancouver ordered that the assassins be killed, and two men were shot, but it is not certain that they were the murderers

W

225

W

(Kuy. 1:44; RC 166). See Pu'u-o-mahuka. *Lit.,* reddish water (as from erosion of red soil).

Wai-naku. Village and land section, Hilo qd., Hawai'i. *Lit.,* pushing water.

Wai-nānā-li'i. Former pond buried by lava flows, North Kona, Hawai'i. Stones standing in the pool in the middle of the lava are supernatural *mo'o* (Kani-kū and Kani-moe), changed to stone by the eruption. Walls are said to have divided the pond into sections for mullet *('anae),* milkfish *(awa),* and *āhole. Lit.,* chief-protected water.

Wai-ne'e. Land division, village, road, church, and cemetery, Lahaina qd., Maui. *Lit.,* moving water.

Wai-neki. Swampy mountains above Wai-mea town, Kaua'i, home of the Menehune (Jarrett 29); also spelled Wai-neke. *Lit.,* bulrush water.

Wai-nēnē. Coastal area, Ka-malō qd., north Moloka'i. *Lit.,* goose water.

Wai-niha. Land section, village, bay, canal, landing, *pali,* river, valley, and canyon, Hanalei district, Kaua'i. (PH 110; UL 135.) *Lit.,* unfriendly water.

Wai-o-'Ahukini. Same as Wai-'Ahukini. *Lit.,* water of 'Ahukini.

Wai-'ōhinu. Village and land division, Honu-'apo and Ka Lae qds., Ka'ū, Hawai'i. *Lit.,* shiny water. Drive, Kāhala, Honolulu.

Wai-o-honu. Stream, gulch, and homesteads near Hāna, Maui. A place between this stream and Papa-hawahawa gulch was called Kiki-manu (bird basket). Here lived Kahuoi, a famous gardener, who had fled from Hawai'i because of his parents' continual scolding; he named his children born here 'Awahua (resentful) and 'Ae'a (wanderer). *Lit.,* water of [the] turtle.

*Wai-oho-o-kalo. Stream, Ka-malō qd., north Moloka'i.

Wai-o-huli. Land division, gulch, and village, Pu'u-o-kali qd., Maui. *Lit.,* water of change.

Wai-o-huli Ke-ō-kea. Homesteads, Pu'u-o-kali qd., Maui.

Wai-'ōkala. Coastal area near Kiki-pua, Hālawa qd., north Moloka'i. *Lit.,* goose-pimple water.

Wai-o-ka-pala'e. Wet cave, Hanalei, Kaua'i. *Lit.,* water of the lace fern.

*Wai-o-keela. Stream, Ka-malō qd., Moloka'i.

Wai-o-ke-ola. Congregational church, Kāhala, Honolulu. *Lit.,* water of the life.

Wai-o-Kila. Gulch, Ka-haku-loa qd., Maui. *Lit.,* water of Kila. (Perhaps this is Kila, a son of Mo'ikeha, who journeyed to Kahiki to fetch La'a-mai-Kahiki.)

Wai-ola. Church and cemetery, Lahaina, Maui. Stream, Kaha-lu'u; valley, Pu'u-kapu qd.; street, Pā-wa'a section, Honolulu; fountain near Liberty House, Ala Moana Center, Honolulu, O'ahu. Sacred pool far inland in Ka-mana Nui Valley, Moana-lua, O'ahu. *Lit.,* water [of] life.

Wai-ōla'i. Gulch, Ka-haku-loa qd., Maui. *Lit.,* earthquake water.

Wai-o-lama. Stream and beach, Hilo, Hawai'i. *Lit.,* water of torch.

Wai-o-lani. Stream, Kāne-'ohe qd., O'ahu. *Lit.,* water of heaven.

Wai-'oli. Land division, stream, and mission house built in 1841 for Abner and Lucy Wilcox, Hanalei, Kaua'i. (UL 155.) See Wilcox.

Tea room operated by the Salvation Army, Mānoa, Honolulu, named for the Kauaʻi mission home in honor of George N. Wilcox, a principal benefactor (Krauss 311). *Lit.,* joyful water.

Wai-ʻōmaʻo. Road, stream, and former land area, Pālolo, Honolulu. *Lit.,* green water.

Wai-ʻōniu. Tidal freshwater spring, Hīlea, Kaʻū, Hawaiʻi; also called Wai-a-niu. *Lit.,* swirling water.

Wai-ʻopa. Gulch, east Lā-naʻi. *Lit.,* crippled water.

Wai-ʻōpai. Land section, gulch, and ranch, Kau-pō qd., Maui. Perhaps a garbled spelling for Wai-ʻōpae (shrimp water).

Wai-o-pipi. Land section, Hālawa qd., Molokaʻi. *Lit.,* pearl-oyster water.

Wai-o-ʻulu. A waterfall, Wai-piʻo, Hawaiʻi. *Lit.,* water of the *maika* stone (water was first made here by a *maika* stone hurled here by a hero).

Wai-pā. Land division and stream, Kō-loa district; stream, Hale-leʻa Forest Reserve, Hanalei district, Kauaʻi. (UL 133.) Lane, Pā-lama, Honolulu, named for Captain Robert Parker Wai-pā, in charge of police during the 1895 insurrection. (TM.) *Lit.,* touched water.

Wai-paheʻe. Trail and waterfall providing a natural slippery-slide, Ka-wai-hau district, Kauaʻi. *Lit.,* slippery water.

Wai-pāhoehoe. Land section and stream, Hilo qd.; gulches, Humuʻula, Mauna Kea, and Kohala qds.; stream, Wai-piʻo qd., Hawaiʻi. *Lit.,* pāhoehoe (smooth lava) water.

Wai-pahu. Quadrangle, land section, city, stream, high school, and field, south central Oʻahu; said to have been originally Wai-pahū. The shark goddess Ka-ʻahu-pāhau lived here. *Lit.,* bursting water (water burst forth from underground).

Wai-pao. Gulch, Wai-mea district, Kauaʻi. Land division near Mākena, East Maui. *Lit.,* scooped water.

Wai-pili. Gulch, Ka-haku-loa qd., Maui. *Lit.,* touching water.

Wai-pilopilo. Land area near the pumping station at King and Hough-tailing streets, Honolulu. *Lit.,* smelly water. (In the battles of 1783 in which Ka-hekili of Maui defeated Ka-hahana of Oʻahu, corpses are said to have dammed the streams; RC 136 and *Aloha Aina,* March 4, 1911.)

Wai-piʻo. *Pali,* Honu-ʻapo qd., Hawaiʻi; quadrangle, valley, land section, bay, gulch, stream, and ancient surfing place, north Hawaiʻi (For. Sel. 138, 170; PH 49–50; Finney and Houston 26). The earth in the upper valley is red because Kanaloa dashed Māui against the rocks and his blood colored the earth there (Westervelt, n.d.:151). Bay, land section, gulch, and school, Haʻi-kū qd., Maui. Land sections, village, golf course, peninsula, point, river, and station, Wai-pahu and Wahi-a-wā qds., south central Oʻahu. *Lit.,* curved water.

Wai-pouli. Land division, beach, and village, Ka-wai-hau district, Kauaʻi. *Lit.,* dark water.

Wai-pū. Coastal area, Ka-malō qd., north Molokaʻi.

Wai-puhia. Upside Down Falls, Nuʻu-anu Valley, Oʻahu. *Lit.,* blown water.

Waipuʻilani. Gulch, Puʻu-o-kali qd., Maui. *Lit.,* waterspout.

Wai-puka. Pools near the mouth of Ka-mana Iki Valley, Moana-lua, O'ahu, where chiefs bathed after games and wrestling. *Lit.,* issuing water.

Wai-puna. Rise, Woodlawn, Mānoa, Honolulu. (TM.) *Lit.,* spring water.

Wai-puna-lei. Land division and gulch, Mauna Kea qd., Hawai'i, where 'Umi lived incognito and in poverty (For. Sel. 124, 150). *Lit.,* lei spring water.

W

Waitā. Reservoir, Grove Farm, Kaua'i. Perhaps *wai-,* water, and *-ta* rice paddy (Japanese). Formerly called Kō-loa.

Waiū. Land area, Līhu'e district, Kaua'i. *Lit.,* female breast.

Waiūbata. See Pu'u-makani.

Wai-welawela. A warm-spring pool near Ka-poho, Hawai'i, covered in the 1960 eruption; also known as Warm Springs. (PH 210.) *Lit.,* warm water.

Wākine. Place, Kuli-'ou'ou, Honolulu, named for the Joaquin family of ranchers who lived in the valley above Kuli-'ou'ou at the time Charles Costa subdivided the tract. (TM.) *Lit.,* Joaquin.

Wā-kiu. Land section near Hāna, Maui. *Lit.,* northwest wind sound.

Waldron. Home of Fred L. Waldron at 2042 Vancouver Drive, Mānoa, Honolulu, built in 1905 and now the Baptist Student Center. See also Mother Waldron.

Waldron Ledge. Small portion of northern rim of Kī-lau-ea caldera, Hawai'i, named for purser of the *Vincennes,* a ship of the U.S. Exploring Expedition in 1840 and 1841.

Walea. Place, Nu'u-anu, Honolulu. *Lit.,* leisure.

Walina. Street, Wai-kīkī, Honolulu. *Lit.,* softness.

Walu. Way, Mānoa, Honolulu. *Lit.,* to scratch *or* eight.

Wanaka. Street, Ālia-manu, Honolulu. (TM.) *Lit.,* Wanda.

Wānana-lua. Land section and Congregational church at Hāna, Maui. *Lit.,* double prophecy.

Wānana-paoa. Island (0.09 acres, 40 feet elevation), Wai-mea Bay, O'ahu. *Lit.,* unsuccessful prophecy.

Wanini. Old name for 'Anini, Kaua'i.

Wao-kanaka. Street and place, upper Nu'u-anu, Honolulu, named for inland inhabited regions *(wao kanaka),* below the uninhabited *wao akua* (god uplands).

Wao-lani. Street, land division, valley, and stream in upper Nu'u-anu Valley, Honolulu. The first Hawaiian *heiau,* built by the gods, was in the area. Kāne and Kanaloa lived here (HM 332) and here the first man, Wākea, was born. In For. 6:408–413 and in Fornander, 1969:280, is the story of Kua-li'i, who crossed the mountains by the Nu'u-anu and Ka-lihi passes, assembled his men at Ke-ana-o-ka-manō ridge that overlooks Wao-lani, then descended to Kawa-luna *heiau* to offer sacrifices, and finally won a victory at Wao-lani. *Lit.,* heavenly mountain area.

Ward. Important avenue leading from Punchbowl to Kewalo Basin, Honolulu, named for Curtis Perry Ward, a Southerner who came to the Islands in the 1860s. He married Victoria Robinson; their home and estate, named Old Plantation, was on King Street at the site now occupied by the Honolulu International Center. The song "Old Plantation" (Elbert and Mahoe 83) honors this place.

Warm Springs. Same as Wai-welawela.

Washington Place. Built in 1847 in downtown Honolulu for merchant and sea captain John Dominis and named by U.S. Commissioner Anthony Ten Eyck, this is the oldest continuously occupied residence in Honolulu. Queen Lili'u-o-ka-lani, wife of John Owen Dominis (son of the captain) inherited the residence and lived in it until her death in 1917. It was purchased by the Territory of Hawai'i in 1921 for a governor's mansion.

Washington Stone. See Ka-hiki-lani.

Watanabe Hall. Physical science building, Mānoa campus, University of Hawai'i, Honolulu, completed in 1970 and named for Dr. Kenichi Watanabe (1910–1969), senior professor of physics.

Waterhouse. Street, Ka-lihi Kai, Honolulu, named for John Thomas Waterhouse, who came to Hawai'i from Tasmania in 1851 and founded the Waterhouse mercantile business. (TM.) The Elizabeth Waterhouse Memorial Swimming Pool on the Puna-hou campus was donated in 1922 by Mr. and Mrs. John Waterhouse in memory of their daughter, who was killed in an auto accident.

Watson. Place, Nu'u-anu, Honolulu, named for Judge Edward M. Watson, who came to Hawai'i in 1901 and was appointed to the Supreme Court in 1913, to the Circuit Court in 1928, and to the U.S. District Court in 1935. (TM.)

Wauke. Street, Diamond Head section, Honolulu. *Lit.,* paper mulberry.

*Wawae-olepe. Land section, Ka-malō qd., Moloka'i.

Wāwā-'ia. Land division and gulch, Ka-malō qd., south Moloka'i. *Lit.,* noisy.

Wāwā-malu. Sandy Beach; formerly Āwawa-malu.

Wawau. Land section near Mo'okini *heiau,* Kohala, Hawai'i. Point near Spreckelsville, Maui. This name is probably cognate with an old name for Ra'i-ātea in the Society Islands, for an inland area at Vai-taha, Tahu'ata, Marquesas, and for Vava'u, an island in the Tongan group. See Appendix 9.

Wawe. Place, Foster Village subdivision, Hālawa, Wai-pahu qd., O'ahu. Name suggested by Mary Kawena Pukui in 1956. *Lit.,* quick, fast.

Weaver. Sister fort to Fort Ka-mehameha at the entrance to Pearl Harbor, established in 1922 and named for Major General Erasmus M. Weaver, chief of the coast artillery, 1911–1918. It is now a naval reservation. (Addleman 34.)

Webling. Elementary school, 'Aiea, O'ahu, named for Gustav Henry Webling (1889–1963), district superintendent of rural schools, O'ahu.

Webster Hall. Building, Mānoa campus, University of Hawai'i, Honolulu, housing the school of nursing, deans' offices, and language departments, completed in 1961 and named for Ernest Charles Webster (1883–1956), professor of mathematics and engineering 1925–1948, and at different times dean of men, dean of student personnel, and acting dean of applied science.

Wēkiu. Land area, northeast central Kaua'i. *Lit.,* top, summit.

Wela. Street, Ka-pahulu section, Honolulu. (TM.) *Lit.,* hot.

Weli. Point, Kō-loa qd., Kaua'i. Fishpond near Ka-hau-iki, Honolulu. *Lit.,* fear.

W

Wells. Ball park, Wai-luku, Maui, named for Charles B. Wells, manager of Wailuku Sugar Company 1893–1908.

Welokā. *Heiau,* Wai-a-lua, Moloka'i, where Ka-mehameha-nui of Maui was reared (Summers 149). See Pākaikai. *Lit.,* hit float.

West Maui Mountains. Mountain mass, West Maui. The principal peaks are Pu'u-kukui (5,788 feet) and Eke (4,480 feet).

Wheeler. Air Force Base, and elementary school, Wahi-a-wā, O'ahu, established in 1922 and named for Air Force Major Sheldon H. Wheeler, who was killed in 1921 when his plane crashed. (Addleman 35.)

Whiting. Street, Punchbowl, Honolulu, named for Judge W.A. Whiting who was first judge of the First Circuit Court of the Republic of Hawai'i at the time of the 1895 insurrection. (TM.)

Whitmore. Dole Company plantation village near Wahi-a-wā, O'ahu.

Whitney. Street, Bingham Tract section, Honolulu, named for Samuel Whitney (1793–1845), member of the first missionary company, 1820. (TM.)

Whittington. Beach park, Honu-'apo qd., southeast Hawai'i, named in 1948 for Richard H. Whittington, road overseer.

Wichman. House on Victoria Street, Honolulu, built in 1902 for Honolulu jeweler H.F. Wichman.

Wilcox. Lane, Ka-lihi Kai, Honolulu, named for Judge William Luther Wilcox (1850–1903), son of the missionary teachers Abner and Lucy Wilcox; he married Chiefess Kahuila of Moloka'i. An elementary school at Lihu'e, Kaua'i, is named for Elsie Hart Wilcox, daughter of Samuel Whitney Wilcox (1847–1929), an older brother of William Luther Wilcox. Miss Wilcox, a civic leader, was commissioner of the Board of Public Instruction 1920–1932. Wilcox Memorial Hospital, Līhu'e, was named for George N. Wilcox (1839–1933). Wilcox Hall, Puna-hou School, Honolulu, was constructed in 1936 as a boys' dormitory with funds left by George N. Wilcox. See Grove Farm, Wai-'oli, Wilikoki.

Wilder. Avenue, Makiki, Honolulu, named for Samuel G. Wilder who arrived in 1858 and established a shipping business. The street was first called Stonewall because of the wall built along it by Hawaiian prisoners at the command of Queen Ka-'ahu-manu in 1830. Clerks in S.G. Wilder's office petitioned to have the name changed. (TM.)

Wilhelmina Rise. Mountain, street, and section 36 of Honolulu (map 6), named for Wilhelmina Tenney, whose father, Edward D. Tenney, was president of Castle and Cooke for many years and associated with the Matson Navigation Company. Many streets on Wilhelmina Rise are named for Matson ships. The old name for the area was Pa'ina.

Wili-ka-'a'i. Name for the old sugar mill at Kua-loa, Wai-kāne qd., O'ahu. *Lit.,* twist the neck. (A one-eyed Hawaiian digger on the excavations, accustomed to the '*ō'ō* digging stick, twisted his neck to follow with his single eye every spadeful of dirt and got a stiff neck as a result; Sterling and Summers 5:12.)

Wilikī. Drive, Ālia-manu, Honolulu. *Lit.,* engineer.

Wilikoki. Place, Kai-lua, O'ahu, site of the former country home of

Gaylord Wilcox (1881–1970), a son of Samuel W. Wilcox (see Wilcox) and a friend of Arthur Rice (see Laiki). *Lit.,* Wilcox.

Wiliwili. Street, McCully section, Honolulu, named for a native tree bearing red seeds.

Wiliwili-nui. Ridge, Wai-'alae, Honolulu. See Wai-'alae Iki. *Lit.,* large Wiliwili.

Williams. Street, Ka-imu-kī, Honolulu, named for Earl Herbert Williams, the realtor who opened the tract. (TM.)

Willows. Restaurant on Hausten Street, Mō-'ili'ili, Honolulu, established in 1944 on family property by Emma A. Hausten and Henry T. Hausten at the site of Ka-pa'akea Pond, which was formerly much larger and was used as a swimming pool.

Wilson. Playground at Papa-kōlea, elementary school on Kī-lau-ea Avenue, and highway tunnels, Ka-lihi Valley, Honolulu, named for John H. Wilson, mayor of Honolulu 1920–1926, 1929–1930, 1947–1954.

Winam. Avenue, Ala-wai section, Honolulu, named in 1870 for Ching Winam, a prominent Chinese merchant in Hawai'i who owned property in this area. (TM.)

Winne Units. Elementary school buildings, Puna-hou School, Honolulu, named for Mary Persis Winne, elementary school teacher 1901–1941.

Wist Hall. College of Education building, Mānoa campus, University of Hawai'i, Honolulu, completed in 1931 and named for Dean Benjamin O. Wist (1889–1951). Dean Wist was the president of the Territorial Normal Training School, and when it merged with the University of Hawai'i in 1931 he became dean of Teachers College.

Wong Ho. Lane, Thomas Square section, Honolulu, named for a prominent Chinese merchant who had a business there before 1900. (TM.)

Wood. Valley, Pāhala and Kī-lau-ea qds., Hawai'i. A mudflow here in 1868 destroyed a village and killed people and cattle (Macdonald and Abbott 192–193); see Ke-aīwa. Street, Nu'u-anu, Honolulu, named for John H. Wood, pioneer merchant who came in 1846 and erected the first brick store building on Fort Street. (TM.) His home was on part of the site of the present Foster Garden. He died in 1892.

Woodland. Site of Hutchinson Plantation, Honu-'apo qd., Ka'ū, Hawai'i, so called because people went there for fuel; formerly called Maka-kupu, and, later, Pua-ka-lehua (the *lehua* blooms), in honor of the pretty girls there.

Woodlawn. The east side of upper Mānoa Valley and a drive in this area, Honolulu, named for the Woodlawn Dairy and Stock Company which had a dairy there in the early 1900s. (TM.)

Woodlawn Terrace. Place, Woodlawn, upper Mānoa, Honolulu.

Woolsey. Place, Mānoa, Honolulu, named for the Woolsey family who live in Mānoa Valley on land granted their ancestors by Ka-mehameha II and deeded them in 1853, after the Great Māhele. (TM.)

Wyllie. Street and place, Nu'u-anu, Honolulu, named for Robert C. Wyllie (1798–1865), a Scottish physician who became foreign minister under Ka-mehameha IV and V. His home, Rosebank, was on

Nu'u-anu Avenue opposite the present Wyllie Street, with the stream at its back. He purchased a coffee plantation at Hanalei, Kaua'i; in 1860 he changed its name to Princeville (in honor of the 2-year-old Prince of Hawai'i) and started sugar production. Once worth a quarter of a million dollars, he was near bankruptcy at his death in 1865 (Daws 175). Kuykendall (2:208) praises his "twenty years of faithful and fruitful service to the government and people of Hawai'i."

YyYyYyY

Yamada. Lane, Lanakila section, Honolulu, named for George Yamada, a contractor. (TM.)

Yokohama Bay. See Ke-awa-'ula.

Yokohama Specie Bank. The building on Merchant Street, Honolulu, built in 1909, was once called the handsomest bank building in Honolulu. It now houses offices.

Yorktown. Avenue, Airport, Honolulu, named for the U.S. aircraft carrier *Yorktown,* that was sunk by the Japanese on December 7, 1941.

Young. Street, Makiki, Honolulu, named for John Young, the English sailor who went ashore at Ke-ala-ke-kua, Hawai'i, in 1790, was detained by Ka-mehameha, and became his companion and trusted adviser (Kuy. 1:25). The street was officially named at the August 30, 1850, Privy Council meeting. (TM.) See Alexander Young Building, Keoniana, 'Olohana.

Yung Hee. Village, Pā'ia qd., Maui.

Y.W.C.A. Building. Built in 1926 on Richards Street, Honolulu, designed and landscaped by women. See Fernhurst.

Note on Style

In the Appendix—but not in the Glossary—prefixes and suffixes are set off from bases by hyphens, whereas all words (including particles) in the names are separated by equal signs. Neither hyphens nor equal signs are pause signals: each entry in the Glossary (and each place name in the Appendix) is pronounced as a single word. Following usual linguistic practice, English glosses in the Appendix are enclosed in single quotation marks. This was not done in the glossary in order to simplify the entries.

1. Previous studies of place names

Place-name studies on the United States mainland have been to some extent anecdotal or unsound linguistically (note Trager's review of Stewart). The domain of place names is viewed here as a branch of lexicography, with the difference that legendary and historical associations of the names take the place of examples of usage found in dictionaries.

The first study of Hawaiian place names was made by W.D. Alexander and was published in 1903. Alexander identified almost 2,000 places (of which many were repeats; Wai=mea, for example, was the name for twelve places and Puna=lu'u for six), and gave the location, type of feature, and sometimes the meaning. No mark was used to indicate the long vowels, and glottal stops were shown only occasionally. Alexander also included a glossary of some 285 words frequently occurring in the place names.

The next study, by Thomas A. Thrum, was published in 1922. This list contains about 1,200 names, but the diacritical marks are haphazard and misleading and the translations unreliable. Using the conventional orthography for each entry Thrum rewrote the name; a few examples follow:

Thrum's phonetic respelling	Appendix spelling
hā'nă-le'i	Hana-lei
hā-wāi'i	Hawai'i
mă'-lă	Māla
mo-i'li-i'li	Mō='ili-'ili
pu-ā-'ā	Pua'a

Thrum's phonetic rendering of Hana=lei contains indications of stress and three degrees of vowel length (ā, ă, e). None are needed because, in Hawaiian, stress is predictably on all long vowels and diphthongs (as -ei in Hana-lei) and otherwise on the next to the last syllable and on alternating preceding syllables. Further, only stressed syllables of unusual length need be marked, as in Māla (but not in Hana-lei). Some final vowels, also, are long and stressed, as in Mānā on Kaua'i (but not in Pua'a), and these, too, are marked with macrons in the present Glossary.

Some of Thrum's translations are questionable. He did not always bother to translate the articles ka and he. For example, he translated Ka=wānana=koa as 'warrior's prophecy' (ka is ignored). Hā-'ena is translated 'sun heat', but actually the name is composed of a base, 'ena 'hot', and a causative prefix hā—nothing at all about the sun.

In compiling this Glossary, Coulter's Gazetteer of the Territory of Hawaii (1935), with some 4,000 entries, was of inestimable value for speedy location of places according to latitude and longitude, but no diacritics are provided in his listing, nor meanings or legendary and historical associations. Moreover, the subdivisions of entries according to islands is inconvenient, tending to conceal the use of the same name on various islands. (This is a striking characteristic of Hawaiian names and has been the despair of the Post Office: Mauna Loa on both Hawai'i and Moloka'i; Wai=mea on Hawai'i, O'ahu, and Kaua'i. Other multiple uses noted in the Glossary are Pōhaku=loa, 17 instances; Kukui, 14 instances; and Pāhoa, Poha=kea, and Puna= lu'u, 9 instances each.)

Few studies have been made of place names in other Oceanic languages. The largest was a compendium by Gifford (1923) of 4,776 Tongan place names and a few place-name songs. He did not indicate glottal stops or phonemic vowel length. Other Polynesian studies were made by Reed (1961) of about 2,200 Maori names and by Barthel (1962) of 1,000 Easter Island names. Neither showed vowel length, and Barthel did not indicate glottal stops. Reed gave meanings but no locations, and Barthel gave neither meanings nor locations. The most linguistically sophisticated study of place names in an Oceanic language is Byron Bender's analysis of 3,313 Marshallese place names (1963). Of these, 54 percent were classified as "grammatical" (coinciding completely or mainly with currently productive patterns), 19 percent as idiomatic, 19 percent as unanalyzable, 5 percent as personal names, and 3 percent as loanwords. Bender gave phonological and grammatical sketches of the difficult Marshallese language, but did not emphasize legendary explanations of the names. Goodenough (1966) listed between 500 and 600 Trukese place names, with meanings if known, variant foreign names of the places, geographic types, and location. A major concern of his study was the development of an orthography. For a brief discussion of Koskinen's comparative study of Polynesian place names, see section 9.

2. Sources consulted

Because the names given to places reflect culture and history, students of Hawaiian place names, like dictionary writers, are confronted by subject matter as diverse as archaeology, folklore, geography, geology, history, language, and surfing.

The relevant literature is voluminous, but certain important works were continually consulted during preparation of the Glossary. These are listed below, grouped according to subject. (See References for complete citations.)

Archaeology: Emory, 1969; McAllister, 1933*a;* Summers.

Folklore: Beckwith, 1919, 1932, 1970; Elbert, 1959; Elbert and Mahoe; Emerson, 1915, 1965; Fornander, 1917–1919; Pukui, unpublished notes; Sterling and Summers; Westervelt, n.d., 1963, 1964*a,* 1964*b.*

Geography: Coulter; United States Geological Survey topographic maps.

Geology: Macdonald and Abbott.

History: Kuykendall, 1947, 1953, 1967; *Missionary Album.*

Honolulu buildings: Jackson, Conrad, and Bannick.

Honolulu streets: Bryan, 1970; Taylor and Miranda.

Language: Pukui and Elbert, 1971.

Surfing: Finney, 1959*a,* 1959*b;* Finney and Houston.

In addition, numerous other works listed in the References were consulted for specialized information, for example, the accounts of early explorers and missionaries, the publications of the Hawaiian Historical Society, and the recent archaeological **237** reports of the anthropology department of the Bishop Museum. It must be emphasized that in no case did time permit the luxury of exhaustive search.

3. Sound changes and the need for salvage

The following example demonstrates the impossibility of determining the meaning of a name whose pronunciation is not known. An isolated beach on the northwest coast of the island of Moloka'i is spelled on maps Kahaiawa. At least six, and possibly more, pronunciations are possible for this spelling, each with a different meaning:

ka=hai=awa 'the sacrifice [in a] bay'
ka=hai='awa 'the sacrifice [of the] kava drink'
ka=ha'i=awa 'the breaking [by the] bay'
ka=ha'i='awa 'the breaking [of the] kava plant'
k-ā=ha'i=awa 'the bay belonging to someone else'
k-ā=ha'i='awa 'the kava plant [or drink] belonging to some-
                  one else'

In the old days, fishermen may have made temporary use of this arid beach, but it probably never supported a permanent agricultural settlement. The people have moved away and died. Present-day Hawaiians have moved into nearby homestead areas, but they, of course, do not know the original pronunciation of this unimportant name.

Important names are well known, of course, as the names of the islands. It is for remote spots such as Kahaiawa that salvage is necessary.

In addition, changes are constantly occurring in the pronunciation of place names, and this raises the question, Do place names change more rapidly or more slowly than other words?

Byron Bender remarked in his Marshallese study that place names are "relatively permanent" (1963:6), presumably because the place themselves are fixed, whereas men, languages, and cultures come and go. Albert Dauzat took the opposite stand and suggested that place names are "isolated" in the language, incomprehensible, and less profoundly anchored in popular conscience than is the general vocabulary; they are, he insisted, more susceptible than ordinary words to ellipsis, false perception, and folk etymology (1957:58–70).

Two years earlier, W.J. Sedgefield had written in the first of a thirteen-volume study of English place names that these names

change more rapidly than the words of ordinary speech because "most place-names are compounds of two or even three words, whereas the proportion of such early compounds still used in ordinary speech is very small. In the second place, place-names, or the majority of them, lost their meaning centuries ago, so that there was not the usual check on change that operates in words that are in every day use with a meaning known to all." (1924:7)

In the absence of ancient written records it is impossible to say whether, in the past, changes in Hawaiian place names occurred more rapidly or more slowly than changes in the general vocabulary. Now, of course, when the daily use of the Hawaiian language is increasingly rare, place names in general are spoken by people who do not know the language, and changes are in the direction of anglicization and are proceeding at an accelerating rate.

However, it is possible to classify the changes as either *(A)* those that occurred some time ago and are observed in the speech of the most fluent speakers of the language, or *(B)* those heard in the speech of persons who do not know the language, especially persons recently arrived from the Mainland.

Some of the first and older types of changes *(A)* follow.

A1. Replacement of long vowels by short ones: Kā=i=nā=liu 'bail out the bilge' to meaningless Kainaliu; Lā=hainā 'day [of] cruelty' to meaningless Lahaina; Māui, name of a demigod, to meaningless Maui; Nā='ā=lehu 'the volcanic ashes', to meaningless Na'alehu; 'Opihi-kāō 'crowd [gathering] limpets' to meaningless 'Opihikao.

A2. Reduction of sequences of vowel + glottal stop + like vowel to a single long vowel: Ka=malo'o 'the dryness' to Kamalō; Mo'o='ili-'ili 'pebble lizard' to Mō='ili-'ili; Pu'u='alaea 'ocherous earth hill' to Pū-'alaea.

A similar shortening occurs in a fast pronounciation of Hawai'i, becoming Hawa'i. This, however, is characteristic only of fast speech, whereas the older pronunciations of the examples mentioned above are never heard. The type of shortening that results in "Hawa'i" is an active morphophonemic process in the language. The common words *loa'a* 'to get, find' and *pua'a* 'pig' are most commonly *lo'a* and *pu'a*.

A3. Replacement of final consonant + vowel by vowel: Moku=kapu 'taboo district' to Mō=kapu; Puna='ahu-'ula 'feather-cloak spring' to Pū='ahu-'ula.

A4. Replacement of a long vowel by a short one, and other reductions: Ke='ā-'ā to Kea'ā.

A5. Loss of the definite article *ka*. This has happened within historic times in the Honolulu place names that were originally Ka=mō=ʻili-ʻili, Ka=pa=lama, Ka=puna=hou.

The second type of change *(B)* in place names, long prevalent in the speech of non-Hawaiians, is now noticed at times in the speech of persons of Hawaiian ancestry—but not, usually, if they know the Hawaiian language. A summary of these changes follows.

B1. Omission of the glottal stop: Kāne=ʻohe, Kauaʻi, Lānaʻi, Molokaʻi.

B2. Shortening and unstressing of long vowels: Ka=lā=kaua, Kū=hiō, Mākaha, Wai=kīkī.

B3. Omission of *-h-* in syllables not receiving primary stress: aloha, Ka=meha-meha, Kāne=ʻohe.

B4. Not distinguishing *-e* and *-i* and replacement of both with the *y* sound in English *pay:* Ānuenue, Kāne=ʻohe, Wai=ʻalae, Wai=ʻanae.

B5. Replacing stressed *a* (the sound in English *far*) by the sound in English *cat:* Kāne=ʻohe, Ka=piʻo=lani, Lani=kai.

B6. Shortening of long vowels in next to the last position: Hāna, Kāne=ʻohe.

B7. Replacement of *oʻo* and *uʻu* by the vowel sounds in English *toad* and *moon:* Na=poʻo-poʻo, Maka=puʻu, Puna=luʻu.

B8. Puffs of breath after *p-* and *k-:* Kai=lua, Kāne=ʻohe, *pali.*[1]

B9. Substitution of English vowel values, as in Kemoʻo (pronounced *kiymuw*), Koʻolau (pronounced *kuulaw*), and Mauna Kea (pronounced *maunə kiyə*).[2]

B10. Addition of *Mount* (as in *Mount Kaʻala*) or *Peak* (as in *Olo=mana Peak*).

B11. Anomalous vowel changes: replacement of stressed *o* in Hono-lulu by *a* (as in *far*); replacement of unstressed *o* in Hono-lulu by the vowel approaching that in English *fun;* replacement of unstressed *a* in Puna=hou by the vowel in *fun.*

B12. Moving primary stress (shown here by a stress mark) in words of three or four syllables from the next to the last, or

1. Recently one of the compilers telephoned an institution directly concerned with the Hawaiian people. A secretary reported that the person sought was at Kʰæni=oi. Note particularly deviations B1, 3, 4, 5, 6, and 8!

2. Turnabout is fair play: at least one English name, Pipeline, is said occasionally to be Hawaiianized as Pi-pe-li-ne, and many people are uncertain as to the street named One—is it Hawaiian ʻsandʼ or an English numeral?

the last, syllable to the first, as Hana-léi to Hánəlei; Maka-púʻu to Makapúw (change B7 above) to Mákəpuw. (This is particularly noticeable in the speech of television announcers; compare pronunciation of *cigarette* with stress on the first syllable.)

A change not heard in Hawaiʻi but prevalent on the Mainland and among people who have never been to the Islands is replacement of the final *-i* in Hawaiʻi by *-ə* (hawayə); an analagous change of final *-i* to *-ə* occurs in common pronunciations of Cincinnati, Miami, and Missouri.

In the speech of some older Caucasian residents, the name of the island was pronounced Háway, with strong stress on the first syllable. Surprisingly, in spite of change B1 noted above (omission of the glottal stop), most people in the Islands today do pronounce the glottal in Hawaʻi or Havaʻi (*v* is a variant of *w*) and some even say Havaiʻian.

4. New names

New names (increments) are mostly deliberate coinages by churches, developers, or county planning boards. In only one domain, that of surfing sites, do the increments arise anonymously, much as they usually do in the general vocabulary.

The names of many churches are examples of such deliberate inventions: Home=laʻi 'peaceful home'; ʻImi=ola 'seek salvation'; Ka=hiku=ō=nā=lani 'the seventh of the kings' (a church helped by Ka=lā=kaua, the seventh king); Ke=alaula-o-ke-mālamala 'the dawn light of enlightenment'; Ke=awa=laʻi 'the tranquil harbor'; Nānā=i=ka=pono 'look to righteousness' (considered a better name for a church than the town's name, Nānā=kuli 'look at knees'); Wai=o=ke=ola 'water of life'.

Many other organizations and developed areas have invented names, sometimes to describe their activities or purposes: Hana=hauʻoli 'happy work' (a children's school with a name that to some, unfortunately, might have sexual connotations); Koko=kahi 'one blood' (a multi-racial YWCA branch); Lani=kai 'sea heaven' (a part of Kai=lua city on Oʻahu; the name, a mistake for Kai=lani 'heavenly sea', was given in 1924, when the area was subdivided); Polapola 'getting well' (the village built for lepers at Ka=lau-papa, Molokaʻi); Ulu=mau 'ever growing' (a model Hawaiian village).

At the present time the most numerous coinages are names of hotels, condominiums, and streets. The names are usually **241** short and easy to say. Effort is made to avoid risqué meanings. (A notable failure is *Le'a-le'a Hale* 'house [of] pleasure' which to Hawaiians often connotes sexual pleasure. This also seems to be ungrammatical, as adjective qualifiers follow nouns in Hawaiian.) Most English words in hotel names lean toward certain semantic rubrics: tropics (surf, sand, coral, isles, palms, tides, seas), royalty (empress, king, queen, regent, dynasty, princess, crown), and vacations (holiday, paradise). Favorite Hawaiian words are Hawai'i, *aloha, ali'i* 'chief', *hale* 'house', *moana* 'open sea', and *ala* 'road, street'. Places charging admission prefer English names: Paradise Park, Polynesian Cultural Center, Sea Life Park, and (Wai=kīkī) Shell. In a few instances English names have replaced Hawaiian ones, for example, Enchanted Lake for Ka='ele=pulu 'the wet blackness', Seven Sacred Pools for a meaningless 'Ohe'o, Cinerama for Pā=wa'a, and Planetarium for Kilo=lani. Some substitutions of English for Hawaiian occurred long ago, as Coconut Island for Moku=ola, Rainbow Falls for Wai=anuenue, and Tantalus for Pu'u='ōhi'a.

Streets in new subdivisions may be named in semantic categories. In Wai='alae Kāhala the streets have names of birds ('Elepaio 'flycatcher', Koloa 'Hawaiian duck', Kolohala 'pheasant', Pueo 'owl', 'Ulili 'tattler', and others). At the Honolulu airport, the streets were named by Mary Kawena Pukui for clouds (Ao=lele 'flying cloud', Ao=lewa 'floating cloud', Ao= loko 'inner cloud', Ao=wena 'glowing cloud'). At Wai=mānalo they are named for fish (Hīhīmanu, Hilu, Hīnālea, Mālolo, Nenue). At Hawai'i=kai (itself an invented name), the names are those of other Island localities (Hana-mā'ulu, Ka=uha=kō, Kau=makani, Wai='ale-'ale).

In some of the new subdivisions, all the street names begin with the same word—an aid, for the informed person, to finding these streets. In 'Āhui=manu 'bird cluster' the names begin with Hui= 'flock': Hui=auku'u 'heron flock', Hui='io 'hawk flock'; Hui='iwa 'frigatebird flock', Hui=nēnē 'goose flock', Hui=palila 'honeycreeper flock'. In Pōhā=kupu 'growing rock' the names are combinations with Ulu= 'grove, growth': Ulu=hala 'pandanus grove', Ulu=kanu 'planted grove', Ulu=lani 'royal grove', Ulu= malu 'peaceful grove', Ulu=nahele 'forest grove'. In Kū=kanono 'stand strike', they begin with Manu= 'bird': Manu=aloha 'love-bird, parrot', Manu=laiki 'ricebird', Manu=mele 'canary', Manu= 'ō'ō 'honeyeater'.

On the island of Hawai'i, streets in areas that are for sale along the Kona coast have names tailored to the convenience of newly arrived visitors or of persons who have never been to Hawai'i and are unable to master Hawaiian words other than *aloha,* Kona, *lehua,* Lei=lani, and *tiki* (from Tuamotuan!). Banal examples are Lei=lani Parkway, Kona Drive, King Ka=meha-meha Boulevard, Ginger Blossom Lane, and Kona Moon Court.

Surfing areas are named informally and spontaneously; more than 1,700 sites have been identified in the Islands. Most commonly, a site is named for its bay or shore area, but considerable imagination is shown in some of the new, short English names. Because many of the surfers are from the Mainland and do not know Hawaiian, English names are much in vogue. Such is the crowding of any good surfing area, that new sites are continually being searched for. Some of the new sites are named for nearby landmarks: Incinerators and adjacent Flies, Irma's (said to be named for a lunch wagon at Sandy Beach), Publics (near the Public Baths), Brown's (for a nearby residence), and Turtles (which are supposedly always there). More interesting are names describing types of waves: Avalanche, Himalayas, Pipeline (or Banzai Pipeline), and Slaughterhouse. Some do not fit any classification: Infinities (infinitely beautiful), Regulars (nearly always a good surf, at Sand Island), and Secrets (most new sites start as "secrets," but at this one the name has stuck). No one knows who first gives the names, and some of them are soon forgotten.

In general the new names for institutions and development areas are short and easy to say. Rarely is an effort made to search in *Indices of Awards* (see References) or in the State archives for the ancient name of a place or for the names of original Hawaiian owners, for fear such names might be hard to say or have unpoetic or risqué meanings.

5. Structural analysis

5.1. The most common frames

On the United States mainland a large proportion of the place names consist of single words (Massachusetts, Fresno, Chicago) or of attribute plus noun (New York, North Dakota, West Virginia). Most of the names are English, although quite a few are of American Indian or other foreign origin (the Indian names are frequently of unclear origin). Of the entries in the **243** present Glossary, some 86 percent are Hawaiian or include Hawaiian words, and two-thirds of them contain more than a single word. (By "word" we mean entities that can stand alone and the particles that are not closely bound to words, most of which indicate grammatical relationship. Here, "words" are separated by spaces or equal signs, not by hyphens. The figures are based on a computer count of 3,906 entries. About a hundred entries were added after the count; these are not included in our computations.)

Following is the count of entries according to number of words comprising the names:

Indivisible names	1,315
Names consisting of two words	1,697
Names consisting of three words	664
Names consisting of four words	179
Names consisting of five words	43
Names consisting of six words	7
Names consisting of seven words	1
Total	3,906

Aside from the indivisible names, most of the entries consist of a noun head, with or without preceding article or following qualifier—that is, a noun phrase. A few consist of two noun phrases. Examples:

Noun: Hawai'i
Article plus noun: Ka=lihi
Article plus noun plus qualifier: Ka=imu=kī
Two noun phrases: Ke=ala   ke=kua
                  Hale   a=ka=lā

The most common frame may be diagrammed as follows (N = noun, V = verb):

$$\left. \begin{array}{l} \pm \text{ article} + \text{N-stem} \pm \text{qualifier(s)} \\ \\ \text{V-stem} \pm \begin{cases} \text{particle} \\ \text{qualifier(s)} \end{cases} \end{array} \right\} \begin{array}{l} \pm \text{ preposition} \pm \text{article} \\ \pm \text{N-stem} \pm \text{qualifier(s)} \end{array}$$

5.2. Affixes

Place names may contain prefixes or suffixes. The prefixes are in two orders: an inner one represented by reduplications, and an outer one with a fixed, mutually exclusive membership.

Reduplications are numerous in the language and have varied shapes and meanings. In the place names, however, they are not frequent and are of two types, complete and partial. In the following examples, the meanings might be glossed *continuing state or activity*.

Complete reduplications: 'Ā=hina-hina 'grayish' from *hina* (gray), Kōlea=li'i-li'i 'little plover' from *li'i* (small), Mauna= lahi-lahi 'thin mountain' from *lahi* (thin), Mō='ili-'ili 'pebbly lizard' from *'ili* (pebble), Wai='ale-'ale 'rippling water' from *'ale* (billow), Wai=ki-ki 'spouting water' from *ki* (to spout forth).

Partial reduplications include: repetition of first syllable, as Ni-nini 'pouring' from *nini* 'to pour'; repetition of first two phonemes of the first syllable, as Ha-hae=ule 'tearing penis' from *hae* 'to tear'; repetition of first syllable and truncated second syllable, as Pu'u=nia-niau 'peaceful mountain' from *niau* 'to move peacefully'.

Not all repeated syllables are reduplications, for example, *nini* (listed above), *lulu* 'protected', *nēnē* 'goose', and *nānā* 'look at'. Such forms are irreducible.

In the place names, bases seem more frequent than their reduplicated derivatives. The contrary may be true in conversation. The following examples were noted (the numerals in parentheses indicate the number of examples in the 3,906 entries that were computer analyzed): *'ala* 'fragrant' (3), *'a-'ala* (1); *'ino* 'stormy, bad' (6), *'ino-'ino* (1); *li'i* 'small' (8), *li'ili'i* (6); *'oli* 'joyous' (4), *'oli-'oli* (1); *'olu* 'cool' (5), *'olu-'olu* (2); *'ula* 'red' (42), *'ula-'ula* (7).

The common meanings of reduplications in the general language (Elbert and Pukui, section 6.2) are frequentative, increased, and plural action, but sometimes there is no difference in meaning between root and reduplicated root. Both statements seem true also of place names, but of the seven shapes of reduplications listed in Elbert and Pukui (section 6.2), only three have been noted in the place names.

The most common outer prefix, but one not now used to form new names, is *Hono-, Hana-* 'bay, place'. (*Hana-* is not to be confused with meaningless Hāna, Maui, or with the verb *hana* 'to work, do', as in Hana=kahi.) The number of each of these prefixes in the Glossary, counted by islands is as follows (schools and streets are excluded; a name occurring twice on the same island is counted twice):

Appendix

	Hana-	Hono-
Northwestern Hawaiian Islands	2	–
Ni'ihau	1	–
Kaua'i	6	1
O'ahu	3	3
Ka=ho'o-lawe	1	1
Moloka'i	1	5
Maui	5	13
Lā=na'i	–	1
Hawai'i	1	21
Total	**20**	**45**

This tabulation according to selection of alternant prefixes shows a continuum of nearly always *Hana-* on the islands to the northwest, to both forms on O'ahu, to usually *Hono-* on Maui, and nearly always *Hono-* on Hawai'i in the southeast. Moloka'i is slightly aberrant in favoring *Hono-* more than does its eastern neighbor Maui.

Hana- is the older form and is cognate with *Hana-* and *Haka-* in the Marquesas, *Hanga-* on Easter Island, *Fa'a-* in Tahiti, *Whanga-* in New Zealand, and *Faga-* (phonetically *fanga-*) in Samoa. This does not mean that the northwesterly islands of Kaua'i and Ni'ihau were settled first, but only that they have been more conservative. At one time the only form may have been *Hana-*. Somehow a change of *-a-a* to *-o-o* may have begun on Hawai'i and moved gradually northwestward. A similar change has occurred in the causative prefix *ha'a-* and *ho'o-* and shorter variants, to be discussed next. (The extreme conservatism of Ni'ihau is also reflected in the continued use of *t* as an allophone of *k;* elsewhere *t* is heard only in chants and occasionally in the speech of elderly people.)

Some well-known examples of *Hana-* and *Hono-* in place names are: Hana-lei 'lei bay', Hana-pē-pē 'crushed bay', Hana-uma[3] 'curved bay', Hono-lulu 'protected bay', Hono-mū 'silent bay'.

---

3. Some non-Hawaiians, having heard that "all the vowels in Hawaiian" are pronounced, assume that diphthongs are lacking, and pronounce this well-known name with a pause or even a glottal stop after *Hana-*, thus *Hana + uma* or *Hana + 'uma* instead of Ha.nau.ma (with the period indicating syllable boundary). This kind of hypercorrection is similar to the insertion of a glottal stop in the word *heiau,* so that the pronunciation becomes—wrongly—*he'iau,* or to the insertion of pauses between the words comprising the name Ka=imu-kī *(ka.imu.kī* instead of Kàimukī). Such errors are due to the imperfect spelling system.

Hana- and *Hono-* most commonly precede single bases or re-duplicated bases, as in the above examples, but occasionally they precede noun phrases and verb phrases: Hono-ke=ana 'the cave bay', Hono-kō=wai 'bay draining water'.

The next most common outer prefix is causative/simulative *ho'o-, hō-, ho-, ho'-, ha'a-, hā-,* as in the following examples:

ho'o- (16 examples), before all consonants except the glottal stop: Ho'o-kipa 'hospitable' from *kipa* 'to visit'.

hō- (3), before the glottal stop plus short vowel: Hō-'eu 'mischievous' from *'eu* 'rascal'.

ho- (1), before the glottal stop plus long vowel: Ho-'ō=pū=loa 'to put together long time' from *'ō* 'to enter'.

ho'- (2), before a vowel (with lengthening of that vowel if it is short): Ho-'ānu-anu 'to make cool' from *anu* 'cool'; Ho-'ēa 'to arrive' from *ea* 'to come up'.

ha'a- (possibly 4), before all consonants except the glottal stop: Ha'a-koa 'warrior-like' from *koa* 'warrior'; Ha'a-kulamanu 'like a bird-gathering place' from *kulamanu* 'bird gathering place'.

hā- (5), before the glottal stop and occasionally other conso-nants: Hā-'ele-'ele 'blackish' from *'ele* 'black'; Hā-la'i 'peaceful' from *la'i* 'peace'.

Other prefixes are:

'a-, general number classifier (2 examples): 'A-kahi 'one'; 'A-kahi=pu'u 'one hill'.

'ā-, 'ō- 'similar to' (7): 'Ā-hina-hina 'grayish' from *hina* 'gray'; 'Ō-lino-lino 'shining' from *lino* 'bright'.

kā-, causative (9): Kā-hea=wai 'water calling' from *hea* 'call'; Kā-hili 'feather standard' from *hili* 'to wave'; Kā=imu=kā-lua= ua 'the rain-baking oven' from *lua* 'pit'; Kā=lepa 'merchant' from *lepa* 'flag' (as raised above their goods by salesmen); Kā-wili 'twist' from *wili* 'twist'; Ke=ana=kā-ko'i 'the adze-making cave' from *ko'i* 'adze'.

kua-, ordinal-number former (3): Ka=holo=kua-iwa 'the ninth run' (probably a reference to an avalanche); Kua-hiku=ka=lapa= o=Anahulu 'seventh of the ridges of Anahulu'; Kua-lua 'twice'.

pā-, distributive and qualifier, noted in new street names in Honolulu: Pā-kahi 'first', Pā-lua 'second', Pā-kolu 'third', and Pā-lima 'fifth'.

The following suffixes have been noted:

-a and *-hia,* passive/imperative markers usually suffixed to **247**

verbs, as Ke'e-ke'ehi-a 'tread upon' from *ke'ehi* 'to tread', and Kukui=walu-hia 'scraped candlenut' from *walu* 'to scratch'.

-hana, a rare nominalizer, as Kilo-hana 'lookout, observatory' from *kilo* 'to look'.

-na, a nominalizer common in the language but rare in place names, as in Kaha-na 'cutting' from *kaha* 'to cut' (the name refers to valleys that have been "cut away" by streams). Also, Palena 'boundary' from *pale* 'to ward off'; Noho-na=o-Hae 'dwelling of Hae' from *noho* 'to stay'.

5.3 Noun phrases

As is shown in the diagram in 5.1, noun phrases in place names contain a maximum of three slots (except when, rarely, more than a single qualifier occurs), this being all, apparently, that speakers choose to use in names repeated as often as are place names. (The potentials in actual speech are much greater; see Diagram 1 in Elbert and Pukui.) All the slots in the noun phrase are optional except that of the noun.

The prepositions noted in the place names may be listed as follows:

a, possession marker, *a*-class (for such acquired objects as spouse, child, and most small possessions, or for objects made by an individual or used by him: compare Ka-wa'a=a=Pele 'the canoe [made] by Pele', and Ka-wa'a=o=Māui 'the canoe [belonging] to Māui').

o, possession marker, *o*-class (for such inherited objects as parents, siblings, gods, chiefs, body parts, and certain important possessions).

i, precise locative/objective marker (14 examples).

For a unique example with the conjunction *mā* 'and', see section 5.5.

Articles are as follows:

ke, singular definite, before nouns beginning with *k, a,* and *e,* and sometimes *m, o,* and the glottal stop.

ka, singular definite, before other nouns and sometimes before nouns beginning with *m, o,* and a glottal stop followed by *a*.

nā, plural definite (about 80 examples).

he, indefinite (3).

Examples:

Ke ana o ke akua pōloli
'the cave of the god hungry'

Ke one kani o Nohili
'the sand sounding of Nohili'

Ke ala i Kahiki
'the road to Tahiti'

Ka wai a Ha'o
'the water [acquired] by Ha'o'

Nā niu o Kāne
'the coconuts of Kāne'

Lili'u o ka lani
'smarting pain of the royal chief'

Hale a ka lā
'house [acquired] by the sun'

Pōhaku o Kaua'i
'stone of Kaua'i'

These names, respectively, are of a cave, a beach, an ocean channel, a spring and nearby church, an offshore islet, the last queen (her name has been given to an avenue, a park, and a building), a mountain, and a stone.

In sequences of noun phrases such as these, the second noun is usually preceded by an article unless it is a proper noun.

A few examples have been found of two qualifiers after a noun: Ke=kā=ulu=ohi 'the vine growing [with] sprouts', Ke=kua=waha='ula-'ula 'the red-mouthed god', Pueo=hulu=nui 'many-feathered owl', Pu'u=maka=kilo 'mountain [with] watching eyes'.

Very common is a noun phrase consisting of article + noun + qualifier, patterning as follows: Ka=lā=kaua 'the day [of] war', Ke=au=hou 'the new era', Nā=pū=mai'a 'the banana trees', He=aka=lani 'a heavenly shadow'.

In the above sequences the article acts as a constituent vis-à-vis the following noun + qualifier. In other, much rarer, article + noun + qualifier sequences, the qualifier is a constituent vis-à-vis preceding article + noun. Thus:

Ko'olau $\begin{Bmatrix} loa & \text{'long} \\ poko & \text{'short} \end{Bmatrix}$ Ko'olau'

249

$$\text{Ka=lihi} \begin{cases} uka & \text{`inland} \\ waena & \text{`central} \\ kai & \text{`seaward} \end{cases} \text{Ka-lihi'}$$

Such names as these are written Ka=lihi Uka, Ka=lihi Waena, and Ko'olau Loa to indicate that the final qualifier modifies all that precedes it. The literal meaning of the constituents in the name Ka-lihi 'the edge' is not applicable inasmuch as there is more than one Ka=lihi.

Similarly, names of people in place names consisting of more than a single base or particle are written as single words, since in such instances the meaning is 'personal name' rather than the literal meaning of the constituents of the name. Thus in the name of the Moloka'i hill Kiha=a=Pi'ilani 'Kiha [son] of Pi'ilani', the sequence *pi'ilani* consists of two bases with a literal meaning 'royal ascent', but in this case Pi'ilani is a chief's name embedded within a name, and hence it is written without hyphens or equal signs.

Certain sequences begin with proper names, for example, Kāne=ana 'Kāne's cave', Ke-ō-ua=hale 'Ke-ō-ua's house', and Hono-lulu=hale 'Honolulu house'. In such sequences the first element is considered the head, because this is a Hawaiian way of honoring a chief or god: important things come first in Hawaiian syntax, and the god Kāne, the chief Ke-ō-ua, and the people of Honolulu precede 'cave' and 'house'.

The two-word sequence article + noun patterns as follows:

$$\left.\begin{array}{l} Ka \\ Ke \\ N\bar{a} \\ He \end{array}\right\} +\text{N} \quad \begin{array}{l} \text{Ka='a'awa 'the 'a'awa fish'} \\ \text{Ke=āhole 'the āhole fish'} \\ \text{Nā=hiku 'the seven'} \\ \text{He=lani 'a royal chief'} \end{array}$$

A few nouns in place names occur with the article in one locality (Ka='ahu-'ula 'the feather cloak') and elsewhere without it ('Ahu-'ula). Certain individual places bear names either with or without the article, as (Ka=) unu=o=Hua '(the) altar of Hua'.

Other common sequences are noun + qualifier: Mauna=loa 'long mountain', Nu'u=anu 'cool height', and Pepeiao=lepo 'dirty ear'.

The longest name consists of three noun phrases: Kōkī=ō=Wai-lau=alapi'i=a=ka='ōpae 'the summit of Wai-lau the shrimp's ladder'. It must be added that the name is usually shortened to **250** Kōkī=o=Wai-lau.

The shortest names consist of one-word noun phrases containing two phonemes apiece, as the streets Nū, Mā, and Ua. Nearly all place names have at least four phonemes (the glottal stop is of course counted as a phoneme). The following contain three phonemes each: Hua, Kau, Kou, Kua, Niu.

Although the nominalyzing particle 'ana is extremely common in the language, it was noted only in the name of a church, Ka=puka='ana 'the Exodus'.

5.4. More possessives

In place names the possessive prepositions *a* and *o*, previously mentioned, do not occur in initial position, but they commonly follow nouns. Only three other possessives have been noted in the place names: *k-ā*, *k-ō*, and *k-a-'u*. *K-ā*, as in the place name K-ā=Hina=wai 'Hina's water' is a contraction of *ka . . . a* 'the . . . of'. The underlying phrase *ka=wai=a=Hina* has the alternate shape *k-ā=Hina=wai: ka . . . a* has become *k-ā*, and *Hina* has been moved up before *wai*. This construction, extremely common in the language, seems to focus on Hina: 'Hina's water'. In the other underlying construction the focus is on 'the water'.

K-ō is noted only in the place name K-ō=ā=uka 'those of the far uplands'. *K-ō=uka*, or its fuller form *k-ō=uka=po'e*, is common in the language and may be interpreted as deriving from an underlying *ka=po'e=o=uka*, with *ka . . . o* contracting to *k-ō* and *uka* moving ahead of *po'e*, with an optional deletion of *po'e*. The unusual part of this construction is the insertion of the locative *ā* 'as far as'.

The third possessive, *k-a-'u*, in the place name K-a-'u=maka 'my eye, [give] me the eye', contains the morpheme *k-*, definite singular; *a*, acquired possession marker; and *-'u*, first person singular. The name derives from a story of two boys excessively greedy for fish eyes; a sorcerer finally killed them for their greed.

5.5. Verb phrases

Verbs are less frequent than nouns in the place names. Many of them are followed by unmarked noun phrases serving as subjects: Pā=ka=lā 'the sun strikes', Pau=walu 'eight are consumed', Pe'ahi=nā=i'a 'the fish beckon', Pili=lua=nu'u 'two high places join' (*lua* is considered an article here).

Rarely, a verb phrase has been noted that is followed by an object/locative phrase introduced by the preposition *i:* Nānā=i=ka=pono 'strive for righteousness'.

251

More commonly an object marker is omitted, just as it is in colloquial conversation: 'Ai=kanaka 'eat man', Nānā=kuli 'look at knees', Ni-nini=wai 'pour water'.

The verb-object sequence may itself qualify a preceding noun: Ka=wai=kilo=kanaka 'the water [for] looking at people', Ka=wai=kilo=kohe 'the water [for] looking at vaginas', Ka=wai=nā'uke=po'o=o=Kahā 'the water delousing [the] head of Kahā', Moku='ai=kaua 'district winning war'.

Verb + particle or qualifier is rare: Pili=wale 'cling for no reason', 'Ai=kanaka 'man eating'.

It is noteworthy that initial verbs are not preceded by verb markers, just as initial nouns are not preceded by prepositions. In short, contentives or bases (whatever one chooses to call them) or article plus noun are the initial parts of place names. (This is evidence that the articles, which are clitics, are intuitively considered a part of the noun.)

Two names are unique: Mā=hā'ule=pū 'and fall together' (here, *mā* is a conjunction), and Mai=poina='oe=i-a'u 'don't you forget me' (the name of a beach park dedicated to World War II servicemen, the only example of the sequence verb + subject + object).

5.6. Particles

Words in Hawaiian may be classified as content words and particles. The latter usually (but not always) indicate grammatical relationship and differ principally from content words in that they cannot be used alone. Five of them occur with great frequency in the place names. Others occur rarely or not at all (see section 10). Common '*o*, a subject marker preceding nouns and pronouns (especially third person singular *ia*) is completely lacking, as are the common verb markers *ua*, perfective; *e . . . ana*, imperfective; and *i* 'if'.

The examples in section 5.3 of articles in article + N + qualifier and article + N sequences do not include all environments in which the articles appear, as they occur also in longer sequences such as Ke=ala=ke=kua, Hale=a=ka=lā, Kā=i=nā=liu, and Hale=o=ka=puni. The total number of examples of each in the Glossary are: *ka,* 555; *ke,* 159; *nā,* 80; *he,* 3.

Other particles not previously mentioned include '*ole*, negative (8); *pū* 'together with' (7); *wale*, limiting (7); '*ia*, passive/imperative marker (4); *i*, marker of completed aspect, in a single name—Ka=maka=i=pō 'the eye that was darkened'.

The content words are classified semantically in section 6.6. They cannot be classified structurally on the basis of the place names because of the lack in this domain of the common noun-phrase-introducing preposition *'o,* and the common verb markers *ua, e . . . ana,* and *i,* as previously mentioned.

For example, the word *mauna* 'mountain' in the general lexicon is a noun because it may follow the article *ka.* In the place names, however, *mauna* does not happen to occur after an article or after the prepositions *'o* or *i.* Thus, relying on the limited data, it can be classified as a noun only on the basis of its meaning.

5.7. Ellipsis

In section 3 we pointed out that ages ago some names were shortened in various ways, most commonly by replacement of long vowels by short ones. In other names, presumably of comparable vintage, particles have been omitted. They have been supplied parenthetically in the following examples: 'Auwai=o= (ka)=limu 'ditch of (the) seaweed', Kau=mai=(i)=luna 'place (on) high', Ke=ala=(o)=ke=kua 'the path (of) the god', Hale=kū=(i=ka) =lani 'house befitting (to the) heaven', Hō=mai=(i)=ka=wa'a 'give me the canoe', Holoi=(i)=nā=wāwae 'wash (object) the feet', Ulu=mā=(ka)=wao 'growing in (the) uplands', 'Ulu=pala= (i=ke)=kua 'breadfruit ripening (on the) back [of carriers]', Wili=(i)=ka='ā'ī 'wring the neck'.

In the above, *hō, holoi,* and *wili* are transitive verbs, and the phrases that follow are considered objects rather than subjects.

6. Semantic analysis

6.1. Folk etymology

In a writing system using only twelve letters, words spelled alike are extremely numerous, and it is difficult to avoid folk etymology. For example, one might think that *he'e* 'squid' and *he'e* 'to slide' were related because of the slipperiness of squids, but *he'e* 'squid' goes back to Proto-Polynesian *heke,* and *he'e* 'slide' to Proto-Polynesian *seke.* Not all folk etymology is as plausible as association of 'squid' and 'slide':

Hana-pē-pē 'crushed bay', a valley on Kaua'i, has been explained as *hana* 'to make' + *pēpē* 'baby'.

Ma'e-ma'e 'clean', a hill and school in Honolulu, is commonly believed to be *Mai! Mai!* 'Come! Come!' as said to children.

253

Papa=one-one 'sandy flat' is said to be 'dancing papa on the sands'. (In this analysis *papa* is from English, and *'oni-'oni* 'to shake' is translated 'dance'.)

6.2. The linguist as a spoilsport

This unflattering term was taken from an important but seldom seen article by Francis Lee Utley, who wrote: "Generally the prosaic is to be preferred to the fanciful or poetic explanation" (1963:154). He quoted (p. 148) George Stewart's history of the evolution of the translations of the name Minnesota from 'Muddy River' to 'Cloudy River' to 'Sky-blue River' to 'Sky-blue Water'. George L. Trager complained that Stewart's book reads like a novel: "For a scientific work must read like what it is, and not like a novel, which it isn't" (1946:110). Stewart is too fascinating, he implied, to be scientific. And a local editor once turned down a manuscript because it was "much too interesting."

In an effort to be truthful we have not prettied up our translations, nor have we been afraid of being prosaic. The following names could never be called glamorous: Ka=haku 'the projection', Ka=lihi 'the edge', Ka=naue 'the rotating', Ke=kaha 'the place', Kino='ole 'no body', Popo=i'a 'fish rot'.

6.3. Homonyms

To choose among possible meanings of homonyms it is necessary to consider the legendary associations and the nature of the geographic feature named. Following are a few examples of homonyms and their several meanings that sometimes cause difficulties (numbers of examples in the computer analyzed Glossary are given in parentheses).

hau

hau 'Hibiscus tiliaceus' (14), as in Hau='ula 'red hibiscus tree', a coastal village on O'ahu.

hau 'cold, ice' (7), as in Hau=ani 'blowing cold', a land section in cold Wai-mea, Hawai'i.

hau 'dew' (2) after *kō* 'to drain', as in Hono-kō=hau 'bay draining dew', and names of various villages, streams, and land divisions.

hau 'to strike' (1) before *ko'i* 'adze': Hau=ko'i 'adze striking', a land division on Hawai'i.

254

kō

kō 'to draw, pull, drain' (9) before a noun, as in Hono-kō=hau (see above) and in Hono-kō=wai 'bay draining water', a Maui stream.

kō 'sugarcane' (6), as in Kō-loa 'long sugarcane', a Kaua'i village and district (but Koloa 'duck', a Hawai'i beach).

lua

lua 'pit, hole' (44) if volcanism or fishing holes are involved, as in Ka=lua=o=Pele 'the pit of Pele' (the volcano goddess), an O'ahu crater, or Ka=lua=puhi 'the eel hole', an O'ahu fishpond.

lua 'two' (27) if counting seems pertinent, and if qualifying a noun, as in Wai-lua 'two streams', a Kaua'i bay.

lua in 'Wai-ka-lua' is either 'water [of] the pit' or 'water [of] the *lua* fighter'.

mō-

mō-, a contraction of *moku* 'cut' (4), as in Mō=iwi 'bone cut'.

mō-, a contraction of *mo'o* 'supernatural lizard' (2), as in Mō='ili-'ili 'pebble lizard', a section of Hono-lulu where a *mo'o* was cut to bits to form a hill.

mō-, a contraction of *moku* 'district' (2), as in Mō=kapu 'taboo or sacred district', an O'ahu peninsula where the first man was created by the gods Kāne, Kū, and Lono.

ō-

ō-, short for *one* 'sand' (4), as in Ke=ō=kea 'the white sand', land divisions of Hawai'i and Maui.

ō-, short for *ao* 'cloud' (3), as in Ke=ō=ua 'the rainy cloud', the father of Ka=meha=meha I for whom a Hono-lulu street is named.

ō-, 'prolonged, as a sound' (3), as in Malu=ō 'continual shade'.

pū

pū-, a contraction of *pu'u* 'hill' (5), as in Pū=o=waina 'hill of placing [sacrifices]', the old name for Punchbowl Crater in Hono-lulu where human sacrifices were offered.

pū-, a contraction of *puna* 'spring' (2), as in Pū=hau 'icy spring'.

pū-, a contraction of *pua* 'young fish' in Pū='ama 'mullet fry'.

pū 'together' (7), as in Ka='ai=pū 'the eating together'.

255

pū 'tree, clump' (3), as in Nā=pū=mai'a 'the banana plants'.
pū 'conch', in Wai=ka=pū 'water [of] the conch'.
pū 'to eat', in Pū=pa'a-kai 'eat salt'.

6.4. Minimal pairs and trios

These are not distinguished in the conventional orthography, as already mentioned.

ala, 'ala, 'alā

ala 'road, path' (23), as in Ke=ala=i=Kahiki 'the path to Tahiti', a channel.

'ala 'fragrant' (3), as in 'Ala='ē 'strange fragrance', a Hawai'i land section and school. (Compare 'Alae 'mudhen', a Hawai'i crater.)

'alā 'basaltic rock' (3), as in Ka='alā=wai 'the basaltic rock [in] water', an area in Hono-lulu.

au, 'au

au 'current' (11), as in Wai=au 'current in water', an O'ahu land division.

'au 'swim, water course' (5), as in Pu'u-'au'au (swimming hill), a Kaua'i hill.

awa, 'awa, a=wā

awa 'milkfish' (3), as in Wahi=awa 'milkfish place', a Kaua'i stream; and 'bay, harbor' (14), as in Ke=awa=nui 'the big harbor', a Kaua'i landing.

'awa '*Piper methysticum*' (4), as in Ka='awa=loa 'the long *'awa*', a Hawai'i land division.

=*a=wā* 'of noise', in Wahi=a=wā 'place of noise', an O'ahu town.

kau, Ka'ū

kau 'to place' (27), as in Kau, a place in the Ka'ū district, Hawai'i, and in Kau=mai=luna 'place above', a Hono-lulu street on a height.

Ka'ū, an important Hawai'i district (the name has no meaning).

lae, la'e

lae 'point' (44), as in Ka=lae, the southernmost point of Hawai'i.

la'e 'clearness' (3), as in Ka=la'e, a Moloka'i village.

mana, mānā

mana 'forked, branched' (12), as in Olo-mana, 'forked hill', a conspicuous O'ahu peak; and 'supernatural power' (3), a Hono-lulu street and a Moloka'i *heiau*.

Mānā 'arid' is the name of a hot and nearly rainless part of western Kaua'i.

Mana also means 'supernatural power' and the interpretation of Ka=mana=kai, a Moloka'i gulch, is uncertain. Is it 'the sea power' or 'the sea branch'?

mano, manō

mano 'many' (11), as in Hale=mano 'many houses', several places on O'ahu.

manō 'shark' (11), as in Pu'u=manō 'shark hill', a Moloka'i hill up which a legendary shark was dragged and beaten.

6.5. Improper segmentation

Many place names could be segmented in various ways, and the acceptable way may not be according to the best-known words:

Alaula 'early dawn light', a Hono-lulu way; not Ala-'ula 'red road'.

Honu='apo 'caught turtle', a Hawai'i village; not Honua=pō 'night land'.

Ka='ai=pū 'the eating together', a Hono-lulu avenue; not Ka'a=ipu 'rolling calabash'.

Kai=mū 'gathering [at] sea'; not Ka=imu (the oven).

Ka=pahulu 'the worn-out soil', a section of Hono-lulu; not Kapa=hulu 'feather bark-cloth'.

Ka=pu'u=lua 'the double hill', a Moloka'i beach; not Kapu=ulua 'crevally fish taboo' (the glottal stop in *pu'u* makes the latter interpretation improbable).

Ka='uiki 'the glimmer', a Maui land point; not K-a-'u=iki 'my little one'.

Kūmimi, a kind of crab, the name of a place on Moloka'i; not Kū-mimi 'stand urinating'.

Pua'a-hala 'passing pig', a Moloka'i land division; not Pū=a'a=hala 'pandanus tree root'.

See also the discussion of Kaua'i in section 6.8.

257

6.6. Semantic classification

The computer analysis showed that about 83 percent of the Hawaiian entries have discernible meanings, a few of these being probable rather than certain. In some instances, alternate translations are given in the Glossary. The Hawaiian words have been classified semantically in the following categories, with the numbers of examples, if ten or more, given for each category, followed in parentheses by the number of items listed fewer than ten times. Some of the assignments to classes are perforce arbitrary and there is some overlapping.

geographic features	831 (20)
inanimate nature	265 (40)
words of size	203 (6)
material culture	170 (36)
plants and plant life	153 (91)
actions	124 (29)
other qualities (except colors)	115 (37)
numbers and words of quantity	71 (10)
colors	69 (27)
birds	68 (22)
body parts	65 (28)
legendary supernaturals	53 (16)
people	44 (24)
sea life	32 (50)
mammals	23 (1)
locatives	10 (6)
smells	(10)
insects	(9)

The individual items found in the computer count to occur ten times or more are given below. The others may be found in Elbert (1971).

Geographic features: *wai* 'stream, river, pond, fresh water' (240); *puʻu* 'hill, mound, elevation, pimple' (219); *moku* 'district, island' (47); *lua* 'pit, crater, hole' (44); *lae* 'cape, point, forehead' (44); *mauna* 'mountain' (32); *pali* 'cliff' (30); *ana* 'cave' (26); *one* 'sand, beach' (23); *papa* 'flats' (21); *puna* 'spring' (19); *ahu* 'heap' (18); *awa* 'bay' (17); *kīpuka* 'green area surrounded by lava' (16); *loko* 'pond, lake' (13); *mana* 'branch, fork' (12); *lapa* 'ridge' (10).

As mentioned in section 3, names of many bays and valleys begin with *Hono-* or *Hana-*. See also *maka* under "body parts."

Inanimate nature: *lani* 'sky, royal chief' (68); *pōhaku* 'stone' (46); *kai* 'sea, seaward' (39); *lā* 'sun, day' (20); *ua* 'rain' (18); *pō* 'night, dark' (14); *kaha* 'place' (13); *ahi* 'fire' (13); *malu* 'shade, shadow' (13); *au* 'current' (11); *ao* 'clouds' (10).

Material culture: *hale* 'house' (58); *pā* 'fence, enclosure, receptacle' (34); *ala* 'road' (23); *lei* 'garland' (17); *wa'a* 'canoe' (15); *lama* 'torch', a kind of tree (12); *ki'i* 'image' (11).

Numbers and words of quantity: *lua* 'two' (19); *kahi* 'one' (14); *kini* '40,000, a great many' (14); *lau* '400, many' (13); *mano* '4,000, a great many' (11).

Words of size: *loa* 'long' (73); *nui* 'large, big, great' (66); *iki* 'small, little' (64).

Colors: *'ula* 'red' (42); *kea* 'white' (27).

Other qualities: *kū* 'upright, resembling' (54); *ola* 'alive, well' (18); *kapu* 'forbidden, sacred' (17); *pili* 'close, related' (15); *nani* 'pretty' (11).

Actions: *lele* 'to fly, jump' (25); *kau* 'to place' (24); *'ai* 'to eat' (16); *ka'a* 'to roll' (14); *hana* 'to work, do' (13); *puka* 'to come out, hole' (12); *kilo* 'to look, watch' (10); *holo* 'to sail, run' (10).

Body parts: *maka* 'eye, face, headland, point' (38); *iwi* 'bone' (15); *po'o* 'head' (12).

Plants and plant life: *kukui* 'candlenut' (27); *lau* 'leaf' (24); *ulu* 'grove, growth' (20); *pua* 'flower' (18); *niu* 'coconut' (15); *hala* 'pandanus' (15); *hau* 'Hibiscus tiliaceus' (13); *maile,* a fragrant vine (11); *lehua, 'ōhi'a* flower' (10).

Birds: *manu* 'bird, insect' (28); *moa* 'chicken' (18); *pueo* 'owl' (12); *'alae* 'mudhen' (10).

Legendary supernaturals: Kāne, god of life and procreation (25); Pele, volcano goddess (17); *mo'o* 'water supernatural' (11).

People: *koa* 'soldier, warrior, brave' (20); *ali'i* 'chief' (14); *kanaka* 'person, human being, commoner' (10).

Sea life: *i'a* 'fish, sea life, food eaten with *poi'* (11); *manō* 'shark' (11); *honu* 'turtle' (10).

Mammals: *pua'a* 'pig' (13); *'īlio* 'dog' (10). (References to 'pig' commonly refer to Kama-pua'a, the pig-man who rooted out valleys, fought Pele and made love to her, and was a symbol of lechery and of the forces of nature that are creative as well as **259**

destructive. The dog references may refer to Kū=ʻīlio=loa or Pupua=lena-lena, a famous dog demigod. See Beckwith, 1970.)

Locative: *uka* 'inland' (10).

The meanings of a large proportion of the place names can be understood if one learns the 86 words listed as occurring ten times or more, as well as the common articles *(ka, ke, nā)*, the prepositions *o* and *a*, and the prefix *Hono-/Hana-*.

6.7. Implications of the semantic classification

The following names, judged on the numbers of examples of the constituents in the semantic categories, might be considered "average" or "typical":

Ka=wai=nui 'the great water': article + geographic entity + word of size.
Pele=ʻula 'red Pele': mythological figure + color.
Puʻu=loa 'long hill': geographic entity + word of size.
Kukui=ʻula 'red candlenut': plant + color.
Hale 'house': material culture.

The semantic ranges of the words are very wide (as *wai, puʻu,* and *moku* under "geographic features") or very narrow *(ʻaʻama* 'black crab', or *ʻama,* young stage of the *ʻama-ʻama* fish under "sea life").

The most frequent geographical entities by far are *wai* and *puʻu,* followed by *moku, lua,* and *lae.* The common land divisions, *ahu-puaʻa, lele,* and *ʻili,* seem unrepresented, as is the word for town, *kū-lana=kau=hale.* This latter is a modern term, but the others have been considered ancient (although perhaps they are not, for the terms are not mentioned often in the legends).

A surprising feature is the total of 100 plant names occurring in the place names; perhaps this can be construed as an indication that one of the primary interests of the early Hawaiians was agriculture, and that this interest seems to have been more compelling than marine life.

The large numbers of names of plants and animals, as well as of geographic entities, reflect the animism of the religion—the association of the supernatural with nature, the *kino lau* (myriad shapes) of the demigods. The pig god, Kama-puaʻa, one of the most important and peculiarly Hawaiian of the many **260** *kupua,* had forms that included, in addition to that of handsome

man, single pigs and dozens of pigs, clouds *(ao)*, plants *(kukui,
'uha=loa, 'āma'uma'u* fern, *kūkae=pua'a* grass [literally 'pig excreta']), the small triggerfish *humu-humu=nuku-nuku=a=pua'a,*
as well as that of the great god Lono.

The culture is reflected in various other ways. *'Ula* 'red' (42
examples), by far the most common of the colors, was the traditional Polynesian sacred color. Kāne (25), considered by Beckwith "the leading god" (1970:42), was god of life and the sea and
the bringer of water, and his name occurs far more frequently
than those of the other great gods—Lono (7), Kū (4), and Kanaloa (3). The frequent occurrence (13 times) of *pua'a* 'pig' is
probably due to the popularity of Kama=pua'a, previously
mentioned, who had erotic adventures on most of the islands but
whose complete name, surprisingly, is found in none of the place
names.

Religious beliefs are reflected in such terms as *akua* (6) and
kua (4) 'god'; *'aumakua* 'family god' (2); *lapu* 'ghost' (1); *kū'ula,*
a fishing god (1); *mana* 'supernatural power' (3); *pueo* 'owl', a
very helpful *'aumakua* (12); *manō* 'shark', also an *'aumakua* (11);
and *'alae* 'mudhen' (its crying at night foretold misfortune) (10).
Maka 'eye, face, headland' (38) and *po'o* 'head' (12) reflect the
belief that spiritual mana was in the head, as is shown in the
exaggerated size of the heads of the images. *Kua* 'back' (90) is
common, perhaps because the backs of very high chiefs were taboo; and *iwi* 'bone' (15), because the bones of chiefs had mana
and were hidden after death. The divinity of chiefs is shown by
the equating of *lani* 'sky' (68) with 'royal chief'. ('Chief' as *lani,*
reflecting this divinity, is more frequent than as *ali'i* (14) or *li'i*
(4), that indicate the chiefs' position on earth.) *Kō* 'sugarcane'
(6) was important as medicine and to bring success to any under-
taking because *kō* also means 'success'.

The low rating of certain cultural items is surprising, for example, mana (3) and *'aumakua* (2), previously mentioned, and of
such important foods as *kalo* 'taro' (3), *'ulu* 'breakfruit' (7),
uhi 'yam' (5), and *'uala* 'sweet potato' (3).

Great numbers of plant and sea-life names occur in the place
names (plants in greater number than sea-life forms), but most
of these are encountered infrequently. Only the *kukui* (27)
ranks high; this may be because of the beauty and commonness
of the tree, and because lights and torches were made of the
oily nuts, the tree thus symbolizing enlightenment and wisdom.

The old culture seems to have had no "four-letter words," **261** and common use of words such as the following probably was quite proper: *ule* 'penis' (9), *kohe* 'vagina' (6), *kūkae* 'feces' (3), *mīana* 'urinal' (2), *aina* 'intercourse' (1), *laho* 'scrotum' (1), *puʻukole* 'vagina' (1), and Puna-wai=kohe=leʻa 'spring [of] orgasm vagina' (1). A beach on crowded Oʻahu called Ule=hawa 'filthy penis' (named for a chief) attracts little attention today— even though the first part of the name is well known—perhaps because the two words in the name are joined: Ulehawa.

6.8. Names without meanings

Many important names are so ancient that no translation at all is possible. These include the names of the inhabited Hawaiian islands (except for Lā=naʻi 'conquest day'). Some persons have attempted to explain Hawaiʻi as meaning 'burning Java' or 'little Java', but as of 1973 no linguist has found evidence for such an etymology. According to present knowledge, the name Hawaiʻi cannot be segmented. Cognates have not been found outside Polynesia. In eastern Polynesia (but not in Hawaiʻi), the ancient homeland (and in the Marquesas, the abode of the dead) was called Hawaiki. The Samoan reflex, Savaiʻi, is merely the name of the largest island in the group.

Equally impossible to explain is Kauaʻi, which some have explained as originally Kau=ʻai 'food season'. But metathesis of glottal stops seems not to have occurred in the history of the Hawaiian language. Instead, the glottal stop, replacing *k* in Proto-Polynesian, is one of the most stable of the Hawaiian consonants. (For one explanation see Elbert and Pukui 8.7.)

Tourists are told that Oʻahu means 'gathering place', and this seems a sensible name for the most populous of the islands. In ancient times, however, Oʻahu was not populous and was distinctly subordinate to Hawaiʻi and Kauaʻi. Alexander (1903), a brilliant scholar, gave no meaning for the name in his article on Hawaiian geographic names. The meaning 'gathering place' may have been suggested first by Thrum, as late as 1922. Thrum, who paid no attention to glottal stops, may have assumed that the initial *O* was the subject marker (ʻo), and that ʻahu meant 'to gather, collect'. ʻAhu (with a glottal stop) means 'garment', and ahu (without a glottal stop) means 'heap, pile, collection' (of objects, rarely of people!). If 'gathering of objects' were the correct translation of the word, the name would be ʻO=ahu (pronounced ʻowahu), with the glottal stop preceding the *o* and not the *a*. That glottal stops are ever transposed in Hawaiian seems to be unattested.

It is safest not to attempt translation of such forms.

7. Words of non-Hawaiian origin and names of streets and buildings

The names with words of non-Hawaiian origin are classified as follows:

English	474
Hawaiianized borrowings from English	63
Non-English and non-Hawaiian ("foreign")	61
Hybrids	
Hawaiian and English	23
English and Hawaiian	11
Hawaiian and borrowings	12
Borrowings and Hawaiian	6
"Foreign" and English	14
"Foreign" and Hawaiian	2
Total	666

For many years new streets have been given Hawaiian names, but streets in the older sections of Honolulu are named for visitors and citizens, as are buildings on the Puna=hou and Ka=meha-meha campuses. Some of these people are listed below according to occupations.

Discoverers and early visitors: Cook, Portlock, Vancouver, John Young.

Missionaries: Andrews, Bachelot, Baldwin, Bingham, Chamberlain, Clark, Cooke, Damien, Eugene, Judd, Maigret.

Business leaders and philanthropists: Alexander, Atherton, Bishop, Castle, Dillingham, Waterhouse.

Educators and scholars: Bachman, Bertram, Brigham, Buck, Donaghho, Moore, Sinclair, Watanabe.

Political leaders: Dole, Farrington, Frear, King, Lee.

Military figures: Bellows, Nimitz, Ruger, Schofield, Shafter, Thomas.

Distinguished Hawaiians for whom streets were named include ʻIo=lani, Ka=hekili, Ka=ʻiu=lani, Ka=lā=kaua, Ka=lani=ana=ʻole, Ka=meha-meha, Ka=piʻo=lani, Keʻeaumoku, Kīnaʻu, Like-like, Liliʻu=o=ka=lani, Luna=lilo.

The buildings of the Ka=meha-meha Schools are named for

Hawaiian notables, most of them suggested by Donald D. Mitchell. Some of these are Ka=ʻahu=manu, Ka=lama, Ka=lani=moku, Ka=lei=o=Papa, Kāne=i=kapōlei, Kapu-āiwa, Ke=awe, Keʻelikōlani, Ke=kā=ulu=ohi, Ke=ola=o=ka=lani, Ke=ō=ua, Konia, Kū=i=Helani, Liho-liho, Nā=ahi=ʻena-ʻena, Pākī, Pau=ahi.

All of these are names of famous persons. Many less well-known figures have also been honored in Honolulu's place names, and their occupations reflect the times: whaler (Lopez), blacksmith (Ka=hanu), sailors (Matzie, Reed, Robinson), fisherman (Lukela), stevedore (Ke=ʻōpua), saloon keepers (Cunha, Houghtailing), hack driver (Quinn), carpenter (Morris), house painter (Enos), street-car conductor (Hayden), auctioneer (Colburn), store owners (Coyne, Emmeluth, Gertz), school teacher (DeCorte), land owners and subdividers and their kin (Coombs, Doris, Ferdinand, Gail, James, Lukepane, Makaleka, Mason, Matlock, McCully, Nā-one, Palani).

Hawaiianized versions of English names (either first or last names) were also used. (For substitutions of Hawaiian sounds for English ones in loanwords, see Elbert and Pukui, section 2.9.) At least 42 Hono-lulu streets were so named (see Elbert, 1971 for a listing), including ʻAnalū 'Andrews' (for the missionary author of a Hawaiian dictionary and grammar) and ʻEmekona 'Emerson' (for a missionary son, a physician who collected and translated Hawaiian legends).[4] No one knows for whom the streets Kale 'Charles' and Kaniela 'Daniel' were named. The only person to rate a title was Mr. Hall (Mikahala), for whom a ship and then a street were named.

A great many place names consist of more than one word, with the individual words from different languages. Such names are hybrids. Some examples from Hawaiian and English follow (the number of names in each category is given in parentheses):

Hawaiian + English (23): Aloha Tower; Moana ('open sea') Hotel.

Hawaiian + Hawaiianized English (13): ʻĀi-na=Haina 'Hind's Land', a section of Honolulu that formerly belonged to the part-Hawaiian Hind family; Kīpuka=Kēkake 'Jackass Kīpuka' (a *kīpuka* is a piece of land surrounded by a lava flow; on this one a donkey was marooned and saved).

English + Hawaiian (11): Princess Ka=ʻiu=lani, a hotel named for the niece of King Ka=lā=kaua.

Hawaiianized English + English (1): Likeke Hall 'Richards

4. Both of these early works are listed in the References.

Hall', a church meeting house named for a benefactor of the church.

Hawaiianized English + Hawaiian (7): Maria Hōkū=o=ke= Kai 'Mary, Star of the Sea', a Catholic church.

Examples from languages other than English follow, with the numbers of occurrences given in parentheses:

Portuguese, anglicized Portuguese, and Portuguese plus English (25): Alencastre Street, named for a bishop; Magellan Street, named for the circumnavigator of the Earth; Cunha's Alley, named for an early immigrant.

French, Belgian French, Hawaiianized French, and French plus English (19): Chaminade College, named for the founder of the Society of Mary; Damien Plaza in Hono-lulu, named for the Belgian martyr; Kaminaka, a Hono-lulu street near Chaminade College named for Bishop Chaminade; La Pérouse Bay, visited by the explorer of that name in 1786.

Chinese, Hawaiianized Chinese, English plus Chinese, and Portuguese Chinese (12): Chun Hoon Lane in Hono-lulu, named for a prominent bookkeeper; Ahana Street, named for a Chinese merchant whose name was Hawaiianized; Sam Sing, a plantation village established for Chinese laborers; Mākao, a land section named for the Portuguese colony.

Japanese and Japanese plus English (12): Watanabe Hall, a University of Hawai'i building named for a distinguished physicist; Yamada Lane, named for a Japanese contractor; Yokohama Bay, frequented by Japanese fishermen.

German (4): Isenberg Street, named for the owner of Wai= 'alae Ranch.

Russian (2): Lisianski, a coral island northwest of Kaua'i named for the Russian discoverer of the island.

Spanish (1): Marin, a Spaniard who came to Hawai'i in the early 1790s.

At least six Hono-lulu streets have Spanish names (Mariposa, Monterey, Paloma, Sierra, Sonoma, Ventura), probably derived from places in California.

Rare sources are Italian (La Pietra), Hawaiianized Tahitian (Niniko), and probably Hindi (Karratti).

It may be asked, in view of present-day population figures, why the Portuguese are so strongly represented, the Japanese so poorly (Yamada Street is the only one in Hono-lulu with a Japanese name), and the Filipinos not at all. The answer is found in dates of immigration of the different groups. The following **265** population figures (in thousands) and dates are from Lind (1967: 28):

	1878	1884	1896	1910	1960
Hawaiian	44	40	31	26	11
Chinese	6	18	22	21	38
Portuguese		10	15	22	–
Japanese			24	80	204
Filipino				2	69

Most of the streets with non-Hawaiian names were named in the last century, especially in the middle years. In the present century, streets have been given Hawaiian names. The Japanese and Filipinos simply arrived too late.

8. Connotative values of place names

8.1. Place names in sayings

Like most Polynesians, Hawaiians are fond of proverbial sayings that are memorized verbatim and are used less for didactic purposes than as displays of wit and as praise of the land. They differ from Euro-American proverbial sayings in that they rely heavily on place names. Rather rare in the West are such phrases as "castles in Spain," "crossing the Rubicon," and "sent to Siberia." These traditional expressions say a great deal in a few words and are elliptic, but they are not encountered frequently and are not particularly admired, being considered by some persons too trite for respectability.

In the traditional Hawaiian culture, however, such expressions were greatly admired, and a few people still use them today. Not many years ago Mary Kawena Pukui found a colleague, Ke=oho=kapu, hard at work. Instead of the banal comment that a *haole* would make, she asked cryptically, *"E kū'o'i a'e ana i ke One=o=Luhi?"* (Are [you] limping along the Beach of Weariness?) Ke=oho=kapu, quick as a flash, said resignedly, *"He pi'i-na kē-ia i mauna Pa'u-pa'u."* ([I'm] just climbing up Drudgery Hill.) Both were pleased, and as a result of this repartee, the work may have seemed less like drudgery. The core of these sayings is the double meaning—in the place names Luhi 'weariness' and Pa'u-pa'u 'drudgery'—a device rarely used in English sayings.

In *The Pilgrim's Progress,* place names are used for their double meanings, but the names are fictitious and didactic (Slough of Despond, Delectable Mountains, Celestial Country, Carnal Policy).

266

Hawaiian sayings also may be didactic. The two quoted above seem to express resignation and patience. The majority, however, are not didactic. Many sayings that use place names describe emotional states or important events, but the largest proportion show *aloha 'āi-na* 'love for the land and the people of the land', and this function, so important in Hawai'i, seems completely lacking in Euro-American proverbial sayings. (It is not noted, for instance, in Archer Taylor's *The Proverb and an Index to the Proverb.)*

The following are examples of proverbial sayings containing place names, each of which describes some type of human emotion or condition.

Anger: *Nā-pele-pele nā pali o Ka=lalau i ka wili 'ia e ka makani* 'crumbling are the cliffs of Astray, twisted by the wind'. *Naue Ka=lalau, pōniu ka Lawakua* 'Astray trembles, the Lawakua wind whirls'. *Ke lau-ahi mai-la 'o Pele iā Puna* 'Pele is pouring lava out on Puna'.

Grief: *Lu'u-lu'u Hana-lei i ka ua nui, kaumaha i ka noe o Alaka'i* 'Hana-lei is downcast with great rains, heavy with the mists of Alaka'i'.

Love: *'O ka ua o Hilo e mao ana, 'o ke aloha i ka ipo, mea pau 'ole* 'the rain of Hilo clears, love of a sweetheart—endless'. *A aloha wale 'ia kā ho'i 'o Ka=unu=o=Hua, he wahi pu'u wale iho nō ia* 'even Ka=unu=o=Hua is loved, it's just a mountain.'

Trouble: *Aia i Kē'ē* 'there at Kē'ē' (a remote cliff difficult or impossible to climb on the Nā=pali coast, Kaua'i).

Hospitality: *Ke ala-nui hele ma-uka o Pu'u=kā-hea* 'the pathway going inland of Calling=hill'.

Coals to Newcastle: *Ho'i hou ka pa'a-kai i Wai=mea* 'the salt goes back again to Wai=mea'. (Lots of salt is already available at Wai=mea in leeward Kaua'i.)

Intelligence: *No Ka=lae nō ka wahine* 'the lady is from The=forehead'.

Stupidity: *He po'e una-unahi he'e 'o Kula; 'o Kula hoe hewa* 'the people of Kula scale squids; the people of Kula paddle badly'. (Kula is high on Hale=a=ka=lā, Maui, where the people don't know how to paddle, and don't know that squids have no scales.) *Mai Ke='ā-'ā mai paha* 'maybe from Dumbness'. (See Ka-lalau in the Glossary.)

Not returning home: *Ua kō'ia paha e ke au o Hala'ea* 'perhaps [he] is dragged away by the current of Hala'ea'. (The currents at Hala'ea, on the Ka'ū side of South Point, Hawai'i, are very strong. A Midas-like story here is of a chief who claimed too many fish. The people piled fish high in his canoe and it was carried away by the current.)

Being poorly dressed: *Aia i Ka'ū i Ka='alu-'alu* 'there in Ka'ū at Sagging' (of baggy, poorly-fitting clothes or a wrinkled body).

Recovery from sickness: *'Ane-'ane e pae aku i Moku=ola* 'almost landed at Isle [of] Life'.

Success: *Ka pi'i nō ia ā Kōkī=o=Wai-lau* 'he has climbed Summit-of-Wai-lau' (a Moloka'i peak that is difficult to climb).

Failure: *Ua pae ka wa'a i Nānā=wale* 'the canoe landed at Profitless=looking'. *Aia akula paha i Wai=kī-kī i Hamo-hamo i ka 'imi 'ahu'awa* 'maybe just at Wai=kī-kī Groping-about (Hamo-hamo) looking for bitter grass'.

Or one may point out, usually in jest, some unpleasant physical characteristic or past happening, or an unpleasant meaning associated with a rival island or place (and place names by extension include the people of the place):

O'ahu: *O'ahu maka 'ewa-'ewa* 'unjust-eyed O'ahu'. (The goddess Hi'iaka of Hawai'i said this when her O'ahu relatives refused to help her mend her canoes. 'Ewa, a district on O'ahu, has the meaning 'crooked'; the saying applies to people who do not welcome and help visitors.)

Puna, Hawai'i: *Lohi'au Puna i ke akua wahine* 'Puna is backward because of the goddess'. *Weli-weli 'ino Puna i ke akua wahine* 'Puna is terrified by the goddess'. (These are references to Pele, the volcano goddess, who still ravages Puna.)

Ka=laoa, Hawai'i: *Ka=laoa 'ai pō 'ele-'ele* 'Ka=laoa eats [in the] dark night'. (The people are stingy and don't want to share their food.)

Maui: *Maui po'o hakahaka* 'empty-headed Mauians'.

Sayings that praise the land may be called *aloha 'āi-na* sayings, a phrase taken from the famous song "Kau-lana nā Pua" 'famous [are] the children' that describes the support of Hawaiians for their last queen, Li-li'u=o=ka=lani, and their sorrow that she was forced to sign "the paper of the enemy" *(ka pepa o ka 'enemi)* brought by the evil-hearted messenger *(ka 'elele o ka loko 'ino)* with its sin of annexation *(ho'o-hui 'āi-na kū'ai hewa)* to America. The song (Elbert and Mahoe 62–63) ends with a salutation to the people who love the land *(ka po'e i aloha i ka 'āi-na).*

There are probably thousands of *aloha 'āi-na* sayings. They name illustrious chiefs and places, important rains, seas, winds, and distinctive features. A speaker of Hawaiian never tires of hearing them over and over again; they recall to him his own grandmother or older relative who used to say them, and songs he heard as a child. They thus reinforce ties to family as well as to places, and are a link with a past that in many ways seems still a glorious never-never land. To the outsider, some of them may sound foolish, and this may be why Kepelino said, more than a hundred years ago, that when the foreigners ask and ask they get only a heap of foolishness *('ahu nā kupaianaha)* (Beckwith, 1932:142–143). Did he mean that Hawaiian lore seems foolish to the foreigners? Or that the Hawaiians refuse to tell the truth and say only foolish things? Either way, outsiders were outsiders, and so they remain today. Even Pele, the volcano goddess, is called a *malihini* (foreigner) because, aeons ago, she came from Kahiki.

Even more cogent than the association of *aloha 'āi-na* sayings with friends and relatives were the ties with the land and the sea, the source of life. The present and the future lay in the gardens, fishing grounds, and surfing sites. This attachment to the land and the sea was reflected in the poetic *aloha 'āi-na* sayings that one heard in conversation and in songs. Poetic? Yes, in the sense that the sayings brought to mind familiar places and cast over them a golden aura of affection.

Only a few of the many *aloha 'āi-na* sayings can be mentioned here, some of the phrases naming chiefs, rains, seas, winds, and famous features associated with the various islands. Each island, for example, is coupled with a chief's name: *Hawai'i o Keawe*, *Kaua'i o Mano=ka=lani=pō* 'multitudes [of] chiefs [from the] gods', *Lāna'i o Ka=ulu=lā'au* 'the forest', *Maui o Kama*, *Moloka'i o Ka=meha-meha=nui*, *Ni'ihau o Mano='ōpū=pa'i-pa'i* 'many belly slappings (as in childbirth)', and *O'ahu o Kākuhihewa*.

Rains, seas, winds, and special features were associated with places on the various islands:

Rains

Hawai'i: *Ka ua kani lehua o Hilo* 'the *lehua* sounding rain of Hilo'.

Kaua'i: *Ka ua loku o Hana-lei* 'the pouring rain of Hana-lei'. **269**

Maui: *Ka ua lani ha'a-ha'a o Hāna* 'the rain of Hāna's low-lying sky'.

O'ahu: *Ka ua Kuahine o Mānoa* 'the Sister rain of Mānoa'. (For songs with a rain name, see Elbert and Mahoe 43, 50.)

Seas

Hawai'i: *Kona kai 'ōpua i ka la'i* 'Kona seas with cloud billows that tell of peace to come'.

Kaua'i: *Ke kai malino mai Ke=kaha a Milo=li'i* 'the quiet seas from Ke=kaha to Milo=li'i'.

O'ahu: *Ka 'ehu kai o Pua='ena* 'the sea spray of Pua='ena'.

Winds

Hawai'i: *'Āpa'apa'a* (Kohala); *Kuehu=lepo* 'dust scattering' (Ka'ū).

Kaua'i: *Ala='oli* 'joyful pathway'.

Maui: *Ka=ua='ula* 'the red rain'.

Moloka'i: *Ala=hou* 'new pathway'.

O'ahu: *Ala='eli* 'eroded pathway' (Mānoa, Hono-lulu).

(For songs with wind names, see Elbert and Mahoe 50, 56. For long lists of winds, see For. 5:92–103.)

Distinctive features

Hawai'i: *I Kala=pana i ka niu moe* 'at Kala=pana, the coconut palms lie flat'. (A traditional way to honor a very high chief was to ask the chief to hold on to the tip of the fronds of a young coconut tree while the people bent the tree over and subsequently trained it to grow flat on the ground. Queen Emma was the last *ali'i* to be honored in this way, at Kala-pana, when she visited there on horseback a short time before the death of Princess Ruth in 1883. Emma died in 1885.)

Kaua'i: *Ka limu kā kanaka o Manu'a=kepa* 'the man-striking moss of Manu'a=kepa' (a slippery moss on which people slip and fall).

Maui: *Kau=pō 'ai loli* 'Kau=pō people eat sea slugs'. (A local chief long ago was so fond of this food that he had a special oven in which to bake all the *loli* that the people brought him.)

Moloka'i: *Ulu kukui o Lani=kāula* 'kukui groves of Lani=kāula'. (Here in this grove the famous prophet, Lani=kāula, was buried by his sons. The grave was believed to have mana.)

270 Ni'ihau: *Kō 'eli lima a'o Halāli'i* 'sugarcane hand-dug at

Halāli'i' (a peculiar sugarcane concealed by wind-blown sand; people saw protruding green leaves and dug out the cane stalks).

O'ahu: *Ka i'a hāmau leo o 'Ewa* 'pearl oysters of 'Ewa that silence voices'. (A taboo of silence was enforced on persons looking for pearl oysters at Pearl Harbor.)

When Ka=meha-meha dreamed of conquest of Kaua'i, he mentioned these places which he wished to enjoy: *E holo a inu i ka wai o Wai=lua, a hume i ka wai o Nā=molo=kama, a 'ai i ka 'anae 'au o Ka=wai=makua i Hā-'ena, a lei ho'i i ka pahapaha o Poli=hale, a laila, ho'i mai a O'ahu, 'oia ka 'āi-na e noho ai (Ka Nupepa Kuokoa,* July 20, 1867, rewritten in the orthography used in this Appendix). The translation by Kamakau (p. 187) has been slightly altered: 'Let [us] go and drink the water of Wai-lua, wear a loincloth in the water of Nā=molo=kama, eat the mullet that swim in Ka=wai=makua at Hā-'ena, wreathe [ourselves] with the seaweed of Poli=hale, then return to O'ahu, the land to dwell upon.'

We have given here only a sampling of the many sayings in which place names appear. Some are remembered because of double meanings, and some are merely tag lines attached to places throughout the Islands. Some are derogatory, but most of them express affection for the land.

8.2. Place names in narratives

Almost all Hawaiian tales are filled with place names—stories in Hawaiian newspapers, in the Fornander collection, and in the semihistorical *Ruling Chiefs of Hawaii* by Kamakau. One of the most interesting legends is Emerson's *Pele and Hiiaka,* an epic describing the journey of Hi'iaka, Pele's younger sister, from Kī=lau=ea volcano on Hawai'i to Kaua'i in order to find Lohi'au, whom Pele had met in her dreams and had fallen in love with. On her long and dangerous journey Hi'iaka encountered a succession of *mo'o* supernaturals whom she fought and vanquished, usually turning them into rocks that still stand. The islet Moko=li'i 'little lizard' (or Chinaman's Hat) in Kāne='ohe Bay, O'ahu, was the tail of a *mo'o* defeated by Hi'iaka, and its body is the long flat section near the shore (Emerson, 1915:91). The rock along the same coast known today as Crouching Lion was a *kupua* 'demigod' already turned to stone who rose to a crouching position and vainly begged Hi'iaka to restore him to life. A cave, Ke=awa='ula, at Yokohama Bay, O'ahu, is said to have been opened by Hi'iaka to get water.

Many gulches and ridges were formed by the rooting of the pig-god, Kama=pua'a, a symbol of erosion and lechery. Some of the stories concerning him are racy. In one account he chased Pele to Pua'a=kanu 'pig planted' in Puna, Hawai'i. He was about to molest her when Pele's sister Kapo=kohe=lele 'flying vagina Kapo' sent her special part flying to lure away the erotic pig-god. He forgot Pele and followed the part to Koko Crater, O'ahu, where it left an imprint. Kama got there too late, however, as the part had already flown off to Ka=lihi.

Places in stories such as these are termed *pana*. In their imaginations people ally the places, with amusement and affection, to the wondrous events of the past.

A second use of place names in narrative is nonpoetic, and the teller becomes a reporter of detail rather than a reteller of adventure. To the outsider, such detailed lists of places are boring, but not so to the narrator or his Hawaiian audience. Listed in travel-guide order, the places are a witness both to the story's veracity and the teller's memory; here again are ties of *aloha 'āi-na*.

The following passage described a swim from Wai='anae, O'ahu, to Puna, Hawai'i, by a female *laenihi* 'labroid fish'. The fish was on a noble mission—to find her brother a wife. Before leaving she told her brother that he would know where she was by natural phenomena (she could create lightning, thunder, and earthquakes when she wished to). In a brief paragraph 18 places are named (if we count Maui twice). They appear here in boldface type, and in the English version are translated when possible. Of the 17 different names, 4 (25 percent) are not listed in Coulter's Gazetteer or the present Glossary: *Hana-ka-'ie'ie, Pōloli=ka=manu, Mahiki, Kukulu;* and 7 of the names are not in the *Atlas of Hawaii* Gazetteer. This may give some idea of the number of places mentioned in the tales that are not recorded on maps.

Holo mai=la 'o Laenihi i ke ahiahi, a hiki i **Hale=o=Lono** *ma* **Pā=lā'au** *i Moloka'i, ua ka ua. Kāhāhā 'o hope no ka hiki=wawe loa. Ma=laila aku a* **Hana-ka-'ie'ie,** *ma* **Kahiki=nui** *i* **Honua-'ula** *ma* **Maui,** *'ōlapa ka uwila. Kāhāhā hou 'o hope no ka 'emo 'ole loa. Mai* **Maui** *aku a* **'Umi=wai,** *ma* **Kohala** *i Hawai'i, ku'i ka hekili; ma=laila aku a* **Pōloli=ka=manu,** *ma=waho o* **Mahiki** *i* **Hāmākua,** *nei ke ōla'i. Ma=laila aku a hala 'o* **Hilo,** *a komo i loko o* **Pana='ewa,** *a hiki i* **Kukulu** *ma=waho o* **Puna,** *kahe ka wai 'ula. A laila, no'o-no'o'o hope nei, ua loa'a 'o Kama=lālā=walu.* [For. Sel. 255]

'Laenihi came in the evening, going to **House=of=Lono** at **Wood-en=fence** on **Moloka'i**—the rain rained. The people behind were astonished at the great speed. From there on to **The-'ie'ie vine=bay** at **Great=Tahiti** at **Red=earth** on **Maui**—the lightning flashed. The people behind were astonished, quick-as-a-flash. From **Maui** to **'Umi's=water,** at **Kohala** on **Hawai'i**—the thunder roared. From there to **The=bird=is=hungry,** beyond **Mahiki** at **Hāmākua**—the earth quaked. From there past **Hilo,** entering within **Pana='ewa** and on to **Kukulu** outside **Puna**—the red rain water ran. Then the people behind thought that Kama=lālā=walu had been found.'

The following passage by Kamakau is from *Ke Au Okoa* of June 10, 1869. It describes the beauties of Hāna, Maui, in the late eighteenth century. A translation appears in Kamakau's *Ruling Chiefs* (1961:385), and recently in Wenkam's *Maui: the Last Hawaiian Place* (1970:34). The Hawaiian text has been re-written in the orthography used in this Appendix, and the translation is slightly altered. An unclear portion is marked with a question mark. Of the 12 places named, only 5 are in the Glossary or in Coulter, and only 2 are in the *Atlas of Hawaii*—another example of the high percentage of names not listed on maps and probably destined soon to be forgotten, if not already so.

A he 'āi-na kaulana 'o Hāna i ka wā kahiko. 'O ka pā kaua ka mea i kaulana ai 'o Hāna, 'o ka nalu o Pūhele ma ka wai 'au'au o Kū=maka, o ka he'e pu'e wai o Wai='ōhinu, o ka lele ma'opu mai a ka wai o Kama, 'o ke kāhuli a ka lau o ka 'ama'u, 'o ka 'awa lau lena o Lanakila. 'O ka momona o ka o (?) Pu'e=kahi, 'o ka poi 'ono o Kua=kahi, 'o nā 'opihi momona o Ka=wai=papa, 'o ka uhu palu-palu momona o Hane=o'o, 'o nā pua'a kū-palu me nā 'īlio nahu maka; aloha nō nā li'i i kē-lā 'āi-na 'olu-'olu, i ho'o-pulu 'ia e ka ua 'Āpua=kea, ka ua wāwahi i luna o ka hala, ka hala mai Wā-kiu a Hono-ka=lani.

'Hāna was in olden days a noted place. Hāna was famous for the fortified hill, the surf at Pūhele, the freshwater bathing pool of Kū=maka, the surfing to the stream mouth at Wai='ōhinu, the leaping to dive in the waters of Kama, the changing color of the fronds of the 'ama'u fern, the yellow-leafed kava of Lanakila, the fat (?) of Pu'e=kahi, the delicious poi of Kua=kahi, the fat limpets of Ka=wai=papa, the fat soft parrotfish of Hane=o'o, and the fattened pigs and eye-biting dogs dear to the memory of chiefs of that pleasant land moistened by the 'Āpua=kea rain, the rain that rattles on the hala trees passing from Wā=kiu to Hono-ka=lani.'

Such an emphasis on place must have seemed dull to Moses Nākuina (1867–1911), the gifted author of the story of Pāka'a and the gourd that controlled the winds. Nākuina's literary style **273** contrasts markedly with that of the legends in the Fornander volumes, collected about a half century earlier. Nākuina's phrases are longer, he piled up sequences of homonyms, and he mentioned only important places. On a long journey made by Pāka'a from Kaua'i to Hilo, only 10 places are mentioned. The reader is not treated to a timetable that tells everywhere the hero slept and took a bath. Nākuina's slighting of place names is similar to that in the literature of the West, and must have pleased his younger readers but left his older ones with the feeling that the story was too meagerly documented to be believed!

8.3. Place names in chants and songs

The most complete discussion of the role of place names in poetry is by Katharine Luomala. She has described with sensitivity and delicacy the emotional effect that place names may have; even when the "specific associations with specific places have blurred ... a halo of happiness or sorrow clings to the poet's recollection ... " (1965:243).

The discussion here begins with examples of the love chants of the legendary antihero, Hale=mano (*antihero,* a currently fashionable term, seems appropriate because Hale=mano is unable to hold his lover and because he himself proves inconstant, a sophistication perhaps rare in the usual folktale). As he sings the chant which begins as follows, Hale=mano has been looking at the summit of the volcanic dome of Hale=a=ka=lā on Maui with clouds flying over, now concealing and now revealing, and he sings of places where he has been with his lover (again the original is rewritten in the orthography of this Appendix):

Kau=pō 'āi-na pali huki i luna,
Huki a'e-la e like me Kahiki=nui,
He nui nō wau nāu, e ke aloha.

(For. Sel. 275)

Kau=pō land of cliffs rising high,
Rising upwards like Great-Tahiti,
Great was I, you [thought], O love.

A Hawaiian poetic device, an echo of the last word of a line in the next line (sometimes known as linked assonance), is found in lines 2 and 3. Kau=pō and Kahiki=nui are places on Maui where Hale=mano shared joy and sorrow with his wife.

Hale=mano then goes on to the next island, Hawai'i, where he and his wife enjoyed the surfing of Kai=mū, but where she deserted him for the chiefs of Hilo and Puna, and he administers the saddest and most gentle of rebukes (For. Sel. 277):

Ke kua 'ia mai la i ke kai ka hala o Puna
E hala 'o'a ana mehe kanaka lā
Lulumi iho=la i ke kai o Hilo—ē.
Hā-nu'u ke kai i luna o Moku=ola.
Ua ola a'e nei loko i kō aloha ē.

Chopped to bits by the sea are the hala trees
Standing up like human beings
Drowned in the Hilo sea.
Rises up the sea of the Isle=of=Life.
This heart lives upon your love.

Later, in the love-matching game of *kilu* (Malo 216–218), another woman makes a sure bet with Hale=mano (if I win you are mine and if you win I am yours); this unsubtle arrangement arouses the heroine's jealousy and she now sings back a love song to Hale=mano (For. Sel. 285).

Auwē ku'u hoa pili, 'o ke kāne ē,
Ku'u hoa o ka hale wai anu o Hilo,
No Hilo ho'i au no ka ipu a Kulukulu'ā
No ke one holu i Wai=o=lama,
No ka ua hehi lau 'ulu o Pi'i=honua.
I noho kā-ua i nā ulu o Mālama ē,
Mālama ke aloha i ka wai-maka.

Alas my dear companion, [my] man,
My companion of the cool waters of the house of Hilo,
From Hilo I and the calabash of Kulukulu'ā
Where sands ripple at Wai=o=lama,
Where rain treads upon breadfruit leaves at Pi'i=honua.
We stayed in the groves of Mālama,
Care for love in tears.

Three places are recalled here with joy and sorrow: the rippling sands of Wai=o=lama (a stream and beach near the town of Hilo), Pi'i=honua (at least five places on the island of Hawai'i have this name), and Mālama, a famous place in the Puna district. The juxtaposition of Mālama and *mālama* is another example of linked assonance.

The following song, given in its entirety, differs from the previously cited extracts in that punning is lacking. Its appeal is in its subtlety and in the repetition of names of places, rains, and winds of the poet's birthplace, together with sayings, mostly of the *aloha 'āi-na* kind. It jumps about from East Maui to West Maui in a seemingly helter-skelter way. This is an example of a **275** song that might seem a heap of foolishness to the outsider but that delights the child of the land.[5] In keeping with the penchant for understatement and veiled meanings, Kula is not mentioned by name, but is identified by the mists and by the derisive reference in the chorus to scaling squids (the saying is given in its entirety in section 6.1).

Place names on East Maui include Honua='ula, Auwahi, and Ka='uiki. Hāna is identified by the *aloha 'āi-na* saying about the low skies (section 9.1). Tributes to West Maui include mention of La'i='e-lua and the *Hono-* bays (Hono-kahua, Hono-ke=ana, Hono-kō=hau, Hono-kō=wai, Hono-lua, Hono-nana) and Koa'e. The skin-stinging rain is at Wai='ehu and the Kili'o'opu wind at Wai=he'e (*'o'opu* fish were caught here). The school at Lahaina Luna is praised as the light of knowledge not blown out by the Red=rain gales. The taboo fish and the famous stones have not been explained.

Honua='ula

Honua='ula kua la'o-la'o,	Honua='ula, pitted back,
Nā pu'u o La'i='e-lua.	Hills of Doubly=peaceful.

Chorus

He aloha wale a'e ana	A greeting
I ku'u 'āi-na kaulana,	For my famous land,
I ka unahi-nahi i ka pika he'e,	For scaling squid suction cups,
I ka uahi kokololio.	Gusty mists.
Ka ua Pe'e=pā=pōhaku,	The rain hiding [behind] stone walls,
Hanohano i ka i'a kapu,	Distinguished by taboo fish,
Nā pōhaku kaulana,	Famous stones,
'O Auwahi wela i ka la'i.	Auwahi hot in the sun.
Ē nā-hono=a=Pi'i-lani	O bays of Pi'ilani
I ka malu hēkuawa.	In the valley shade.
Ē ka ua hō'eha 'ili	O rain that stings the skin
A me ka ua Kili'o'opu.	And the rain and Kili'o'opu wind.
Ālai 'oe e Ka='uiki,	You block, Ka='uiki,
I ka wai 'āwili me ke kai	Streams mingling with seas
I ka ua Lani=ha'a-ha'a	In the Low=lying rain
Ma nā pali o Ko'olau.	And windward cliffs.

5. Koana Wilcox, who contributed the song, said that its composer, David K. Ka=poha=kimo=hewa, lived at Kula, high on Hale=a=ka=lā on East Maui, in the first decades of this century.

Moloka'i nui a Hina,	Great Moloka'i, [child] of Hina,
E ka pu'u o Koa'e,	O hill, Koa'e,
I ka ipu kukui pio 'ole	Light never extinguished
I ka makani Ka=ua='ula.	By the Red=rain gales.

The many sayings in this song raise the question, Which comes first, the saying or the song? According to Mrs. Pukui, the senior author, either may be first. She tells of a famous chant that later became a saying. A colleague at the Bishop Museum many years ago became suddenly angry. Seeing this, Mrs. Pukui chanted: *"Ua pau k-o-'u lihi hoi-hoi i ka nani o Poka 'Ailana."* (My pleasure in the beauty of Ford Island is no more.)

That was all, but the angry one's wrath vanished and she burst into laughter. She well knew the story of the person for whose anger the chant was composed, a person from 'Ewa. The chant was a mild rebuke for a loss of temper and has long been admired for several reasons:

(1) It is indirect. One never calls an adze by its own name. And the incident is thinly disguised by change of locale from 'Ewa to nearby Ford Island.

(2) It is understated. This is a favorite rhetorical device not unrelated to the fondness for indirection.

(3) It recalls stories and jokes from the past, and suggests one's own childhood and a generation older than one's own; to hear it might bring tears as well as laughter.

9. Names found elsewhere in Polynesia

The only comparative study of Polynesian place names made thus far is by Koskinen (1963). He compared names in 15 languages. The number of names available to him ranged from 2,410 for Tongan to 107 for Niue. None of the lists other than those for Hawai'i and Rennell/Bellona indicated all the phonemes. Koskinen concluded that the greatest number of Hawaiian place names are shared with Maori (23 percent), Tahitian (21 percent), Rarotongan and Tupuai (18 percent), Samoan, Marquesan, and Tongan (each 17 percent). He believed that Hawaiian shared 281 names with Tongan. How he arrived at such a high number is not clear, as he does not give his data. He did attempt to compare ancient rather than present-day forms of the names. (He would have disdained equation of today's Moloka'i and the island of Morotai in the Moluccas; the Proto-Polynesian form of Moloka'i is *Molotaki[6] or *Morotaki.)

6. Names preceded by an asterisk are Proto-Polynesian reconstructions.

Appendix

Certain generic names are found nearly everywhere in Polynesia, including reflexes of *'awa 'bay, anchorage', *fale 'house, building', *fanga 'bay', *la'e 'point, cape', *maunga 'mountain', *tahi 'sea', and *wai 'fresh water'. A question that the comparativist is bound to raise is this: Are compound names formed with such bases to be considered cognate, or may one assume that some of them may have originated independently? The pairs of words in the following list seem to have coincidental correspondence rather than genetic correspondence (names other than Hawaiian are written as single words), especially if we consider that they are isolated examples found, in some instances, in only two areas. In the general vocabulary usually more than two reflexes are available.

Hawai'i: *Hono-uli-uli*
Samoa: *Fangauli* [7]
⎱ 'black bay'

Maori: *Whanganui*
Easter Island: *Hanganui*
⎱ 'large bay'

Hawai'i: *Mauna Kea*
Easter Island: *Maungateatea*
⎱ 'white mountain'

Hawai'i: *Mauna=pōhaku*
Maori: *Maungapohatu*
⎱ 'stony mountain'

Hawai'i: *Wai=lele*
Niue: *Vailele*
⎱ 'waterfall'

These names, which we tentatively reject as cognate because they could have originated independently, have at least similarity in meaning, but many place names old enough to go back to Proto-Polynesian are without meaning. Thus a comparativist working with place names does not have the tool of meaning (other than the vague gloss 'place name') to check hypotheses based on phonemic similarity. Still, even without the tool of meaning, we feel that occurrence of the meaningless and unusual name *Takuu in various shapes over broad expanses of the Pacific Ocean cannot be due to coincidence.

The comparison of Polynesian place names attempted here is largely exploratory; it seems impossible to make a definitive comparative study until certain theoretical problems are ironed out, and until rather lengthy phonemic lists of numerous places are available. In Table 1 we list only a few Hawaiian names that

7. The Samoan "g," pronounced *ng,* is written here as it is sounded.

TABLE 1. Proto-Polynesian Reflexes of Hawaiian Place Names

Proto-Polynesian	Tongan	Samoan	Maori	Hawaiian	Other[†]
*Kupolu	Kupolu	'Upolu	Kuporu	'Upolu	
*Langiatea	Langiatea		Rangiatea	Lani=ākea	Ra'iatea (T)
*Manuka	Manuka	Manu'a	Manuka	Manu'a	
				Manu'a=Kepa	
*Sa'akupu	Ha'akupu			Hā-'upu	Hakupu (N)
*Sa'amoa	Ha'amoa	Sāmoa		Hāmoa	Ha'amoa (R)
*Savaiki	Hawaiki	Savai'i	Hawaiki	Hawai'i	Falehawaiki (N)
*Tafitinui	Tahisi		Tawhitinui	Kahiki=nui	Tahitinui (T)
*Takuu	Toku (?)	Ta'ū		Ka'ū	Takuu (Tk)
*Tokelau	Tokelau	To'elau	Tokerau	Ko'olau	Tokenggau (R)
*Tonga	Tonga	Tonga	Tongariroriro	Kona	Tonga (R)
*Waimea	Waimea	Vaimea	Waimea	Wai=mea	
*Wava'u	Vava'u	Vavau		Wawau	Vavau (T)
					Vevau (M)
					Vava'u (R)

[†]The languages in which these names occur are identified here by the following abbreviations: T, Tahitian; N, Niue; Tk, Takuu (Mortlocks); R, Rennellese; M, Marquesan.

279

seem unquestionably to date back to Proto-Polynesian. For such an assumption, cognates of Hawaiian names must occur in Tongan or Niue.

10. Representation of the lexicon and the grammar in the place names

The Pukui and Elbert *Hawaiian Dictionary* (1971), contains approximately 26,000 entries, but only 1,836 different Hawaiian words and particles occur in the 3,359 Hawaiian place names counted by computer—only a small fraction of the total. Frequency counts were given in section 6; however, it was not mentioned there that many of the names, such as Kukui 'candlenut', occur many times. The conclusion seems to be that for place names, even though most of them have discernible meanings, only a fraction of the possibilities are utilized. The dictionary, for example, lists about 2,200 plant names and 120 fish names, but only 99 and 54 are included in the place names.

Table 2 provides a hint as to the grammatical apparatus included in the place names. The abbreviation EP refers to the Elbert and Pukui *Hawaiian Grammar*. Allomorphs have not been counted in the totals except in the verb suffixes.

TABLE 2. Representation of Hawaiian Grammar in the Place Names

Grammatical Elements	EP grammar	Present Study	EP grammar (section no.)
Prefixes to verbs other than reduplications	12	5	6.1
Suffixes to verbs	2	2	6.5
Nominalizing suffixes	3	2	8.9
Other affixes	3	1	8.9
Pre-verb markers	11	0	5.1
Post-verb particles	27	0	7
Prepositions	13	3	9.1
Articles	3	3	10.3
Plural markers	3	0	10.5
Substitutes			
Pronouns	13	1	8.2
Demonstratives	8	0	8.3
Possessives	20	2	8.4
Interrogatives	3	0	8.5
Locative nouns	16	11	8.6
Numeral affixes	7	3	10.4
Conjunctions	5	1	11.1
Interjections	16	0	4.7

Books and Articles

Addleman, William C. n.d. "History of the United States Army in Hawaii 1849–1939." Mimeographed. (Archives of Hawaii)

Adler, Jacob. 1970. "Elias Abraham Rosenberg, King Kalakaua's Soothsayer." *The Hawaiian Journal of History* 4:57n.

Alexander, W.D. 1891. *A Brief History of the Hawaiian People.* New York.

———— 1903. *Hawaiian Geographic Names.* U.S. Coast and Geodetic Survey, Appendix no. 7. Washington, D.C.

Andrade, Ernest, Jr. 1962. *Our Heritage, Commemorating the Seventy-fifth Anniversary of Central Union Church.* Honolulu: Published by the church.

Barthel, Thomas S. 1962. "Easter-Island Place-Names," *Journal de la Société des Océanistes* 18:100–107.

Beckwith, Martha Warren. 1919. "The Hawaiian Romance of Laieikawai" [by S.N. Haleole, 1863], with introduction and translation. Bureau of American Ethnology Annual Report 33 (for 1911–1912), pp. 285–677. Washington, D.C.

———— 1932. *Kepelino's* Traditions of Hawaii. Bernice P. Museum Bulletin 95. Honolulu.

———— 1970. *Hawaiian Mythology.* Honolulu: University of Hawaii Press. (First published in 1940 by Yale University Press.)

Bender, Byron Wilbur. 1963. "A Linguistic Analysis of the Place-Names of the Marshall Islands." Ph.D. dissertation, Indiana University.

Bryan, E.H., Jr. 1942. *American Polynesia and the Hawaiian Chain.* Honolulu: Tongg Publishing Co.

———— 1970. *Bryan's Sectional Maps of Honolulu, Rural Oahu, and the Hawaiian Islands.* Honolulu.

Buck, Peter H. See Te Rangi Hiroa.

References

Clark, T. Blake. 1939. "Honolulu's Streets." *Papers of the Hawaiian Historical Society,* no. 20, pp. 4–25. Honolulu.

Cook, James. 1785. *A Voyage to the Pacific Ocean, Undertaken by the Command of His Majesty, for Making Discoveries in the Northern Hemisphere.* Vol. 3. London.

Cooke, George P. 1949. *Moolelo o Molokai, a Ranch Story of Molokai.* Honolulu: Honolulu Star-Bulletin.

Coulter, John Wesley. 1935. *A Gazetteer of the Territory of Hawaii.* University of Hawaii Research Publications, no. 11. Honolulu.

Cox, J. Halley, with Edward Stasack. 1970. *Hawaiian Petroglyphs.* Bernice P. Bishop Museum Special Publication 60. Honolulu.

Dauzat, Albert. 1957. *Les Noms de Lieux, Origine et Evolution, Villes et Villages, Pays, Cours d'eau, Montagnes, Lieuxdits.* Paris: Librairie Delagrave. (First printed in 1926.)

Daws, Gavan. 1968. *Shoal of Time, a History of the Hawaiian Islands.* New York: Macmillan Co.

Decisions on Names in Hawaii. 1954. Cumulative Decision List no. 5403. U.S. Board on Geographic Names, Dept. of the Interior. Washington, D.C.

Department of Geography, University of Hawaii. 1973. *Atlas of Hawaii.* Honolulu: The University Press of Hawaii.

Elbert, Samuel H., ed. 1959. *Selections from Fornander's Hawaiian Antiquities and Folk-lore.* Honolulu: University of Hawaii Press.

———— 1971. "Hawaiian Place Names." Working Papers in Linguistics, University of Hawaii, vol. 3, no. 7. Honolulu.

Elbert, Samuel H., and Noelani Mahoe. 1970. *Nā Mele o Hawai'i Nei, 101 Hawaiian Songs.* Honolulu: University of Hawaii Press.

Elbert, Samuel H., and Mary Kawena Pukui. *Hawaiian Grammar.* Honolulu: The University Press of Hawaii, forthcoming.

Ellis, William. 1963. *Journal of William Ellis, Narrative of a Tour of Hawaii, or Owhyhee; with Remarks on the History, Traditions, Manners, Customs and Language of the Inhabitants of the Sandwich Islands.* Honolulu: Advertiser Publishing Company. (First printed in 1827.)

Emerson, Nathaniel B. 1915. *Pele and Hiiaka, a Myth of Hawaii.* Honolulu: Honolulu Star-Bulletin.

———— 1965. *Unwritten Literature of Hawaii: The Sacred Songs of the Hula, Collected and Translated with Notes and an Account of the Hula.* Rutland, Vt.: Charles E. Tuttle Co. (First published in 1909 as Bureau of American Ethnology Bulletin 38, Washington, D.C.)

Emory, Kenneth P. 1928. *Archaeology of Nihoa and Necker Islands.* Bernice P. Bishop Museum Bulletin 53. Honolulu.

———— 1969. *The Island of Lanai: a Survey of Native Culture.* Bishop Museum Reprints. Honolulu. (First published in 1924 as Bernice P. Bishop Museum Bulletin 12.)

Emory, Kenneth P., and Lloyd J. Soehren. 1971. *Archaeological and Historical Survey, Honokohau Area, North Kona, Hawaii.* Rev. ed. Department of Anthropology report 61-61, Bernice P. Bishop Museum, Honolulu.

Feher, Joseph, Edward Joesting, and O.A. Bushnell. 1969. *Hawaii, a Pictorial History.* Bernice P. Bishop Museum Special Publication 58. Honolulu.

Finney, Ben R. 1959*a*. "Hawaiian Surfing, a Study of Cultural Change." Master of Arts thesis, University of Hawaii.

———— 1959*b*. "Surfing in Ancient Hawaii." *Journal of the Polynesian Society* 68:327–347.

Finney, Ben R., and James D. Houston. 1966. *Surfing: The Sport of Hawaiian Kings.* Rutland, Vt.: Charles E. Tuttle Co.

Fornander, Abraham. 1917, 1918. "Hawaiian Antiquities and Folk-lore." *Bernice P. Bishop Museum Memoirs,* vols. 4, 5. Honolulu.

———— 1969. *An Account of the Polynesian Race, its Origin and Migrations and the Ancient History of the Hawaiian People to the Times of Kamehameha I.* Rutland, Vt.: Charles E. Tuttle Co. (First published in London in 1880.)

Frankenstein, Alfred and Norman Carlson. 1961. *Angels Over the Altar: Christian Folk Art in Hawaii and the South Seas.* Honolulu: University of Hawaii Press.

Freitas, J.F. 1930. *Portuguese-Hawaiian Memories.* Honolulu: Printshop Co.

Gassner, Julius S., trans. 1969. *Voyages and Adventures of La Pérouse.* Honolulu: University of Hawaii Press.

Gay, Lawrence Kainoahou. 1965. *True Stories of the Island of Lanai.* Honolulu: Mission Press.

Gifford, Edward Winslow. 1923. *Tongan Place Names.* Bernice P. Bishop Museum Bulletin 6. Honolulu.

Goodenough, Ward H. 1960. "Notes on Truk's Place Names." *Micronesica* 2(2): 95–129.

References

Greer, Richard A. 1969. "The Founding of Queen's Hospital." *Hawaiian Journal of History* 3:110–145.

Greer, Richard A., and others. 1968. "I Remember Cunha's Alley—The Anatomy of a Landmark." *Hawaiian Journal of History* 2:142–150.

Gudde, Erwin G. 1969. *California Place Names.* Berkeley: University of California Press.

Handy, E. S. Craighill. 1923. *The Native Culture in the Marquesas.* Bernice P. Bishop Museum Bulletin 9. Honolulu.

"Hawaii Natural History Association Guide to the Kalapana Chain of Craters Road." 1965. Manuscript. (Sinclair Library, University of Hawaii)

Hawaiian Place Names. 1929. Headquarters, Hawaiian Department, Fort Shafter, Honolulu.

Healy, John R. 1959. "The Mapping of the Hawaiian Islands from 1778 to 1848." Master's thesis, University of Hawaii.

Historical Glimpses of Central Union Church, 1887-1937. 1937. Honolulu: Published by the church.

History of Manoa School, Honolulu. 1952. Manoa School Parent-Teacher Association Historical Committee. Honolulu.

Howay, F.W. 1939. "Captain Henry Barber of Barber's Point." *Hawaiian Historical Society Annual Report for 1938,* pp. 39–49. Honolulu.

Ii, John Papa. 1959. *Fragments of Hawaiian History.* Honolulu: Bernice P. Bishop Museum Press.

Indices of Awards Made by the Board of Commissioners to Quiet Land Titles in the Hawaiian Islands. 1929. Honolulu: Star-Bulletin Press.

Jackson, Frances, Agnes Conrad, and Nancy Bannick, eds. 1969. *Old Honolulu, A Guide to Oahu's Historic Buildings.* Honolulu: Historic Buildings Task Force.

Jarrett, Lorna H. 1930. "A Source Book in Hawaiian Geography." Master of Arts thesis, University of Hawaii.

Jones, Davis, and W.C. Addleman. 1938. *Directory of Hawaiian Place Names Including the Islands of Oahu, Hawaii, Kahoolawe, Kauai, Lanai, Maui, and Niihau. Also Beacon Lights and Channels.* Revised by Sgt. Addleman. Honolulu: U.S. Army.

Kamakau, S.M. 1961. *Ruling Chiefs of Hawaii.* Honolulu: Kamehameha Schools Press.

King, William H.D. 1954. "A Son of Hawaii in the Civil War,

Samuel Chapman Armstrong." *The Hawaii Guardsman* 5(2).

Knowlton, Edgar C., Jr. 1960. "The Portuguese Language Press in Hawaii." *Social Process in Hawaii* 24:88–99.

Koskinen, Aarne A. 1963. "A Preliminary Statistical Study of Polynesian Place Names." *Studia Missiologica Fennica II* (Publications of the Finnish Society for Missionary Research) 8:7–11.

Krauss, Bob, with William P. Alexander. 1965. *Grove Farm Plantation, the Biography of a Hawaiian Sugar Plantation.* Palo Alto: Pacific Books.

Kuykendall, Ralph S. 1938. *The Hawaiian Kingdom [Vol. 1] 1778–1854: Foundation and Transformation.* Honolulu: University of Hawaii. (Reprinted 1947, 1957, 1968 by the University of Hawaii Press.)

———— 1953. *The Hawaiian Kingdom. Vol. 2. 1854–1874: Twenty Critical Years.* Honolulu: University of Hawaii Press.

———— 1967. *The Hawaiian Kingdom. Vol. 3. 1874–1893: the Kalakaua Dynasty.* Honolulu: University of Hawaii Press.

LeBarron, Russell. 1970. "Hawaii's Sandalwoods." *Aloha Aina* (May 1970). State Dept. of Land and Natural Resources, Honolulu.

Lind, Andrew. 1967. *Hawaii's People.* 3rd ed. Honolulu: University of Hawaii Press.

Luomala, Katharine. 1965. "Creative Processes in Hawaiian Use of Place Names in Chants." *In* Lectures and Reports 4th International Congress for Folk-Narrative Research in Athens, Athens, 1964. *Laographia* 22:234–237.

Macdonald, Gordon A., and Agatin T. Abbott. 1970. *Volcanoes in the Sea: the Geology of Hawaii.* Honolulu: University of Hawaii Press.

Macdonald, Gordon A., and Will Kyselka. 1967. *Anatomy of an Island: a Geological History of Oahu.* Honolulu: Bishop Museum Press.

Malo, David. 1971. *Hawaiian Antiquities (Moolelo Hawaii).* Translated by Nathaniel B. Emerson, 1898. Bernice P. Bishop Museum Special Publication 2. Honolulu.

McAllister, J. Gilbert. 1933a. *Archaeology of Oahu.* Bernice P. Bishop Museum Bulletin 104. Honolulu.

———— 1933b. *Archaeology of Kahoolawe.* Bernice P. Bishop Museum Bulletin 115. Honolulu.

References

Missionary Album: Portraits and Biographical Sketches of the American Protestant Missionaries to the Hawaiian Islands, enlarged from the Edition of 1937. 1969. Honolulu: Hawaiian Mission Children's Society.

Nakuina, Moses. n.d. *Moolelo Hawaii o Pakaa a me Ku-a-Pakaa, na Kahu Iwikuamoo o Keawenuiaumi, ke Alii o Hawaii, a o na Moopuna hoi a Laamaomao* [Hawaiian story of Pāka'a and Ku-ā-Pāka'a, the high attendants of Ke-awe-nui-a-'umi, the chief of Hawai'i and the grandchildren also of La'ama'oma'o]. (Sinclair Library, University of Hawaii)

Newman, T. Stell. 1968. *Hawaiian Fishing and Farming on the Island of Hawaii in A.D. 1778.* Honolulu: Department of Land and Natural Resources, Division of State Parks.

—————— 1970. "Huilua Fishpond." *Aloha Aina* (April 1970). State Dept. of Land and Natural Resources, Honolulu.

Olson, Gunder E., ed. 1941. *The Story of the Volcano House.* Hilo: Hilo Tribune Herald.

Paulin, Eugene, and Joseph A. Bender. 1959. *New Wars: the History of the Brothers of Mary (Marianists) in Hawaii 1883–1958.* Milwaukee: Bruce Press.

Pierce, Richard A. 1965. *Russia's Hawaiian Adventure, 1815–1817.* Berkeley: University of California Press.

Pukui, Mary Kawena. "Hawaiian Chants." Manuscript, private collection.

Pukui, Mary Kawena, and Samuel H. Elbert. 1966. *Place Names of Hawaii.* Honolulu: University of Hawaii Press.

—————— 1971. *Hawaiian Dictionary: Hawaiian-English, English-Hawaiian.* Honolulu: University of Hawaii Press. (First, second, and third editions of the *Hawaiian-English Dictionary* were published in 1957, 1961, and 1965; first edition of the *English-Hawaiian Dictionary,* in 1964.)

Reed, A.W. 1961. *A Dictionary of Maori Place Names.* Wellington: A.H. and A.W. Reed.

Restarick, Henry B. 1927. "Historic Kealakekua Bay." *Papers of the Hawaiian Historical Society,* no. 15, pp. 5–20.

Rice, William Hyde. 1923. *Hawaiian Legends.* Bernice P. Bishop Museum Bulletin 3. Honolulu.

Richards, Mary A. 1937. *The Hawaiian Chiefs' Children's School: a Record Compiled from the Diary and Letters of Amos Starr Cooke and Juliette Montague Cooke.* Rutland, Vt.: Charles E. Tuttle Co. (First published in Honolulu in 1837.)

Rockwood, Paul C., and Dorothy B. Barrère. *Map of Honolulu, 1810.* 1957. Honolulu: Bernice P. Bishop Museum Press.

Scudder, Doremus, and others. 1909. *Edward G. Beckwith.* Honolulu: Honolulu Mercantile Print.

Sedgefield, W.J. 1924. "Methods of Place-name Study." In *Introduction to the Study of English Place-names.* Vol. 1, part 1. Cambridge: At the University Press.

Statistical Boundaries of Cities, Towns and Villages, as Approved through December 31, 1971. 1972. Report SB-A7. Department of Planning and Economic Development, State of Hawaii, Honolulu.

Stearns, Harold T. 1939. *Geologic Map and Guide of the Island of Oahu, Hawaii (with a Chapter on Mineral Resources).* Hawaii Division of Hydrography, Bulletin 2. Honolulu.

Stearns, H.T., and Gordon A. Macdonald. 1942. *Geology and Ground-water Resources of the Island of Maui, Hawaii.* Hawaii Division of Hydrography, Bulletin 7. Honolulu.

———— 1947. *Geology and Ground-water Resources of the Island of Molokai, Hawaii.* Hawaii Division of Hydrography, Bulletin 11. Honolulu.

Sterling, Elspeth P., and Catherine C. Summers. 1962. "The Sites of Oahu." 5 vols. Loose leaf. Bernice P. Bishop Museum, Honolulu.

Stewart, George R. 1967. *Names on the Land.* Boston: Houghton, Mifflin. (First published in 1945.)

Stroup, Elaine Fogg. 1950. *The Ports of Hawaii.* [Honolulu]: Propeller Club of the United States.

Summers, Catherine C. 1971. *Molokai: a Site Survey.* Bernice P. Bishop Museum, Pacific Anthropological Records, no. 14, Honolulu.

Taylor, Archer. 1962. *The Proverb and an Index to the Proverb.* Hatboro, Pennsylvania: Folklore Associates. (First printed in 1931.)

Taylor, Clarice B., in collaboration with George Miranda. 1956. "Honolulu Street Names." *Honolulu Star-Bulletin,* January–February 1956.

Te Rangi Hiroa [Peter H. Buck]. 1957. *Arts and Crafts of Hawaii.* Bernice P. Bishop Museum Special Publication 45. Honolulu.

Thrum, Thos. G. 1904. *The Hawaiian Almanac and Annual for 1904.* Honolulu: Thos. G. Thrum.

———— 1907. *Hawaiian Folktales.* Chicago: A.C. McClurg and Co.

References

_____ 1922. "Hawaiian Place Names." In *A Dictionary of the Hawaiian Language,* by Lorrin Andrews, revised by Henry H. Parker. Honolulu: Board of Commissioners of the Public Archives of the Territory of Hawaii.

Titcomb, Margaret, and Mary Kawena Pukui. 1969. *Dog and Man in the Ancient Pacific, with Special Attention to Hawaii.* Bishop Museum Special Publication 59. Honolulu.

Trager, George L. 1946. Review of *Names on the Land,* by George R. Stewart. *International Journal of American Linguistics* 12:108–110.

United States Department of the Interior, Geological Survey. Topographic maps.

Utley, Francis Lee. 1963. "The Linguistic Component of Onomastics." *Names* 11:145–176.

Vancouver, George. 1798. *A Voyage of Discovery to the North Pacific Ocean, and Round the World . . .* Vol. I. London.

Wallace, William J., and Edith Taylor Wallace. 1969. *Pinao Bay Site (H24): A Small Prehistoric Fishing Settlement near South Point (Ka Lae), Hawaii.* Bernice P. Bishop Museum, Pacific Anthropological Records, no. 2. Honolulu.

Wenkam, Robert G. 1970. *Maui: the Last Hawaiian Place.* San Francisco: Friends of the Earth.

Westervelt, W.D. n.d. *Legends of Maui—a Demigod of Polynesia and of his Mother Hina.* Melbourne: George Robertson and Company. (First published in Honolulu in 1910.)

_____ 1963. *Hawaiian Legends of Volcanoes, Collected and Translated from the Hawaiian.* Rutland, Vt.: Charles E. Tuttle Co. (First published in 1916.)

_____ 1964a. *Hawaiian Legends of Ghosts and Ghost-Gods, Collected and Translated from the Hawaiian.* Rutland, Vt.: Charles E. Tuttle Co. (First published in 1915 under the title *Legends of Gods and Ghosts.)*

_____ 1964b. *Hawaiian Legends of Old Honolulu, Collected and Translated from the Hawaiian.* Rutland, Vt.: Charles E. Tuttle Co. (First published in 1916.)

Wilkes, Charles. 1845. *Narrative of the United States Exploring Expedition during the Years 1838, 1839, 1840, 1841, 1842.* Vol. 4. Philadelphia.

Yzendoorn, Father Reginald. 1927. *History of the Catholic Mission in the Hawaiian Islands.* Honolulu: Honolulu Star-Bulletin.

Newspapers and Magazines

The Friend. Honolulu, 1843–1954
Honolulu Advertiser. Honolulu, 1921–
Honolulu Star-Bulletin. Honolulu, 1912–
Pacific Commercial Advertiser. Honolulu, 1856–1921

Aloha Aina (Love of Land). Honolulu, 1895–1920
Hawaii Holomua (Hawaii Progress). Honolulu, 1891–1895
Ka Elele Poakolu (The Wednesday Messenger). Honolulu, 1880–1881
Ka Lahui Hawaii (The Hawaiian Nation). Honolulu, 1875–1877
Ka Leo o ka Lahui (The Voice of the Nation). Honolulu, 1889–1896
Ka Nupepa Elele Poakolu (The Wednesday Messenger Newspaper). Honolulu, 1883–1885
Ka Nupepa Kuokoa (The Independent Newspaper). Honolulu, 1861–1927
Ke Au Hou (The New Era). Honolulu, 1910–1912
Ke Au Okoa (The Independent Era). Honolulu, 1865–1873
Puka La Kuokoa (Daily Independence). Honolulu, 1893–1919 (?)